HOUGHTON MIFFLIN LITERATURE SERIES

MOMENTS IN LITERATURE

EXPLORATIONS IN LITERATURE

REFLECTIONS IN LITERATURE

PERCEPTIONS IN LITERATURE

THEMES IN AMERICAN LITERATURE

FORMS IN ENGLISH LITERATURE

THEMES IN WORLD LITERATURE

PHILIP McFARLAND

LINDA KONICHEK

JEANNE KING

WILLIAM JAMISON

MORSE PECKHAM

EXPLORATIONS IN LITERATURE

HOUGHTON
MIFFLIN
COMPANY

BOSTON
New York
Atlanta

Geneva, Illinois
Dallas
Palo Alto

Library of Congress Catalog Card Number: 75–153157

ISBN: 0–395–11198–6

ABOUT THE EDITORS

Philip McFarland is a novelist and a teacher of English at Concord (Mass.) Academy. A graduate of Oberlin, he holds a master's degree from Cambridge University, where he received First Honors in English Literature. Before becoming a teacher, Mr. McFarland edited textbooks for classes in secondary English.

Linda Konichek taught junior high and high school English in Atascosa, Texas, and West Allis and New Berlin, Wisconsin. She holds a lifetime certification in secondary school English, and attended Luther College, Decorah, Iowa, receiving her undergraduate degree at Trinity University, San Antonio, Texas. She attended the Institute for Advanced Study in English at Lawrence University, and has worked at the Youth Opportunity Center, Milwaukee.

Jeanne King teaches English at Parkway Junior High School in South San Francisco. She has her undergraduate and graduate degrees from San Francisco State College, where she also taught journalism. In addition, she has studied the humanities at Oxford.

William A. Jamison is teaching in the Humanities Division of Kirkland College, Clinton, New York, and has taught in the Department of English, University of Rochester. Dr. Jamison did his undergraduate work at the University of Pittsburgh, and has his M.A. and Ph.D. in English from Princeton. His background includes extensive experience in publishing, and he is the author of the critical study, *Arnold and the Romantics*.

Morse Peckham has spent many years studying the relationship among the arts of literature, painting, and music, and evolving a new theory of art. The result can be seen in two recent volumes—*Beyond the Tragic Vision* and *Man's Rage for Chaos*. Dr. Peckham has taught at the Citadel, Rutgers, the University of Pennsylvania, and the University of South Carolina, where he now serves as Distinguished Professor of English and Comparative Literature.

CONTENTS

ALIENATION

POEMS

CONFLICT

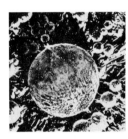

MANY TOMORROWS

INSIGHTS

DRAMA

EXPLORATIONS
IN
LITERATURE

SUSPENSE

S USPENSE IS A KIND OF TORTURE. Everyone has felt the discomforts it can produce: breath held, mouth dry, muscles stiffened. The score in the final seconds of a football game is 13–13. Eighty thousand people, all of them tense, watch the place kicker lope onto the field to try to kick a field goal. He takes his position. A heart-stopping pause, then the snap, the rush of the line, the foot meeting the ball that rises to sail toward the goal posts thirty-two yards away. . . .

Occasionally, comparable reactions of stress can be stirred by nothing more outwardly dramatic than words on a page. A murder story artfully written may do it. Such a story may have one of those same spectators at the football game tense again that same evening, with fingers gripping the book and eyes hurrying forward through the chapters, in search of a killer's identity and fate.

It may seem strange that stories and poems like the ones that follow have such wide appeal, even though they strive to produce the sometimes unpleasant responses that accompany suspense. Why do we enjoy such reading? Surely for reasons more complicated than the feeling of relief we have when the suspense ends. That would be like banging our hand with a hammer because it feels good when we stop. Maybe accounts of others in danger provide a pleasant sense of our own cozy security by contrast. We feel all the more comfortable and grateful to be where we are. Or if in fact we have known what it is to be under great stress ourselves, we welcome a chance to understand other people's ordeals. They remind us of a truth that can be reassuring: not even the most sheltered life is—or would even want to be—entirely free from risk or tension.

Philip McFarland

And his eyes have all the seeming of a demon's that is dreaming,
And the lamplight o'er him streaming throws his shadow on the floor.

"The Raven"

THE TELLTALE HEART
EDGAR ALLAN POE

TRUE!—nervous—very, very dreadfully nervous I had been and am; but why *will* you say that I am mad? The disease had sharpened my senses—not destroyed, not dulled them. Above all was the sense of hearing acute. I heard all things in the heaven and in the earth. I heard many things in hell. How, then, am I mad? Hearken! and observe how healthily, how calmly I can tell you the whole story.

It is impossible to say how first the idea entered my brain; but once conceived, it haunted me day and night. Object there was none. Passion there was none. I loved the old man. He had never wronged me. He had never given me insult. For his gold I had no desire. I think it was his eye! Yes, it was this! He had the eye of a vulture—a pale blue eye, with a film over it. Whenever it fell upon me, my blood ran cold; and so by degrees—very gradually—I made up my mind to take the life of the old man, and thus rid myself of the eye forever.

Now this is the point. You fancy me mad. Madmen know nothing. But you should have seen *me*. You should have seen how wisely I proceeded—with what caution, with what foresight, with what dissimulation[1] I went to work! I was never kinder to the old man than during the whole week before I killed him. And every night, about midnight, I turned the latch of his door and opened it—oh, so gently! And then, when I had made an opening sufficient for my head, I put in a dark lantern, all closed, closed, so that no light shone out, and then I thrust in my head. Oh, you would have laughed to see how cunningly I thrust it in! I moved it slowly—very, very slowly, so that I might not disturb the old man's sleep. It took me an hour to place my whole head within the opening so far that I could see him as he lay upon his bed. Ha!—would a madman have been so wise as this? And then, when my head was well in the room, I undid the lantern cautiously—oh, so cautiously—cautiously (for the hinges creaked), I undid it just so much that a single thin ray fell upon the vulture eye. And this I did for seven long nights—every night just at midnight—but I found the eye always closed; and so it was impossible to do the work, for it was not the old man who vexed me, but his Evil Eye. And every morning, when the day broke, I went boldly into the chamber, and spoke courageously to him, calling him by name in a hearty tone, and inquiring how he had passed the night. So you see he would have been a very profound old man, indeed, to suspect that every night, just at twelve, I looked in upon him while he slept.

---

[1] DISSIMULATION: pretense in order to deceive.

Upon the eighth night I was more than usually cautious in opening the door. A watch's minute hand moves more quickly than did mine. Never before that night had I *felt* the extent of my own powers, of my sagacity. I could scarcely contain my feelings of triumph. To think that there I was, opening the door, little by little, and he not even to dream of my secret deeds or thoughts. I fairly chuckled at the idea; and perhaps he heard me, for he moved on the bed suddenly, as if startled. Now you may think that I drew back—but no. His room was as black as pitch with the thick darkness (for the shutters were close fastened, through fear of robbers), and so I knew that he could not see the opening of the door, and I kept pushing it on steadily, steadily.

I had my head in, and was about to open the lantern, when my thumb slipped upon the tin fastening, and the old man sprang up in bed, crying out, "Who's there?"

I kept quite still and said nothing. For a whole hour I did not move a muscle, and in the meantime I did not hear him lie down. He was still sitting up in the bed, listening—just as I have done night after night, hearkening to the deathwatches[1] in the wall.

Presently I heard a slight groan, and I knew it was the groan of mortal terror. It was not a groan of pain or of grief—oh no! —it was the low, stifled sound that arises from the bottom of the soul when overcharged with awe. I knew the sound well. Many a night, just at midnight, when all the world slept, it has welled up from my own bosom, deepening with its dreadful echo the terrors that distracted me. I say I knew it well. I knew what the old man felt, and pitied him, although I chuckled at heart. I knew that he had been lying awake ever since the first slight noise, when he had turned in the bed. His fears had been ever since growing upon him. He had been trying to fancy them causeless, but could not. He had been saying to himself, "It is nothing but the wind in the chimney—it is only a mouse crossing the floor," or "It is merely a cricket which has made a single chirp." Yes, he had been trying to comfort himself with these suppositions, but he had found all in vain. *All in vain*, because Death, in approaching him, had stalked with his black shadow before him and enveloped the victim. And it was the mournful influence of the unperceived shadow that caused him to feel—although he neither saw nor heard—to *feel* the presence of my head within the room.

When I had waited a long time, very patiently, without hearing him lie down, I resolved to open a little—a very, very little —crevice in the lantern. So I opened it— you cannot imagine how stealthily, stealthily—until, at length, a single dim ray, like the thread of the spider, shot from out the crevice and fell full upon the vulture eye.

It was open—wide, wide open—and I grew furious as I gazed upon it. I saw it with perfect distinctness—all a dull blue, with a hideous veil over it that chilled the very marrow in my bones; but I could see nothing else of the old man's face or person, for I had directed the ray, as if by instinct, precisely upon the damned spot.

And now—have I not told you that what you mistake for madness is but overacuteness of the senses?—now, I say, there came to my ears a low, dull, quick sound,

[1] DEATHWATCHES: beetles that live in old woodwork. Their ticking sound was thought to be a warning of death.

such as a watch makes when enveloped in cotton. I knew *that* sound well, too. It was the beating of the old man's heart. It increased my fury, as the beating of a drum stimulates the soldier into courage.

But even yet I refrained and kept still. I scarcely breathed. I held the lantern motionless. I tried how steadily I could maintain the ray upon the eye. Meantime the hellish tattoo of the heart increased. It grew quicker and quicker, and louder and louder every instant. The old man's terror *must* have been extreme! It grew louder, I say, louder every moment!—Do you mark me well? I have told you that I am nervous; so I am.—And now at the dead hour of the night, amid the dreadful silence of that old house, so strange a noise as this excited me to uncontrollable terror. Yet, for some minutes longer I refrained and stood still. But the beating grew louder, louder! I thought the heart must burst. And now a new anxiety seized me—the sound would be heard by a neighbor! The old man's hour had come! With a loud yell, I threw open the lantern and leaped into the room. He shrieked once—once only. In an instant I dragged him to the floor and pulled the heavy bed over him. I then smiled gaily, to find the deed so far done. But, for many minutes, the heart beat on with a muffled sound. This, however, did not vex me; it would not be heard through the wall. At length it ceased. The old man was dead. I removed the bed and examined the corpse. Yes, he was stone, stone dead. I placed my hand upon the heart and held it there many minutes. There was no pulsation. He was stone dead. His eye would trouble me no more.

If still you think me mad, you will think so no longer when I describe the wise precautions I took for the concealment of the body. The night waned, and I worked hastily but in silence. First of all I dismembered the corpse. I cut off the head and the arms and the legs.

I then took up three planks from the flooring of the chamber and deposited all between the scantlings.[1] I then replaced the boards so cleverly, so cunningly, that no human eye—not even *his*—could have detected anything wrong. There was nothing to wash out—no stain of any kind, no blood spot whatever. I had been too wary for that. A tub had caught all—ha! ha!

When I had made an end of these labors, it was four o'clock—still dark as midnight. As the bell sounded the hour, there came a knocking at the street door. I went down to open it with a light heart—for what had I *now* to fear? There entered three men, who introduced themselves, with perfect suavity, as officers of the police. A shriek had been heard by a neighbor during the night; suspicion of foul play had been aroused; information had been lodged at the police office, and they (the officers) had been deputed to search the premises.

I smiled—for *what* had I to fear? I bade the gentlemen welcome. The shriek, I said, was my own in a dream. The old man, I mentioned, was absent in the country. I took my visitors all over the house. I bade them search—search *well*. I led them, at length, to *his* chamber. I showed them his treasures, secure, undisturbed. In the enthusiasm of my confidence I brought chairs into the room, and desired them *here* to rest from their fatigues, while I myself, in the wild audacity of my perfect triumph, placed my own seat upon the very spot

---

[1] SCANTLINGS: timbers.

beneath which reposed the corpse of the victim.

The officers were satisfied. My *manner* had convinced them. I was singularly at ease. They sat, and while I answered cheerily, they chatted of familiar things. But ere long I felt myself getting pale and wished them gone. My head ached, and I fancied a ringing in my ears; but still they sat and still chatted. The ringing became more distinct; it continued and became more distinct. I talked more freely to get rid of the feeling, but it continued and gained definitiveness—until at length I found that the noise was *not* within my ears.

No doubt I now grew *very* pale—but I talked more fluently, and with a heightened voice. Yet the sound increased—and what could I do? It was a *low, dull, quick sound—much such a sound as a watch makes when enveloped in cotton.* I gasped for breath—and yet the officers heard it not. I talked more quickly, more vehemently—but the noise steadily increased. I arose and argued about trifles, in a high key and with violent gesticulations, but the noise steadily increased. Why *would* they not be gone? I paced the floor to and fro with heavy strides, as if excited to fury by the observations of the men—but the noise steadily increased. Oh, God! What *could* I do? I foamed—I raved—I swore! I swung the chair upon which I had been sitting, and grated it upon the boards, but the noise arose over all and continually increased. It grew louder—louder—*louder!* And still the men chatted pleasantly, and smiled. Was it possible they heard not? Almighty God! No, no! They heard!—They suspected!—They *knew!*—They were making a mockery of my horror!—This I thought, and this I think. But anything was better than this agony! Anything was more tolerable than this derision! I could bear those hypocritical smiles no longer! I felt that I must scream or die! And now—Again!—Hark! —Louder! Louder! Louder! *Louder!*

"Villains!" I shrieked, "dissemble[1] no more! I admit the deed! Tear up the planks! —here, here!—It is the beating of his hideous heart!"

[1] DISSEMBLE: pretend.

FOR DISCUSSION

1. Does the murderer really hear his victim's heart beating? If not, what do you think he hears?

2. In the first sentence the narrator denies that he is mad. Discuss details within the story that confirm or contradict his statement.

3. *Mood* in fiction describes the particular emotional effect a story or poem makes upon its reader. Poe is considered a master at creating a mood of horror and suspense. For instance, Poe makes use of light in his description; in our imagination we can see the garish effect of the dim lantern light on the sleeping face of the soon-to-be-murdered man. What other senses does Poe use to create the mood he wants?

4. The story is told from the point of view of the murderer, who is obviously excited and afraid. How does this device add to the mood of the story? Do you think that the story would have had the same intensity of emotion if it had been related by the policeman, for instance? Explain your answer.

The roses bloomed green on Mars, and the grass grew purple. Everything was different; everything was changing. And Bittering was afraid.

DARK THEY WERE AND GOLDEN-EYED

RAY BRADBURY

THE ROCKET METAL COOLED in the meadow winds. Its lid gave a bulging *pop.* From its clock interior stepped a man, a woman, and three children. The other passengers whispered away across the Martian meadow, leaving the man alone among his family.

The man felt his hair flutter and the tissues of his body draw tight as if he were standing at the center of a vacuum. His wife, before him, seemed almost to whirl away in smoke. The children, small seeds, might at any instant be sown to all the Martian climes.

The children looked up at him, as people look to the sun to tell what time of their life it is. His face was cold.

"What's wrong?" asked his wife.

"Let's get back on the rocket."

"Go back to Earth?"

"Yes! Listen!"

The wind blew as if to flake away their identities. At any moment the Martian air might draw his soul from him, as marrow comes from a white bone. He felt submerged in a chemical that could dissolve his intellect and burn away his past.

They looked at Martian hills that time had worn with a crushing pressure of years. They saw the old cities, lost in their meadows, lying like children's delicate bones among the blowing lakes of grass.

"Chin up, Harry," said his wife. "It's too late. We've come over sixty million miles."

The children with their yellow hair hollered at the deep dome of Martian sky. There was no answer but the racing hiss of wind through the stiff grass.

He picked up the luggage in his cold hands. "Here we go," he said—a man standing on the edge of a sea, ready to wade in and be drowned.

They walked into town.

Their name was Bittering. Harry and his wife Cora; Dan, Laura, and David. They built a small white cottage and ate good breakfasts there, but the fear was never gone. It lay with Mr. Bittering and Mrs. Bittering, a third unbidden partner at every midnight talk, at every dawn awakening.

"I feel like a salt crystal," he said, "in a mountain stream, being washed away. We don't belong here. We're Earth people. This is Mars. It was meant for Martians. For heaven's sake, Cora, let's buy tickets for home!"

But she only shook her head. "One day the atom bomb will fix Earth. Then we'll be safe here."

"Safe and insane!"

Tick-tock, seven o'clock sang the voice-clock; *time to get up*. And they did.

Something made him check everything each morning—warm hearth, potted blood-geraniums—precisely as if he expected something to be amiss. The morning paper was toast-warm from the 6 A.M. Earth rocket. He broke its seal and tilted it at his breakfast place. He forced himself to be convivial.

"Colonial days all over again," he declared. "Why, in ten years there'll be a million Earthmen on Mars. Big cities, everything! They said we'd fail. Said the Martians would resent our invasion. But did we find any Martians? Not a living soul! Oh, we found their empty cities, but no one in them. Right?"

A river of wind submerged the house. When the windows ceased rattling Mr. Bittering swallowed and looked at the children.

"I don't know," said David. "Maybe there're Martians around we don't see. Sometimes nights I think I hear 'em. I hear the wind. The sand hits my window. I get scared. And I see those towns way up in the mountains where the Martians lived a long time ago. And I think I see things moving around those towns, Papa. And I wonder if those Martians *mind* us living here. I wonder if they won't do something to us for coming here."

"Nonsense!" Mr. Bittering looked out the windows. "We're clean, decent people." He looked at his children. "All dead cities have some kind of ghosts in them. Memories, I mean." He stared at the hills. "You see a staircase and you wonder what Mar-

tians looked like climbing it. You see Martian paintings and you wonder what the painter was like. You make a little ghost in your mind, a memory. It's quite natural. Imagination." He stopped. "You haven't been prowling up in those ruins, have you?"

"No, Papa." David looked at his shoes.

"See that you stay away from them. Pass the jam."

"Just the same," said little David, "I bet something happens."

Something happened that afternoon.

Laura stumbled through the settlement, crying. She dashed blindly onto the porch.

"Mother, Father—the war, Earth!" she sobbed. "A radio flash just came. Atom bombs hit New York! All the space rockets blown up. No more rockets to Mars, ever!"

"Oh, Harry!" The mother held onto her husband and daughter.

"Are you sure, Laura?" asked the father quietly.

Laura wept. "We're stranded on Mars, forever and ever!"

For a long time there was only the sound of the wind in the late afternoon.

Alone, thought Bittering. Only a thousand of us here. No way back. No way. No way. Sweat poured from his face and his hands and his body; he was drenched in the hotness of his fear. He wanted to strike Laura, cry, "No, you're lying! The rockets will come back!" Instead, he stroked Laura's head against him and said, "The rockets will get through someday."

"Father, what will we do?"

"Go about our business, of course. Raise crops and children. Wait. Keep things going until the war ends and the rockets come again."

The two boys stepped out onto the porch.

"Children," he said, sitting there, looking beyond them, "I've something to tell you."

"We know," they said.

In the following days, Bittering wandered often through the garden to stand alone in his fear. As long as the rockets had spun a silver web across space, he had been able to accept Mars. For he had always told himself: Tomorrow, if I want, I can buy a ticket and go back to Earth.

But now: The web gone, the rockets lying in jigsaw heaps of molten girder and unsnaked wire. Earth people left to the strangeness of Mars, the cinnamon dusts and wine airs, to be baked like gingerbread shapes in Martian summers, put into harvested storage by Martian winters. What would happen to him, the others? This was the moment Mars had waited for. Now it would eat them.

He got down on his knees in the flower bed, a spade in his nervous hands. Work, he thought, work and forget.

He glanced up from the garden to the Martian mountains. He thought of the proud old Martian names that had once been on those peaks. Earthmen, dropping from the sky, had gazed upon hills, rivers, Martian seas left nameless in spite of names. Once Martians had built cities, named cities; climbed mountains, named mountains; sailed seas, named seas. Mountains melted, seas drained, cities tumbled. In spite of this, the Earthmen had felt a silent guilt at putting new names to these ancient hills and valleys.

Nevertheless, man lives by symbol and label. The names were given.

Mr. Bittering felt very alone in his gar-den under the Martian sun, anachronism[1] bent here, planting Earth flowers in a wild soil.

Think. Keep thinking. Different things. Keep your mind free of Earth, the atom war, the lost rockets.

He perspired. He glanced about. No one watching. He removed his tie. Pretty bold, he thought. First your coat off, now your tie. He hung it neatly on a peach tree he had imported as a sapling from Massachusetts.

He returned to his philosophy of names and mountains. The Earthmen had changed names. Now there were Hormel Valleys, Roosevelt Seas, Ford Hills, Vanderbilt Plateaus, Rockefeller Rivers, on Mars. It wasn't right. The American settlers had shown wisdom, using old Indian prairie names: Wisconsin, Minnesota, Idaho, Ohio, Utah, Milwaukee, Waukegan, Osseo. The old names, the old meanings.

Staring at the mountains wildly, he thought: Are you up there? All the dead ones, you Martians? Well, here we are, alone, cut off! Come down, move us out! We're helpless!

The wind blew a shower of peach blossoms.

He put out his sun-browned hand, gave a small cry. He touched the blossoms, picked them up. He turned them, he touched them again and again. Then he shouted for his wife.

"Cora!"

She appeared at a window. He ran to her.

"Cora, these blossoms!"

She handled them.

"Do you see? They're different. They've

---

[1] ANACHRONISM: that which is out of its regular time or place.

changed! They're not peach blossoms any more!"

"Look all right to me," she said.

"They're not. They're *wrong!* I can't tell how. An extra petal, a leaf, something, the color, the smell!"

The children ran out in time to see their father hurrying about the garden, pulling up radishes, onions, and carrots from their beds.

"Cora, come look!"

They handled the onions, the radishes, the carrots among them.

"Do they look like carrots?"

"Yes . . . no." She hesitated. "I don't know."

"They're changed."

"Perhaps."

"You know they have! Onions but not onions, carrots but not carrots. Taste: the same but different. Smell: not like it used to be." He felt his heart pounding, and he was afraid. He dug his fingers into the earth. "Cora, what's happening? What is it? We've got to get away from this." He ran across the garden. Each tree felt his touch. "The roses. The roses. They're turning green!"

And they stood looking at the green roses.

And two days later Dan came running. "Come see the cow. I was milking her and I saw it. Come on!"

They stood in the shed and looked at their one cow.

It was growing a third horn.

And the lawn in front of their house very quietly and slowly was coloring itself like spring violets. Seed from Earth but growing up a soft purple.

"We must get away," said Bittering.

"We'll eat this stuff and then we'll change —who knows to what? I can't let it happen. There's only one thing to do. Burn this food!"

"It's not poisoned."

"But it is. Subtly, very subtly. A little bit. A very little bit. We mustn't touch it."

He looked with dismay at their house. "Even the house. The wind's done something to it. The air's burned it. The fog at night. The boards, all warped out of shape. It's not an Earthman's house any more."

"Oh, your imagination!"

He put on his coat and tie. "I'm going into town. We've got to do something now. I'll be back."

"Wait, Harry!" his wife cried.

But he was gone.

In town, on the shadowy step of the grocery store, the men sat with their hands on their knees, conversing with great leisure and ease.

Mr. Bittering wanted to fire a pistol in the air.

What are you doing, you fools! he thought. Sitting here! You've heard the news—we're stranded on this planet. Well, move! Aren't you frightened? Aren't you afraid? What are you going to do?

"Hello, Harry," said everyone.

"Look," he said to them. "You did hear the news, the other day, didn't you?"

They nodded and laughed. "Sure. Sure, Harry."

"What are you going to do about it?"

"Do, Harry, do? What *can* we do?"

"Build a rocket, that's what!"

"A rocket, Harry? To go back to all that trouble? Oh, Harry!"

"But you *must* want to go back. Have you noticed the peach blossoms, the onions, the grass?"

"Why, yes, Harry, seems we did," said one of the men.

"Doesn't it scare you?"

"Can't recall that it did much, Harry."

"Idiots!"

"Now, Harry."

Bittering wanted to cry. "You've got to work with me. If we stay here, we'll all change. The air. Don't you smell it? Something in the air. A Martian virus, maybe; some seed, or a pollen. Listen to me!"

They stared at him.

"Sam," he said to one of them.

"Yes, Harry?"

"Will you help me build a rocket?"

"Harry, I got a whole load of metal and some blueprints. You want to work in my metal shop on a rocket, you're welcome. I'll sell you that metal for five hundred dollars. You should be able to construct a right pretty rocket, if you work alone, in about thirty years."

Everyone laughed.

"Don't laugh."

Sam looked at him with quiet good humor.

"Sam," Bittering said. "Your eyes—"

"What about them, Harry?"

"Didn't they used to be gray?"

"Well now, I don't remember."

"They were, weren't they?"

"Why do you ask, Harry?"

"Because now they're kind of yellow-colored."

"Is that so, Harry?" Sam said, casually.

"And you're taller and thinner—"

"You might be right, Harry."

"Sam, you shouldn't have yellow eyes."

"Harry, what color eyes have *you* got?" Sam said.

"My eyes? They're blue, of course."

"Here you are, Harry." Sam handed him a pocket mirror. "Take a look at yourself."

Mr. Bittering hesitated, and then raised the mirror to his face.

There were little, very dim flecks of new gold captured in the blue of his eyes.

"Now look what you've done," said Sam a moment later. "You've broken my mirror."

Harry Bittering moved into the metal shop and began to build the rocket. Men stood in the open door and talked and joked without raising their voices. Once in a while they gave him a hand on lifting something. But mostly they just idled and watched him with their yellowing eyes.

"It's suppertime, Harry," they said.

His wife appeared with his supper in a wicker basket.

"I won't touch it," he said. "I'll eat only food from our Deepfreeze. Food that came from Earth. Nothing from our garden."

His wife stood watching him. "You can't build a rocket."

"I worked in a shop once, when I was twenty. I know metal. Once I get it started, the others will help," he said, not looking at her, laying out the blueprints.

"Harry, Harry," she said, helplessly.

"We've got to get away, Cora. We've *got* to!"

The nights were full of wind that blew down the empty moonlit sea meadows past the little white chess cities lying for their twelve-thousandth year in the shallows. In the Earthmen's settlement, the Bittering house shook with a feeling of change.

Lying abed, Mr. Bittering felt his bones shifted, shaped, melted like gold. His wife, lying beside him, was dark from many

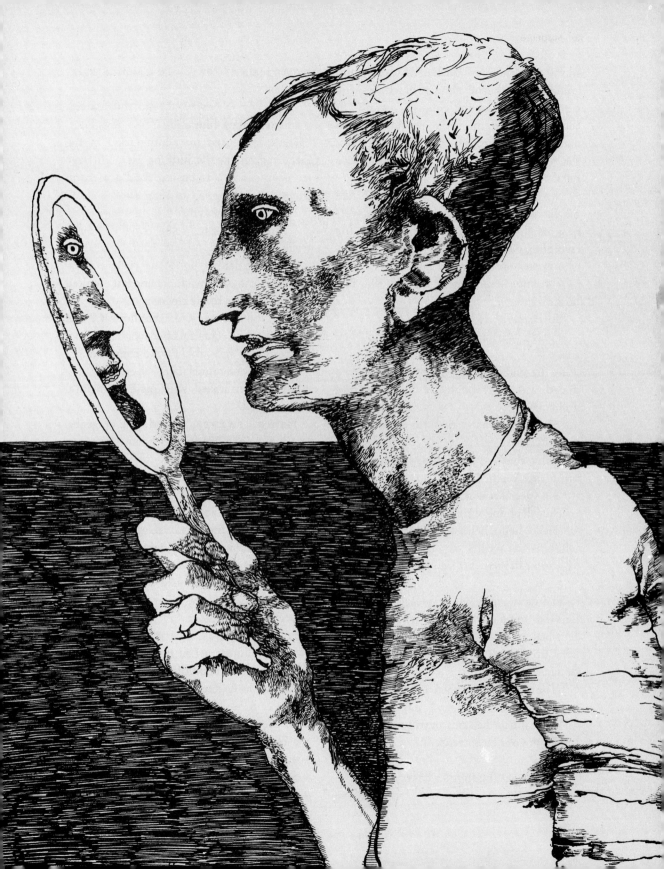

sunny afternoons. Dark she was, and golden-eyed, burnt almost black by the sun, sleeping, and the children metallic in their beds, and the wind roaring forlorn and changing through the old peach trees, the violet grass, shaking out green rose petals.

The fear would not be stopped. It had his throat and heart. It dripped in a wetness of the arm and the temple and the trembling palm.

A green star rose in the east.

A strange word emerged from Mr. Bittering's lips.

"*Iorrt. Iorrt.*" He repeated it.

It was a Martian word. He knew no Martian.

In the middle of the night he arose and dialed a call through to Simpson, the archeologist.

"Simpson, what does the word *Iorrt* mean?"

"Why that's the old Martian word for our planet Earth. Why?"

"No special reason."

The telephone slipped from his hand.

"Hello, hello, hello, hello," it kept saying while he sat gazing out at the green star. "Bittering? Harry, are you there?"

The days were full of metal sound. He laid the frame of the rocket with the reluctant help of three indifferent men. He grew very tired in an hour or so and had to sit down.

"The altitude," laughed a man.

"Are you *eating*, Harry?" asked another.

"I'm eating," he said, angrily.

"From your Deepfreeze?"

"Yes!"

"You're getting thinner, Harry."

"I'm not!"

"And taller."

"Liar!"

His wife took him aside a few days later. "Harry, I've used up all the food in the Deepfreeze. There's nothing left. I'll have to make sandwiches using food grown on Mars."

He sat down heavily.

"You must eat," she said. "You're weak."

"Yes," he said.

He took a sandwich, opened it, looked at it, and began to nibble at it.

"And take the rest of the day off," she said. "It's hot. The children want to swim in the canals and hike. Please come along."

"I can't waste time. This is a crisis!"

"Just for an hour," she urged. "A swim'll do you good."

He rose, sweating. "All right, all right. Leave me alone. I'll come."

"Good for you, Harry."

The sun was hot, the day quiet. There was only an immense staring burn upon the land. They moved along the canal, the father, the mother, the racing children in their swim suits. They stopped and ate meat sandwiches. He saw their skin baking brown. And he saw the yellow eyes of his wife and his children, their eyes that were never yellow before. A few tremblings shook him, but were carried off in waves of pleasant heat as he lay in the sun. He was too tired to be afraid.

"Cora, how long have your eyes been yellow?"

She was bewildered. "Always, I guess."

"They didn't change from brown in the last three months?"

She bit her lips. "No. Why do you ask?"

"Never mind."

They sat there.

"The children's eyes," he said. "They're yellow, too."

"Sometimes growing children's eyes change color."

"Maybe *we're* children, too. At least to Mars. That's a thought." He laughed. "Think I'll swim."

They leaped into the canal water, and he let himself sink down and down to the bottom like a golden statue and lie there in green silence. All was water-quiet and deep, all was peace. He felt the steady, slow current drift him easily.

If I lie here long enough, he thought, the water will work and eat away my flesh until the bones show like coral. Just my skeleton left. And then the water can build on that skeleton—green things, deep water things, red things, yellow things. Change. Change. Slow, deep, silent change. And isn't that what it is up *there?*

He saw the sky submerged above him, the sun made Martian by atmosphere and time and space.

Up there, a big river, he thought, a Martian river, all of us lying deep in it, in our pebble houses, in our sunken boulder houses, like crayfish hidden, and the water washing away our old bodies and lengthening the bones and—

He let himself drift up through the soft light.

Dan sat on the edge of the canal, regarding his father seriously.

"*Utha,*" he said.

"What?" asked his father.

The boy smiled. "You know. *Utha's* the Martian word for 'father.' "

"Where did you learn it?"

"I don't know. Around. *Utha!*"

"What do you want?"

The boy hesitated. "I—I want to change my name."

"Change it?"

"Yes."

His mother swam over. "What's wrong with Dan for a name?"

Dan fidgeted. "The other day you called Dan, Dan, Dan. I didn't even hear. I said to myself, That's not my name. I've a new name I want to use."

Mr. Bittering held to the side of the canal, his body cold and his heart pounding slowly. "What is this new name?"

"Linnl. Isn't that a good name? Can I use it? Can't I, please?"

Mr. Bittering put his hand to his head. He thought of the silly rocket, himself working alone, himself alone even among his family, so alone.

He heard his wife say, "Why not?"

He heard himself say, "Yes, you can use it."

"Yaaa!" screamed the boy. "I'm Linnl, Linnl!"

Racing down the meadowlands, he danced and shouted.

Mr. Bittering looked at his wife. "Why did we do that?"

"I don't know," she said. "It just seemed like a good idea."

They walked into the hills. They strolled on old mosaic paths, beside still pumping fountains. The paths were covered with a thin film of cool water all summer long. You kept your bare feet cool all the day, splashing as in a creek, wading.

They came to a small deserted Martian villa with a good view of the valley. It was on top of a hill. Blue marble halls, large murals, a swimming pool. It was refreshing in this hot summertime. The Martians hadn't believed in large cities.

"How nice," said Mrs. Bittering, "if we could move up here to this villa for the summer."

"Come on," he said. "We're going back to town. There's work to be done on the rocket."

But as he worked that night, the thought of the cool blue marble villa entered his mind. As the hours passed, the rocket seemed less important.

In the flow of days and weeks, the rocket receded and dwindled. The old fever was gone. It frightened him to think he had let it slip this way. But somehow the heat, the air, the working conditions—

He heard the men murmuring on the porch of his metal shop.

"Everyone's going. You heard?"

"All going. That's right."

Bittering came out. "Going where?" He saw a couple of trucks, loaded with children and furniture, drive down the dusty street.

"Up to the villas," said the man.

"Yeah, Harry. I'm going. So is Sam. Aren't you, Sam?"

"That's right, Harry. What about you?"

"I've got work to do here."

"Work! You can finish that rocket in the autumn, when it's cooler."

He took a breath. "I got the frame all set up."

"In the autumn is better." Their voices were lazy in the heat.

"Got to work," he said.

"Autumn," they reasoned. And they sounded so sensible, so right.

"Autumn would be best," he thought. "Plenty of time, then."

No! cried part of himself, deep down, put away, locked tight, suffocating. No! No!

"In the autumn," he said.

"Come on, Harry," they all said.

"Yes," he said, feeling his flesh melt in the hot liquid air. "Yes, in the autumn. I'll begin work again then."

"I got a villa near the Tirra Canal," said someone.

"You mean the Roosevelt Canal, don't you?"

"Tirra. The old Martian name."

"But on the map—"

"Forget the map. It's Tirra now. Now I found a place in the Pillan mountains—"

"You mean the Rockefeller range," said Bittering.

"I mean the Pillan mountains," said Sam.

"Yes," said Bittering, buried in the hot, swarming air. "The Pillan mountains."

Everyone worked at loading the truck in the hot, still afternoon of the next day.

Laura, Dan, and David carried packages. Or, as they preferred to be known, Ttil, Linnl, and Werr carried packages.

The furniture was abandoned in the little white cottage.

"It looked just fine in Boston," said the mother. "And here in the cottage. But up at the villa? No. We'll get it when we come back in the autumn."

Bittering himself was quiet.

"I've some ideas on furniture for the villa," he said after a time. "Big, lazy furniture."

"What about your encyclopedia? You're taking it along, surely?"

Mr. Bittering glanced away. "I'll come and get it next week."

They turned to their daughter. "What about your New York dresses?"

The bewildered girl stared. "Why, I don't want them any more."

They shut off the gas, the water, they locked the doors and walked away. Father peered into the truck.

"Gosh, we're not taking much," he said. "Considering all we brought to Mars, this is only a handful!"

He started the truck.

Looking at the small white cottage for a long moment, he was filled with a desire to rush to it, touch it, say good-bye to it, for he felt as if he were going away on a long journey, leaving something to which he could never quite return, never understand again.

Just then Sam and his family drove by in another truck.

"Hi, Bittering! Here we go!"

The truck swung down the ancient highway out of town. There were sixty others traveling the same direction. The town filled with a silent, heavy dust from their passage. The canal waters lay blue in the sun, and a quiet wind moved in the strange trees.

"Good-bye, town!" said Mr. Bittering.

"Good-bye, good-bye," said the family, waving to it.

They did not look back again.

Summer burned the canals dry. Summer moved like flame upon the meadows. In the empty Earth settlement, the painted houses flaked and peeled. Rubber tires upon which children had swung in back yards hung suspended like stopped clock pendulums in the blazing air.

At the metal shop, the rocket frame began to rust.

In the quiet autumn Mr. Bittering stood, very dark now, very golden-eyed, upon the slope above his villa, looking at the valley.

"It's time to go back," said Cora.

"Yes, but we're not going," he said quietly. "There's nothing there any more."

"Your books," she said. "Your fine clothes."

"Your *Illes* and your fine *ior uele rre*," she said.

"The town's empty. No one's going back," he said. "There's no reason to, none at all."

The daughter wove tapestries and the sons played songs on ancient flutes and pipes, their laughter echoing in the marble villa.

Mr. Bittering gazed at the Earth settlement far away in the low valley. "Such odd, such ridiculous houses the Earth people built."

"They didn't know any better," his wife mused. "Such ugly people. I'm glad they've gone."

They both looked at each other, startled by all they had just finished saying. They laughed.

"Where did they go?" he wondered. He glanced at his wife. She was golden and slender as his daughter. She looked at him, and he seemed almost as young as their eldest son.

"I don't know," she said.

"We'll go back to town maybe next year, or the year after, or the year after that," he said, calmly. "Now—I'm warm. How about taking a swim?"

They turned their backs to the valley. Arm in arm they walked silently down a path of clear-running spring water.

Five years later a rocket fell out of the sky. It lay steaming in the valley. Men leaped out of it, shouting.

"We won the war on Earth! We're here to rescue you! Hey!"

But the American-built town of cottages, peach trees, and theaters was silent. They found a flimsy rocket frame rusting in an empty shop.

The rocket men searched the hills. The

captain established headquarters in an abandoned bar. His lieutenant came back to report.

"The town's empty, but we found native life in the hills, sir. Dark people. Yellow eyes. Martians. Very friendly. We talked a bit, not much. They learn English fast. I'm sure our relations will be most friendly with them, sir."

"Dark, eh?" mused the captain. "How many?"

"Six, eight hundred, I'd say, living in those marble ruins in the hills, sir. Tall, healthy. Beautiful women."

"Did they tell you what became of the men and women who built this Earth settlement, Lieutenant?"

"They hadn't the foggiest notion of what happened to this town or its people."

"Strange. You think those Martians killed them?"

"They looked surprisingly peaceful. Chances are a plague did this town in, sir."

"Perhaps. I suppose this is one of those mysteries we'll never solve. One of those mysteries you read about."

The captain looked at the room, the dusty windows, the blue mountains rising beyond, the canals moving in the light, and he heard the soft wind in the air. He shivered. Then, recovering, he tapped a large fresh map he had thumbtacked to the top of an empty table.

"Lots to be done, Lieutenant." His voice droned on and quietly on as the sun sank behind the blue hills. "New settlements. Mining sites, minerals to be looked for. Bacteriological specimens taken. The work, all the work. And the old records were lost. We'll have a job of remapping to do, renaming the mountains and rivers and such. Calls for a little imagination.

"What do you think of naming those mountains the Lincoln Mountains, this canal the Washington Canal, those hills— we can name those hills for you, Lieutenant. Diplomacy. And you, for a favor, might name a town for me. Polishing the apple. And why not make this the Einstein Valley, and further over . . . are you *listening*, Lieutenant?"

The lieutenant snapped his gaze from the blue color and the quiet mist of the hills far beyond the town.

"What? Oh, *yes*, sir!"

FOR DISCUSSION

1. What physical changes do the earthlings on Mars undergo? What other kinds of changes? What explanation does Bradbury suggest for these changes?

2. Bittering is afraid of the Martian ways, and he fights to maintain old earth ways. But he and his family, we are told, had come to Mars to escape the atomic war that the earth ways had made inevitable. Can you explain why Harry finally changes his attitude? Do you agree with the settlers' decision that the Martian way of life is preferable? Why or why not?

3. You will notice that the author uses a series of images to express Bittering's growing sense of fear. The children, for example, are described as "small seeds" which "might at any minute be sown to all the Martian climes." What other images can you find that describe the relationship between the earth settlers and their new home? How do these images help us to understand what is happening to these settlers? How do they help us to understand the fear that Bittering feels?

4. The narrator comments that "man lives by symbol and label," and names do play an important role in this story, tracing the changing relationship between the earthlings and their Martian home. What hint about the future is suggested by the captain's desire to re-name the mountains and hills in the last part of the story? What is suggested by the lieutenant's lack of attention to the captain's recommendations?

"I haven't been bitten," he whispered. "Not yet. It's on my stomach. Lying there asleep."

POISON
ROALD DAHL

IT MUST HAVE BEEN around midnight when I drove home, and as I approached the gates of the bungalow I switched off the headlamps of the car so the beam wouldn't swing in through the window of the side bedroom and wake Harry Pope. But I needn't have bothered. Coming up the drive I noticed his light was still on, so he was awake anyway—unless perhaps he'd dropped off while reading.

I parked the car and went up the five steps to the balcony, counting each step carefully in the dark so I wouldn't take an extra one which wasn't there when I got to the top. I crossed the balcony, pushed through the screen doors into the house itself and switched on the light in the hall. I went across to the door of Harry's room, opened it quietly, and looked in.

He was lying on the bed and I could see he was awake. But he didn't move. He didn't even turn his head toward me, but I heard him say, "Timber, Timber, come here."

He spoke slowly, whispering each word carefully, separately, and I pushed the door right open and started to go quickly across the room.

"Stop. Wait a moment, Timber." I could hardly hear what he was saying. He seemed to be straining enormously to get the words out.

"What's the matter, Harry?"

"Sshhh!" he whispered. "Sshhh! For God's sake don't make a noise. Take your shoes off before you come nearer. *Please* do as I say, Timber."

The way he was speaking reminded me of George Barling after he got shot in the stomach, when he stood leaning against a crate containing a spare airplane engine, holding both hands on his stomach and saying things about the German pilot in just the same hoarse straining half whisper Harry was using now.

"Quickly, Timber, but take your shoes off first."

I couldn't understand about taking off the shoes but I figured that if he was as ill as he sounded I'd better humor him, so I bent down and removed the shoes and left them in the middle of the floor. Then I went over to his bed.

"Don't touch the bed! For God's sake don't touch the bed!" He was still speaking like he'd been shot in the stomach and I could see him lying there on his back with a single sheet covering three quarters of his body. He was wearing a pair of pajamas with blue, brown, and white stripes, and he was sweating terribly. It was a hot night and I was sweating a little myself, but not like Harry. His whole face was wet and the pillow around his head was sodden with moisture. It looked like a bad go of malaria to me.

"What is it, Harry?"

"A krait,"[1] he said.

"A *krait!* Oh, my God! Where'd it bite you? How long ago?"

"Shut up," he whispered.

"Listen, Harry," I said, and I leaned forward and touched his shoulder. "We've got to be quick. Come on now, quickly, tell me where it bit you." He was lying there very still and tense as though he were holding on to himself hard because of sharp pain.

"I haven't been bitten," he whispered. "Not yet. It's on my stomach. Lying there asleep."

I took a quick pace backward; I couldn't help it, and I stared at his stomach or rather at the sheet that covered it. The sheet was rumpled in several places and it was impossible to tell if there was anything underneath.

[1] KRAIT: a poisonous snake.

"You don't really mean there's a krait lying on your stomach now?"

"I swear it."

"How did it get there?" I shouldn't have asked the question because it was easy to see he wasn't fooling. I should have told him to keep quiet.

"I was reading," Harry said, and he spoke very slowly, taking each word in turn and speaking it carefully so as not to move the muscles of his stomach. "Lying on my back reading and I felt something on my chest, behind the book. Sort of tickling. Then out of the corner of my eye saw this little krait sliding over my pajamas. Small, about ten inches. Knew I mustn't move. Couldn't have anyway. Lay there watching it. Thought it would go over top of the sheet." Harry paused and was silent for a few moments. His eyes looked down along his body toward the place where the sheet covered his stomach, and I could see he was watching to make sure his whispering wasn't disturbing the thing that lay there.

"There was a fold in the sheet," he said, speaking more slowly than ever now and so softly I had to lean close to hear him. "See it, it's still there. It went under that. I could feel it through my pajamas, moving on my stomach. Then it stopped moving and now it's lying there in the warmth. Probably asleep. I've been waiting for you." He raised his eyes and looked at me.

"How long ago?"

"Hours," he whispered. "Hours and bloody hours and hours. I can't keep still much longer. I've been wanting to cough."

There was not much doubt about the truth of Harry's story. As a matter of fact it wasn't a surprising thing for a krait to do. They hang around people's houses and they go for the warm places. The surprising thing was that Harry hadn't been bitten. The bite is quite deadly except sometimes when you catch it at once, and they kill a fair number of people each year in Bengal, mostly in the villages.

"All right, Harry," I said, and now I was whispering too. "Don't move and don't talk any more unless you have to. You know it won't bite unless it's frightened. We'll fix it in no time."

I went softly out of the room in my stocking feet and fetched a small sharp knife from the kitchen. I put it in my trouser pocket ready to use instantly in case something went wrong while we were still thinking out a plan. If Harry coughed or moved or did something to frighten the krait and got bitten, I was going to be ready to cut the bitten place and try to suck the venom out. I came back to the bedroom and Harry was still lying there very quiet and sweating all over his face. His eyes followed me as I moved across the room to his bed and I could see he was wondering what I'd been up to. I stood beside him, trying to think of the best thing to do.

"Harry," I said, and now when I spoke I put my mouth almost on his ear so I wouldn't have to raise my voice above the softest whisper, "I think the best thing to do is for me to draw the sheet back very, very gently. Then we could have a look first. I think I could do that without disturbing it."

"Don't be a damn fool." There was no expression in his voice. He spoke each word too slowly, too carefully, and too softly for that. The expression was in the eyes and around the corners of the mouth.

"Why not?"

"The light would frighten him. It's dark under there now."

"Then how about whipping the sheet back quick and brushing it off before it has time to strike?"

"Why don't you get a doctor?" Harry said. The way he looked at me told me I should have thought of that myself in the first place.

"A doctor. Of course. That's it. I'll get Ganderbai."

I tiptoed out to the hall, looked up Ganderbai's number in the book, lifted the phone and told the operator to hurry.

"Doctor Ganderbai," I said. "This is Timber Woods."

"Hello, Mr. Woods. You not in bed yet?"

"Look, could you come round at once? And bring serum—for a krait bite."

"Who's been bitten?" The question came so sharply it was like a small explosion in my ear.

"No one. No one yet. But Harry Pope's in bed and he's got one lying on his stomach—asleep under the sheet on his stomach."

For about three seconds there was silence on the line. Then speaking slowly, not like an explosion now but slowly, precisely, Ganderbai said, "Tell him to keep quite still. He is not to move or to talk. Do you understand?"

"Of course."

"I'll come at once!" He rang off and I went back to the bedroom. Harry's eyes watched me as I walked across to his bed.

"Ganderbai's coming. He said for you to lie still."

"What in God's name does he think I'm doing!"

"Look, Harry, he said no talking. Absolutely no talking. Either of us."

"Why don't you shut up then?" When

he said this, one side of his mouth started twitching with rapid little downward movements that continued for a while after he finished speaking. I took out my handkerchief and very gently I wiped the sweat off his face and neck, and I could feel the slight twitching of the muscle—the one he used for smiling—as my fingers passed over it with the handkerchief.

I slipped out to the kitchen, got some ice from the icebox, rolled it up in a napkin, and began to crush it small. That business of the mouth, I didn't like that. Or the way he talked, either. I carried the ice pack back to the bedroom and laid it across Harry's forehead.

"Keep you cool."

He screwed up his eyes and drew breath sharply through his teeth. "Take it away," he whispered. "Make me cough." His smiling-muscle began to twitch again.

The beam of a headlamp shone through the window as Ganderbai's car swung around to the front of the bungalow. I went out to meet him, holding the ice pack with both hands.

"How is it?" Ganderbai asked, but he didn't stop to talk; he walked on past me across the balcony and through the screen doors into the hall. "Where is he? Which room?"

He put his bag down on a chair in the hall and followed me into Harry's room. He was wearing soft-soled bedroom slippers and he walked across the floor noiselessly, delicately, like a careful cat. Harry watched him out of the sides of his eyes. When Ganderbai reached the bed he looked down at Harry and smiled, confident and reassuring, nodding his head to tell Harry it was a simple matter and he was not to worry but just to leave it to Doctor Gan-

derbai. Then he turned and went back to the hall and I followed him.

"First thing is to try to get some serum into him," he said, and he opened his bag and started to make preparations. "Intravenously. But I must do it neatly. Don't want to make him flinch."

We went into the kitchen and he sterilized a needle. He had a hypodermic syringe in one hand and a small bottle in the other and he stuck the needle through the rubber top of the bottle and began drawing a pale yellow liquid up into the syringe by pulling out the plunger. Then he handed me the syringe.

"Hold that till I ask for it."

He picked up the bag and together we returned to the room. Harry's eyes were bright now and wide open. Ganderbai bent over Harry and very cautiously, like a man handling sixteenth-century lace, he rolled up the pajama sleeve to the elbow without moving the arm. I noticed he stood well away from the bed.

He whispered, "I'm going to give you an injection. Serum. Just a prick but try not to move. Don't tighten your stomach muscles. Let them go limp."

Harry looked at the syringe.

Ganderbai took a piece of red rubber tubing from his bag and slid one end under and up and around Harry's bicep; then he tied the tubing tight with a knot. He sponged a small area of the bare forearm with alcohol, handed the swab to me and took the syringe from my hand. He held it up to the light, squinting at the calibrations, squirting out some of the yellow fluid. I stood still beside him, watching. Harry was watching too and sweating all over his face so it shone like it was smeared thick with face cream melting on his skin

and running down onto the pillow.

I could see the blue vein on the inside of Harry's forearm, swollen now because of the tourniquet, and then I saw the needle above the vein, Ganderbai holding the syringe almost flat against the arm, sliding the needle in sideways through the skin into the blue vein, sliding it slowly but so firmly it went in smooth as into cheese. Harry looked at the ceiling and closed his eyes and opened them again but he didn't move.

When it was finished Ganderbai leaned forward putting his mouth close to Harry's ear. "Now you'll be all right even if you *are* bitten. But don't move. Please don't move. I'll be back in a moment."

He picked up his bag and went out to the hall and followed.

"Is he safe now?" I asked.

"No."

"How safe is he?"

The little Indian doctor stood there in the hall rubbing his lower lip.

"It must give some protection, mustn't it?" I asked.

He turned away and walked to the screen doors that led onto the veranda. I thought he was going through them but he stopped this side of the doors and stood looking out into the night.

"Isn't the serum very good?" I asked.

"Unfortunately not," he answered without turning round. "It might save him. It might not. I am trying to think of something else to do."

"Shall we draw the sheet back quick and brush it off before it has time to strike?"

"Never! We are not entitled to take a risk." He spoke sharply and his voice was pitched a little higher than usual.

"We can't very well leave him lying there," I said. "He's getting nervous."

"Please! Please!" he said, turning round, holding both hands up in the air. "Not so fast, please. This is not a matter to rush into bald-headed." He wiped his forehead with his handkerchief and stood there, frowning, nibbling his lip.

"You see," he said at last. "There is a way to do this. You know what we must do—we must administer an anesthetic to the creature where it lies."

It was a splendid idea.

"It is not safe," he continued, "because a snake is cold-blooded and anesthetic does not work so well or so quick with such animals, but it is better than any other thing to do. We could use ether . . . chloroform . . ." He was speaking slowly and trying to think the thing out while he talked.

"Which shall we use?"

"Chloroform," he said suddenly. "Ordinary chloroform. That is best. Now quick!" He took my arm and pulled me toward the balcony. "Drive to my house! By the time you get there I will have waked up my boy on the telephone and he will show you my poisons cupboard. Here is the key of the cupboard. Take a bottle of chloroform. It has an orange label and the name is printed on it. I stay here in case anything happens. Be quick now, hurry! No, no, you don't need your shoes!"

I drove fast and in about fifteen minutes I was back with the bottle of chloroform. Ganderbai came out of Harry's room and met me in the hall. "You got it?" he said. "Good, good. I just been telling him what we are going to do. But now we must hurry. It is not easy for him in there like that all this time. I am afraid he might move."

He went back to the bedroom and I followed, carrying the bottle carefully with both hands. Harry was lying on the bed in precisely the same position as before with the sweat pouring down his cheeks. His face was white and wet. He turned his eyes toward me, and I smiled at him and nodded confidently. He continued to look at me. I raised my thumb, giving him the okay signal. He closed his eyes. Ganderbai was squatting down by the bed, and on the floor beside him was the hollow rubber tube that he had previously used as a tourniquet, and he'd got a small paper funnel fitted into one end of the tube.

He began to pull a little piece of the sheet out from under the mattress. He was working directly in line with Harry's stomach, about eighteen inches from it, and I watched his fingers as they tugged gently at the edge of the sheet. He worked so slowly it was almost impossible to discern any movement either in his fingers or in the sheet that was being pulled.

Finally he succeeded in making an opening under the sheet and he took the rubber tube and inserted one end of it in the opening so that it would slide under the sheet along the mattress toward Harry's body. I do not know how long it took him to slide that tube in a few inches. It may have been twenty minutes, it may have been forty. I never once saw the tube move. I knew it was going in because the visible part of it grew gradually shorter, but I doubted that the krait could have felt even the faintest vibration. Ganderbai himself was sweating now, large pearls of sweat standing out all over his forehead and along his upper lip. But his hands were steady and I noticed that his eyes were watching, not the tube in his hands, but the area of crumpled sheet above Harry's stomach.

Without looking up, he held out a hand to me for the chloroform. I twisted out the ground-glass stopper and put the bottle right into his hand, not letting go till I was sure he had a good hold on it. Then he jerked his head for me to come closer and he whispered, "Tell him I'm going to soak the mattress and that it will be very cold under his body. He must be ready for that and he must not move. Tell him now."

I bent over Harry and passed on the message.

"Why doesn't he get on with it?" Harry said.

"He's going to now, Harry. But it'll feel very cold, so be ready for it."

"Oh, God Almighty, get on!" For the first time he raised his voice, and Ganderbai glanced up sharply, watched him for a few seconds, then went back to his business.

Ganderbai poured a few drops of chloroform into the paper funnel and waited while it ran down the tube. Then he poured some more. Then he waited again, and the heavy sickening smell of chloroform spread out over the room bringing with it faint unpleasant memories of white-coated nurses and white surgeons standing in a white room around a long white table. Ganderbai was pouring steadily now and I could see the heavy vapor of the chloroform swirling slowly like smoke above the paper funnel. He paused, held the bottle up to the light, poured one more funnelful and handed the bottle back to me. Slowly he drew out the rubber tube from under the sheet; then he stood up.

The strain of inserting the tube and pouring the chloroform must have been great, and I recollect that when Ganderbai turned and whispered to me, his voice was small and tired. "We'll give it fifteen minutes. Just to be safe."

I leaned over to tell Harry. "We're going to give it fifteen minutes, just to be safe. But it's probably done for already."

"Then why for God's sake don't you look and see!" Again he spoke loudly and Ganderbai sprang round, his small brown face suddenly very angry. He had almost pure black eyes and he stared at Harry and Harry's smiling-muscle started to twitch. I took my handkerchief and wiped his wet face, trying to stroke his forehead a little for comfort as I did so.

Then we stood and waited beside the bed, Ganderbai watching Harry's face all the time in a curious intense manner. The little Indian was concentrating all his will power on keeping Harry quiet. He never once took his eyes from the patient and although he made no sound, he seemed somehow to be shouting at him all the time, saying: Now listen, you've got to listen, you're not going to go spoiling this now, d'you hear me; and Harry lay there twitching his mouth, sweating, closing his eyes, opening them, looking at me, at the sheet, at the ceiling, at me again, but never at Ganderbai. Yet somehow Ganderbai was holding him. The smell of chloroform was oppressive and it made me feel sick, but I couldn't leave the room now. I had the feeling someone was blowing up a huge balloon and I could see it was going to burst, but I couldn't look away.

At length Ganderbai turned and nodded and I knew he was ready to proceed. "You go over to the other side of the bed," he said. "We will each take one side of the sheet and draw it back together, but very slowly please, and very quietly."

"Keep still now, Harry," I said and I went around to the other side of the bed and took hold of the sheet. Ganderbai stood opposite me, and together we began to draw back the sheet, lifting it up clear of Harry's body, taking it back very slowly, both of us standing well away but at the same time bending forward, trying to peer underneath it. The smell of chloroform was awful. I remember trying to hold my breath and when I couldn't do that any longer I tried to breathe shallow so the stuff wouldn't get into my lungs.

The whole of Harry's chest was visible now, or rather the striped pajama top which covered it, and then I saw the white cord of his pajama trousers, neatly tied in a bow. A little farther and I saw a button, a mother-of-pearl button, and that was something I had never had on my pajamas, a fly button, let alone a mother-of-pearl one. This Harry, I thought, he is very refined. It is odd how one sometimes has frivolous thoughts at exciting moments, and I distinctly remember thinking about Harry being very refined when I saw that button.

Apart from the button there was nothing on his stomach.

We pulled the sheet back faster then, and when we had uncovered his legs and feet we let the sheet drop over the end of the bed onto the floor.

"Don't move," Ganderbai said, "don't move, Mr. Pope"; and he began to peer around along the side of Harry's body and under his legs.

"We must be careful," he said. "It may be anywhere. It could be up the leg of his pajamas."

When Ganderbai said this, Harry quickly raised his head from the pillow and looked down at his legs. It was the first time he had moved. Then suddenly he jumped up, stood on his bed and shook his legs one after the other violently in the air. At that moment we both thought he had been bitten and Ganderbai was already reaching down into his bag for a scalpel and a tourniquet when Harry ceased his caperings and stood still and looked at the mattress he was standing on and shouted, "It's not there!"

Ganderbai straightened up and for a moment he too looked at the mattress; then he looked up at Harry. Harry was all right. He hadn't been bitten and now he wasn't going to get bitten and he wasn't going to be killed and everything was fine. But that didn't seem to make anyone feel any better.

"Mr. Pope, you are of course *quite* sure you saw it in the first place?" There was a note of sarcasm in Ganderbai's voice that he would never have employed in ordinary circumstances. "You don't think you might possibly have been dreaming, do you, Mr. Pope?" The way Ganderbai was looking at Harry, I realized that the sarcasm was not seriously intended. He was only easing up a bit after the strain.

Harry stood on his bed in his striped pajamas, glaring at Ganderbai, and the color began to spread out over his cheeks.

"Are you telling me I'm a liar?" he shouted.

Ganderbai remained absolutely still, watching Harry. Harry took a pace forward on the bed and there was a shining look in his eyes.

"Why, you dirty little Hindu sewer rat!"

"Shut up, Harry!" I said.

"You dirty black—"

"Harry!" I called. "Shut up, Harry!" It was terrible, the things he was saying.

Ganderbai went out of the room as though neither of us was there and I followed him and put my arm around his shoulder as he walked across the hall and out onto the balcony.

"Don't you listen to Harry," I said. "This thing's made him so he doesn't know what he's saying."

We went down the steps from the balcony to the drive and across the drive in the darkness to where his old Morris car was parked. He opened the door and got in.

"You did a wonderful job," I said. "Thank you so very much for coming."

"All he needs is a good holiday," he said quietly, without looking at me, then he started the engine and drove off.

FOR DISCUSSION

1. At what point in the story did you begin to suspect that there was no snake?

2. Timber remarks, "He hadn't been bitten and now he wasn't going to get bitten and he wasn't going to be killed and everything was fine. But that didn't seem to make anyone feel any better." Explain why there still seems to be tension among the three men.

3. Dr. Ganderbai did everything in his power to help Harry through his crisis. Ganderbai even risked his own life. In view of these circumstances, why did Harry insult his benefactor?

Emotions may severely limit our senses, causing us to see only those things for which we are looking.

PHONE CALL

BERTON ROUECHÉ

I GOT OUT of the truck and got down on my knees and twisted my neck and looked underneath. Everything looked O.K. There wasn't anything hanging down or anything. I got up and opened the hood and looked at the engine. I don't know too much about engines—only what I picked up working around Lindy's Service Station the summer before last. But the engine looked O.K., too. I slammed down the hood and lighted a cigarette. It really had me beat. A school bus from that convent over in Sag Harbor came piling around the bend, and all the girls leaned out the windows and yelled. I just waved. They didn't mean anything by it—just a bunch of kids going home. The bus went on up the road and into the woods and out of sight. I got back in the truck and started it up again. It sounded fine. I put it in gear and let out the clutch and gave it the gas, and nothing happened. It just sat there. So it was probably the transmission. I shut it off and got out. There was nothing to do but call the store. I still had three or four deliveries that had to be made, and it was getting kind of late. I knew what Mr. Lester would say, but this was one time when he couldn't blame me. It wasn't my fault. It was him himself that told me to take this truck.

There was a house just up the road—a big white house at the edge of the woods, with a white Rambler station wagon standing in the drive. I dropped my cigarette in a pothole puddle and started up the road, and stopped. A dog was laying there in the grass beside the station wagon. It put up its head and—oh, man! it was one of those German police dogs. I turned around and headed the other way. There was another house back there around the bend. I remembered passing it. I went by the truck and walked down the road and around the bend, and the house was there. It was a brown shingle house with red shutters, and there was a sign in one of the windows: "Piano Lessons." The name on the mailbox was Timothy. I couldn't tell if there was anybody home or not. There wasn't any car around, but there was a garage at the end of the drive, and it could be parked in there. I went up the drive and around to the kitchen door, and when I got close, I could hear a radio talking and laughing inside. I knocked on the door.

The radio went off. Then the door opened a crack and a woman looked out. She had bright blonde hair and little black eyes, and she was forty years old at least. "Yes?" she said.

"Mrs. Timothy?" I said. "I work for the market over in Bridgehampton, Mrs. Timothy, and my truck—"

"How do you know my name?" she said.

"What?" I said. "Why—it's on the mailbox. I just read it on the mailbox."

"Oh," she said. She licked her lips. "And you say you work for a market?"

"That's right," I said. "The market over in Bridgehampton. And my truck's broke down. So I wondered—"

"What market?" she said.

"Why, Lester's Market," I said. "You know—over in Bridgehampton?"

"I see," she said.

"That's right," I said. "And my truck's broke down. I wondered could I use your phone to call the store and tell them?"

"Well," she said. She looked at me for about a minute. Then she stepped back and opened the door. She had on a pink sweater and one of those big, wide skirts with big, wide pockets, and she was nothing but skin and bones. "The telephone's in the living room. I'll show you."

I followed her through the kitchen and across a hall into the living room. I guess that was where she gave her music lessons,

too. There was a piano there against the wall and a music stand and a couple of folding chairs, and on top of the piano was a clarinet and one of those metronomes[1] and a big pile of sheet music. The telephone was on a desk between the windows.

"I don't suppose you need the book?" Mrs. Timothy said.

"What?" I said.

"The telephone book," she said. "You know the number of your store, I hope?"

"Oh, sure," I said.

"Very well," she said. She reached up and straightened the "Piano Lessons" sign in the window. "Then go ahead and make your—"

She turned around, and she had the funniest look on her face. I mean, it was real strange. It was like she was scared or something.

"I thought you said you had a truck?" she said. "I don't see any truck out there."

"My truck?" I said. "Oh, it's up around the bend. That's where it broke down. You can't see it from here."

"I see," she said, and looked at me. She still had that funny look on her face. Even her voice sounded funny. "I'm here alone, but I want you to know something," she said. "I don't live alone. I'm married. I've got a husband, and he'll be home any minute. He gets off work early today." She came away from the window. "So my advice to you is to make your call just as quickly as you can."

"O.K.," I said, but I didn't get it. I watched her go across the room and through the hall to the kitchen. I didn't get it at all. She acted almost like I'd done something. I heard a car on the road and

looked out. I thought maybe it might be her husband, but it was only some guys in a beat-up '59 Impala. But so what if it was her husband? I mean, man—she really had me going. I turned back to the desk and picked up the phone. A woman's voice said, "But, of course, I never let on. I simply—"

I put down the phone and lighted a cigarette, and wandered down the room. I stopped at the piano and looked at the pile of sheet music. They were none of them songs I ever heard of. I looked around for an ashtray, and I found a big white clamshell. It looked like they used it for that. It was on a little table next to an easy chair. Then I went back and tried the phone again. The woman was still talking. I listened for a moment, but it sounded like she was still going strong. I was beginning to get kind of worried. I looked at my watch. It was already almost four o'clock. I went over to the clamshell and punched out my cigarette, but I guess I was in too big of a hurry. I punched too hard or something, and the clamshell flipped off the table. I made a grab, but I only touched it, and it skidded across the rug. I squatted down and picked it up, and, thank God, it wasn't broken. I must have broke its fall. It wasn't even cracked.

I heard Mrs. Timothy coming. The cigarette butt had rolled under the chair, and I brushed the ashes after it. Mrs. Timothy came through the door, and stopped. Her mouth fell open.

"It's O.K.," I said. "It didn't even—"

"What were you doing in that table drawer?" she said.

"What?" I said.

---

[1] METRONOMES: devices to mark time at a steady beat.

Continued on page 41

IDEAS AND THE ARTS

A feeling of suspense comes from not knowing what to expect. We can be in situations or circumstances that create suspense because the outcome is unknown. Similarly, a movie, a book, or a short story can be suspenseful. Even if the outcome is known in advance (the hero always wins), there may still be elements of suspense present. It is the manner or the method of the presentation which then creates the mystery or tension, rather than the known outcome.

The subjects of the first painting in this group were certainly well known, but it is the treatment of the artist which adds suspense and tension to the familiar. The painting is *Madonna of the Rocks,* by Leonardo da Vinci. There are obviously some relationships understood or portrayed between the woman, the two young children, and the young man at the right. A kind of tension is created by the actions of the figures, and certainly by the looming landscape in the background. The woman, as the people of Leonardo's time would have known, is the Virgin Mary, whose left hand is raised above the infant Jesus. He in turn is blessing the other child, St. John the Baptist. The young man who is pointing at St. John to indicate that he is the one who will prepare the way for Christ is actually an angel. The threatening rocks in the background foreshadow the crucifixion of Christ. Like other elements in the painting, they contribute to a well-known story aspects of tension and eventual tragedy.

The subject of the next painting, *The Temptation of St. Anthony* by Matthias Grünewald, was also familiar to its early viewers. St. Anthony was one of the first Christian hermits. He lived in the Egyptian desert and devoted his long life to fasting and holiness. Among the legends about St. Anthony was that he was tempted by devils to give up his faith in Christianity. But everyone knew the devils had failed. Therefore the artist makes the devils unspeakably horrible and frightening. He shows the saint almost completely at their mercy. By creating horrible and convincing devils, he makes it seem all the more impossible for the saint to resist them. And thus the artist adds suspense and conflict to an old legend.

On the other hand the entire atmosphere of Winslow Homer's painting, *Life Line,* might be said to be suspenseful. Shipping and sailing one hundred years ago could be very dangerous occupations. Today, when all kinds of electronic aids exist to assure the safety of shipping, it is easy to forget the element of danger that in Homer's time was often present. There were only lighthouses and unreliable charts—no weather information and, of course, no radio or radar. As a consequence, wrecks on uncharted reefs and rocks were far more common. This picture was painted only a few years after a lifesaving service had been established on the New England coast. A life line was shot from the station to the ship in distress. In the painting some of the ship's sails are shown at the left. On the right is the rocky coast and the lifesaving station. The whole rescue operation was extremely dangerous because the ship might easily change its position and plunge rescuer and rescued into the ocean. Suspense is present in the very subject of the painting.

Jan Vermeer's *The Letter* portrays a different kind of suspense, one that is domestic and not uncommon. The young lady playing a lute has been brought a letter by a servant. The servant has come from her laundry work, and stands by her mistress with what looks like a comforting

33

expression on her face. But what does the lady's look mean? Is it one of anxiety, surprise, suffering, even of despair? The unanswered questions bring a certain tension to the observer of this scene. In Homer's picture at least we can predict a happy ending to the suspense. Vermeer gives us no such security.

The next painting, *The Sleeping Gypsy* by Henri Rousseau, is in a style known as "primitive." Although the artist had no formal training, his talent and excellence as a painter are considerable. The scene of Rousseau's painting is a desert. Since there is a lion in the picture, this could be the Sahara Desert in Africa. The sleeping figure could be a nomad or wandering tribesman. He has been drinking some wine and playing his lute under the desert moon, and then has fallen asleep. Sniffing at him is the lion. Perhaps if he moves, the lion will attack. There is no way of knowing or even guessing what will happen. The lion may even go away, although the dark colors suggest the worst. Rousseau has left his painting full of unresolved suspense.

René Magritte's *Castle of the Pyrenees* is still a different style of painting known as "surrealistic," as Rousseau's is primitive. Surrealistic literally means "beyond realistic." Objects or scenes may be recognizable, but they are portrayed unlike anything seen in the real world. The appearance of things is altered to reveal emotions or attitudes. If you cover the lower half of Magritte's painting, the upper half is simply a picture of a castle on a very steep and rocky mountaintop. Covering the upper half shows a huge rock falling into the sea. When seen as a whole, each half of the picture denies the possibility of the other half. Rocks can fall into the sea, and castles can be built on rocks, but——. This is tension or suspense based upon a contradiction of logic and reason, and it is a contradiction that cannot be resolved.

Morse Peckham

LEONARDO DA VINCI (1452-1519) *MADONNA OF THE ROCKS*. Musée du Louvre.

MATTHIAS GRÜNEWALD (c. 1480-1528) *THE TEMPTATION OF ST. ANTHONY.* Musée d'Unterlinden, Colmar, France.

WINSLOW HOMER (1836-1910) *LIFE LINE.* Philadelphia Museum of Art.

JAN VERMEER (1632-1675) *THE LETTER*. Rijksmuseum, Amsterdam.

HENRI ROUSSEAU (1844-1910) *THE SLEEPING GYPSY.* Museum of Modern Art, New York.

RENÉ MAGRITTE (1898-1967) *CASTLE OF THE PYRENEES.* Collection of Harry Torczyner, New York.

"I said what were you doing in that table drawer?" she said.

I shook my head. "Nothing," I said. "What drawer? I mean, I wasn't doing anything in any drawer. I just accidentally dropped this ashtray. I dropped it, and I was just picking it up."

Mrs. Timothy didn't say anything. She just stood there and looked at me. Then she cleared her throat. "Well," she said. "Did you make your call?"

"Not yet," I said. "The line was busy."

"Oh?" she said. "And how do you know that? I didn't hear you dial or even say a word."

"I don't mean the store," I said. "I mean the party line. It was your line was busy."

She gave me one of those looks. Something sure was eating her. She walked over to the desk and picked up the phone and listened. Then she held it out. I could hear the buzz of the empty line. She put down the phone. "I suppose they just this minute hung up," she said. "Is that what I'm supposed to believe?"

"There was somebody talking before," I said. "I tried it twice."

"I don't know what you have in mind, but I advise you to forget it," she said. "I'm not that easily fooled. I'm really not as

41

stupid as you seem to think. I know what's going on these days. I read the papers, you know. I hear the news, and I've heard about boys like you. I know all about them. I didn't want to let you in. I only did it against my better judgment. I had a feeling about you the minute I opened the door." She stood back against the desk. "I don't believe you had a breakdown. I don't believe it for a minute. If you broke down where you say you did, you were practically in front of the Millers', so that's where you would have gone to phone. You wouldn't have come all the way down here. I don't think you even *have* a truck. I think you came through the woods." She took a deep breath. "And now I want you to leave. I want you to get out of my house."

"I don't know what you're talking about, Mrs. Timothy," I said. "I just want to call the store. I've *got* to call the store."

"I said get out of my house," she said.

"O.K.," I said. "O.K., but—"

"I said get out," she said. She reached in one of the pockets of her big skirt and brought out a knife. It was a kitchen knife, with a long blade honed down thin. She pointed it at me like a gun.

"Hey!" I said.

"Oh, I see," she said. "That changes things. It's a different story now, isn't it? You didn't know I could take care of myself, did you? That never occurred to you." She came away from the desk. "You thought I was just another helpless woman, didn't you?"

I stepped back a couple of steps.

"Hey," I said. "Wait a minute."

"What's the matter?" she said. "You're not afraid of me, are you?" She moved the knife. "A big, strong, tough boy like you?"

I stepped back again.

"Hey," I said. "For God's sake, what do you—"

"You *are* a big, strong, tough boy," she said. "Aren't you?"

"For God's sake, Mrs. Timothy," I said. "I don't know what you're talking about. I wasn't doing anything."

She kind of smiled. "A great, big, strong, tough boy," she said.

I didn't say anything. The way she was looking at me, I couldn't hardly think, I couldn't hardly even believe it. It was like it was all a dream. I took another step, and stumbled into one of the folding chairs. Then I was up against the piano. I looked at that knife coming at me and my heart began to jump. She meant it. She really meant it, but that didn't mean I had to just stand there and let her. I slid along the front of the piano and reached up and touched the metronome and pushed it away and stretched and found the clarinet and grabbed it.

She let out a kind of yell. "Don't you dare!" she said. "You put that down!" She raised the knife. "Put that clarinet down."

But I had a good grip on it now. I looked at that knife with the point coming at me, and swung. I swung at it as hard as I could. I felt it connect, it tingled all the way up my arm. The knife went sailing across the room and I heard it hit the wall. Mrs. Timothy didn't move. She just stood there, and she was holding her wrist. It wasn't bleeding or anything, but it looked kind of funny and loose. Then she began to scream.

FOR DISCUSSION

1. From the moment that Mrs. Timothy opens her screen door, it is obvious that she is looking for something. Does she find the thing for which she is looking? Explain your answer.

2. Point out statements made by Mrs. Timothy that show how her sight was limited by her emotions. What emotions or inner drives seem to be guiding her perceptions and her resulting actions?

3. Why do you think that the boy attacks Mrs. Timothy at the end of story? Describe the boy as clearly as you can through the things he says, things said about him, and things he has done so far in the story. Is his final act the kind of behavior you would consider typical of the boy as you have come to know him? If not, how do you account for his action?

In German folklore an Erl-King was an evil goblin who wandered through the forests in search of children.

THE ERL-KING

JOHANN WOLFGANG VON GOETHE

Who rides so late in a night so wild?
A father is riding with his child.
He clasps the boy close in his arm;
He holds him tightly, he keeps him warm.

"My son, you are trembling. What do you fear?"   5
"Look, father, the Erl-King! He's coming near!
With his crown and his shroud!* Yes, that is he!"
"My son, it's only the mist you see."

"O lovely child, oh, come with me,
Such games we'll play! So glad we'll be!   10
Such flowers to pick! Such sights to behold!
My mother will make you clothes of gold!"

---

7 SHROUD: a burial garment; a veil.

"O father, my father, did you not hear
The Erl-King whispering in my ear?"
"Lie still, my child, lie quietly.   15
It's only the wind in the leaves of the tree."

"Dear boy, if you will come away,
My daughters will wait on you every day;
They'll give you the prettiest presents to keep;
They'll dance when you wake and they'll sing you asleep." 20

"My father! My father! Do you not see
The Erl-King's pale daughters waiting for me?"
"My son, my son, I see what you say—
The willow is waving its branches of gray."

"I love you—so come without fear or remorse.*   25
And if you're not willing, I'll take you by force!"
"My father! My father! Tighten your hold!
The Erl-King has caught me—his fingers are cold!"

The father shudders. He spurs on his steed.
He carries the child with desperate speed.   30
He reaches the courtyard, and looks down with dread.
There in his arms the boy lies dead.

25 REMORSE: bitter regret.

FOR DISCUSSION

1. How many voices do you hear in the poem and to whom do these voices belong? What changes are there in the sound of the poetry when different characters speak?

2. How many people in the poem can see the Erl-King? How do you know this?

3. Goethe uses the traditional concept of the Erl-King, but he also embroiders it with ideas of his own. What else might the Erl-King in this poem represent?

Suppose someone offered you a magic charm that would grant you three wishes.
Would you accept it?

THE MONKEY'S PAW

W. W. JACOBS

I

WITHOUT, the night was cold and wet; but in the small parlor of Laburnam Villa the blinds were drawn and the fire burned brightly. Father and son were at chess, the former, who possessed ideas about the game involving radical chances, putting his king into such sharp and unnecessary perils that it even provoked comment from the white-haired old lady knitting placidly by the fire.

"Hark at the wind," said Mr. White, who, having seen a fatal mistake after it was too late, was amiably desirous of preventing his son from seeing it.

"I'm listening," said the latter, grimly surveying the board as he stretched out his hand. "Check."

"I should hardly think that he'd come tonight," said his father, with his hand poised over the board.

"Mate," replied the son.

"That's the worst of living so far out," bawled Mr. White, with sudden and un-looked-for violence; "of all the beastly, slushy, out-of-the-way places to live in, this is the worst. Pathway's a bog, and the road's a torrent. I don't know what people are thinking about. I suppose because only two houses in the road are let, they think it doesn't matter."

"Never mind, dear," said his wife soothingly; "perhaps you'll win the next one."

Mr. White looked up sharply, just in time to intercept a knowing glance between mother and son. The words died away on his lips, and he hid a guilty grin in his thin gray beard.

"There he is," said Herbert White, as the gate banged to loudly and heavy footsteps came toward the door.

The old man rose with hospitable haste, and opening the door, was heard condoling[1] with the new arrival. The new arrival also condoled with himself, so that Mrs. White said, "Tut, tut!" and coughed gently as her husband entered the room, followed by a tall, burly man, beady of eye and rubicund of visage.[2]

"Sergeant Major Morris," he said, introducing him.

The sergeant major shook hands, and taking the proffered seat by the fire, watched contentedly while his host got out whiskey and tumblers and stood a small copper kettle on the fire.

At the third glass his eyes got brighter, and he began to talk, the little family circle regarding with eager interest this visitor from distant parts, as he squared his broad shoulders in the chair and spoke of wild

"The Monkey's Paw" reprinted by permission of Dodd, Mead & Company, Inc., from *The Lady of the Barge* by W. W. Jacobs.

[1] CONDOLING: expressing sympathy.
[2] RUBICUND OF VISAGE: rosy of face.

scenes and doughty[1] deeds; of wars and plagues and strange peoples.

"Twenty-one years of it," said Mr. White, nodding at his wife and son. "When he went away, he was a slip of a youth in the warehouse. Now look at him."

"He don't look to have taken much harm," said Mrs. White politely.

"I'd like to go to India myself," said the old man, "just to look round a bit, you know."

"Better where you are," said the sergeant major, shaking his head. He put down the empty glass, and sighing softly, shook it again.

"I should like to see those old temples and fakirs[2] and jugglers," said the old man. "What was that you started telling me the other day about a monkey's paw or something, Morris?"

"Nothing," said the soldier hastily. "Leastways nothing worth hearing."

"Monkey's paw?" said Mrs. White curiously.

"Well, it's just a bit of what you might call magic, perhaps," said the sergeant major offhandedly.

His three listeners leaned forward eagerly. The visitor absent-mindedly put his empty glass to his lips and then set it down again. His host filled it for him.

"To look at," said the sergeant major, fumbling in his pocket, "it's just an ordinary little paw, dried to a mummy."

He took something out of his pocket and proffered it. Mrs. White drew back with a grimace, but her son, taking it, examined it curiously.

"And what is there special about it?" inquired Mr. White as he took it from his son, and having examined it, placed it upon the table.

"It had a spell put on it by an old fakir," said the sergeant major, "a very holy man. He wanted to show that fate ruled people's lives and that those who interfered with it did so to their sorrow. He put a spell on it so that three separate men could each have three wishes from it."

His manner was so impressive that his hearers were conscious that their light laughter jarred somewhat.

"Well, why don't you have three, sir?" said Herbert White cleverly.

The soldier regarded him in the way that middle age is wont to regard presumptuous youth. "I have," he said quietly, and his blotchy face whitened.

"And did you really have the three wishes granted?" asked Mrs. White.

"I did," said the sergeant major, and his glass tapped against his strong teeth.

"And has anybody else wished?" persisted the old lady.

"The first man had his three wishes, yes," was the reply; "I don't know what the first two were, but the third was for death. That's how I got the paw."

His tones were so grave that a hush fell upon the group.

"If you've had your three wishes, it's no good to you now, then, Morris," said the old man at last. "What do you keep it for?"

The soldier shook his head. "Fancy, I suppose," he said slowly. "I did have some idea of selling it, but I don't think I will. It has caused enough mischief already. Besides, people won't buy. They think it's a fairy tale, some of them; and those who do think anything of it want to try it first and pay me afterward."

---

[1] DOUGHTY: courageous.
[2] FAKIRS: magicians.

"If you could have another three wishes," said the old man, eyeing him keenly, "would you have them?"

"I don't know," said the other. "I don't know."

He took the paw, and dangling it between his forefinger and thumb, suddenly threw it upon the fire. White, with a slight cry, stooped down and snatched it off.

"Better let it burn," said the soldier solemnly.

"If you don't want it, Morris," said the other, "give it to me."

"I won't," said his friend doggedly. "I threw it on the fire. If you keep it, don't blame me for what happens. Pitch it on the fire again like a sensible man."

The other shook his head and examined his new possession closely. "How do you do it?" he inquired.

"Hold it up in your right hand and wish aloud," said the sergeant major, "but I warn you of the consequences."

"Sounds like the *Arabian Nights*," said Mrs. White, as she rose and began to set the supper. "Don't you think you might wish for four pairs of hands for me?"

Her husband drew the talisman[1] from his pocket, and then all three burst into laughter as the sergeant major, with a look of alarm on his face, caught him by the arm.

"If you must wish," he said gruffly, "wish for something sensible."

Mr. White dropped it back in his pocket, and placing chairs, motioned his friend to the table. In the business of supper the talisman was partly forgotten, and afterward the three sat listening in an enthralled fashion to a second installment of the soldier's adventures in India.

"If the tale about the monkey's paw is not more truthful than those he has been telling us," said Herbert, as the door closed behind their guest just in time for him to catch the last train, "we shan't make much out of it."

"Did you give him anything for it, Father?" inquired Mrs. White, regarding her husband closely.

"A trifle," said he, coloring slightly. "He didn't want it, but I made him take it. And he pressed me again to throw it away."

"Likely," said Herbert with pretended horror. "Why, we're going to be rich and famous and happy. Wish to be an emperor, Father, to begin with; then you can't be henpecked."

He darted round the table, pursued by the maligned[2] Mrs. White armed with an antimacassar.[3]

Mr. White took the paw from his pocket and eyed it dubiously. "I don't know what to wish for, and that's a fact," he said slowly. "It seems to me I've got all I want."

"If you only cleared the house, you'd be quite happy, wouldn't you?" said Herbert, with his hand on his father's shoulder. "Well, wish for two hundred pounds, then; that'll just do it."

His father, smiling shamefacedly at his own credulity,[4] held up the talisman as his son, with a solemn face, somewhat marred by a wink at his mother, sat down at the piano and struck a few impressive chords.

"I wish for two hundred pounds," said the old man distinctly.

---

[1] TALISMAN: magical charm.

[2] MALIGNED: injured; slandered; (*here,* used jokingly).

[3] ANTIMACASSAR: protective covering for backs of chairs and sofas.

[4] CREDULITY: willingness to believe unproved statements.

A fine crash from the piano greeted the words, interrupted by a shuddering cry from the old man. His wife and son ran toward him.

"It moved," he cried, with a glance of disgust at the object as it lay on the floor. "As I wished, it twisted in my hand like a snake."

"Well, I don't see the money," said his son as he picked it up and placed it on the table, "and I bet I never shall."

"It must have been your fancy, Father," said his wife, regarding him anxiously.

He shook his head. "Never mind, though; there's no harm, but it gave me a shock all the same."

They sat down by the fire again while the two men finished their pipes. Outside, the wind was higher than ever, and the old man started nervously at the sound of a door banging upstairs. A silence unusual and depressing settled upon all three, which lasted until the old couple rose to retire for the night.

"I expect you'll find the cash tied up in a big bag in the middle of your bed," said Herbert, as he bade them good night, "and something horrible squatting up on top of the wardrobe watching you as you pocket your ill-gotten gains."

He sat alone in the darkness, gazing at the dying fire and seeing faces in it. The last face was so horrible and so simian[1] that he gazed at it in amazement. It got so vivid that, with a little uneasy laugh, he felt on the table for a glass containing a little water to throw over it. His hand grasped the monkey's paw, and with a little shiver he wiped his hand on his coat and went up to bed.

---

[1] SIMIAN: resembling an ape or monkey.

II

In the brightness of the wintry sun next morning as it streamed over the breakfast table he laughed at his fears. There was an air of prosaic wholesomeness about the room which it had lacked on the previous night, and the dirty, shriveled little paw was pitched on the sideboard with a carelessness which betokened no great belief in its virtues.

"I suppose all old soldiers are the same," said Mrs. White. "The idea of our listening to such nonsense! How could wishes be granted in these days? And if they could, how could two hundred pounds hurt you, Father?"

"Might drop on his head from the sky," said the frivolous Herbert.

"Morris said the things happened so naturally," said his father, "that you might if you so wished attribute it to coincidence."

"Well, don't break into the money before I come back," said Herbert, as he rose from the table. "I'm afraid it'll turn you into a mean, avaricious[2] man, and we shall have to disown you."

His mother laughed, and following him to the door, watched him down the road; and returning to the breakfast table, was very happy at the expense of her husband's credulity. All of which did not prevent her from scurrying to the door at the postman's knock, nor prevent her from referring somewhat shortly to retired sergeants major of bibulous[3] habits when she found that the post brought a tailor's bill.

"Herbert will have some more of his funny remarks, I expect, when he comes home," she said as they sat at dinner.

---

[2] AVARICIOUS: greedy for money.
[3] BIBULOUS: given to social drinking.

"I dare say," said Mr. White, pouring himself out some beer; "but for all that, the thing moved in my hand; that I'll swear to."

"You thought it did," said the old lady soothingly.

"I say it did," replied the other. "There was no thought about it; I had just— What's the matter?"

His wife made no reply. She was watching the mysterious movements of a man outside, who, peering in an undecided fashion at the house, appeared to be trying to make up his mind to enter. In mental connection with the two hundred pounds, she noticed that the stranger was well dressed and wore a silk hat of glossy newness. Three times he paused at the gate, and then walked on again. The fourth time he stood with his hand upon it, and then with sudden resolution flung it open and walked up the path. Mrs. White at the same moment placed her hands behind her, and hurriedly unfastening the strings of her apron, put that article of apparel beneath the cushion of her chair.

She brought the stranger, who seemed ill at ease, into the room. He gazed at her furtively and listened in a preoccupied fashion as the old lady apologized for the appearance of the room, and her husband's coat, a garment which he usually reserved for the garden. She then waited as patiently as her sex would permit, for him to broach his business, but he was at first strangely silent.

"I—was asked to call," he said at last, and stooped and picked a piece of cotton from his trousers. "I come from Maw and Meggins."

The old lady started. "Is anything the matter?" she asked breathlessly. "Has any-thing happened to Herbert? What is it? What is it?"

Her husband interposed. "There, there, Mother," he said. "Sit down, and don't jump to conclusions. You've not brought bad news, I'm sure, sir"; and he eyed the other wistfully.

"I'm sorry—," began the visitor.

"Is he hurt?" demanded the mother wildly.

The visitor bowed in assent. "Badly hurt," he said quietly, "but he is not in any pain."

"Oh, thank God!" said the old woman, clasping her hands. "Thank God for that! Thank—"

She broke off suddenly as the sinister meaning of the assurance dawned upon her and she saw the awful confirmation of her fears in the other's averted face. She caught her breath, and turning to her slower-witted husband, laid her trembling old hand upon his. There was a long silence.

"He was caught in the machinery," said the visitor at length in a low voice.

"Caught in the machinery," repeated Mr. White in a dazed fashion, "yes."

He sat staring blankly out at the window, and taking his wife's hand between his own, pressed it, as he had been wont to do in their old courting days nearly forty years before.

"He was the only one left to us," he said, turning gently to the visitor. "It is hard."

The other coughed, and rising, walked slowly to the window. "The firm wished me to convey their sincere sympathy with you in your great loss," he said, without looking round. "I beg that you will understand I am only their servant and merely obeying orders."

There was no reply; the old woman's face was white, her eyes staring, and her breath inaudible; on the husband's face was a look such as his friend the sergeant might have carried into his first action.

"I was to say that Maw and Meggins disclaim all responsibility," continued the other. "They admit no liability at all; but in consideration of your son's services, they wish to present you with a certain sum as compensation."

Mr. White dropped his wife's hand, and rising to his feet, gazed with a look of horror at his visitor. His dry lips shaped the words, "How much?"

"Two hundred pounds," was the answer.

Unconscious of his wife's shriek, the old man smiled faintly, put out his hands like a sightless man, and dropped, a senseless heap, to the floor.

III

In the huge new cemetery, some two miles distant, the old people buried their dead, and came back to a house steeped in shadow and silence. It was all over so quickly that at first they could hardly realize it and remained in a state of expectation as though of something else to happen—something else which was to lighten this load, too heavy for old hearts to bear.

But the days passed, and expectation gave place to resignation[1]—the hopeless resignation of the old, sometimes miscalled apathy.[2] Sometimes they hardly exchanged a word, for now they had nothing to talk about, and their days were long to weariness.

It was about a week after that the old man, waking suddenly in the night, stretched out his hand and found himself alone. The room was in darkness, and the sound of subdued weeping came from the window. He raised himself in bed and listened.

"Come back," he said tenderly. "You will be cold."

"It is colder for my son," said the old woman, and wept afresh.

The sound of her sobs died away on his ears. The bed was warm, and his eyes heavy with sleep. He dozed fitfully and then slept until a sudden wild cry from his wife awoke him with a start.

"*The paw!*" she cried wildly. "The monkey's paw!"

He started up in alarm. "Where? Where is it? What's the matter?"

She came stumbling across the room toward him. "I want it," she said quietly. "You've not destroyed it?"

"It's in the parlor, on the bracket," he replied, marveling. "Why?"

She cried and laughed together, and bending over, kissed his cheek.

"I only just thought of it," she said hysterically. "Why didn't I think of it before? Why didn't *you* think of it?"

"Think of what?" he questioned.

"The other two wishes," she replied rapidly. "We've only had one."

"Was not that enough?" he demanded fiercely.

"No," she cried triumphantly; "we'll have one more. Go down and get it quickly, and wish our boy alive again."

The man sat up in bed and flung the bedclothes from his quaking limbs. "Good God, you are mad!" he cried, aghast.

"Get it," she panted; "get it quickly, and wish—Oh, my boy, my boy!"

---

[1] RESIGNATION: unresisting acceptance.
[2] APATHY: lack of interest; indifference.

Her husband struck a match and lit the candle. "Get back to bed," he said unsteadily. "You don't know what you are saying."

"We had the first wish granted," said the old woman feverishly; "why not the second?"

"A coincidence," stammered the old man.

"Go and get it and wish," cried his wife, quivering with excitement.

The old man turned and regarded her, and his voice shook. "He has been dead ten days, and besides he—I would not tell you else, but—I could only recognize him by his clothing. If he was too terrible for you to see then, how now?"

"Bring him back," cried the old woman and dragged him toward the door. "Do you think I fear the child I have nursed?"

He went down in the darkness and felt his way to the parlor and then to the mantelpiece. The talisman was in its place, and a horrible fear that the unspoken wish might bring his mutilated son before him ere he could escape from the room seized upon him, and he caught his breath as he found that he had lost the direction of the door. His brow cold with sweat, he felt his way round the table and groped along the wall until he found himself in the small passage with the unwholesome thing in his hand.

Even his wife's face seemed changed as he entered the room. It was white and expectant and to his fears seemed to have an unnatural look upon it. He was afraid of her.

"*Wish!*" she cried in a strong voice.

"It is foolish and wicked," he faltered.

"*Wish!*" repeated his wife.

He raised his hand. "I wish my son alive again."

The talisman fell to the floor, and he regarded it fearfully. Then he sank trembling into a chair as the old woman, with burning eyes, walked to the window and raised the blind.

He sat until he was chilled with the cold, glancing occasionally at the figure of the old woman peering through the window. The candle end, which had burned below the rim of the china candlestick, was throwing pulsating shadows on the ceilings and walls, until, with a flicker larger than the rest, it expired. The old man, with an unspeakable sense of relief at the failure of the talisman, crept back to his bed, and a minute or two afterward the old woman came silently and apathetically beside him.

Neither spoke but lay silently listening to the ticking of the clock. A stair creaked, and a squeaky mouse scurried noisily through the wall. The darkness was oppressive, and after lying for some time screwing up his courage, he took the box of matches, and striking one, went downstairs for a candle.

At the foot of the stairs the match went out, and he paused to strike another; and at the same moment a knock, so quiet and stealthy as to be scarcely audible, sounded on the front door.

The matches fell from his hand and spilled in the passage. He stood motionless, his breath suspended until the knock was repeated. Then he turned and fled swiftly back to his room and closed the door behind him. A third knock sounded through the house.

"*What's that?*" cried the old woman, starting up.

"A rat," said the old man in shaking tones—"A rat. It passed me on the stairs."

His wife sat up in bed listening. A loud knock resounded through the house.

"It's Herbert!" she screamed. "It's

Herbert!"

She ran to the door, but her husband was before her, and catching her by the arm, held her tightly.

"What are you going to do?" he whispered hoarsely.

"It's my boy; it's Herbert!" she cried, struggling mechanically. "I forgot it was two miles away. What are you holding me for? Let go. I must open the door."

"For God's sake don't let it in," cried the old man, trembling.

"You're afraid of your own son," she cried, struggling. "Let me go. I'm coming, Herbert; I'm coming."

There was another knock, and another. The old woman with a sudden wrench broke free and ran from the room. Her husband followed to the landing and called after her appealingly as she hurried downstairs. He heard the chain rattle back and the bottom bolt drawn slowly and stiffly from the socket. Then the old woman's voice, strained and panting.

"The bolt," she cried loudly. "Come down. I can't reach it."

But her husband was on his hands and knees groping wildly on the floor in search of the paw. If he could only find it before the thing outside got in. A perfect fusillade[1] of knocks reverberated through the house, and he heard the scraping of a chair as his wife put it down in the passage against the door. He heard the creaking of the bolt as it came slowly back, and at the same moment he found the monkey's paw and frantically breathed his third and last wish.

The knocking ceased suddenly, although the echoes of it were still in the house. He heard the chair drawn back, and the door opened. A cold wind rushed up the staircase, and a long loud wail of disappointment and misery from his wife gave him courage to run down to her side and then to the gate beyond. The street lamp flickering opposite shone on a quiet and deserted road.

[1] FUSILLADE: series of sharp sounds like gunfire.

FOR DISCUSSION

1. Account for the "fusillade of knocks" which "reverberated through the house."

2. What clues does the author give that suggest Mr. White will not be pleased with the outcome of his wishes?

3. What was the fakir's purpose in putting the charm on the paw? Is that purpose important in relation to the story as a whole? Explain your answer.

His head ached, his nose bled, and he was so tired he could hardly stand.
Still Jerry dove into the wild bay.

THROUGH THE TUNNEL
DORIS LESSING

GOING TO THE SHORE on the first morning of the vacation, the young English boy stopped at a turning of the path and looked down at a wild and rocky bay, and then over to the crowded beach he knew so well from other years. His mother walked on in front of him, carrying a bright striped bag in one hand. Her other arm, swinging loose, was very white in the sun. The boy watched that white, naked arm, and turned his eyes, which had a frown behind them, toward the bay and back again to his mother. When she felt he was not with her, she swung around. "Oh, there you are, Jerry!" she said. She looked impatient, then smiled. "Why, darling, would you rather not come with me? Would you rather—" She frowned, conscientiously worrying over what amusements he might secretly be longing for, which she had been too busy or too careless to imagine. He was very familiar with that anxious, apologetic smile. Contrition[1] sent him running after her. And yet, as he ran, he looked back over his shoulder at the wild bay; and all morning, as he played on the safe beach, he was thinking of it.

[1] CONTRITION: sincere regret for having hurt another.

"Through the Tunnel" by Doris Lessing, originally published in *The New Yorker*, copyright © 1955 by Doris Lessing; from *The Habit of Loving*, Thomas Y. Crowell Company, New York (copyright © 1957 by Doris Lessing).

Next morning, when it was time for the routine of swimming and sunbathing, his mother said, "Are you tired of the usual beach, Jerry? Would you like to go somewhere else?"

"Oh, no!" he said quickly, smiling at her out of that unfailing impulse of contrition—a sort of chivalry. Yet, walking down the path with her, he blurted out, "I'd like to go and have a look at those rocks down there."

She gave the idea her attention. It was a wild-looking place, and there was no one there; but she said, "Of course, Jerry. When you've had enough, come to the big beach. Or just go straight back to the villa, if you like." She walked away, that bare arm, now slightly reddened from yesterday's sun, swinging. And he almost ran after her again, feeling it unbearable that she should go by herself, but he did not.

She was thinking, Of course he's old enough to be safe without me. Have I been keeping him too close? He mustn't feel he ought to be with me. I must be careful.

He was an only child, eleven years old. She was a widow. She was determined to be neither possessive nor lacking in devotion. She went worrying off to her beach.

As for Jerry, once he saw that his mother had gained her beach, he began the steep descent to the bay. From where he was, high up among red-brown rocks, it was a scoop of moving bluish green fringed with white. As he went lower, he saw that it spread among small promontories[1] and inlets of rough, sharp rock, and the crisping, lapping surface showed stains of purple and darker blue. Finally, as he ran sliding and scraping down the last few yards, he saw an edge of white surf and the shallow, luminous movement of water over white sand, and, beyond that, a solid, heavy blue.

He ran straight into the water and began swimming. He was a good swimmer. He went out fast over the gleaming sand, over a middle region where rocks lay like discolored monsters under the surface, and then he was in the real sea—a warm sea where irregular cold currents from the deep water shocked his limbs.

When he was so far out that he could look back not only on the little bay but past the promontory that was between it and the big beach, he floated on the buoyant surface and looked for his mother. There she was, a speck of yellow under an umbrella that looked like a slice of orange peel. He swam back to shore, relieved at being sure she was there, but all at once very lonely.

On the edge of a small cape that marked the side of the bay away from the promontory was a loose scatter of rocks. Above them, some boys were stripping off their clothes. They came running, naked, down to the rocks. The English boy swam toward them, but kept his distance at a stone's throw. They were of that coast; all of them were burned smooth dark brown and speaking a language he did not understand. To be with them, of them, was a craving that filled his whole body. He swam a little closer; they turned and watched him with narrowed, alert dark eyes. Then one smiled and waved. It was enough. In a minute, he had swum in and was on the rocks beside them, smiling with a desperate, nervous supplication.[2] They shouted cheerful greetings at him; and then, as he preserved his nervous, uncomprehending smile, they understood that he was a foreigner strayed from his own beach, and they proceeded to forget him. But he was happy. He was with them.

They began diving again and again from a high point into a well of blue sea between rough, pointed rocks. After they had dived and come up, they swam around, hauled themselves up, and waited their turn to dive again. They were big boys—men, to Jerry. He dived, and they watched him; and when he swam around to take his place, they made way for him. He felt he was accepted and he dived again, carefully, proud of himself.

Soon the biggest of the boys poised himself, shot down into the water, and did not come up. The others stood about, watching. Jerry, after waiting for the sleek brown head to appear, let out a yell of warning; they looked at him idly and turned their eyes back toward the water. After a long time, the boy came up on the other side of a big dark rock, letting the air out of his lungs in a sputtering gasp and a shout of triumph. Immediately the rest of them dived in. One moment, the morning seemed full of chattering boys; the next, the air and the surface of the water were empty. But through the heavy blue, dark shapes could be seen moving and groping.

Jerry dived, shot past the school of

[1] PROMONTORIES: high ridges of rock jutting out into the sea.

[2] SUPPLICATION: act of asking for earnestly and humbly.

underwater swimmers, saw a black wall of rock looming at him, touched it, and bobbed up at once to the surface, where the wall was a low barrier he could see across. There was no one visible; under him, in the water, the dim shapes of the swimmers had disappeared. Then one, and then another of the boys came up on the far side of the barrier of rock, and he understood that they had swum through some gap or hole in it. He plunged down again. He could see nothing through the stinging salt water but the blank rock. When he came up the boys were all on the diving rock, preparing to attempt the feat again. And now, in a panic of failure, he yelled up, in English, "Look at me! Look!" and he began splashing and kicking in the water like a foolish dog.

They looked down gravely, frowning. He knew the frown. At moments of failure, when he clowned to claim his mother's attention, it was with just this grave, embarrassed inspection that she rewarded him. Through his hot shame, feeling the pleading grin on his face like a scar that he could never remove, he looked up at the group of big brown boys on the rock and shouted, "*Bonjour! Merci! Au revoir! Monsieur, monsieur!*" while he hooked his fingers round his ears and waggled them.

Water surged into his mouth; he choked, sank, came up. The rock, lately weighted with boys, seemed to rear up out of the water as their weight was removed. They were flying down past him, now, into the water; the air was full of falling bodies. Then the rock was empty in the hot sunlight. He counted one, two, three. . . .

At fifty, he was terrified. They must all be drowning beneath him, in the watery caves of the rock! At a hundred, he stared around him at the empty hillside, wondering if he should yell for help. He counted faster, faster, to hurry them up, to bring them to the surface quickly, to drown them quickly—anything rather than the terror of counting on and on into the blue emptiness of the morning. And then, at a hundred and sixty, the water beyond the rock was full of boys blowing like brown whales. They swam back to the shore without a look at him.

He climbed back to the diving rock and sat down, feeling the hot roughness of it under his thighs. The boys were gathering up their bits of clothing and running off along the shore to another promontory. They were leaving to get away from him. He cried openly, fists in his eyes. There was no one to see him, and he cried himself out.

It seemed to him that a long time had passed, and he swam out to where he could see his mother. Yes, she was still there, a yellow spot under an orange umbrella. He swam back to the big rock, climbed up, and dived into the blue pool among the fanged and angry boulders. Down he went, until he touched the wall of rock again. But the salt was so painful in his eyes that he could not see.

He came to the surface, swam to shore and went back to the villa to wait for his mother. Soon she walked slowly up the path, swinging her striped bag, the flushed, naked arm dangling beside her. "I want some swimming goggles," he panted, defiant and beseeching.

She gave him a patient, inquisitive look as she said casually, "Well, of course, darling."

But now, now, now! He must have them this minute, and no other time. He nagged and pestered until she went with him to a shop. As soon as she had bought the goggles, he grabbed them from her hand as if she were going to claim them for herself, and was off, running down the steep path to the bay.

Jerry swam out to the big barrier rock, adjusted the goggles, and dived. The impact of the water broke the rubber-enclosed vacuum, and the goggles came loose. He understood that he must swim down to the base of the rock from the surface of the water. He fixed the goggles tight and firm, filled his lungs, and floated, face down, on the water. Now, he could see. It was as if he had eyes of a different kind—fish eyes that showed everything clear and delicate and wavering in the bright water.

Under him, six or seven feet down, was a floor of perfectly clean, shining white sand, rippled firm and hard by the tides. Two grayish shapes steered there, like long, rounded pieces of wood or slate. They were fish. He saw them nose toward each other, poise motionless, make a dart forward, swerve off, and come around again. It was like a water dance. A few inches above them the water sparkled as if sequins[1] were dropping through it. Fish again—myriads of minute fish, the length of his fingernail, were drifting through the water, and in a moment he could feel the innumerable tiny touches of them against his limbs. It was like swimming in flaked silver. The great rock the big boys had swum through rose sheer out of the white sand—black, tufted lightly with greenish weed. He could see no gap in it. He swam down to its base.

Again and again he rose, took a big chestful of air, and went down. Again and again he groped over the surface of the

---

[1] SEQUINS: small, shiny, ornamental disks.

rock, feeling it, almost hugging it in the desperate need to find the entrance. And then, once, while he was clinging to the black wall, his knees came up and he shot his feet out forward and they met no obstacle. He had found the hole.

He gained the surface, clambered about the stones that littered the barrier rock until he found a big one, and, with this in his arms, let himself down over the side of the rock. He dropped, with the weight, straight to the sandy floor. Clinging tight to the anchor of stone, he lay on his side and looked in under the dark shelf at the place where his feet had gone. He could see the hole. It was an irregular, dark gap; but he could not see deep into it. He let go of his anchor, clung with his hands to the edges of the hole, and tried to push himself in.

He got his head in, found his shoulders jammed, moved them in sidewise, and was inside as far as his waist. He could see nothing ahead. Something soft and clammy touched his mouth; he saw a dark frond moving against the grayish rock, and panic filled him. He thought of octopuses, of clinging weed. He pushed himself out backward and caught a glimpse, as he retreated, of a harmless tentacle of seaweed drifting in the mouth of the tunnel. But it was enough. He reached the sunlight, swam to shore, and lay on the diving rock. He looked down into the blue well of water. He knew he must find his way through that cave, or hole, or tunnel, and out the other side.

First, he thought, he must learn to control his breathing. He let himself down into the water with another big stone in his arms, so that he could lie effortlessly on the bottom of the sea. He counted. One, two, three. He counted steadily. He could hear the movement of blood in his chest. Fifty-one, fifty-two. . . . His chest was hurting. He let go of the rock and went up into the air. He saw that the sun was low. He rushed to the villa and found his mother at her supper. She said only "Did you enjoy yourself?" and he said "Yes."

All night the boy dreamed of the water-filled cave in the rock, and as soon as breakfast was over he went to the bay.

That night, his nose bled badly. For hours he had been underwater, learning to hold his breath, and now he felt weak and dizzy. His mother said, "I shouldn't overdo things, darling, if I were you."

That day and the next, Jerry exercised his lungs as if everything, the whole of his life, all that he would become, depended upon it. Again his nose bled at night, and his mother insisted on his coming with her the next day. It was a torment to him to waste a day of his careful self-training, but he stayed with her on that other beach, which now seemed a place for small children, a place where his mother might lie safe in the sun. It was not his beach.

He did not ask for permission, on the following day, to go to his beach. He went, before his mother could consider the complicated rights and wrongs of the matter. A day's rest, he discovered, had improved his count by ten. The big boys had made the passage while he counted a hundred and sixty. He had been counting fast, in his fright. Probably now, if he tried, he could get through that long tunnel, but he was not going to try yet. A curious, most unchildlike persistence, a controlled impatience, made him wait. In the meantime, he lay underwater on the white sand, littered now by stones he had brought down from the upper air, and studied the entrance to the tunnel. He knew every jut and corner of it, as far as it was possible to see. It was as if he already felt its sharpness about his shoulders.

He sat by the clock in the villa, when his mother was not near, and checked his time. He was incredulous and then proud to find he could hold his breath without strain for two minutes. The words "two minutes," authorized by the clock, brought close the adventure that was so necessary to him.

In another four days, his mother said casually one morning, they must go home. On the day before they left, he would do it. He would do it if it killed him, he said defiantly to himself. But two days before they were to leave—a day of triumph when he increased his count by fifteen—his nose bled so badly that he turned dizzy and had to lie limply over the big rock like a bit of seaweed, watching the thick red blood flow on to the rock and trickle slowly down to the sea. He was frightened. Supposing he turned dizzy in the tunnel? Supposing he died there, trapped? Supposing—his head went around, in the hot sun, and he almost gave up. He thought he would return to the house and lie down, and next summer, perhaps, when he had another year's growth in him—*then* he would go through the hole.

But even after he had made the decision, or thought he had, he found himself sitting up on the rock and looking down into the water; and he knew that now, this moment, when his nose had only just stopped bleeding, when his head was still sore and throbbing—this was the moment when he would try. If he did not do it now, he never would. He was trembling with fear that he would not go; and he was trembling with horror at that long, long tunnel under the rock, under the sea. Even in the open sunlight, the barrier rock seemed very wide and very heavy; tons of rock pressed down on where he would go. If he died there, he would lie until one day—perhaps not before next year—those big boys would swim into it and find it blocked.

He put on his goggles, fitted them tight, tested the vacuum. His hands were shaking. Then he chose the biggest stone he could carry and slipped over the edge of the rock until half of him was in the cool, enclosing water and half in the hot sun. He looked up once at the empty sky, filled his lungs once, twice, and then sank fast to the bottom with the stone. He let it go and began to count. He took the edges of the hole in his hands and drew himself into it, wriggling his shoulders in sidewise as he remembered he must, kicking himself along with his feet.

Soon he was clear inside. He was in a small rockbound hole filled with yellowish-gray water. The water was pushing him up against the roof. The roof was sharp and pained his back. He pulled himself along with his hands—fast, fast—and used his legs as levers. His head knocked against something; a sharp pain dizzied him. Fifty, fifty-one, fifty-two. . . . He was without light, and the water seemed to press upon him with the weight of rock. Seventy-one, seventy-two. . . . There was no strain on his lungs. He felt like an inflated balloon, his lungs were so light and easy, but his head was pulsing.

He was being continually pressed against the sharp roof, which felt slimy as well as sharp. Again he thought of octopuses, and wondered if the tunnel might be filled with weed that could tangle him. He gave himself a panicky, convulsive kick forward, ducked his head, and swam. His feet and hands moved freely, as if in open water. The hole must have widened out. He thought he must be swimming fast, and he was frightened of banging his head if the tunnel narrowed.

A hundred, a hundred and one. . . . The water paled. Victory filled him. His lungs were beginning to hurt. A few more strokes and he would be out. He was counting wildly; he said a hundred and fifteen, and then, a long time later, a hundred and fifteen again. The water was a clear jewel-green all around him. Then he saw, above his head, a crack running up through the rock. Sunlight was falling through it, showing the clean, dark rock of the tunnel, a single mussel shell, and darkness ahead.

He was at the end of what he could do. He looked up at the crack as if it were filled with air and not water, as if he could put his mouth to it to draw in air. A hundred and fifteen, he heard himself say inside his head—but he had said that long ago. He must go on into the blackness ahead, or he would drown. His head was swelling, his lungs cracking. A hundred and fifteen, a hundred and fifteen pounded through his head, and he feebly clutched at rocks in the dark, pulling himself forward, leaving the brief space of sunlit water behind. He felt he was dying. He was no longer quite conscious. He struggled on in the darkness between lapses into unconsciousness. An immense, swelling pain filled his head, and then the darkness cracked with an explosion of green light. His hands, groping forward, met nothing; and his feet, kicking

back, propelled him out into the open sea.

He drifted to the surface, his face turned up to the air. He was gasping like a fish. He felt he would sink now and drown; he could not swim the few feet back to the rock. Then he was clutching it and pulling himself up on to it. He lay face down, gasping. He could see nothing but a red-veined, clotted dark. His eyes must have burst, he thought; they were full of blood. He tore off his goggles and a gout of blood went into the sea. His nose was bleeding, and the blood had filled the goggles.

He scooped up handfuls of water from the cool, salty sea, to splash on his face, and did not know whether it was blood or salt water he tasted. After a time, his heart quieted, his eyes cleared, and he sat up. He could see the local boys diving and playing half a mile away. He did not want them. He wanted nothing but to get back home and lie down.

In a short while, Jerry swam to shore and climbed slowly up the path to the villa. He flung himself on his bed and slept, waking at the sound of feet on the path outside. His mother was coming back. He rushed to the bathroom, thinking she must not see his face with bloodstains, or tearstains, on it. He came out of the bathroom and met her as she walked into the villa, smiling, her eyes lighting up.

"Have a nice morning?" she asked, laying her hand in his warm brown shoulder a moment.

"Oh, yes, thank you," he said.

"You look a bit pale." And then, sharp and anxious, "How did you bang your head?"

"Oh, just banged it," he told her.

She looked at him closely. He was strained; his eyes were glazed-looking. She was worried. And then she said to herself, Oh, don't fuss! Nothing can happen. He can swim like a fish.

They sat down to lunch together.

"Mummy," he said, "I can stay under water for two minutes—three minutes, at least." It came bursting out of him.

"Can you, darling?" she said. "Well, I shouldn't overdo it. I don't think you ought to swim any more today."

She was ready for a battle of wills, but he gave in at once. It was no longer of the least importance to go to the bay.

FOR DISCUSSION

1. Why does Jerry feel he has to go through the tunnel? At the end of the story, why does he feel that it is "no longer of the least importance to go to the bay"?

2. After the native boys swim through the tunnel, their feelings toward Jerry appear to change. Describe and account for their change in attitude.

3. Jerry's actions finally reach a point of desperation after the boys leave. Find details in the story which indicate his feelings at this point. Why does he feel this way?

4. Describe as precisely as you can the changing relationship between Jerry and his mother, using details from the story to support your observations. How do the events in the story change this relationship?

Through an open window disappear a man, two boys, and a brown dog.

THE OPEN WINDOW
SAKI

MY AUNT WILL be down presently, Mr. Nuttel," said a very self-possessed young lady of fifteen. "In the meantime you must try and put up with me."

Framton Nuttel endeavored to say the correct something which should duly flatter the niece of the moment without unduly discounting the aunt that was to come. Privately he doubted more than ever whether these formal visits on a succession of total strangers would do much toward helping the nerve cure which he was supposed to be undergoing.

"I know how it will be," his sister had said when he was preparing to migrate to this rural retreat. "You will bury yourself down there and not speak to a living soul, and your nerves will be worse than ever from moping. I shall just give you letters of introduction to all the people I know there. Some of them, as far as I can remember, were quite nice."

Framton wondered whether Mrs. Sappleton, the lady to whom he was presenting one of the letters of introduction, came into the nice division.

"Do you know many of the people round here?" asked the niece, when she judged that they had had sufficient silent com-

munion.

"Hardly a soul," said Framton. "My sister was staying here, at the rectory,[1] you know, some four years ago, and she gave me letters of introduction to some of the people here."

He made the last statement in a tone of distinct regret.

"Then you know practically nothing about my aunt?" pursued the self-possessed young lady.

"Only her name and address," admitted the caller. He was wondering whether Mrs. Sappleton was in the married or widowed state. An indefinable something about the room seemed to suggest masculine habitation.

"Her great tragedy happened just three years ago," said the child. "That would be since your sister's time."

"Her tragedy?" asked Framton. Somehow in this restful country spot tragedies seemed out of place.

"You may wonder why we keep that window wide open on an October afternoon," said the niece, indicating a large French window that opened onto a lawn.

"It is quite warm for the time of the year," said Framton; "but has that window got anything to do with the tragedy?"

"Out through that window, three years ago to a day, her husband and her two

SAKI: pronounced sä′kē.

"The Open Window" from *The Short Stories of Saki* by H. H. Munro. Reprinted by permission of The Viking Press, Inc.

[1] RECTORY: house in which a minister lives.

young brothers went off for their day's shooting. They never came back. In crossing the moor to their favorite snipe-shooting ground they were all three engulfed in a treacherous piece of bog. It had been that dreadful wet summer, you know, and places that were safe in other years gave way suddenly without warning. Their bodies were never recovered. That was the dreadful part of it." Here the child's voice lost its self-possessed note and became falteringly human. "Poor Aunt always thinks that they will come back some day, they and the little brown spaniel that was lost with them, and walk in at that window just as they used to do. That is why the window is kept open every evening till it is quite dusk. Poor dear Aunt! She has often told me how they went out, her husband with his white waterproof coat over his arm, and Ronnie, her youngest brother, singing 'Bertie, why do you bound?' as he always did to tease her, because she said it got on her nerves. Do you know, sometimes on still, quiet evenings like this, I almost get a creepy feeling that they will all walk in through that window—"

She broke off with a little shudder. It was a relief to Framton when the aunt bustled into the room with a whirl of apologies for being late in making her appearance.

"I hope Vera has been amusing you?" she said.

"She has been very interesting," said Framton.

"I hope you don't mind the open window," said Mrs. Sappleton briskly. "My husband and brothers will be home directly from shooting, and they always come in this way. They've been out for snipe in the marshes today, so they'll make a fine mess over my poor carpets. So like you menfolk, isn't it?"

She rattled on cheerfully about the shooting and the scarcity of birds and the prospects for duck in the winter. To Framton it was all purely horrible. He made a desperate but only partially successful effort to turn the talk onto a less ghastly topic. He was conscious that his hostess was giving him only a fragment of her attention, and her eyes were constantly straying past him to the open window and the lawn beyond. It was certainly an unfortunate coincidence that he should have paid his visit on this tragic anniversary.

"The doctors agree in ordering me complete rest, an absence of mental excitement, and avoidance of anything in the nature of violent physical exercise," announced Framton, who labored under the tolerably widespread delusion that total strangers and chance acquaintances are hungry for the least detail of one's ailments and infirmities, their cause and cure. "On the matter of diet they are not so much in agreement," he continued.

"No?" said Mrs. Sappleton, in a voice which only replaced a yawn at the last moment. Then she suddenly brightened into alert attention—but not to what Framton was saying.

"Here they are at last!" she cried. "Just in time for tea, and don't they look as if they were muddy up to the eyes!"

Framton shivered slightly and turned toward the niece with a look intended to convey sympathetic comprehension. The child was staring out through the open window with dazed horror in her eyes. In a chill shock of nameless fear Framton swung round in his seat and looked in the same direction.

In the deepening twilight three figures were walking across the lawn towards the window. They all carried guns under their arms, and one of them was additionally burdened with a white coat hung over his shoulders. A tired brown spaniel kept close at their heels. Noiselessly they neared the house, and then a hoarse young voice chanted out of the dusk: "I say, Bertie, why do you bound?"

Framton grabbed wildly at his stick and hat. The hall door, the gravel drive, and the front gate were dimly noted stages in his headlong retreat. A cyclist coming along the road had to run into the hedge to avoid imminent collision.

"Here we are, my dear," said the bearer of the white mackintosh, coming in through the window; "fairly muddy, but most of it's dry. Who was that who bolted out as we came up?"

"A most extraordinary man, a Mr. Nuttel," said Mrs. Sappleton. "Could only talk about his illness, and dashed off without a word of good-bye or apology when you arrived. One would think he had seen a ghost."

"I expect it was the spaniel," said the niece calmly. "He told me he had a horror of dogs. He was once hunted into a cemetery somewhere on the banks of the Ganges by a pack of pariah[1] dogs, and had to spend the night in a newly dug grave with the creatures snarling and grinning and foaming just above him. Enough to make anyone lose their nerve."

Romance at short notice was her specialty.

[1] PARIAH: outcast; wild.

FOR DISCUSSION

1. What is Vera's last fantasy? Why does the author wait until the last line to mention that "romance at short notice was her specialty"?

2. What motive would you ascribe to Vera's question to Mr. Nuttel: "Then you know practically nothing about my aunt?"

3. What are your feelings toward Mr. Nuttel? Do you feel, for example, sympathy or contempt? Justify your reaction by points in the story that support it.

4. To what extent is your attitude toward Vera determined by the answer to the previous question?

The highwaymen of eighteenth-century England were bold outlaws who held up riders and stagecoach passengers along lonely stretches of road. This ballad tells the story of one unusually daring highwayman who chose to ride by moonlight over the treeless moor country that afforded no cover from the King's soldiers.

THE HIGHWAYMAN
ALFRED NOYES

PART ONE

The wind was a torrent of darkness among the gusty trees,
The moon was a ghostly galleon* tossed upon cloudy seas,
The road was a ribbon of moonlight over the purple moor,
And the highwayman came riding—
    Riding—riding—   5
The highwayman came riding, up to the old inn-door.

He'd a French cocked hat on his forehead, a bunch of lace at his chin,
A coat of the claret velvet, and breeches of brown doeskin;
They fitted with never a wrinkle, his boots were up to the thigh.
And he rode with a jeweled twinkle,   10
    His pistol butts a-twinkle,
His rapier hilt a-twinkle, under the jeweled sky.

Over the cobbles he clattered and clashed, in the dark innyard.
He tapped with his whip on the shutters, but all was locked and barred.
He whistled a tune to the window, and who should be waiting there   15
But the landlord's black-eyed daughter,
    Bess, the landlord's daughter,
Plaiting a dark red love-knot into her long black hair.

And dark in the dark old innyard, a stable-wicket* creaked
Where Tim the ostler* listened. His face was white and peaked;   20
His eyes were hollows of madness, his hair like moldy hay;
But he loved the landlord's daughter,

---

2 GALLEON: old-time sailing vessel.   19 STABLE-WICKET: stable-gate.   20 OSTLER (os′lər): stableman.

"The Highwayman" from the book *Collected Poems* by Alfred Noyes. Reprinted by permission of J. B. Lippincott Company.

The landlord's red-lipped daughter.
Dumb as a dog he listened, and he heard the robber say,

"One kiss, my bonny sweetheart. I'm after a prize tonight,   25
But I shall be back with the yellow gold before the morning light;
Yet, if they press me sharply and harry me through the day,
Then look for me by moonlight,
      Watch for me by moonlight,
I'll come to thee by moonlight, though hell should bar the way!"   30

He rose upright in the stirrups; he scarce could reach her hand,
But she loosened her hair in the casement!* His face burnt like a brand*
As the black cascade of perfume came tumbling over his breast,
And he kissed its waves in the moonlight
      (O sweet black waves in the moonlight!);   35
Then he tugged at his rein in the moonlight and galloped away to the west.

32 CASEMENT: hinged window opening outward.   BRAND: firebrand, a flaming
piece of wood.

PART TWO

He did not come in the dawning; he did not come at noon.
And out of the tawny sunset, before the rise of the moon,
When the road was a gypsy's ribbon, looping the purple moor,
A redcoat troop came marching—   40
     Marching—marching—
King George's men came marching, up to the old inn-door.

They said no word to the landlord; they drank his ale instead;
But they gagged his daughter and bound her to the foot of her narrow bed.
Two of them knelt at her casement, with muskets at their side.   45
There was death at every window,
     And hell at one dark window,
For Bess could see through her casement the road that *he* would ride.

They had bound her up to attention, with many a sniggering jest;
They had bound a musket beside her, with the muzzle beneath her breast.   50
"Now keep good watch!" and they kissed her. She heard the dead man say,
Look for me by moonlight,
     Watch for me by moonlight,
I'll come to thee by moonlight, though hell should bar the way!

She twisted her hands behind her, but all the knots held good.   55
She writhed her hands till her fingers were wet with sweat or blood.
They stretched and strained in the darkness, and the hours crawled by like
     years,
Till now, on the stroke of midnight,
     Cold on the stroke of midnight,
The tip of one finger touched it! The trigger at least was hers!   60

The tip of one finger touched it; she strove no more for the rest!
Up she stood to attention, with the muzzle beneath her breast.
She would not risk their hearing; she would not strive again;
For the road lay bare in the moonlight,
     Blank and bare in the moonlight,   65
And the blood of her veins in the moonlight throbbed to her love's refrain.

Tlot-tlot, tlot-tlot! Had they heard it? The horse-hoofs ringing clear!
Tlot-tlot, tlot-tlot in the distance! Were they deaf that they did not hear?
Down the ribbon of moonlight, over the brow of the hill,
The highwayman came riding—   70

Riding—riding—
The redcoats looked to their priming!* She stood up, straight and still.

Tlot-tlot in the frosty silence! *Tlot-tlot* in the echoing night!
Nearer he came and nearer! Her face was like a light.
Her eyes grew wide for a moment; she drew one last deep breath.   75
Then her finger moved in the moonlight,
      Her musket shattered the moonlight,
Shattered her breast in the moonlight, and warned him—with her death.

He turned; he spurred to the west; he did not know who stood
Bowed, with her head o'er the musket, drenched with her own blood.   80
Not till the dawn he heard it, and his face grew gray to hear
How Bess, the landlord's daughter,
      The landlord's black-eyed daughter,
Had watched for her love in the moonlight, and died in the darkness there.

Back he spurred like a madman, shouting a curse to the sky,   85
With the white road smoking behind him and his rapier brandished high!
Blood-red were his spurs in the golden noon, wine-red was his velvet coat,
When they shot him down on the highway,
      Down like a dog on the highway,
And he lay in his blood on the highway, with a bunch of lace at his throat.   90

[72] PRIMING: preparing guns for firing.

And still of a winter's night, they say, when the wind is in the trees,
When the moon is a ghostly galleon tossed upon cloudy seas,
When the road is a ribbon of moonlight over the purple moor,
A highwayman comes riding—
  Riding—riding—   95
A highwayman comes riding, up to the old inn-door.

Over the cobbles he clatters and clangs, in the dark innyard.
He taps with his whip on the shutters, but all is locked and barred.
He whistles a tune to the window, and who should be waiting there
But the landlord's black-eyed daughter,   100
  Bess, the landlord's daughter,
Plaiting a dark red love-knot into her long black hair.

FOR DISCUSSION

1. Tell briefly the story of "The Highwayman."

2. No matter how good your prose summary, it is far inferior to the poem. Discuss the patterned flow of sound (*rhythm*) that makes the poem come alive. How does the rhythm suggest the galloping of a horse, for example?

What do words like *Tlot-Tlot* add? How effective is the repetition in the last two stanzas?

3. With her death Bess warned the highwayman to stay away from the inn. Why, then, do you think he returned to the inn in the morning?

In Summary

FOR DISCUSSION

1. One way an author builds up a reader's suspense is through *foreshadowing,* which is the technique of dropping clues or suggesting events before they actually occur in a story. Choose the story you think was most suspenseful and find as many examples of foreshadowing as you can.

2. An eerie or unusual setting often helps create suspense or heightens the suspense of a story. In which stories did you feel the setting contributed a great deal to the suspense of the story? In which stories was setting relatively unimportant to the suspense? Be specific—try to explain your answer by referring directly to the stories.

3. Edgar Allan Poe has long been considered a master of suspense. Carefully re-examine "The Telltale Heart." How many different techniques do you recognize that make this such a successful suspense story?

4. Fear is an important element in suspense stories. Usually something unfamiliar or unknown causes a more fearful reaction in a person than anything else. What proof for this statement can you find in each story of this unit?

OTHER THINGS TO DO

1. Try to imagine that you possess the monkey's paw. Write a well-organized composition in which you cover the following questions: What three wishes would you make? Do you think your three wishes have been planned carefully enough to keep you from an unhappy fate similar to that of the keepers of the paw described in Jacobs' story?

2. Imagine some everyday setting that is very familiar to you. Remember all the sights, sounds, smells, tastes, and feelings that are a part of it. Then write a basic description of this place in one or two paragraphs. Next, study the descriptions of setting in these suspense stories. Finally, use the techniques you have observed in these stories to rewrite your description of the setting, trying to make it ominous and eerie.

3. In "Phone Call" Mrs. Timothy becomes a victim of her own emotions. Poll the class and see how many different situations have occurred in the lives of students where fear has affected judgment or actions. What really causes fear? How do suspense writers appeal to a reader's basic fears?

4. Another important element in suspense is the action of the story, or the *plot*. Choose your three favorite stories in this unit and write out the plot for each of the three. Remember that plot is only the action of the story; don't include any other parts of the story in your summary.

The World of Words

THE TELLTALE HEART

The narrator of "The Telltale Heart" insists that he is not *mad*, that is, "not insane." We know what the word *mad* means here because of the words around it. These surrounding words in which the word appears we call its "context," and it is the context that tells us what a word means. Explain the meaning of the word *mad* as it is used in each of the following sentences: (1) John is *mad* about football; (2) He was so *mad* he tried to knock me down; (3) After the fumble there was a *mad* scramble for the ball; (4) He rode like *mad* to get to the ranch on time; (5) We ran into the house when the *mad* dog came down the street. What other uses of *mad* can you think of?

DARK THEY WERE AND GOLDEN-EYED

1. Names play a large part in Bradbury's story.

The word *name* has been in English for a long time, but other words from the same original source came into English later. Some of these words are *nominate, noun, renown*. What do these words mean? Do their meanings suggest any connection with the word *name*? Explain.

2. Mars and the other planets are named after figures from Roman mythology. These names are *Mars, Mercury, Venus, Jupiter, Saturn, Uranus, Neptune,* and *Pluto*. Look up these names, and explain what each figure was famous for.

POISON

When people of different languages are brought together, there is always an exchange of words from one language to another. During the years when the British ruled India, many Indian words came into English. One of these words—*bungalow*—appears in the first sentence of Dahl's story (page 20). Some others are *coolie, jungle, jodhpurs, rajah.* What meanings can you find for these words? The meaning of the word *jungle* has changed over the years. Use your dictionary to find what the original meaning of *jungle* was.

PHONE CALL

Other people characterize us by the way we speak or write. The narrator of Berton Roueché's story uses language in a way that enables us to characterize him. Look at what he says. "There wasn't anything hanging down or anything" (page 30). "It really had me beat" (page 30). "It was him himself that told me to take this truck" (page 30). "A dog was laying there" (page 30). On the basis of these remarks, how would you describe the narrator of the story?

THE MONKEY'S PAW

"Hark at the wind," says Mr. White as the story opens (page 46). The word *hark* means "to listen attentively" and it goes back to an early word root meaning "to pay attention." Other words that come from this same root are *acoustic, caution,* and *scavenge.* At first glance these words appear to have little in common, yet they all go back to the same source. Examine their meanings and explain how they could have come from a root meaning "to pay attention."

THROUGH THE TUNNEL

The word *tunnel* is an example of how a word can develop an entirely different meaning from its source. This source, it is believed, is an Old Irish word *tonn,* meaning "skin," which came to be used for a wineskin, a skin that was used to store wine. When barrels replaced wineskins, the word *tonn* became the name for the barrels. (Later the word became changed to *tun* which is the name for a large cask or barrel.) During the Middle Ages people constructed arches of wire over hoops or traps to catch birds. They called this trap a "tonel." This name gradually became *tunnel,* the name for any kind of arched passageway or shaft. The word *ton* is also related to *tun.* Considering that *tun* refers to a very large cask or barrel to be filled with wine, how might *ton* be related to *tun?*

THE OPEN WINDOW

On page 67 we read that Framton Nuttel "made a desperate . . . effort to turn the talk onto a less ghastly topic." And later Mrs. Sappleton says, "One would think he had seen a ghost." The words *ghastly* and *ghost,* or *ghostly,* come from an Old English word *gast* that means "spirit" or "soul." How do *ghastly* and *ghostly* differ in meaning? Do they share any qualities that would suggest their common origin?

Reader's Choice

Come Along with Me, *by Shirley Jackson.*

An ordinary town with ordinary people becomes the setting for one of the most deadly and terrifying games ever played. The trick ending in this and other stories will leave you squirming—and wondering about a lot of things you usually take for granted.

The Complete Sherlock Holmes, *by Arthur Conan Doyle.*

The most famous detective of all times has an amazing knowledge about odd subjects—weapons, poisons, the ashes of various brands of tobacco, soils—and all this information proves useful to him in solving the most unusual crimes. The reader, like Holmes' assistant Watson, will be continually amazed at the cleverness of this master sleuth.

Guns in the Heather, *by Amerman Lockhart.*

Jonathan may think he is going on a vacation with his secret agent father, but instead he is to be met by a stranger, who blindfolds him. This spy thriller begins in a boys' private school and ends, many gasps and heartbeats later, on a perilous peak of the Scottish West Highlands.

The Moonstone, *by Wilkie Collins.*

The Moonstone, an enormous yellow diamond stolen from the forehead of an Indian statue, puts a curse on those who possess it. When the stone is stolen from the household of a wealthy English family, panic follows.

Nine Coaches Waiting, *by Mary Stewart.*

After Linda Martin becomes governess to the nine-year-old Phillipe, strange "accidents" lead her to believe that the young count is the intended victim of a murder plot.

Runway Zero-Eight, *by Arthur Hailey and John Castle.*

Food poisoning hits the passengers and the pilots on a transcontinental flight. There is taut suspense and excitement as George Spencer, an ordinary salesman, is forced to take the controls and land the plane.

The Strange Case of Dr. Jekyll and Mr. Hyde, *by Robert Louis Stevenson.*

Through the use of mysterious drugs, a doctor is able to alternate between the personalities of a decent and respectable doctor and a brutal criminal. The exciting struggle for the domination of this man's spirit by the evil half makes both a gripping adventure story and a compelling allegory of every man's battles with his evil impulses.

Tales and Poems of Edgar Allan Poe, *by Edgar Allan Poe.*

The nightmare ingredients of these haunted stories come from Poe's own brilliant and tormented mind. This book brings together Poe's stories of cellars, dungeons, and tombs, as well as several of his poems.

We Die Alone, *by David Howarth.*

A Nazi informer has betrayed the band of Norwegian refugees who have returned to their native land. Jan Baalsrud is the only man to escape the Germans, and this true story follows his perilous journeys as he carries on the fight against the Nazi invaders on his own.

HEROES

WHEN JOHN KENNEDY was elected President in 1960, he was still in his early forties, and a generation that had been used to seeing Chief Executives much older than that—Franklin Roosevelt and Harry Truman and Dwight Eisenhower—had some trouble getting used to youth in the White House. At first it didn't seem right. But after a while, just as his fellow citizens adjusted to the new title before Kennedy's name, they grew accustomed to images of that same young man deftly answering questions at press conferences or presiding effectively over cabinet meetings.

For many, President Kennedy was an authentic hero of his time. As a hero, he extended the possibilities of being human. Henceforth it would be possible not only for a Roman Catholic to be President (Kennedy was the first), but also—if he was good enough—for a young man, who to earlier voters would have looked immature, to hold the most important job in the world. And during his brief tenure Kennedy did seem to be establishing a new style in office. He bore heavier burdens than the rest of us, yet bore them gracefully, seemed to have more self-control, to have more imagination in the same way that he had more authority than the rest of us. Or many people felt that he did. And to those people Kennedy was heroic, inspiring them through his accomplishments and example.

That is what a hero does, living or dead, real or fictional. His superiority doesn't discourage or belittle us. On the contrary, through the example of his life he sets ideals—of courage, or sacrifice, or devotion—to which the rest of us may aspire.

Philip McFarland

DANIEL

BELSHAZZAR[1] THE KING made a great feast to a thousand of his lords, and drank wine before the thousand. Belshazzar, while he tasted the wine, commanded to bring the golden and silver vessels which his father Nebuchadnezzar had taken out of the temple which was in Jerusalem; that the king and his princes, his wives and his concubines, might drink therein. Then they brought the golden vessels that were taken out of the house of God which was at Jerusalem; and the king and his princes, his wives and his concubines, drank in them. They drank wine, and praised the gods of gold, and of silver, of brass, of iron, of wood, and of stone.

In the same hour came forth fingers of a man's hand, and wrote over against the candlestick upon the plaster of the wall of the king's palace: and the king saw the part of the hand that wrote. Then the king's countenance[2] was changed, and his thoughts troubled him, so that the joints of his loins were loosed, and his knees smote one against the other. The king cried aloud to bring in the astrologers, the Chaldeans, and the soothsayers. And the king spake, and said to the wise men of Babylon, Whosoever shall read this writing, and show me the interpretation thereof, shall be clothed with scarlet, and have a chain of gold about his neck, and shall be the third ruler in the kingdom. Then came in all the king's wise men: but they could not read the writing, nor make known to the king the interpretation thereof. Then was king Belshazzar greatly troubled, and his countenance was changed in him, and his lords were astonished.

Now the queen, by reason of the words of the king and his lords, came into the banquet house: and the queen spake and said, O king, live for ever: let not thy thoughts trouble thee, nor let thy countenance be changed: There is a man in thy kingdom, in whom is the spirit of the holy gods; and in the days of thy father light and understanding and wisdom, like the wisdom of the gods, was found in him; whom the king Nebuchadnezzar thy father, the king, I say, thy father, made master of the magicians, astrologers, Chaldeans, and soothsayers; Forasmuch as[3] an excellent spirit, and knowledge, and understanding, interpreting of dreams, and showing of hard sentences, and dissolving of doubts, were found in the same Daniel, whom the king named Belteshazzar: now let Daniel be called, and he will show the interpretation.

Then was Daniel brought in before the king. And the king spake and said unto

---

[1] BELSHAZZAR (bel·shaz′ər): the last king of Babylon; son of Nebuchadnezzar II.

[2] COUNTENANCE: appearance, especially the expression of the face.

[3] FORASMUCH AS: because.

Daniel, Art thou that Daniel, which art of the children of the captivity of Judah, whom the king my father brought out of Jewry? I have even heard of thee, that the spirit of the gods is in thee, and that light and understanding and excellent wisdom is found in thee. And now the wise men, the astrologers, have been brought in before me, that they should read this writing, and make known unto me the interpretation thereof, but they could not show the interpretation of the thing. And I have heard of thee, that thou canst make interpretations, and dissolve doubts: now if thou canst read the writing, and make known to me the interpretation thereof, thou shalt be clothed with scarlet, and have a chain of gold about thy neck, and shalt be the third ruler in the kingdom.

Then Daniel answered and said before the king, Let thy gifts be to thyself, and give thy rewards to another; yet I will read the writing unto the king and make known to him the interpretation. O thou king, the most high God gave Nebuchadnezzar thy father a kingdom, and majesty, and glory, and honor: And for the majesty that he gave him, all people, nations, and languages trembled and feared before him: whom he would he slew; and whom he would he kept alive; and whom he would he set up; and whom he would he put down. But when his heart was lifted up, and his mind hardened in pride, he was deposed from his kingly throne, and they took his glory from him: And he was driven from the sons of men: and his heart was made like the beasts, and his dwelling was with the wild asses: they fed him with grass like oxen, and his body was wet with the dew of heaven; till he knew that the most high God ruled in the kingdom of men, and that he appointeth over it whomsoever he will.

And thou his son, O Belshazzar, hast not humbled thine heart, though thou knewest all this; But hast lifted up thyself against the Lord of heaven; and they have brought the vessels of his house before thee, and thou and thy lords, thy wives and thy concubines, have drunk wine in them; and thou hast praised the gods of silver, and gold, of brass, iron, wood, and stone, which see not, nor hear, nor know: and the God in whose hand thy breath is, and whose are all thy ways, hast thou not glorified: Then was the part of the hand sent from him; and this writing was written.

And this is the writing that was written, MENE, MENE, TEKEL, UPHARSIN.[1] This is the interpretation of the thing: MENE; God hath numbered thy kingdom, and finished it. TEKEL; Thou art weighed in the balances, and art found wanting. PERES,[2] Thy kingdom is divided, and given to the Medes and Persians.

Then commanded Belshazzar, and they clothed Daniel with scarlet, and put a chain of gold about his neck, and made a proclamation concerning him, that he should be the third ruler in the kingdom.

In that night was Belshazzar the king of the Chaldeans slain. And Darius the Median took the kingdom, being about threescore and two years old.

It pleased Darius to set over the kingdom a hundred and twenty princes, which should be over the whole kingdom; And over these three presidents; of whom Daniel was first: that the princes might

---

[1] MENE . . . UPHARSIN: Aramaic words, literally meaning "numbered, numbered, weighed, divided."
[2] PERES: singular form of *upharsin.*

give accounts unto them, and the king should have no damage. Then this Daniel was preferred above the presidents and princes, because an excellent spirit was in him; and the king thought to set him over the whole realm. Then the presidents and princes sought to find occasion against Daniel concerning the kingdom; but they could find none occasion nor fault; forasmuch as he was faithful, neither was there any error or fault found in him. Then said these men, We shall not find any occasion against this Daniel, except we find it against him concerning the law of his God.

Then these presidents and princes assembled together to the king, and said thus unto him, King Darius, live for ever. All the presidents of the kingdom, the governors, and the princes, the counselors, and the captains, have consulted together to establish a royal statute, and to make a firm decree, that whosoever shall ask a petition of any God or man for thirty days, save of thee, O king, he shall be cast into the den of lions. Now, O king, establish the decree, and sign the writing, that it be not changed, according to the law of the Medes and Persians, which altereth not. Wherefore king Darius signed the writing and the decree.

Now when Daniel knew that the writing was signed, he went into his house; and, his windows being open in his chamber toward Jerusalem, he kneeled upon his knees three times a day, and prayed, and gave thanks before his God, as he did aforetime. Then these men assembled, and found Daniel praying and making supplication before his God.

Then they came near, and spake before the king concerning the king's decree; Hast thou not signed a decree, that every man that shall ask a petition of any God or man within thirty days, save of thee, O king, shall be cast into the den of lions?

The king answered and said, The thing is true, according to the law of the Medes and Persians, which altereth not.

Then answered they and said before the king, That Daniel, which is of the children of the captivity of Judah, regardeth not thee, O king, nor the decree that thou hast signed, but maketh his petition three times a day. Then the king, when he heard these words, was sore displeased with himself, and set his heart on Daniel to deliver him: and he labored till the going down of the sun to deliver him.

Then these men assembled unto the king, and said unto the king, Know, O king, that the law of the Medes and Persians is, That no decree nor statute which the king establisheth may be changed. Then the king commanded, and they brought Daniel, and cast him into the den of lions. Now the king spake and said unto Daniel, Thy God whom thou servest continually, he will deliver thee. And a stone was brought, and laid upon the mouth of the den; and the king sealed it with his own signet[1] and with the signet of his lords; that the purpose might not be changed concerning Daniel.

Then the king went to his palace, and passed the night fasting: neither were instruments of music brought before him: and his sleep went from him. Then the king arose very early in the morning, and went in haste unto the den of lions. And when he came to the den, he cried with a lamentable voice unto Daniel: and the king spake

[1] SIGNET: ring which makes a particular, unique impression upon wax; if the stone were to be moved, the mark of the signet could not be duplicated, and the fraud would be discovered.

and said to Daniel, O Daniel, servant of the living God, is thy God, whom thou servest continually, able to deliver thee from the lions?

Then said Daniel unto the king, O king, live for ever. My God hath sent his angel, and hath shut the lions' mouths, that they have not hurt me: forasmuch as before him innocency was found in me; and also before thee, O king, have I done no hurt. Then was the king exceeding glad for him, and commanded that they should take Daniel up out of the den.

So Daniel was taken up out of the den, and no manner of hurt was found upon him, because he believed in his God. And the king commanded, and they brought those men which had accused Daniel, and they cast them into the den of lions, them,

their children, and their wives; and the lions had the mastery of them, and brake all their bones in pieces or ever they came at the bottom of the den.

Then king Darius wrote unto all people, nations, and languages, that dwell in all the earth; Peace be multiplied unto you. I make a decree, That in every dominion of my kingdom men tremble and fear before the God of Daniel: for he is the living God, and steadfast for ever, and his kingdom that which shall not be destroyed, and his dominion shall be even unto the end. He delivereth and rescueth, and he worketh signs and wonders in heaven and in earth, who hath delivered Daniel from the power of the lions. So this Daniel prospered in the reign of Darius, and in the reign of Cyrus the Persian.

FOR DISCUSSION

1. Do you feel Daniel's faith was truly tested by this incident? Would you define his behavior as heroic? Explain. How do you know that the king did not have the same type of faith as Daniel?

2. Daniel's interpretation of the writing on the wall reveals that Belshazzar has committed the same sins that his father committed. What were they? Why do you think Belshazzar's punishment was so immediate? Were his sins actually worse than his father's?

3. Why do the presidents and princes desire Daniel's death? Was he neglectful of his duties? Unfair?

4. What flaw in the king caused him to sign the decree? Why did Daniel disobey the king's command?

"Although the winds blow upon him, and the sun streams upon him, and the vulture tears at his liver, Prometheus will not cry out his repentance to heaven."

PROMETHEUS
PADRAIC COLUM

THE GODS more than once made a race of men; the first was a Golden Race. Very close to the gods who dwell on Olympus[1] was this Golden Race; they lived justly, although there were no laws to compel them. In the time of the Golden Race the earth knew only one season, and that season was everlasting spring. The men and women of the Golden Race lived through a span of life that was far beyond that of the men and women of our day, and when they died, it was as though sleep had become everlasting with them. They had all good things, and that without labor, for the earth without any forcing bestowed fruits and crops upon them. They had peace all through their lives, this Golden Race, and after they had passed away, their spirits remained above the earth, inspiring the men of the race that came after them to do great and gracious things and to act justly and kindly to one another.

After the Golden Race had passed away, the gods made for the earth a second race— a Silver Race. Less noble in spirit and in body was this Silver Race, and the seasons that visited them were less gracious. In the time of the Silver Race the gods made the seasons—summer and spring, and autumn and winter. They knew parching heat, and the bitter winds of winter, and snow and rain and hail. It was the men of the Silver

PROMETHEUS: pronounced prō·mēth′yüs.
[1] OLYMPUS: Mt. Olympus, in Greece, was at one time thought to be the home of the gods.

"Prometheus" by Padraic Colum reprinted by permission of The Macmillan Company from *The Golden Fleece* by Padraic Colum. Copyright 1921 by The Macmillan Company, renewed 1949 by Padraic Colum.

Race who first built houses for shelter. They lived through a span of life that was longer than our span, but it was not long enough to give wisdom to them. Children were brought up at their mothers' sides for a hundred years, playing at childish things. And when they came to years beyond a hundred, they quarreled with one another and wronged one another, and did not know enough to give reverence to the immortal gods. Then, by the will of Zeus, the Silver Race passed away as the Golden Race had passed away. Their spirits stay in the Underworld, and they are called by men the blessed spirits of the Underworld.

And then there was made the third race —the Race of Bronze. They were a race great of stature, terrible and strong. Their armor was of bronze, their swords were of bronze, their implements were of bronze, and of bronze, too, they made their houses. No great span of life was theirs, for with the weapons that they took in their terrible hands they slew one another. Thus they passed away and went down under the earth to Hades,[1] leaving no name that men might know them by.

Then the gods created a fourth race— our own: a Race of Iron. We have not the justice that was amongst the men of the Golden Race, nor the simpleness that was amongst the men of the Silver Race, nor the stature nor the great strength that the men of the Bronze Race possessed. We are of iron that we may endure. It is our doom that we must never cease from labor and that we must very quickly grow old.

But miserable as we are today, there was a time when the lot of men was more miserable. With poor implements they had to labor on a hard ground. There was less justice and kindliness amongst men in those days than there is now.

Once, it came into the mind of Zeus that he would destroy the fourth race and leave the earth to the nymphs and the satyrs.[2] He would destroy it by a great flood. But Prometheus, the Titan god who had given aid to Zeus against the other Titans—Prometheus, who was called the Foreseer—could not consent to the race of men being destroyed utterly, and he considered a way of saving some of them. To a man and a woman, Deucalion and Pyrrha,[3] just and gentle people, he brought word of the plan of Zeus, and he showed them how to make a ship that would bear them through what was about to be sent upon the earth.

Then Zeus shut up in their cave all the winds but the wind that brings rain and clouds. He bade this wind, the South Wind, sweep over the earth, flooding it with rain. He called upon Poseidon[4] and bade him to let the sea pour in upon the land. And Poseidon commanded the rivers to put forth all their strength, and sweep dikes away, and overflow their banks.

The clouds and the sea and the rivers poured upon the earth. The flood rose higher and higher, and in the places where the pretty lambs had played the ugly sea calves now gamboled; men in their boats drew fishes out of the tops of elm trees, and the water nymphs were amazed to come on men's cities under the waves.

Soon even the men and women who had boats were overwhelmed by the rise

[1] HADES: the underworld kingdom believed to be the abode of the spirits of the dead.

[2] NYMPHS . . . SATYRS: Nymphs were nature goddesses; satyrs, part human and part goat.
[3] DEUCALION, PYRRHA: dü·kāl'yən, pir'ə.
[4] POSEIDON (pə·sīd'ən): god of the sea.

of water; all perished then except Deucalion and Pyrrha, his wife—them the waves had not overwhelmed, for they were in a ship that Prometheus had shown them how to build. The flood went down at last, and Deucalion and Pyrrha climbed up to a high and a dry ground. Zeus saw that two of the race of men had been left alive. But he saw that these two were just and kindly and had a right reverence for the gods. He spared them, and he saw their children again peopling the earth.

Prometheus, who had saved them, looked on the men and women of the earth with compassion. Their labor was hard, and they wrought much to gain little. They were chilled at night in their houses, and the winds that blew in the daytime made the old men and women bend double like a wheel. Prometheus thought to himself that if men and women had the element that only the gods knew of—the element of fire—they could make for themselves implements for labor; they could build houses that would keep out the chilling winds, and they could warm themselves at the blaze.

But the gods had not willed that men should have fire, and to go against the will of the gods would be impious.[1] Prometheus went against the will of the gods. He stole fire from the altar of Zeus, and he hid it in a hollow fennel stalk, and he brought it to men.

Then men were able to hammer iron into tools, and cut down forests with axes, and sow grain where the forests had been. Then were they able to make houses that the storms could not overthrow, and they were able to warm themselves at hearth fires. They had rest from their labor at

times. They built cities; they became beings who no longer had heads and backs bent but were able to raise their faces even to the gods.

And Zeus spared the race of men who had now the sacred element of fire. But he knew that Prometheus had stolen this fire even from his own altar and had given it to men. And he thought on how he might punish the great Titan god for his impiety.

He brought back from the Underworld the giants that he had put there to guard the Titans that had been hurled down to Tartarus.[2] He brought back Gyes, Cottus, and Briareus, and he commanded them to lay hands upon Prometheus and to fasten him with fetters to the highest, blackest crag upon Caucasus.[3] And Briareus, Cottus, and Gyes seized upon the Titan god, and carried him to Caucasus, and fettered him with fetters of bronze to the highest, blackest crag—with fetters of bronze that may not be broken. There they have left the Titan stretched, under the sky, with the cold winds blowing upon him, and with the sun streaming down on him. And that his punishment might exceed all other punishments, Zeus had sent a vulture to prey upon him—a vulture that tears at his liver each day.

And yet Prometheus does not cry out that he has repented of his gift to man; although the winds blow upon him, and the sun streams upon him, and the vulture tears at his liver, Prometheus will not cry out his repentance to heaven. And Zeus may not utterly destroy him. For Prometheus the Foreseer knows a secret that Zeus would fain have him disclose. He knows

[1] IMPIOUS: not reverent.

[2] TARTARUS: part of the Underworld.
[3] CAUCASUS: mountain chain in what is now southwestern Russia.

that even as Zeus overthrew his father and made himself the ruler in his stead, so, too, another will overthrow Zeus. And one day Zeus will have to have the fetters broken from around the limbs of Prometheus, and will have to bring from the rock and the vulture, and into the Council of the Olympians, the unyielding Titan god.

FOR DISCUSSION

1. Prometheus was severely punished for giving fire to mankind. Why did he defy the gods? Did Prometheus ever do anything else for mankind in defiance of the gods?

2. What were the basic differences in the four races of man? To which race do we belong? How did fire improve the life of our race?

3. Why couldn't Zeus overlook Prometheus' impiety? How did he go about capturing Prometheus? What prevents Zeus from completely destroying Prometheus?

"I do not know where I shall go. I am in trouble, but I cannot tell you now what it is."

SCARFACE

GEORGE BIRD GRINNELL

IN THE EARLIEST TIMES there was no war. All the tribes were at peace. In those days there was a man who had a daughter, a very beautiful girl. Many young men wanted to marry her, but every time she was asked, she only shook her head and said she did not want a husband.

"How is this?" asked her father. "Some of these young men are rich, handsome, and brave."

"Why should I marry?" replied the girl. "I have a rich father and mother. Our lodge is good. The parfleches[1] are never empty. There are plenty of tanned robes

[1] PARFLECHES (pär′flesh·əz): rawhide pouches.

and soft furs for winter. Why worry me, then?"

The Raven Bearers held a dance; they all dressed carefully and wore their ornaments, and each one tried to dance the best. Afterwards some of them asked for this girl, but still she said no. Then the Bulls, the Kit-foxes, and others of the *I-kun-uh'-kah-tsi* held their dances, and all those who were rich, many great warriors, asked this man for his daughter, but to every one of them she said no. Then her father was angry and said, "Why, now, this way? All the best men have asked for you, and still you say no. I believe you have a secret lover."

"Ah!" said her mother. "What shame for us should a child be born and our daughter still unmarried!" "Father! mother!" replied the girl. "Pity me. I have no secret lover, but now hear the truth. That Above Person, the Sun, told me, 'Do not marry any of those men, for you are mine; thus you shall be happy, and live to great age'; and again he said, 'Take heed. You must not marry. You are mine.'"

"Ah!" replied her father. "It must always be as he says." And they talked no more about it.

There was a poor young man, very poor. His father, mother, all his relations, had gone to the Sand Hills. He had no lodge, no wife to tan his robes or sew his moccasins. He stopped in one lodge today, and tomorrow he ate and slept in another; thus he lived. He was a good-looking young man, except that on his cheek he had a scar, and his clothes were always old and poor.

After those dances some of the young men met this poor Scarface, and they laughed at him and said, "Why don't you ask that girl to marry you? You are so rich

and handsome!" Scarface did not laugh; he replied, "Ah! I will do as you say. I will go and ask her." All the young men thought this was funny. They laughed a great deal. But Scarface went down by the river. He waited by the river, where the women came to get water, and by and by the girl came along. "Girl," he said, "wait. I want to speak with you. Not as a designing person do I ask you, but openly where the Sun looks down, and all may see."

"Speak then," said the girl.

"I have seen the days," continued the young man. "You have refused those who are young and rich and brave. Now, today, they laughed and said to me, 'Why do you not ask her?' I am poor, very poor. I have no lodge, no food, no clothes, no robes and warm furs. I have no relations; all have gone to the Sand Hills; yet now, today, I ask you, take pity, be my wife."

The girl hid her face in her robe and brushed the ground with the point of her moccasin, back and forth, back and forth, for she was thinking. After a time she said, "True. I have refused all those rich young men, yet now the poor one asks me, and I am glad. I will be your wife, and my people will be happy. You are poor, but it does not matter. My father will give you dogs. My mother will make us a lodge. My people will give us robes and furs. You will be poor no longer."

Then the young man was happy, and he started to kiss her, but she held him back, and said: "Wait! The Sun has spoken to me. He says I may not marry; that I belong to him. He says if I listen to him, I shall live to great age. But now I say: Go to the Sun. Tell him, 'She whom you spoke with heeds your words. She has never done wrong, but now she wants to marry. I want her for my wife.' Ask him to take that scar from your face. That will be his sign. I will know he is pleased. But if he refuses, or if you fail to find his lodge, then do not return to me."

"Oh!" cried the young man, "at first your words were good. I was glad. But now it is dark. My heart is dead. Where is that far-off lodge? Where the trail, which no one yet has traveled?"

"Take courage, take courage!" said the girl, and she went to her lodge.

Scarface was very sad. He sat down and covered his head with his robe and tried to think what to do. After a while he got up and went to an old woman who had been kind to him. "Pity me," he said. "I am very poor. I am going away now on a long journey. Make me some moccasins."

"Where are you going?" asked the old woman. "There is no war; we are very peaceful here."

"I do not know where I shall go," replied Scarface. "I am in trouble, but I cannot tell you now what it is."

So the old woman made him some moccasins, seven pairs, with parfleche soles, and also she gave him a sack of food— pemmican[1] of berries, pounded meat, and dried back fat; for this old woman had a good heart. She liked the young man.

All alone and with a sad heart, he climbed the bluffs and stopped to take a last look at the camp. He wondered if he would ever see his sweetheart and the people again. "*Hai'-yu!* Pity me, O Sun," he prayed, and turning, he started to find the trail.

For many days he traveled on, over great

---

[1] PEMMICAN: form of concentrated food used by the Indians.

prairies, along timbered rivers, and among the mountains, and every day his sack of food grew lighter; but he saved it as much as he could, and ate berries and roots, and sometimes he killed an animal of some kind. One night he stopped by the home of a wolf. "*Hai-yah!*" said that one, "what is my brother doing so far from home?"

"Ah!" replied Scarface, "I seek the place where the Sun lives: I am sent to speak with him."

"I have traveled far," said the wolf. "I know all the prairies, the valleys, and the mountains, but I have never seen the Sun's home. Wait; I know one who is very wise. Ask the bear. He may tell you."

The next day the man traveled on again, stopping now and then to pick a few berries, and when night came, he arrived at the bear's lodge.

"Where is your home?" asked the bear. "Why are you traveling alone, my brother?"

"Help me! Pity me!" replied the young man; "because of her words I seek the Sun. I go to ask him for her."

"I know not where he stops," replied the bear. "I have traveled by many rivers, and I know the mountains, yet I have never seen his lodge. There is someone beyond, that striped-face, who is very smart. Go and ask him."

The badger was in his hole. Stooping over, the young man shouted, "Oh, cunning striped-face! Oh, generous animal! I wish to speak with you."

"What do you want?" said the badger, poking his head out of the hole.

"I want to find the Sun's home," replied Scarface. "I want to speak with him."

"I do not know where he lives," replied the badger. "I never travel very far. Over there in the timber is a wolverine. He is always traveling around, and is of much knowledge. Maybe he can tell you."

Then Scarface went to the woods and looked all around for the wolverine, but could not find him. So he sat down to rest. *"Hai'-yu! Hai'-yu!"* he cried. "Wolverine, take pity on me. My food is gone, my moccasins worn out. Now I must die."

"What is it, my brother?" he heard, and looking around, he saw the animal sitting near.

"She whom I would marry," said Scarface, "belongs to the Sun; I am trying to find where he lives, to ask him for her."

"Ah!" said the wolverine. "I know where he lives. Wait; it is nearly night. Tomorrow I will show you the trail to the big water. He lives on the other side of it."

Early in the morning, the wolverine showed him the trail, and Scarface followed it until he came to the water's edge. He looked out over it, and his heart almost stopped. Never before had anyone seen such a big water. The other side could not be seen, and there was no end to it. Scarface sat down on the shore. His food was all gone, his moccasins worn out. His heart was sick. "I cannot cross this big water," he said. "I cannot return to the people. Here, by this water, I shall die."

Not so. His Helpers were there. Two swans came swimming up to the shore. "Why have you come here?" they asked him. "What are you doing? It is very far to the place where your people live."

"I am here," replied Scarface, "to die. Far away, in my country, is a beautiful girl. I want to marry her, but she belongs to the Sun. So I started to find him and ask for her. I have traveled many days. My food is gone. I cannot go back. I cannot cross this big water, so I am going to die."

"No," said the swans, "it shall not be so. Across this water is the home of that Above Person. Get on our backs, and we will take you there."

Scarface quickly arose. He felt strong again. He waded out into the water and lay down on the swans' backs, and they started off. Very deep and black is that fearful water. Strange people live there, mighty animals which often seize and drown a person. The swans carried him safely, and took him to the other side. Here was a broad, hard trail leading back from the water's edge.

"*Kyi*," said the swans. "You are now close to the Sun's lodge. Follow that trail, and you will soon see it."

Scarface started up the trail, and pretty soon he came to some beautiful things lying in it. There was a war shirt, a shield, and a bow and arrows. He had never seen such pretty weapons; but he did not touch them. He walked carefully around them, and traveled on. A little way further on he met a young man, the handsomest person he had ever seen. His hair was very long, and he wore clothing made of strange skins. His moccasins were sewn with bright-colored feathers. The young man said to him, "Did you see some weapons lying on the trail?"

"Yes," replied Scarface, "I saw them."

"But did you not touch them?" asked the young man.

"No; I thought someone had left them there, so I did not take them."

"You are not a thief," said the young man. "What is your name?"

"Scarface."

"Where are you going?"

"To the Sun."

"My name," said the young man, "is A-pi-su'-ahts.[1] The Sun is my father; come, I will take you to our lodge. My father is not now at home, but he will come in at night."

Soon they came to the lodge. It was very large and handsome; strange medicine animals were painted on it. Behind, on a tripod, were strange weapons and beautiful clothes—the Sun's. Scarface was ashamed to go in, but Morning Star said, "Do not be afraid, my friend; we are glad you have come."

They entered. One person was sitting there, Ko-ko-mik'-e-is,[2] the Sun's wife, Morning Star's mother. She spoke to Scarface kindly and gave him something to eat. "Why have you come so far from your people?" she asked.

Then Scarface told her about the beautiful girl he wanted to marry. "She belongs to the Sun," he said. "I have come to ask him for her."

When it was time for the Sun to come home, the Moon hid Scarface under a pile of robes. As soon as the Sun got to the doorway, he stopped and said, "I smell a person."

"Yes, father," said Morning Star, "a good young man has come to see you. I know he is good, for he found some of my things on the trail and did not touch them."

Then Scarface came out from under the robes, and the Sun entered and sat down. "I am glad you have come to our lodge," he

[1] A-pi-su'-ahts: Early riser; that is, the Morning Star.
[2] Ko-ko-mik'-e-is: Night Red Light; the Moon.

said. "Stay with us as long as you think best. My son is lonesome sometimes; be his friend."

The next day the Moon called Scarface out of the lodge and said to him, "Go with Morning Star where you please, but never hunt near that big water; do not let him go there. It is the home of great birds which have long, sharp bills; they kill people. I have had many sons, but these birds have killed them all. Morning Star is the only one left."

So Scarface stayed there a long time and hunted with Morning Star. One day they came near the water and saw the big birds.

"Come," said Morning Star, "let us go and kill those birds."

"No, no!" replied Scarface; "we must not go there. Those are very terrible birds; they will kill us."

Morning Star would not listen. He ran towards the water, and Scarface followed. He knew that he must kill the birds and save the boy. If not, the Sun would be angry and might kill him. He ran ahead and met the birds, which were coming towards him to fight, and killed every one of them with his spear: not one was left. Then the young men cut off their heads and carried them home. Morning Star's mother was glad when they told her what they had done, and showed her the birds' heads. She cried and called Scarface "my son." When the Sun came home at night, she told him about it, and he too was glad. "My son," he said to Scarface, "I will not forget what you have this day done for me. Tell me now, what can I do for you?"

"*Hai'-yu*," replied Scarface, "*Hai'-yu*, pity me. I am here to ask you for that girl. I want to marry her. I asked her, and she was glad; but she says you own her, that

you told her not to marry."

"What you say is true," said the Sun. "I have watched the days, so I know it. Now, then, I give her to you; she is yours. I am glad she has been wise. I know she has never done wrong. The Sun pities good women. They shall live a long time. So shall their husbands and children. Now you will soon go home. Let me tell you something. Be wise and listen: I am the only chief. Everything is mine. I made the earth, the mountains, prairies, rivers, and forests. I made the people and all the animals. This is why I say I alone am the chief. I can never die. True, the winter makes me old and weak, but every summer I grow young again."

Then said the Sun, "What one of all animals is smartest? The raven is, for he always finds food. He is never hungry. Which one of all the animals is most Nat-o'-ye?[1] The buffalo is. Of all animals, I like him best. He is for the people. He is your food and your shelter. What part of his body is sacred? The tongue is. That is mine. What else is sacred? Berries are. They are mine too. Come with me and see the world." He took Scarface to the edge of the sky, and they looked down and saw it. It is round and flat, and all around the edge is the jumping-off place (or walls straight down).

Then said the Sun, "When any man is sick or in danger, his wife may promise to build me a lodge, if he recovers. If the woman is pure and true, then I will be pleased and help the man. But if she is bad, if she lies, then I will be angry. You shall build the lodge like the world, round with

[1] NAT-O'-YE: "of the Sun" or "having Sun power"; thus, sacred.

walls, but first you must build a sweat-house[1] of a hundred sticks. It shall be like the sky (a hemisphere), and half of it shall be painted red. That is me. The other half you will paint black. That is the night."

Further said the Sun, "Which is the best, the heart or the brain? The brain is. The heart often lies, the brain never." Then he

[1] SWEATHOUSE: lodge used by Indians for sweating, either as a ritual or in the treatment of a disease.

told Scarface everything about making the Medicine Lodge, and when he had finished, he rubbed a powerful medicine on his face, and the scar disappeared. Then he gave him two raven feathers, saying, "These are the sign for the girl, that I give her to you. They must always be worn by the husband of the woman who builds a Medicine Lodge."

The young man was now ready to return home. Morning Star and the Sun gave him

many beautiful presents. The Moon cried and kissed him, and called him "my son." Then the Sun showed him the short trail. It was the Wolf Road (Milky Way). He followed it, and soon reached the ground.

It was a very hot day. All the lodge skins were raised, and the people sat in the shade. There was a chief, a very generous man, and all day long people kept coming to his lodge to feast and smoke with him. Early in the morning this chief saw a person sitting out on a butte[1] nearby, close wrapped in his robe. The chief's friends came and went, the sun reached the middle, and passed on down towards the mountains. Still this person did not move. When it was almost night, the chief said, "Why does that person sit there so long? The heat has been strong, but he has never eaten nor drunk. He may be a stranger; go and ask him in."

So some young men went up to him and said, "Why do you sit here in the great heat all day? Come to the shade of the lodges. The chief asks you to feast with him."

---

[1] BUTTE (byüt): isolated hill.

Then the person arose and threw off his robe, and they were surprised. He wore beautiful clothes. His bow, shield, and other weapons were of strange make. But they knew his face, although the scar was gone, and they ran ahead shouting, "The scarface poor young man has come. He is poor no longer. The scar on his face is gone."

All the people rushed out to see him. "Where have you been?" they asked. "Where did you get all these pretty things?" He did not answer. There in the crowd stood that young woman; and taking the two raven feathers from his head, he gave them to her and said, "The trail was very long, and I nearly died, but by those Helpers, I found his lodge. He is glad. He sends these feathers to you. They are the sign."

Great was her gladness then. They were married, and made the first Medicine Lodge, as the Sun had said. The Sun was glad. He gave them great age. They were never sick. When they were very old, one morning their children said, "Awake! Rise and eat." They did not move. In the night, in sleep, without pain, their shadows had departed for the Sand Hills.

FOR DISCUSSION

1. Upon his triumphant return, Scarface does not answer the excited questions of the crowd; instead, he brings the two feathers to the young maiden. Why?

2. The beautiful girl had many suitors before Scarface. Why had she refused to marry? Is more than one reason suggested in the story?

3. The Indians' great respect for animals and their religious importance is clearly seen in this story. Which animals are able to help Scarface? Which animal does the Sun claim is the smartest? Which animal is most Nat-o'-ye?

4. The maiden's last words to Scarface before his journey were, "Take courage, take courage." What incidents on the journey reveal Scarface's courage? What other admirable traits does he possess?

A SONG OF GREATNESS
TRADITIONAL CHIPPEWA SONG

When I hear the old men
Telling of heroes,
Telling of great deeds
Of ancient days—
When I hear that telling,   5
Then I think within me
I, too, am one of these.

When I hear the people
Praising great ones,
Then I know that I too   10
Shall be esteemed;
I, too, when my time comes
Shall do mightily.

FOR DISCUSSION

1. What effect do heroic tales have upon the speaker of this poem?

2. The speaker in this poem is an Indian. What words does the poet use that make you think of Indians?

3. Do you think the great deeds of ancestors are often responsible for the creation of heroes? Was this more true for Indians than it would be for modern man?

"A Song of Greatness" from *The Children Sing in the Far West* by Mary Austin. Copyright 1956 by Kenneth M. Chapman and Mary C. Wheelright.

"Will you turn back on the very threshold of heaven for a dog?"

YUDHISTHIR AND HIS BROTHERS
MABEL ASHE BELING

AGES AND AGES AGO there was a war in India, as fiercely fought, as nobly sung, as that war which Homer made immortal.[1] It was the war between the five Pandav princes and their hundred cousins, the Kurus, and this is the way it came to pass.

YUDHISTHIR: pronounced yŭ·dĭs′tĭr.

[1] THAT WAR . . . IMMORTAL: that is, the Trojan War, which the Greek poet Homer described in the *Iliad*.

"Yudhisthir and His Brothers" by Mabel Ashe Beling, from *The Wicked Goldsmith*, copyright 1941 by Mabel Ashe Beling, published by Harper & Brothers. Reprinted by permission of Lurton Blassingame, agent.

King Pandu lay dying. Beside his couch knelt his blind brother, and the King whispered feebly, "I leave this world before my sons are old enough to take my place. Rule the land so long as you live, brother, and see to it that my sons are trained as kings should be. To you I trust them, my kingdom and my sons."

So a blind king came to the throne, and faithfully he bore the trust laid on him. He ruled justly; he had the five Pandav princes instructed in all that warrior princes should know.

Yudhisthir was eldest. Over his birth the god of Justice presided—Yudhisthir was just and generous in heart. Bhima, the second, was godchild of the Wind, swift to think and swift to act. Arjun, the third, born under the sign of Indra,[1] was a mighty archer like the god who speeds the arrows of the rain and the bolts of thunder. The youngest two were twins, godsons of the starry Aswin Twins[2] who shine together in the night sky.

The blind King did not fail in the up-bringing of his nephews, but he had a blind spot to the faults of his own sons—they were bad as sons could be. Perhaps the King failed because there were so many of them. One hundred sons he had—and all were evil.

Eldest, proudest, cruelest was Duryodhan. By right of age and force he led the clan of Kuru princes and fostered in them a bitter jealousy of the five Pandavs, their cousins.

When Yudhisthir came of age, he shone in all the qualities his father had desired his sons to have. The five Pandav princes all were brave, wise, noble in spirit, but Yudhisthir was noblest of them all. Proudly the good blind King proclaimed him heir apparent to the throne.

His own sons raged. Never, the Kurus vowed, would they submit to be ruled by a Pandav prince. But they raged in secret. Duryodhan counseled them to hide their hate. He had a plan to be rid of these rivals forever. The Kurus took the oath of fealty[3] with smiling lips, while they waited a chance to slay their cousins.

The chance came soon. There was a festival in a town far distant from the capital city. The King was old and feeble, so he sent the Pandav princes with their mother to take his place at the festivities. As if to honor their visit, a special dwelling was built for them. Duryodhan ordered its building—every piece of wood which went into it was dry as tinder and soaked in oil.

As soon as the princes and their mother slept on the night of their arrival, one of the Kurus set fire to the house, and the Pandavs woke to the roar of flames about them.

But they were not to die. Workmen who built the house—perhaps they knew the plot and wished to save their rightful lords—had made an underground passage which led from the building to the jungle just behind it. Through this secret way the brothers escaped, carrying their old mother to safety.

Once in the jungle they considered what was best for them to do. They had no doubt the Kurus had planned their death, and the oath of fealty had been but a trick to lull suspicion. The Pandavs knew no fear for themselves—they feared for their mother. The Kurus had not scrupled to include her in the death they planned. What were five against one hundred? Five who would stoop to no shameful deed, against one hundred who had no honor, who felt no shame!

Only in the jungles and the forests, and only so long as the Kurus thought them dead in the flames, were they and their mother safe. They built in the forest a little house, well thatched against the weather. Then they joined an order of Brahmins[4]

---

[1] INDRA (in′drə): Hindu god of the sun, of rain and thunder, and of battle.
[2] ASWIN TWINS: gods of light.
[3] FEALTY (fēl′tē): faithfulness.

[4] BRAHMINS: Hindu priests.

nearby and gave up the life of warrior princes to put on the robes of humble mendicants.[1] Day by day along the dusty roads they begged their bread according to the rule of the order, and each night they took food home to their mother.

One day they met on the road a group of strangers, Brahmin mendicants like themselves, who hailed them with a great piece of news.

"Come along with us, brothers!" the Brahmins urged. "We are on our way to Panchala. The King has proclaimed 'Bride's Choice.' He will give his fair daughter as prize in the test of the bow. Any man not baseborn[2] may try his skill. All the kings and princes of India will be there."

Arjun's heart leaped at thought of drawing bow again, but he shook his head. "We cannot go. We are five poor brothers with a mother to care for; we must stay here."

"Bring your mother with you. We travel but slowly, begging as we go. There are aged women and holy sisters among our number. Come, there will be feasts for all and gifts for all. There will be dancers and wrestlers, actors and storytellers. You will see all the chieftains and kings try their mightiest for the hand of fair Draupadi.[3]

"Who knows? You are all handsome as princes—the princess may lose her heart to one of you; perhaps to this tall youth with arms stout as a bowman's," and they pointed to stalwart Arjun, standing with his arm about his old mother. "At least he may contend in some of the feats of valor, and perhaps win one of the thousand prizes."

So the five brothers and their mother joined the band of Brahmins, and slowly, on foot and begging their food along the way, they came after many days to the noble city of Panchala. It seemed all India had moved to the same place, humble folk afoot, great ones on horseback, in chariot, or swaying in howdahs[4] on the broad back of an elephant. No place was to be found in the crowded city for the Pandavs and their mother, but a kindly potter offered them room in his cottage outside the city gates, and they were grateful.

Every morning they left their mother to rest in this humble shelter and went forth to beg food and to see the wonders of the festive city. Beyond the wall and moat, a level field had been enclosed for the festivities. Around it, for the royal guests, were new-built mansions which shone in the sunshine white as silver swans.

Minstrels and dancers, strolling players and famous storytellers swarmed thick as honeybees, and plied their arts to entertain the multitude.

Music, feasting, contests at sport and arms, gaiety for fifteen days, and at last came the great day of "Bride's Choice." The people surged about the field of contest, thousands upon thousands of them. Under red canopies sat kings, queens, nobles, to watch the proudest youths of India contend for the hand of its fairest princess.

She came, Draupadi, in bridal dress, with the golden garland of bridal on her arm. That garland she would hang around the neck of the victor, and him she would wed. The Prince, her brother, led her to the altar where an aged priest kindled the holy fire and spoke the holy mantras.[5]

---

[1] MENDICANTS: members of a religious order who live by begging.
[2] BASEBORN: of humble parentage.
[3] DRAUPADI: drou'pə·dē.

[4] HOWDAHS: seats, usually covered by canopies, on the backs of elephants.
[5] MANTRAS: in the Hindu religion, prayer formulas to be sung or recited.

Then brother and sister turned to face the multitude, and the Prince made proclamation, saluting first his aged father, King Drupad, sitting on a throne high above them. The Prince held aloft for all to see the huge war bow of the King.

"Behold the bow of Drupad, my father. By the ancient custom of our fathers, today we celebrate Bride's Choice. Far down the field shines the high-hung target. Mark well the ring of brass which whirls before it. Whoever, born of Arya[1] blood, be he rich or be he poor, shall send five arrows from this bow through that whirling ring and hit the target, may stand forth and claim for his bride my sister, the Princess Draupadi."

A roar of applause went up from the throng. The Prince held up his hand for silence. He turned to the Princess and named aloud the roll call of her suitors. Like a herald he proclaimed the lineage and name of each, and the famous deeds he had done.

"Behold, my sister, these monarchs and princes who come to seek thy hand. Here are brave Duryodhan and his brothers of the house of Kuru. Here are Kalinga and Tamra from the eastern ocean. Here is Pattan who rules the western shore. . . ." On he went down the long list of jewel-decked monarchs from north, east, south, and west—and each, as his name and fame were spoken, sought a look from the lovely Draupadi.

"And now, my sister," he ended, "these suitors abide thy choice! Whoso hits the target, choose him for thy husband, Draupadi, if he please thy heart, and if he be of noble blood!"

The crowd cheered. One by one the noble suitors stepped forward to the test. In

[1] ARYA: noble.

haughtiness and pride, they stepped forth. In shame, they slunk back. Most of them had not strength to bend the mighty bow, one was challenged as baseborn, the three whose arms were strong enough to nock the arrow and bend the bow, saw each his arrow strike the whirling ring, rebound, and fall to earth. Not a single shaft reached the target shining far down the field.

From under the red canopies, women's laughter rang at each defeat. The populace roared and jeered.

The defeated suitors stormed angrily to each other, "We have been tricked! The test is impossible. Indra himself could not bend that bow, nor strike that target with his thunderbolts! Drupad has shamed us before great queens, and made us a laughingstock for the populace!"

The five brothers, standing among the Brahmins, watched trials and failures. Arjun trembled like a hunting leopard held on leash, and looked to Yudhisthir. At last the older brother nodded, and Arjun, tall, calm now as a god, strode from the rank of mendicants and walked to the dais[2] where the great bow lay. All eyes followed as he lifted it and took five arrows in his hand.

He bent his head to the fair Draupadi, then he nocked the arrow, and his mighty arm drew the bow full arc. With a long hiss, the arrow sped its way. Another, another, another—five arrows in air at the same time, like wild geese following their leader—flew through the whirling ring and struck the target with a clang! It fell to earth with a sound of thunder, and a roar like thunder echoed from the multitude. Draupadi looked deep into Arjun's eyes,

[2] DAIS (dā'əs): raised platform.

Continued on page 113

IDEAS AND THE ARTS

A hero is a person who does more than anyone has a right to expect. Through his actions he usually expresses the aspirations and desires of a particular group of people at a particular time. Since he performs on a larger scale than others, he is always open to the risk of failure. But if he succeeds he becomes a symbol of those aspirations and desires. Artists celebrate his deeds, and he becomes a legend.

The first painting in this group presents one of the most famous heroes of English and European legend, King Arthur. We have no information about King Arthur that could be called fact. But we have many stories, and these stories suggest that he lived fourteen or fifteen centuries ago. The picture we see here is of a stained glass window from a church in England. It shows Arthur kneeling in prayer in the private chapel of his castle. All around him angels play music. In this setting Arthur is presented as a religious hero. Whatever else he did, Arthur created a kingdom out of social confusion and conflicting forces. He did so in the name of God and in cooperation with the church. His deeds were important for social and political reasons, but this picture in a church recognizes their religious importance.

The next picture, by the Italian artist Bonaventura Berlinghieri, was painted to be placed above the altar in a church. It is a picture of St. Francis of Assisi. The scenes around St. Francis represent events from his life. At the middle left, for example, we see St. Francis preaching to the birds. St. Francis was the son of a wealthy family who gave up all his wealth and lived in poverty. He wanted to live a life of true Christian piety, and he wanted to preach to the poor, who were neglected by everyone, including the church. His action may not seem very heroic according to our usual notions of heroism, but it was strikingly heroic in his own time. It was so unusual that it shocked a great many people, and it was a long time before the church recognized his greatness. Here the artist presents St. Francis as a heroic figure—noble, determined, and dedicated.

The third picture is taken from a tapestry woven during the Middle Ages. People in the Middle Ages did not have the same sense of history that we have today. Whatever action he was presenting, the medieval artist presented it as if it were happening in his own time. Here we see the arming of Hector as if he were a medieval knight instead of a warrior from a much earlier time. Hector was the son of Priam, King of Troy. The Greeks set out to conquer and destroy Troy because Paris, also a son of Priam, had stolen Helen from her Greek husband. During the Middle Ages sympathy was on the side of the Trojans. They were regarded as the heroes. This picture shows Hector putting on his armor with the aid of a servant. He is bidding farewell to his wife, Andromache, and to his little son. Hector appears again in the scene below. Here his father is wishing him well in the coming battle. Hector, the greatest hero and the hope of Troy, was to be killed in a duel with Achilles, the Greek hero.

Benozzo Gozzoli's *Procession of the Magi* shows a very different kind of heroism. The Magi were the three kings, or wise men, who by watching the stars foretold the birth of Jesus Christ, the savior of man. The heroism of the Magi lay in their setting out to discover a miraculous child solely on the basis of their wisdom. They were heroic in recognizing the truth when there was no other evidence but the stars. This picture was painted for the chapel in the palace of the Medici of

Florence. The Medici were the rulers of Florence who led this small medieval Italian city to great power and prosperity. In the eyes of their followers they were both wise and heroic. Thus Gozzoli uses the faces of the Medici in painting the Magi.

The last two pictures deal in different ways with efforts to make heroes out of people who were not heroic. William Dobson's *Charles II as the Prince of Wales* is a portrait of an unheroic king. Charles' father, Charles I of England, was overthrown in the English Civil War of the seventeenth century and was finally put to death. Charles himself (who later became King under the name of Charles II) fought in these wars, but he was neither successful nor heroic. The face at the lower left of the picture is the face of the civil war. It is meant to suggest envy of Charles. The pose, the design, and the entire composition of this painting are intended to make an undistinguished man seem heroic.

The last painting is a satire on heroism. It is *Gangster Funeral,* painted by Jack Levine. A gangster is not at all heroic because what he does—through stealth, theft, and murder—works to destroy society instead of supporting it. Yet to his followers who share his ambitions he may appear heroic. In this painting the artist expresses contempt for those who would make a hero out of a man of evil.

Morse Peckham

STAINED GLASS WINDOW (1501) *KING ARTHUR* from the *MAGNIFICAT WINDOW*. Priory Church, Great Malvern, England.

108   BONAVENTURA BERLINGHIERI (early 13th century) *THE ST. FRANCIS ALTARPIECE*. Church of San Francesco, Pescia, Italy.

FRANCO-FLEMISH TAPESTRY (15th century) *HECTOR AND ANDROMACHE* from the *DESTRUCTION OF TROY.* Metropolitan Museum of Art, New York.

BENOZZO GOZZOLI (1420-1497) *PROCESSION OF THE MAGI.* Palazzo Medici-Riccardi, Florence.

WILLIAM DOBSON (1610-1646) *CHARLES II AS THE PRINCE OF WALES*. Scottish National Portrait Gallery, Edinburgh.

JACK LEVINE (born 1915) *GANGSTER FUNERAL*. Whitney Museum of American Art. New York.

then she stepped toward him, flung the golden garland of Bride's Choice round his neck, and stood beside him before the multitude.

The people went mad with delight, the Brahmins screamed and shook their deerskins, the heralds blew their trumpets.

But the suitors, stung by defeat, shouted a battle cry. This was the last insult, not to be borne. To have a beggar outdo them! To see the fairest princess in India won by a ragged mendicant!

They leaped to attack the old King, his son, and Draupadi herself! They yelled she was a shameless woman, she scorned kings and warriors for a beggar. Let her be burned on a blazing pyre to wipe out this insult she had put upon them!

But the Pandav brothers were ready to meet the maddened monarchs. At the first sign of attack, they dashed from their place and stood before old Drupad and his children, a mighty guard. Bhima was weaponless, but he snatched a living tree from its roots and wielded it before him like a mace.[1]

There was a battle, but it was brief. The suitors could not pass that barrier of brothers who stood like a wall before the old King. At last the King was able to make his voice heard, and calm the tumult.

"Hear me, ye monarchs!" Drupad called. "Calm your rage and hear me. You have naught to vex your pride. This lad whom you think a beggar is one of yourselves! I knew him the moment he drew bow. He is Arjun, son of Pandu, and these are his four brothers. How they came here in this guise I know not, but warriors they are and princes, not priests nor baseborn. I am

proud to give my daughter to any son of the house of Pandu."

There was nothing for the suitors then but to make the best of their disappointment and withdraw with what grace they could. The Kuru princes were confounded. To them it was as if the dead had risen to face their murderers. They slunk quietly away, lest the brothers accuse them to King Drupad. But the brothers had no thought of vengeance on this day of their triumph. Like good sons, they thought first of their mother. She would rejoice that the weary exile was over. With Drupad to support the Pandav cause, the Kurus would not dare withhold their rightful kingdom.

And Draupadi! Their mother would welcome the lovely princess to her heart. They must take Draupadi to her now, in the very moment of victory.

In triumph the five brothers led Draupadi to the humble cottage outside the gates where their mother awaited them. Joyously they called out to her before entering. "Mother, Mother! Come see! We have won a noble prize this day!"

And the mother, answering from within, called back, "Share it as brothers should!" Seeing Draupadi, she trembled lest her words cause dissension among her sons. One princess-bride to be disputed among five princes! Yet the words of a mother cannot be recalled, nor disobeyed.

Arjun spoke. It was he who had won Draupadi, and he loved her, but nothing must come between him and his brothers, nothing must prevent obedience to a mother's command.

"Yudhisthir is eldest," Arjun said, "and he is to be king. He shall wed Draupadi, and yet she shall be queen to all of us. When the time comes for us to wed, each

---

[1] MACE: club.

shall choose a bride, yet hold Draupadi always his First Queen."

Thus was the command obeyed, and thus it came about that Draupadi was wife to one brother, and queen to five. . . .

Yudhisthir, with his four truehearted brothers and Draupadi, queen of them all, were enthroned at last and reigned over a happy people. Sons grew up about them, tall and good, worthy to carry on the name and the labor. Wherever the Pandav brothers looked they saw their work done,

their earthly duty ended. The time had come for them to seek a higher conquest.

Queen Draupadi laid aside her silken robes, the five brothers their kingly state, they bade farewell to sons and daughters and loyal subjects. These six, who had suffered together and conquered together, undertook the hardest quest of all. They set out to cross the burning deserts and find the City of the Gods.

And after them, unnoticed, there trailed a dog—Yudhisthir's faithful hound.

Now where this City of the Gods lay, and how far distant, they were not sure. They knew its general direction—a glimmer of its light had shone out to them once in a while on the far horizon of the desert. This was enough to set their course by.

Over the frightful distances they looked and were not afraid. The sands burned their feet by day, the winds chilled them to the bone by night. Yudhisthir tried in vain to order the old hound home—to leave his master was the only command to which he was deaf. In the daytime the dog followed humbly in the rear, when night came he crept close and warmed his master's body with his own. Yudhisthir shared his scanty food with the poor creature.

Daily the way grew harder, the travelers weaker. One day at dawn when they rose, the Queen lay wan and smiling. Bhima bent over her and looked at Yudhisthir with tears in his eyes. "She is dead. Why should our dear queen, who never did a wrong in all her life, why should she fail to reach the City of the Gods with us?"

Yudhisthir, with anguished lips, answered him. "Because she was too true she dies. She could rule her deeds, but not her inner heart. It was our brother Arjun she loved from the day his arrows won her—better than heaven itself she loved him."

And the brothers left their lady to the burial of the sands, and strode on, the hound trailing after their weary feet.

Then Bhima passed, Arjun, the twins, one by one they died, each for some fault so generous that it was near to a virtue—some fault borne lightly on the roadways of the world, but too heavy a weight to bear on one's shoulders in the desert.

Only Yudhisthir was left—Yudhisthir

and the hound. In a timeless dream, the King strode on—and on, and on . . . alone, yet not alone, for always the dog was at his heels.

And on the horizon, the light shone clearer, and the horizon seemed not so far away.

The deadly sands were passed, a mountain rose before the King. He felt new strength in his limbs as he set foot to the rising slope. Then came a sudden thunder of chariot wheels, and lo, at Yudhisthir's side, Lord Indra appeared in a blaze of light. The hound, trembling, pressed close to his master's knee.

"Mount the chariot," the Lord said, smiling. "I have come to take you the rest of the way."

But Yudhisthir answered with a sick heart. "What is the City of the Gods to me now? My brothers have fallen by the way. My wife, too, my kind and faithful love—what is heaven without her?"

"They are there, Yudhisthir, they are there before you. What was earthly of them has been stripped away. But you alone of all men shall enter heaven in your own flesh!"

Still the King delayed. "There is one more I must have with me, Lord. This hound has followed me. I cannot leave him here."

Indra's face darkened, as the sun is darkened by a cloud passing over.

"You are a man no more. You have become as we, the gods. What need have you of this beast here?"

Yudhisthir groaned. "I cannot leave him, this hound has eaten my food, has shared my hardships, has loved me. . . ."

"He is unclean!" Indra's voice was stern. "Angels sweep away the prayers of one

whom a dog has touched while praying. Why did you leave your queen on the way, and all your brothers? And yet you will not leave this brute. Have you conquered your faults and reached the mount of heaven to yield to a foolish fondness for this unclean beast? Will you turn back on the very threshold of heaven for a dog?"

The King lifted his face. "When I was king on earth, men called me true and just. I never turned a suppliant[1] away. Look at this hound of mine. Shall I be less faithful to him? Shall I turn away and leave him to die alone, who has no friend but me? I left my brothers and my queen—I could do

[1] SUPPLIANT: one who begs for a favor.

nothing for the dead. But not for heaven itself will I leave a living thing that looks to me for love."

And the King turned his face back again toward the desert.

A great light shone as Indra smiled. "Mount the chariot, my son, and bring with you the hound. True king are you, Yudhisthir, who would not enter heaven, and fail one humble soul who trusted you. You have met the last test. You have not failed even a poor dog who loved you."

And Yudhisthir, in his worn human flesh, the hound in his own shaggy hide, mounted the car of Indra and ascended with him into life immortal.

FOR DISCUSSION

1. Actually the reader doesn't know much about Yudhisthir as an individual until he makes his journey to the City of the Gods. What do the incidents that occur on the trip tell you about him as a person?

2. How did the war between the Pandav princes and the Kurus come about? Why did the plot against the Pandavs fail? What fear made the Pandavs stay in hiding?

3. What were the conditions of the contest for Princess Draupadi's hand in marriage? What was the attitude of the suitors before Arjun drew the bow? Afterward? Why didn't the Pandavs seek revenge on the Kuru princes?

4. All the Pandav princes might be described as heroic. List their heroic deeds and traits as they occur throughout the story.

"Whoso Pulleth Out This Sword of this Stone and Anvil, is Rightwise King Born of All England."

THE SWORD IN THE STONE
T. H. WHITE

I

KING PELLINORE arrived for the important week-end, in a high state of flurry.

"I say," he exclaimed. "Do you know? Have you heard? Is it a secret, what?"

"Is what a secret, what?" they asked him.

"Why, the King," cried his majesty. "You know, about the King?"

"What's the matter with the King?" inquired Sir Ector. "You don't say he's comin' down to hunt with those dratted hounds of his or anythin' like that?"

"He's dead," cried King Pellinore tragically. "He's dead, poor fellah, and can't hunt any more."

Sir Grunmore stood up respectfully and took off his helm.

"The King is dead," he said. "Long live the King."

Everybody else felt they ought to stand up too, and the boys' nurse burst into tears.

"There, there," she sobbed. "His loyal highness dead and gone, and him such a respectful gentleman. Many's the illuminated[1] picture I've cut out of him, from the illustrated Missals,[2] aye, and stuck up over the mantel. From the time when he was in swaddling bands,[3] right through them world towers till he was a-visiting the dispersed areas as the world's Prince Charming, there wasn't a picture of 'im but I had it out, aye, and give 'im a last thought o' nights."

"Compose yourself, Nannie," said Sir Ector.

"It's solemn, isn't it," said King Pellinore, "what?"

"A solemn moment," said Sir Grunmore. "The King is dead. Long live the King."

"We ought to pull down the blinds," said Kay, who was always a stickler for good form, "or half-mast the banners."

"That's right," said Sir Ector. "Somebody go and tell the sergeant-at-arms."

It was obviously the Wart's duty to execute this command, for he was now the junior of all the noblemen present, and so he ran out cheerfully to find the sergeant. Soon those who were left in the solar could hear a voice crying out, "Nah then, one-two, special mourning fer 'is lite majesty, lower awai on the command Two!" and then the flapping of all standards, ban-

---

[1] ILLUMINATED: decorated with ornamental designs.

[2] MISSALS: prayer books.

[3] SWADDLING BANDS: strips of cloth wound about a newborn infant.

Reprinted by permission of G. P. Putnam's Sons from *The Sword in the Stone* by T. H. White. Copyright 1939 by T. H. White. Copyright renewed © 1965 by Lloyds Bank, Executor and Trustee, (Channel Islands) Ltd.

ners, pennons, pennoncells, banderolls, guidons, streamers and cognizances which made gay the snowy turrets of the Forest Sauvage.

"How did you hear?" asked Sir Ector.

"I was just pricking through the purlieus of the forest after that Beast, you know, when I met with a solemn friar of orders gray, and he told me. It's the very latest news."

"Poor old Pendragon," said Sir Ector.

"The King is dead," said Sir Grummore solemnly. "Long live the King."

"It's all very well for you to keep on mentioning that, my dear Grummore," exclaimed King Pellinore petulantly, "but who is this King, what, that is to live so long, what, accordin' to you?"

"Well, his heir," said Sir Grummore, rather taken aback.

"Our blessed monarch," said the Nurse tearfully, "never had no hair. Anybody that studied the loyal family knowed that."

"Good gracious!" exclaimed Sir Ector. "But he must have had a next-of-kin?"

"That's just it," cried King Pellinore in high excitement. "That's the excitin' part about it, what? No hair and no next of skin, and who's to succeed to the throne? That's what my friar was so excited about, what, and why he was asking who could succeed to what, what? What?"

"Do you mean to tell me," exclaimed Sir Grummore indignantly, "that there ain't no King of England?"

"Not a scrap of one," cried King Pellinore, feeling most important. "And there have been signs and wonders of no mean might."

"I think it's a scandal," said Sir Grummore. "God knows what the dear old country is comin' to. It's these bolshevists, no doubt."

"What sort of signs and wonders?" asked Sir Ector.

"Well, there has appeared a sort of sword in a stone, what, in a sort of a church. Not in the church, if you see what I mean, and not in the stone, but that sort of thing, what, like you might say."

"I don't know what the Church is coming to," said Sir Grummore.

"It's in an anvil," explained the King.

"The church?"

"No, the sword."

"But I thought you said the sword was in the stone?"

"No," said King Pellinore. "The stone is outside the church."

"Look here, Pellinore," said Sir Ector. "You have a bit of a rest, old boy, and start again. Here, drink up this horn of mead and take it easy."

"The sword," said King Pellinore, "is stuck through an anvil which stands on a stone. It goes right through the anvil and into the stone. The anvil is stuck to the stone. The stone stands outside a church. Give me some more mead."

"I don't think that's much of a wonder," remarked Sir Grummore. "What I wonder at is that they should allow such things to happen. But you can't tell nowadays, what with all these socialists."

"My dear fellah," cried Pellinore, getting excited again, "it's not where the stone is, what, that I'm trying to tell you, but what is written on it, what, where it is."

"What?"

"Why, on its pommel."[1]

"Come on, Pellinore," said Sir Ector. "You just sit quite still with your face to the wall for a minute, and then tell us what you are talkin' about. Take it easy,

---

[1] POMMEL: knob on the hilt (handle) of a sword.

old fruit. No need for hurryin'. You sit still and look at the wall, there's a good chap, and talk as slow as you can."

"There are words written on this sword in this stone outside this church," cried King Pellinore piteously, "and these words are as follows. Oh, do try to listen to me, you two, instead of interruptin' all the time about nothin', for it makes a man's head go ever so."

"What are these words?" asked Kay.

"These words say this," said King Pellinore, "so far as I can understand from that old friar of orders gray."

"Go on, do," said Kay, for the King had come to a halt.

"Go on," said Sir Ector, "what do these words on this sword in this anvil in this stone outside this church, say?"

"Some red propaganda, no doubt," remarked Sir Grummore.

King Pellinore closed his eyes tight, extended his arms in both directions, and announced in capital letters, "Whoso Pulleth Out This Sword of this Stone and Anvil, is Rightwise King Born of All England."

"Who said that?" asked Sir Grummore.

"But the sword said it, like I tell you."

"Talkative weapon," remarked Sir Grummore skeptically.

"It was written on it," cried the King angrily. "Written on it in letters of gold."

"Why didn't you pull it out then?" asked Sir Grummore.

"But I tell you that I wasn't there. All this that I am telling you was told to me by that friar I was telling you of, like I tell you."

"Has this sword with this inscription been pulled out?" inquired Sir Ector.

"No," whispered King Pellinore dramatically. "That's where the whole excitement comes in. They can't pull this sword out

at all, although they have all been tryin' like fun, and so they have had to proclaim a tournament all over England, for New Year's Day, so that the man who comes to the tournament and pulls out the sword can be King of all England for ever, what, I say?"

"Oh, father," cried Kay. "The man who pulls that sword out of the stone will be the King of England. Can't we go to this tournament, father, and have a shot?"

"Couldn't think of it," said Sir Ector.

"Long way to London," said Sir Grummore, shaking his head.

"My father went there once," said King Pellinore.

Kay said, "Oh, surely we could go? When I am knighted I shall have to go to a tournament somewhere, and this one happens at just the right date. All the best people will be there, and we should see the famous knights and great kings. It doesn't matter about the sword, of course, but think of the tournament, probably the greatest there has ever been in England, and all the things we should see and do. Dear father, let me go to this tourney, if you love me, so that I may bear away the prize of all, in my maiden[1] fight."

"But Kay," said Sir Ector, "I have never been to London."

"All the more reason to go. I believe that anybody who doesn't go for a tournament like this, will be proving that he has no noble blood in his veins. Think what people will say about us, if we don't go and have a shot at that sword. They will say that Sir Ector's family was too vulgar and knew it had no chance."

"We all know the family has no chance," said Sir Ector, "that is, for the sword."

---

[1] MAIDEN: *here*, first.

"Lot of people in London," remarked Sir Grummore, with a wild surmise.[1] "So they say."

He took a deep breath and goggled at his host with eyes like marbles.

"And shops," added King Pellinore suddenly, also beginning to breathe heavily.

"Dang it!" cried Sir Ector, bumping his horn mug on the table so that it spilled. "Let's all go to London, then, and see the new King!"

They rose up as one man.

"Why shouldn't I be as good a man as my father?" exclaimed King Pellinore.

"Dash it all," cried Sir Grummore. "After all, dash it all, it is the capital."

"Hurray!" shouted Kay.

"Lord have mercy," said the nurse.

At this moment the Wart came in with Merlyn, and everybody was too excited to notice that, if he had not now been grown up, he would have been on the verge of tears.

"Oh, Wart," cried Kay, forgetting for the moment that he was only addressing his squire,[2] and slipping back into the familiarity of their boyhood. "What do you think? We are all going to London for a great tournament on New Year's Day!"

"Are we?"

"Yes, and you will carry my shield and spears for the jousts, and I shall win the palm[3] of everybody and be a great knight!"

"Well, I am glad we are going," said the Wart, "for Merlyn is leaving us too."

"Oh, we shan't need Merlyn."

"He is leaving us," repeated the Wart.

"Leavin' us?" asked Sir Ector. "I thought it was we that were leavin'."

"He is going away from the Forest Sauvage."

Sir Ector said, "Oh, come now, Merlyn, what's all this about? I don't understand all this a bit."

"I have come to say Good-by, Sir Ector," said the old magician. "Tomorrow my pupil Kay will be knighted, and the next week my other pupil will be away as his squire. I have outlived my usefulness here, and it is time to go."

"Now, now, don't say that," said Sir Ector. "I think you're a jolly useful chap whatever happens. You just stay here and teach me, or be the librarian or something. Don't you leave an old man alone, after the children have flown."

"We shall all meet again," said Merlyn. "There is no cause to be sad."

"Don't go," said Kay.

"I must go," replied their tutor. "We have had a good time while we were young, but it is in the nature of Time to fly. There are many things in other parts of the kingdom which I ought to be attending to just now: and it is a specially busy time for me. Come, Archimedes,[4] say Good-by to the company."

"Good-by," said Archimedes tenderly to the Wart.

"Good-by," said the Wart without looking up at all.

"But you can't go," cried Sir Ector, "not without a month's notice."

"Can't I?" replied Merlyn, taking up the position always assumed by philosophers who propose to dematerialize. He stood on his toes, while Archimedes held tight to his shoulder: began to spin on them slowly like a top: spun faster and faster till he was only a blur of grayish light: and in a

---

[1] SURMISE: idea formed in the imagination.
[2] SQUIRE: young nobleman who acts as a servant to a knight.
[3] PALM: prize.

[4] ARCHIMEDES: Merlin's pet owl.

few seconds there was no one there at all.

"Good-by, Wart," cried two faint voices outside the solar window.

"Good-by," said the Wart for the last time; and the poor fellow went quickly out of the room.

II

The knighting took place in a whirl of preparations. Kay's sumptuous bath had to be set up in the box-room, between two towel-horses and an old box of selected games which contained a worn-out straw dart-board—it was called flechette in those days—because all the other rooms were full of packing. The nurse spent the whole time constructing new warm pants for everybody, on the principle that the climate of any place outside the Forest Sauvage must be treacherous to the extreme, and, as for the sergeant, he polished all the armor till it was quite brittle and sharpened the swords till they were almost worn away.

At last it was time to set out.

Perhaps, if you happen not to have lived in the old England of the fifteenth century, or whenever it was, and in a remote castle on the borders of the Marches at that, you will find it difficult to imagine the wonders of their journey.

The road, or track, ran most of the time along the high ridges of the hills or downs, and they could look down on either side of them upon the desolate marshes where the snowy reeds sighed, and the ice crackled, and the duck in the red sunsets quacked loud on the winter air. The whole country was like that. Perhaps there would be a moory marsh on one side of the ridge, and a forest of thirty thousand acres on the other, with all the great branches weighted in white. They could sometimes see a wisp of smoke among the trees, or a huddle of buildings far out among the impassable reeds, and twice they came to quite respectable towns which had several inns to boast of; but on the whole it was an England without civilization. The better roads were cleared of cover for a bow-shot on either side of them, lest the traveler should be slain by hidden thieves.

They slept where they could, sometimes in the hut of some cottager who was prepared to welcome them, sometimes in the castle of a brother knight who invited them to refresh themselves, sometimes in the firelight and fleas of a dirty little hovel with a bush tied to a pole outside it—this was the sign-board used at that time by inns—and once or twice on the open ground, all huddled together for warmth between their grazing chargers. Wherever they went and wherever they slept, the east wind whistled in the reeds, and the geese went over high in the starlight, honking at the stars.

London was full to the brim. If Sir Ector had not been lucky enough to own a little land in Pie Street, on which there stood a respectable inn, they would have been hard put to it to find a lodging. But he did own it, and as a matter of fact drew most of his dividends from this source, so that they were able to get three beds between the five of them. They thought themselves fortunate.

On the first day of the tournament, Sir Kay managed to get them on the way to the lists at least an hour before the jousts could possibly begin. He had lain awake all night, imagining how he was going to beat the best barons in England, and he had not been able to eat his breakfast. Now he rode at the front of the cavalcade,[1] with

[1] CAVALCADE: ceremonial procession.

pale cheeks, and Wart wished there was something he could do to calm him down.

For country people who only knew the dismantled tilting ground of Sir Ector's castle, the scene which now met their eyes was really ravishing. It was a huge green pit in the earth, about as big as the arena at a football match. It lay about ten feet lower than the surrounding country, with sloping banks, and all the snow had been swept off it. It had been kept warm with straw, which had been cleared off that morning, and now all the close-mown grass sparkled green in the white landscape. Round the arena there was a world of color so dazzling and moving and twinkling as to make you blink your eyes. The wooden grandstands were painted in scarlet and white. The silk pavilions of famous people, pitched on every side, were azure and green and saffron and chequered. The pennons and pennoncells which floated everywhere in the sharp wind were flapping with every color of the rainbow, as they strained and slapped at their flag-poles, and the barrier down the middle of the arena itself was done in chessboard squares of black and white. Most of the combatants and their friends had not yet arrived, but you could see from those few who had arrived how the very people would turn the scene into a bank of flowers, and how the armor would flash, and the scalloped sleeves of the heralds jig in the wind, as they raised their brazen trumpets to their lips to shake the fleecy clouds of winter with joyances and fanfares.

"Good heavens!" cried Sir Kay. "I have left my sword at home."

"Can't joust without a sword," said Sir Grummore. "Quite irregular."

"Better go and fetch it," said Sir Ector.

"You have time."

"My squire will do," said Sir Kay. "What a dashed mistake to make. Here, squire, ride hard back to the inn and fetch my sword. You shall have a shilling if you fetch it in time."

The Wart went as pale as Sir Kay was, and looked as if he were going to strike him. Then he said, "It shall be done, master," and turned his stupid little ambling palfrey[1] against the stream of newcomers. He began to push his way towards their hostelry as best he might.

"To offer me money!" cried the Wart to himself. "To look down at this beastly little donkey-affair off his great charger and to call me Squire! Oh, Merlyn, give me patience with the brute, and stop me from throwing his filthy shilling in his face."

When he got to the inn it was closed. Everybody had thronged out to see the famous tournament, and the entire household had followed after the mob. Those were lawless days and it was not safe to leave your house—or even to go to sleep in it—unless you were certain that it was impregnable.[2] The wooden shutters bolted over the downstairs windows were two inches thick, and the doors were double-barred.

"Now what do I do," said the Wart, "to earn my shilling?"

He looked ruefully at the blind little inn, and began to laugh.

"Poor Kay," he said. "All that shilling stuff was only because he was scared and miserable, and now he has good cause to be. Well, he shall have a sword of some sort if I have to break into the Tower of London."

[1] PALFREY: saddle horse.
[2] IMPREGNABLE: able to resist attack.

"How does one get hold of a sword?" he continued. "Where can I steal one? Could I waylay some knight, even if I am mounted on an ambling pad, and take his weapons by force? There must be some swordsmith or armorer in a great town like this, whose shop would be still open."

He turned his mount and cantered off along the street.

There was a quiet churchyard at the end of it, with a kind of square in front of the church door. In the middle of the square there was a heavy stone with an anvil on it, and a fine new sword was struck through the anvil.

"Well," said the Wart, "I suppose it's some sort of war memorial, but it will have to do. I am quite sure nobody would grudge Kay a war memorial, if they knew his desperate straits."

He tied his reins round a post of the lych-gate, strode up the gravel path, and took hold of the sword.

"Come, sword," he said. "I must cry your mercy[1] and take you for a better cause."

"This is extraordinary," said the Wart. "I feel queer when I have hold of this sword, and I notice everything much more clearly. Look at the beautiful gargoyles of this church, and of the monastery which it belongs to. See how splendidly all the famous banners in the aisle are waving. How nobly that yew holds up the red flakes of its timbers to worship God. How clean the snow is. I can smell something like fetherfew and sweet briar—and is that music that I hear?"

It was music, whether of pan-pipes or of recorders, and the light in the churchyard was so clear, without being dazzling, that

[1] CRY YOUR MERCY: ask your pardon.

you could have picked a pin out twenty yards away.

"There is something in this place," said the Wart. "There are people here. Oh, people, what do you want?"

Nobody answered him, but the music was loud and the light beautiful.

"People," cried the Wart. "I must take this sword. It is not for me, but for Kay. I will bring it back."

There was still no answer, and Wart turned back to the sword. He saw the golden letters on it, which he did not read, and the jewels on its pommel, flashing in the lovely light.

"Come, sword," said the Wart.

He took hold of the handles with both hands, and strained against the stone. There was a melodious consort on the recorders, but nothing moved.

The Wart let go of the handles, when they were beginning to bite into the palms of his hands, and stepped back from the anvil, seeing stars.

"It is well fixed," said the Wart.

He took hold of it again and pulled with all his might. The music played more and more excitedly, and the light all about the churchyard glowed like amethysts; but the sword still stuck.

"Oh, Merlyn," cried the Wart, "help me to get this sword."

There was a kind of rushing noise, and a long chord played along with it. All round the churchyard there were hundreds of old friends. They rose over the church wall all together, like the Punch and Judy ghosts of remembered days, and there were otters and nightingales and vulgar crows and hares and serpents and falcons and fishes and goats and dogs and dainty unicorns and newts and solitary wasps and goat-moth

caterpillars and corkindrills and volcanoes and mighty trees and patient stones. They loomed round the church wall, the lovers and helpers of the Wart, and they all spoke solemnly in turn. Some of them had come from the banners in the church, where they were painted in heraldry, some from the waters and the sky and the fields about, but all, down to the smallest shrew mouse, had come to help on account of love. Wart felt his power grow.

"Remember my biceps," said the Oak, "which can stretch out horizontally against Gravity, when all the other trees go up or down."

"Put your back into it," said a Luce[1] (or pike) off one of the heraldic banners. "Remember that all power springs from the nape of the neck."

"What about those forearms," asked a Badger gravely, "that are held together by a chest? Come along, my dear, and find your tool."

A Merlin sitting at the top of the yew tree cried out, "Now then, Captain Wart, what is the first law of the foot? I thought I once heard something about never letting go?"

"Don't work like a stalling woodpecker," urged a Tawny Owl affectionately. "Keep up a steady effort, my duck, and you will have it yet."

"Cohere," said a Stone in the church wall.

A Snake, slipping easily along the coping which bounded the holy earth, said, "Now then, Wart, surely you can co-ordinate a few little muscles here and there? Make everything work together, as you have been learning to do ever since God let the amphibia crawl out of the sea. Fold your

[1] LUCE: type of fish.

powers together, with the spirit of your mind, and it will come out like butter. Come along, homo sapiens, for all we humble friends of yours are waiting here to cheer."

The Wart walked up to the great sword for the third time. He put out his right hand softly and drew it out as gently as from a scabbard.

There was a lot of cheering, a noise like a hurdy-gurdy which went on and on. In the middle of this noise, after a very long time, he saw Kay and gave him the sword. The people at the tournament were making a frightful row.

"But this isn't my sword," said Sir Kay.

"It was the only one I could get," said the Wart. "The inn was locked."

"It is a nice-looking sword. Where did you get it?"

"I found it stuck in a stone, outside a church."

Sir Kay had been watching the tilting nervously, waiting for his turn. He had not paid much attention to his squire.

"That's a funny place to find a sword," he said.

"Yes, it was stuck through an anvil."

"What?" cried Sir Kay, suddenly rounding upon him. "Did you just say this sword was stuck in a stone?"

"It was," said the Wart. "It was a sort of war memorial."

Sir Kay stared at him for several seconds in amazement, opened his mouth, shut it again, licked his lips, then turned his back and plunged through the crowd. He was looking for Sir Ector, and the Wart followed after him.

"Father," cried Sir Kay, "come here a moment."

"Yes, my boy," said Sir Ector. "Splendid falls these professional chaps do manage. Why, what's the matter, Kay? You look as white as a sheet."

"Do you remember that sword which the King of England would pull out?"

"Yes."

"Well, here it is. I have it. It is in my hand. I pulled it out."

Sir Ector did not say anything silly. He looked at Kay and he looked at the Wart. Then he stared at Kay again, long and lovingly, and said, "We will go back to the church."

"Now then, Kay," he said, when they were at the church door. He looked at his first-born again, kindly, but straight between the eyes. "Here is the stone, and you have the sword. It will make you the King of England. You are my son that I am proud of, and always will be, whatever happens. Will you promise me that you took it out by your own might?"

Kay looked at his father. He also looked at the Wart and at the sword.

Then he handed the sword to the Wart quite quietly.

He said, "I am a liar. Wart pulled it out."

As far as the Wart was concerned, there was a time after this in which Sir Ector kept telling him to put the sword back into the stone—which he did—and in which Sir Ector and Kay then vainly tried to take it out. The Wart took it out for them, and stuck it back again once or twice. After this, there was another time which was more painful.

He saw that his dear guardian Sir Ector was looking quite old and powerless, and that he was kneeling down with difficulty on a gouty old knee.

"Sir," said poor old Sir Ector, without looking up, although he was speaking to his own boy.

"Please don't do this, father," said the Wart, kneeling down also. "Let me help you up, Sir Ector, because you are making me unhappy."

"Nay, nay, my lord," said Sir Ector, with some very feeble old tears. "I was never your father nor of your blood, but I wote well ye are of an higher blood than I wend ye were."

"Plenty of people have told me you are not my father," said the Wart, "but it doesn't matter a bit."

"Sir," said Sir Ector humbly, "will ye be my good and gracious lord when ye are King?"

"Don't!" said the Wart.

"Sir," said Sir Ector, "I will ask no more of you but that you will make my son, your foster-brother, Sir Kay, seneschal[1] of all your lands."

Kay was kneeling down too, and it was more than the Wart could bear.

"Oh, do stop," he cried. "Of course he can be seneschal, if I have got to be this King, and, oh, father, don't kneel down like that, because it breaks my heart. Please get up, Sir Ector, and don't make everything so horrible. Oh, dear, oh, dear, I wish I had never seen that filthy sword at all."

And the Wart also burst into tears.

III

Perhaps there ought to be one more chapter about the coronation. The barons naturally kicked up a dreadful fuss, but as the Wart was prepared to go on putting the sword into the stone and pulling it out again till Doomsday, and as there was nobody else

---

[1] SENESCHAL: official who represents a lord or king in the management of his estate.

who could do the thing at all, in the end they had to give in. A few revolted, who were quelled later, but in the main the people of England were glad to settle down.

The coronation was a splendid ceremony, and, what was still more splendid, it was like a birthday or Christmas Day. Everybody sent presents to the Wart, for his prowess in having learned to pull swords out of stones, and several burghers of the City of London asked him to help them in taking stoppers out of unruly bottles, unscrewing taps which had got stuck, and in other household emergencies which had got beyond their control. The Dog Boy and Wat clubbed together and sent him a mixture for the distemper, which contained quinine and was absolutely priceless. Goat sent him a watchchain plaited out of his own beard. Cavall came quite simply, and gave him his heart and soul. The Nurse of the Forest Sauvage sent a cough mixture, thirty dozen handkerchiefs all marked, and a pair of combinations with a double chest. The sergeant sent him his medals, to be preserved in the British Museum. Hob lay awake in agony all night, and sent off Cully with brand-new white leather jesses, silver varvels and silver bell. Robin and Marian went out on an expedition which took them six weeks, and sent a whole gown made out of the skins of pine martens. Little John added a yew bow, seven feet long, which he was quite unable to draw. An anonymous hedgehog sent four or five dirty leaves with some fleas on them. The Questing Beast and King Pellinore put their heads together and sent some of their most perfect fewmets, all wrapped up in the green leaves of spring in a golden horn with a red velvet baldrick. Sir Grummore sent a gross of spears, with the old school crest on all of them. The vicar chose a work called *De*

Clericali Disciplina, attributed to Petrus Alphonsus, which could be read at nights and did not have to be explained. The cooks, tenants, villeins and retainers of the Castle of the Forest Sauvage, who were all given an angel each and sent up for the ceremony in a char-a-banc at Sir Ector's charge, brought an enormous silver model of cow Crumbocke, who had won the championship for the third time, and Ralph Passelewe to sing at the coronation banquet. Archimedes sent his own great-great-grandson, so that he could sit on the back of the King's throne at dinner, and make messes in the soup. The Lord Mayor and Aldermen of the City of London subscribed for a spacious aquarium-mews-cum-menagerie in which all the creatures were starved one day a week for the good of their stomachs; and here, for the fresh food, good bedding, constant attention, and every modern convenience, all the Wart's friends resorted in their old age, on wing and foot and fin, for the sunset of their happy lives. The citizens of London sent fifty million pounds, to keep the menagerie up, and the Ladies of Britain constructed a pair of black velvet carpet slippers with the Wart's initials embroidered on in gold. Kay sent his own record griffin, with honest love. There were many other tasteful presents, from various barons, archbishops, princes, landgraves, tributary kings, corporations, popes, sultans, royal commissions, urban district councils, czars, beys, mahatmas, and so forth, but the nicest present of all was sent most affectionately by his own guardian, old Sir Ector. This present was a dunce's cap, rather like a pharaoh's serpent, which you lit at the top end. The Wart lit it, and watched it grow. When the flame had quite gone out, Merlin was standing before him in his magic hat.

"Well, Wart," said Merlyn, "here we are—or were—again. How nice you look in your crown. I was not allowed to tell you before, or since, but your father was, or will be, King Uther Pendragon, and it was I myself, disguised as a beggar, who first carried you to Sir Ector's castle, in your golden swaddling bands. I know all about your birth and parentage and who gave you your real name. I know the sorrows before you, and the joys, and how there will never again be anybody who dares to call you by the friendly name of Wart. In fu-ture it will be your glorious doom to take up the burden and to enjoy the nobility of your proper name: so now I shall crave the privilege of being the very first of your subjects to address you with it—as my dear liege lord, King Arthur."

"Will you stay with me for a long time?" asked the Wart, not understanding much of this.

"Yes, Wart," said Merlyn. "Or rather, as I should say (or is it have said?), Yes, King Arthur."

FOR DISCUSSION

1. This portrayal of King Arthur as a boy is quite different from the historic portrayal of King Arthur. What do you learn about Arthur's birth and boyhood? Why are Sir Ector and Sir Kay important to him? Who is Merlyn?

2. In a certain sense, the Wart had help removing the sword from the stone. Who helped him? Why? What can you learn about Wart in this episode?

3. Examine the relationship between Sir Kay and the Wart. What incidents suggest that the Wart already possesses more noble qualities than Sir Kay?

4. Among the legendary traits that made King Arthur great were his kindness and compassion. What evidence of these traits do you find in this story?

Every man wishes he could be a hero. Walter Mitty, for instance, believed that he was someone quite extraordinary—even if no one else seemed to notice.

THE SECRET LIFE OF WALTER MITTY

JAMES THURBER

"WE'RE GOING THROUGH!" The Commander's voice was like thin ice breaking. He wore his full-dress uniform, with the heavily braided white cap pulled down rakishly over one cold gray eye. "We can't make it, sir. It's spoiling for a hurricane, if you ask me." "I'm not asking you, Lieutenant Berg," said the Commander. "Throw on the power lights! Rev her up to 8,500! We're going through!" The pounding of the cylinders increased: ta-pocketa-pocketa-pocketa-*pocketa-pocketa*. The Commander stared at the ice forming on the pilot window. He walked over and twisted a row of complicated dials. "Switch on No. 8 auxiliary!" he shouted. "Switch on No. 8 auxiliary!" repeated Lieutenant Berg. "Full strength in No. 3 turret!" shouted the Commander. "Full strength in No. 3 turret!" The crew, bending to their various tasks in the huge, hurtling eight-engined Navy hydroplane[1] looked at each other and grinned. "The Old Man'll get us through," they said to one another. "The Old Man ain't afraid of Hell!" . . .

"Not so fast! You're driving too fast!" said Mrs. Mitty. "What are you driving so fast for?"

[1] HYDROPLANE: seaplane.

"Hmm?" said Walter Mitty. He looked at his wife, in the seat beside him, with shocked astonishment. She seemed grossly unfamiliar, like a strange woman who had yelled at him in a crowd. "You were up to fifty-five," she said. "You know I don't like to go more than forty. You were up to fifty-five." Walter Mitty drove on toward Waterbury in silence, the roaring of the SN202 through the worst storm in twenty years of Navy flying fading in the remote, intimate airways of his mind. "You're tensed up again," said Mrs. Mitty. "It's one of your days. I wish you'd let Dr. Renshaw look you over."

Walter Mitty stopped the car in front of the building where his wife went to have her hair done. "Remember to get those overshoes while I'm having my hair done," she said. "I don't need overshoes," said Mitty. She put her mirror back into her bag. "We've been all through that," she said, getting out of the car. "You're not a young man any longer." He raced the engine a little. "Why don't you wear your gloves? Have you lost your gloves?" Walter Mitty reached in a pocket and brought out the gloves. He put them on, but after she had turned and gone into the building and he had driven on to a red light, he took them off again. "Pick it up, brother!" snapped a cop as the light changed, and Mitty hastily pulled on his gloves and lurched ahead. He drove around the streets aimlessly for a time, and then he drove past the hospital on his way to the parking lot.

. . . "It's the millionaire banker, Wellington McMillan," said the pretty nurse. "Yes?" said Walter Mitty, removing his gloves slowly. "Who has the case?" "Dr. Renshaw and Dr. Benbow, but there are two specialists here, Dr. Remington from New York and Dr. Pritchard-Mitford from London. He flew over." A door opened down a long, cool corridor and Dr. Renshaw came out. He looked distraught[1] and haggard.[2] "Hello, Mitty," he said. "We're having the devil's own time with McMillan, the millionaire banker and close personal friend of Roosevelt. Obstreosis of the ductal tract. Tertiary. Wish you'd take a look at him." "Glad to," said Mitty.

In the operating room there were whispered introductions: "Dr. Remington. Dr. Mitty. Dr. Pritchard-Mitford, Dr. Mitty." "I've read your book on streptothricosis," said Pritchard-Mitford, shaking hands. "A brilliant performance, sir." "Thank you." said Walter Mitty. "Didn't know you were in the States, Mitty," grumbled Remington. "Coals to Newcastle,[3] bringing Mitford and me up here for a tertiary." "You are very kind," said Mitty. A huge, complicated machine, connected to the operating table, with many tubes and wires, began at this moment to go pocketa-pocketa-pocketa. "The new anaesthetizer is giving way!" shouted an intern. "There is no one in the East who knows how to fix it!" "Quiet, man!" said Mitty, in a low, cool voice. He sprang to the machine, which was now going pocketa-pocketa-queep-pocketa-queep. He began fingering delicately a row of glistening dials. "Give me a fountain pen!" he snapped. Someone handed him a fountain pen. He pulled a faulty piston out of the machine and inserted the pen in its place. "That will hold for ten minutes," he said. "Get on with the operation." A

[1] DISTRAUGHT (dis·trôt′): anxious, worried.
[2] HAGGARD (hag′ərd): exhausted.

[3] COALS TO NEWCASTLE: Newcastle is one of the chief coal producing centers of England; thus, the phrase means "unnecessary effort."

nurse hurried over and whispered to Renshaw, and Mitty saw the man turn pale. "Coreopsis has set in," said Renshaw nervously. "If you would take over, Mitty?" Mitty looked at him and at the craven[1] figure of Benbow, who drank, and at the grave, uncertain faces of the two great specialists. "If you wish," he said. They slipped a white gown on him; he adjusted a mask and drew on thin gloves; nurses handed him shining . . .

"Back it up, Mac! Look out for that Buick!" Walter Mitty jammed on the brakes. "Wrong lane, Mac," said the parking lot attendant, looking at Mitty closely. "Gee. Yeh," muttered Mitty. He began cautiously to back out of the lane marked "Exit Only." "Leave her sit there," said the attendant. "I'll put her away." Mitty got out of the car. "Hey, better leave the key."

"Oh," said Mitty, handing the man the ignition key. The attendant vaulted into the car, backed it up with insolent skill, and put it where it belonged.

[1] CRAVEN: cowardly.

They're so damn cocky, thought Walter Mitty, walking along Main Street; they think they know everything. Once he had tried to take his chains off, outside New Milford, and he had got them wound around the axles. A man had had to come out in a wrecking car and unwind them, a young, grinning garageman. Since then Mrs. Mitty always made him drive to a garage to have the chains taken off. The next time, he thought, I'll wear my right arm in a sling; they won't grin at me then. I'll have my right arm in a sling and they'll see I couldn't possibly take the chains off myself. He kicked at the slush on the sidewalk. "Overshoes," he said to himself, and he began looking for a shoe store.

When he came out into the street again, with the overshoes in a box under his arm, Walter Mitty began to wonder what the other thing was his wife had told him to get. She had told him twice before they set out from their house for Waterbury. In a way he hated these weekly trips to town —he was always getting something wrong. Kleenex, he thought, Squibb's, razor

blades? No. Toothpaste, toothbrush, bicarbonate, carborundum, initiative and referendum? He gave it up. But she would remember it. "Where's the what's-its-name?" she would ask. "Don't tell me you forgot the what's-its-name." A newsboy went by shouting something about the Waterbury trial.

. . . "Perhaps this will refresh your memory." The District Attorney suddenly thrust a heavy automatic at the quiet figure on the witness stand. "Have you ever seen this before?" Walter Mitty took the gun and examined it expertly. "This is my Webley-Vickers 50.80," he said calmly. An excited buzz ran around the courtroom. The Judge rapped for order. "You are a crack shot with any sort of firearms, I believe?" said the District Attorney, insinuatingly. "Objection!" shouted Mitty's attorney. "We have shown that the defendant could not have fired the shot. We have shown that he wore his right arm in a sling on the night of the fourteenth of July." Walter Mitty raised his hand briefly and the bickering attorneys were stilled. "With any known make of gun," he said evenly, "I could have killed Gregory Fitzhurst at three hundred feet *with my left hand*." Pandemonium broke loose in the courtroom. A woman's scream rose above the bedlam and suddenly a lovely, dark-haired girl was in Walter Mitty's arms. The District Attorney struck at her savagely. Without rising from his chair, Mitty let the man have it on the point of the chin. "You miserable cur!" . . .

"Puppy biscuit," said Walter Mitty. He stopped walking and the buildings of Waterbury rose up out of the misty courtroom and surrounded him again. A woman who was passing laughed. "He said 'Puppy biscuit,' " she said to her companion. "That

man said 'Puppy biscuit' to himself." Walter Mitty hurried on. He went into an A. & P., not the first one he came to but a smaller one farther up the street. "I want some biscuit for small, young dogs," he said to the clerk. "Any special brand, sir?" The greatest pistol shot in the world thought a moment. "It says 'Puppies Bark for It' on the box," said Walter Mitty.

His wife would be through at the hairdresser's in fifteen minutes, Mitty saw in looking at his watch, unless they had trouble drying it; sometimes they had trouble drying it. She didn't like to get to the hotel first; she would want him to be there waiting for her as usual. He found a big leather chair in the lobby, facing a window, and he put the overshoes and the puppy biscuit on the floor beside it. He picked up an old copy of *Liberty* and sank down into the chair. "Can Germany Conquer the World Through the Air?" Walter Mitty looked at the pictures of bombing planes and of ruined streets.

. . . "The cannonading has got the wind up in[1] young Raleigh, sir," said the sergeant. Captain Mitty looked up at him through tousled hair. "Get him to bed," he said wearily. "With the others. I'll fly alone." "But you can't, sir," said the sergeant anxiously. "It takes two men to handle that bomber and the Archies[2] are pounding hell out of the air. Von Richtman's circus[3] is between here and Saulier." "Somebody's got to get that ammunition dump," said Mitty. "I'm going over. Spot of brandy?" He poured a drink for the ser-

[1] GOT THE WIND UP IN: frightened, panicked.
[2] ARCHIES: antiaircraft.
[3] VON RICHTMAN'S CIRCUS: Baron von Richthofen's "Flying Circus," a squadron of German fighter planes in World War I.

geant and one for himself. War thundered and whined around the dugout and battered at the door. There was a rending of wood, and splinters flew through the room. "A bit of a near thing," said Captain Mitty carelessly. "The box barrage is closing in," said the sergeant. "We only live once, Sergeant," said Mitty, with his faint, fleeting smile. "Or do we?" He poured another brandy and tossed it off. "I never see a man could hold his brandy like you, sir," said the sergeant. "Begging your pardon, sir." Captain Mitty stood up and strapped on his huge Webley-Vickers automatic. "It's forty kilometers through hell, sir," said the sergeant. Mitty finished one last brandy. "After all," he said softly, "what isn't?" The pounding of the cannon increased; there was the rat-tat-tatting of machine guns, and from somewhere came the menacing pocketa-pocketa-pocketa of the new flame-throwers. Walter Mitty walked to the door of the dugout humming "Auprès de Ma Blonde."[1] He turned and waved to the sergeant. "Cheerio!" he said. . . .

Something struck his shoulder. "I've been looking all over this hotel for you," said Mrs. Mitty. "Why do you have to hide in this old chair? How did you expect me to find you?" "Things close in," said Walter Mitty vaguely. "What?" Mrs. Mitty said. "Did you get the what's-its-name? The puppy biscuit? What's in that box?" "Overshoes," said Mitty. "Couldn't you have put them on in the store?" "I was thinking," said Walter Mitty. "Does it ever occur to you that I am sometimes thinking?" She looked at him. "I'm going to take your temperature when I get you home," she said.

They went out through the revolving doors that made a faintly derisive whistling sound when you pushed them. It was two blocks to the parking lot. At the drugstore on the corner she said, "Wait here for me. I forgot something. I won't be a minute." She was more than a minute. Walter Mitty lighted a cigarette. It began to rain, rain with sleet in it. He stood up against the wall of the drugstore, smoking. . . . He put his shoulders back and his heels together. "To hell with the handkerchief," said Walter Mitty scornfully. He took one last drag on his cigarette and snapped it away. Then, with that faint, fleeting smile playing about his lips, he faced the firing squad; erect and motionless, proud and disdainful, Walter Mitty the Undefeated, inscrutable[2] to the last.

---

[1] "Auprès de Ma Blonde": a French drinking song popular in World War I.

[2] INSCRUTABLE (in·skroo'tə·bəl): not able to be fathomed or understood; mysterious.

FOR DISCUSSION

1. Study each of Mitty's roles in his "secret life." What similarities do you find in each one? What do these daydreams tell you about Walter Mitty?

2. Notice the differences between Mitty and his wife. Most people dislike Mrs. Mitty when they finish this story—do you? Why? How responsible is she for Walter's daydreams?

3. What evidence do you have that Mitty's daydreams interfere with his daily life to the extent that they prevent him from functioning normally? Would he be better off without them?

*November 22, 1963—An assassin's bullet snuffed out the life of the young
and popular President, John Fitzgerald Kennedy.*

A TRIBUTE TO J. F. K.

ZACK GILBERT

Who would disgrace
The tragic majesty of his passing
With words so weak
And worn as these we know?
Let us invent   5
A new nobler tongue:
Sky tall,
Proud as the sweeping winds,
Reverend as the sea,
Necessary as the oxygen   10
We breathe.

Let us explore for him
A new frontier of speech.
If we cannot,
Let us be silent then,   15
And let our silence
Speak.

FOR DISCUSSION

1. What does the poet say would disgrace Kennedy's death?

2. To pay tribute to J.F.K., the poet claims something new must be invented. What?

3. The poet does not actually praise Kennedy, but the words he chooses suggest Kennedy's greatness. Which words do you feel help you create a mental picture of Kennedy?

4. Can silence speak? What do you think the poet means to express by using this phrase?

"A Tribute to J. F. K." by Zack Gilbert, reprinted from *Negro Digest*, January 1964, with permission of the author.

"Martin Luther King, Jr. taught us, all of us, black men and white men, Jews and Gentiles, not only how to die, but also, and more importantly, how to live."

EPILOGUE: MARTIN LUTHER KING, JR.
LERONE BENNETT, JR.

THERE WAS an air of inevitability about it.

First there was the rain, then the snow, then the blood.

Blood called to blood, and there was a convulsion of coast-to-coast violence unprecedented in the civil history of America.

In more than one hundred cities, black people exploded in rebellion.

Ten thousand plate glass windows were broken.

A thousand fires blazed.

Federal troops were deployed to protect the White House and the U.S. Capitol.

There was irony in this.

Martin Luther King, Jr., was a man of peace and nonviolence—and in the first five days after his death, forty-three men, women, and children died in his name.

After the screams, after the smashing of idols, after the purification of fire, there was a funeral in a red-brick Atlanta church, smelling of chrysanthemums and lilies, and the rhythmic benediction of a Baptist choir and, out in the audience, women in black, their eyes red from weeping, and the powerful and the famous sitting and standing shoulder to shoulder with the meek and the unknown.

It was a funeral the likes of which has never been seen in this land.

One has to go back ten decades, back to the traveling Lincoln bier, to find an analogue[1] to the marching King catafalque[2] and the rivers of people following his body in misery.

A half-million people were in and of and around this funeral.

Tens of thousands filed past his bier, weeping.

Hundreds of thousands followed the plain wagon and the two Georgia mules which bore him to a second service amid the azaleas and the dogwoods—the crucifixion flower—on the campus of his alma mater, Morehouse College.

Late in the afternoon, when the shadows were long on the new grass, it ended for Martin Luther King, Jr., in the silence of a crypt on a hillside in South View Cemetery.

Something within him had known that it would come to this, to the chrysanthemums and crowds and silence. He had foreseen it all, had thought about it, the weight and the sound and the feel of his own funeral—the long lines and the tears and the immortal silence of a closed casket on the other side of the world.

"Epilogue: Martin Luther King, Jr." by Lerone Bennett, Jr., from *What Manner of Man: A Biography of Martin Luther King, Jr.* Published by Johnson Publishing Co., Inc. Copyright © 1964 and 1968 by Johnson Publishing Co., Inc.

[1] ANALOGUE: something which is similar and comparable.
[2] CATAFALQUE: raised structure upon which a coffin rests.

Something deep inside him *knew*.

But nothing inside him or outside him, neither the snow nor the rain nor the thunder and lightning, warned him against the specific web the spider of racism was spinning in the last days of his life.

When, on Lincoln's birthday, the garbage workers went out on strike, he was far away, deep in plans for tomorrows that would never come. All that day— February 12, 1968—he sat in his Atlanta office planning for April days he would not see. Two months before, in December, 1967, he had announced plans to go to Washington, to the seat of Caesar, with a Poor People's Campaign; and now, in Memphis, he was closeted with aides in an all-day strategy session. In this meeting, King and his aides made plans for every contingency,[1] save one. They decided what they would do in Washington in April if X did Y and how they would respond if Y did X. They decided many things of moment, but they did not decide what they would do about the garbage workers, who were going out on strike now in Memphis, Tennessee.

This strike grew out of an earlier decision, which was made in the rain. Because of the rain, which fell on Memphis on January 31, city officials made a decision which would lead, web by web, to the martyrdom of Martin Luther King, Jr. They didn't plan it that way. But a pattern of racism, as old as the slave ships which brought King's ancestors to this country, worked in them and through them. It was this pattern which spun the first web of death. It was this pattern which led Memphis officials to separate garbage collectors on the basis of race, sending the black workers home with two hours pay and

keeping the white men for a full day's work. This decision, which would change so many lives, which would lead to so many graves, angered the black garbage collectors who held a meeting and decided to go out on strike. The strike catalyzed[2] the black community of Memphis and sent ripples of red across the land.

The Memphis strike did not immediately engage King's attention. He was involved just then in a struggle for his very existence as a national leader. Although he was still the foremost symbol of the struggle for racial justice, he was being pressed by Stokely Carmichael and Rap Brown and other leaders who stressed Black Power and militant self-defense. More ominously, his moral authority as a champion of nonviolence was being eroded[3] by a new mood rising from the despair and determination of the very young and the very defiant. This new mood was behind the annual summer seasons of riots and rebellions. In 1966, King moved to meet this new challenge by organizing his first Northern campaign in Chicago, Illinois. He rented an apartment in the city, organized tenants' unions, and staged marches which attracted national attention. On one of these marches, angry white racists stoned King and dispersed his supporters. King redoubled his efforts, winning a paper agreement on open housing from Chicago's white power structure. In 1967, he organized a second Northern campaign in Cleveland; but the economic roots of racism resisted his nonviolent approach, and black people, in despair, exploded in rebellion after rebellion. The awesome insurrection of Watts in 1965 was followed by Cleveland and Chicago

[1] CONTINGENCY: possible event.

[2] CATALYZED: *here*, aroused.
[3] ERODED: worn away, weakened.

and scores of other cities in 1966 and the 1967 cataclysm[1] of Newark and Detroit.

King's Poor People's Campaign was designed, in part, to answer his critics and to reverse the drift toward violence. He planned to take thousands of blacks, Puerto Ricans, and poor whites to the capital and camp there until Congress passed a multibillion program of national reconstruction. In King's view, the Poor People's Campaign was going to be a litmus test for nonviolence. It was going to prove, once and for all, whether nonviolence could attack the structural roots of racism and provide an alternative to violence. And so, while the garbage collectors of Memphis marched, King crisscrossed the country, seeking resources and bodies for the Washington campaign. During this same period, he moved into the leadership of the forces opposing the Vietnam War, which he considered immoral and irresponsible.

As the calendar moved toward the ides of March,[2] King made a whirlwind People-to-People pilgrimage which takes on

new meaning in the light of subsequent events. For what he did now, with no inkling of the unfolding web which was pulling him toward his death, was to make one last triumphant tour of the scenes of his greatest nonviolent campaigns. On Thursday night, February 15, he spoke in Birmingham, the scene of the massive demonstrations of 1963. The next morning, Friday, February 16, he spoke to a large and enthusiastic group in Selma, the focal point of the famous Selma-to-Montgomery March. That same afternoon, he visited Montgomery, where thirteen years before he had started his rise to worldwide acclaim. This eerily meaningful journey into the past gave King new hope and he flew off to Jamaica with his wife Coretta and his aide, Andrew Young, for his final vacation.

By the time King returned to America, the web of fate was tightening. The Memphis garbage strike had moved from the periphery[3] to the center of the civil rights movement, and King decided to lead a mass march in Memphis on March 22. But on

---

[1] CATACLYSM: violent upheaval.

[2] IDES OF MARCH: fifteenth of March; suggests tragedy, as Julius Caesar was assassinated then.

[3] PERIPHERY: outer edge.

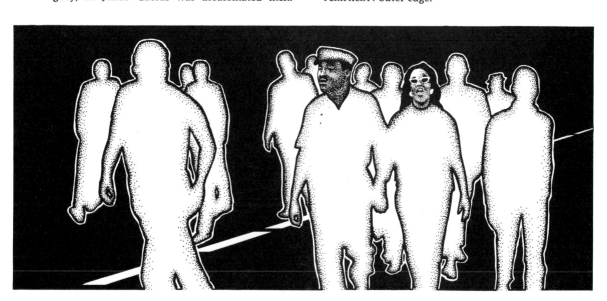

that Friday, a massive snowfall blanketed Memphis in a shroud of white. And the march was postponed until Thursday, March 28. On this date King led a march of six thousand protestors. As it turned out, this was one of the major miscalculations of King's life. For, as he himself later admitted, the march was poorly planned and insufficiently monitored. Worse, King committed his name to a venture over which he had little control. This became apparent soon after the march began. Young militants, disdainful of King's methods, broke away and started smashing windows and looting stores. Within a few minutes, a full-scale riot was under way, and National Guardsmen were rushed to the city. Before the turbulence subsided, one person had been killed and sixty-two had been injured.

King missed the excitement. When the rioting began, his aides, fearful for his life, pushed him into a passing car and sped to the Rivermont Motel on the banks of the Mississippi. Here, in a posh and depressingly white setting, King, who had less than a week to live, spent what one of his associates later called the worst night of his life.

Outside the Rivermont, men were saying that Martin Luther King, Jr., the apostle of nonviolence, had led a march that degenerated into violence. Some men were demanding cancellation of the projected Poor People's Campaign in Washington. Others were saying that it was all over for King, that history had passed him by.

Inside the Rivermont, King studied the reports and lapsed into an intense depression which lasted, his aides say, for most of the last week of his life. Jesse Jackson, a top King aide, said, "Some of us didn't understand, and he was going through

this extreme tension; he was in the Garden of Gethsemane[1] making a decision trying to see which way to go." Chauncey Eskridge, King's tax consultant and personal advisor, said: "He could agonize himself so. He couldn't help feeling that agony. Riots depressed him, and he would say that it was his fault. He would ask himself, 'Am I doing any good?'" Rev. Ralph Abernathy, who was with King throughout that terrible night, said later: "I had never seen him so depressed." According to Abernathy, King spoke of the possibility of going on a personal retreat for meditation and reflection. Jesse Jackson says King spoke of the possibility of imitating Gandhi by going on a prolonged fast until black people abandoned violence "and the Stokelys and the Raps and the Youngs and the Wilkins united."

King was still in a state of indecision and depression when he flew back to Atlanta on the day after the riot. Rev. Abernathy, King's constant companion and successor, rode with him from the Atlanta airport to the West Side of Atlanta. When the car reached King's home on Sunset Avenue, Abernathy got out and tried to comfort his friend. He suggested a movie or a session at the health club of the Butler Street YMCA. King shook Abernathy off. He was in no mood for diversions. "I'll pull out of it, Ralph," Abernathy recalls King saying. "I might call you later on."

Later that night, King and his wife dined at the Abernathys. They had an entrée of pig ears and pig feet and a main course of fried kroker fish. The soul food, King's

[1] GARDEN OF GETHSEMANE: scene of the agony and arrest of Jesus; thus, any occasion of great spiritual suffering.

favorite, revived his spirit; and the two couples sat up until the wee hours of the morning, joshing[1] and whiling away the time.

The next day, Saturday, March 30, King called a staff meeting in the pastor's study at Ebenezer Baptist Church. But he seemed somehow detached from the proceedings. He sat on the edge of the group and, at one point, denounced the tensions and dissensions[2] within the staff. According to Abernathy, he said: "Before we can go to Washington, something has to happen within this staff." Jesse Jackson has a similar recollection of this crucial staff meeting. "I had never seen him under such a spiritual cloud before," he said. "He talked with us and at one point he left the meeting because he didn't feel the staff was as intellectually and as spiritually involved in the Washington project as we should have been. . . . He was calling the roll, just going around the room until he got all of us to feeling bad. Then he left. . . ." Abernathy followed King out of the meeting. "I didn't like the way he was acting," Abernathy said later. "I was worried about him. But he told me he would be all right and said: 'I'll pull out of it, Ralph.' "

King pulled out of it; so did the staff. Within a few minutes after King's departure, the staff was caught up in an extraordinary emotional fervor which led to a number of concrete proposals. The most important of these proposals was that it was necessary for Dr. King to go to Washington with the Poor People's Campaign, but that it was necessary for him to go by way of Memphis. This idea was relayed to King by staff members who told

him that it was important for him to return to the meeting. "Doc," one staff member said, "The Holy Spirit is in this room." King returned to the meeting and decided to turn disaster into triumph by going to Memphis and proving that nonviolence was not dead.

King had, at that point, only five days to live. At some point within these five days, according to close associates, he transcended[3] the agony of doubt and reached a new plateau[4] of understanding and acceptance. "The ordeal," Chauncey Eskridge said, "strengthened him." Jesse Jackson said. "He made the decision after he saw the mountain there."

The mountain was there waiting, on Wednesday, April 3, when Martin Luther King, Jr., returned to Memphis to lead a second march. He checked into Room 306 —a twelve-dollar-a-day double room on the second floor of the Lorraine Motel—and went into a series of conferences with lawyers and aides over a court injunction which banned the proposed march. He was still conferring late that afternoon when a tornado roared over the city. Wind from the tornado ripped off roofs, shook windows, and sprayed the city with uncollected garbage. Rain came down in sheets. A local radio personality regarded the natural disaster with foreboding and said on the air: "Maybe God is trying to tell us something."

The rain came down, lightning rent the sky, thunder spoke—and men and institutions moved with the inexorability[5] of a Greek tragedy toward the eye of a national disaster.

[3] TRANSCENDED: rose above.
[4] PLATEAU (pla·tō): elevated and stable period.
[5] INEXORABILITY: incapability of being changed or softened.

[1] JOSHING: joking.
[2] DISSENSIONS: disagreements; conflicts.

Somewhere in Memphis at that moment, National Guardsmen, who had been on duty since the riot, were returning to their homes to prepare for the Easter season.

Somewhere in Memphis, a white man or a group of white men were studying murder.

Somewhere in Memphis, Martin Luther King's aides were recruiting nonviolent marshals for a march King would never lead.

At that moment, King was regarding the rain with disquiet. He was scheduled to speak at a mass meeting that night and his aides were advising him not to go. The rain, they reasoned, would limit the crowd; and if King spoke to an empty house, reporters would write another spate of stories about the death of nonviolence. King listened to the advisors and decided to send a substitute speaker. But a few minutes later, Ralph Abernathy called King and told him there were two thousand people in Mason Temple and that they wanted to see and hear him.

King put on his coat and went out into the driving rain to deliver the last speech of his life. No one knows really what went on in his mind that night. No one knows why he decided to talk about death. But men sometimes *know* more than they know. And the words, which came from deep within King this night, were words of death; and it would seem twenty-four hours later that he knew precisely what was going to happen and why it was going to happen. He had lived now for a long time in the shadow of death, had the taste of it in his mouth. There had been many attempts on his life and he knew that there would be others and he knew that someday somebody would succeed. He had spoken of these things many times before to intimates. Now he said it out loud, taking the audience into his confidence, telling them about mountains and valleys, about the good days and the bad.

"We've got some difficult days ahead," he said. "But it really doesn't matter with me now. Because I've been to the mountaintop. I won't mind. Like anybody, I would like to live a long life. Longevity has its place. But I'm not concerned about that now. I just want to do God's will. And He's allowed me to go up to the mountain. And I've looked over, and I've seen the Promised Land. I may not get there with you, but I want you to know tonight that we as a people will get to the Promised Land. So I'm happy tonight. I'm not fearing any man. *Mine eyes have seen the glory of the coming of the Lord!*"

King went out into the rain, buoyed up[1] by the cheers of thousands. He spent almost all of the next day—Thursday, April 4—in his room, challenging his staff to live up to the principles of nonviolence.

While he talked, the web tightened around him. Between 3 and 3:30 P.M., a white man slipped into a rooming house on a rise overlooking the motel. He had binoculars and a rifle. He took up a position in the common bathroom facing Room 306—and he waited.

When King emerged from his room to go to dinner, he was centered in the crosshairs of the telescopic sight of a high-powered rifle. King tarried for a moment in the eye of death. He leaned over the green railing of the balcony and chatted with aides on the ground below. As he started to straighten up, a shot rang out. He fell backwards, blood flowing from gaping wounds in his right jaw and neck.

There was an icy moment of silence, then a woman screamed for all her life.

King lay on the walkway concrete, his legs propped up on the railing, his eyes wide open. He did not speak; and apparently he did not suffer. The single bullet severed his spinal cord. He died at 7:02 P.M. in St. Joseph's Hospital at the age of thirty-nine.

Now began the rites of martyrdom, the eulogies and memorials, the riots and the tears.

Now began the unprecedented tributes, the postponement of the baseball season, the shutting down of the docks, the lowering of all U.S. flags to half-staff.

Now began the marches which extended from one end of the country to the other and ended five days later on Tuesday, April 9, 1968, when Martin Luther King, Jr., was laid to rest in an Atlanta cemetery green with new grass and the promise of new life.

It is true, as Carl Sandburg has so eloquently said, that "a tree is measured best when it is down." And in April, in the Easter Season, when the tall, young tree fell in the United States of America, men vied with each other in describing its size.

The World Council of Churches said King was one of the first citizens of the world.

Paul Douglas, former U.S. Senator, said King ranked with Gandhi and Pope John as outstanding religious leaders of the century.

---

[1] BUOYED UP: cheered, heartened.

William Stringfellow said that future historians will call him "the best friend the white American ever had."

And Benjamin E. Mays, in an eloquent eulogy, said King was "called of God," adding: "If Amos and Micah were prophets in the eighth century B.C., Martin Luther King, Jr. was a prophet in the twentieth century. If Isaiah was called of God to prophesy in his day, Martin Luther was called of God to prophesy in his day. If Hosea was sent to preach love and forgiveness centuries ago, Martin Luther was sent to expound the doctrine of nonviolence and forgiveness in the third quarter of the twentieth century."

In the Niagara of tributes, King's voice was heard. In a sense, one can say that he preached his own funeral. For at the private services at Ebenezer Baptist Church, a tape was played of the sermon he had preached at Ebenezer on Sunday, February 4, 1968. In this sermon, King said:

If any of you are around when I have to meet my day, I don't want a long funeral. And if you get somebody to deliver the eulogy, tell him not to talk too long. . . . Tell them not to mention that I have a Nobel Peace Prize. That isn't important. Tell them not to mention that I have three or four hundred other awards. That's not important. Tell them not to mention where I went to school. I'd like

somebody to mention that day, that Martin Luther King, Jr. tried to give his life serving others. I'd like for somebody to say that day, that Martin Luther King, Jr. tried to love somebody. I want you to say that day that I tried to be right on the war question. I want you to be able to say that day, that I did try to feed the hungry. And I want you to be able to say that day that I did try in my life to clothe those who were naked. I want you to say on that day, that I did try in my life to visit those who were in prison. I want you to say that I tried to love and serve humanity.

All this—and more—was said of Martin Luther King, Jr. on the day of his interment.[1] And men will undoubtedly say for years to come that he was an exemplary servant of humanity. For, in death, as in life, King bypassed cerebral[2] centers and attacked the archetypal[3] roots of man. His grace, like Gandhi's, grew out of a complicated relation not to oppression but to the ancient scourges of man, to pain, to suffering, to death. Men who conquer the fear of these things in themselves acquire extraordinary power over themselves and over others.

"A man who won't die for something," King said, "is not fit to live."

By resurrecting that truth and flinging it into the teeth of our fears, by saying it repeatedly and by living it, Martin Luther King, Jr. taught us, all of us, black men and white men, Jews and Gentiles, not only how to die, but also, and more importantly, how to live.

[1] INTERMENT: burial
[2] CEREBRAL: intellectual.

[3] ARCHETYPAL: *here*, earliest, most primitive.

FOR DISCUSSION

1. King stated, "A man who won't die for something is not fit to live." What did he mean?

2. What caused the strike in Memphis? How did King become involved? What was the cause of the violence on the March 28 march in Memphis?

3. What problems were involved in King's struggle to exist as a national leader? What was the main purpose of the Poor People's Campaign? Why did King, at one point, consider fasting like Gandhi?

4. Examine the excerpt from King's sermon pertaining to his death. What does it tell you about him? How important was religion to him?

WE NEVER KNOW HOW HIGH

EMILY DICKINSON

We never know how high we are
   Till we are called to rise;
And then, if we are true to plan,
   Our statures* touch the skies.

The heroism we recite
   Would be a daily thing,
Did not ourselves the cubits* warp
   For fear to be a king.

4 STATURES: heights; levels of achievement.   7 CUBITS: ancient units of linear measure.

FOR DISCUSSION

1. Have you ever been surprised by one of your accomplishments? Why? What explanation does the poet offer for such an occurrence?

2. What does the poet mean by "the heroism we recite . . ."? Can you apply your answer to the class studies of this unit?

3. What do we do that prevents our becoming heroes?

4. Does the poet think everyone could be a "king"?

In Summary

FOR DISCUSSION

1. The story of Daniel and the life of Martin Luther King, Jr. both contain examples of heroism motivated by religious faith. How are the two men similar? How are they different? Which of the two seems to you to be the most "heroic" according to your own conception of the term? Defend your answers, supporting them with evidence from the text of each selection.

2. Fictional heroes are often as important to people as real-life heroes. Which heroes in this unit were fictional? Which ones actually lived? What is the value of studying both types of heroes, instead of merely studying heroes who actually lived?

3. Courage is often measured in terms of physical daring and strength; however, there are also other types of courage. Which heroes in this unit showed courage by performing great deeds of daring and physical strength? Which heroes exhibited other types of courage? Be specific.

4. Any study of heroes will reveal that each one has undergone some supreme task or hardship which brought out his heroic traits. Carefully review the unit; then describe the supreme test that confronted each hero.

OTHER THINGS TO DO

1. Select some famous historic figure whom you admire for his or her heroic traits. After choosing your real-life hero or heroine, consult an encyclopedia or other source to increase your knowledge of his life. Then write a well-organized composition describing this person's heroism and explaining your choice.

2. Mythology has played an important part in man's cultural development. Consult an encyclopedia or other resource book for information on Greek or Roman mythology. Prepare a report for class presentation on your favorite myth. Be sure to explain the myth carefully, as well as any types of heroism it contains.

3. Study the newspaper or a current news magazine. Try to find one example of heroism and write a good summary of the article or news story. Be sure to include all the important facts. Is the hero or heroine a famous person? What supreme test or hardship confronted him? What particular heroic traits did his actions reveal?

The World of Words

DANIEL

The story of Daniel in the lion's den is a familiar story of a man whose faith gives him courage to face great danger. Because of his power and dignified appearance, the lion is referred to as the "king of beasts." His name is also used in a number of common phrases and expressions, such as "to beard the lion in his den," "the lion's share," "to twist the lion's tail." What do these expressions mean? We sometimes see the lion referred to as *Leo the Lion*. How is the name *Leo* related to *lion*?

PROMETHEUS

1. From the idea of various races of man, as expressed in the story of Prometheus, we get several rather commonly used phrases. You might see the phrases *golden age* and *iron age* or *age of iron*. Someone looking back at an earlier time in his life might say, "That was a golden age." What would he mean? And if someone says, "We live in an iron age," what might he mean?

2. The word *Promethean* is used as an adjective. Judging by what you know of the actions of Prometheus, what do you think *Promethean* means? Does your dictionary give the same meaning?

SCARFACE

The Indians of North America had many languages, but they were spoken languages, not written. The early settlers imitated these sounds as best they could and made them into words that became written in English. Only experts in Indian languages know how accurately these words represent the original spoken words. Two of these words are *moccasin* (page 90) and *pemmican* (page 91).

What do they mean today? Other words from Indian language are *toboggan, tomahawk, totem*. What do these words mean?

YUDHISTHIR AND HIS BROTHERS

When Yudhisthir was first made king, his enemies "took the oath of fealty" (page 101). That is, they promised to be faithful to the new king. The word *fealty* comes from the Latin word *fides*, meaning "faith." Other words from the same source are *fidelity, perfidy*, and *infidel*. What is the difference between *fealty* and *fidelity*? Can they be used interchangeably, as if they were the same word? Does Yudhisthir's dog show *fealty* or *fidelity*? What is the meaning of *perfidy*, and how does it relate to *fides* or *faith*? Where could the word *perfidy* be used in this story? What does *infidel* mean? Find two meanings for it.

THE SWORD IN THE STONE

The Sword in the Stone is filled with what are called "anachronisms," that is, references to things that did not exist at the time in which the story is set. For example, the nurse speaks of having cut out illuminated pictures of the King from some missals (page 118). No such pictures would have been available to her before the coming of newspapers, and it is to these that she refers. Later the various knights refer to "bolshevists" (page 120), "socialists" (page 120), and "red propaganda" (page 121) —terms from the twentieth century. And when Merlyn says he is leaving, Sir Ector protests that he cannot leave "without a month's notice" (page 122), a phrase that refers to much more recent customs. What other examples of anachronism can you find?

THE SECRET LIFE OF WALTER MITTY

The word "secret" in the title has a number of synonyms, words which have similar (but not exactly the same) meanings. Some of these are *stealthy, covert, clandestine,* and *furtive.* How would the meaning of the title of this story be affected if we were to substitute one of these words for *secret?* Look up the meanings of *secret, stealthy, covert, clandestine,* and *furtive,* and explain how their meanings are similar and how they differ.

EPILOGUE: MARTIN LUTHER KING, JR.

The author refers to the "martyrdom" of Dr. King. The word *martyr* is often used loosely, in ways that distort, or at least stretch, its precise meaning. *Martyr* comes from a Greek word meaning "witness," in the sense of testifying, or standing up for, one's beliefs. Examine carefully the meanings of the word *martyr,* and on the basis of Mr. Bennett's account, decide how the word can be applied to Dr. King.

Reader's Choice

Abe Lincoln Grows Up, *by Carl Sandburg.*

Abe Lincoln knew when he left home at the age of nineteen that he had a great deal to learn about people and himself. He was a small town boy with little education. Who could say what he might become?

The Black Athlete: His Story in American History, *by Jack Orr.*

This book tells the story of the black athlete in sports history from the days of the plantation slave through the black power of the 1968 Olympics. It tells the accomplishments of such athletes as Wilt Chamberlain, Arthur Ashe, Joe Louis, and Althea Gibson.

The Book of King Arthur and His Noble Knights, *by Mary MacLeod.*

The author unfolds the famous stories of King Arthur and the knights of the Round Table. We see adventure follow adventure as King Arthur obtains his enchanted sword and loses it, Sir Tristam and La Belle Iseult drink a potion from a flask of gold, and a young knight dares to accept a challenge and fulfills a prophecy.

Damien the Leper, *by John Farrow.*

Over 100 years ago, a Belgian monk received his long-awaited orders for assignment to the Sandwich Islands. From that time on, Father Damien worked in the leper colony of Molokai, ignoring the danger that he might become infected himself. But finally came the moment when he addressed his congregation, "We lepers. . . ."

Doctor Tom Dooley: My Story, *by Thomas A. Dooley.*

"Over half of the people on God's earth are born and live and die and never see a physician. Half! Half of the people on the face of the earth tonight will go to bed just a little hungry. This is the half with whom I live." So speaks young Dr. Dooley, a courageous man who devoted his life to combating starvation, disease and ignorance in Southeast Asia.

Greek Gods and Heroes, *by Robert Graves.*

When angered or otherwise aroused, the Greek gods had special weapons and powers at hand. They were all too eager to use these powers to meddle in the affairs of others, both on Mt. Olympus and on earth. The gods of love, war, and wisdom are only a part of the large, quarrelsome family of gods that Robert Graves describes in these exciting myths.

Man in Space to the Moon, *by Franklyn M. Branley.*

This is a detailed and interesting account of the first landing on the moon by Armstrong, Aldrin, and Collins. Branley works to give the reader the real "feel" of space.

Nigger, *by Dick Gregory.*

Dick Gregory is out to change "a system where a white man can destroy a black man with a single word. Nigger." This is a frank and witty account of Dick Gregory's youth.

Profiles in Courage, *by John F. Kennedy.*

Good readers will enjoy these stories of men who faced crises with courage. The group includes Sam Houston, John Quincy Adams, Daniel Webster, and others.

ALIENATION

ALIENS ARE FOREIGNERS, with allegiances to some nation other than the one in which they live at present. A Spaniard is an alien in England; a German citizen is an alien in the United States.

In a broader sense, we use the word *alienation,* which is the state of being an alien, to mean any condition that separates a person from his community or society. The separation is not a physical one, however. An alien lives in the midst of others from whom he feels isolated—and fundamentally so. A blind person among people who can see must inevitably feel different from others, alienated from them. And what he does about that alienation will measure the character of the man. If he gives in to discouragement, he may let his difference defeat him. But if he reacts to his handicap with a determination to master it, he may end by reducing the distance between himself and his fellows so that it hardly exists at all. People stop thinking of him as blind. He gets about by himself. He holds a job. He leads a full life and contributes to the welfare of others. Such a man has triumphed over the causes of his alienation.

What is sometimes difficult to realize is just how many conditions can make a person feel alienated. The boy who has trouble in school can feel alienated from his more gifted classmates. A poor man in the midst of people who have plenty, a fat woman among slender people, someone of a race or religion different from the majority: all those people may feel like aliens. Indeed, as the following selections suggest, so numerous are the sources of alienation that each of us at times must feel alone, coping with life in our own foreign land.

Philip McFarland

THE FORECAST

DAN JAFFE

Perhaps our age has driven us indoors.
We sprawl in the semi-darkness, dreaming sometimes
Of a vague world spinning in the wind.
But we have snapped our locks, pulled down our shades,
Taken all precautions. We shall not be disturbed.
If the earth shakes, it will be on a screen;
And if the prairie wind spills down our streets
And covers us with leaves, the weatherman will tell us.

FOR DISCUSSION

1. The situation the poet presents us with is a familiar one, watching a television weather forecast. Why does the poet find this common occurrence one that is worth examining? What conclusions about modern life in general does he draw from this occurrence?

2. The "precautions" mentioned in line 5 describe on a literal level how modern man shuts out the weather. On another level, what is the poem suggesting that we have shut out from our lives? Consider carefully additional meaning for "semi-darkness," "vague world," "snapped our locks," and "pulled down our shades."

His blindness set him apart from the world of sight. But Ved was ready to prove that he did not need to be pitied or pampered.

A DONKEY IN A WORLD OF HORSES
VED MEHTA

AFTER THE INITIAL few weeks of school, when everything seemed gloomy and I still brooded a great deal about having left home, things started to get easier. I stopped going to the elementary-grade arithmetic class, and with a little coaching from our high school math teacher now and then, I could keep up with my own class quite handsomely. I sometimes even got better marks than Ray in English and civics. Whereas before I had spent hours on homework, I could now finish it all in thirty or forty minutes. Often, however, I felt discouraged that the classes were not hard enough, that most of the time in the classrooms was spent just talking rather than learning.

Big Jim once remarked, "What good does it do us to keep on learning about adjustment, when we are around blind people in school all the time and might even end up working in workshops for the blind, where no one could tell whether you ate with hands or silverware, wiped your mouth with a shirt sleeve or a napkin, or wore a navy-blue shirt with brown pants?" Indeed, the program for "social adjustment" got more attention than our academic edu-

MEHTA: pronounced mā′tä.

"A Donkey in a World of Horses" from *Face to Face* by Ved Mehta, copyright © 1957 by Ved Mehta. By permission of Atlantic-Little, Brown and Co.

cation. We met in classes, sometimes twice, sometimes four times a week, to learn about social graces and adjustment to a sighted society, which, at least at our school for the blind, would not have been represented at all were it not for some of our seeing teachers.

Mr. Chiles, almost totally blind himself, introducing one of the social adjustment classes, had remarked, "To be blind is an uphill struggle. You've got to sell yourself to every seeing man. You've got to show him that you can do things that he thinks you can't possibly do."

It was true enough—if you were a donkey in a world of horses, you had to justify your worth and existence to the horses. You had, somehow, to prove to them that you could carry as much weight as they could, and if you couldn't move as fast, you at least were willing to work harder and put in longer hours.

"Anything you do wrong in the world of the seeing," Mr. Chiles had said, "like dressing untidily or putting your elbows on the table while eating—even if half the sighted world themselves commit these sins, people around you will chalk it up to your blindness. They'll call you poor wretches, feel sorry for you, and they will commit the worst sin of all by excusing it because you're blind."

So we were marshaled in groups and marched into classes where we were given good common-sense lessons—that you had to introduce young to old, rather than vice versa; that it was good to avoid wearing brown and blue together, even if you did not know what brown or blue signified; and that if you could not eat an orange-half with a spoon, it was better not to eat oranges at all. At the same time, we were told that no matter how independent blind people became, they must always accept help from the sighted graciously, recognizing that the feeling for helping the blind was the result of a generous impulse.

When Ernest asked, "If you went to a restaurant and they served you oranges in halves and you couldn't eat them and the waitress offered to feed you, should you accept the help?" he was abruptly told not to make light of serious matters. . . .

The more serious side of the social adjustment program was concerned with facial vision and the teaching of "mobility." One day early in spring, all the totally blind students were herded into the gymnasium and asked to run through an obstacle course. Plastic and wooden slabs of all sizes and weights were suspended from the ceiling around the gymnasium. Some of them hung as low as the waist; others barely came down to the forehead. These slabs were rotated at varying speeds, and the blind were asked to walk through the labyrinth[1] at as great a speed as possible without bumping into the obstacles. The purpose of keeping the slabs moving was to prevent the students from getting accustomed to their position and to force them to strain every perceptory ability to

sense the presence of the obstacles. The thinner the slab and the higher its position, the harder it was to feel or hear it—that is to say, to sense the pressure of the object against the skin, a pressure felt by the myriad of pores above, below, and next to our ears. Some of the slabs were of an even fainter mass than the slimmest solitary lamppost on a street corner. This obstacle course helped gauge how well an individual could distinguish one shadow-mass from another and, having located the one closest to him, circumvent[2] it without running into yet another. Here was where the wheat was separated from the chaff.

A person who has knocked about fearlessly—and it is a help if he was blinded in his childhood—will do much better in this test of facial vision than an individual who either lost his sight late in life or has been restrained from developing the full range of his coordinated senses. Having, of course, during my childhood jumped from banister to banister, from roof to roof, and ridden my bicycle through unfamiliar places crowded with unlocated objects—and that, too, at a much faster rate of speed—for me, going through this obstacle course was child's play. The gymnasium was kept quiet so that the blind people could hear the obstacles, although I could not help feeling that I could have run through the labyrinth with a jet buzzing overhead. When someone cracked his head against one of the slabs, and the others discovered who had done it, they would laugh mercilessly, until of course, they themselves ran smack into one.

After we had spent three or four class sessions running through this obstacle course, we were given a theoretical briefing

---

[1] LABYRINTH: complex arrangement of objects through which it is difficult to pass.

[2] CIRCUMVENT: avoid by passing around.

on the importance of facial vision—that the blind ought to put the same emphasis on it as sighted do on seeing, and that the way to develop it was through abandonment of fear and through complete relaxation. We were also briefed on a few stock secrets of the trade, such as that the head should always be held high in order to more easily walk a straight line, that some found that a hardly perceptible arching of the back helped to minimize any injuries frontally received, and that compass directions—determined sometimes by the sun against the cheek—were better than remembering lefts and rights. In time, one would get the knack of such things as going into unfamiliar stores and finding the right counter or finding an elevator in a strange building.

We were also advised that in crossing streets it was safer to walk with the traffic rather than to follow pedestrians, as they might be crossing against the light. In crossing streets without lights, safety depended entirely upon the ingenuity of the blind individual in gauging the distance of the cars correctly, although it was helpful in crossing wider streets to take them in parts or in halves. Above all, one must never get panicky and run across a street.

Each instructor then was assigned two or three students, and with cane in hand, bus token in pocket, we separated for downtown. My instructor gave me a list of trifling, if not embarrassing, things to purchase from scattered counters in a Rexall drugstore, and then asked me to meet him at the coffee shop of a department store for a milkshake, the treat being dependent upon my success in making the purchases. I was specifically told not to ask for help, and even if it were volun-

tarily offered, I should try to decline, provided I could do so gracefully. I did not know whether the instructor would keep his watchful eye on me, but whether he did or not, it was important to me that I should do well on this first day of independence.

I started out by tapping the cane in front of each foot before taking a step, as I had been taught. This was supposed to ward off tripping over a curb, dropping into a manhole, or meeting some other such obstacle, inclining or declining. I found that the noise of the cane made me very self-conscious and was quite distracting, so I flung it into the gutter at the end of the driveway in front of the school, and having made a mental note of the spot so that I might pick up the cane on my return, I started walking rapidly toward the bus stop, with my hands thrust into my pockets. Rather than wait at the nearest bus stop, I decided I would walk three or four blocks to the next one. Just to test my facial vision, I counted the lampposts and tried to guess the distance from which I first perceived them.

The sun was out in its full noon glory, although there was just the right proportion of breeze, making the heat not severe, but pleasant. In fact, the breeze was so gentle that it disturbed my facial vision not at all, and I could even perceive the curves and slight upgrades on the street, though that street was totally unfamiliar to me. However, when I unexpectedly stepped off a curb, that fraction of a second between the curb and the street was so frightening I almost wished I had my cane back —that cane which my instructor called the third leg of a blind man, although Big Jim had remarked that it was more like a displaced tail. I found, though, that soon my foot started registering a slight indentation before the end of the sidewalk, and that was clue enough. To my left, on the street, there was a steady stream of cars going both ways at, I guessed, about forty miles an hour. There were sounds of Ford motors, Chevrolets, and I even remember hearing a few Buick engines. Walking on that street, I felt as confident and happy as I imagined a driver would feel with a ton of machine at the command of his feet. Then I heard the clanging vibration of the electric wire just above the traffic. My instructor had told me to listen for it as a sign of the approaching trackless trolley. Then, almost a block behind me, I distinguished the sound of the trolley motor from the rest of the traffic. The bus stop was still a block and a half ahead of me, and I knew I had to catch that trolley, because it would be twenty minutes before the next one. With the ever-increasing sound of the trolley motor in my ears, I started running as fast as I could to the bus stop. I wished there were the shadow of a wall or a fence to my right, to run by. As it was, there was empty space to my right and the hindering noise of the traffic to my left, a narrow sidewalk with a string of lampposts, and heaven knew what other hazards. I skirted one lamppost by a hair's breadth, and another actually caught my shoulder, but not my head.

When I got to the next intersection, the trolley was almost abreast. If I waited to listen for the sound of the traffic, I could not possibly make it, so I dashed across the street, thinking of what I had repeated to my mother a long time ago:

"Death comes only once," I had said.

"But," she had said, "what if you lose a leg?"

That had been frightening, all right. "After that I wouldn't want to live. I don't mind being blind, but a wheel chair. . . ."

Maybe if I had a white cane in my hand, I wouldn't have to worry as much about the traffic, and the bus driver would know I was blind and would wait for me. But it is better this way, I thought.

Just when I perceived the looming shadow of the bench at the bus stop, about ten or fifteen feet away from me, the trolley passed me. If only someone would be waiting there, I wished, so that the trolley will at least stop. But no one was, and I missed the trolley.

With a discouraged heart I slowly walked up to the bench, out of breath, and sat down. It would be twenty minutes more, twenty whole long minutes, and maybe I wouldn't get my milkshake after all. I took out my Braille watch[1] and kept my fingers fixed on the hands, and I heard car after car pass by. I felt as envious of the drivers inside as a man standing in a rainstorm trying to thumb a ride, although I myself had no intention of flagging down a car.

At last there was another trolley. I heard its door open a few feet ahead of me. Walking parallel to the shadow of the trolley, I felt the gap of the door and climbed the three steps, slightly nervous, wondering if I could drop my coins in the box without having to be shown. I found the box, and the driver must have thought I could see some, because he did not say anything about a vacant seat. The trolley was moving already. I walked down the aisle, feeling the vague shadows of the people, hearing the crackling sounds of packages or newspapers, until I felt the

[1] Braille (brāl) watch: a watch designed for blind people, on which time can be told by touch.

shadow of an empty seat and sat down. All of a sudden I was trembling all over.

I was glad I did not have a cane, because this way probably no one was watching me. No, I assured myself, I would rather be blind than deaf, any day. I was surer about it at that time than ever before.

I did not pay any attention to the half bends of the trolley. My instructor had told me, "Just wait for the second right-angle turn, where the trolley goes from Markham to Main Street." It was such an obvious turn that I could not miss it. We were going south now (I always oriented myself with the direction of one street), and the Rexall drugstore was on Fifth Street. My instructor had said, "Don't bank on the bus halting at every bus or light stop. Try to get used to the distance of a block, and that way you can't go wrong."

I got off on Fifth all right, and crossing Main, I went into the Rexall drugstore. Since it was my first time, I asked the man in the front where I could pick up some shoelaces.

"Straight to the back," he said, "and the second counter to the right."

After five minutes I had bought all that my instructor had asked for, and I started walking rapidly a block up to the department store, dodging the window-shoppers by using facial vision to keep a proper distance between the windows and myself, and the luncheon crowd, by a watchful ear. By counting the gaps in the sustained shadow of the windows, I knew how many stores there were on that block. Next time I came to town, I would get the various stores located by keeping track of how many doors up they were from the street corner. It was as simple as that.

My instructor had said that there were a number of ways of telling when you got

to the street corner. It could be done by the noise of the traffic, the draft of air, or the receding shadow of the windows. At last I was at the double doors of the department store. I went in and started walking back toward the elevator, listening for the sound of its door. Inside the elevator I found my instructor.

As soon as we sat down in the restaurant, he said laughingly, "You shouldn't have asked that man for the shoelace counter."

"And how was I to know where to find it?" I retorted. "By the smell of it?"

"You gave me the slip," he said, "that is, until I saw you running, from inside the trolley that you missed. But I picked you up again at the drugstore." So he had watched me!

"The first thing," he was saying admonishingly, "is that you've got to admit to yourself that you are blind and that there are certain things you just can't do, like throwing away your cane and crossing streets without listening for traffic."

He was right, of course, I wouldn't make a habit of crossing streets that way, but the cane—that was another matter. I had never hooked a cane in front of my bicycle when I rode it, so I did not see why I had to carry one when walking, if I did not mind taking the chance of falling into a manhole. As for letting drivers know I was blind, I felt safer relying on myself than on their judgment. Maybe it was all rationalization,[1] like that of Benjamin Franklin when he stopped being a vegetarian because he saw a little fish in the open stomach of a big fish about to be cooked.

"You'll carry that cane," my instructor

---

[1] RATIONALIZATION (rash·ən·əl·ə·zā′shən): explaining one's behavior reasonably while concealing one's real motives.

said threateningly. "If not, you won't be allowed to leave campus."

"Yes, sir," I replied.

The milkshake was there now, and putting the straw between my teeth, I let it drain down my throat. It was cool and delicious, and I forgot about the cane. All of a sudden I felt weak, weak and empty. "It must have been tougher than I admitted," I said.

"It always is the first day you are on the road by yourself," the instructor agreed. After we had finished the milkshakes, he asked, "Can you find your way home? I have some other business in town."

"Yes," I said.

We walked out of the department store together, and then separated. I could have caught the bus on that corner, but I decided I would walk all the way down to Markham (or First) Street. I must have passed a nut shop on the way, because there was the smell of roasting peanuts. And from the next open door, a fresh smell of leather. Must be a shoe store, I thought, or maybe a luggage shop. Then there was a swinging door which creaked as it was opened and closed, letting out a burst of air which breathed of dime store. At Markham Street there were three or four buses standing. I knew which was a trolley because of the motor. A number of people were getting on it, and I got in line. I felt in my pocket and there were two bus tokens. I had been given one extra for the trip, just in case I lost one or took the wrong bus. They would be good for another trip downtown, I thought—that is, if I did not use one now. So I left the line, crossed Main Street, and started walking west on Markham. I could not think of walking home, because the dis-

tance was at least a couple of miles. Besides, I did not know the way.

Halfway down the block, I stepped off the curb and, standing about a foot away from it, tried to thumb a ride. The trolley whizzed past in front of me. Cars kept on passing me until finally a woman stopped.

"Are you going toward Stiff Station?" I asked.

"Going right there," she said.

I climbed in.

"I bet you go to the school for the blind," she said. Why did my eyes always give me away? I thought. Maybe if I had glass eyes and kept my eyes open all the time, no one would ever know. But that was useless. My mother wouldn't think of it, and from my left eye everyone would always know that I was blind.

"How much can you see?" she asked.

"Just enough to get around," I replied. That way, I thought, there would be no fuss about her taking me right to the door of the school and helping me in.

"You know," she said—we had just overtaken the trolley—"you half-sighted people are the link between the world of the blind and the world of the seeing."

"Yes, ma'am," I said. That was the first time the words "half-sighted" had ever sounded good to me.

"The blind must have a world of their own, don't you think?" she asked.

"It's just a world minus eyes," I said. "It's what one might call a world of four senses, instead of five."

"But you have developed your senses so much more acutely, and to see a blind person get around is so amazing to me, until, of course, I remind myself that they have extra senses."

"They don't have any extra senses,

ma'am," I said, "unless you call facial vision that. Sometime try to find a door in the dark, and believe me, ma'am, you'll find even you have some facial vision."

"They must have extra senses," she said emphatically. She probably had not even listened to what I had said. "If you were totally blind, you would know what I am talking about."

I was too tired to argue, and leaning back against the seat, I relaxed while she lectured me about the extra senses of the blind, the car all the time moving swiftly through traffic.

Bringing the car to a stop, she said, "Here we are." I thanked her and got out of the car right in front of the long driveway leading to the school. She drove away.

I found my cane where I had left it. It had a spring at the tip so that when you tapped it, the cane would automatically spring up. I stood there, just springing the cane up and down, listening to the tapping sound. The more I tapped, the less I liked it. I knew I couldn't get used to it even if I wanted to. The spring made it worse rather than better.

I heard then, above the roar of the traffic, a clattering noise, beginning a block away. Clack, clack, clack, and I could almost forecast the next one. Some blind man was walking on the sidewalk, finding his way with the help of a cane. He must have very bad facial vision, I thought, to have to locate every wretched lamppost with a cane. Clack, clack, clack. I stood there, running my hand up and down my new long, thin cane, with a fancy strap instead of a handle at the top. I took the two ends of the cane in my hands, and putting my foot at the center, pulled hard and broke it in two. And flinging it back into the gutter, I walked rapidly toward the school building.

FOR DISCUSSION

• His instructor warns Ved that he simply cannot do certain things, like throwing away his cane. Yet the boy does just that. What does the cane represent to him? Why does he break it?

Sometimes trouble can bring a family closer together, but for Jenny's family the crisis was one that each member faced alone.

PLACES WE LOST

MARY HEDIN

THAT HOUSE was more than ordinarily loved. My father had built and sold houses all over the south side of Minneapolis. Almost every year, we had moved into and out of one of them. Move in, fix it up, sell it. That was the pattern. But that house was built just for us. It was a high-gabled, English country-style house, and when we moved in, Mother announced that that was it. She had had her fill of moving, and she had things just the way she wanted them there, from the clever limed-oak phone niche[1] in the hall to the breakfast nook with its trestle table and built-in benches.

Four years later, we were in the middle of the Depression. My father no longer built houses. He worked at intervals for a sash-and-door shop. Mostly he was home. In those days, shabby-looking men knocked on our door and asked for food, and abandoned cats howled in the alleys at night.

In spite of that, we children did not understand. Buddy was still a baby, and Jenny and I were fed. We were clothed. We heard the words—Depression, bread-lines, WPA,[2] Mecklenburg scrip.[3] They had a grand and mysterious sound, and we did not comprehend them. When Father announced, one day, that the sash-and-door shop had closed, it meant less to us than the quick change in weather that was moving March from winter into spring.

Then, on a Friday night in May, an evening warmer than the calendar allowed, Jenny and I grew keenly aware of the change and loss threatening us all. That it came then, on the same night that Jenny came to something else, launching the risk and deceit which harmed us all, was not, perhaps, entirely coincidental.

Usually, Jenny and I were among the first to be called home from the evening games. That night, no one called us. We marveled, at first, at our unexpected freedom. We played Kick the Can furiously as the evening turned dusky, crowding the last minutes with the greatest amount of pleasure. Even after most of the children had gone home and we were much too tired, we played on. At last, there were just three of us—Jenny and I and Carrie Bergman, whose parents had gone to church and

[1] NICHE: pronounced nĕsh.

[2] WPA: Works Progress Administration, government agency providing jobs for the unemployed.
[3] MECKLENBURG SCRIP: local currency used in place of normal money during the Depression when banks were shut down.

didn't know she was out.

We huddled by the telephone pole that had been goal and watched the final excessive blooming of stars in the altogether darkened skies. Still no one called. Jenny looked at me, caught between wanting to be called and wanting to stay there in the dew-sharpened, strange night air. The trees were high black shadows against the lighted sky. Beneath them, fireflies scudded[1] over an unseen earth. Down the avenue, the houses in formal rows were large and remote from us. At last, our sense of freedom grew so immense that we were strange in it, unsure of it, and wanted to escape before it swept us toward things we only sensed and did not wish to know.

"Let's go," Jenny whispered. "Let's go," Carrie agreed.

We turned and ran our separate ways. I clutched Jenny's hand and pulled her as fast as I could down the alley, across the grass, up the concrete walk to our back door. The house was still there. The kitchen windows facing the alley were dark, but the double windows of the dining room gave out an old light. Seeing that, I knew that part of the thumping of my chest, there in the enlarged darkness, was caused by the notion that house and parents might have disappeared into the great, dark night.

But I stopped when we reached the steps. We were out too late. I knew that. "Jenny, did you hear Mother calling us?" I whispered.

"No, she didn't," Jenny warbled. "She never called us."

"Jenny, we're going to get spanked." I was gloomily sure of it.

Jenny stood still, considering. The crickets' warnings riddled[2] the dark. Finally, she tugged like a fish at the hand in which I still held hers. "Come on," she said carelessly. "Let's go in."

"We'll get spanked," I repeated.

Jenny tossed her head. The fair hair moved like wind in the scant light. "Well, I don't care. I'm going in. Come on, Berit. Let's go." She started up the steps; but on the second one, she stopped. Her hand left mine. Her head leaned toward the night. "Shh," she whispered. "Listen."

I stopped. I waited. I heard nothing. "What? What do you hear?"

"Shh," Jenny whispered again.

Then I heard it, the faint, fine tissue of sound, a thin belling of woe, moving without source into and out of the night.

The sound came again, and we both knew it for what it was. Tenderness quavered out of Jenny's throat in a whispered half-sung cry. "A kitten. It's a kitten." She went blindly from me towards whatever dark place she thought the sound came from, crooning. "Here, kitty, kitty. Here, kitty." I could hear, in the quick, breathless callings, that extravagance of love which was Jenny's gift and liability[3] and which poured from her toward any small furred thing she ever saw.

Plaintive, haunting mews were coming in answer to her calls. Then both murmurs and mewing ceased, and Jenny stood beside me, holding something against her chest. "Look at him, Berit. Oh, look at him, how tiny he is."

I could not see the kitten in the darkness but she couldn't keep him, anyway. She knew that. She was always bringing home hungry cats, and Father never let her keep

---

[1] SCUDDED: skimmed swiftly and easily.

[2] RIDDLED: pierced.

[3] LIABILITY: handicap.

one. "Put him down, Jenny. Come on. We have to go in."

"He's so tiny, Berit. Look. He's lost, Berit, poor little thing."

I heard the small, rich thrum, the purring. I started up the steps saying, "Put him down, Jenny," and she came after me and didn't put the kitten down. I stopped outside the door, the knob cold and damp in my hand.

"I'm going to ask," Jenny said. The dark prevented seeing; but I knew from the sound of her slow, soft words that in her wide eyes there was that look of determination I was never able to defeat. I wiped my palm against my skirt and pulled open the door.

The weathers of my father's nature blew violently from sublimity and joy to outrage and despair. His knobby, sharp-boned face was seamed and creased by his moods, as lands are marked by their climates' demands. To hear my father angry did not astonish. To hear him shouting at Mother gave room for apprehension. But she, who usually would not speak to him unless he was calm, was answering his anger with anger equal to his own, her voice raised to a near shout. In bewilderment, we both stopped on the dark side of the dining room door.

"Don't be so unreasonable, Emma!" he shouted. "It has to be done."

"No. I will not let you."

"We have to live. It's that simple. What do you think we'll eat? Leaves off the trees, perhaps?"

"Not the house," Mother cried in a loud, sharp voice. "We don't have to sell the house. We're eating. We're not starving. Not the house!" She sat at the table, the light of the dining room fixture falling on her coppery hair, her face now lowered into her covering hands.

My father paced around her, circling the round oak table, stopping to lean over her bowed body, and shouting into her ears. "Not starving! Not starving, she says!" With each word, he stabbed the air in front of her with a thrust-out forefinger. "Women! Masters of logic! We'll live in a nice house. We'll walk around with empty bellies, and then, when it's too late, we'll lose the house, anyway. We'll see the day the bank forecloses,[1] that's how it will be!"

From the dark kitchen we watched, trying to find meaning in the storm of words. Why would we sell the house? How could you lose a house? Where would we be if we were not there in that house?

My mother dropped her hands from a pale face in which her eyes were two places of darkness. Then she stood up and put that white face close to my father's red knotted one and shouted, "No. No. No."

His mouth snapped like a trap. His lids slitted down against his eyes' fury. His brows were one black streak across a blazing forehead. Overhead, the light fixture still trembled with the shouts, which had frozen now into total silence. Under the flickering, fragmented light, they stood dumbly unyielding, unforgiving, sudden hate flung up between them that grew into a wall of silence, from which neither could move and which neither could destroy.

In that cold, walled silence, the breaths I drew shook past a thick tongue and a closed throat. Against my arm, Jenny's arm trembled with dismay, and we stood locked, two small girls caught on the outer edge of their anger.

[1] FORECLOSES: claims property because mortgage payments have not been met.

Then, in Jenny's arms, the kitten stirred; lifted a small, sleepy head; mewed faintly.

Both faces turned toward the door, turned from anger to remembrance and surprise.

"What are you girls doing here?" My father's bellow was a lesser anger. "Why aren't you in bed?" Then his black brows rode up, up on his corrugated[1] forehead. His eyes pulled wide open. "What's that?" he shouted. "Get that cat out of here!"

In spite of all, Jenny's desire gave sufficient courage. "I thought we could keep—" she ventured, on a high, frail note.

"Get that cat out of here!" He plunged around the table toward us.

We stumbled back toward the safe dark behind us.

But Mother had already wheeled from her place, and she came to us with her arms spread, like a winged, red-haired angel. She swept both of us away in the white arc of her arms, away from my black-browed, bellowing father, crying over her turned, sharply defying shoulder, "Stop shouting at the children." His huge fist crashed upon the shining table as she herded us through the kitchen to the back door, where Jenny lowered her arms and gave up the tiny kitten to the larger, cold night.

Upstairs in our bed, we lay cradled in each other's comfortless arms. Jenny's tears dampened the pillow beneath my cheek. Her questions—"Berit, where will the kitten go? How will we lose the house, Berit? Foreclosure, does that hurt much? Berit, do you think the kitten will die?"—went with us unanswered, threatening, even as we moved hopeless, helpless, into the distance of sleep.

[1] CORRUGATED: wrinkled.

I awakened to total quiet. The light of a late-rising moon had taken our room. Black shadows of quivering leaves flickered in changing patterns against the white wall. Even before I reached out, I knew that the place beside me was empty. Jenny was gone. I listened. I felt the empty space. I raised up on one elbow, looked about the room. "Jenny?" I whispered.

No answer. Had she gone for a drink? To the bathroom? I listened for the sound of running water, for the flush. I heard no sound. I shook the sheet from my legs. I got up. Gooseflesh fled along my arms, between my shoulders. I tiptoed around the bed. My shadow grew long and strange upon the white wall and moved before me as I left the room. I went along the hall, down the stairs, stopped at the bottom. From my parents' room, the usual deep-drawn breaths issued in forgetful counterpoint.

"Jenny?" The whisper met with consuming silence. I dared once more. "Jenny?"

There was a tick of noise in the kitchen. A door? Opening? Closing? Then I heard the tiny, singing wire of sound. The kitten. I slipped over the smooth, moon-sheathed linoleum floor to the back door.

The moonlight lay like water upon the concrete steps. Its light made a clearness deprived of detail, sharper than reality. Jenny crouched on the step, her long hair fallen past her face so that its ends swept the glittering steps. Her arms were lifted from her sides, and the curve of her hands was shaped to the saucer's circle. The tiny kitten, spraddle-legged and quivering, looked frail and blue in the moon's light, fumbling at the offered milk.

She had not heard me. I looked down on her and the kitten, set there like a carving in the wash of light. I gave up a giggle. "Jenny," I scolded, "what are you doing?"

She turned her face to me, looked at me, not surprised, but with absolute assurance, as though getting up in a deserted, half-finished night to feed a stray kitten she could not keep was an entirely reasonable and expected action. "He's hungry." Her lips fluttered between smiles and woe. As she turned back to the kitten, the silvered sheath of her hair fell again over the curve of her cheek, hiding the look on her face as whispered petals of love and comfort fell from the kitten's peaked, attentive ears. The fear and unhappiness from which we had taken our sleep were gone. Watching her there, sturdy and strange in the moon-whitened gown that covered even her human feet, I took from her the tiny blue kitten, the lapping tides of stirring moon-watered air, forgetfulness and wonder for myself.

But in the day that followed, and in the long, tense days following it, there was little such relief. A great silence stood between my mother and my father, and it was not peace. Whatever occasional dialogue went between them began abruptly, ended impotently.[1]

Each day, Father walked the long way to the Loop. Late in the afternoon, he pulled open the back door, shrugged his coat from weary, humped shoulders, and dropped it to the bench in the breakfast nook. Like someone very old, cautious of his aches, he lowered himself down beside it. Mother set a dishpan full of water on the green linoleum floor in front of him. He tugged at stiff shoes, sticky socks. He dropped his hot, abused feet into the water,

[1] IMPOTENTLY: weakly.

moved his toes, groaned. He leaned his elbows on the table, his head on his hands, and growled out tales of jobs gone, homes lost, businesses closed. "America, America," he muttered, with contempt and bitterness clogging his throat. "Land of broken promise." On the radio, Father Coughlin's speeches, dreary stock quotations, glum news reports fed his despair.

And Mother turned only silence against his words. Hearing his grim, unpatriotic speeches, she suffered, perhaps, the pain and embarrassment burning in me. When he was away, she attacked her chores as though she were fighting a battle involving dust mops and laundry tubs and vacuum cleaners. She didn't walk; she ran, as if victory depended on vigilance,[2] and I knew the battle she waged somehow involved her differences with my father. Buddy was cutting his molars, and when she sang comforting, foolish rhymes to him, rocking him toward rest he could not find, her own face held weariness and pain.

But that she hid from Father. She turned toward him a cool, impersonal mask, and he showed her a constant, impersonal and frowning bitterness. They remained if not enemies, antagonists, keeping mind and flesh and soul to resistance.

Jenny paid no attention to their warfares. The kitten had claimed her, and there was room in her thoughts only for it, how to care for it, how to keep it for her own. The Saturday morning after that moonlit night, she found a cardboard box in the basement. She sneaked rags out of Mother's ragbag. She tucked the box with its nest of rags in a green hollow of the wild honeysuckle crowding the corner of the empty lot next door. She smuggled milk out to it.

[2] VIGILANCE: watchfulness.

From then on, each morning when we started down the alley to school, I had to wait on the damp concrete, shivers riding up and down my legs, while she crept through the dew-wet branches to see the kitten and leave it bits of her lunch.

When we got home in the afternoon, she poured herself a glass of milk and went out on the back steps to drink it. In a few minutes, she brought the emptied glass back to the sink, and then she was gone. I knew she was going to the kitten's hiding place with a jar of milk held against her stomach. And the kitten seemed to know. At least, it made that bush its home and did not betray Jenny by following her home, as kittens usually do.

At first, the necessary deception cost Jenny something. There were fever and shyness in her darkened eyes; a deepened color burned her cheeks, and it seemed that the demands of conscience gave off the same signs of danger as disease. Or perhaps the burning of cheek and eye was, even in the beginning, not the mark of guilt, but only a sign of the heart's whole mission. At any rate, she was changed, and I thought someone ought to notice other than me. No one did.

The passions my parents themselves were enduring took from them their ordinary perceptions. Jenny went her dedicated, deceitful way. I warned her, and scolded her, and worried, and Jenny ignored all that.

On the last Sunday in May, I went down the stairs into the kitchen full of morning sun. I felt at once, in spite of that wealth of brilliant light, that the air was drained and empty. My mother stood by the stove as though she leaned on the spoon moving slowly through the pan of oatmeal. In the heaviness of lids lying over her inward-looking eyes, in the droop of her head, there was defeat.

My father leaned over the Sunday paper, spread out upon the trestle table. He looked up; his brows lifted; his teeth gleamed in a showy smile. "Well, there's a fine sleepy-head!" His laugh was loud and not free.

I knew the fine show was for Mother and she was getting no comfort or amusement from it. I could not laugh and only blushed. Father picked up the funnies he never allowed us to see until after we were home from church. He gave them to me, and I held them and looked at the gaudy, foolish colors and didn't feel like reading them.

"When is he coming?" my mother said, her eyes not lifting from the spoon.

I looked up from the funnies and out the window at the quiet yellow morning and saw Jenny wandering down the alley in her red sweater, her head bent toward the kitten in her arms.

"This afternoon," Father answered, and he looked out the window and saw Jenny, too. "Whose cat is that?" he shouted, his anger easier and truer than his joy had been.

I jumped, hesitated, and found deception easy enough to practice. "I think it's Carrie Wallstrom's," I murmured, and, suffering, went and took Buddy, where he leaned from Mother's hip, drooling on his fresh shirt. "Stop that, Buddy," I fussed, and wiped away the bubbles he blew from his wet, laughing mouth.

My father studied the paper again. "Stop acting as though it's my fault!" he suddenly shouted.

My mother's hand dropped the spoon and fell to her side. She stood with her head lowered to her chest and turned away from us. My father stood up, looked at her, and stomped out of the kitchen, down the basement stairs, banging the doors behind him. . . .

It was noon, and we were eating lunch in the breakfast nook when the doorbell rang.

"That will be Johnson," Father announced. There was warning in the river of his voice. His brown eyes shone at Mother.

She did not look up to see it, but the spoonful of custard she was lifting toward Buddy's wide-open mouth stopped in mid-air. Buddy's mouth stretched a wide and wider O. Suddenly it blared out a great, wounded bellow. Mother jumped. She popped the spoon into Buddy's mouth. The howl split off. Father went from the kitchen, and Mother began to shovel the filled spoon at Buddy's mouth faster than he could swallow.

"Hurry, girls," she rushed us. Her red head dipped toward the dining room door. "Shush, girls," she hushed us.

The voice joining my father's was a high-pitched man's voice, with a singsong motion to it that hid its sense.

But Father's bugle-noted words came clear. "The floors," he said. "The floors are of first-grade oak. And the hardware. Throughout the house, the finest. Look at that fireplace. Wisconsin stone. Had the best mason in the business lay that fireplace. See how those edges join? Beautiful. The dining room," he said. "Fourteen by sixteen."

They came into the kitchen, my father walking with arms folded across his chest, the rolled sleeves of his shirt showing the muscle lying smooth and heavy beneath the browned skin, his jaw out, his mouth stern and glad. Beside him was a taller man, thin in the body and loose-looking under the pin-striped cloth of his suit. His long legs lifted and dropped in a slow, light step, like the legs of a water spider. His oiled cap of gray hair lay flat and smooth over a crown that was as oval as an egg.

"Mr. Johnson, my wife." My father's smile was for Johnson, his frown for Mother.

"How do you do," my mother answered, and her tone was light and armored. She moved from table to sink like a dancer, with dirty dishes in her hands.

Mr. Johnson looked down from his high place. His face slipped into and out of a quick, promising, unreliable smile. His small, light eyes ran from corner to corner, taking in the whole room.

"Inlaid linoleum," my father said, looking coldly at my mother's straight back.

"Ah, yes." Mr. Johnson paused. "The stove should go with, of course," he said. "It fits so nicely there."

There was a jerk in the arc of my mother's arm as she lifted plates from the table. "We'll keep the stove," she said.

Johnson looked at my father. His smile, tolerant and fluid, slid over his face.

A band of red flared across my father's high-boned cheeks and took his ears. "There are plenty of cupboards," he said. "Look at this large storage closet."

"That comfy breakfast nook should catch someone's fancy." Johnson's chant was comforting.

They went to tour the bedrooms.

Afterward, my father came back to the kitchen. He sat down on one of the benches by the trestle table in the nook and looked out the white-curtained window at the leaves of the one great oak tree, holding the sun sharply on their scalloped edges. He looked at the leaves as though he needed to study the intricacies of their twined and shadowed shapes. And he said nothing at all.

My mother went to the table. She put her hands on the table's edge. Now she looked down on Father as though she were a teacher and he a recalcitrant[1] student. "Well, what did he say?"

My father looked not at her, but only into the dense clusters of leaves. "Forty-five hundred. He says forty-five hundred."

My mother's hands dropped from the table's edge, went to her sides, came up again, and sat on her hipbones in the shape of fists. Her lips pouted with contempt. Her chin lifted. She stared down at Father. The light in her eyes snapped out at him. Her hair and cheeks looked on fire. She stood there growing straighter and taller and blazing more vividly with each short moment until she burst into rocketing words.

"Forty-five hundred? Forty-five hundred dollars? Why, that's ridiculous! It cost that much to build. That doesn't even allow for labor! What about that? Isn't your labor worth anything? If that Mr. Johnson thinks we're going to sell this house at a price like that, he's mistaken, that's what he is! Why, I'll sit here till doomsday, before I let you give away this house for forty-five hundred dollars!"

But her indignation didn't touch Father. Neither the day's heat nor the last of her words affected him. He sat on the bench, looking out at leaves, as though some cold winter had frozen him to the spot, and

when the flare of Mother's words faded, it seemed that gray, dreary smoke drifted down over us all, darkening my mother's face so that what had been marvelously brilliant became paled and drained before our eyes. But Father didn't see that, either.

"Axel, you can't sell for forty-five hundred," my mother whispered at last.

"Mortgage, twenty-seven hundred." (He was counting only to himself.) "Rent, probably twenty-five a month. That's three hundred. Food, a hundred a month. Fifteen hundred. One year. It'll do for one year. Perhaps stretch it some. By then, maybe—"

And then he turned from the window and looked at Mother; but she bent from his haunted, calculating look, down to Buddy squeezing her knees. She lifted him up and went away with him, murmuring, "Don't cry, Buddy. There, now. Don't cry."

Johnson came and went at irregular intervals. He brought one or two prospective buyers, who went through the house in a desultory[2] way and did not return. My father still walked to town each day and returned with hurt feet and a bad temper. Jenny was in the empty lot almost all the time. She named the kitten Tiger, though he had a gray coat with a white bib. Mother was quiet and remote. The frown between her fair brows seemed a permanent record.

Then it was late June, and we were out of school. The blue days were long and unseasonably hot. Mornings we played in the shade of the oak in the back yard, and afternoons we retired to the damp coolness of the basement and played there. Mother answered an ad in the paper and began to do piecework for a knitting mill. She got twenty-five cents for each finished sleeve.

[1] RECALCITRANT (ri·kal′sə·trənt): stubbornly resistant to authority.

[2] DESULTORY: *here,* showing little interest.

It took her six hours to knit one sleeve. Father forecast total disaster. "Democracy," he intoned. "A beautiful intention. Failed!"

We went to Powderhorn Park on the Fourth of July. We sat on high hills ringing the small pond and watched the fireworks spray across the close, dark sky. At the end, a box of fireworks blew up, and the show ended precipitously[1] in a wild spatter of sound and brilliant, confused flares, rockets, Roman candles, and fire fountains. "Fourth of July," Father shouted. "Last rites."

In the middle of July, the middle of the day, we were in the basement, canning peaches. Jenny and I had slipped the wet, limp skins from the fruit. Mother had halved them, stoned them, slid the yellow rounds into the green Mason jars that stood in rows on the newspaper-covered table. On the small, two-burner gas stove, sugar syrup simmered over a blue flame. The cool air was heavy with sweetness. Mother lifted the pot of syrup from the stove.

The doorbell rang.

"Shoot. Who can that be?" She set the pot back on the stove, lifted the corner of her wet, stained apron, and wiped the fine beads from her forehead. "Berit, run up and see."

I ran up the stairs, through the shade-drawn rooms to the front door. As I reached the door, the flat, dull buzz repeated. I pushed down the latch, pulled at the heavy door with both hands, and almost fell forward into the blast of white light.

"Well, hello, little girl, is your mother home?"

I recognized that high voice. I peered

into the sun and up. Behind Mr. Johnson I saw another form, a large bulk of darkness, someone strange, a woman. A buyer. Important.

I banged the door shut and ran back through the dim rooms and down the stairs, shouting, "Mother, it's Mr. Johnson. And someone else."

Upstairs, the doorbell buzzed. Mother dropped her hot pad and towel, ran ahead of me up the stairs, through the house to the front door. "Excuse me," she said, when I pulled the door open again. "Please come in."

Mr. Johnson looked at my mother as though he towed behind him a cargo of untold value. His face was several shades brighter than usual, his grin wider and looser. "This is Mrs. Faulk." He flapped his hand like a flag.

She had a forward-thrusting, presumptuous bosom, a chin tucked forbiddingly back toward a stiff neck. Her black eyes looked all around coldly, possessively, taking everything in and giving nothing out. She swayed into the living room behind the shelf of her bosom like a captain looking over a ship's bridge. "The shades," she commanded.

Mr. Johnson rushed to a window and jerked at the hoop on the string of the shade.

"I'll do that, Mr. Johnson." My mother's voice was new, and I turned and saw that she had learned in one swift lesson the art of condescension.[2] She went from window to window, her back and mouth stiff. The hot sunlight broke into the room's summer shade.

"Wisconsin stone." Mr. Johnson gestured grandly toward the fireplace.

---

[1] PRECIPITOUSLY: abruptly.

[2] CONDESCENSION: acting as though one is coming down to the level of one's inferiors.

Mrs. Faulk exhaled audibly through her thin nose. She pushed at the carpet with the perforated toe of her black oxford.

Mr. Johnson stooped and flung the carpet back. "Good—excellent condition, the floors," he cried. "Fine housekeeper, fine, fine."

Red spots marred my mother's cheeks. Her lips closed in upon themselves. "I will leave you, Mr. Johnson. Excuse me." She turned away with her chin high, signaling indifference. She shooed us children down the stairs ahead of her into the basement. She lifted the syrup from the burner and poured it into the jars filled with mounded peaches. White steam rose around her. She blew a long breath up toward her hair, lifted an arm, wiped her forehead.

"Is she going to buy the house, Momma?" Jenny looked toward the stairs, as if she expected to find those cold black eyes staring down on her.

Mother didn't answer. . . .

We were to move to a duplex on Cedar Avenue. It was a high, narrow, scabby-looking building. Its brown paint was flaking. Black screens on the windows and front porch gave it a sinister aspect. The patch of ground that was its front yard was burned dry, and the bushes flanking the steps were woody and tangled. Traffic was steady down Cedar Avenue. At regular intervals, streetcars roared through its steady hum.

"It's temporary," Father repeated, as we toured the empty, high-ceilinged rooms.

My mother eyed inadequate closets; high, narrow windows.

"I can put shelves over the stove," Father said, as we trailed through a small kitchen. "The children can sleep three in one room for a while," he asserted, standing in the center of a lightless bedroom. "After all," he shouted at my silent mother in the small, square living room, where dark woodwork looked soft and disintegrating under too many coats of varnish and stain, "what do you expect for twenty dollars a month?"

"Who's complaining?" my mother said, and walked out the door and out to the car at the curb.

But whatever anxiety and pain touched the rest of us still did not touch Jenny. She went about with her face looking like a flower with sun on it. As long as she had the kitten to be sometimes cuddled, sometimes played with and murmured to, nothing else affected her.

But I knew, if Jenny did not, that her strange impregnability[1] was doomed. Time, which she ignored, was still inexorable.[2] Days dawned and turned and passed into swift, forgotten nights. When six or seven more had gone, Jenny would have to abandon her kitten to his makeshift home in the empty lot, and her present happiness would shatter into loss.

On the last day of July, early in the morning, Father's friend Lars arrived at the house with an old truck. Draperies were down, folded into huge cardboard cartons and covered with sheets. The rugs were rolled into cylinders. The house echoed when we spoke.

Father was furious with energy. He shouted at all of us. "Get that box out of there. Berit, open that door. Let's get that chest next, Lars. Emma, bring the hammer. Berit, get Buddy out of the way."

Everyone but Jenny hauled and shoved and carried and ran. She was not around.

It was past noon when they went off with the first load. Lars was driving. My mother sat beside him, smudged and disheveled,[3] holding Buddy on her knees. My father stood on the crowded platform of the truck, leaning his elbows on the cab's roof. I was left behind to watch the house.

As soon as the truck rumbled out of sight, I ran to the empty lot to find Jenny. The high, covering weeds were dry. They scraped at my legs as I ran. At the far corner of the lot, the tumble of honeysuckle shimmered where sun touched it. The tiny yellow blossoms gave off light as though of sun themselves, and as I came near the lit place, the air was suffused with fragrance.

"Jenny?" I whispered, as though the place would be marred by ordinary sound. She did not answer. "Jenny?" I moved a branch, and in the deeper light, I saw her there, lying face down on the patch of ground smoothed with use. Her long fair hair was tumbled over her neck and face. The gray kitten jumped about her, hissing softly and clawing at the strands of her hair. The light was golden upon them, and in its dapple,[4] they seemed private and privileged.

---

[1] IMPREGNABILITY: *here,* inner strength or peace that cannot be shaken.
[2] INEXORABLE: inevitable; unyielding.

[3] DISHEVELED: disarranged, untidy.
[4] DAPPLE: spotted marking (from the play of sunlight and shade).

"Jenny!" I said harshly, though why I scolded her I was not sure.

She flung back her hair and looked at me.

"Jenny, come on home," I commanded, though when I came, I had no plans for ordering her away. The sight of that much happiness somehow made it seem necessary to save her from it.

Jenny sat up and took the kitten into her arms. It lay in the folds of her smooth arms, a soft gray bundle collapsed into comfort. The kitten's wide eyes narrowed down, and a lush rumble of purring filled the shady den. Jenny looked at me, her own eyes grown heavy-lidded with secrecy and willfulness. She shook her head. "I'm not coming. I'm going to stay here."

"Jenny, come on. They're coming back. You can't stay here forever."

Jenny looked only at her kitten. She stroked it, and her face began to assume a look of dreams and separation. Then she stopped, shook the hair from her face, sighed. "I'm hungry, Berit."

I could do nothing but go back across the burned grasses to the disordered kitchen and make peanut-butter sandwiches and take them to her with a glass of milk.

I watched while she ate the sandwiches and drank the milk. She stopped drinking before the milk was gone. She held the kitten and tilted the glass, so that he could lap up what was left. I sat and rested and did not say all the things I had already said too often. Now, even more than ever, she would not listen to what I said, and if I felt sorrowful and full of foreboding, perhaps by now I also envied her for being able to give so wholly what I, possibly, could never give—a desire and love so entire that it could not conceive disaster, though what it risked challenged all realities.

Perhaps I guessed, too, that for one like Jenny, so much more possessed by what she found within herself than I, that it was not a matter of choice. Even if she admitted that she would lose her kitten and her believed-in unreality within a few short hours, that knowledge would not diminish or alter her commitment, and she would have to accept and endure the suffering which was the price of her gift.

Then I heard the truck's faulty motor clattering up the avenue. I left Jenny in the honeysuckle and ran back to the half-emptied house before Father and the gloomy-faced Lars climbed out of the truck.

I ran with them from room to room, as they heaved and hauled the rest of the afternoon.

It was after five, and the hot day was dulling down toward a ruddy evening when Father wearily brushed his hands on his haunches, looked around the emptied rooms, said, "Well, I guess that's it. Let's go."

He closed and locked windows and doors, strode out to the truck, and was halfway up on the seat behind the steering wheel when I grabbed his sleeve.

"Jenny. We have to get Jenny."

Surprise sent his eyebrows high up his sweaty forehead. "Jenny? Where is she?"

I pointed to the empty-looking lot. "Over there."

"Well, go get her." He pulled his leg up and settled down behind the wheel. I shook my head. "Hurry up," he shouted, and I ran again over the weeds, knowing what would happen.

After he called the third time, I trudged back to the truck. "She won't come."

"What do you mean, she won't come? Where is that girl?" Father demanded.

I pointed to the corner of the lot. "Over there. In the honeysuckle bush."

He jumped out of the cab and went down the walk and across the vacant lot, shouting, "Jenny, Jenny," in a huge voice, his long legs pumping furiously. I ran after him and saw him rummage through the tangle of branches and stand tall and momentarily arrested[1] when he uncovered her there.

[1] ARRESTED: stopped.

Color and weariness and anger deepened in his face as he looked. He took it all in at once—the nest in the box, the tin for food, the look of custom within the den, Jenny kneeling there on her cleared ground, her kitten against her breast, her eyes at last barren with fear. There was that moment of silence, each one looking, disbelieving, upon the other.

Then Father burst into rage. "What in God's name are you doing here?"

With that shout, Jenny changed, stiffened, turned adamant with desire. In eye and mouth and uptilted chin, her will was pitted against his own. "Go away," she shouted. "Go away!"

A snarl like anguish rolled from Father's throat. With flaming face and burned eyes, he bent and grabbed the animal from Jenny's arms. He held it by the neck in one hand. The kitten's body arched and twisted. It spit and clawed. Its pointed teeth yearned in the arched red mouth. The claws whipped at Father's arm.

Jenny flew at Father. She beat on his chest with hard fists, kicked wildly at his legs. Leaves and light shook over the three of them in a whistling, spattering storm.

The fury on Father's face became a look I had never seen. That snarling sound repeated in his throat. He wrapped a large, wrenching hand around the kitten's wild, twisting form and turned it fiercely away from the hand that held the kitten's head.

The tiny crack broke through the spitting and the hissing and Jenny's crying, and, in immense silence, the kitten fell from its single, violent shudder and lay broken, looking only like a dirty rag, upon the ground.

With one long cry, Jenny fell upon it there. Father reached down and grabbed her and flung her over his shoulder. He plunged through the fragrant, blossoming branches and ran toward the truck.

We were not what we had been. What was known was gone. What was new was strange. The darker light and limited space of the place in which we lived robbed even the furniture of familiarity. But if the place in which we lived was bleak, it was less than the bleakness each of us found within himself. For Jenny and I could not forget. We would never forget; we knew that. And we could not understand at all.

Those summer days, Jenny sat on the chipped concrete steps in front of the duplex and looked at the paper-littered, track-scarred street and did not see what she looked at. Not even the abrupt, paining roar of the streetcars changed the flat disinterest on her face.

If Father saw her there, her small round chin held on one upturned palm, unwilling or unable to play, his frown pulled blackly across his face. "Let her sit," he'd say roughly. "She'll get over it." But in his eyes there was a distance that had not been there before.

On a leaf-strewn day in October, Jenny and I walked home from our new school. Early evening already blended shadow to dusk. A skinny, half-wild cat darted out at us from the shelter of a low tree. Jenny screamed when she saw it, and ran, terrorized and sobbing, the long block home.

When I went into the kitchen, she stood in Mother's arms, crying and shaking, her dropped books scattered across the floor. Mother looked at me for the explanation Jenny could not give, and Father turned the same mystified and worried look from where he was, half up from his chair at the table.

"A cat. She saw a cat."

The look then that went from Father to Mother, and from her to him, was so stunned and so cold, so knowing and so burdened with recognition, that I stood in the center of it, a prisoner in its harsh winter.

Then my father turned away. He laid his arms and head upon the table. His shoulders heaved and humped; but I would not have known those shaking sounds were sobs had he not suddenly pushed away the chair and fled from the house out into the fallen dark. When he rushed by, I saw the tears runneling his face.

And so there was, in time, forgiveness. We lived through those years to years more comfortable. We knew again times of happiness, and of love. Looking back, one can say if Mother had needed that house less, or if Jenny had been a less willful child, or Father a less passionate man, or the times easier, there would have been less hurt. But where we live and where we love, we must, it seems, bear a plenitude[1] of pain.

[1] PLENITUDE: abundance.

FOR DISCUSSION

1. Both Jenny and her father are faced with the same terrible awareness: that they do not have the power to save those that they love from hurt. Discuss this statement in the light of the father's cruel behavior to Jenny and her kitten.

2. When the girls' parents are arguing about selling the house, "sudden hate flung up between them that grew into a wall of silence from which neither could move and which neither could destroy." What other family relationship is affected this way? Do you think that the members of Jenny's family care for each other? Why or why not? Why do you think that both Jenny and her mother try to hide their deepest feelings from their family?

3. *Setting* is the time or place in which a story happens. The setting in this story, the Depression and the move that it makes necessary, does far more than just provide an interesting and colorful background for the adventure of the kitten. How would the story be different if the same incident had taken place in a calm and prosperous setting? How would our judgment of Jenny's father change? Does the setting of this story help us to understand better the actions of the characters? Why or why not?

is people and
have friend
ing and world
other ways.—CARMEN oth
Look out your window and look at the
ople faces and see sadness in their eyes.

there is noth
My friend
friend in the est
person. She sick
. . . Yes me an son
each other no ect

Even if you d
sometimes rich that
play wild. While and
yish-

dren

News Sun and Index

see that I try to help pick

Maud Martha could live with empty Christmas boxes and nothing on the shelf, but there was one thing in life she couldn't do without.

AT THE BURNS-COOPERS'

GWENDOLYN BROOKS

IT WAS a little red and white and black woman who appeared in the doorway of the beautiful house in Winnetka.

About, thought Maud Martha, thirty-four.

"I'm Mrs. Burns-Cooper," said the woman, "and after this, well, it's all right this time, because it's your first time, but after this time always use the back entrance."

There is a pear in my icebox, and one end of rye bread. Except for three Irish potatoes and a cup of flour and the empty Christmas boxes, there is absolutely nothing on my shelf. My husband is laid off. There is newspaper on my kitchen table instead of oilcloth. I can't find a filing job in a hurry. I'll smile at Mrs. Burns-Cooper and hate her just some.

"First, you have the beds to make," said Mrs. Burns-Cooper. "You either change the sheets or air the old ones for ten minutes. I'll tell you about the changing when the time comes. It isn't any special day. You are to pull my sheets, and pat and pat and pull till all's tight and smooth. Then shake the pillows into the slips, carefully. Then punch them in the middle.

"Next, there is the washing of the midnight snack dishes. Next, there is the scrubbing. Now, I know that your other ladies have probably wanted their floors scrubbed after dinner. I'm different. I like to enjoy a bright clean floor all the day. You can just freshen it up a little before you leave in the evening, if it needs a few more touches. Another thing. I disapprove of mops. You can do a better job on your knees.

"Next is dusting. Next is vacuuming—that's for Tuesdays and Fridays. On Wednesdays, ironing and silver cleaning.

"Now about cooking. You're very fortunate in that here you have only the evening meal to prepare. Neither of us has breakfast, and I always step out for lunch. Isn't that lucky?"

"It's quite a kitchen, isn't it?" Maud Martha observed. "I mean, big."

Mrs. Burns-Cooper's brows raced up in amazement.

"Really? I hadn't thought so. I'll bet"— she twinkled indulgently—"you're comparing it to your *own* little kitchen." And why do that, her light eyes laughed. Why talk of beautiful mountains and grains of alley sand in the same breath?

"Once," mused Mrs. Burns-Cooper, "I had a girl who botched up the kitchen. Made a botch out of it. But all I had to do was just sort of cock my head and say, 'Now, now, Albertine!' Her name was Albertine. Then she'd giggle and scrub and scrub and she was *so* sorry about trying to take advantage."

It was while Maud Martha was peeling potatoes for dinner that Mrs. Burns-Cooper laid herself out to prove that she was not a snob. Then it was that Mrs. Burns-Cooper came out to the kitchen and, sitting, talked and talked at Maud Martha. In my college days. At the time of my debut. The imported lace on my lingerie. My brother's rich wife's Stradivarius.[1] When I was in Madrid. The charm of the Nile. Cost fifty dollars. Cost one hundred dollars. Cost one thousand dollars. Shall I mention, considered Maud Martha, my own social triumphs, my own education, my travels to Gary and Milwaukee and Columbus, Ohio? Shall I mention my collection of fancy pink satin bras? She decided against it. She went on listening, in silence, to the confidences until the arrival of the lady's mother-in-law (large-eyed, strong, with hair of a mighty white, and with an eloquent, angry bosom). Then the junior Burns-Cooper was very much the mistress, was stiff, cool, authoritative.

There was no introduction, but the elder Burns-Cooper boomed, "Those potato parings are entirely too thick!"

The two of them, richly dressed, and each with that health in the face that bespeaks,[2] or seems to bespeak, much milk drinking from earliest childhood, looked at Maud Martha. There was no remonstrance;[3] no firing! They just looked. But for the first time, she understood what Paul endured daily. For so—she could gather from a Paul-word here, a Paul-curse there—his Boss! when, squared, upright, terribly upright, superior to the President, commander of the world, he wished to underline Paul's lacks, to indicate soft shock, controlled incredulity.[4] As his boss looked at Paul, so these people looked at her. As though she were a child, a ridiculous one, and one that ought to be given a little shaking, except that shaking was —not quite the thing, would not quite do. One held up one's finger (if one did anything), cocked one's head, was arch.[5] As in the old song, one hinted, "Tut tut! now now! come come!" Metal rose, all built, in one's eye.

I'll never come back, Maud Martha assured herself, when she hung up her apron at eight in the evening. She knew Mrs. Burns-Cooper would be puzzled. The wages were very good. Indeed, what could be said in explanation? Perhaps that the hours were long. I couldn't explain *my* explanation, she thought.

One walked out from that almost perfect wall, spitting at the firing squad. What difference did it make whether the firing squad understood or did not understand the manner of one's retaliation[6] or why one had to retaliate?

Why, one was a human being. One wore clean nightgowns. One loved one's baby. One drank cocoa by the fire—or the gas range—come the evening, in the wintertime.

---

[1] Stradivarius: one of the famous and very valuable violins made in the workshop of Antonio Stradivari.

[2] bespeaks: indicates.

[3] remonstrance: speech or gesture of protest and reproof.

[4] incredulity (in·krə·dü′lə·tē): disbelief.

[5] arch: *here*, playful.

[6] retaliation: paying back in kind.

FOR DISCUSSION

1. What does Maud Martha mean by her statement concerning the firing squad? Does the last paragraph clarify this statement in any way? What basic ingredient in life does Maud Martha find she can't live without?

2. From whose point of view is this story told? How does this influence our understanding of the events? Imagine, for example, that Mrs. Burns-Cooper is telling her husband about her encounter with the new maid. How different would the story be? Explain your answer.

BLACKBIRD

JOHN LENNON AND PAUL McCARTNEY

Blackbird singing in the dead of night,
Take these broken wings and learn to fly.
All your life
You were only waiting for this moment
to arise.   5

Blackbird singing in the dead of night,
Take these sunken eyes and learn to see.
All your life
You were only waiting for this moment
to be free.   10

Blackbird fly. Blackbird fly.
Into the light of the dark black night.

Blackbird fly. Blackbird fly.
Into the light of the dark black night.

Blackbird singing in the dead of night,   15
Take these broken wings and learn to fly.
All your life
You were only waiting for this moment
to arise.
You were only waiting for this moment   20
to arise.
You were only waiting for this moment
to arise.

FOR DISCUSSION

1. The blackbird is used in this poem as a *symbol*—that is, it means the bird itself and it also suggests additional meanings. What else do you imagine the blackbird might represent? Why is the bird described as having broken wings and sunken eyes? What symbolic meaning might these characteristics have?

2. The blackbird is urged to fly "into the light of the dark black night." Can you explain how a dark black night might be light?

Dropping out of school at sixteen, a boy finds himself adrift on a sea of loneliness.

A SUMMER'S READING

BERNARD MALAMUD

GEORGE STOYONOVICH was a neighborhood boy who had quit high school on an impulse when he was sixteen, run out of patience, and though he was ashamed every time he went looking for a job, when people asked him if he had finished and he had to say no, he never went back to school. This summer was a hard time for jobs, and he had none. Having so much time on his hands, George thought of going to summer school, but the kids in his classes would be too young. He also considered registering in a night high school, only he didn't like the idea of the teachers always telling him what to do. He felt they had not respected him. The result was he stayed off the streets and in his room most of the day. He was close to twenty and had needs with the neighborhood girls, but no money to spend, and he couldn't get more than an occasional few cents because his father was poor, and his sister Sophie, who resembled George, a tall bony girl of twenty-three, earned very little and what she had she kept for herself. Their mother was dead, and Sophie had to take care of the house.

Very early in the morning George's father got up to go to work in a fish market. Sophie left at about eight for her long ride in the subway to a cafeteria in the Bronx. George had his coffee by himself, then hung around in the house. When the house, a five-room railroad flat[1] above a butcher store, got on his nerves he cleaned it up—mopped the floors with a wet mop and put things away. But most of the time he sat in his room. In the afternoons he listened to the ball game. Otherwise he had a couple of old copies of the *World Almanac* he had bought long ago, and he liked to read in them and also the magazines and newspapers that Sophie brought home, that had been left on the tables in the cafeteria. They were mostly picture magazines about movie stars and sports figures, also usually the *News* and *Mirror*. Sophie herself read whatever fell into her hands, although she sometimes read good books.

She once asked George what he did in his room all day, and he said he read a lot too.

"Of what besides what I bring home? Do you ever read any worthwhile books?"

"Some," George answered, although he really didn't. He had tried to read a book or two that Sophie had in the house but found he was in no mood for them. Lately he couldn't stand made-up stories; they got on his nerves. He wished he had some hobby to work at—as a kid he was good in carpentry, but where could he work at it? Sometimes during the day he went for

"A Summer's Reading" by Bernard Malamud, from *The Magic Barrel*, reprinted by permission of Farrar, Straus & Giroux, Inc. Copyright © 1965 by Bernard Malamud; first published in *The New Yorker*.

[1] RAILROAD FLAT: apartment of narrow rooms arranged in a straight line.

walks, but mostly he did his walking after the hot sun had gone down and it was cooler in the streets.

In the evening after supper George left the house and wandered in the neighborhood. During the sultry days some of the storekeepers and their wives sat in chairs on the thick, broken sidewalks in front of their shops, fanning themselves, and George walked past them and the guys hanging out on the candy store corner. A couple of them he had known his whole life, but nobody recognized each other. He had no place special to go, but generally, saving it till the last, he left the neighborhood and walked for blocks till he came to a darkly lit little park with benches and trees and an iron railing, giving it a feeling of privacy. He sat on a bench here, watching the leafy trees and the flowers blooming on the inside of the railing, thinking of a better life for himself. He thought of the jobs he had had since he had quit school —delivery boy, stock clerk, runner, lately working in a factory—and he was dissatisfied with all of them. He felt he would someday like to have a good job and live in a private house with a porch, on a street with trees. He wanted to have some dough in his pocket to buy things with, and a girl to go with, so as not to be so lonely, especially on Saturday nights. He wanted people to like and respect him. He thought about these things often but mostly when he was alone at night. Around midnight he got up and drifted back to his hot and stony neighborhood.

One time while on his walk George met Mr. Cattanzara coming home very late from work. He wondered if he was drunk but then could tell he wasn't. Mr. Cattanzara, a stocky, bald-headed man who worked in a change booth on an IRT[1] station, lived on the next block after George's, above a shoe repair store. Nights, during the hot weather, he sat on his stoop[2] in an undershirt, reading the *New York Times* in the light of the shoemaker's window. He read it from the first page to the last, then went up to sleep. And all the time he was reading the paper, his wife, a fat woman with a white face, leaned out of the window, gazing into the street, her thick white arms folded under her loose breast, on the window ledge.

Once in a while Mr. Cattanzara came home drunk, but it was a quiet drunk. He never made any trouble, only walked stiffly up the street and slowly climbed the stairs into the hall. Though drunk, he looked the same as always, except for his tight walk, the quietness, and that his eyes were wet. George liked Mr. Cattanzara because he remembered him giving him nickels to buy lemon ice with when he was a squirt. Mr. Cattanzara was a different type than those in the neighborhood. He asked different questions than the others when he met you, and he seemed to know what went on in all the newspapers. He read them, as his fat sick wife watched from the window.

"What are you doing with yourself this summer, George?" Mr. Cattanzara asked. "I see you walkin' around at nights."

George felt embarrassed. "I like to walk."

"What are you doin' in the day now?"

"Nothing much just right now. I'm waiting for a job." Since it shamed him to admit he wasn't working, George said, "I'm staying home—but I'm reading a lot

---

[1] IRT: Interborough Rapid Transit, one of New York's public transportation systems.
[2] STOOP: stairway or platform outside the front door.

to pick up my education."

Mr. Cattanzara looked interested. He mopped his hot face with a red handkerchief.

"What are you readin'?"

George hesitated, then said, "I got a list of books in the library once, and now I'm gonna read them this summer." He felt strange and a little unhappy saying this, but he wanted Mr. Cattanzara to respect him.

"How many books are there on it?"

"I never counted them. Maybe around a hundred."

Mr. Cattanzara whistled through his teeth.

"I figure if I did that," George went on earnestly, "it would help me in my education. I don't mean the kind they give you in high school. I want to know different things than they learn there, if you know what I mean."

The change maker nodded. "Still and all, one hundred books is a pretty big load for one summer."

"It might take longer."

"After you're finished with some, maybe you and I can shoot the breeze about them?" said Mr. Cattanzara.

"When I'm finished," George answered.

Mr. Cattanzara went home and George continued on his walk. After that, though he had the urge to, George did nothing different from usual. He still took his walks at night, ending up in the little park. But one evening the shoemaker on the next block stopped George to say he was a good boy, and George figured that Mr. Cattanzara had told him all about the books he was reading. From the shoemaker it must have gone down the street, because George saw a couple of people smiling kindly at

him, though nobody spoke to him personally. He felt a little better around the neighborhood and liked it more, though not so much he would want to live in it forever. He had never exactly disliked the people in it, yet he had never liked them very much either. It was the fault of the neighborhood. To his surprise, George found out that his father and Sophie knew about his reading too. His father was too shy to say anything about it—he was never much of a talker in his whole life—but Sophie was softer to George, and she showed him in other ways she was proud of him.

As the summer went on George felt in a good mood about things. He cleaned the house every day, as a favor to Sophie, and he enjoyed the ball games more. Sophie gave him a buck a week allowance, and though it still wasn't enough and he had to use it carefully, it was a helluva lot better than just having two bits now and then. What he bought with the money—cigarettes mostly, an occasional beer or movie ticket—he got a big kick out of. Life wasn't so bad if you knew how to appreciate it. Occasionally he bought a paperback book from the newsstand, but he never got around to reading it, though he was glad to have a couple of books in his room. But he read thoroughly Sophie's magazines and newspapers. And at night was the most enjoyable time, because when he passed the storekeepers sitting outside their stores, he could tell they regarded him highly. He walked erect, and though he did not say much to them, or they to him, he could feel approval on all sides. A couple of nights he felt so good that he skipped the park at the end of the evening. He just wandered in the neighborhood, where people had known him from the time he was a kid playing punchball whenever there was a game of it going; he wandered there, then came home and got undressed for bed, feeling fine.

For a few weeks he had talked only once with Mr. Cattanzara, and though the change maker had said nothing more about the books, asked no questions, his silence made George a little uneasy. For a while George didn't pass in front of Mr. Cattanzara's house anymore, until one night, forgetting himself, he approached it from a different direction than he usually did when he did. It was already past midnight. The street, except for one or two people, was deserted, and George was surprised when he saw Mr. Cattanzara still reading his newspaper by the light of the street lamp overhead. His impulse was to stop at the stoop and talk to him. He wasn't sure what he wanted to say, though he felt the words would come when he began to talk; but the more he thought about it, the more the idea scared him, and he decided he'd better not. He even considered beating it home by another street, but he was too near Mr. Cattanzara, and the change maker might see him as he ran, and get annoyed. So George unobtrusively[1] crossed the street, trying to make it seem as if he had to look in a store window on the other side, which he did, and then went on, uncomfortable at what he was doing. He feared Mr. Cattanzara would glance up from his paper and call him a dirty rat for walking on the other side of the street, but all he did was sit there, sweating through his undershirt, his bald head shining in the dim light as he read his *Times*, and upstairs

[1] UNOBTRUSIVELY: without drawing attention to himself.

his fat wife leaned out of the window, seeming to read the paper along with him. George thought she would spy him and yell out to Mr. Cattanzara, but she never moved her eyes off her husband.

George made up his mind to stay away from the change maker until he had got some of his softback books read, but when he started them and saw they were mostly story books, he lost his interest and didn't bother to finish them. He lost his interest in reading other things too. Sophie's magazines and newspapers went unread. She saw them piling up on a chair in his room and asked why he was no longer looking at them, and George told her it was because of all the other reading he had to do. Sophie said she had guessed that was it. So for most of the day, George had the radio on, turning to music when he was sick of the human voice. He kept the house fairly neat, and Sophie said nothing on the days when he neglected it. She was still kind and gave him his extra buck, though things weren't so good for him as they had been before.

But they were good enough, considering. Also his night walks invariably picked him up, no matter how bad the day was. Then one night George saw Mr. Cattanzara coming down the street toward him. George was about to turn and run but he recognized from Mr. Cattanzara's walk that he was drunk, and if so, probably he would not even bother to notice him. So George kept on walking straight ahead until he came abreast of Mr. Cattanzara and though he felt wound up enough to pop into the sky, he was not surprised when Mr. Cattanzara passed him without a word, walking slowly, his face and body stiff. George drew a breath in relief at his narrow escape, when he heard his name called, and there stood Mr. Cattanzara at his elbow, smelling like the inside of a beer barrel. His eyes were sad as he gazed at George, and George felt so intensely uncomfortable he was tempted to shove the drunk aside and continue on his walk.

But he couldn't act that way to him, and, besides, Mr. Cattanzara took a nickel out of his pants pocket and handed it to him.

"Go buy yourself a lemon ice, Georgie."

"It's not that time anymore, Mr. Cattanzara," George said, "I am a big guy now."

"No, you ain't," said Mr. Cattanzara, to which George made no reply he could think of.

"How are all your books comin' along now?" Mr. Cattanzara asked. Though he tried to stand steady, he swayed a little.

"Fine, I guess," said George, feeling the red crawling up his face.

"You ain't sure?" The change maker smiled slyly, a way George had never seen him smile.

"Sure I'm sure. They're fine."

Though his head swayed in little arcs, Mr. Cattanzara's eyes were steady. He had small blue eyes which could hurt if you looked at them too long.

"George," he said, "name me one book on that list that you read this summer, and I will drink to your health."

"I don't want anybody drinking to me."

"Name me one so I can ask you a question on it. Who can tell, if it's a good book maybe I might wanna read it myself."

George knew he looked passable on the outside, but inside he was crumbling apart.

Unable to reply, he shut his eyes, but when—years later—he opened them, he saw that Mr. Cattanzara had, out of pity, gone away, but in his ears he still heard the words he had said when he left: "George, don't do what I did."

The next night he was afraid to leave his room, and though Sophie argued with him he wouldn't open the door.

"What are you doing in there?" she asked.

"Nothing."

"Aren't you reading?"

"No."

She was silent a minute, then asked, "Where do you keep the books you read? I never see any in your room outside of a few cheap trashy ones."

He wouldn't tell her.

"In that case you're not worth a buck of my hard-earned money. Why should I break my back for you? Go on out, you bum, and get a job."

He stayed in his room for almost a week, except to sneak into the kitchen when nobody was home. Sophie railed at[1] him, then begged him to come out, and his old father wept, but George wouldn't budge, though the weather was terrible and his small room stifling. He found it very hard to breathe, each breath was like drawing a flame into his lungs.

One night, unable to stand the heat anymore, he burst into the street at one A.M., a shadow of himself. He hoped to sneak to the park without being seen, but there were people all over the block, wilted and listless, waiting for a breeze. George lowered his eyes and walked, in disgrace, away from them, but before long he discovered they were still friendly to him. He figured Mr. Cattanzara hadn't told on him. Maybe

[1] RAILED AT: angrily scolded.

when he woke up out of his drunk the next morning he had forgotten all about meeting George. George felt his confidence slowly come back to him.

That same night a man on a street corner asked him if it was true that he had finished reading so many books, and George admitted he had. The man said it was a wonderful thing for a boy his age to read so much.

"Yeah," George said, but he felt relieved. He hoped nobody would mention the books anymore, and when, after a couple of days, he accidentally met Mr. Cattanzara again, *he* didn't, though George had the idea he was the one who had started the rumor that he had finished all the books.

One evening in the fall, George ran out of his house to the library, where he hadn't been in years. There were books all over the place, wherever he looked, and though he was struggling to control an inward trembling, he easily counted off a hundred, then sat down at a table to read.

FOR DISCUSSION

1. Do you think that George really will read the hundred books he chooses at the end of the story? What kind of books do you imagine were included in George's "one hundred"? How do you imagine that reading these books would affect the future course of George's life?

2. Discuss the changes in the other characters' attitude toward George throughout the story. To what extent do their attitudes govern George's actions?

3. The most obvious difference between George and Mr. Cattanzara is one of age. Discuss other significant differences. Are there any similarities? If so, explain them. What does Mr. Cattanzara mean when he tells George, "don't do what I did"?

I AM A CHILD IN THESE HILLS

JACKSON BROWNE

I am a child in these hills
I am away, I am alone
I am a child in these hills
And looking for water
And looking for water.   5

Who will show me the river
And ask me my name
There's nobody near me to do that
I have come to these hills
I will come to the river   10
As I choose to be gone
From the house of my father
I am a child in these hills
I am a child in these hills.

Chased from the gates of the city   15
By no one who touched me
I am away, I am alone
I am a child in these hills
And looking for water
And looking for life.   20

Who will show me the river
And ask me my name
There's nobody near me to do that
I have come to these hills
I will come to the river   25
As I choose to be gone
From the house of my father
I am a child in these hills
I am a child in these hills.

FOR DISCUSSION

1. In some parts of the poem, the speaker's motive in leaving seems to be a simple desire to be alone. In what stanza does this situation change? How does it become different? What word signals the change?

2. Repetition follows a pattern in all stanzas except one. Which is this? Why do you suppose the poem deviates from its usual pattern of repetition at this point?

3. If the speaker is running from "no one" as the poem suggests, then what *is* he running from? Why is he running to the hills?

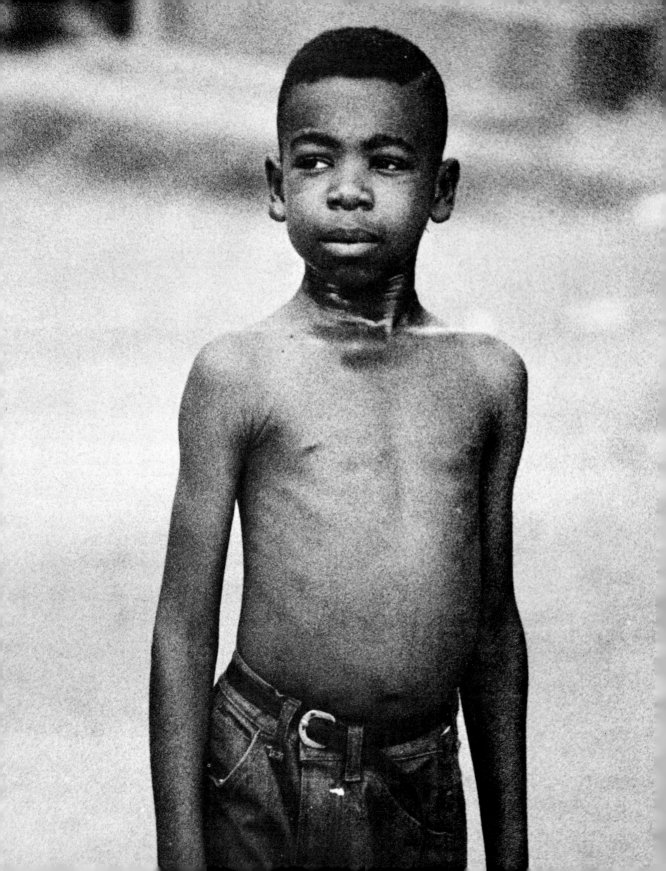

An overheard conversation brings a terrible awareness and a difficult challenge to a young boy.

BEFORE THE END OF SUMMER

GRANT MOSS, JR.

WHEN DR. FRAZIER CAME, Bennie's grandmother told him to run down to the spring and wade in the stream that flowed from it across the pasture field to Mr. Charley Miller's pond, or play under the big oak tree that stood between her field and Mr. Charley Miller's. He started along the path, but when he was about midway to the spring he stopped. He had waded in the stream and caught minnows all that morning. He had played under the oak tree all yesterday afternoon. He had asked his grandmother to let him walk the mile and a half down the road to James and Robert Lee Stewart's to play, but she had not let him go. There was nothing he wanted to do alone. He wanted someone to play with. He turned and went back and crept under the window of his grandmother's room. Their voices floated low and quiet out into the cool shade that lay over the house.

"How long will it be?" he heard his grandmother say.

"Before the end of summer."

"Are you sure?"

"Yes. You should have sent for me long ago."

"I've passed my threescore and ten[1] years. I'm eighty-four."

[1] THREESCORE AND TEN: seventy.

"Before the End of Summer" by Grant Moss, Jr., © 1960 by The New Yorker Magazine, Inc. Reprinted by permission.

What did they mean? Perhaps he ought not to be listening.

"How will it come? Tell me, Doctor. I can stand it."

"There will be sharp, quick pains like the ones you've been having. Your heart cannot stand many more attacks. It grows weaker with each one, even though you're able to go about your work as you did before the attack came. I'm going to leave you a prescription for some pills that will kill the pain almost instantly. But that's about all they will do. When an attack comes, take two with a glass of water. They'll make you drop off to sleep. One time you won't wake up."

Now Bennie understood. But he could not turn and run away.

There was a brief silence. Then his grandmother said, "Don't tell Birdie nor anybody else."

"But you can't stay here alone with the child all day long. Why, he's only ten years old."

"I know. . . . Doctor, there ain't anyone to come stay with me. Birdie must go the Fieldses' to work. You know it's just Birdie, the boy, and me. I got no close kin. My husband, my three sons, and my other daughter's been dead for years now. You see, I know death, Doctor, I know it well. I'm just not use to it."

"No one is," Dr. Frazier said.

"Here's what I want to do. I'll go on just like before. There ain't nothin' else for me to do. When an attack comes, I'll take the two pills and I'll send Bennie runnin' down the road for May Mathis. She'll come. May will come. I know nobody I'd rather have set beside me than May. I knowed her all my life. Me and her done talked about this thing many times. It's July now. July the seventh. Then August—then September. But here I go runnin' on and on. Let me get your money. You've got to be paid. You've got to live."

"Please," Dr. Frazier said.

"No harm meant."

In a moment, Bennie heard them walking out onto the porch through the door of her room. Then he could see them as they crossed the yard to the gate, where Dr. Frazier's horse and buggy stood. He was a little man, with a skin that was almost black. He climbed into his buggy and started up the road toward the town, which was three miles away, and she stood and looked after him. Her back was to the house. People said that Bennie's grandmother had Indian blood in her veins, for she had high cheekbones and her nose was long and straight, but her mouth was big. Her eyes seemed as though they were buried way back in her head, in a mass of wrinkles. They danced and twinkled whenever they looked at him. She was a big woman, and she wore long full skirts that came all the way to the ground.

She closed the gate and started back to the house, and it came to Bennie that he was alone with her, and that she was going to die soon. He turned and ran noiselessly across the back yard, through the gate, and down the path to the spring.

When he reached the spring, he kept running. He ran across the pasture field and up the hill to the barbed-wire fence that divided his grandmother's land from Mr. Charley Miller's. He threw himself to the ground and rolled under the fence, picked himself up on the other side, and ran through Mr. Charley Miller's field of alfalfa and into the woods, until at last he fell exhausted in the cool damp grass of a shaded clearing.

His grandmother was going to die. She might even be dead now. She was going to lie cold and still, in a long black casket that would be put into a hearse that would take her to church in town. The Reverend Isaiah Jones would preach her funeral. People would cry, because people liked his grandmother. His mother would cry. He would cry. And now he was crying, and he could not stop crying.

But at last he did, and he sat up and took from his pocket the clean white rag that his grandmother had given him to use as a handkerchief and dried his eyes. He must get up and go back to the house. He would have to be alone with his grandmother until his mother came home from the Fieldses' after she had cooked their supper. And he must tell no one what he had heard Dr. Frazier say to his grandmother.

He found her sitting in her big rocking chair, her hands clasped in her lap. "You been gone a long time," she said. "The water bucket's empty. Take it and go fill it at the spring. Time for me to be gettin' up from here and cookin' supper."

When he got back from the spring, he found her laying a fire in the kitchen stove.

It was nearly dark when he saw his

mother coming, and he ran to meet her. She looked at him closely and said, "Bennie, why on earth did you run so fast?"

He could only say breathlessly, "I don't know." He added quickly, "What did you bring me?" Sometimes she brought him a piece of cake or pie, or the leg of chicken from the Fieldses'. Today she did not have anything.

It was a long time before he went to sleep that night.

The next day, he stayed outdoors and only went into the house when his grandmother called him to do something for her. She did not notice.

On Sunday his mother did not go to the Fieldses'. In the morning they went to church. That afternoon, Mr. Joe Bailey drove up to the house in his horse and buggy to take Bennie's mother for a buggy ride. She had put on her pretty blue-flowered dress and her big wide-brimmed black straw hat with the red roses around its crown and the black ribbon that fell over the brim and down her back. She looked very pretty and as pleased as she could be. Bennie wanted to go riding with them. Once he had asked Mr. Joe if he could go along, and Mr. Joe had grinned and said yes, but Bennie's mother had not been pleased at all, for some reason. This Sunday, after they had gone, his grandmother let him walk the mile and half down the road to play with James and Robert Lee Stewart.

He knew that his grandmother was preparing to die. He came upon her kneeling in prayer beside her bed with its high headboard that almost touched the ceiling. As she sat in her rocking chair, she said the Twenty-third Psalm. He knew only the first verse: "The Lord is my shepherd; I shall not want."

Now he felt toward his grandmother the way he felt toward certain people, only more so. There was a feeling that made people seem strange—a feeling that came from them to you—that made you stand away from them. There was Miss Sally Cannon, his teacher. You did not go close to Miss Sally. She made you sit still and always keep your reader or your spelling book open on your desk, or do your arithmetic problems. If she caught you whispering or talking, she called you up to the front of the room and gave you several stinging lashes on your leg or across your back with one of the long switches that always lay across her desk. You did not go close to Miss Sally unless you had to. You did not go close to Dr. Frazier or the Reverend Isaiah Jones. Teachers, doctors, and preachers were special people.

You did not go close to white people, either. Sometimes when he and his grandmother went to town, they would stop at the Fieldses'. They would walk up the long green yard and go around the big red brick house, with its tall white columns, to the kitchen, where his mother was; it always seemed a nice place to be, even on a hot summer day. His mother and his grandmother would chuckle over something that Miss Marion Fields or Mr. Ridley Fields had done. They would stop smiling the minute Miss Marion came into the room, and they would become like people waiting in the vestibule of a church for the prayer to be finished so they could go in. He knew that he acted the same way.

Miss Marion had light-brown hair and light-brown eyes. His grandmother said that she was like a sparrow, for she was a tiny woman. She always wore a dress that was pretty enough to wear to church. The last time he was at the Fieldses', Miss Marion came into the kitchen. After she had spoken to his grandmother, she turned to him. He was sitting in a chair near the window, and he felt himself stiffen both inside and outside. She said, "I declare, Birdie, Bennie's the prettiest colored child I ever did see. Lashes long as a girl's. Is he a good boy, Hannah?"

"He's a quiet child," his grandmother said. "Sometimes I think he's too quiet, but he's a good child—at least when I got my eyes on him." They all laughed.

"I'm sure Bennie's good," Miss Marion said. "Be a good boy, Bennie. Eat plenty and grow strong, and when you're big enough to work, Mr. Ridley will be glad to give you work here on his place. We're so glad to have your mother here with us. Now, be good, won't you?"

"Yes, Ma'am," he answered.

"Birdie, give him a piece of that lemon pie you baked for supper. Well, Hannah, it's been nice talking with you again. Always stop on your way to town."

Two weeks to the day after Dr. Frazier's visit, Miss May Mathis came to see his grandmother. She was much shorter than his grandmother—a plump woman, who always wore long black-and-white checked gingham dresses that fell straight down from her high full breasts to her knees and then flared outward. Her chin was sharp, with folds of flesh around it. Her nose was wide and flat. She had small, snapping black eyes. Her skin was like cream that had been kept too long and into which hundreds of tiny black specks had fallen.

As she came into the yard, she asked Bennie if his grandmother was at home.

She said she would sit on the porch, where it was cool. He ran into the house to tell his grandmother that she was there.

His grandmother put away her sewing and went out on the porch. "May, I'm glad you come. I've been lookin' for you," she said.

"I'd been here sooner, but my stomach's been givin' me trouble lately. Sometimes I think my time ain't long."

"Hush—hush! You'll live to see me put under the ground."

"Well, the day before yesterday I spent half the day in bed. I thought I'd have to send John for you," Miss May answered, and she went into a long account of the illness that troubled her.

Bennie got up from the edge of the porch and ran around the house. The two old women paid no attention to his going. He knew what his grandmother would say to Miss May. She would tell Miss May how she wanted to be dressed for burial. She would name the song she wanted to be sung over her. He had heard the same conversation many times. Now it was different. What they were talking about would soon "come to pass," as his grandmother would say. Miss May did not know, but he knew.

He went out of the back gate and down the path to the spring. He waded in the stream awhile, catching minnows in his hands and then letting them go. He went across the pasture field. He broke off a persimmon bush to use as a switch, and he chased his grandmother's cow about the pasture a bit. But the cow was old and soon grew tired of moving when he hit her with the switch. Then he went to the big oak tree that stood between the fields and sat down. He stayed there until he saw Miss May Mathis going out of the front gate.

The July days went slowly by, one much

like another. It grew hotter and hotter.

One day when he walked into the house after playing a long time in the stream and the pasture field, he found his grandmother quietly sleeping in her big rocking chair. He saw a bottle full of big white pills on the dresser. It had not been there when he left the house. An empty glass stood beside the pills. He felt too frightened to move. Her breast was rising and falling evenly. She stirred and then opened her eyes.

She seemed dazed and not to see him for a moment. Then her lips curved into a queer smile, and a twinkle came into her eyes. "Must have dropped off to sleep like a baby," she said. "Run outdoors and play. I'll set here awhile, and then I'll get up and start supper."

Later on, she called him and asked if he could make out with milk and cold food from dinner. She left the milking for his mother to do when she came home from the Fieldses'. But the next morning his grandmother was all right, and he thought she was not going to die that summer, after all.

One morning, a little after his mother had gone to the Fieldses', Mr. John Mathis drove up. He turned his horse and buggy around to face the way he had come. Then he walked up the path to the house. He was a tall, rawboned man with a bullet-shaped head, and he looked exactly like what he was—a deacon[1] in a church.

"What is it, John?" Bennie's grandmother asked.

"It's May. She was sick all day yesterday. Last night I had to get the doctor for her. Jennie Stewart's there now."

"I'll be ready to go in a minute," his grandmother said.

[1] DEACON: clergyman's assistant.

On the way to the Mathises', Bennie sat on the back of the buggy. His grandmother and Mr. John said only a few words. When they reached the house, his grandmother told him to keep very quiet and to be good, and she went inside at once. There were people on the porch, and people continued to come and go. It was midafternoon, and still his grandmother had not come from within the house. A Ford car drove up to the gate. In it were Philomena Jones and her mother. Philomena was a year younger than Bennie. She had a sharp little yellow face, big black eyes that went everywhere, and she wore her hair in two long plaits. "Come on," she said, "and let's play something." When they were out of hearing of the grown-up people, she said, "Miss May going to die."

"How do you know?"

"I heard my mama say she was. She's old. When you're old you have to die."

Next Philomena said, "Your mama's tryin' to catch Mr. Joe Bailey for a husband. Mama said it's time she's getting another husband if she's ever going to get one."

"You stop talkin'!" Bennie told her.

"She said your pa's been dead nine years now and if your mama don't hurry and take Mr. Joe Bailey—that is, if she can get him—she may never get a chance to marry again."

"If you don't stop talkin', I'll hit you!"

"No, you won't. I'm not scared of you, even if you are a boy, and I'll say what I want to. Mama said, 'Birdie Wilson's in her forties, if she's a day, and if a woman lets herself get into her forties without marryin', her chances are mighty slim after that.' I'm goin' to marry when I'm twenty."

Continued on page 217

IDEAS AND THE ARTS

An alienated person is one who can no longer accept the standards, the values, and the beliefs of the society he lives in. He might be alienated only from one group but not from others, or from most people but not from a few. Or he might be completely alienated, feeling himself separate from all mankind, and even from the entire natural world.

Alienation has often been the concern of painters, though it has rarely been their main subject. Sometimes the theme of alienation appears as the subject of a painting, and sometimes it is expressed indirectly through the artist's treatment of a subject. In Pieter Bruegel's painting *The Fall of Icarus* (page 211), the alienation theme appears in the subject of the painting, rather than expressing the artist's own feelings of alienation. Icarus was the son of Daedalus, a legendary artist and inventor in Greek mythology. When Daedalus and Icarus were imprisoned on the island of Crete, Daedalus made them wings of feather and wax so that they could escape. Daedulus warned Icarus not to fly close to the sun, but Icarus, in a gesture of alienation from his father's authority, disobeyed. His wings melted, and he fell into the sea and drowned. In the painting he can barely be seen at the lower right. Meanwhile the rest of the world goes about its business, indifferent to his fate, as it often is to the fates and feelings of those who are alienated.

Two kinds of alienation are present in Philip Otto Runge's *Rest on the Flight into Egypt.* First, there is the alienation present in its subject. Mary and Joseph are shown fleeing from Palestine into Egypt with the baby Jesus to escape the order of King Herod that all infants were to be killed.

Herod had been told that a new king had been born, and he feared that he would lose his power. Herod, however, misunderstood what he had been told. Jesus was not to be a political king but a religious and spiritual leader. Jesus and his family were, of course, completely alienated from the values of Herod, but Jesus was also alienated from the Jewish people among whom he had been born. The second kind of alienation in the picture is that of Runge, the painter, who was himself alienated from the standards and values of his age. He developed a style of painting so different from those of his contemporaries in the early nineteenth century that his work was misunderstood and neglected.

The next painting, entitled *Man and Woman Gazing at the Moon,* is by a friend of Runge's, Caspar David Friedrich. In almost all of Friedrich's paintings in which human figures appear, the figures have their backs to the observer of the painting. In this painting, a man and a woman stand together, facing away from us. They are united, but only in their alienation and loneliness. They are facing away from the society from which they are alienated, and are gazing at nature. But the fantastic shapes of the trees, which seem both dead and threatening, and the appearance of the immensely distant moon, suggest that nature offers them no acceptable substitute for the society of their fellow human beings. The painting reflects Friedrich's own feelings; he himself was completely alienated from the values and beliefs of his time which he saw as dead or dying, and he used his art to examine and express that alienation.

In the next painting, *Self-Portrait with Masks,* alienation appears in the vision of the artist. James Ensor sees the world from the point of view of the alienated individual who is convinced that he is right in rejecting his society and its culture. In this painting, Ensor portrays himself as the only face that is not a mask. He looks out of the painting, viewing the world he lives in. The people in that world are masks— they are not real people who are wearing masks. They are masks, and there is nothing behind them. Ensor presents a world in which the humanity of people no longer exists. It is a world of things that are made, not things that are alive.

Runge, Friedrich, and Ensor painted during the nineteenth century, and they were often misunderstood because most people did not recognize their alienated visions. The painter of the next picture, Giorgio de Chirico, painted during the twentieth century. He did not have the same difficulties as the earlier artists because many more people had themselves become alienated from society. They recognized what he was doing and bought his paintings. In this painting, *Delight of a Poet,* the artist is concerned with the alienation of the human mind from the world in which it finds itself. We see an arcaded street in distorted perspective which is disturbing and foreboding in its stillness. The hard light creates elongated and mysterious shadows which suggest late afternoon and the passage of time. The fountain in the center which barely trickles, the clock which seems frozen at two o'clock, and the train in the distance all suggest time irretrievably lost. The tiny human figure seems dwarfed by the overpowering universe around him. The painting emphasizes the isolation of man even among the objects he himself has created.

Max Ernst's *Epiphany* deals with a far-reaching sense of alienation. In his vision, nature has become strange and dangerous. The natural world that man once thought was made for him, for his well-being and enjoyment, is here seen in a different light. It is not simply indifferent to man. It is hostile to man, with a life of its own. Strange monsters are fused with tree and organic shapes and the landscape seems to threaten the human figure. In this painting Ernst expresses alienation from one of mankind's oldest basic beliefs. Nature, called "Mother Nature," was for many generations considered the one certain good, the faithful and comforting nurturer of man, but for Ernst this traditional view was not consistent with his own perception of life. Ernst here expresses what well may be considered the ultimate in alienation—that man is neither welcome nor at home in his only home.

Morse Peckham

PIETER BRUEGEL THE ELDER (c. 1525-1569) *THE FALL OF ICARUS.* Musées Royaux des Beaux-Arts de Belgique, Brussels.

PHILIP OTTO RUNGE (1777-1810), *REST ON THE FLIGHT INTO EGYPT*. Kunsthalle, Hamburg.

CASPAR DAVID FRIEDRICH (1774-1840) *MAN AND WOMAN GAZING AT THE MOON.* Nationalgalerie, Berlin.

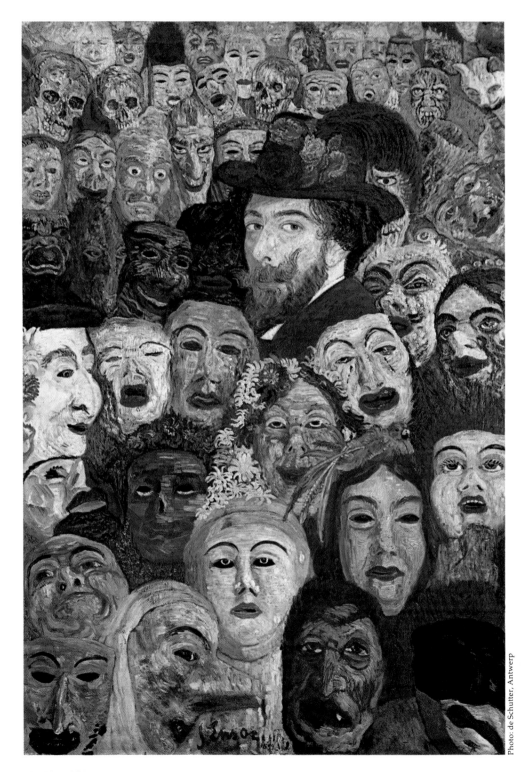

214   JAMES ENSOR (1860-1949) *SELF-PORTRAIT WITH MASKS.* Collection of Cleomire Jussiant, Ansers, Belgium.

GIORGIO DE CHIRICO (born 1888) *DELIGHT OF A POET*. Mr. and Mrs. Leonard C. Yaseen, Larchmont, New York.

MAX ERNST (born 1891) *EPIPHANY*. Collection of Mr. David Lloyd Kreeger, Washington, D.C.

"Nobody'd want you. You talk too much."

"I don't, neither."

"I won't play with you. I'm goin' back to the porch," he said.

Philomena stayed in the yard a little longer. She carried on an imaginary conversation with a person who seemed as eager to talk as she. After a while, she ran back to the porch and sat down and gave her attention to what the grown-up people were saying, now and then putting in a word herself.

Then his grandmother came out from the house. People stopped talking at the sight of her. "May's gone," she said.

The people on the porch bowed their heads, and their faces became as though they were already at Miss May Mathis's funeral.

His grandmother looked very tired. After a moment she said, "The Lord giveth and the Lord taketh. Blessed be the name of the Lord." There was a silence. Then she spoke again. "I thought May would do for me what I have to do for her now." She turned and went back into the house. Some of the women rose and followed her.

The people who remained on the porch spoke in low voices. Someone wondered when the funeral would be. Someone wondered if Miss May's sister Ethel, who lived in St. Louis, would come. Someone hoped it would not rain the day of the funeral.

Then Mr. John Mathis and Bennie's grandmother came out on the porch. Mr. John said, "Hannah, you done all you could do. May couldn't have had a better friend. You're tired now. I'll send you home."

At home, his grandmother seemed not to notice him. Her eyes seemed to be taking a great sad rest. She sent him to the spring to get water to cook supper.

As he walked down the path, he thought about his grandmother. He felt more sorry for her than he felt fear of her. Miss May Mathis was dead; he could not run and get her now.

On Sunday afternoon at two o'clock at the Baptist Church, Miss May Mathis's funeral service was held. There was a procession of buggies, surreys, and even a few automobiles from the house to the church. Mr. Joe Bailey came and took Bennie's mother, his grandmother, and him to church. The funeral was a long one. He sat beside his grandmother and listened to the prayers, the songs, and the sermon, all the time dreading the moment when the flowers would be taken from the gray casket, the casket would be opened, and the people would file by to see the body for the last time.

The Reverend Isaiah Jones described Heaven as a land flowing with milk and honey, a place where people ate fruit from the tree of life, wore golden slippers, long white robes, and starry crowns, and rested forever. The Reverend Isaiah Jones was certain that Miss May Mathis was there, resting in the arms of Jesus, done with the sins and sorrows of this world. Bennie wondered why Mr. John covered his face with his hands, and why Miss May's sister Ethel, who had come all the way from St. Louis, cried out, and why people cried, if Miss May was so happy in this land. It seemed that they should be glad for her, so glad they would not cry. Or did they cry because they were glad? He could not understand. The Reverend Jones said that they would see Miss May on the Resurrection morning.[1] Bennie could not understand this, either.

---

[1] RESURRECTION MORNING: Judgment Day, when all the dead would come to life again.

At last the gray casket was opened, and people began to file by it. And at last he was close. His mother went by, and then Mr. Joe. Now his grandmother. The line of people stopped, waiting expectantly. His grandmother stood and looked down on Miss May for a long time. She did not cry out. She simply stood there and looked down, and finally she moved on. Now he was next. Miss May Mathis looked as though she had simply combed her hair and piled it on top of her head, put on her best black silk dress, pinned her big old pearl brooch to its lace collar, picked up a white handkerchief with one hand, and then decided that instead of going to church she would sleep a little while. As he looked down on her, he was not as afraid as he'd thought he would be.

Outside the church, as the procession was forming to go to the graveyard, Dr. Frazier came up to his grandmother and asked how she was.

"As well as could be expected, Doctor," his grandmother said. And then, in a low voice, "I've had only one."

"You got through it all right."

"Yes."

"And this?"

"I've managed to get through it."

"You will be careful."

"Yes."

"Now?"

"He'll have to go to the Stewarts'."

They did not know that he understood what they were talking about, even if none of the other people around them did. He heard two women whispering. One said to the other, "It's wonderful the way Aunt Hannah took it." He felt very proud of his grandmother.

Now his grandmother's footsteps were slower as she moved about the house and yard. He kept the garden and the flower beds along the yard fences weeded; the stove box full of wood, the water bucket full all the time, without her having to ask him to do these things for her. He overheard her say to his mother, "Child does everything without being told. It ain't natural."

"Reckon he's not well?" his mother asked anxiously.

"Don't think so. He eats well. Maybe the trouble is the child don't have nobody to play with every day. He'll be all right when fall comes and school starts."

August came, and it grew hotter. The sun climbed up the sky in the morning and down the sky in the evening like a tired old man with a great load on his back going up and down a hill. Then one hot mid-August day dawned far hotter and sultrier than the one just past. It grew still hotter during the early part of the morning, but by midday there was a change, for there was a breeze, and in the west a few dark clouds gathered in the sky. His grandmother said, "I believe the rain will come at last."

About three o'clock the wind rose suddenly. It bent the top of the big oak tree that stood in the yard. There were low rumbles of thunder.

"Bennie, Bennie, come! Let's get the chickens up!" his grandmother called to him.

By the time all the chickens were safe in the henhouse and chicken coops, it was time to go into the house and put the windows down. The wind lifted the curtains almost to the ceiling. They got the windows down. His grandmother went into the kitchen. He went out on the porch. He wanted to watch the clouds, for he had never seen any bigger or blacker or quite so low to the earth—he was sure they must be touching the ground somewhere. He wanted to see what the wind did to the trees, the corn, and the grass.

At last the rain fell, first in great drops that were blown onto the edge of the porch by the wind and felt cool and good as they touched his face. They made him want to run out into the yard. Then the rain came so quickly and so heavily, and with it so much wind, that it came up on the porch and almost pushed him back into the house. The thunder roared and there were flashes of lightning.

"Bennie, Bennie, where are you?" his grandmother called, and when he went inside she said, "Set down—set down in the big chair there or come into my room if you want to. I'm goin' to just set in my rocker."

"I'll stay here," he said, and he went to the big chair near the fireplace and sat down.

"There—there—just set there. I'll leave the door open."

He tried to keep from thinking what might happen if his grandmother had one of her spells, but he could not. He went to the fireplace. The back of the fireplace was wet; water stood on it in drops that looked like tears on a face. He stood and looked at it awhile, then he sat down in the big chair. There was nothing else to do but to sit there.

He heard her cry out. The cry was sharp and quick. Then it was cut off.

She called him. "Bennie! Bennie!" Her voice was thick.

He could not move.

"Bennie!"

He went into the room where she was.

She sat on the side of her bed. She was breathing hard, and in one hand she had the bottle of white pills. "Get me a glass of water. One of my spells done come over me."

He went into the kitchen and got a glass from the kitchen safe[1] and filled it with water from the bucket that sat on the side table. Then he went back to her and gave her the water.

She took it and put two pills in her mouth and gulped them down with the water. She was breathing hard. "Pull off my shoes," she said.

As he was unlacing the high-top shoes she always wore, she gave a little cry. He felt her body tremble. "Just a bit of pain. Don't worry. I'm all right," she said. "It's gone," she added a moment later.

When he got her shoes off, he lifted her legs onto the bed, and she lay back and closed her eyes. "Go into the front room," she said, "and close the door behind you and stay there until the storm is past. I'm goin' to drop off to sleep—and if I'm still asleep when the storm is over, just let me sleep until your mama comes. Don't come in here. Don't try to wake me. 'Twon't do me no harm to take me a long good sleep."

He could not move. He could only stand and stare at her.

"Hear me? Go on, I tell you. Go on—don't, I'll get up from here and skin you alive."

He crept from the room, closing the door after him.

He went to the big chair and sat down. He must not cry. Crying could not help him. There was nothing to do but to sit there until the storm was past.

[1] SAFE: cupboard.

The rain and the wind came steadily now. He sat back in the big chair. He wondered about his mother. Was she safe at the Fieldses'? He wondered if the water had flowed into the henhouse and under the chicken coops, where the little chickens were. If it had, some of the little chickens might get drowned. The storm lasted so long that it began to seem to him that it had always been there.

At last he became aware that the room was growing lighter and the rain was not so hard. The thunder and lightning were gone. Then, almost as suddenly as it had begun, the storm was over.

He got up and went out on the porch. Everything was clean. Everything looked new. There were little pools of water everywhere, and it was cool. There were a few clouds in the sky, but they were white and light gray. He looked across the field toward Mr. Charley Miller's, and he opened his eyes wide when he saw that the storm had blown down the big oak tree. He started to run back into the house to tell his grandmother that the storm had blown the tree down, and then he stopped. After a minute he stepped down from the porch. The wet grass felt good on his bare feet.

He felt his grandmother in the doorway even before he heard her call. He turned and looked at her. She had put on her shoes and the long apron she always wore. She came out on the porch, and he decided that she looked as though her sleep had done her good.

He remembered the tree, and he cried, "Look—look, Grannie! The storm blowed down the tree between your field and Mr. Charley Miller's."

"That tree was there when me and your grandpa came here years and years ago,"

she said. "The Lord saw fit to let it be blowed down in this storm. I—I—" She broke off and went back into the house.

He ran into the house and said to her, "I'm going down to the spring. I bet the stream's deep as a creek."

"Don't you get drowned like old Pharaoh's army,"[1] she said.

The storm drove away the heat, for the days were now filled with cool winds that came and rattled the cornstalks and the leaves on the oak tree in the yard. There were showers. The nights were long and cool; the wind came into the rooms, gently pushing aside the neat white curtains to do so. One morning when he went into the kitchen to get hot water and soap to take to the back porch to wash his face and hands, he found his mother and grandmother busy talking. They stopped the moment they saw him. His mother's face seemed flushed and uncomfortable, but her eyes were very bright.

"Done forgot how to say good mornin' to a body?" his grandmother said.

"Good mornin', Grannie. Good mornin', Mama."

"That's more like it."

"Good mornin', Bennie," his mother said. She looked at him, and he had a feeling that she was going to come to him and take him in her arms the way she used to do when he was a little boy. But she did not.

His grandmother laughed. "Well, son, Mr. Joe Bailey went and popped the question to your mama last night."

His mother blushed. He did not know what to say to either of them. He just stood and looked at them.

[1] Don't . . . army: a reference to the biblical account of the Israelites' escape from the Egyptians (Exodus 14:12–28).

"What are you goin' to say to that?" his mother said.

All he could think to say was, "It's all right."

His grandmother laughed again, and his mother smiled at him the way she did when he ran down the road to meet her and asked her to let him carry the packages that she had.

"When will they be married?" he asked.

"Soon," his mother said.

"Where will they live—here?"

"That ain't been settled yet," his grandmother said. "Nothin' been settled. They just got engaged last night while they were settin' in the front room and you was sleepin' in your bed. Things can be settled later." She gave a sigh that his mother did not hear. But he heard it.

He poured water from the teakettle into the wash pan and took the pan out on the back porch and washed and dried his hands. He looked across the fields and hills. The sun had not come up yet, but the morning lay clear and soft and quiet as far as his eyes could see.

His mother was going to marry Mr. Joe Bailey. He did mind a little. He knew that was what she wanted. He liked Mr. Joe. When Mr. Joe smiled at him, he always had to smile back at him; something seemed to make him do so.

After his mother had gone to the Fieldses', he and his grandmother sat down to breakfast at the table in the kitchen. His grandmother never ate a meal without saying grace. Usually she gave thanks just for the food that they were about to eat. This morning she asked the Lord to bless his mama, Mr. Joe, and him, and she thanked the Lord for answering all her prayers.

As they ate, she talked to him. She spoke as though she were talking to herself, expecting no answer from him, but he knew that she meant for him to listen to her words, and he knew why she was talking to him. "Joe Bailey will make your mama a good husband and you a good father to take the place of your father who you never knew. The Lord took your father when your father was still young, but that was the Lord's will. Joe Bailey will be good to you, for he is a good man. Mind him. Don't make trouble between him and your mama. Hear me?"

"Yes, Ma'am."

"Don't you worry about where you'll stay. You'll be with your mama. Hear me?"

"Yes'm."

She sat silent for a moment, and then she added, "Well, no matter if your mama is going to marry Mr. Joe Bailey. We got to work today just like we always has. No matter what comes, we have to do the little things that our hands find to do. Soon as you finish eatin', go to the spring and get water and fill the pot and the tubs."

August drew toward its close, but the soft cool days stayed on, and they were calm and peaceful. His grandmother cooked the meals, and washed and ironed their own clothes and those that his mother brought home from the Fieldses' and Mr. Charley Miller's. Sometimes Bennie wondered if she had put from her mind the things that Dr. Frazier had said to her that day he listened under the window. Sometimes it seemed to him that he had never crept close to the window and listened to her and Dr. Frazier. The summer seemed just like last summer and the summer before that.

One day near the end of the month, Mr. John Mathis stopped by the house on his way to town. He was on horseback, riding a big black horse whose sides glistened. He hailed Bennie's grandmother, and she came out on the porch to pass the time of day with him.

"Ever see such a fine summer day, John?" she said.

"It's not a summer day, Hannah. It's a fall day. It's going to be an early fall this year."

"Think so?" his grandmother asked. Her face changed, but Mr. John did not notice.

"I can feel it. I can feel it in the air. The smell of fall is here already." Then they fell to talking about the church and people they knew.

She stood on the porch and watched Mr. John ride up the road on his big black horse. Often that day she came out on the porch and stood and looked across the fields and hills.

When Bennie went outside for the first time the next morning and looked around him, he did not see a single cloud in the sky. The quiet that lay about him felt like a nice clean sheet you pull over your head before you go to sleep at night that shuts out everything to make a space both warm and cool just for you. The day grew warm. A little after midday, clouds began to float across the sky, but for the most part it remained clear and very blue. He played in the yard under the oak tree, and then he went down to the spring and played. In the afternoon, he rolled his hoop up and down the road in front of the house. He grew tired of this and went and sat under the tree.

He was still sitting under the tree when his grandmother cried out. She gave a sharp sudden cry, like the cry people make when they've been stung by a bee or a wasp. He got to his feet. Then he heard her call. "Bennie! Bennie!"

He ran into the house and into her room.

She sat in her big rocking chair, leaning forward a little, her hands clutching the arms of the chair. She was breathing hard. He had never seen her eyes as they were now. "Water—the pills—in the dresser."

He ran into the kitchen and got a glass of water and ran back to the room and gave it to her and then went to the dresser and got the bottle of pills. He unscrewed the top and took out two of them and gave them to her.

She put the pills in her mouth and gulped them down with water. Then she leaned back and closed her eyes. At last she breathed easier, and in a few moments she opened her eyes. "Run and get—get Miss—no, go get your mama. Hurry! Your grandmother is very sick."

It was a long way to the Fieldses'—even longer than to the Stewarts'! He stood still and looked at her. She was a big woman, and the chair was a big chair. Now she seemed smaller—lost in the chair.

"Hurry—hurry, child."

"Grannie, I'll stay with you until you go to sleep, if you want me to," he heard himself say.

"No! No! Hurry!"

"I heard you and Dr. Frazier talking that day."

"Child! Child! You knew all the time?"

"Yes, Grannie."

"When I drop off to sleep, I won't wake up. Your grandmother won't wake up here."

"I know."

"You're not afraid?"

He shook his head.

She seemed to be thinking hard, and at last she said, "Set down, child. Set down beside me."

He pulled up the straight chair and sat down facing her.

"Seems like I don't know what to say to you, Bennie. Be a good boy. Seems like I can't think any more. Everything leavin' me—leavin' me."

"I'll set here until you go to sleep, and then I'll go and get Mama."

"That's a good boy," she said, and she closed her eyes.

He sat still and quiet until her breath came softly and he knew that she was asleep. It was not long. Then he got up and walked from the room and out of the house.

He did not look back, and he did not run until he was a good way down the road. Then suddenly he began to run, and he ran as fast as he could.

FOR DISCUSSION

1. Bennie believes there are certain "special" people from whom you separate yourself because of a certain feeling that comes "from them to you." Name these "special" people and tell what it is about them that might make them seem strange and untouchable to Bennie.

2. Several episodes involve Bennie's running: when he runs to the woods after overhearing the doctor, when he runs to meet his mother, and when he runs to her at the end of the story. Compare his motives and feelings in the first two instances and the final one.

3. At different points in the story, Bennie feels fear, pride, and sympathy for his grandmother. What occasions these feelings? Which of these feelings does he seem to have toward her at the end? Explain your answer.

4. Edna St. Vincent Millay has spoken of childhood as "the kingdom where nobody dies." How would you interpret this statement in relation to the story you have just read? In what sense do Bennie's final moments with his grandmother make him, regardless of what his chronological age is, no longer a child?

I YEARS HAD BEEN FROM HOME

EMILY DICKINSON

I years had been from home,
And now, before the door
I dared not open, lest a face
I never saw before

Stare vacant into mine   5
And ask my business there.
My business,—just a life I left,
Was such still dwelling there?

I fumbled at my nerve,
I scanned the windows near;   10
The silence like an ocean rolled,
And broke against my ear.

I laughed a wooden laugh
That I could fear a door,
Who danger and the dead had faced,   15
But never quaked before.

I fitted to the latch
My hand, with trembling care,
Lest back the awful door should spring,
And leave me standing there.   20

I moved my fingers off
As cautiously as glass,
And held my ears, and like a thief
Fled gasping from the house.

FOR DISCUSSION

• What does the speaker fear in going home? Why do you think that the speaker flees "gasping from the house" at the end of the poem?

Each lives alone in a world of dark,
Crossing the skies in a lonely arc,
Save when love leaps out like a leaping spark
Over thousands, thousands of miles!

    Kurt Weill

THE SURVIVORS

ELSIE SINGMASTER

IN THE YEAR 1868, when Memorial Day was instituted, Fosterville had thirty-five men in its parade. Fosterville was a border town; in it enthusiasm had run high, and many more men had enlisted than those required by the draft. All the men were on the same side but Adam Foust, who, slipping away, joined himself to the troops of his mother's Southern State. It could not have been any great trial for Adam to fight against most of his companions in Fosterville, for there was only one of them with whom he did not quarrel. That one was his cousin Henry, from whom he was inseparable,[1] and of whose friendship for any other boys he was intensely jealous. Henry was a frank, open-hearted lad who would have lived on good terms with the whole world if Adam had allowed him to.

[1] INSEPARABLE (in·sep′·ə·bəl): incapable of being separated.

Adam did not return to Fosterville until the morning of the first Memorial Day, of whose establishment he was unaware. He had been ill for months, and it was only now that he had earned enough to make his way home. He was slightly lame, and he had lost two fingers of his left hand. He got down from the train at the station, and found himself at once in a great crowd. He knew no one, and no one seemed to know him. Without asking any questions, he started up the street. He meant to go, first of all, to the house of his cousin Henry, and then to set about making arrangements to resume his long-interrupted business, that of a saddler, which he could still follow in spite of his injury.

As he hurried along he heard the sound of band music, and realized that some sort of a procession was advancing. With the throng about him he pressed to the curb. The tune was one which he hated; the colors he hated also; the marchers, all but one, he had never liked. There was Newton Towne, with a sergeant's stripe on his blue sleeve; there was Edward Green, a captain; there was Peter Allinson, a color-bearer. At their head, taller, handsomer, dearer than ever to Adam's jealous eyes, walked Henry Foust. In an instant of forgetfulness Adam waved his hand. But Henry did not see; Adam chose to think that he saw and would not answer. The veterans passed, and Adam drew back and was lost in the crowd.

But Adam had a parade of his own. In the evening, when the music and the speeches were over and the half-dozen graves of those of Fosterville's young men who had been brought home had been heaped with flowers, and Fosterville sat on doorsteps and porches talking about the day, Adam put on a gray uniform and walked from one end of the village to the other. These were people who had known him always; the word flew from step to step. Many persons spoke to him, some laughed, and a few jeered. To no one did Adam pay any heed. Past the house of Newton Towne, past the store of Ed Green, past the wide lawn of Henry Foust, walked Adam, his hands clasped behind his back, as though to make more perpendicular[1] than perpendicularity itself that stiff backbone. Henry Foust ran down the steps and out to the gate.

"Oh, Adam!" cried he.

Adam stopped, stock-still. He could see Peter Allinson and Newton Towne, and even Ed Green, on Henry's porch. They were all having ice cream and cake together.

"Well, what?" said he, roughly.

"Won't you shake hands with me?"

"No," said Adam.

"Won't you come in?"

"Never."

Still Henry persisted.

"Some one might do you harm, Adam."

"Let them!" said Adam.

[1] PERPENDICULAR: straight, upright.

Then Adam walked on alone. Adam walked alone for forty years.

Not only on Memorial Day did he don his gray uniform and make the rounds of the village. When the Fosterville Grand Army Post met on Friday evenings in the post room, Adam managed to meet most of the members either going or returning. He and his gray suit became gradually so familiar to the village that no one turned his head or glanced up from book or paper to see him go by. He had from time to time a new suit, and he ordered from somewhere in the South a succession of gray, broad-brimmed military hats. The farther the war sank into the past, the straighter grew old Adam's back, the prouder his head. Sometimes, early in the forty years, the acquaintances of his childhood, especially the women, remonstrated with him.

"The war's over, Adam," they would say. "Can't you forget it?"

"Those G.A.R. fellows don't forget it," Adam would answer. "They haven't changed their principles. Why should I change mine?"

"But you might make up with Henry."

"That's nobody's business but my own."

"But when you were children you were never separated. Make up, Adam."

"When Henry needs me, I'll help him," said Adam.

"Henry will never need you. Look at all he's got!"

"Well, then, I don't need him," declared Adam, as he walked away. He went back to his saddler shop, where he sat all day stitching. He had ample time to think of Henry and the past.

"Brought up like twins!" he would say. "Sharing like brothers! Now he has a fine business and a fine house and fine children, and I have nothing. But I have my principles. I ain't never truckled[1] to him. Some day he'll need me, you'll see!"

As Adam grew older, it became more and more certain that Henry would never need him for anything. Henry tried again and again to make friends, but Adam would have none of him. He talked more and more to himself as he sat at his work.

"Used to help him over the brook and bait his hook for him. Even built corn-cob houses for him to knock down, that much littler he was than me. Stepped out of the race when I found he wanted Annie. He might ask me for *something!*" Adam seemed often to be growing childish.

By the year 1875 fifteen of Fosterville's thirty-five veterans had died. The men who survived the war were, for the most part, not strong men, and weaknesses established in prisons and on long marches asserted themselves. Fifteen times the Fosterville Post paraded to the cemetery and read its committal[2] service and fired its salute. For these parades Adam did not put on his gray uniform.

During the next twenty years deaths were fewer. Fosterville prospered as never before; it built factories and an electric car line. Of all its enterprises Henry Foust was at the head. He enlarged his house and bought farms and grew handsomer as he grew older. Everybody loved him; all Fosterville, except Adam, sought his company. It seemed sometimes as though Adam would almost die from loneliness and jealousy.

"Henry Foust sittin' with Ed Green!" said Adam to himself, as though he could never accustom his eyes to this phenomenon.[3] "Henry consortin' with Newt Towne!"

The Grand Army Post also grew in importance. It paraded each year with more ceremony; it imported fine music and great speakers for Memorial Day.

Presently the sad procession to the cemetery began once more. There was a long, cold winter, with many cases of pneumonia, and three veterans succumbed; there was an intensely hot summer, and twice in one month the Post read its committal service and fired its salute. A few years more, and the Post numbered but three. Past them still on Post evenings walked Adam, head in air, hands clasped behind his back. There was Edward Green, round, fat, who puffed and panted; there was Newton Towne, who walked, in spite of palsy, as though he had won the battle of Gettysburg; there was, last of all, Henry Foust, who at seventy-five was hale[4] and strong. Usually a tall son walked beside him, or a grandchild clung to his hand. He was almost never alone; it was as though everyone who knew him tried to have as much as possible of his company. Past him with a grave nod walked Adam. Adam was two years older than Henry; it required more and more stretching of arms behind his back to keep his shoulders straight.

In April Newton Towne was taken ill and died. Edward Green was terrified, though he considered himself, in spite of his shortness of breath, a strong man.

---

[1] TRUCKLED: weakly submitted.
[2] COMMITTAL: *here*, memorial.

[3] PHENOMENON (fĭ·nŏm′ə·nŏn): unusual or significant occurrence.
[4] HALE: healthy.

"Don't let anything happen to you, Henry," he would say. "Don't let anything get you, Henry. I can't march alone."

"I'll be there," Henry would reassure him. Only one look at Henry, and the most alarmed would have been comforted.

"It would kill me to march alone," said Edward Green.

As if Fosterville realized that it could not continue long to show its devotion to its veterans, it made this year special preparations for Memorial Day. The Fosterville Band practiced elaborate music, the children were drilled in marching. The children were to precede the veterans to the cemetery and were to scatter flowers over the graves. Houses were gaily decorated, flags and banners floated in the pleasant spring breeze. Early in the morning carriages and wagons began to bring in the country folk.

Adam Foust realized as well as Fosterville that the parades of veterans were drawing to their close.

"This may be the last time I can show my principles," said he, with grim setting of his lips. "I will put on my gray coat early in the morning."

Though the two veterans were to march to the cemetery, carriages were provided to bring them home. Fosterville meant to be as careful as possible of its treasures.

"I don't need any carriage to ride in, like Ed Green," said Adam proudly. "I could march out and back. Perhaps Ed Green will have to ride out as well as back."

But Edward Green neither rode nor walked. The day turned suddenly warm, the heat and excitement accelerated[1] his already rapid breathing, and the doctor forbade his setting foot to the ground.

[1] ACCELERATED: quickened.

"But I will!" cried Edward, in whom the spirit of war still lived.

"No," said the doctor.

"Then I will ride."

"You will stay in bed," said the doctor.

So without Edward Green the parade was formed. Before the courthouse waited the band, and the long line of school children, and the burgess,[2] and the fire company, and the distinguished stranger who was to make the address, until Henry Foust appeared, in his blue suit, with his flag on his breast and his bouquet in his hand. On each side of him walked a tall, middle-aged son, who seemed to hand him over reluctantly to the marshal, who was to escort him to his place. Smilingly he spoke to the marshal, but he was the only one who smiled or spoke. For an instant men and women broke off in the middle of their sentences, a husky something in their throats; children looked up at him with awe. Even his own grandchildren did not dare to wave or call from their places in the ranks. Then the storm of cheers broke.

Round the next corner Adam Foust waited. He was clad in his gray uniform—those who looked at him closely saw with astonishment that it was a new uniform; his brows met in a frown, his gray moustache seemed to bristle.

"How he hates them!" said one citizen of Fosterville to another. "Just look at poor Adam!"

"Used to bait his hook for him," Adam was saying. "Used to carry him pick-a-back! Used to go halves with him on everything. Now he walks with Ed Green!"

Adam pressed forward to the curb. The band was playing "Marching Through

[2] BURGESS: a county official.

Georgia," which he hated; everybody was cheering. The volume of sound was deafening.

"Cheering Ed Green!" said Adam. "Fat! Lazy! Didn't have a wound. Dare say he hid behind a tree! Dare say—"

The band was in sight now, the back of the drum-major appeared, then all the musicians swung round the corner. After them came the little children with their flowers and their shining faces.

"Him and Ed Green next," said old Adam.

But Henry walked alone. Adam's whole body jerked in his astonishment. He heard someone say that Edward Green was sick, that the doctor had forbidden him to march, or even to ride. As he pressed nearer the curb he heard the admiring comments of the crowd.

"Isn't he magnificent!"

"See his beautiful flowers! His grandchildren always send him his flowers."

"He's our first citizen."

"He's mine!" Adam wanted to cry out. "He's mine!"

Never had Adam felt so miserable, so jealous, so heartsick. His eyes were filled with the great figure. Henry was, in truth, magnificent, not only in himself, but in what he represented. He seemed symbolic of a great era of the past, and at the same time of a new age which was advancing. Old Adam understood all his glory.

"He's mine!" said old Adam again, foolishly.

Then Adam leaned forward with startled, staring eyes. Henry had bowed and smiled in answer to the cheers. Across the street his own house was a mass of color—red, white, and blue over windows and doors,

gay dresses on the porch. On each side the pavement was crowded with a shouting multitude. Surely no hero had ever had a more glorious passage through the streets of his birthplace!

But old Adam saw that Henry's face blanched,[1] that there appeared suddenly upon it an expression of intolerable pain. For an instant Henry's step faltered and grew uncertain.

Then old Adam began to behave like a wild man. He pushed himself through the crowd, he flung himself upon the rope as though to tear it down, he called out, "Wait! wait!" Frightened women, fearful of some sinister purpose, tried to grasp and hold him. No man was immediately at hand, or Adam would have been seized and taken away. As for the feeble women— Adam shook them off and laughed at them.

"Let me go, you geese!" said he.

A mounted marshal saw him and rode down upon him; men started from under the ropes to pursue him. But Adam eluded them or outdistanced them. He strode across an open space with a surety which gave no hint of the terrible beating of his heart, until he reached the side of Henry. Him he greeted, breathlessly and with terrible eagerness.

"Henry," said he, gasping, "Henry, do you want me to walk along?"

Henry saw the alarmed crowds, he saw the marshal's hand stretched to seize Adam, he saw most clearly of all the tearful eyes under the beetling brows. Henry's voice shook, but he made himself clear.

"It's all right," said he to the marshal. "Let him be."

"I saw you were alone," said Adam. "I

[1] BLANCHED: turned pale.

said, 'Henry needs me.' I know what it is to be alone. I—"

But Adam did not finish his sentence. He found a hand on his, a blue arm linked tightly in his gray arm, he felt himself moved along amid thunderous roars of sound. "Of course I need you!" said Henry.

"I've needed you all along."

Then, old but young, their lives almost ended, but themselves immortal, united, to be divided no more, amid an ever-thickening sound of cheers, the two marched down the street.

FOR DISCUSSION

1. Was it really the fact that they fought on different sides in the war which alienated Adam from Henry and the others in Fosterville, or was it something different? Explain.

2. On page 234, Adam states, "I know what it is to be alone." How does this comment reflect on what we know of his life?

3. Why does Adam tell the women "when Henry needs me, I'll help him"? Does Henry really need Adam at the end of the story? Explain why or why not.

In Summary

FOR DISCUSSION

1. In "Places We Lost" Jenny's sister concludes, "But where we live and where we love, we must, it seems, bear a plenitude of pain." Find evidence to support this conclusion in the stories of this unit and from your own experience.

2. Childhood often causes a type of alienation that disappears as a child matures and gains more understanding and knowledge. What evidence do you find to support this statement in this unit?

3. In the story "At the Burns-Coopers'" and the story "Before the End of Summer" we learn something about the alienation a black person feels in a white society. Re-examine these two stories; is there anything different about this type of alienation and the other types of alienation portrayed in the unit? Explain your conclusions.

4. In "A Summer's Reading" George's own actions—first his quitting school and later his lies about reading the books—set him apart from those people whose admiration and affection he most desires. A similar observation might be made about old Adam Foust. Using the insights you may have gained from reading these two stories, as well as your own experiences, suggest what kinds of feelings might make a person set himself apart from those he most cares about.

OTHER THINGS TO DO

1. Ved Mehta gives us some idea of what it must be like to be blind in "A Donkey in a World of Horses" but clearly it is very hard for people who have always been sighted to imagine what it is like to live in a world of darkness. Invent your own simple exercises to help you understand what it is to be blind, as well as to sharpen your other senses by "seeing" with them as blind people must. You might want to take Ved's own suggestion for a start, trying to find a door in a dark room. Or try to eat a meal with your eyes closed.

Report on your experiments to the class.

2. We hear the story of what happened to the family in "Places We Lost" from Berit, but it is obvious that she could not have known exactly what the experiences she describes meant to the other members of her family. Re-create Jenny's family by dividing the class into groups of four and assigning the roles of father, mother, Jenny, and the kitten to the members of each group. Have each character in the "family" in turn retell the same events as they experienced them. In assuming your role, try to imagine and then to show the others how your character's point of view might both clarify some aspects of the situation and also alienate him or her from the feelings and motives of the others.

The World of Words

A DONKEY IN A WORLD OF HORSES

The words *sense* and *perceive* are used in Ved Mehta's story (pages 162 and 163). The word *sense* refers to the functions of hearing, sight, smell, taste, and touch, but it also has other meanings. How else is the word *sense* used? What does the word *perceive* mean? How does it relate to the senses? What do we mean when we say that something is *perceptible*? How does the word *perceptible* relate to *sense* and *perceive*?

PLACES WE LOST

An important part of Mary Hedin's story is the selling of the house that the mother loved. One of the meanings of *house* is "a place where people live." The word *home* has much the same meaning. This meaning we call the "denotation" of the word. This is the meaning you find in a dictionary. But the word *home* has many other meanings that come from our thoughts and feelings about what we call "home." These meanings cannot be put into a dictionary because they are not the same for each person. They depend on our experience with the people and the place where we live. This kind of meaning we call the "connotation" of a word. If our experience has been happy, the word *home* will have a pleasant connotation for us. If we have been unhappy, it can have an unpleasant connotation. Or, as often happens, our feelings can be mixed, and the connotation can be complex. What do you think the connotation of the word *home* would be for Berit, Jenny, their mother and father?

AT THE BURNS-COOPERS'

Mrs. Burns-Cooper tries to show that she is not a "snob" (page 188), but the word clearly fits her behavior. What is the meaning of the word *snob*, and how does it fit Mrs. Burns-Cooper? The origin of the word *snob* is not known, but it resembles the word *snub*. Do you find any connection between the two words? The word *snub* goes back to an early root for words that have to do with the nose, such as *snub, snout, snuffle, sniff, snoop*. Although no clear connection has been found between the word *snob* and words having to do with the nose, do you feel that there ought to be a connection? Explain.

A SUMMER'S READING

The word *book* goes back to an early word root meaning "beech tree" that came into Old English more than a thousand years ago as *boc*, meaning "written document." The connection between the tree and the book is that beech wood was used to carve runes on, runes being a very early form of writing. When writing was later put on paper, the word for the beech tree came along with it. One dictionary lists fifteen uses of the word *book,* used as a noun. What are five of these uses, or meanings?

BEFORE THE END OF SUMMER

When Bennie's grandmother calls him to ask for a glass of water, she says, "One of my spells done come over me" (page 219). In English *spell* is three separate words with three separate meanings, and each of the three words comes from a different source. The use of *spell* in this story is an informal, or special, use of one of the three words. What are the meanings of the three separate words that are *spell?* Write three sentences that will illustrate these three meanings.

THE SURVIVORS

1. The meaning of the word *survive* is similar to the meanings of *outlive* and *outlast.* The words are synonyms, but they are not equally appropriate for all situations. What differences in meaning do you find among the three words? Is *survive* the most accurate word to use for this story? Why, or why not?

2. "But I have my principles," says Adam (page 231). The words *principle* and *principal* are often confused although their meanings and uses are quite different. Explain the differences between these two words, and write a sentence using each word to illustrate its meaning.

Reader's Choice

Black Like Me, *by John Griffin.*

Can a white man understand how it feels to be black? In this true story, John Griffin decides to find out. With the help of a doctor, he darkens his skin chemically and steps into the life of a Southern black man for three months. Griffin is shocked at what he learns from within "someone else's skin."

A Christmas Memory, *by Truman Capote.*

A small boy and his elderly cousin make their own Christmas traditions, since they are shunned by the other relatives with whom they live. We share the sounds and smells of Christmas with the boy and his dear but eccentric friend as they chop their own Christmas tree and prepare a fantastic fruit-cake.

Coming of Age in Mississippi, *by Anne Moody.*

Anne tells her own story about growing up in the black South. Born of sharecropper parents, Anne goes on from school to college and participates in sit-ins and black voter registration drives. It is a history of our times, seen from the viewpoint of someone who has decided to change things.

I Never Promised You a Rose Garden, *by Hannah Green.*

Young Deborah Blair decides that the real world is too painful, and gradually withdraws into her own imaginary kingdom of Yr. This novel concerns her life after she is committed to a mental institution at the age of sixteen. An understanding doctor makes contact with the girl, but explains that the real world is no rose garden.

The Light in the Forest, *by Conrad Richter.*

Fifteen-year-old True Son hates being a white man. He has been raised as an Indian since the age of four, but now must go back to the family of his birth. He has heard tales of the white man's savagery and cruelty. Soon, however, he must make a choice between two cultures, and betray one of them.

North Town, *by Lorenz Graham.*

David Williams, a black student from the South, begins a new life at a Northern high school. He must overcome many obstacles as he learns that both blacks and whites can be unfair in their judgments.

The Old Man and the Sea, *by Ernest Hemingway.*

The old man had been fishing eighty-four days without a nibble when suddenly there was a tug on the line. In the story that follows, Santiago battles a fish the size of his boat which means everything to him. To release the line would mean safety—and defeat; to catch the prize might mean a dream of greatness and respect realized.

The Peanuts Treasury, *by Charles Schulz.*

Good ol' Charlie Brown, manager of the world's most defeated baseball team, Lucy, the number-one fussbudget, and Snoopy, the only canine flying ace, fill this book with their wit and wisdom as they attempt to cope with the complex problems of modern life.

The Witch of Blackbird Pond, *by Elizabeth George Speare.*

High-spirited Kit feels out of place when she comes north from Barbados to visit her Puritan relatives. She rebels at the bigotry in her surroundings and befriends Hannah, who is suspected by the Puritans of being a witch. Their friendship eventually results in a terrifying witch hunt and trial.

POEMS

A POET CAN write poems about anything: about a dead kitten or a filling station or a town dump or a bicycle. Indeed, poems about those very subjects appear among the selections that follow. What makes a poem a poem is not so much what it is about as how it says what it has to say.

In other words, poetry is by no means exclusively a matter of pretty words about sunrises or surf along the shore. Good poems have been written about sunrises, to be sure. (So have a lot of bad poems.) But good poems—poems that are effective because of the freshness and truth of what they say and the appealing way they say it—have been written about ugliness as well as beauty, about the ordinary as well as the extraordinary, about the humble and real as well as the ideal and exalted.

Whatever the subject of a memorable poem, the method of expressing that subject will almost invariably differ from the methods of prose. For one thing, poetry generally sounds better than prose. Moreover, the moods of poetry, whether of grief or joy or outrage or ecstasy, are usually more intense. The intensity comes in part from the greater compression a poem exhibits. More meaning is carried in each word and line of a poem than is generally borne by prose sentences such as these.

As a result, poems must be considered attentively and repeatedly, for good poetry goes on yielding new meanings. In a line of verse that follows, Langston Hughes has a woman say much in a few words: "Life for me ain't been no crystal stair." The word *crystal* conveys a wealth of meaning that a hasty reader might overlook. One word evokes an envied life of splendor, against which the rest of Hughes's poem is contrasted. The result is verse that is memorable.

Philip McFarland

Glimpses of People

The poet is such an alert, keen observer that he is able to choose just the right details to give us a second, sharper look at the people we've passed in life—Or is it a second, sharper look at ourselves?

AT THE AQUARIUM

MAX EASTMAN

Serene the silver fishes glide,
Stern-lipped, and pale, and wonder-eyed;
As through the agèd deeps of ocean,
They glide with wan and wavy motion.
They have no pathway where they go,   5
They flow like water to and fro.
They watch with never-winking eyes,
They watch with staring, cold surprise,
The level people in the air,
The people peering, peering there,   10
Who also wander to and fro,
And know not why or where they go,
Yet have a wonder in their eyes,
Sometimes a pale and cold surprise.

FOR DISCUSSION

1. Is this poem about fish or people? How are the two alike? How are they different?

2. What does the image "cold surprise" suggest to you?

3. What words has the poet used to help you feel the movements of the water? How does the sound of the poem, its rhythm and its pattern of rhyme, duplicate the "wan and wavy motion" of the fish and the water?

THEM LUNCH TOTERS
MASON WILLIAMS

How about Them Lunch Toters,
Ain't they a bunch?
Goin' off to work,
A-totin' they lunch.

Totin' them vittles,   5
Totin' that chow,
Eatin' it later,
But a-totin' it now.

Look at Them Lunch Toters,
Ain't they funny?   10
Some use a paper sack,
Some use a gunny.

Them food-frugal Lunch Toters,
Ain't they wise?
Totin' they lunch,   15
Made by they wives.

How to be a Lunch Toter?
Iffa may emote* it,
Gitchy wife to fix it,
Go to work and tote it!   20

18 EMOTE: express.

FOR DISCUSSION

• The poet uses slang words to create humor in this poem. How many examples can you find? Does the poet make up any words?

THIS IS JUST TO SAY

WILLIAM CARLOS WILLIAMS

I have eaten
the plums
that were in
the icebox

and which   5
you were probably
saving
for breakfast

Forgive me
they were delicious   10
so sweet
and so cold

FOR DISCUSSION

• In this short sketch we are able to relive a common, everyday experience with the poet. He doesn't use any big words or unusual images, but each word has been carefully chosen for effect. Can you imagine why the man may have eaten the plums? What is it that the poet does with words to make you understand?

"I AM CHERRY ALIVE," THE LITTLE GIRL SANG

DELMORE SCHWARTZ

"I am cherry alive," the little girl sang,
"Each morning I am something new:
I am apple, I am plum, I am just as excited
As the boys who made the Hallowe'en bang:
I am tree, I am cat, I am blossom too: 5
When I like, if I like, I can be someone new,
Someone very old, a witch in a zoo:
I can be someone else whenever I think who,
And I want to be everything sometimes too:
And the peach has a pit and I know that too,   10
And I put it in along with everything
To make the grown-ups laugh whenever I sing:
And I sing: *It is true; It is untrue;*
I know, I know, the true is untrue,
The peach has a pit, the pit has a peach: 15
And both may be wrong when I sing my song,
But I don't tell the grown-ups: because it is sad,
And I want them to laugh just like I do
Because they grew up and forgot what they knew
And they are sure I will forget it some day too.   20
They are wrong. They are wrong. When I sang my song, I knew, I knew!
I am red, I am gold, I am green, I am blue,
I will always be me, I will always be new!"

FOR DISCUSSION

1. Upon a first reading, this poem might seem rather silly and meaningless, but in fact it shares several important meanings with the reader. What is the mood that this poem shares with its readers? Use words from the poem to support your idea of how the poem makes you feel.

2. The little girl wants grown-ups to laugh like she does: why don't they? Do you think that she will "forget some day too"?

3. The image in the title is really a perfect picture of the main idea in the poem. Why? What does each word suggest or bring to mind?

SUMMONS

ROBERT FRANCIS

Keep me from going to sleep too soon
Or if I go to sleep too soon
Come wake me up. Come any hour
Of night. Come whistling up the road.
Stomp on the porch. Bang on the door.   5
Make me get out of bed and come
And let you in and light a light.
Tell me the northern lights are on
And make me look. Or tell me clouds
Are doing something to the moon   10
They never did before, and show me.
See that I see. Talk to me till
I'm half as wide awake as you
And start to dress wondering why
I ever went to bed at all.   15
Tell me the walking is superb.
Not only tell me but persuade me.
You know I'm not too hard persuaded.

FOR DISCUSSION

• Sometimes poets use the word "sleep" as a symbol of something else. What else might sleep mean in this poem? Compare this poem to Delmore Schwartz's " 'I Am Cherry Alive,' the Little Girl Sang" on page 245. Do you think that Schwartz's little girl would be a good person for Francis's sleeper to address his request to? Explain your answer.

MILLIONS OF STRAWBERRIES
GENEVIEVE TAGGARD

Marcia and I went over the curve,
Eating our way down
Jewels of strawberries we didn't deserve,
Eating our way down.
Till our hands were sticky, and our lips painted,   5
And over us the hot day fainted,
And we saw snakes,
And got scratched,
And a lust overcame us for the red unmatched
Small buds of berries,   10
Till we lay down—
Eating our way down—
And rolled in the berries like two little dogs.
Rolled
In the late gold.   15
And gnats hummed,
And it was cold,
And home we went, home without a berry,
Painted red and brown,
Eating our way down.   20

FOR DISCUSSION

• Marcia and her friend have gone "over the curve" in more senses than one. What words or phrases in the poem help to express that the children's response to the good taste of the strawberries is more intense than is usual? How do the children try to involve themselves completely with the strawberries?

Moods

One of the greatest skills the poet possesses is an extraordinary ability to create and share different moods with the reader. Through the poet's artistry with images and techniques a reader can actually come to feel what the poet feels, whether it is the marvelous freedom and newness of early spring, the tense excitement of a hurricane, or the terrible loneliness of a foggy night. All that is needed is a small response from the reader's imagination, and a whole world of moods can be shared and relived.

FIXER OF MIDNIGHT
REUEL DENNEY

He went to fix the awning,
Fix the roping,
In the middle of the night,
On the porch;
He went to fix the awning,   5
In pajamas went to fix it,
Fix the awning,
In the middle of the moonlight,
On the porch;
He went to fix it yawning;   10
The yawing of this awning
In the moonlight
Was his problem of the night;
It was knocking,
And he went to fix its flight.   15

"Fixer of Midnight" from *In Praise of Adam* by Reuel Denney, copyright 1961. Reprinted by permission of The University of Chicago Press.

He went to meet the moonlight
In the porch-night
Where the awning was up dreaming
Dark and light;
It was shadowy and seeming;   20
In the night, the unfixed awning,
In his nightmare,
Had been knocking dark and bright.
It seemed late
To stop it in its dark careening. 25
The yawner went to meet it,
Meet the awning,
By the moon of middle night,
On his porch;
And he went to fix it right.   30

FOR DISCUSSION

1. Look up the different meanings of the word "fix." How do both definitions fit this poem? What did the awning have to do with the man's nightmare? Why do you think he did not wait until morning to fix it?

2. A good poet will make the *sound* of the words in his poem help us to understand the *sense* of the poem. What kind of feeling does the regularly repeated "aw" sound in the words "yawning" and "awning" give to the poem? Can you find other patterns of sound which the poet uses to express a sense of what is happening in his words?

3. Another technique the poet uses to help create the mood and meaning of this poem is *contrast*. How many words can you find that suggest the contrast between light and dark? The combination and confusion of dark and light is described as "shadowy and seeming"; do you think it is more than a coincidence that this phrase also describes what dreams are like?

APRIL

MARCIA LEE MASTERS

It's lemonade, it's lemonade, it's daisy.
It's a roller-skating, scissor-grinding day;
It's gingham-waisted, chocolate flavored, lazy,
With the children flower-scattered at their play.

It's the sun like watermelon,   5
And the sidewalks overlaid
With a glaze of yellow yellow
Like a jar of marmalade.

It's the mower gently mowing,
And the stars like startled glass,   10
While the mower keeps on going
Through a waterfall of grass.

Then the rich magenta evening
Like a sauce upon the walk,
And the porches softly swinging   15
With a hammockful of talk.

It's the hobo at the corner
With his lilac-sniffing gait,
And the shy departing thunder
Of the fast departing skate.   20

It's lemonade, it's lemonade, it's April!
A water sprinkler, puddle winking time,
When a boy who peddles slowly, with a smile remote and holy,
Sells you April chocolate flavored for a dime.

FOR DISCUSSION

• An important reason for the rich, strong impression this poem makes on us is the way the poet forces us to respond to the scene with all our senses. What images appeal primarily to our sense of sight? Of sound? Of touch? Of taste? Of smell?

HURRICANE

ARCHIBALD MacLEISH

Sleep at noon. Window blind
rattle and bang. Pay no mind.
Door go jump like somebody coming:
let him come. Tin roof drumming:
drum away—she's drummed before.   5
Blinds blow loose: unlatch the door.
Look up sky through the manchineel:*
black show through like a hole in your heel.
Look down shore at the old canoe:
rag-a-tag sea turn white, turn blue,   10
kick up dust in the lee* of the reef,
wallop around like a loblolly* leaf.
Let her wallop—who's afraid?
Gale from the north-east: just the Trade* . . .

And that's when you hear it: far and high—   15
sea-birds screaming down the sky
high and far like screaming leaves;
tree-branch slams across the eaves;
rain like pebbles on the ground . . .

and the sea turns white and the wind goes round.   20

7 MANCHINEEL (man·chi·nēl′): type of tropical tree.   11 LEE: shelter from the wind.   12 LOBLOLLY: type of tropical tree having tough, leathery leaves. 14 TRADE: that is, trade winds, a system of winds which prevail in a consistent northeasterly pattern in the tropics of the Northern Hemisphere.

FOR DISCUSSION

1. Which of your senses responds most to this poem? Why?

2. There is a sudden change of mood in the poem. Where? What are the two different moods? Support your answer by referring to the poem itself.

3. How important is rhyme to the poem? How do you think the poem would be different if the rhyme pattern were changed so that every other line rhymed?

LOST

CARL SANDBURG

Desolate and lone
All night long on the lake
Where fog trails and mist creeps,
The whistle of a boat
Calls and cries unendingly,
Like some lost child
In tears and trouble
Hunting the harbor's breast
And the harbor's eyes.

FOR DISCUSSION

1. This whole poem is a comparison; it says that a boat's whistle is like a child's cry. How does the poet use his art to expand this simple comparison to a point where we as readers can experience in our imagination those qualities of feeling which both the boat's whistle and the child's crying have in common? Find examples in the text of the poem that show how the poet uses his words to express that feeling.

2. Alliteration is the repetition of sounds—usually initial sounds—in a series of words. Where in this poem do you find examples of this technique? Do the words that are connected by alliteration belong together in any other sense?

Love

Love has always been the most popular subject of poetry throughout history. One explanation for this interest in talking about love
may be that for every person, no matter how much he has heard of
love before, the actual experience of love itself appears to be quite
a fresh and new and completely surprising discovery. In the poems
that follow, three poets speak in very different ways about their
own adventures in feeling.

A SPACE IN THE AIR

JON SILKIN

The first day he had gone
I barely missed him. I was glad almost he had left
    Without a bark or flick of his tail,
        I was content he had slipped

Out into the world. I felt,   5
Without remarking, it was nearly a relief
    From his dirty habits. Then, the second
        Day I noticed the space

He left behind him. A hole
Cut out of the air. And I missed him suddenly,   10
    Missed him almost without knowing
        Why it was so. And I grew

Afraid he was dead, expecting death
As something I had grown used to. I was afraid
    The clumsy children in the street   15
        Had cut his tail off as

A souvenir of the living and
I did not know what to do. I was fearing
    Somebody had hurt him. I called his name
        But the hole in the air remained.   20

I have grown accustomed to death
Lately. But his absence made me sad,
    I do not know how he should do it
        But his absence frightened me.

It was not only his death I feared,   25
Not only his but as if all of those
    I loved, as if all those near me
        Should suddenly go

Into the hole in the light
And disappear. As if all of them should go   30
  Without barking, without speaking,
    Without noticing me there

  But go; and going as if
The instrument of pain were a casual thing
    To suffer, as if they should suffer so,   35
      Casually and without greatness,

  Without purpose even. But just go.
I should be afraid to lose all those friends like this.
    I should fear to lose those loves. But mostly
      I should fear to lose you.   40

  If you should go
Without affliction, but even so, I should tear
    The rent you would make in the air
      And the bare howling

  Streaming after your naked hair.   45
I should feel your going down more than my going down.
    My own death I bear everyday
      More or less

  But your death would be something else,
Something else beyond me. It would not be   50
    Your death or my death, love,
      But our rose-linked dissolution.*

  So I feared his going,
His death, not our death, but a hint at our death. And I shall always fear
    The death of those we love as   55
      The hint of your death, love.

^{52} DISSOLUTION: reduction into fragments; melting away.

FOR DISCUSSION

1. What is it that really frightens the poet about his missing dog?

2. The most unusual image in the poem is that of the "hole cut out of the air." Why is air (which is invisible, and something we take for granted without question) an appropriate symbol here? What does the image as a whole suggest about death and grief? Do you find this description a realistic one?

3. The poem changes mood and purpose twice. Where does it stop talking primarily about a lost dog? In what stanza does it become a poem addressed to just one person?

4. This poem appears in the category of poems about love, yet it seems to talk mainly of losses and death. What makes it a love poem?

THE RIVER-MERCHANT'S WIFE:
A LETTER
EZRA POUND
AFTER RIHAKU

While my hair was still cut straight across my forehead
I played about the front gate, pulling flowers.
You came by on bamboo stilts, playing horse,
You walked about my seat, playing with blue plums.
And we went on living in the village of Chokan: 5
Two small people, without dislike or suspicion.

At fourteen I married My Lord you.
I never laughed, being bashful.
Lowering my head, I looked at the wall.
Called to, a thousand times, I never looked back.   10

At fifteen I stopped scowling,
I desired my dust to be mingled with yours
Forever and forever and forever.
Why should I climb the lookout?

At sixteen you departed,   15
You went into far Ku-to-yen, by the river of swirling eddies,
And you have been gone five months.
The monkeys make sorrowful noise overhead.

You dragged your feet when you went out.
By the gate now, the moss is grown, the different mosses,   20
Too deep to clear them away!

The leaves fall early this autumn, in wind.
The paired butterflies are already yellow with August
Over the grass in the West garden;
They hurt me. I grow older.   25
If you are coming down through the narrows of the river Kiang,
Please let me know beforehand,
And I will come out to meet you
            As far as Cho-fu-sa.

FOR DISCUSSION

1. This poem speaks simply and directly of an arranged marriage, one that began without love or feeling. What evidence do you have that the marriage has become one of mutual love and respect?

2. In most love poetry, nature and the various seasons are important in setting the mood of the poem. What time of year is it here? How do the natural seasonal events described here suggest the feelings of the young wife?

PERMANENTLY

KENNETH KOCH

One day the Nouns were clustered in the street.
An Adjective walked by, with her dark beauty.
The Nouns were struck, moved, changed.
The next day a Verb drove up, and created the Sentence.

Each Sentence says one thing—for example, "Although it was a dark
    rainy day when the Adjective walked by, I shall remember the pure
    and sweet expression on her face until the day I perish from the green,
    effective earth."   5
Or, "Will you please close the window, Andrew?"
Or, for example, "Thank you, the pink pot of flowers on the window sill
    has changed color recently to a light yellow, due to the heat from the
    boiler factory which exists nearby."

In the springtime the Sentences and the Nouns lay silently on the grass.
A lonely Conjunction here and there would call, "And! But!"
But the Adjective did not emerge.   10

As the adjective is lost in the sentence,
So I am lost in your eyes, ears, nose, and throat—
You have enchanted me with a single kiss
Which can never be undone
Until the destruction of language.   15

FOR DISCUSSION

1. *Personification* is a poetic technique in which nonhuman things are described as having human qualities. This poet has used personification in a very fresh and unusual way to describe the kind of effect falling in love can have on ordinary people. Does each part of speech personified here act in a way that is consistent with its actual grammatical function? Find examples from the poem to support your answers.

2. How does the sample sentence quoted in line 5 enrich the meaning of the poem as a whole? What effect does the contrast of this sample sentence with the other two quoted in lines 6 and 7 create?

3. At what point does this poem stop telling a story and start using the feeling and meaning which that story has created to speak in another way about love? What lines in the final stanza of the poem explain why the poem is titled as it is?

The Animal World

A trip to any zoo will uncover the insight that there is a deep bond between man and his brother animals. The fascination and delight with which we regard our fellow creatures are highlighted in these poems as they bring us a closer look at the various personalities in the animal world.

PUPPY
ROBERT L. TYLER

Catch and shake the cobra garden hose.
Scramble on panicky paws and flee
The hiss of tensing nozzle nose,
Or stalk that snobbish bee.

The back yard world is vast as park
With belly-tickle grass and stun
Of sudden sprinkler squalls that arc
Rainbows to the yap yap sun.

FOR DISCUSSION

1. Whose activities are described in the first stanza? What do we learn about him from this description?

2. In the second stanza the world is pictured through whose eyes? How do you know?

3. Why is the final image of "the yap yap sun" an appropriate one? Explain how the image helps you to imagine the subject and the scene the poet is describing.

"Puppy" from *The Deposition of Don Quixote and Other Poems* by Robert L. Tyler, copyright 1964. Reprinted with the permission of Golden Quill Press.

POEM

WILLIAM CARLOS WILLIAMS

As the cat
climbed over
the top of

the jamcloset
first the right   5
forefoot

carefully
then the hind
stepped down

into the pit of   10
the empty
flowerpot.

FOR DISCUSSION

• How is the poet able to re-create the exact movements of the cat for us? Find examples in the poem showing how the poet creates the impression of carefully selecting each word and placing it precisely on the paper in such a way as to demonstrate the cat's movements with the rhythm and pace of the poetry.

SOME BROWN SPARROWS
BRUCE FEARING

Some brown sparrows who live
in the Bronx Zoo visit often
the captive Victoria Crested
Pheasant, visit captive Peacocks,
Cockatoos. They fly through bars   5
to visit also monkeys, jackals,
bears. They delouse themselves in
cage dust, shaking joyously;
they hunt for bread crumbs, seeds
or other tidbits. Briefly,   10
they lead free sparrow lives
and fly free.

FOR DISCUSSION

• What is the obvious difference between the sparrows and the other birds at the zoo? What other differences are there? The sparrows seem to be getting the best out of both worlds. Could there be any advantage in living at the zoo? What word suggests a possible advantage?

FOR A DEAD KITTEN

SARA HENDERSON HAY

Put the rubber mouse away,
Pick the spools up from the floor,
What was velvet-shod, and gay,
Will not want them any more.

What was warm, is strangely cold.
Whence dissolved the little breath?
How could this small body hold
So immense a thing as Death?

FOR DISCUSSION

• Although this poem is very short, it offers a rich and complete picture of death and the small creature it came upon. The poet's artistry lies primarily in choosing just the right word or detail to create an immediate response in the reader. Here, the poet has made particular use of the device of contrast to express the vast differences between what it is like to be alive and what it is like to be dead. What images or details express the feeling of life? Which words suggest death? Why is the last word in the poem capitalized?

OGDEN NASH

THE EEL

I don't mind eels
Except as meals.
And the way they feels.

THE PIG

The pig, if I am not mistaken,
Supplies us sausage, ham, and bacon.
Let others say his heart is big—
I call it stupid of the pig.

THE WASP

The wasp and all his numerous family
I look upon as a major calamily.
He throws open his nest with prodigality,
But I distrust his waspitality.

THE KITTEN

The trouble with a kitten is
THAT
Eventually it becomes a
CAT.

THE DOG

The truth I do not stretch or shove
When I state the dog is full of love.
I've also proved, by actual test,
A wet dog is the lovingest.

THE CLAM

The clam, esteemed by gourmets highly,
Is said to live the life of Riley;
When you are lolling on a piazza
It's what you are as happy as a.

FOR DISCUSSION

• Ogden Nash writes poetry just for fun, and that is how we are meant to read it. Nash uses his rhymes as a way of creating humor. What examples of this technique do you find in his poems?

Conflict

Poems are not only written about things we enjoy and understand. Sometimes the most interesting talk can be about things we do not fully understand, about problems that puzzle and bother us. In the same way, many poets use their art to try to make some sense out of the conflicts which trouble their thoughts.

DIRGE WITHOUT MUSIC
EDNA ST. VINCENT MILLAY

I am not resigned to the shutting away of loving hearts in the hard ground.
So it is, and so it will be, for so it has been, time out of mind:
Into the darkness they go, the wise and the lovely. Crowned
With lilies and with laurel they go; but I am not resigned.

Lovers and thinkers, into the earth with you.   5
Be one with the dull, the indiscriminate* dust.
A fragment of what you felt, or what you knew,
A formula, a phrase remains,—but the best is lost.

The answers quick & keen, the honest look, the laughter, the love,
They are gone. They have gone to feed the roses. Elegant and curled   10
Is the blossom. Fragrant is the blossom. I know. But I do not approve.
More precious was the light in your eyes than all the roses in the world.

Down, down, down into the darkness of the grave
Gently they go, the beautiful, the tender, the kind;
Quietly they go, the intelligent, the witty, the brave.   15
I know. But I do not approve. And I am not resigned.

DIRGE: funeral hymn; lament. [6] INDISCRIMINATE: not capable of making distinctions between more or less valuable things.

FOR DISCUSSION

1. Why do you think the speaker of the poem has decided to recite her dirge without the accompaniment of music?

2. If you were to read this poem aloud, what tone of voice would you choose as most appropriate to the meanings and feelings of the poem? How does the poet indicate to you what tone she intends here? Find evidence within the text of the poem to explain your answer.

3. Why do you think that the speaker in the poem talks so much about flowers?

4. For the most part, this poem seems to be about the experience of losing loved ones in general. Which line in the poem suggests that the speaker is thinking of a specific death as she speaks her dirge?

FORGIVE MY GUILT

ROBERT P. TRISTRAM COFFIN

Not always sure what things called sins may be,
I am sure of one sin I have done.
It was years ago, and I was a boy,
I lay in the frostflowers with a gun,
The air ran blue as the flowers, I held my breath,   5
Two birds on golden legs slim as dream things
Ran like quicksilver on the golden sand,
My gun went off, they ran with broken wings
Into the sea, I ran to fetch them in,
But they swam with their heads high out to sea,   10
They cried like two sorrowful high flutes,
With jagged ivory bones where wings should be.

For days I heard them when I walked that headland
Crying out to their kind in the blue,
The other plovers* were going over south   15
On silver wings leaving these broken two.
The cries went out one day; but I still hear them
Over all the sounds of sorrow in war or peace
I ever have heard, time cannot drown them,
Those slender flutes of sorrow never cease.   20
Two airy things forever denied the air!
I never knew how their lives at last were spilt,
But I have hoped for years all that is wild,
Airy, and beautiful will forgive my guilt.

15 PLOVERS: type of birds.

FOR DISCUSSION

1. Although this poem is concerned with shooting and death, the poet does not choose the words one would expect to describe the incident. For example, he uses only a few colors in his description. Why do you think he chooses the colors he does? What happens to your mental picture of the birds?

2. The images appealing to the sense of sound are very important to the mood of this poem. What words appeal primarily to the sense of sound? What kind of feeling do these sounds suggest to you?

3. Suggest reasons why the speaker in the poem still hears the cries of the wounded birds. Why do you imagine that these sounds seem to affect him "over all the sounds of sorrow in war or peace"?

DIRECTIONS TO THE ARMORER

ELDER OLSON

All right, armorer,
Make me a sword—
Not too sharp,
A bit hard to draw,
And of cardboard, preferably.   5
On second thought, stick
An eraser on the handle.
Somehow I always
Clobber the wrong guy.

Make me a shield with   10
Easy-to-change
Insignia. I'm often
A little vague
As to which side I'm on,
What battle I'm in.   15
And listen, make it
A trifle flimsy,
Not too hard to pierce.
I'm not absolutely sure
I want to win.   20

Make the armor itself
As tough as possible,
But on a reverse
Principle: don't
Worry about its   25
Saving my hide;
Just fix it to give me
Some sort of protection—
Any sort of protection—
From a possible enemy   30
Inside.

FOR DISCUSSION

1. The title of this poem suggests that it will be about a knight or warrior of some sort and his requirements for a suit of armor and other battle equipment. Is this poem primarily concerned with knights and warfare, as the title suggests? Refer directly to the poem to support your answer.

2. What are some enemies "inside" from whom a person might need protection?

Lessons

Sometimes a young person feels his whole world is filled with advice and rules. The poet, perhaps better than anyone else, is able to reveal the love and genuine concern that is often behind the lessons adults seem so eager to teach.

FIRST LESSON
PHILIP BOOTH

Lie back, daughter, let your head
be tipped back in the cup of my hand.
Gently, and I will hold you. Spread
your arms wide, lie out on the stream
and look high at the gulls. A dead-   5
man's float is face down. You will dive
and swim soon enough where this tidewater
ebbs to the sea. Daughter, believe
me, when you tire on the long thrash
to your island, lie up, and survive.   10
As you float now, where I held you
and let go, remember when fear
cramps your heart what I told you:
lie gently and wide to the light-year
stars, lie back, and the sea will hold you.   15

FOR DISCUSSION

• The obvious lesson the poet is teaching his daughter (and his readers) is a swimming lesson. What other kind of lesson is suggested? Many people would say that this suggested "first lesson" which teaches what to do "when fear cramps your heart" is really the most important lesson in a man's life. Do you agree? Explain your answer.

MOTHER TO SON
LANGSTON HUGHES

Well, son, I'll tell you:
Life for me ain't been no crystal stair.
It's had tacks in it,
And splinters,
And boards torn up,   5
And places with no carpet on the floor—
Bare.
But all the time
I'se been a-climbin' on,
And reachin' landin's,   10
And turnin' corners,
And sometimes goin' in the dark
Where there ain't been no light.
So boy, don't you turn back.
Don't you set down on the steps   15
'Cause you finds it's kinder hard.
Don't you fall now—
For I'se still goin', honey,
I'se still climbin',
And life for me ain't been no crystal stair.   20

FOR DISCUSSION

• The poet relies on images to involve us in a poem. What do you "see" in your mind when you read the words "crystal stair"? This mother's stairway hasn't been of crystal; what was her life like? Use words from the poem to support your description. Why is this comparison of life to a stairway a good one?

PRIMER LESSON
CARL SANDBURG

Look out how you use proud words.
When you let proud words go, it is not easy to call them back.
They wear long boots, hard boots; they walk off proud; they can't hear you
        calling—
Look out how you use proud words.

FOR DISCUSSION

1. What is a primer? Why should the idea in this poem be a "primer lesson" for everyone?

2. What do you think the poet means by "proud words"? Suggest specific examples from your own experience.

3. The poet has used the techniques of personification in this poem; what type of person does he suggest that proud words are like? Why can't proud words hear you calling?

CLAMMING

REED WHITTEMORE

I go digging for clams every two or three years
Just to keep my hand in (I usually cut it),
And whenever I do so I tell the same story: how,
At the age of four,
I was trapped by the tide as I clammed a vanishing sandbar.   5
It's really no story at all, but I keep telling it
(Seldom adding the end, the commonplace rescue).
It serves my small lust to be thought of as someone who's lived.

I've a war, too, to fall back on, and some years of flying,
As well as a staggering quota of drunken parties,   10
A wife and children; but somehow the clamming thing
Gives me an image of me that soothes my psyche*
As none of the louder events—me helpless,
Alone with my sand pail,
As fate in the form of soupy Long Island Sound   15
Comes stalking me.

My youngest son is that age now.
He's spoiled. He's been sickly.
He's handsome and bright, affectionate and demanding.
I think of the tides when I look at him.   20
I'd have him alone and seagirt,* poor little boy.

The self, what a brute it is. It wants, wants.
It will not let go of its even most fictional grandeur,
But must grope, grope down in the muck of its past
For some little squirting life and bring it up tenderly   25
To the lo and behold of death, that it may weep
And pass on the weeping, keep it all going.

        Son, when you clam,
Watch out for the tides, take care of yourself,
Yet no great care,   30

---

12 PSYCHE (sī′kē): spirit.   21 SEAGIRT: encircled by the sea.

Lest you care too much and talk too much of the caring
And bore your best friends and inhibit* your children and sicken
At last into opera on somebody's sandbar.

When you clam, Son,

Clam.   35

³² INHIBIT: restrain from free expression.

FOR DISCUSSION

• This poem tells a story within a story. At first, the speaker in the poem recounts the story of his dangerous childhood experience on a sandbar. But as the poem progresses we watch the speaker as he reaches toward another experience—that is, finally coming to terms with his own reasons for enjoying the story so much. What does the speaker discover that those reasons are? Why does the speaker seldom add the "commonplace rescue" to the story he tells? Why does he, in the final stanza of the poem, reject his earlier desire (expressed in stanza 3) to have his son repeat his own experience? How does the speaker's newly found understanding of himself change his wishes for his child?

The Environment

The poet does not concern himself only with a special, "poetical" world of beauty and love. With the rest of mankind, he looks around him and sees much that is ugly and dirty; this is his world, too, and he uses his art to bring even that aspect of man's experience into sharper and more sensitive focus.

RURAL DUMPHEAP
MELVILLE CANE

This rusty mound of cans,
This scatter of tires and pans,
This litter of mattresses and twisted springs,
This rotting refuse, these abandoned things
Malodorously* flung—this impudent pile   5
That dares to choke the current, to defile
The innocent season—all are man's.

Man's inhumanity to sod
Makes countless snowdrops mourn,
And every gentle seed that's born   10
Gives battle for a dishonored god.

Within the heap and darkly, heaves
The growing mutiny of leaves,
While down the valley bird to bird
Relays the rallying word,   15
And courage calls on every breeze
To armies of anemones,*

⁵ MALODOROUSLY: smelling badly.   ¹⁷ ANEMONES (ə·nem′ə·nēz): type of purple flower.

And triumph scales the parapet,
A host* of violet.

O man, where is thy victory?   20
Despite this blight of tins,
The fern persists and cleaves* and wins,
And, gladly, spring begins.

¹⁹ HOST: army.   ²² CLEAVES: holds fast.

FOR DISCUSSION

1. The poet's use of contrast is very important in describing for our imaginations the scene this poem concerns itself with. What kinds of things are contrasted? How does this pattern of contrasting images enrich the meaning of the poem?

2. In line 11, reference is made to "battle." Find other words from the vocabulary associated with war in the poem. If there is a war, what weapons are being used? Who is fighting whom? Who does the poem suggest is winning?

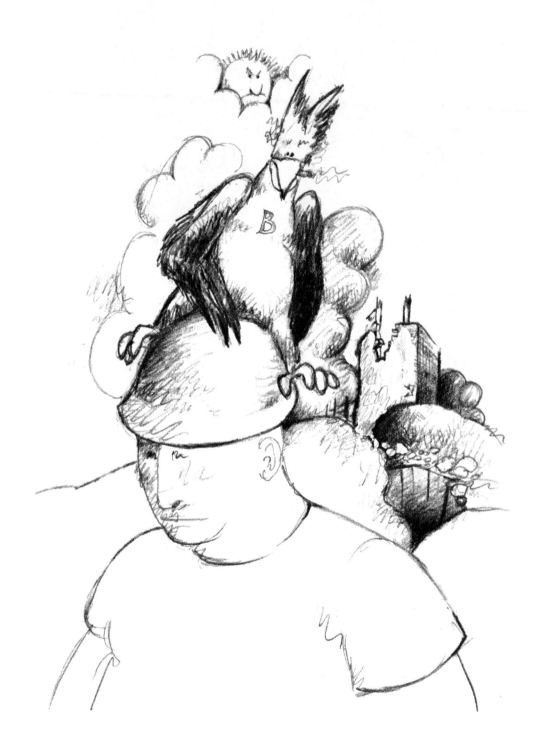

BAY-BREASTED BARGE BIRD

WILLIAM JAY SMITH

The bay-breasted barge bird delights in depressions
And simply flourishes during slumps;
It winters on hummocks* near used-car lots
    And summers near municipal dumps.

It nests on the coils of old bed springs,   5
And lines its nest with the labels from cans;
It feeds its young on rusty red things,
    And bits of pots and pans.

The bay-breasted barge bird joyfully passes
Where bulldozers doze and wreckers rumble,   10
Gazing bug-eyed, when traffic masses,
    At buildings that feather and crumble.

It wheels and dips to the glare and thunder
Of blasted rock and burning fuel
While the red-hot riveted* sun goes under   15
    On every urban renewal.

It flaps long wings the color of soot,
It cranes a neck dotted with purple bumps;
And lets out a screech like a car in a crack-up
    As it slowly circles the dumps.   20

3 HUMMOCKS: hills of ice.   15 RIVETED: firmly fastened (that is, to the sky).

FOR DISCUSSION

• Melville Cane's "Rural Dumpheap" suggests that the beauty of natural things and the blight of a mismanaged industrial technology cannot easily exist together. This poem is also based on that idea, but the poet here uses quite a different method of making a similar point. How does Smith describe the imaginary bird which "flourishes" in a polluted, junkyard environment? Does the bird sound more or less appealing than the real creatures whose existence is now being threatened by pollution?

FILLING STATION
ELIZABETH BISHOP

Oh, but it is dirty!
—this little filling station,
oil-soaked, oil-permeated
to a surprising, over-all
black translucency.   5
Be careful with that match!

Father wears a dirty,
oil-soaked monkey suit
that cuts him under the arms,
and several quick and saucy   10
and greasy sons assist him
(it's a family filling station),
all quite thoroughly dirty.

Do they live in the station?
It has a cement porch   15
behind the pumps, and on it
a set of crushed and grease-
impregnated wickerwork;
on the wicker sofa
a dirty dog, quite comfy.   20

Some comic books provide
the only note of color—
of certain color. They lie
upon a big dim doily
draping a taboret*   25
(part of a set), beside
a big hirsute* begonia.

Why the extraneous* plant?
Why, oh why, the table?
Why, oh why, the doily?   30
(Embroidered in daisy stitch
with marguerites, I think,
and heavy with gray crochet.)

Somebody embroidered the doily.
Somebody waters the plant,   35
or oils it, maybe. Somebody
arranges the rows of cans
so that they softly say:
ESSO—SO—SO—SO
to high-strung automobiles.   40
Somebody loves us all.

[25] TABORET: a low stand. [27] HIRSUTE (hèr′soot): hairy. [28] EXTRANEOUS: present, but not essential.

FOR DISCUSSION

1. Because of the poet's skill in selecting details and images, one almost feels greasy at the end of this poem. How many different words can you find that are associated with dirt or grease? What word is repeated most often to emphasize this effect?

2. The poet asks three questions in the fifth stanza. What prompts her to ask them? Is an answer ever suggested for these questions? Quote from the text of the poem to explain the real significance of these questions and any answers the poem may suggest.

Special Visions

Sometimes the poet's imagination can so transform his perceptions that he can dream of worlds which the rest of us might never know except for his telling. The world he offers us might be a desolate vision of a time beyond hope, or a shining wonder of a world where grace and greatness await the most humble, but, whether happy or sad, the vision is precious and special because it expands our own ability to dream and see.

VISION OF A PAST WARRIOR
PETER LA FARGE

I have within me such a dream of pain
That all my silver horseman hopes rust still,
Beyond quicksilver mountains,
On the plain,
The buffalo are gone,   5
None left to kill,

I see the plains grow blackened with that dawn,
No robes for winter warmth
No meat to eat,
The ghost white buffalos' medicine gone,   10
No hope for Indians then,
I see defeat.

Then there will be changes to another way,
We will fight battles that are legends long.
But of all our glory   15
None will stay,
Who will remember
That I sang this song.

FOR DISCUSSION

1. In many Indian religions, dreams were believed to be prophetic messages from the gods which could accurately foretell the future. According to the title of this poem, when did the speaker have his dream? Was the vision an accurate one?

2. What does the speaker mean when he says "We will fight battles that are legends long"?

Are these battles still being fought by Indians? Explain your answer.

3. Sometimes, greater understanding can bring despair. Why does the Indian's vision destroy his "silver horseman hopes"? Do you think that for most people seeing far into the future might be an experience which would make them change their ideas about themselves and their accomplishments? Explain your conclusions.

THE BICYCLE

JERZY HARASYMOWICZ

TRANSLATED BY EDMUND ORDON

once
forgotten by tourists
a bicycle joined
a herd
of mountain goats   5

with its splendidly turned
silver horns
it became
their leader

with its bell   10
it warned them
of danger

with them
it partook
in romps   15
on the snow covered
glade

the bicycle
gazed from above
on people walking;   20
with the goats

it fought
over a goat,
with a bearded buck

it reared up at eagles   25
enraged
on its back wheel

"The Bicycle" by Jerzy Harasymowicz, translated from the Polish by Edmund Ordon, appeared in *San Francisco Review Annual #1*. Reprinted by permission of the San Francisco Review Annual.

it was happy
though it never
nibbled at grass   30

or drank
from a stream

until once
a poacher
shot it   35

tempted
by the silver trophy
of its horns

and then
above the Tatras* was seen   40
against the sparkling
January sky

the angel of death erect
slowly
riding to heaven   45
holding the bicycle's
dead horns.

---

40 TATRAS: the Tatra Mountains, located on the border between Poland and
Czechoslovakia.

FOR DISCUSSION

1. Why do you imagine the bicycle is so happy among the mountain goats? What kind of a life do you think it might have lived before it was abandoned?

2. What one quality of the bicycle represents its greatest glory, as well as the cause of its downfall?

3. Notice how important the last two stanzas are to the overall mood of the poem. If these stanzas had been omitted, how would the mood and meaning of the poem be changed?

In Summary

FOR DISCUSSION

1. For emphasis and comparison, the poems in this section have been grouped under a number of headings—"Glimpses of People," "Conflict," and "Moods," for example. But a poem is seldom so limited to one category or idea. Rearrange this unit; find several poems which you think might fit equally as well under another of the headings. Defend your suggestions by referring directly to the words of the poem to support your ideas.

2. Since a poem is of necessity somewhat brief and limited in its scope, a poet will often include important clues or concepts in the title of his poem. In fact, the meaning of some poems would be quite obscure or altered if their titles were omitted. Which poems in this unit would be changed in scope or meaning if their titles were removed?

3. One very good way to appreciate a poet's unique talents is to paraphrase a poem. Paraphrase means to put into your own words. Review the unit and select your favorite poem; then paraphrase it. Be sure you don't leave out any important details. What happens to the poem as soon as you begin to write it as prose? What kind of words has the poet omitted that you cannot omit when you "re-write" the poem? What other changes do you notice?

OTHER THINGS TO DO

1. Most poetry should be read aloud so that the full effect of rhythm and rhyme can be appreciated. However, it is not easy to present a poem to an audience. Select a poem that you especially like and practice reading it aloud. Be prepared to present your poem dramatically to the class. Try to pronounce words with the emphasis and emotion of an actor so that the audience can "feel" the poem with you. Sometimes it is helpful to play an appropriate recording as background music for your presentation.

2. People who read poetry regularly develop a fondness for the work of certain poets. Generally, a poet's works reveal his preference for certain techniques, subjects, or settings which a reader can easily identify. Furthermore, after reading a number of poems by the same poet you will find that you understand his techniques more easily and respond more quickly to them. Find and read a number of poems by an individual poet until you begin to "see" the world as he does. Then write a three or four page report on the results of your reading. Explain the settings, ideas, and techniques the poet uses most frequently. Support your ideas by quoting directly from the poems you have read and studied.

3. Many people like to memorize their favorite poems so that the lines become a part of their thoughts and lives. Another advantage in memorizing a poem is the way a person doing so is forced to become conscious of each word in it. As he repeats the words to himself, he gains new understanding and appreciation. The poet's love for words and images will add a new dimension to anyone's life. Select the poem in this unit that you enjoyed the most. Memorize it carefully so that it will always be at your command.

Reader's Choice

Beyond the High Hills: A Book of Eskimo Poems, *collected by Knud Rasmussen.*

This book, beautifully illustrated with color photographs, contains the songs and chants of the Eskimos. The poems describe the hunt and other adventures, the sorrow and happiness of a strong people.

The Birds and the Beasts Were There: Animal Poems, *selected by William Cole.*

"Slitherers, creepers, and hardshells, buzzers, leapers, and flyers" fill this anthology of poems about animals. Verses by Robert Burns, Elizabeth Coatsworth, Gerard Manley Hopkins, Vachel Lindsay and others show the sober and comic sides of birds and beasts.

Cricket Songs: Japanese Haiku, *translated by Harry Behn.*

"An old silent pond/ A frog jumps into the pond,/ splash! Silence again." This little poem conveys sound, silence, and a keen perception of nature in only three lines and seventeen syllables. It is an example of haiku, a Japanese form of poetry, which often describes cameos of experience that will be quickly read but long remembered.

Don't Cry, Scream, *by Don L. Lee.*

"Super-cool/ultrablack"—This is the poetry of Don Lee, who describes the events of our times from the viewpoint of an angry young black. There is nothing "elegant" about the poetry; it is a screaming appeal for justice.

The Dream Keeper and Other Poems, *by Langston Hughes.*

Langston Hughes uses poetry to convey his black pride, his concern for people, and his sense of beauty. Particularly interesting is his use of the rhythms of black speech to express the unique "soul" feeling central to black experience.

Poems to Solve, *by May Swenson.*

"A poem, read for the first time, can offer the same pleasure as opening a wrapped box. There is the anticipation of untying an intriguing knot of words, of unloosening all their intimations like loops, of lifting out . . . an unexpected idea or fresh sensation." This is the way May Swenson describes these delightful poems, all of which contain a puzzle or riddle.

The Poetry of Rock, *edited by Richard Goldstein.*

This anthology is a comprehensive collection of representative rock lyrics from 1952 to 1968. The composers range from Chuck Berry to the Beatles, from Bob Dylan to the Jefferson Airplane.

Some Haystacks Don't Even Have Any Needle, *compiled by Stephen Dunning, Edward Lueders and Hugh Smith.*

These are poems with fresh images about today's world. Be prepared for the unexpected and the unusual. These poems reflect real life —they show that sometimes love has flaws, that war is never glorious. Look for poems about shortstops, power mowers, bagels, and flat tires.

Sounds and Silences, *edited by Richard Peck.*

In the introduction to this book, Richard Peck writes, "Once upon a time poetry knew its place: the schoolroom, the tombstone, and the love letter. But that was before the poetry explosion." This anthology deals with that explosion—the poetry of now. Here are poems about topics that make today's headlines: dissent, sonic booms, migrant workers, psychedelic images, and revolution.

CONFLICT

LIFE IS FULL OF CONFLICT, not only in places where we would normally expect to find it—battlefields, prizefight rings—but in places where its presence might not at first be suspected: in a sleepy Mexican coastal village, for instance, where days seem to go on pretty much the same year after year. Consider the conflicts that a poor man in such a village faces. He is a humble fisherman. Each day brings only the poorest catches, or none at all, of the pearls he fishes for to furnish his family a livelihood. Each night he goes to bed hearing his child in the sparse room with him and knowing that the infant is condemned to grow into a life no better than his father's. The struggle of such a man against heavy odds re-enacts the plight of millions of people since the beginning of time: the peasant in barren fields, the unskilled worker crippled by accident or age, the unneeded or overlooked wherever they may be found.

Such a man, in conflict with his fate, is Kino, the Mexican fisherman in John Steinbeck's impressive novel *The Pearl*.

Suppose, though, that for every man as unfortunate as Kino apparently is, a way should suddenly open out of his predicament. Suppose the factory worker, whose wife is ill and needing care, should one day hit the jackpot. Or suppose the pauper should be told, with many bows and apologies, that all this time he has really been a prince. Suppose a man in Kino's seemingly hopeless situation should suddenly find something of great value that would make him rich overnight. Wouldn't all his struggles end with that discovery? Or would new conflicts arise, more heartrending and complex than any he has known before?

Philip McFarland

"In the town they tell the story of the great pearl—how it was found and how it was lost again. They tell of Kino, the fisherman, and of his wife, Juana, and of the baby, Coyotito. And because the story has been told so often, it has taken root in every man's mind. And, as with all retold tales that are in people's hearts, there are only good and bad things and black and white things and good and evil things and no in-between anywhere.

"If this story is a parable, perhaps everyone takes his own meaning from it and reads his own life into it. In any case, they say in the town that . . ."

THE PEARL

JOHN STEINBECK

CHAPTER 1

KINO[1] AWAKENED in the near dark. The stars still shone and the day had drawn only a pale wash of light in the lower sky to the east. The roosters had been crowing for some time, and the early pigs were already beginning their ceaseless turning of twigs and bits of wood to see whether anything to eat had been overlooked. Outside the brush house in the tuna clump, a covey of little birds chittered and flurried with their wings.

Kino's eyes opened, and he looked first at the lightening square which was the door and then he looked at the hanging box where Coyotito[2] slept. And last he turned his head to Juana,[3] his wife, who lay beside him on the mat, her blue head shawl over her nose and over her breasts and around the small of her back. Juana's eyes were open too. Kino could never remember seeing them closed when he awakened. Her dark eyes made little reflected stars. She was looking at him as she was always looking at him when he awakened.

Kino heard the little splash of morning waves on the beach. It was very good—Kino closed his eyes again to listen to his music. Perhaps he alone did this and perhaps all of his people did it. His people had once been great makers of songs so that everything they saw or thought or did or heard became a song. That was very long ago. The songs remained; Kino knew them, but no new songs were added. That does not mean that there were no personal songs. In Kino's head there was a song now, clear and soft, and if he had been able to speak it, he would have called it the Song of the Family.

His blanket was over his nose to protect him from the dank air. His eyes flicked to a rustle beside him. It was Juana arising,

[1] KINO: pronounced kē′nō.
[2] COYOTITO: pronounced koi·ō·tē′tō.
[3] JUANA: pronounced hwä′nä.

almost soundlessly. On her hard bare feet she went to the hanging box where Coyotito slept, and she leaned over and said a little reassuring word. Coyotito looked up for a moment and closed his eyes and slept again.

Juana went to the fire pit and uncovered a coal and fanned it alive while she broke little pieces of brush over it.

Now Kino got up and wrapped his blanket about his head and nose and shoulders. He slipped his feet into his sandals and went outside to watch the dawn.

Outside the door he squatted down and gathered the blanket ends about his knees. He saw the specks of Gulf[1] clouds flame high in the air. And a goat came near and sniffed at him and stared with its cold yellow eyes. Behind him Juana's fire leaped into flame and threw spears of light through the chinks of the brush-house wall and threw a wavering square of light out the door. A late moth blustered in to find the fire. The Song of the Family came now from behind Kino. And the rhythm of the family song was the grinding stone where Juana worked the corn for the morning cakes.

The dawn came quickly now, a wash, a glow, a lightness, and then an explosion of fire as the sun arose out of the Gulf. Kino looked down to cover his eyes from the glare. He could hear the pat of the corn-cakes in the house and the rich smell of them on the cooking plate. The ants were busy on the ground, big black ones with shiny bodies, and little dusty quick ants. Kino watched with the detachment of God while a dusty ant frantically tried to escape the sand trap an ant lion had dug for him. A thin, timid dog came close and, at a soft word from Kino, curled up, arranged its tail neatly over its feet, and laid its chin delicately on the pile. It was a black dog with yellow-gold spots where its eyebrows should have been. It was a morning like other mornings and yet perfect among mornings.

Kino heard the creak of the rope when Juana took Coyotito out of his hanging box and cleaned him and hammocked him in her shawl in a loop that placed him close to her breast. Kino could see these things without looking at them. Juana sang softly an ancient song that had only three notes and yet endless variety of interval. And this was part of the family song too. It was all part. Sometimes it rose to an aching chord that caught the throat, saying this is safety, this is warmth, this is the *Whole*.

Across the brush fence were other brush houses, and the smoke came from them too, and the sound of breakfast, but those were other songs, their pigs were other pigs, their wives were not Juana. Kino was young and strong and his black hair hung over his brown forehead. His eyes were warm and fierce and bright and his mustache was thin and coarse. He lowered his blanket from his nose now, for the dark poisonous air was gone and the yellow sunlight fell on the house. Near the brush fence two roosters bowed and feinted at each other with squared wings and neck feathers ruffed out. It would be a clumsy fight. They were not game chickens.[2] Kino watched them for a moment, and then his eyes went up to a flight of wild doves twinkling inland to the hills. The world

---

[1] GULF: the Gulf of California. The story is set in La Paz, capital of Baja California Sur Territory in Mexico.

[2] GAME CHICKENS: birds specially bred and trained for fighting.

was awake now, and Kino arose and went into his brush house.

As he came through the door Juana stood up from the glowing fire pit. She put Coyotito back in his hanging box and then she combed her black hair and braided it in two braids and tied the ends with thin green ribbon. Kino squatted by the fire pit and rolled a hot corncake and dipped it in sauce and ate it. And he drank a little pulque[1] and that was breakfast. That was the only breakfast he had ever known outside of feast days and one incredible fiesta on cookies that had nearly killed him. When Kino had finished, Juana came back to the fire and ate her breakfast. They had spoken once, but there is not need for speech if it is only a habit anyway. Kino sighed with satisfaction—and that was conversation.

The sun was warming the brush house, breaking through its crevices in long streaks. And one of the streaks fell on the hanging box where Coyotito lay, and on the ropes that held it.

It was a tiny movement that drew their eyes to the hanging box. Kino and Juana froze in their positions. Down the rope that hung the baby's box from the roof support a scorpion moved slowly. His stinging tail was straight out behind him, but he could whip it up in a flash of time.

Kino's breath whistled in his nostrils and he opened his mouth to stop it. And then the startled look was gone from him and the rigidity from his body. In his mind a new song had come, the Song of Evil, the music of the enemy, of any foe of the family, a savage, secret, dangerous melody, and underneath, the Song of the Family cried plaintively.

[1] PULQUE (pool'kā): fermented drink made in Mexico from various plants.

The scorpion moved delicately down the rope toward the box. Under her breath Juana repeated an ancient magic to guard against such evil, and on top of that she muttered a Hail Mary between clenched teeth. But Kino was in motion. His body glided quietly across the room, noiselessly and smoothly. His hands were in front of him, palms down, and his eyes were on the scorpion. Beneath it in the hanging box Coyotito laughed and reached up his hand toward it. It sensed danger when Kino was almost within reach of it. It stopped, and its tail rose up over its back in little jerks and the curved thorn on the tail's end glistened.

Kino stood perfectly still. He could hear Juana whispering the old magic again, and he could hear the evil music of the enemy. He could not move until the scorpion moved, and it felt for the source of the death that was coming to it. Kino's hand went forward very slowly, very smoothly. The thorned tail jerked upright. And at that moment the laughing Coyotito shook the rope and the scorpion fell.

Kino's hand leaped to catch it, but it fell past his fingers, fell on the baby's shoulder, landed and struck. Then, snarling, Kino had it, had it in his fingers, rubbing it to a paste in his hands. He threw it down and beat it into the earth floor with his fist, and Coyotito screamed with pain in his box. But Kino beat and stamped the enemy until it was only a fragment and a moist place in the dirt. His teeth were bared and fury flared in his eyes and the Song of the Enemy roared in his ears.

But Juana had the baby in her arms now. She found the puncture with redness starting from it already. She put her lips down over the puncture and sucked hard and spat and sucked again while Coyotito screamed.

Kino hovered; he was helpless, he was in the way.

The screams of the baby brought the neighbors. Out of their brush houses they poured—Kino's brother Juan Tomás and his fat wife Apolonia and their four children crowded in the door and blocked the entrance, while behind them others tried to look in, and one small boy crawled among legs to have a look. And those in front passed the word back to those behind—"Scorpion. The baby has been stung."

Juana stopped sucking the puncture for a moment. The little hole was slightly enlarged and its edges whitened from the sucking, but the red swelling extended farther around it in a hard lymphatic mound. And all of these people knew about the scorpion. An adult might be very ill from the sting, but a baby could easily die from the poison. First, they knew, would come swelling and fever and tightened throat, and then cramps in the stomach, and then Coyotito might die if enough of the poison had gone in. But the stinging pain of the bite was going away. Coyotito's screams turned to moans.

Kino had wondered often at the iron in his patient, fragile wife. She, who was obedient and respectful and cheerful and patient, she could arch her back in child pain with hardly a cry. She could stand fatigue and hunger almost better than Kino himself. In the canoe she was like a strong man. And now she did a most surprising thing.

"The doctor," she said. "Go to get the doctor."

The word was passed out among the neighbors where they stood close packed in the little yard behind the brush fence. And they repeated among themselves, "Juana wants the doctor." A wonderful thing, a memorable thing, to want the doctor. To get him would be a remarkable thing. The doctor never came to the cluster of brush houses. Why should he, when he had more than he could do to take care of the rich people who lived in the stone and plaster houses of the town.

"He would not come," the people in the yard said.

"He would not come," the people in the door said, and the thought got into Kino.

"The doctor would not come," Kino said to Juana.

She looked up at him, her eyes as cold as the eyes of a lioness. This was Juana's first baby—this was nearly everything there was in Juana's world. And Kino saw her determination and the music of the family sounded in his head with a steely tone.

"Then we will go to him," Juana said, and with one hand she arranged her dark blue shawl over her head and made of one end of it a sling to hold the moaning baby and made of the other end of it a shade over his eyes to protect him from the light. The people in the door pushed against those behind to let her through. Kino followed her. They went out of the gate to the rutted path and the neighbors followed them.

The thing had become a neighborhood affair. They made a quick soft-footed procession into the center of the town, first Juana and Kino, and behind them Juan Tomás and Apolonia, her big stomach jiggling with the strenuous pace, then all the neighbors with the children trotting on the flanks. And the yellow sun threw their black shadows ahead of them so that they walked on their own shadows.

They came to the place where the brush houses stopped and the city of stone and plaster began, the city of harsh outer walls and inner cool gardens where a little water played and the bougainvillaea crusted the walls with purple and brick-red and white. They heard from the secret gardens the singing of caged birds and heard the splash of cooling water on hot flagstones. The procession crossed the blinding plaza and passed in front of the church. It had grown now, and on the outskirts the hurrying newcomers were being softly informed how the baby had been stung by a scorpion, how the father and mother were taking it to the doctor.

And the newcomers, particularly the beggars from the front of the church who were great experts in financial analysis, looked quickly at Juana's old blue skirt, saw the tears in her shawl, appraised the green ribbon on her braids, read the age of Kino's blanket and the thousand washings of his clothes, and set them down as poverty people and went along to see what kind of drama might develop. The four beggars in front of the church knew everything in the town. They were students of the expressions of young women as they went into confession, and they saw them as they came out and read the nature of the sin. They knew every little scandal and some very big crimes. They slept at their posts in the shadow of the church so that no one crept in for consolation without their knowledge. And they knew the doctor. They knew his ignorance, his cruelty, his avarice,[1] his appetites, his sins. They knew his clumsy operations and the little brown pennies he gave sparingly for alms.

They had seen his corpses go into the church. And, since early Mass was over and business was slow, they followed the procession, these endless searchers after perfect knowledge of their fellow men, to see what the fat lazy doctor would do about an indigent[2] baby with a scorpion bite.

The scurrying procession came at last to the big gate in the wall of the doctor's house. They could hear the splashing water and the singing of caged birds and the sweep of the long brooms on the flagstones. And they could smell the frying of good bacon from the doctor's house.

Kino hesitated a moment. This doctor was not of his people. This doctor was of a race which for nearly four hundred years had beaten and starved and robbed and despised Kino's race, and frightened it too, so that the indigene came humbly to the door. And as always when he came near to one of this race, Kino felt weak and afraid and angry at the same time. Rage and terror went together. He could kill the doctor more easily than he could talk to him, for all of the doctor's race spoke to all of Kino's race as though they were simple animals. And as Kino raised his right hand to the iron ring knocker in the gate, rage swelled in him, and the pounding music of the enemy beat in his ears, and his lips drew tight against his teeth—but with his left hand he reached to take off his hat. The iron ring pounded against the gate. Kino took off his hat and stood waiting. Coyotito moaned a little in Juana's arms and she spoke softly to him. The procession crowded close the better to see and hear.

---

[1] AVARICE: greed.

[2] INDIGENT (in′də·jənt): poor.

After a moment the big gate opened a few inches. Kino could see the green coolness of the garden and little splashing fountain through the opening. The man who looked out at him was one of his own race. Kino spoke to him in the old language. "The little one—the first born—has been poisoned by the scorpion," Kino said. "He requires the skill of the healer."

The gate closed a little, and the servant refused to speak in the old language. "A little moment," he said. "I go to inform myself," and he closed the gate and slid the bolt home. The glaring sun threw the bunched shadows of the people blackly on the white wall.

In his chamber the doctor sat up in his high bed. He had on his dressing gown of red watered silk that had come from Paris, a little tight over the chest now if it was buttoned. On his lap was a silver tray with a silver chocolate pot and a tiny cup of eggshell china, so delicate that it looked silly when he lifted it with his big hand, lifted it with the tips of thumb and forefinger and spread the other three fingers wide to get them out of the way. His eyes rested in puffy little hammocks of flesh and his mouth drooped with discontent. He was growing very stout, and his voice was hoarse with the fat that pressed on his throat. Beside him on a table was a small Oriental gong and a bowl of cigarettes. The furnishings of the room were heavy and dark and gloomy. The pictures were religious, even the large tinted photograph of his dead wife, who, if Masses willed and paid for out of her own estate could do it, was in Heaven. The doctor had once for a short time been a part of the great world and his whole subsequent life was memory and longing for France. "That," he said, "was civilized living"—by which he meant that on a small income he had been able to keep a mistress and eat in restaurants. He poured his second cup of chocolate and crumbled a sweet biscuit in his fingers. The servant from the gate came to the open door and stood waiting to be noticed.

"Yes?" the doctor asked.

"It is a little Indian with a baby. He says a scorpion stung it."

The doctor put his cup down gently before he let his anger rise.

"Have I nothing better to do than cure insect bites for 'little Indians'? I am a doctor, not a veterinary."

"Yes, Patron,"[1] said the servant.

"Has he any money?" the doctor demanded. "No, they never have any money. I, I alone in the world am supposed to work for nothing—and I am tired of it. See if he has any money!"

At the gate the servant opened the door a trifle and looked out at the waiting people. And this time he spoke in the old language.

"Have you money to pay for the treatment?"

Now Kino reached into a secret place somewhere under his blanket. He brought out a paper folded many times. Crease by crease he unfolded it, until at last there came to view eight small misshapen seed pearls, as ugly and gray as little ulcers, flattened and almost valueless. The servant took the paper and closed the gate again, but this time he was not gone long. He opened the gate just wide enough to pass the paper back.

"The doctor has gone out," he said. "He was called to a serious case." And he shut the gate quickly out of shame.

And now a wave of shame went over the whole procession. They melted away. The

[1] PATRON (pä·trōn′): sir, master.

beggars went back to the church steps, the stragglers moved off, and the neighbors departed so that the public shaming of Kino would not be in their eyes.

For a long time Kino stood in front of the gate with Juana beside him. Slowly he put his suppliant hat on his head. Then, without warning, he struck the gate a crushing blow with his fist. He looked down in wonder at his split knuckles and at the blood that flowed down between his fingers.

FOR DISCUSSION

1. At the end of the chapter, the reader is almost as surprised as Kino when he smashes his fist into the doctor's gate. What conflict in Kino caused this action? What things has he done and said up to this point that give the reader important insights into his character? Notice, for example, his relationship with Juana, his treatment of the dog, and his actions when Coyotito is threatened.

2. Kino's people had "once been the makers of great songs." Songs and music are usually very important in cultures where people can-not read or write. Why do you imagine this might be so? Steinbeck uses Kino's personal songs in several ways. Explain how they portray the culture of Kino's people, how they are used to reveal Kino's thoughts, how they contain foreshadowing, and how they affect the mood of the story.

3. The author's skillful writing enables the reader to "see" the doctor. What is revealed about him through his physical description? Things he says? Things he does? Things others say about him? How do you know that he thinks of the Indians as animals?

CHAPTER 2

The town lay on a broad estuary,[1] its old yellow plastered buildings hugging the beach. And on the beach the white and blue canoes that came from Nayarit[2] were drawn up, canoes preserved for generations by a hard shell-like waterproof plaster whose making was a secret of the fishing people. They were high and graceful canoes with curving bow and stern and a braced section midships where a mast could be stepped to carry a small lateen sail.

The beach was yellow sand, but at the water's edge a rubble of shell and algae took its place. Fiddler crabs bubbled and sputtered in their holes in the sand, and in the shallows little lobsters popped in and out of their tiny homes in the rubble and sand. The sea bottom was rich with crawling and swimming and growing things. The brown algae waved in the gentle currents and the green eel grass swayed and little sea horses clung to its stems. Spotted botete, the poison fish, lay on the bottom in the eel-grass beds, and the bright-colored swimming crabs scampered over them.

On the beach the hungry dogs and the hungry pigs of the town searched endlessly for any dead fish or sea bird that might have floated in on a rising tide.

[1] ESTUARY: the part of the sea which extends in-land to join the mouth of a river.
[2] NAYARIT: Mexican state situated on the Pacific coast.

Although the morning was young, the hazy mirage was up. The uncertain air that magnified some things and blotted out others hung over the whole Gulf so that all sights were unreal and vision could not be trusted; so that sea and land had the sharp clarities and the vagueness of a dream. Thus it might be that the people of the Gulf trust things of the spirit and things of the imagination, but they do not trust their eyes to show them distance or clear outline or any optical exactness. Across the estuary from the town one section of mangroves stood clear and telescopically defined, while another mangrove clump was a hazy black-green blob. Part of the far shore disappeared into a shimmer that looked like water. There was no certainty in seeing, no proof that what you saw was there or was not there. And the people of the Gulf expected all places were that way, and it was not strange to them. A copper haze hung over the water, and the hot morning sun beat on it and made it vibrate blindingly.

The brush houses of the fishing people were back from the beach on the right-hand side of the town, and the canoes were drawn up in front of this area.

Kino and Juana came slowly down to the beach and to Kino's canoe, which was the one thing of value he owned in the world. It was very old. Kino's grandfather had brought it from Nayarit, and he had given it to Kino's father, and so it had come to Kino. It was at once property and source of food, for a man with a boat can guarantee a woman that she will eat something. It is the bulwark[1] against starvation. And every year Kino refinished his canoe with the hard shell-like plaster by the secret method that had also come to him from his father. Now he came to the canoe and touched the bow tenderly as he always did. He laid his diving rock and his basket and the two ropes in the sand by the canoe. And he folded his blanket and laid it in the bow.

Juana laid Coyotito on the blanket, and she placed her shawl over him so that the hot sun could not shine on him. He was quiet now, but the swelling on his shoulder had continued up his neck and under his ear and his face was puffed and feverish. Juana went to the water and waded in. She gathered some brown seaweed and made a flat damp poultice[2] of it, and this she applied to the baby's swollen shoulder, which was as good a remedy as any and probably better than the doctor could have done. But the remedy lacked his authority because it was simple and didn't cost anything. The stomach cramps had not come to Coyotito. Perhaps Juana had sucked out the poison in time, but she had not sucked out her worry over her first-born. She had not prayed directly for the recovery of the baby —she had prayed that they might find a pearl with which to hire the doctor to cure the baby, for the minds of people are as unsubstantial as the mirage of the Gulf.

Now Kino and Juana slid the canoe down the beach to the water, and when the bow floated, Juana climbed in, while Kino pushed the stern in and waded beside it until it floated lightly and trembled on the little breaking waves. Then in coordination Juana and Kino drove their double-bladed paddles into the sea, and the canoe creased the water and hissed with speed. The other pearlers were gone out long since. In a few moments Kino could see

[1] BULWARK: defense.

[2] POULTICE: soft mixture spread on cloth and applied to a wound to soothe or medicate it.

them clustered in the haze, riding over the oyster bed.

Light filtered down through the water to the bed where the frilly pearl oysters lay fastened to the rubbly bottom, a bottom strewn with shells of broken, opened oysters. This was the bed that had raised the King of Spain to be a great power in Europe in past years, had helped to pay for his wars, and had decorated the churches for his soul's sake. The gray oysters with ruffles like skirts on the shells, the barnacle-crusted oysters with little bits of weed clinging to the skirts and small crabs climbing over them. An accident could happen to these oysters, a grain of sand could lie in the folds of muscle and irritate the flesh until in self-protection the flesh coated the grain with a layer of smooth cement. But once started, the flesh continued to coat the foreign body until it fell free in some tidal flurry or until the oyster was destroyed. For centuries men had dived down and torn the oysters from the beds and ripped them open, looking for the coated grains of sand. Swarms of fish lived near the bed to live near the oysters thrown back by the searching men and to nibble at the shining inner shells. But the pearls were accidents, and the finding of one was luck, a little pat on the back by God or the gods or both.

Kino had two ropes, one tied to a heavy stone and one to a basket. He stripped off his shirt and trousers and laid his hat in the bottom of the canoe. The water was oily smooth. He took his rock in one hand and his basket in the other, and he slipped feet first over the side and the rock carried him to the bottom. The bubbles rose behind him until the water cleared and he could see. Above, the surface of the water was an undulating[1] mirror of brightness, and he could see the bottoms of the canoes sticking through it.

Kino moved cautiously so that the water would not be obscured with mud or sand. He hooked his foot in the loop on his rock and his hands worked quickly, tearing the oysters loose, some singly, others in clusters. He laid them in his basket. In some places the oysters clung to one another so that they came free in lumps.

Now, Kino's people had sung of everything that happened or existed. They had made songs to the fishes, to the sea in anger and to the sea in calm, to the light and the dark and the sun and the moon, and the songs were all in Kino and in his people—every song that had ever been made, even the ones forgotten. And as he filled his basket the song was in Kino, and the beat of the song was his pounding heart as it ate the oxygen from his held breath, and the melody of the song was the gray-green water and the little scuttling animals and the clouds of fish that flitted by and were gone. But in the song there was a secret little inner song, hardly perceptible, but always there, sweet and secret and clinging, almost hiding in the counter-melody and this was the Song of the Pearl That Might Be, for every shell thrown in the basket might contain a pearl. Chance was against it, but luck and the gods might be for it. And in the canoe above him Kino knew that Juana was making the magic of prayer, her face set rigid and her muscles hard to force the luck, to tear the luck out of the god's hands, for she needed the luck for the swollen shoulder of Coyotito. And because the need was great and the desire

[1] UNDULATING: rippling.

was great, the little secret melody of the pearl that might be was stronger this morning. Whole phrases of it came clearly and softly into the Song of the Undersea.

Kino, in his pride and youth and strength, could remain down over two minutes without strain, so that he worked deliberately, selecting the largest shells. Because they were disturbed, the oyster shells were tightly closed. A little to his right a hummock[1] of rubbly rock stuck up, covered with young oysters not ready to take. Kino moved next to the hummock, and then, beside it, under a little overhang, he saw a very large oyster lying by itself, not covered with its clinging brothers. The shell was partly open, for the overhang protected this ancient oyster, and in the lip-like muscle Kino saw a ghostly gleam, and then the shell closed down. His heart beat out a heavy rhythm and the melody of the maybe pearl shrilled in his ears. Slowly he forced the oyster loose and held it tightly against his breast. He kicked his foot free from the rock loop, and his body rose to the surface and his black hair gleamed in the sunlight. He reached over the side of the canoe and laid the oyster in the bottom.

Then Juana steadied the boat while he climbed in. His eyes were shining with excitement, but in decency he pulled up his rock, and then he pulled up his basket of oysters and lifted them in. Juana sensed his excitement, and she pretended to look away. It is not good to want a thing too much. It sometimes drives the luck away. You must want it just enough, and you must be very tactful with God or the gods. But Juana stopped breathing. Very deliberately Kino opened his short strong knife.

[1] HUMMOCK: ridge.

He looked speculatively[2] at the basket. Perhaps it would be better to open *the* oyster last. He took a small oyster from the basket, cut the muscle, searched the folds of flesh, and threw it in the water. Then he seemed to see the great oyster for the first time. He squatted in the bottom of the canoe, picked up the shell and examined it. The flutes were shining black to brown, and only a few small barnacles adhered to the shell. Now Kino was reluctant to open it. What he had seen, he knew, might be a reflection, a piece of flat shell accidentally drifted in or a complete illusion. In this Gulf of uncertain light there were more illusions than realities.

But Juana's eyes were on him and she could not wait. She put her hand on Coyotito's covered head. "Open it," she said softly.

Kino deftly slipped his knife into the edge of the shell. Through the knife he could feel the muscle tighten hard. He worked the blade lever-wise and the closing muscle parted and the shell fell apart. The lip-like flesh writhed up and then subsided. Kino lifted the flesh, and there it lay, the great pearl, perfect as the moon. It captured the light and refined it and gave it back in silver incandescence.[3] It was as large as a sea-gull's egg. It was the greatest pearl in the world.

Juana caught her breath and moaned a little. And to Kino the secret melody of the maybe pearl broke clear and beautiful, rich and warm and lovely, glowing and gloating and triumphant. In the surface of the great pearl he could see dream forms. He picked the pearl from the dying flesh and held it in

[2] SPECULATIVELY: thoughtfully.
[3] INCANDESCENCE: glow.

his palm, and he turned it over and saw that its curve was perfect. Juana came near to stare at it in his hand, and it was the hand he had smashed against the doctor's gate, and the torn flesh of the knuckles was turned grayish white by the sea water.

Instinctively Juana went to Coyotito where he lay on his father's blanket. She lifted the poultice of seaweed and looked at the shoulder. "Kino," she cried shrilly.

He looked past his pearl, and he saw that the swelling was going out of the baby's shoulder, the poison was receding from its body. Then Kino's fist closed over the pearl and his emotion broke over him. He put back his head and howled. His eyes rolled up and he screamed and his body was rigid. The men in the other canoes looked up, startled, and then they dug their paddles into the sea and raced toward Kino's canoe.

FOR DISCUSSION

1. Kino's canoe was the one thing of value he owned. How valuable was it? What slight action on the part of Kino suggests his deep feelings toward the canoe?

2. It is ironic that at the moment Kino finds the great pearl the swelling in Coyotito's shoulder was beginning to go down, and the poison was leaving his body. Why? Steinbeck comments that Juana's poultice of seaweed was probably as good a remedy as any the doctor could propose. Why wouldn't this thought have occurred to Juana?

3. The author spends time explaining the phenomenon of mirages and uncertainties in the air of the Gulf. How does this explanation enrich our understanding of the story? Why, for example, did Kino's people trust things of the spirit and imagination before they trusted their own eyes to show them distance or outlines? How does this trait suggest in a general way their philosophy of life? How might this trait be used against them?

CHAPTER 3

A town is a thing like a colonial animal. A town has a nervous system and a head and shoulders and feet. A town is a thing separate from all other towns, so that there are no two towns alike. And a town has a whole emotion. How news travels through a town is a mystery not easily to be solved. News seems to move faster than small boys can scramble and dart to tell it, faster than women can call it over the fences.

Before Kino and Juana and the other fishers had come to Kino's brush house, the nerves of the town were pulsing and vibrating with the news—Kino had found the Pearl of the World. Before panting little boys could strangle out the words, their mothers knew it. The news swept on past the brush houses, and it washed in a foaming wave into the town of stone and plaster. It came to the priest walking in his garden, and it put a thoughtful look in his eyes and a memory of certain repairs necessary to the church. He wondered what the pearl would be worth. And he wondered whether he had baptized Kino's baby, or married him for that matter. The news came to the shopkeepers, and they looked at men's clothes that had not sold so well.

The news came to the doctor where he sat with a woman whose illness was age, though neither she nor the doctor would admit it. And when it was made plain who Kino was, the doctor grew stern and judicious[1] at the same time. "He is a client of mine," the doctor said. "I'm treating his child for a scorpion sting." And the doctor's eyes rolled up a little in their fat hammocks and he thought of Paris. He remembered the room he had lived in there as a great and luxurious place, and he remembered the hard-faced woman who had lived with him as a beautiful and kind girl, although she had been none of these three. The doctor looked past his aged patient and saw himself sitting in a restaurant in Paris and a waiter was just opening a bottle of wine.

The news came early to the beggars in front of the church, and it made them giggle a little with pleasure, for they knew that there is no almsgiver in the world like a poor man who is suddenly lucky.

Kino had found the Pearl of the World. In the town, in little offices, sat the men who bought pearls from the fishers. They waited in their chairs until the pearls came in, and then they cackled and fought and shouted and threatened until they reached the lowest price the fisherman would stand. But there was a price below which they dared not go, for it had happened that a fisherman in despair had given his pearls to the church. And when the buying was over, these buyers sat alone and their fingers played restlessly with the pearls, and they wished they owned the pearls. For there were not many buyers really—there was only one, and he kept these agents in separate offices to give a semblance of competition. The news came to these men, and their eyes squinted and their fingertips burned a little, and each one thought how the patron could not live forever and someone had to take his place. And each one thought how with some capital he could get a new start.

All manner of people grew interested in Kino—people with things to sell and people with favors to ask. Kino had found the Pearl of the World. The essence of pearl mixed with essence of men and a curious dark residue[2] was precipitated.[3] Every man suddenly became related to Kino's pearl, and Kino's pearl went into the dreams, the speculations, the schemes, the plans, the futures, the wishes, the needs, the lusts, the hungers, of everyone, and only one person stood in the way and that was Kino, so that he became curiously every man's enemy. The news stirred up something infinitely black and evil in the town; the black distillate[4] was like the scorpion, or like hunger in the smell of food, or like loneliness when love is withheld.

---

[1] JUDICIOUS (joo·dish'əs): wise; showing good judgment.

[2] RESIDUE: matter remaining after completion of a chemical process.

[3] PRECIPITATED: separated from a solution.

[4] DISTILLATE: extracted matter, in a purified form.

The poison sacs of the town began to manufacture venom, and the town swelled and puffed with the pressure of it.

But Kino and Juana did not know these things. Because they were happy and excited they thought everyone shared their joy. Juan Tomás and Apolonia did, and they were the world too. In the afternoon, when the sun had gone over the mountains of the Peninsula to sink in the outward sea, Kino squatted in his house with Juana beside him. And the brush house was crowded with neighbors. Kino held the great pearl in his hand, and it was warm and alive in his hand. And the music of the pearl had merged with the music of the family so that one beautified the other. The neighbors looked at the pearl in Kino's hand and they wondered how such luck could come to any man.

And Juan Tomás, who squatted on Kino's right hand because he was his brother, asked, "What will you do now that you have become a rich man?"

Kino looked into his pearl, and Juana cast her eyelashes down and arranged her shawl to cover her face so that her excitement could not be seen. And in the incandescence of the pearl the pictures formed of the things Kino's mind had considered in the past and had given up as impossible. In the pearl he saw Juana and Coyotito and himself standing and kneeling at the high altar, and they were being married now that they could pay. He spoke softly, "We will be married—in the church."

In the pearl he saw how they were dressed—Juana in a shawl stiff with newness and a new skirt, and from under the long skirt Kino could see that she wore shoes. It was in the pearl—the picture glowing there. He himself was dressed in new white clothes, and he carried a new hat—not of straw but of fine black felt—and he too wore shoes—not sandals but shoes that laced. But Coyotito—he was the one—he wore a blue sailor suit from the United States and a little yachting cap such as Kino had seen once when a pleasure boat put into the estuary. All of these things Kino saw in the lucent[1] pearl and he said, "We will have new clothes."

And the music of the pearl rose like a chorus of trumpets in his ears.

Then to the lovely gray surface of the pearl came the little things Kino wanted: a harpoon to take the place of one lost a year ago, a new harpoon of iron with a ring in the end of the shaft; and—his mind could hardly make the leap—a rifle—but why not, since he was so rich. And Kino saw Kino in the pearl, Kino holding a Winchester carbine. It was the wildest daydreaming and very pleasant. His lips moved hesitantly over this— "A rifle," he said. "Perhaps a rifle."

It was the rifle that broke down the barriers. This was an impossibility, and if he could think of having a rifle whole horizons were burst and he could rush on. For it is said that humans are never satisfied, that you give them one thing and they want something more. And this is said in disparagement,[2] whereas it is one of the greatest talents the species has and one that has made it superior to animals that are satisfied with what they have.

The neighbors, close pressed and silent in the house, nodded their heads at his wild imaginings. And a man in the rear murmured, "A rifle. He will have a rifle."

---

[1] LUCENT: giving off light; glowing.
[2] DISPARAGEMENT: belittling, discrediting.

But the music of the pearl was shrilling with triumph in Kino. Juana looked up, and her eyes were wide at Kino's courage and at his imagination. And electric strength had come to him now the horizons were kicked out. In the pearl he saw Coyotito sitting at a little desk in a school, just as Kino had once seen it through an open door. And Coyotito was dressed in a jacket, and he had on a white collar and a broad silken tie. Moreover, Coyotito was writing on a big piece of paper. Kino looked at his neighbors fiercely. "My son will go to school," he said, and the neighbors were hushed. Juana caught her breath sharply. Her eyes were bright as she watched him, and she looked quickly down at Coyotito in her arms to see whether this might be possible.

But Kino's face shone with prophecy. "My son will read and open the books, and my son will write and will know writing. And my son will make numbers, and these things will make us free because he will know—he will know and through him we will know." And in the pearl Kino saw himself and Juana squatting by the little fire in the brush hut while Coyotito read from a great book. "This is what the pearl will do," said Kino. And he had never said so many words together in his life. And suddenly he was afraid of his talking. His hand closed down over the pearl and cut the light away from it. Kino was afraid as a man is afraid who says, "I will," without knowing.

Now the neighbors knew they had witnessed a great marvel. They knew that time would now date from Kino's pearl, and that they would discuss this moment for many years to come. If these things came to pass, they would recount how Kino looked and what he said and how his eyes shone, and they would say, "He was a man transfigured.[1] Some power was given to him, and there it started. You see what a great man he has become, starting from that moment. And I myself saw it."

And if Kino's planning came to nothing, those same neighbors would say, "There it started. A foolish madness came over him so that he spoke foolish words. God keep us from such things. Yes, God punished Kino because he rebelled against the way things are. You see what has become of him. And I myself saw the moment when his reason left him."

Kino looked down at his closed hand and the knuckles were scabbed over and tight where he had struck the gate.

Now the dusk was coming. And Juana looped her shawl under the baby so that he hung against her hip, and she went to the fire hole and dug a coal from the ashes and broke a few twigs over it and fanned a flame alive. The little flames danced on the faces of the neighbors. They knew they should go to their own dinners, but they were reluctant to leave.

The dark was almost in, and Juana's fire threw shadows on the brush walls when the whisper came in, passed from mouth to mouth. "The Father is coming—the priest is coming." The men uncovered their heads and stepped back from the door, and the women gathered their shawls about their faces and cast down their eyes. Kino and Juan Tomás, his brother, stood up. The priest came in—a graying, aging man with an old skin and a young sharp eye. Children, he considered these people, and he treated them like children.

"Kino," he said softly, "thou art named after a great man—and a great Father of

[1] TRANSFIGURED: changed so as to become glorified and exalted.

the Church." He made it sound like a benediction.[1] "Thy namesake tamed the desert and sweetened the minds of thy people, didst thou know that? It is in the books."

Kino looked quickly down at Coyotito's head, where he hung on Juana's hip. Some day, his mind said, that boy would know what things were in the books and what things were not. The music had gone out of Kino's head, but now, thinly, slowly, the melody of the morning, the music of evil, of the enemy sounded, but it was faint and weak. And Kino looked at his neighbors to see who might have brought this song in.

But the priest was speaking again. "It has come to me that thou hast found a great fortune, a great pearl."

Kino opened his hand and held it out, and the priest gasped a little at the size and beauty of the pearl. And then he said, "I hope thou wilt remember to give thanks, my son, to Him who has given thee this treasure, and to pray for guidance in the future."

Kino nodded ·dumbly, and it was Juana who spoke softly. "We will, Father. And we will be married now. Kino has said so." She looked at the neighbors for confirmation, and they nodded their heads solemnly.

The priest said, "It is pleasant to see that your first thoughts are good thoughts. God bless you, my children." He turned and left quietly, and the people let him through.

But Kino's hand had closed tightly on the pearl again, and he was glancing about suspiciously, for the evil song was in his ears, shrilling against the music of the pearl.

The neighbors slipped away to go to their houses, and Juana squatted by the fire

---

[1] BENEDICTION : blessing.

and set her clay pot of boiled beans over the little flame. Kino stepped to the doorway and looked out. As always, he could smell the smoke from many fires, and he could see the hazy stars and feel the damp of the night air so that he covered his nose from it. The thin dog came to him and threshed itself in greeting like a wind-blown flag, and Kino looked down at it and didn't see it. He had broken through the horizons into a cold and lonely outside. He felt alone and unprotected, and scraping crickets and shrilling tree frogs and croaking toads seemed to be carrying the melody of evil. Kino shivered a little and drew his blanket more tightly against his nose. He carried the pearl still in his hand, tightly closed in his palm, and it was warm and smooth against his skin.

Behind him he heard Juana patting the cakes before she put them down on the clay cooking sheet. Kino felt all the warmth and security of his family behind him, and the Song of the Family came from behind him like the purring of a kitten. But now, by saying what his future was going to be like, he had created it. A plan is a real thing, and things projected are experienced. A plan once made and visualized becomes a reality along with other realities—never to be destroyed but easily to be attacked. Thus Kino's future was real, but having set it up, other forces were set up to destroy it, and this he knew, so that he had to prepare to meet the attack. And this Kino knew also—that the gods do not love men's plans, and the gods do not love success unless it comes by accident. He knew that the gods take their revenge on a man if he be successful through his own efforts. Consequently Kino was afraid of plans, but having made one, he could never destroy it. And to meet the attack, Kino was already making a hard skin for himself against the world. His eyes and his mind probed for danger before it appeared.

Standing in the door, he saw two men approach; and one of them carried a lantern which lighted the ground and the legs of the men. They turned in through the opening of Kino's brush fence and came to his door. And Kino saw that one was the doctor and the other the servant who had opened the gate in the morning. The split knuckles on Kino's right hand burned when he saw who they were.

The doctor said, "I was not in when you came this morning. But now, at the first chance, I have come to see the baby."

Kino stood in the door, filling it, and hatred raged and flamed in back of his eyes, and fear too, for the hundreds of years of subjugation[1] were cut deep in him.

"The baby is nearly well now," he said curtly.

The doctor smiled, but his eyes in their little lymph-lined hammocks did not smile.

He said, "Sometimes, my friend, the scorpion sting has a curious effect. There will be apparent improvement, and then without warning—pouf!" He pursed his lips and made a little explosion to show how quick it could be, and he shifted his small black doctor's bag about so that the light of the lamp fell upon it, for he knew that Kino's race love the tools of any craft and trust them. "Sometimes," the doctor went on in a liquid tone, "sometimes there will be a withered leg or a blind eye or a crumpled back. Oh, I know the sting of the scorpion, my friend, and I can cure it."

Kino felt the rage and hatred melting toward fear. He did not know, and perhaps this doctor did. And he could not take the

¹ SUBJUGATION: enslavement, control.

chance of putting his certain ignorance against this man's possible knowledge. He was trapped as his people were always trapped, and would be until, as he had said, they could be sure that the things in the books were really in the books. He could not take a chance—not with the life or with the straightness of Coyotito. He stood aside and let the doctor and his man enter the brush hut.

Juana stood up from the fire and backed away as he entered, and she covered the baby's face with the fringe of her shawl. And when the doctor went to her and held out his hand, she clutched the baby tight and looked at Kino where he stood with the fire shadows leaping on his face.

Kino nodded, and only then did she let the doctor take the baby.

"Hold the light," the doctor said, and when the servant held the lantern high, the doctor looked for a moment at the wound on the baby's shoulder. He was thoughtful for a moment and then he rolled back the baby's eyelid and looked at the eyeball. He nodded his head while Coyotito struggled against him.

"It is as I thought," he said. "The poison has gone inward and it will strike soon. Come look!" He held the eyelid down. "See —it is blue." And Kino, looking anxiously, saw that indeed it was a little blue. And he didn't know whether or not it was always a little blue. But the trap was set. He couldn't take the chance.

The doctor's eyes watered in their little hammocks. "I will give him something to try to turn the poison aside," he said. And he handed the baby to Kino.

Then from his bag he took a little bottle of white powder and a capsule of gelatine. He filled the capsule with the powder and

closed it, and then around the first capsule he fitted a second capsule and closed it. Then he worked very deftly. He took the baby and pinched its lower lip until it opened its mouth. His fat fingers placed the capsule far back on the baby's tongue, back of the point where he could spit it out, and then from the floor he picked up the little pitcher of pulque and gave Coyotito a drink, and it was done. He looked again at the baby's eyeball and he pursed his lips and seemed to think.

At last he handed the baby back to Juana, and he turned to Kino. "I think the poison will attack within the hour," he said. "The medicine may save the baby from hurt, but I will come back in an hour. Perhaps I am in time to save him." He took a deep breath and went out of the hut, and his servant followed him with the lantern.

Now Juana had the baby under her shawl, and she stared at it with anxiety and fear. Kino came to her, and he lifted the shawl and stared at the baby. He moved his hand to look under the eyelid, and only then saw that the pearl was still in his hand. Then he went to a box by the wall, and from it he brought a piece of rag. He wrapped the pearl in the rag, then went to the corner of the brush house and dug a little hole with his fingers in the dirt floor, and he put the pearl in the hole and covered it up and concealed the place. And then he went to the fire where Juana was squatting, watching the baby's face.

The doctor, back in his house, settled into his chair and looked at his watch. His people brought him a little supper of chocolate and sweet cakes and fruit, and he stared at the food discontentedly.

In the houses of the neighbors the subject that would lead all conversations for a long time to come was aired for the first time to see how it would go. The neighbors showed one another with their thumbs how big the pearl was, and they made little caressing gestures to show how lovely it was. From now on they would watch Kino and Juana very closely to see whether riches turned their heads, as riches turn all people's heads. Everyone knew why the doctor had come. He was not good at dissembling[1] and he was very well understood.

Out in the estuary a tight woven school of small fishes glittered and broke water to escape a school of great fishes that drove in to eat them. And in the houses the people could hear the swish of the small ones and the bouncing splash of the great ones as the slaughter went on. The dampness arose out of the Gulf and was deposited on bushes and cacti and on little trees in salty drops. And the night mice crept about on the ground and the little night hawks hunted them silently.

The skinny black puppy with flame spots over his eyes came to Kino's door and looked in. He nearly shook his hind quarters loose when Kino glanced up at him, and he subsided when Kino looked away. The puppy did not enter the house, but he watched with frantic interest while Kino ate his beans from the little pottery dish and wiped it clean with a corncake and ate the cake and washed the whole down with a drink of pulque.

Kino was finished and was rolling a cigarette when Juana spoke sharply. "Kino." He glanced at her and then got up and went quickly to her for he saw fright in her eyes. He stood over her, looking down, but the light was very dim. He kicked a pile

---

[1] DISSEMBLING: concealing his true nature and motives.

of twigs into the fire hole to make a blaze, and then he could see the face of Coyotito. The baby's face was flushed and his throat was working and a little thick drool of saliva issued from his lips. The spasm of the stomach muscles began, and the baby was very sick.

Kino knelt beside his wife. "So the doctor knew," he said, but he said it for himself as well as for his wife, for his mind was hard and suspicious and he was remembering the white powder. Juana rocked from side to side and moaned out the little Song of the Family as though it could ward off the danger, and the baby vomited and writhed in her arms. Now uncertainty was in Kino, and the music of evil throbbed in his head and nearly drove out Juana's song.

The doctor finished his chocolate and nibbled the little fallen pieces of sweet cake. He brushed his fingers on a napkin, looked at his watch, arose, and took up his little bag.

The news of the baby's illness traveled quickly among the brush houses, for sickness is second only to hunger as the enemy of poor people. And some said softly, "Luck, you see, brings bitter friends." And they nodded and got up to go to Kino's house. The neighbors scuttled with covered noses through the dark until they crowded into Kino's house again. They stood and gazed, and they made little comments on the sadness that this should happen at a time of joy, and they said, "All things are in God's hands." The old women squatted down beside Juana to try to give her aid if they could and comfort if they could not.

Then the doctor hurried in, followed by his man. He scattered the old women like chickens. He took the baby and examined it and felt its head. "The poison it has

worked," he said. "I think I can defeat it. I will try my best." He asked for water, and in the cup of it he put three drops of ammonia, and he pried open the baby's mouth and poured it down. The baby spluttered and screeched under the treatment, and Juana watched him with haunted eyes. The doctor spoke a little as he worked. "It is lucky that I know about the poison of the scorpion, otherwise—" and he shrugged to show what could have happened.

But Kino was suspicious, and he could not take his eyes from the doctor's open bag, and from the bottle of white powder there. Gradually the spasms subsided and the baby relaxed under the doctor's hands. And then Coyotito sighed deeply and went to sleep, for he was very tired with vomiting.

The doctor put the baby in Juana's arms. "He will get well now," he said. "I have won the fight." And Juana looked at him with adoration.

The doctor was closing his bag now. He said, "When do you think you can pay this bill?" He said it even kindly.

"When I have sold my pearl I will pay you," Kino said.

"You have a pearl? A good pearl?" the doctor asked with interest.

And then the chorus of the neighbors broke in. "He has found the Pearl of the World," they cried, and they joined forefinger with thumb to show how great the pearl was.

"Kino will be a rich man," they clamored. "It is a pearl such as one has never seen."

The doctor looked surprised. "I had not heard of it. Do you keep this pearl in a safe place? Perhaps you would like me to put it in my safe?"

Kino's eyes were hooded now, his cheeks were drawn taut. "I have it secure," he said. "Tomorrow I will sell it and then I will pay you."

The doctor shrugged, and his wet eyes never left Kino's eyes. He knew the pearl would be buried in the house, and he thought Kino might look toward the place where it was buried. "It would be a shame to have it stolen before you could sell it," the doctor said, and he saw Kino's eyes flick involuntarily to the floor near the side post of the brush house.

When the doctor had gone and all the neighbors had reluctantly returned to their houses, Kino squatted beside the little glowing coals in the fire hole and listened to the night sound, the soft sweep of the little waves on the shore and the distant barking of dogs, the creeping of the breeze through the brush house roof and the soft speech of his neighbors in their houses in the village. For these people do not sleep soundly all night; they awaken at intervals and talk a little and then go to sleep again. And after a while Kino got up and went to the door of his house.

He smelled the breeze and he listened for any foreign sound of secrecy or creeping, and his eyes searched the darkness, for the music of evil was sounding in his head and he was fierce and afraid. After he had probed the night with his senses he went to the place by the side post where the pearl was buried, and he dug it up and brought it to his sleeping mat, and under his sleeping mat he dug another little hole in the dirt floor and buried his pearl and covered it up again.

And Juana, sitting by the fire hole, watched him with questioning eyes, and when he had buried his pearl she asked, "Who do you fear?"

Kino searched for a true answer, and at last he said, "Everyone." And he could feel a shell of hardness drawing over him.

After a while they lay down together on the sleeping mat, and Juana did not put the baby in his box tonight, but cradled him on her arms and covered his face with her head shawl. And the last light went out of the embers in the fire hole.

But Kino's brain burned, even during his sleep, and he dreamed that Coyotito could read, that one of his own people could tell him the truth of things. And in his dream, Coyotito was reading from a book as large as a house, with letters as big as dogs, and the words galloped and played on the book. And then darkness spread over the page, and with the darkness came the music of evil again, and Kino stirred in his sleep; and when he stirred, Juana's eyes opened in the darkness. And then Kino awakened, with the evil music pulsing in him, and he lay in the darkness with his ears alert.

Then from the corner of the house came a sound so soft that it might have been simply a thought, a little furtive movement, a touch of a foot on earth, the almost inaudible purr of controlled breathing. Kino held his breath to listen, and he knew that whatever dark thing was in his house was holding its breath too, to listen. For a time no sound at all came from the corner of the brush house. Then Kino might have thought he had imagined the sound. But Juana's hand came creeping over to him in warning, and then the sound came again! the whisper of a foot on dry earth and the scratch of fingers in the soil.

And now a wild fear surged in Kino's

breast, and on the fear came rage, as it always did. Kino's hand crept into his breast where his knife hung on a string, and then he sprang like an angry cat, leaped striking and spitting for the dark thing he knew was in the corner of the house. He felt cloth, struck at it with his knife and missed, and struck again and felt his knife go through cloth, and then his head crashed with lightning and exploded with pain. There was a soft scurry in the doorway, and running steps for a moment, and then silence.

Kino could feel warm blood running down from his forehead, and he could hear Juana calling to him. "Kino! Kino!" And there was terror in her voice. Then coldness came over him as quickly as the rage had, and he said, "I am all right. The thing has gone."

He groped his way back to the sleeping mat. Already Juana was working at the fire. She uncovered an ember from the ashes and shredded little pieces of cornhusk over it and blew a little flame into the cornhusks so that a tiny light danced through the hut. And then from a secret place Juana brought a little piece of consecrated candle and lighted it at the flame and set it upright on a fireplace stone. She worked quickly, crooning as she moved about. She dipped the end of her head shawl in water and swabbed the blood from Kino's bruised forehead. "It is nothing," Kino said, but his eyes and his voice were hard and cold and a brooding hate was growing in him.

Now the tension which had been growing in Juana boiled up to the surface and her lips were thin. "This thing is evil," she cried harshly. "This pearl is like a sin! It

will destroy us," and her voice rose shrilly. "Throw it away, Kino. Let us break it between stones. Let us bury it and forget the place. Let us throw it back into the sea. It has brought evil. Kino, my husband, it will destroy us." And in the firelight her lips and her eyes were alive with her fear.

But Kino's face was set, and his mind and his will were set. "This is our one chance," he said. "Our son must go to school. He must break out of the pot that holds us in."

"It will destroy us all," Juana cried. "Even our son."

"Hush," said Kino. "Do not speak any more. In the morning we will sell the pearl, and then the evil will be gone, and only the good remain. Now hush, my wife." His dark eyes scowled into the little fire, and for the first time he knew that his knife was still in his hands, and he raised the blade and looked at it and saw a little line of blood on the steel. For a moment he seemed about to wipe the blade on his trousers but then he plunged the knife into the earth and so cleansed it.

The distant roosters began to crow and the air changed and the dawn was coming. The wind of the morning ruffled the water of the estuary and whispered through the mangroves, and the little waves beat on the rubbly beach with an increased tempo. Kino raised the sleeping mat and dug up his pearl and put it in front of him and stared at it.

And the beauty of the pearl, winking and glimmering in the light of the little candle, cozened his brain with its beauty. So lovely it was, so soft, and its own music came from it—its music of promise and delight, its guarantee of the future, of comfort, of security. Its warm lucence promised a poultice against illness and a wall against insult. It closed a door on hunger. And as he stared at it Kino's eyes softened and his face relaxed. He could see the little image of the consecrated candle reflected in the soft surface of the pearl, and he heard again in his ears the lovely music of the undersea, the tone of the diffused green light of the sea bottom. Juana, glancing secretly at him, saw him smile. And because they were in some way one thing and one purpose, she smiled with him.

And they began this day with hope.

FOR DISCUSSION

1. Kino and his people instinctively recognize the treachery of the doctor, and hate him. What conflict forces Kino to allow the doctor to treat Coyotito? After the doctor has given Coyotito the white powder, Steinbeck pauses in the narrative to comment on a school of fish that slaughters smaller fish and night hawks that hunt little mice. Why do you think he does this?

2. Kino's discovery affected everyone with whom he came in contact. How did it affect the priest? The shopkeepers? The doctor? The beggars? How does the discovery of the pearl cause Kino to become "every man's enemy"?

3. A person's dreams can reveal a great deal about him. What does each of Kino's dreams suggest about him as a person? These dreams are also important because they indicate a complete change in the pattern of Kino's life, and the resulting change in Kino himself. What change in Kino occurs as soon as he makes his plans for the future?

4. Kino's neighbors and friends recognize that future time would date from the discovery of the pearl. What two distinct possibilities do they see in Kino's dreams and plans?

CHAPTER 4

It is wonderful the way a little town keeps track of itself and of all its units. If every single man and woman, child and baby, acts and conducts itself in a known pattern and breaks no walls and differs with no one and experiments in no way and is not sick and does not endanger the ease and peace of mind or steady unbroken flow of the town, then that unit can disappear and never be heard of. But let one man step out of the regular thought or the known and trusted pattern, and the nerves of the townspeople ring with nervousness and communication travels over the nerve lines of the town. Then every unit communicates to the whole.

Thus, in La Paz, it was known in the early morning through the whole town that Kino was going to sell his pearl that day. It was known among the neighbors in the brush huts, among the pearl fishermen; it was known among the Chinese grocery-store owners; it was known in the church, for the altar boys whispered about it. Word of it crept in among the nuns; the beggars in front of the church spoke of it, for they would be there to take the tithe[1] of the first fruits of the luck. The little boys knew about it with excitement, but most of all the pearl buyers knew about it, and when the day had come, in the offices of the pearl buyers, each man sat alone with his little black velvet tray, and each man rolled the pearls about with his fingertips and considered his part in the picture.

It was supposed that the pearl buyers were individuals acting alone, bidding against one another for the pearls the fishermen brought in. And once it had been so. But this was a wasteful method, for often, in the excitement of bidding for a fine pearl, too great a price had been paid to the fishermen. This was extravagant and not to be countenanced.[2] Now there was only one pearl buyer with many hands, and the men who sat in their offices and waited for Kino knew what price they would offer, how high they would bid, and what method each one would use. And although these men would not profit beyond their salaries, there was excitement among the pearl buyers, for there was excitement in the hunt, and if it be a man's function to break down a price, then he must take joy and satisfaction in breaking it as far down as possible. For every man in the world functions to the best of his ability, and no one does less than his best, no matter what he may think about it. Quite apart from any reward they might get, from any word of praise, from any promotion, a pearl buyer was a pearl buyer, and the best and happiest pearl buyer was he who bought for the lowest prices.

The sun was hot yellow that morning, and it drew the moisture from the estuary and from the Gulf and hung it in shimmering scarves in the air so that the air vibrated and vision was insubstantial. A vision hung in the air to the north of the city —the vision of a mountain that was over two hundred miles away, and the high slopes of this mountain were swaddled with pines and a great stone peak arose above the timber line.

And the morning of this day the canoes lay lined up on the beach; the fishermen did not go out to dive for pearls, for there would be too much happening, too many things to see when Kino went to sell the great pearl.

In the brush houses by the shore Kino's neighbors sat long over their breakfasts, and they spoke of what they would do if they had found the pearl. And one man said that he would give it as a present to the Holy Father in Rome. Another said that he would buy Masses for the souls of his family for a thousand years. Another thought he might take the money and distribute it among the poor of La Paz; and a fourth thought of all the good things one could do with the money from the pearl, of all the charities, benefits, of all the rescues one could perform if one had money. All of the neighbors hoped that sudden wealth would not turn Kino's head, would not make a rich man of him, would not graft onto him the evil limbs of greed and hatred and coldness. For Kino was a well-liked man; it would be a shame if the pearl destroyed him. "That good wife Juana," they said, "and the beautiful baby Coyotito, and the others to come. What a pity it would be if the pearl should destroy them all."

---

[1] TITHE (tīth): part of one's income contributed to charity.

[2] COUNTENANCED: approved of.

For Kino and Juana this was the morning of mornings of their lives, comparable only to the day when the baby was born. This was to be the day from which all other days would take their arrangement. Thus they would say, "It was two years before we sold the pearl," or, "It was six weeks after we sold the pearl." Juana, considering the matter, threw caution to the winds, and she dressed Coyotito in the clothes she had prepared for his baptism, when there would be money for his baptism. And Juana combed and braided her hair and tied the ends with two little bows of red ribbon, and she put on her marriage skirt and waist. The sun was quarter high when they were ready. Kino's ragged white clothes were clean at least, and this was the last day of his raggedness. For tomorrow, or even this afternoon, he would have new clothes.

The neighbors, watching Kino's door through the crevices in their brush houses, were dressed and ready too. There was no self-consciousness about their joining Kino and Juana to go pearl selling. It was expected, it was an historic moment, they would be crazy if they didn't go. It would be almost a sign of unfriendship.

Juana put on her head shawl carefully, and she draped one end under her right elbow and gathered it with her right hand so that a hammock hung under her arm, and in this little hammock she placed Coyotito, propped up against the head shawl so that he could see everything and perhaps remember. Kino put on his large straw hat and felt it with his hand to see that it was properly placed, not on the back or side of his head, like a rash, unmarried, irresponsible man, and not flat as an elder would wear it, but tilted a little forward to show aggressiveness and seriousness and vigor. There is a great deal to be seen in the tilt of a hat on a man. Kino slipped his feet into his sandals and pulled the thongs up over his heels. The great pearl was wrapped in an old soft piece of deerskin and placed in a little leather bag, and the leather bag was in a pocket in Kino's shirt. He folded his blanket carefully and draped it in a narrow strip over his left shoulder, and now they were ready.

Kino stepped with dignity out of the house, and Juana followed him, carrying Coyotito. And as they marched up the freshet-washed alley toward the town, the neighbors joined them. The houses belched people; the doorways spewed out children. But because of the seriousness of the occasion, only one man walked with Kino, and that was his brother, Juan Tomás.

Juan Tomás cautioned his brother. "You must be careful to see they do not cheat you," he said.

And, "Very careful," Kino agreed.

"We do not know what prices are paid in other places," said Juan Tomás. "How can we know what is a fair price, if we do not know what the pearl buyer gets for the pearl in another place."

"That is true," said Kino, "but how can we know? We are here, we are not there."

As they walked up toward the city the crowd grew behind them, and Juan Tomás, in pure nervousness, went on speaking.

"Before you were born, Kino," he said, "the old ones thought of a way to get more money for their pearls. They thought it would be better if they had an agent who took all the pearls to the capital and sold them there and kept only his share of the profit."

Kino nodded his head. "I know," he said.

"It was a good thought."

"And so they got such a man," said Juan Tomás, "and they pooled the pearls, and they started him off. And he was never heard of again and the pearls were lost. Then they got another man, and they started him off, and he was never heard of again. And so they gave the whole thing up and went back to the old way."

"I know," said Kino. "I have heard our father tell of it. It was a good idea, but it was against religion, and the Father made that very clear. The loss of the pearl was a punishment visited on those who tried to leave their station. And the Father made it clear that each man and woman is like a soldier sent by God to guard some part of the castle of the Universe. And some are in the ramparts and some far deep in the darkness of the walls. But each one must remain faithful to his post and must not go running about, else the castle is in danger from the assaults of Hell."

"I have heard him make that sermon," said Juan Tomás. "He makes it every year."

The brothers, as they walked along, squinted their eyes a little, as they and their grandfathers and their great-grandfathers had done for four hundred years, since first the strangers came with arguments and authority and gunpowder to back up both. And in the four hundred years Kino's people had learned only one defense—a slight slitting of the eyes and a slight tightening of the lips and a retirement. Nothing could break down this wall, and they could remain whole within the wall.

The gathering procession was solemn, for they sensed the importance of this day, and any children who showed a tendency to scuffle, to scream, to cry out, to steal hats and rumple hair, were hissed to silence by their elders. So important was this day that an old man came to see, riding on the stalwart shoulders of his nephew. The procession left the brush huts and entered the stone and plaster city where the streets were a little wider and there were narrow pavements beside the buildings. And as before, the beggars joined them as they passed the church; the grocers looked out at them as they went by; the little saloons lost their customers and the owners closed up shop and went along. And the sun beat down on the streets of the city and even tiny stones threw shadows on the ground. The news of the approach of the procession ran ahead of it, and in their little dark offices the pearl buyers stiffened and grew alert. They got out papers so that they could be at work when Kino appeared, and they put their pearls in the desks, for it is not good to let an inferior pearl be seen beside a beauty. And word of the loveliness of Kino's pearl had come to them. The pearl buyers' offices were clustered together in one narrow street, and they were barred at the windows, and wooden slats cut out the light so that only a soft gloom entered the offices.

A stout slow man sat in an office waiting. His face was fatherly and benign, and his eyes twinkled with friendship. He was a caller of good mornings, a ceremonious shaker of hands, a jolly man who knew all the jokes and yet who hovered close to sadness, for in the midst of a laugh he could remember the death of your aunt, and his eyes could become wet with sorrow for your loss. This morning he had placed a flower in a vase on his desk, a single scarlet hibiscus, and the vase sat beside the black velvet-lined pearl tray in front of him. He was shaved close to the blue roots of his beard, and his hands were clean and his nails polished. His door stood open to the morning, and he hummed under his breath while his right hand practiced legerdemain.[1] He rolled a coin back and forth over his knuckles and made it appear and disappear, made it spin and sparkle. The coin winked into sight and as quickly slipped out of sight, and the man did not even watch his own performance. The fingers did it all mechanically, precisely, while the man hummed to himself and peered out the door. Then he heard the tramp of feet of the approaching crowd, and the fingers of his right hand worked faster and faster until, as the figure of Kino filled the doorway, the coin flashed and disappeared.

"Good morning, my friend," the stout man said. "What can I do for you?"

Kino stared into the dimness of the little office, for his eyes were squeezed from the outside glare. But the buyer's eyes had become as steady and cruel and unwinking as a hawk's eyes, while the rest of his face smiled in greeting. And secretly, behind his desk, his right hand practiced with the coin.

"I have a pearl," said Kino. And Juan Tomás stood beside him and snorted a little at the understatement. The neighbors peered around the doorway, and a line of little boys clambered on the window bars and looked through. Several little boys, on their hands and knees, watched the scene around Kino's legs.

"You have a pearl," the dealer said. "Sometimes a man brings in a dozen. Well, let us see your pearl. We will value it and give you the best price." And his fingers worked furiously with the coin.

Now Kino instinctively knew his own

dramatic effects. Slowly he brought out the leather bag, slowly took from it the soft and dirty piece of deerskin, and then let the great pearl roll into the black velvet tray, and instantly his eyes went to the buyer's face. But there was no sign, no movement, the face did not change, but the secret hand behind the desk missed in its precision. The coin stumbled over a knuckle and slipped silently into the dealer's lap. And the fingers behind the desk curled into a fist. When the right hand came out of hiding, the forefinger touched the great pearl, rolled it on the black velvet; thumb and forefinger picked it up and brought it near to the dealer's eyes and twirled it in the air.

Kino held his breath, and the neighbors held their breath, and the whispering went back through the crowd. "He is inspecting it—No price has been mentioned yet—They have not come to a price."

Now the dealer's hand had become a personality. The hand tossed the great pearl back to the tray, the forefinger poked and insulted it, and on the dealer's face there came a sad and contemptuous smile.

"I am sorry, my friend," he said, and his shoulders rose a little to indicate that the misfortune was no fault of his.

"It is a pearl of great value," Kino said.

The dealer's fingers spurned the pearl so that it bounced and rebounded softly from the sides of the velvet tray.

"You have heard of fool's gold," the dealer said. "This pearl is like fool's gold. It is too large. Who would buy it? There is no market for such things. It is a curiosity only. I am sorry. You thought it was a thing of value, and it is only a curiosity."

Now Kino's face was perplexed and worried. "It is the Pearl of the World," he cried. "No one has ever seen such a pearl."

[1] LEGERDERMAIN (lej·ər·də·mān´): sleight of hand trickery.

"On the contrary," said the dealer, "it is large and clumsy. As a curiosity it has interest; some museum might perhaps take it to place in a collection of seashells. I can give you, say, a thousand pesos."

Kino's face grew dark and dangerous. "It is worth fifty thousand," he said. "You know it. You want to cheat me."

And the dealer heard a little grumble go through the crowd as they heard his price. And the dealer felt a little tremor of fear.

"Do not blame me," he said quickly. "I am only an appraiser. Ask the others. Go to their offices and show your pearl—or better let them come here, so that you can see there is no collusion. Boy," he called. And when his servant looked through the rear door, "Boy, go to such a one, and such another one and such a third one. Ask them to step in here and do not tell them why. Just say that I will be pleased to see them." And his right hand went behind the desk and pulled another coin from his pocket, and the coin rolled back and forth over his knuckles.

Kino's neighbors whispered together. They had been afraid of something like this. The pearl was large, but it had a strange color. They had been suspicious of it from the first. And after all, a thousand pesos was not to be thrown away. It was comparative wealth to a man who was not wealthy. And suppose Kino took a thousand pesos. Only yesterday he had nothing.

But Kino had grown tight and hard. He felt the creeping of fate, the circling of wolves, the hover of vultures. He felt the evil coagulating[1] about him, and he was helpless to protect himself. He heard in his ears the evil music. And on the black velvet the great pearl glistened, so that

[1] COAGULATING: gathering and thickening.

the dealer could not keep his eyes from it.

The crowd in the doorway wavered and broke and let the three pearl dealers through. The crowd was silent now, fearing to miss a word, to fail to see a gesture or an expression. Kino was silent and watchful. He felt a little tugging at his back, and turned and looked in Juana's eyes, and when he looked away he had renewed strength.

The dealers did not glance at one another nor at the pearl. The man behind the desk said, "I have put a value on this pearl. The owner here does not think it fair. I will ask you to examine this—this thing and make an offer. Notice," he said to Kino, "I have not mentioned what I have offered."

The first dealer, dry and stringy, seemed now to see the pearl for the first time. He took it up, rolled it quickly between thumb and forefinger, and then cast it contemptuously back into the tray.

"Do not include me in the discussion," he said dryly. "I will make no offer at all. I do not want it. This is not a pearl—it is a monstrosity." His thin lips curled.

Now the second dealer, a little man with a shy soft voice, took up the pearl, and he examined it carefully. He took a glass from his pocket and inspected it under magnification. Then he laughed softly.

"Better pearls are made of paste," he said. "I know these things. This is soft and chalky, it will lose its color and die in a few months. Look—" He offered the glass to Kino, showed him how to use it, and Kino, who had never seen a pearl's surface magnified, was shocked at the strange-looking surface.

The third dealer took the pearl from Kino's hands. "One of my clients likes such things," he said. "I will offer five hundred pesos, and perhaps I can sell it to my client for six hundred."

Kino reached quickly and snatched the pearl from his hand. He wrapped it in the deerskin and thrust it inside his shirt.

The man behind the desk said, "I'm a fool, I know, but my first offer stands. I still offer one thousand. What are you doing?" he asked, as Kino thrust the pearl out of sight.

"I am cheated," Kino cried fiercely. "My pearl is not for sale here. I will go, perhaps even to the capital."

Now the dealers glanced quickly at one another. They knew they had played too hard; they knew they would be disciplined for their failure, and the man at the desk said quickly, "I might go to fifteen hundred."

But Kino was pushing his way through the crowd. The hum of talk came to him dimly, his rage blood pounded in his ears, and he burst through and strode away. Juana followed, trotting after him.

When the evening came, the neighbors in the brush houses sat eating their corncakes and beans, and they discussed the great theme of the morning. They did not know, it seemed a fine pearl to them, but they had never seen such a pearl before, and surely the dealers knew more about the value of pearls than they. "And mark this," they said. "Those dealers did not discuss these things. Each of the three knew the pearl was valueless."

"But suppose they had arranged it before?"

"If that is so, then all of us have been cheated all of our lives."

Perhaps, some argued, perhaps it would have been better if Kino took the one thousand five hundred pesos. That is a great deal of money, more than he has ever seen. Maybe Kino is being a pigheaded fool. Suppose he should really go to the capital and find no buyer for his pearl. He would never live that down.

And now, said other fearful ones, now that he had defied them, those buyers will not want to deal with him at all. Maybe Kino has cut off his own head and destroyed himself.

And others said, Kino is a brave man, and a fierce man; he is right. From his courage we may all profit. These were proud of Kino.

In his house Kino squatted on his sleeping mat, brooding. He had buried his pearl under a stone of the fire hole in his house, and he stared at the woven tules of his sleeping mat until the crossed design danced in his head. He had lost one world and had not gained another. And Kino was afraid. Never in his life had he been far from home. He was afraid of strangers and of strange places. He was terrified of that monster of strangeness they called the capital. It lay over the water and through the mountains, over a thousand miles, and every strange terrible mile was frightening. But Kino had lost his old world and he must clamber[1] on to a new one. For his dream of the future was real and never to be destroyed, and he had said "I will go," and that made a real thing too. To determine to go and to say it was to be halfway there.

Juana watched him while he buried his pearl, and she watched him while she cleaned Coyotito and nursed him, and Juana made the corncakes for supper.

Juan Tomás came in and squatted down beside Kino and remained silent for a long

[1] CLAMBER: climb with difficulty.

time, until at last Kino demanded, "What else could I do? They are cheats."

Juan Tomás nodded gravely. He was the elder, and Kino looked to him for wisdom. "It is hard to know," he said. "We do know that we are cheated from birth to the overcharge on our coffins. But we survive. You have defied not the pearl buyers, but the whole structure, the whole way of life, and I am afraid for you."

"What have I to fear but starvation?" Kino asked.

But Juan Tomás shook his head slowly. "That we must all fear. But suppose you are correct—suppose your pearl is of great value—do you think then the game is over?"

"What do you mean?"

"I don't know," said Juan Tomás, "but I am afraid for you. It is new ground you are walking on, you do not know the way."

"I will go. I will go soon," said Kino.

"Yes," Juan Tomás agreed. "That you must do. But I wonder if you will find it any different in the capital. Here, you have friends and me, your brother. There, you will have no one."

"What can I do?" Kino cried. "Some deep outrage is here. My son must have a chance. That is what they are striking at. My friends will protect me."

"Only so long as they are not in danger or discomfort from it," said Juan Tomás. He arose, saying, "Go with God."

And Kino said, "Go with God," and did not even look up, for the words had a strange chill in them.

Long after Juan Tomás had gone Kino sat brooding on his sleeping mat. A lethargy[1] had settled on him, and a little gray hopelessness. Every road seemed blocked

---

[1] LETHARGY: tiredness, indifference.

against him. In his head he heard only the dark music of the enemy. His senses were burningly alive, but his mind went back to the deep participation with all things, the gift he had from his people. He heard every little sound of the gathering night, the sleepy complaint of settling birds, the love agony of cats, the strike and withdrawal of little waves on the beach, and the simple hiss of distance. And he could smell the sharp odor of exposed kelp from the receding tide. The little flare of the twig fire made the design on his sleeping mat jump before his entranced eyes.

Juana watched him with worry, but she knew him and she knew she could help him best by being silent and by being near. And as though she too could hear the Song of Evil, she fought it, singing softly the melody of the family, of the safety and warmth and wholeness of the family. She held Coyotito in her arms and sang the song to him, to keep the evil out, and her voice was brave against the threat of the dark music.

Kino did not move nor ask for his supper. She knew he would ask when he wanted it. His eyes were entranced, and he could sense the wary, watchful evil outside the brush house; he could feel the dark creeping things waiting for him to go out into the night. It was shadowy and dreadful, and yet it called to him and threatened him and challenged him. His right hand went into his shirt and felt his knife; his eyes were wide; he stood up and walked to the doorway.

Juana willed to stop him; she raised her hand to stop him, and her mouth opened with terror. For a long moment Kino looked out into the darkness and then he stepped outside. Juana heard the little rush, the grunting struggle, the blow. She froze with terror for a moment, and then her lips drew back from her teeth like a cat's lips. She set Coyotito down on the ground. She seized a stone from the fireplace and rushed outside, but it was over by then. Kino lay on the ground, struggling to rise, and there was no one near him. Only the shadows and the strike and rush of waves and the hiss of distance. But the evil was all about, hidden behind the brush fence, crouched beside the house in the shadow, hovering in the air.

Juana dropped her stone, and she put her arms around Kino and helped him to his feet and supported him into the house. Blood oozed down from his scalp and there was a long deep cut in his cheek from ear to chin, a deep, bleeding slash. And Kino was only half conscious. He shook his head from side to side. His shirt was torn open and his clothes half pulled off. Juana sat him down on his sleeping mat and she wiped the thickening blood from his face with her skirt. She brought him pulque to drink in a little pitcher, and still he shook his head to clear out the darkness.

"Who?" Juana asked.

"I don't know," Kino said. "I didn't see."

Now Juana brought her clay pot of water and she washed the cut on his face while he stared dazed ahead of him.

"Kino, my husband," she cried, and his eyes stared past her. "Kino, can you hear me?"

"I hear you," he said dully.

"Kino, this pearl is evil. Let us destroy it before it destroys us. Let us crush it between two stones. Let us—let us throw it back in the sea where it belongs. Kino, it is evil, it is evil!"

And as she spoke the light came back in Kino's eyes so that they glowed fiercely and his muscles hardened and his will hardened.

"No," he said. "I will fight this thing. I will win over it. We will have our chance." His fist pounded the sleeping mat. "No one shall take our good fortune from us," he said. His eyes softened then and he raised a gentle hand to Juana's shoulder. "Believe me," he said. "I am a man." And his face grew crafty.

"In the morning we will take our canoe and we will go over the sea and over the mountains to the capital, you and I. We will not be cheated. I am a man."

"Kino," she said huskily, "I am afraid. A man can be killed. Let us throw the pearl back into the sea."

"Hush," he said fiercely. "I am a man. Hush." And she was silent, for his voice was command. "Let us sleep a little," he said. "In the first light we will start. You are not afraid to go with me?"

"No, my husband."

His eyes were soft and warm on her then, his hand touched her cheek. "Let us sleep a little," he said.

FOR DISCUSSION

1. After Kino is attacked, Juana says, "This thing is evil . . . . This pearl is like a sin!" She urges him to throw the pearl away before it destroys her family. What instinctive feelings seem to be at work in Juana? Is her belief merely superstition, or is there some basis for her conclusions?

2. What system had developed in the town that kept the fishermen from receiving a fair price for their pearls? Had Kino's people ever tried to go against the system? What part did the priest play in shaping their attitudes toward the matter?

3. What is the neighbors' reaction when Kino refuses the offer of the pearl buyers? What does Juan Tomás fear? Does Kino seem to realize what his refusal means? Do you think that his actions are motivated only by stubbornness, or does Steinbeck suggest that more complex motives are also involved? Explain your answer.

CHAPTER 5

The late moon arose before the first rooster crowed. Kino opened his eyes in the darkness, for he sensed movement near him, but he did not move. Only his eyes searched the darkness, and in the pale light of the moon that crept through the holes in the brush house Kino saw Juana arise silently from beside him. He saw her move toward the fireplace. So carefully did she work that he heard only the lightest sound when she moved the fireplace stone. And then like a shadow she glided toward the door. She paused for a moment beside the hanging box where Coyotito lay, then for a second she was back in the doorway, and then she was gone.

And rage surged in Kino. He rolled up to his feet and followed her as silently as she had gone, and he could hear her quick footsteps going toward the shore. Quietly he tracked her, and his brain was red with anger. She burst clear of the brush line and stumbled over the little boulders toward the water, and then she heard him coming and she broke into a run. Her arm was up to throw when he leaped at her and caught her arm and wrenched the pearl from her. He struck her in the face with his clenched fist and she fell among the boulders, and he kicked her in the side. In the pale light he could see the little waves break over her, and her skirt floated about and clung to her legs as the water receded.

Kino looked down at her and his teeth were bared. He hissed at her like a snake, and Juana stared at him with wide unfrightened eyes, like a sheep before the butcher. She knew there was murder in him, and it was all right; she had accepted it, and she would not resist or even protest. And then the rage left him and a sick disgust took its place. He turned away from her and walked up the beach and through the brush line. His senses were dulled by his emotion.

He heard the rush, got his knife out and lunged at one dark figure and felt his knife go home, and then he was swept to his knees and swept again to the ground. Greedy fingers went through his clothes, frantic fingers searched him, and the pearl, knocked from his hand, lay winking behind a little stone in the pathway. It glinted in the soft moonlight.

Juana dragged herself up from the rocks on the edge of the water. Her face was a dull pain and her side ached. She steadied herself on her knees for a while and her wet skirt clung to her. There was no anger in her for Kino. He had said, "I am a man," and that meant certain things to Juana. It meant that he was half insane and half god.

It meant that Kino would drive his strength against a mountain and plunge his strength against the sea. Juana, in her woman's soul, knew that the mountain would stand while the man broke himself; that the sea would surge while the man drowned in it. And yet it was this thing that made him a man, half insane and half god, and Juana had need of a man; she could not live without a man. Although she might be puzzled by these differences between man and woman, she knew them and accepted them and needed them. Of course she would follow him, there was no question of that. Sometimes the quality of woman, the reason, the caution, the sense of preservation, could cut through Kino's manness and save them all. She climbed painfully to her feet, and she dipped her cupped palms in the little waves and washed her bruised face with the stinging salt water, and then she went creeping up the beach after Kino.

A flight of herring clouds had moved over the sky from the south. The pale moon dipped in and out of the strands of clouds so that Juana walked in darkness for a moment and in light the next. Her back was bent with pain and her head was low. She went through the line of brush when the moon was covered, and when it looked through she saw the glimmer of the great pearl in the path behind the rock. She sank to her knees and picked it up, and the moon went into the darkness of the clouds again. Juana remained on her knees while she considered whether to go back to the sea and finish her job, and as she considered, the light came again, and she saw two dark figures lying in the path ahead of her. She leaped forward and saw that one was Kino and the other a stranger with dark shiny fluid leaking from his throat.

Kino moved sluggishly, arms and legs stirred like those of a crushed bug, and a thick muttering came from his mouth. Now, in an instant, Juana knew that the old life was gone forever. A dead man in the path and Kino's knife, dark bladed beside him, convinced her. All of the time Juana had been trying to rescue something of the old peace, of the time before the pearl. But now it was gone, and there was no retrieving it. And knowing this, she abandoned the past instantly. There was nothing to do but to save themselves.

Her pain was gone now, her slowness. Quickly she dragged the dead man from the pathway into the shelter of the brush. She went to Kino and sponged his face with her wet skirt. His senses were coming back and he moaned.

"They have taken the pearl. I have lost it. Now it is over," he said. "The pearl is gone."

Juana quieted him as she would quiet a sick child. "Hush," she said. "Here is your pearl. I found it in the path. Can you hear me now? Here is your pearl. Can you understand? You have killed a man. We must go away. They will come for us, can you understand? We must be gone before the daylight comes."

"I was attacked," Kino said uneasily. "I struck to save my life."

"Do you remember yesterday?" Juana asked. "Do you think that will matter? Do you remember the men of the city? Do you think your explanation will help?"

Kino drew a great breath and fought off his weakness. "No," he said. "You are right." And his will hardened and he was a man again.

"Go to our house and bring Coyotito," he said, "and bring all the corn we have. I will drag the canoe into the water and we will go."

He took his knife and left her. He stumbled toward the beach and he came to his canoe. And when the light broke through again he saw that a great hole had been knocked in the bottom. And a searing rage came to him and gave him strength. Now the darkness was closing in on his family; now the evil music filled the night, hung over the mangroves, skirled in the wave beat. The canoe of his grandfather, plastered over and over, and a splintered hole broken in it. This was an evil beyond thinking. The killing of a man was not so evil as the killing of a boat. For a boat does not have sons, and a boat cannot protect itself, and a wounded boat does not heal. There was sorrow in Kino's rage, but this last thing had tightened him beyond breaking. He was an animal now, for hiding, for attacking, and he lived only to preserve himself and his family. He was not conscious of the pain in his head. He leaped up the beach, through the brush line toward his brush house, and it did not occur to him to take one of the canoes of his neighbors. Never once did the thought enter his head, any more than he could have conceived breaking a boat.

The roosters were crowing and the dawn was not far off. Smoke of the first fires seeped out through the walls of the brush houses, and the first smell of cooking corn-cakes was in the air. Already the dawn birds were scampering in the bushes. The weak moon was losing its light and the clouds thickened and curdled to the southward. The wind blew freshly into the estuary, a nervous, restless wind with the smell of storm on its breath, and there was change and uneasiness in the air.

Kino, hurrying toward his house, felt a surge of exhilaration. Now he was not confused, for there was only one thing to do, and Kino's hand went first to the great pearl in his shirt and then to his knife hanging under his shirt.

He saw a little glow ahead of him, and then without interval a tall flame leaped up in the dark with a crackling roar, and a tall edifice[1] of fire lighted the pathway. Kino broke into a run; it was his brush house, he knew. And he knew that these houses could burn down in a very few moments. And as he ran a scuttling figure ran toward him—Juana, with Coyotito in her arms and Kino's shoulder blanket clutched in her hand. The baby moaned with fright, and Juana's eyes were wide and terrified. Kino could see the house was gone, and he did not question Juana. He knew, but she said, "It was torn up and the floor dug—even the baby's box turned out, and as I looked they put the fire to the outside."

The fierce light of the burning house lighted Kino's face strongly. "Who?" he demanded.

"I don't know," she said. "The dark ones."

The neighbors were tumbling from their houses now, and they watched the falling sparks and stamped them out to save their own houses. Suddenly Kino was afraid. The light made him afraid. He remembered the man lying dead in the brush beside the the path, and he took Juana by the arm and drew her into the shadow of a house away from the light, for light was danger to him. For a moment he considered and then he worked among the shadows until he came to the house of Juan Tomás, his brother, and he slipped into the doorway and drew

[1] EDIFICE: large, impressive structure.

Juana after him. Outside, he could hear the squeal of children and the shouts of the neighbors, for his friends thought he might be inside the burning house.

The house of Juan Tomás was almost exactly like Kino's house; nearly all the brush houses were alike, and all leaked light and air, so that Juana and Kino, sitting in the corner of the brother's house, could see the leaping flames through the wall. They saw the flames tall and furious, they saw the roof fall and watched the fire die down as quickly as a twig fire dies. They heard the cries of warning of their friends, and the shrill, keening[1] cry of Apolonia, wife of Juan Tomás. She, being the nearest woman relative, raised a formal lament for the dead of the family.

Apolonia realized that she was wearing her second-best head shawl and she rushed to her house to get her fine new one. As she rummaged in a box by the wall, Kino's voice said quietly, "Apolonia, do not cry out. We are not hurt."

"How do you come here?" she demanded.

"Do not question," he said. "Go now to Juan Tomás and bring him here and tell no one else. This is important to us, Apolonia."

She paused, her hands helpless in front of her, and then, "Yes, my brother-in-law," she said.

In a few moments Juan Tomás came back with her. He lighted a candle and came to them where they crouched in a corner and he said, "Apolonia, see to the door, and do not let anyone enter." He was older, Juan Tomás, and he assumed the authority. "Now, my brother," he said.

"I was attacked in the dark," said Kino. "And in the fight I have killed a man."

"Who?" asked Juan Tomás quickly.

[1] KEENING: wailing.

"I do not know. It is all darkness—all darkness and shape of darkness."

"It is the pearl," said Juan Tomás. "There is a devil in this pearl. You should have sold it and passed on the devil. Perhaps you can still sell it and buy peace for yourself."

And Kino said, "Oh, my brother, an insult has been put on me that is deeper than my life. For on the beach my canoe is broken, my house is burned, and in the brush a dead man lies. Every escape is cut off. You must hide us, my brother."

And Kino, looking closely, saw deep worry come into his brother's eyes and he forestalled[2] him in a possible refusal. "Not for long," he said quickly. "Only until a day has passed and the new night has come. Then we will go."

"I will hide you," said Juan Tomás.

"I do not want to bring danger to you," Kino said. "I know I am like a leprosy. I will go tonight and then you will be safe."

"I will protect you," said Juan Tomás, and he called, "Apolonia, close up the door. Do not even whisper that Kino is here."

They sat silently all day in the darkness of the house, and they could hear the neighbors speaking of them. Through the walls of the house they could watch their neighbors raking the ashes to find the bones. Crouching in the house of Juan Tomás, they heard the shock go into their neighbors' minds at the news of the broken boat. Juan Tomás went out among the neighbors to divert their suspicions, and he gave them theories and ideas of what had happened to Kino and to Juana and to the baby. To one he said, "I think they have gone south along the coast to escape the evil that was on them." And to another, "Kino would

[2] FORESTALLED: prevented by delaying.

never leave the sea. Perhaps he found another boat." And he said, "Apolonia is ill with grief."

And in that day the wind rose up to beat the Gulf and tore the kelps[1] and weeds that lined the shore, and the wind cried through the brush houses and no boat was safe on the water. Then Juan Tomás told among the neighbors, "Kino is gone. If he went to the sea, he is drowned by now." And after each trip among the neighbors Juan Tomás came back with something borrowed. He brought a little woven straw bag of red beans and a gourd full of rice. He borrowed a cup of dried peppers and a block of salt, and he brought in a long working knife, eighteen inches long and heavy, as a small ax, a tool and a weapon. And when Kino saw this knife his eyes lighted up, and he fondled the blade and his thumb tested the edge.

The wind screamed over the Gulf and turned the water white, and the mangroves plunged like frightened cattle, and a fine sandy dust arose from the land and hung in a stifling cloud over the sea. The wind drove off the clouds and skimmed the sky clean and drifted the sand of the country like snow.

Then Juan Tomás, when the evening approached, talked long with his brother.

[1] KELPS: seaweed.

"Where will you go?"

"To the north," said Kino. "I have heard that there are cities in the north."

"Avoid the shore," said Juan Tomás. "They are making a party to search the shore. The men in the city will look for you. Do you still have the pearl?"

"I have it," said Kino. "And I will keep it. I might have given it as a gift, but now it is my misfortune and my life and I will keep it." His eyes were hard and cruel and bitter.

Coyotito whimpered and Juana muttered little magics over him to make him silent.

"The wind is good," said Juan Tomás. "There will be no tracks."

They left quietly in the dark before the moon had risen. The family stood formally in the house of Juan Tomás. Juana carried Coyotito on her back, covered and held in by her head shawl, and the baby slept, cheek turned sideways against her shoulder. The head shawl covered the baby, and one end of it came across Juana's nose to protect her from the evil night air. Juan Tomás embraced his brother with the double embrace and kissed him on both cheeks. "Go with God," he said, and it was like a death. "You will not give up the pearl?"

"This pearl has become my soul," said Kino. "If I give it up I shall lose my soul. Go thou also with God."

FOR DISCUSSION

1. At the end of chapter four, Kino says, "I am a man." What do these words mean to Kino? Juana reflects on these words after Kino attacks her; what do they mean to her?

2. Kino finally realizes what the pearl is doing to him and refers to it as his "misfortune."

Then he says, "This pearl has become my soul. If I give it up I shall lose my soul." What does he mean? Are the two evaluations of the pearl contradictory? Explain your answer.

3. When Kino discovers the destruction of his boat, the transformation of his character is complete. What role is he forced to adopt?

Find examples of foreshadowing by which the author has suggested that this would occur. Review the story up to this point; at what times is Kino compared to an animal? What does this suggest?

CHAPTER 6

The wind blew fierce and strong, and it pelted them with bits of sticks, sand, and little rocks. Juana and Kino gathered their clothing tighter about them and covered their noses and went out into the world. The sky was brushed clean by the wind and the stars were cold in a black sky. The two walked carefully, and they avoided the center of town where some sleeper in a doorway might see them pass. For the town closed itself in against the night, and anyone who moved about in the darkness would be noticeable. Kino threaded his way around the edge of the city and turned north, north by the stars, and found the rutted sandy road that led through the brushy country toward Loreto where the miraculous Virgin has her station.[1]

Kino could feel the blown sand against his ankles and he was glad, for he knew there would be no tracks. The little light from the stars made out for him the narrow road through the brushy country. And Kino could hear the pad of Juana's feet behind him. He went quickly and quietly, and Juana trotted behind him to keep up.

Some ancient thing stirred in Kino. Through his fear of dark and the devils that haunt the night, there came a rush of exhilaration; some animal thing was moving in him so that he was cautious and wary and dangerous; some ancient thing out of the past of his people was alive in

[1] STATION: shrine.

him. The wind was at his back and the stars guided him. The wind cried and whisked in the brush, and the family went on monotonously, hour after hour. They passed no one and saw no one. At last, to their right, the waning moon arose, and when it came up the wind died down, and the land was still.

Now they could see the little road ahead of them, deep cut with sand-drifted wheel tracks. With the wind gone there would be footprints, but they were a good distance from the town and perhaps their tracks might not be noticed. Kino walked carefully in a wheel rut, and Juana followed in his path. One big cart, going to the town in the morning, could wipe out every trace of their passage.

All night they walked and never changed their pace. Once Coyotito awakened, and Juana shifted him in front of her and soothed him until he went to sleep again. And the evils of the night were about them. The coyotes cried and laughed in the brush, and the owls screeched and hissed over their heads. And once some large animal lumbered away, crackling the undergrowth as it went. And Kino gripped the handle of the big working knife and took a sense of protection from it.

The music of the pearl was triumphant in Kino's head, and the quiet melody of the family underlay it, and they wove themselves into the soft padding of sandaled

feet in the dusk. All night they walked, and in the first dawn Kino searched the roadside for a covert to lie in during the day. He found his place near to the road, a little clearing where deer might have lain, and it was curtained thickly with the dry brittle trees that lined the road. And when Juana had seated herself and had settled to nurse the baby, Kino went back to the road. He broke a branch and carefully swept the footprints where they had turned from the roadway. And then, in the first light, he heard the creak of a wagon, and he crouched beside the road and watched a heavy two-wheeled cart go by, drawn by slouching oxen. And when it had passed out of sight, he went back to the roadway and looked at the rut and found that the footprints were gone. And again he swept out his traces and went back to Juana.

She gave him the soft corncakes Apolonia had packed for them, and after a while she slept a little. But Kino sat on the ground and stared at the earth in front of him. He watched the ants moving, a little column of them near to his foot, and he put his foot in their path. Then the column climbed over his instep and continued on its way, and Kino left his foot there and watched them move over it.

The sun arose hotly. They were not near the Gulf now, and the air was dry and hot so that the brush cricked with heat and a good resinous smell came from it. And when Juana awakened, when the sun was high, Kino told her things she knew already.

"Beware of that kind of tree there," he said, pointing. "Do not touch it, for if you do and then touch your eyes, it will blind you. And beware of the tree that bleeds. See, that one over there. For if you break

it the red blood will flow from it, and it is evil luck." And she nodded and smiled a little at him, for she knew these things.

"Will they follow us?" she asked. "Do you think they will try to find us?"

"They will try," said Kino. "Whoever finds us will take the pearl. Oh, they will try."

And Juana said, "Perhaps the dealers were right and the pearl has no value. Perhaps this has all been an illusion."

Kino reached into his clothes and brought out the pearl. He let the sun play on it until it burned in his eyes. "No," he said, "they would not have tried to steal it if it had been valueless."

"Do you know who attacked you? Was it the dealers?"

"I do not know," he said. "I didn't see them."

He looked into his pearl to find his vision. "When we sell it at last, I will have a rifle," he said, and he looked into the shining surface for his rifle, but he saw only a huddled dark body on the ground with shining blood dripping from its throat. And he said quickly, "We will be married in a great church." And in the pearl he saw Juana with her beaten face crawling home through the night. "Our son must learn to read," he said frantically. And there in the pearl Coyotito's face, thick and feverish from the medicine.

And Kino thrust the pearl back into his clothing, and the music of the pearl had become sinister in his ears and it was interwoven with the music of evil.

The hot sun beat on the earth so that Kino and Juana moved into the lacy shade of the brush, and small gray birds scampered on the ground in the shade. In the heat of the day Kino relaxed and covered his eyes with his hat and wrapped his blanket about his face to keep the flies off, and he slept.

But Juana did not sleep. She sat quiet as a stone and her face was quiet. Her mouth was still swollen where Kino had struck her, and big flies buzzed around the cut on her chin. But she sat as still as a sentinel, and when Coyotito awakened she placed him on the ground in front of her and watched him wave his arms and kick his feet, and he smiled and gurgled at her until she smiled too. She picked up a little twig from the ground and tickled him, and she gave him water from the gourd she carried in her bundle.

Kino stirred in a dream, and he cried out in a guttural[1] voice, and his hand moved in symbolic fighting. And then he moaned and sat up suddenly, his eyes wide and his nostrils flaring. He listened and heard only the cricking heat and the hiss of distance.

"What is it?" Juana asked.

"Hush," he said.

"You were dreaming."

"Perhaps." But he was restless, and when she gave him a corncake from her store he paused in his chewing to listen. He was uneasy and nervous; he glanced over his shoulder; he lifted the big knife and felt its edge. When Coyotito gurgled on the ground Kino said, "Keep him quiet."

"What is the matter?" Juana asked.

"I don't know."

He listened again, an animal light in his eyes. He stood up then, silently; and crouched low, he threaded his way through the brush toward the road. But he did not step into the road; he crept into the cover of a thorny tree and peered out along the way he had come.

And then he saw them moving along. His body stiffened and he drew down his head and peeked out from under a fallen branch. In the distance he could see three figures, two on foot and one on horseback. But he knew what they were, and a chill of fear went through him. Even in the distance he could see the two on foot moving slowly along, bent low to the ground. Here, one would pause and look at the earth, while the other joined him. They were the trackers, they could follow the trail of a bighorn sheep in the stone mountains. They were as sensitive as hounds. Here, he and Juana might have stepped out of the wheel rut, and these people from the inland, these hunters, could follow, could read a broken straw or a little tumbled pile of dust. Behind them, on a horse, was a dark man, his nose covered with a blanket, and across his saddle a rifle gleamed in the sun.

Kino lay as rigid as the tree limb. He barely breathed, and his eyes went to the place where he had swept out the track. Even the sweeping might be a message to the trackers. He knew these inland hunters. In a country where there is little game they managed to live because of their ability to hunt, and they were hunting him. They scuttled over the ground like animals and found a sign and crouched over it while the horseman waited.

The trackers whined a little, like excited dogs on a warming trail. Kino slowly drew his big knife to his hand and made it ready. He knew what he must do. If the trackers found the swept place, he must leap for the horseman, kill him quickly and take the rifle. That was his only chance in the world.

---

[1] GUTTURAL: deep-throated.

And as the three drew nearer on the road, Kino dug little pits with his sandaled toes so that he could leap without warning, so that his feet would not slip. He had only a little vision under the fallen limb.

Now Juana, back in her hidden place, heard the pad of the horse's hoofs, and Coyotito gurgled. She took him up quickly and put him under her shawl and gave him her breast and he was silent.

When the trackers came near, Kino could see only their legs and only the legs of the horse from under the fallen branch. He saw the dark horny feet of the men and their ragged white clothes, and he heard the creak of leather of the saddle and the clink of spurs. The trackers stopped at the swept place and studied it, and the horseman stopped. The horse flung his head up against the bit and the bit-roller clicked under his tongue and the horse snorted. Then the dark trackers turned and studied the horse and watched his ears.

Kino was not breathing, but his back arched a little and the muscles of his arms and legs stood out with tension and a line of sweat formed on his upper lip. For a long moment the trackers bent over the road, and then they moved on slowly, studying the ground ahead of them, and the horseman moved after them. The trackers scuttled along, stopping, looking, and hurrying on. They would be back, Kino knew. They would be circling and searching, peeping, stooping, and they would come back sooner or later to his covered track.

He slid backward and did not bother to cover his tracks. He could not; too many little signs were there, too many broken twigs and scuffed places and displaced stones. And there was a panic in Kino now, a panic of flight. The trackers would find his trail, he knew it. There was no escape, except in flight. He edged away from the road and went quickly and silently to the hidden place where Juana was. She looked up at him in question.

"Trackers," he said. "Come!"

And then a helplessness and a hopelessness swept over him, and his face went black and his eyes were sad. "Perhaps I should let them take me."

Instantly Juana was on her feet and her hand lay on his arm. "You have the pearl," she cried hoarsely. "Do you think they would take you back alive to say they had stolen it?"

His hand strayed limply to the place where the pearl was hidden under his clothes. "They will find it," he said weakly.

"Come," she said. "Come!"

And when he did not respond, "Do you think they would let me live? Do you think they would let the little one here live?"

Her goading struck into his brain; his lips snarled and his eyes were fierce again. "Come," he said. "We will go into the mountains. Maybe we can lose them in the mountains."

Frantically he gathered the gourds and the little bags that were their property. Kino carried a bundle in his left hand, but the big knife swung free in his right hand. He parted the brush for Juana and they hurried to the west, toward the high stone mountains. They trotted quickly through the tangle of the undergrowth. This was panic flight. Kino did not try to conceal his passages; he trotted, kicking the stones, knocking the telltale leaves from the little trees. The high sun streamed down on the

Continued on page 353

IDEAS AND THE ARTS

Conflict is a universal part of human experience. It is always present, even in the most casual and relaxed human situations. To get along with other people, we must conceal conflict. But when it appears in games, sports, and art, we can both acknowledge it and enjoy it.

The first painting in this group, *The Hippopotamus Hunt* by Peter Paul Rubens, presents a double conflict. Its subject is hunting, and hunting offers an enjoyable form of the conflict with nature. But there is another kind of conflict here that is not so obvious. It is social conflict. The men on horseback are masters; the men on the ground are servants, or perhaps slaves. In hunting it is exciting to take risks, but it is more comfortable, and often just as exciting, if someone else can be hired or owned to take the risks for you. One man, an archer, is already dead or mortally wounded. The other, with a knife, is half crushed by the crocodile. He is frightened and perhaps dying. The masters are enjoying the conflict as they close in for the kill.

Although European painters have painted thousands of battle scenes, Paolo Uccello's *The Battle of San Romano* is one of the great battle scenes in European art. Uccello was fascinated by perspective, the techniques of giving depth to figures painted on a flat surface. He was delighted to have the opportunity to paint foreshortened figures, such as the man in the left foreground, the black horse on the right, and the many broken spears. The battle itself was so unimportant that few historians know or care about it. It was important, however, to the people who fought in it and to their descendants. It was probably at their request that Uccello

painted this memorial picture of the battle. Bloody as they were, medieval battles were almost enjoyable, compared to those of later times. They were much closer to sporting events, providing more conflict than destruction. One reason the nobles of Europe loved to hunt was that hunting provided training for their battles.

The third painting is from an Indian manuscript. It shows the great emperor Akbar watching an armed conflict of religious ascetics. Akbar, who ruled in India in the sixteenth century, was a noble, just, and peace-loving monarch. Few monarchs of any land have been so admirable. An ascetic is a religious or "holy" man who has given up all worldly pleasures to devote himself to religious meditation. Here, however, two groups of ascetics have started a terrible hand-to-hand fight over some religious principle. Akbar, mounted on his horse, has stopped on a hillside. The people of the community have knelt before him, perhaps appealing for his aid in stopping the fight. This painting tells us that conflict is present even in deeply religious men.

The next picture, *The Triumph of Death* by Pieter Bruegel, is very grim indeed. The conflict of man with death, which cannot be avoided, is the basic human conflict. Unless man keeps up that struggle, no other conflict can exist. In this picture Bruegel has imagined innumerable kinds of death. The armies of death are drawn up at the right, ready for action. Many of the forces of death are already at work. At the upper left two are ringing the funeral bell. In the distance are fires. At the right, still-living human beings are driven into a vast coffin. At the left, a cart and a horse are collecting those dead from the plague. The strange wheels on poles are a means of execution. Criminals are tied to these wheels and exposed to the elements. Bruegel uses every means he can imagine to support the title of his painting.

The last two pictures present psychological conflict. This is the kind of conflict a person feels within himself. Francisco de Goya's *The Colossus,* or *Panic,* shows people in flight from a terrible monster who has appeared above the mountains in the sky. But this is not a real monster. It is what is called a ''projection'' of the people's own fears. When someone feels a conflict within himself, he often believes that the source of that conflict is something outside himself. This painting shows how many people interpret inner conflicts.

Salvador Dali's *Soft Construction with Boiled Beans: Premonition of Civil War* presents a psychological conflict that is fully experienced as internal. Dali gives us a dramatic portrayal of a man tearing himself apart. Or is it two men? If it is two, neither is complete. They are both parts of one, just as civil war (indicated in the title) tears one country into two parts. The reference in the title to boiled beans is puzzling until we realize that the landscape is Spanish, that the civil war is the Spanish Civil War of the 1930's, and that beans are a staple of the Spanish diet. Food which gives life is ignored in this conflict which brings death.

Morse Peckham

PETER PAUL RUBENS (1577-1640) *THE HIPPOPOTAMUS HUNT*. Alte Pinakothek. Munich.

PAOLO UCCELLO (1397-1475) *THE BATTLE OF SAN ROMANO.* National Gallery, London.

BASĀWAN (16th century) *AKBAR PRESENT AT AN ARMED COMBAT OF CONTENDING ASCETICS,* from a manuscript of the *AKBAR-NĀMA.* Victoria and Albert Museum, London.

PIETER BRUEGEL THE ELDER (c. 1525-1569) *THE TRIUMPH OF DEATH.* Prado Museum, Madrid.

FRANCISCO DE GOYA (1746-1828) *THE COLOSSUS OR PANIC*. Prado Museum, Madrid.

SALVADOR DALI (born 1904) *SOFT CONSTRUCTION WITH BOILED BEANS: PREMONITION OF CIVIL WAR.*   Philadelphia Museum of Art.

dry creaking earth so that even vegetation ticked in protest. But ahead were the naked granite mountains, rising out of erosion rubble and standing monolithic[1] against the sky. And Kino ran for the high place, as nearly all animals do when they are pursued.

This land was waterless, furred with the cacti which could store water and with the great-rooted brush which could reach deep into the earth for a little moisture and get along on very little. And underfoot was not soil but broken rock, split into small cubes, great slabs, but none of it water-rounded. Little tufts of sad dry grass grew between the stones, grass that had sprouted with one single rain and headed, dropped its seed, and died. Horned toads watched the family go by and turned their little pivoting dragon heads. And now and then a great jackrabbit, disturbed in his shade, bumped away and hid behind the nearest rock. The singing heat lay over this desert country, and ahead the stone mountains looked cool and welcoming.

And Kino fled. He knew what would happen. A little way along the road the trackers would become aware that they had missed the path, and they would come back, searching and judging, and in a little while they would find the place where Kino and Juana had rested. From there it would be easy for them—these little stones, the fallen leaves and the whipped branches, the scuffed places where a foot had slipped. Kino could see them in his mind, slipping along the track, whining a little with eagerness, and behind them, dark and half disinterested, the horseman with the rifle. His work would come last, for he would not take them back. Oh, the music of evil sang loud in Kino's head now, it sang with the whine of heat and with the dry ringing of snake rattles. It was not large and overwhelming now, but secret and poisonous, and the pounding of his heart gave it undertone and rhythm.

The way began to rise, and as it did the rocks grew larger. But now Kino had put a little distance between his family and the trackers. Now, on the first rise, he rested. He climbed a great boulder and looked back over the shimmering country, but he could not see his enemies, not even the tall horseman riding through the brush. Juana had squatted in the shade of the boulder. She raised her bottle of water to Coyotito's lips; his little dried tongue sucked greedily at it. She looked up at Kino when he came back; she saw him examine her ankles, cut and scratched from the stones and brush, and she covered them quickly with her skirt. Then she handed the bottle to him, but he shook his head. Her eyes were bright in her tired face. Kino moistened his cracked lips with his tongue.

"Juana," he said, "I will go on and you will hide. I will lead them into the mountains, and when they have gone past, you will go north to Loreto or to Santa Rosalia. Then, if I can escape them, I will come to you. It is the only safe way."

She looked full into his eyes for a moment. "No," she said. "We go with you."

"I can go faster alone," he said harshly. "You will put the little one in more danger if you go with me."

"No," said Juana.

"You must. It is the wise thing and it is my wish," he said.

"No," said Juana.

He looked then for weakness in her face, for fear or irresolution, and there was none. Her eyes were very bright. He shrugged his shoulders helplessly then, but he had taken

[1] MONOLITHIC: massive and solid.

strength from her. When they moved on it was no longer panic flight.

The country, as it rose toward the mountains, changed rapidly. Now there were long outcroppings of granite with deep crevices between, and Kino walked on bare unmarkable stone when he could and leaped from ledge to ledge. He knew that wherever the trackers lost his path they must circle and lose time before they found it again. And so he did not go straight for the mountains any more; he moved in zigzags, and sometimes he cut back to the south and left a sign and then went toward the mountains over bare stone again. And the path rose steeply now, so that he panted a little as he went.

The sun moved downward toward the bare stone teeth of the mountains, and Kino set his direction for a dark and shadowy cleft in the range. If there were any water at all, it would be there where he could see, even in the distance, a hint of foliage. And if there were any passage through the smooth stone range, it would be by this same deep cleft. It had its danger, for the trackers would think of it too, but the empty water bottle did not let that consideration enter. And as the sun lowered, Kino and Juana struggled wearily up the steep slope toward the cleft.

High in the gray stone mountains, under a frowning peak, a little spring bubbled out of a rupture in the stone. It was fed by shade-preserved snow in the summer, and now and then it died completely and bare rocks and dry algae were on its bottom. But nearly always it gushed out, cold and clean and lovely. In the times when the quick rains fell, it might become a freshet[1] and

[1] FRESHET: stream of fresh water emptying into a body of salt water.

send its column of white water crashing down the mountain cleft, but nearly always it was a lean little spring. It bubbled out into a pool and then fell a hundred feet to another pool, and this one, overflowing, dropped again, so that it continued, down and down, until it came to the rubble of the upland, and there it disappeared altogether. There wasn't much left of it then anyway, for every time it fell over an escarpment the thirsty air drank it, and it splashed from the pools to the dry vegetation. The animals from miles around came to drink from the little pools, and the wild sheep and the deer, the pumas and raccoons, and the mice—all came to drink. And the birds which spent the day in the brushland came at night to the little pools that were like steps in the mountain cleft. Beside this tiny stream, wherever enough earth collected for root-hold, colonies of plants grew, wild grape and little palms, maidenhair fern, hibiscus, and tall pampas grass with feathery rods raised above the spike leaves. And in the pool lived frogs and water skaters, and waterworms crawled on the bottom of the pool. Everything that loved water came to these few shallow places. The cats took their prey there, and strewed feathers and lapped water through their bloody teeth. The little pools were places of life because of the water, and places of killing because of the water, too.

The lowest step, where the stream collected before it tumbled down a hundred feet and disappeared into the rubbly desert, was a little platform of stone and sand. Only a pencil of water fell into the pool, but it was enough to keep the pool full and to keep the ferns green in the underhang of the cliff, and wild grape climbed the stone mountain and all manner of little plants found comfort here. The freshets had made a small sandy beach through which the pool flowed, and bright green watercress grew in the damp sand. The beach was cut and scarred and padded by the feet of animals that had come to drink and to hunt.

The sun had passed over the stone mountains when Kino and Juana struggled up to the steep broken slope and came at last to the water. From this step they could look out over the sunbeaten desert to the blue Gulf in the distance. They came utterly weary to the pool, and Juana slumped to her knees and first washed Coyotito's face and then filled her bottle and gave him a drink. And the baby was weary and petulant,[1] and he cried softly until Juana gave him her breast, and then he gurgled and clucked against her. Kino drank long and thirstily at the pool. For a moment, then, he stretched out beside the water and relaxed all his muscles and watched Juana feeding the baby, and then he got to his feet and went to the edge of the step where the water slipped over, and he searched the distance carefully. His eyes set on a point and he became rigid. Far down the slope he could see the two trackers; they were little more than dots or scurrying ants and behind them a larger ant.

Juana had turned to look at him and she saw his back stiffen.

"How far?" she asked quietly.

"They will be here by evening," said Kino. He looked up the long steep chimney of the cleft where the water came down. "We must go west," he said, and his eyes searched the stone shoulder behind the cleft. And thirty feet up on the gray

[1] PETULANT: cranky.

shoulder he saw a series of little erosion caves. He slipped off his sandals and clambered up to them, gripping the bare stone with his toes, and he looked into the shallow caves. They were only a few feet deep, wind-hollowed scoops, but they sloped slightly downward and back. Kino crawled into the largest one and lay down and knew that he could not be seen from the outside. Quickly he went back to Juana.

"You must go up there. Perhaps they will not find us there," he said.

Without question she filled her water bottle to the top, and then Kino helped her up to the shallow cave and brought up the packages of food and passed them to her. And Juana sat in the cave entrance and watched him. She saw that he did not try to erase their tracks in the sand. Instead, he climbed up the brush cliff beside the water, clawing and tearing at the ferns and wild grape as he went. And when he had climbed a hundred feet to the next bench, he came down again. He looked carefully at the smooth rock shoulder toward the cave to see that there was no trace of passage, and last he climbed up and crept into the cave beside Juana.

"When they go up," he said, "we will slip away, down to the lowlands again. I am afraid only that the baby may cry. You must see that he does not cry."

"He will not cry," she said, and she raised the baby's face to her own and looked into his eyes and he stared solemnly back at her.

"He knows," said Juana.

Now Kino lay in the cave entrance, his chin braced on his crossed arms, and he watched the blue shadow of the mountain move out across the brushy desert below until it reached the Gulf, and the long twilight of the shadow was over the land.

The trackers were long in coming, as though they had trouble with the trail Kino had left. It was dusk when they came at last to the little pool. And all three were on foot now, for a horse could not climb the last steep slope. From above they were thin figures in the evening. The two trackers scurried about on the little beach, and they saw Kino's progress up the cliff before they drank. The man with the rifle sat down and rested himself, and the trackers squatted near him, and in the evening the points of their cigarettes glowed and receded. And then Kino could see that they were eating, and the soft murmur of their voices came to him.

Then darkness fell, deep and black in the mountain cleft. The animals that used the pool came near and smelled men there and drifted away again into the darkness.

He heard a murmur behind him. Juana was whispering, "Coyotito." She was begging him to be quiet. Kino heard the baby whimper, and he knew from the muffled sounds that Juana had covered his head with her shawl.

Down on the beach a match flared, and in its momentary light Kino saw that two of the men were sleeping, curled up like dogs, while the third watched, and he saw the glint of the rifle in the match light. And then the match died, but it left a picture on Kino's eyes. He could see it, just how each man was, two sleeping curled and the third squatting in the sand with the rifle between his knees.

Kino moved silently back into the cave. Juana's eyes were two sparks reflecting a low star. Kino crawled quietly close to her and he put his lips near to her cheek.

"There is a way," he said.

"But they will kill you."

"If I get first to the one with the rifle," Kino said, "I must get to him first, then I will be all right. Two are sleeping."

Her hand crept out from under her shawl and gripped his arm. "They will see your white clothes in the starlight."

"No," he said. "And I must go before moonrise."

He searched for a soft word and then gave it up. "If they kill me," he said, "lie quietly. And when they are gone away, go to Loreto."

Her hand shook a little, holding his wrist.

"There is no choice," he said. "It is the only way. They will find us in the morning."

Her voice trembled a little. "Go with God," she said.

He peered closely at her and he could see her large eyes. His hand fumbled out and found the baby, and for a moment his palm lay on Coyotito's head. And then Kino raised his hand and touched Juana's cheek, and she held her breath.

Against the sky in the cave entrance Juana could see that Kino was taking off his white clothes, for dirty and ragged though they were they would show up against the dark night. His own brown skin was a better protection for him. And then she saw how he hooked his amulet[1] neck-string about the horn handle of his great knife, so that it hung down in front of him and left both hands free. He did not come back to her. For a moment his body was black in the cave entrance, crouched and slient, and then he was gone.

Juana moved to the entrance and looked

[1] AMULET: object worn as a charm against injury or evil.

out. She peered like an owl from the hole in the mountain, and the baby slept under the blanket on her back, his face turned sideways against her neck and shoulders. She could feel his warm breath against her skin, and Juana whispered her combination of prayer and magic, her Hail Marys and her ancient intercession,[1] against the black unhuman things.

The night seemed a little less dark when she looked out, and to the east there was a lightening in the sky, down near the horizon where the moon would show. And, looking down, she could see the cigarette of the man on watch.

Kino edged like a slow lizard down the smooth rock shoulder. He had turned his neck-string so that the great knife hung down from his back and could not clash against the stone. His spread fingers gripped the mountain, and his bare toes found support through contact, and even his chest lay against the stone so that he would not slip. For any sound, a rolling pebble or a sigh, a little slip of flesh on rock, would rouse the watchers below. Any sound that was not germane[2] to the night would make them alert. But the night was not silent; the little tree frogs that lived near the stream twittered like birds, and the high metallic ringing of the cicadas[3] filled the mountain cleft. And Kino's own music was in his head, the music of the enemy, low and pulsing, nearly asleep. But the Song of the Family had become as fierce and sharp and feline[4] as the snarl of a female puma.[5] The family song was alive now and driving

him down on the dark enemy. The harsh cicada seemed to take up its melody, and the twittering tree frogs called little phrases of it.

And Kino crept silently as a shadow down the smooth mountain face. One bare foot moved a few inches and the toes touched the stone and gripped, and the other foot a few inches, and then the palm of one hand a little downward, and then the other hand, until the whole body, without seeming to move, had moved. Kino's mouth was open so that even his breath would make no sound, for he knew that he was not invisible. If the watcher, sensing movement, looked at the dark place against the stone which was his body, he could see him. Kino must move so slowly he would not draw the watcher's eyes. It took him a long time to reach the bottom and to crouch behind the little dwarf palm. His heart thundered in his chest and his hands and face were wet with sweat. He crouched and took slow long breaths to calm himself.

Only twenty feet separated him from the enemy now, and he tried to remember the ground between. Was there any stone which might trip him in his rush? He kneaded his legs against cramp and found that his muscles were jerking after their long tension. And then he looked apprehensively to the east. The moon would rise in a few moments now, and he must attack before it rose. He could see the outline of the watcher, but the sleeping men were below his vision. It was the watcher Kino must find—must find quickly and without hesitation. Silently he drew the amulet string over his shoulder and loosened the loop from the horn handle of his great knife.

[1] INTERCESSION: prayer that others be spared.
[2] GERMANE: naturally related.
[3] CICADAS: cricket-like insects.
[4] FELINE: cat-like.
[5] PUMA: mountain lion.

He was too late, for as he rose from his crouch the silver edge of the moon slipped above the eastern horizon, and Kino sank back behind his bush.

It was an old and ragged moon, but it threw hard light and hard shadow into the mountain cleft, and now Kino could see the seated figure of the watcher on the little beach beside the pool. The watcher gazed full at the moon, and then he lighted another cigarette, and the match illumined his dark face for a moment. There could be no waiting now; when the watcher turned his head, Kino must leap. His legs were as tight as wound springs.

And then from above came a little murmuring cry. The watcher turned his head to listen and then he stood up, and one of the sleepers stirred on the ground and awakened and asked quietly, "What is it?"

"I don't know," said the watcher. "It sounded like a cry, almost like a human —like a baby."

The man who had been sleeping said, "You can't tell. Some coyote bitch with a litter. I've heard a coyote pup cry like a baby."

The sweat rolled in drops down Kino's forehead and fell into his eyes and burned them. The little cry came again and the watcher looked up the side of the hill to the dark cave.

"Coyote maybe," he said, and Kino heard the harsh click as he cocked the rifle.

"If it's a coyote, this will stop it," the watcher said as he raised the gun.

Kino was in mid-leap when the gun crashed and the barrel-flash made a picture on his eyes. The great knife swung and crunched hollowly. It bit through neck and deep into chest, and Kino was a terrible machine now. He grasped the rifle even as he wrenched free his knife. His strength and his movement and his speed were a machine. He whirled and struck the head of the seated man like a melon. The third man scrabbled away like a crab, slipped into the pool, and then he began to climb frantically, to climb up the cliff where the water penciled down. His hands and feet threshed in the tangle of the wild grapevine, and he whimpered and gibbered as he tried to get up. But Kino had become as cold and deadly as steel. Deliberately he threw the lever of the rifle, and then he raised the gun and aimed deliberately and fired. He saw his enemy tumble backward into the pool, and Kino strode to the water. In the moonlight he could see the frantic frightened eyes, and Kino aimed and fired between the eyes.

And then Kino stood uncertainly. Something was wrong, some signal was trying to get through to his brain. Tree frogs and cicadas were silent now. And then Kino's brain cleared from its red concentration and he knew the sound—the keening, moaning, rising hysterical cry from the little cave in the side of the stone mountain, the cry of death.

Everyone in La Paz remembers the return of the family; there may be some old ones who saw it, but those whose fathers and whose grandfathers told it to them remember it nevertheless. It is an event that happened to everyone.

It was late in the golden afternoon when the first little boys ran hysterically in the town and spread the word that Kino and Juana were coming back. And everyone hurried to see them. The sun was settling toward the western mountains and the shadows on the ground were long. And

perhaps that was what left the deep impression on those who saw them.

The two came from the rutted country road into the city, and they were not walking in single file, Kino ahead and Juana behind, as usual, but side by side. The sun was behind them and their long shadows stalked ahead, and they seemed to carry two towers of darkness with them. Kino had a rifle across his arm and Juana carried her shawl like a sack over her shoulder. And in it was a small limp heavy bundle. The shawl was crusted with dried blood, and the bundle swayed a little as she walked. Her face was hard and lined and leathery with fatigue and with the tightness with which she fought fatigue. And her wide eyes stared inward on herself. She was as remote and as removed as Heaven. Kino's lips were thin and his jaws tight, and the people say that he carried fear with him, that he was as dangerous as a rising storm. The people say that the two seemed to be removed from human experience; that they had gone through pain and had come out on the other side; that there was almost a magical protection about them. And those people who had rushed to see them crowded back and let them pass and did not speak to them.

Kino and Juana walked through the city as though it were not there. Their eyes glanced neither right nor left nor up nor down, but stared only straight ahead. Their legs moved a little jerkily, like well-made wooden dolls, and they carried pillars of black fear about them. And as they walked through the stone and plaster city brokers peered at them from barred windows and servants put one eye to a slitted gate and mothers turned the faces of their youngest children inward against their skirts. Kino

and Juana strode side by side through the stone and plaster city and down among the brush houses, and the neighbors stood back and let them pass. Juan Tomás raised his hand in greeting and did not say the greeting and left his hand in the air for a moment uncertainly.

In Kino's ears the Song of the Family was as fierce as a cry. He was immune and terrible, and his song had become a battle cry. They trudged past the burned square where their house had been without even looking at it. They cleared the brush that edged the beach and picked their way down the shore toward the water. And they did not look toward Kino's broken canoe.

And when they came to the water's edge they stopped and stared out over the Gulf. And then Kino laid the rifle down, and he dug among his clothes, and then he held the great pearl in his hand. He looked into its surface and it was gray and ulcerous. Evil faces peered from it into his eyes, and he saw the light of burning. And in the surface of the pearl he saw the frantic eyes of the man in the pool. And in the surface of the pearl he saw Coyotito lying in the little cave with the top of his head shot away. And the pearl was ugly; it was gray, like a malignant growth. And Kino heard the music of the pearl, distorted and insane. Kino's hand shook a little, and he turned slowly to Juana and held the pearl out to her. She stood beside him, still holding her dead bundle over her shoulder. She looked at the pearl in his hand for a moment and then she looked into Kino's eyes and said softly, "No, you."

And Kino drew back his arm and flung the pearl with all his might. Kino and Juana watched it go, winking and glimmering

under the setting sun. They saw the little splash in the distance, and they stood side by side watching the place for a long time.

And the pearl settled into the lovely green water and dropped toward the bottom. The waving branches of the algae called to it and beckoned to it. The lights on its surface were green and lovely. It settled down to the sand bottom among the fern-like plants. Above, the surface of the water was a green mirror. And the pearl lay on the floor of the sea. A crab scampering over the bottom raised a little cloud of sand, and when it settled the pearl was gone.

And the music of the pearl drifted to a whisper and disappeared.

FOR DISCUSSION

1. Upon their return Kino and Juana "were not walking in single file, Kino ahead and Juana behind, as usual, but side by side." Why?

2. Kino and Juana could have thrown the pearl away anywhere on their journey; why did they return to La Paz to throw the pearl into the ocean? What prompts Kino to offer the pearl to Juana to throw? Why does Juana refuse and tell Kino that he should be the one to do it? Why doesn't Kino just give the pearl to one of his neighbors instead of throwing it away?

3. The setting is important to the development of mood and action throughout this story. It also acts in several instances as foreshadowing. Reread the description of the mountain spring where the trackers and Coyotito are later killed. Do you find anything that foreshadows their deaths?

In Summary

FOR DISCUSSION

1. The theme of this unit is conflict. Conflict usually occurs in one of three areas in a novel: man against man, man against nature or natural forces, or man against himself. How many different kinds of conflict do you recognize in *The Pearl?*

2. In the preface to his novel, Steinbeck states, "And, as with all retold tales that are in people's hearts, there are only good and bad things and black and white things and good and evil things and no in-between anywhere." What evidence do you find that Steinbeck has followed this formula in portraying the characters and incidents in *The Pearl?* Where does he deviate from the formula? For example, are all the characters portrayed as either good or bad or are some "in-between"?

3. Throughout the novel, Steinbeck describes the pearl as a mirror or reflector of images— that is, people seem to see the things they dream of in the shiny surface of the pearl. Why do you imagine the author describes the pearl in this manner? Consider carefully the relationship this description suggests between the physical appearance of the pearl and its significance in the lives of the characters.

OTHER THINGS TO DO

1. Steinbeck calls his story a parable, explaining that "everyone takes his own meaning from it and reads his own life into it." In a well-organized essay explain what you think *The Pearl* means. Can you support your interpretation by referring to evidence in the novel? How does the meaning you have found apply to your own life?

2. Reference is made at several points in the story to the music of the pearl. Reread these passages, and look through your record collection to find passages of music that seem to be the kind of "mood music" the pearl is described as making at various points in the story. Have the class listen to the selections that various students have chosen, and comment on the differences and similarities in each individual's imaginative interpretation of the music Steinbeck describes.

The World of Words

THE PEARL

1. Each of the following words appears in *The Pearl: gulf, estuary, pool, spring,* and *freshet.* What do all five words have in common? How do they differ from each other? Are they synonyms? What is a *strait?* A *bay?* A *channel?* A *canal?*

2. The national language of Mexico, where *The Pearl* takes place, is Spanish. The influence of that language on our own culture has been strong ever since Spanish adventurers in the sixteenth century first explored the region that was to become the American Southwest. In addition to such Spanish-American words as *pulque, puma,* and *pampas,* all three of which appear in *The Pearl,* standard English contains many other words that were originally borrowed from the Spanish, or filtered through Spanish from early Indian languages spoken in the Western Hemisphere. What is a *pueblo*? A *mesa*? A *canyon*? A *patio*? The following American place names are all Spanish: *Los Angeles* (city of the angels), *Las Vegas* (the meadows), *Nevada* (snow-covered), *Colorado* (red), *Santa Fe* (holy faith), *San Francisco* (St. Francis), and *Arizona* (dry region). What other place names from Spanish do you find on a map of the United States? In what parts of the United States would you be most likely to find them?

Reader's Choice

The Call of the Wild, *by Jack London.*

Buck had to forget his domestic days on a California ranch, for now he was lead dog of a team in the Yukon, pulling provisions for the men of the Alaskan gold rush. As the whip stung his back, Buck grew in cunning and savagery. A primitive urge, as old as the first dog in the world, would drive him to answer the call of the wild—and his love for one man would call him back.

Captains Courageous, *by Rudyard Kipling.*

No one on a Gloucester fishing boat cares whether or not you are going to inherit thirty million dollars. Spoiled and sassy Harvey Cheyne finds this out the hard way. After being swept off a luxury liner bound for Europe, Harvey is saved by fishermen who insist that he earn his keep aboard ship. The stern sea and the men who live with it make a man out of a silly and swaggering boy.

The Good Earth, *by Pearl Buck.*

Through persistent labor and a bit of luck, a Chinese peasant rises slowly to become a wealthy landowner. Battling the forces of nature, fate, and his fellow man in the forms of drought, famine, and revolution, he works on to accumulate land and attain his dream.

The Hobbit, *by J. R. R. Tolkien.*

Bilbo Baggins is a hobbit, one of a race of small, round, furry-toed creatures who love comfort and homey pleasures more than anything else. But Gandalf the wizard sees the stuff of heroes in Bilbo, and sends him off on a grand adventure to befriend dwarfs and elves, battle a dragon, win magic treasure, and discover his own greatness in this classic fantasy tale.

Jane Eyre, *by Charlotte Bronte.*

Orphaned and unwanted in her relative's home, young Jane Eyre is sent off to a grim boarding school and later leaves to be a governess at mysterious Thornfield Hall. Her employer, Mr. Rochester, is deeply drawn to Jane, but there are things about himself and his unhappy home that he will not explain. What is the cause of the fire in Mr. Rochester's room? And why does eerie laughter echo down the halls? Fear leads to faith and mystery to romance in this exciting novel.

The Mysterious Island, *by Jules Verne.*

Perhaps the mysterious being who waited in the grotto could answer the questions of the shipwrecked crew. Who had provided the chest filled with tools? Who floated a message in the bottle? Who fired the gun? A group of men survive a Pacific storm and the collapse of their passenger balloon only to be marooned on a mysterious island where they must deal with these and other riddles.

Shane, *by Jack Schaefer.*

The summer of 1889 was a time of conflict

—often deadly conflict—in Wyoming as the cattlemen tried to force the homesteaders off the range. Not surprisingly, the appearance of a quiet, handsome stranger put the whole town on edge.

"There's something about him. Something under the gentleness . . . Something . . . ."

"Mysterious?"

"Yes, of course. Mysterious. But more than that. Dangerous."

In the days to follow, the townspeople found that they were right; Shane was a dangerous enemy. But to young Bob Starrett and his family, the lonely and haunted man proved himself to be a wonderful friend as well.

Travels with Charley, *by John Steinbeck.*

The author, winner of a Nobel Prize for his literature, sets off in a trailer-truck accompanied only by his pet poodle Charley to reexamine human nature and the land in which he has lived his life. From Long Island to Maine to California to Texas, Steinbeck travels and looks and talks with many sorts of people, and paints this appealing portrait of the people of America.

The Yearling, *by Marjorie Kinnan Rawlings.*

Jody Baxter, growing up in the backwoods during pioneer days, is kept busy with farmwork. Without brothers and sisters, Jody finds his only companionship in an orphan fawn which he raises as a pet. The young deer becomes a nuisance on the farm, and Jody's conflicting responsibilities force him to make a difficult decision.

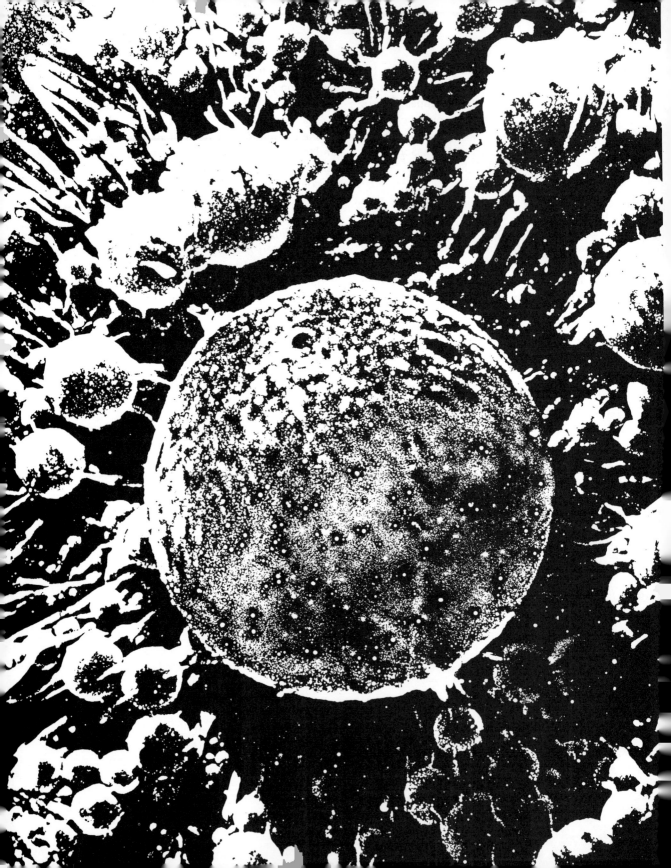

MANY TOMORROWS

JUST AS every day we live is destined to become the past, every tomorrow is destined to become the present. There will be a November 12, 1996, and a March 13, 1999, and a January 1, 2100. When that last-named day rolls around, will people still be putting on funny hats and singing *Auld Lang Syne* and generally whooping it up to usher the new year in? Or will that custom, familiar to us on New Year's Eve, have faded into oblivion, like forgotten customs that the ancient Egyptians faithfully observed and assumed were vital?

The present, of course, is made up of many todays. The day that lay before you as you woke this morning, somewhere in America, was different from the day of the Peruvian boy with his llamas to tend in the Andes, or the Japanese girl on her way to school in Tokyo, or the Laplander in the Arctic or the Bushman in Africa. And as there are many kinds of todays, there will be many tomorrows—some in cities, some in the country, some above ground, others perhaps underwater, some on this planet and no doubt others on extraterrestrial bodies like the moon.

"I have but one lamp by which my feet are guided," said Patrick Henry, "and that is the lamp of experience." To imagine the future, most of us can draw only on what we have already seen. Yet so radically different is the present—with computers, satellites, moon-landings, heart transplants—from anything that has gone before that it becomes increasingly difficult to imagine tomorrow on the basis of today.

The following selections probe what lies ahead of us from different angles, sometimes locating worlds of challenge, sometimes worlds of dread. But each of the futures here envisaged throws light back on the present, from which all of them will emerge.

Philip McFarland

Mr. Leonard Mead's favorite pastime was walking. But in the world of 2131 A.D. a harmless stroll could very quickly turn into a crisis.

THE PEDESTRIAN

RAY BRADBURY

TO ENTER out into that silence that was the city at eight o'clock of a misty evening in November, to put your feet upon that buckling[1] concrete walk, to step over grassy seams and make your way, hands in pockets, through the silences, that was what Mr. Leonard Mead most dearly loved to do. He would stand upon the corner of an intersection and peer down long moonlit avenues of sidewalk in four directions, deciding which way to go, but it really made no difference; he was alone in this world of A.D. 2131, or as good as alone; and with a final decision made, a path selected, he would stride off sending patterns of frosty air before him like the smoke of a cigar.

Sometimes he would walk for hours and miles and return only at midnight to his house. And on his way he would see the cottages and homes with their dark windows, and it was not unequal to walking through a graveyard, because only the faintest glimmers of firefly light appeared in flickers behind the windows. Sudden gray phantoms seemed to manifest[2] themselves upon inner room walls where a curtain was still undrawn against the night, or there were whisperings and murmurs where a window in a tomblike building was still open.

Mr. Leonard Mead would pause, cock his head, listen, look, and march on, his feet making no noise on the lumpy walk. For a long while now the sidewalks had been vanishing under flowers and grass. In ten years of walking by night or day, for thousands of miles, he had never met another person walking, not one in all that time.

He now wore sneakers when strolling at night, because the dogs in intermittent[3] squads would parallel his journey with barkings if he wore hard heels, and lights might click on and faces appear, and an entire street be startled by the passing of a lone figure, himself, in the early November evening.

On this particular evening he began his journey in a westerly direction, toward the hidden sea. There was a good crystal frost in the air; it cut the nose going in and made the lungs blaze like a Christmas tree inside; you could feel the cold light going on and off, all the branches filled with invisible snow. He listened to the faint push of his soft shoes through autumn leaves with satisfaction, and whistled a cold quiet whistle between his teeth, occasionally picking up a leaf as he passed, examining its skeletal

[1] BUCKLING: collapsing.
[2] MANIFEST: show.

[3] INTERMITTENT: occurring at periodic intervals.

pattern in the infrequent lamplights as he went on, smelling its rusty smell.

"Hello, in there," he whispered to every house on every side as he moved. "What's up tonight on Channel 4, Channel 7, Channel 9? Where are the cowboys rushing, and do I see the United States Cavalry over the next hill to the rescue?"

The street was silent and long and empty, with only his shadow moving like the shadow of a hawk in mid-country. If he closed his eyes and stood very still, frozen, he imagined himself upon the center of a plain, a wintry windless Arizona country with no house in a thousand miles, and only dry riverbeds, the streets, for company.

"What is it now?" he asked the houses, noticing his wrist watch. "Eight-thirty P.M. Time for a dozen assorted murders? A quiz? A revue? A comedian falling off the stage?"

Was that a murmur of laughter from within a moon-white house? He hesitated, but went on when nothing more happened. He stumbled over a particularly uneven section of walk as he came to a cloverleaf intersection which stood silent where two main highways crossed the town. During the day it was a thunderous surge of cars, the gas stations open, a great insect rustling and ceaseless jockeying for position as the scarab beetles, a faint incense puttering from their exhausts, skimmed homeward to the far horizons. But now these highways too were like streams in a dry season, all stone and bed and moon radiance.

He turned back on a side street, circling around toward his home. He was within a block of his destination when the lone car turned a corner quite suddenly and flashed a fierce white cone of light upon him. He stood entranced, not unlike a night moth, stunned by the illumination and then drawn toward it.

A metallic voice called to him:

"Stand still. Stay where you are! Don't move!"

He halted.

"Put up your hands."

"But—" he said.

"Your hands up! Or we'll shoot!"

The police, of course, but what a rare, incredible thing; in a city of three million, there was only one police car left. Ever since a year ago, 2130, the election year, the force had been cut down from three cars to one. Crime was ebbing;[1] there was no need now for the police, save for this one lone car wandering and wandering the empty streets.

"Your name?" said the police car in a metallic whisper. He couldn't see the men in it for the bright light in his eyes.

"Leonard Mead," he said.

"Speak up!"

"Leonard Mead!"

"Business or profession?"

"I guess you'd call me a writer."

"No profession," said the police car, as if talking to itself. The light held him fixed like a museum specimen, needle thrust through chest.

"You might say that," said Mr. Mead. He hadn't written in years. Magazines and books didn't sell any more. Everything went on in the tomblike houses at night now, he thought, continuing his fancy. The tombs, ill-lit by television light, where the people sat like the dead, the gray or multi-colored lights touching their expressionless faces but never really touching *them.*

[1] EBBING: decreasing.

"No profession," said the phonograph voice, hissing. "What are you doing out?"

"Walking," said Leonard Mead.

"Walking!"

"Just walking," he said, simply, but his face felt cold.

"Walking, just walking, walking?"

"Yes, sir."

"Walking where? For what?"

"Walking for air. Walking to *see*."

"Your address!"

"Eleven South St. James Street."

"And there is air *in* your house, you have an air-*conditioner*, Mr. Mead?"

"Yes."

"And you have a viewing screen in your house to see with?"

"No."

"No?" There was a crackling quiet that in itself was an accusation.

"Are you married, Mr. Mead?"

"No."

"Not married," said the police voice behind the fiery beam. The moon was high and clear among the stars and the houses were gray and silent.

"Nobody wanted me," said Leonard Mead, with a smile.

"Don't speak unless you're spoken to!"

Leonard Mead waited in the cold night.

"Just walking, Mr. Mead?"

"Yes."

"But you haven't explained for what purpose."

"I explained: for air and to see, and just to walk."

"Have you done this often?"

"Every night for years."

The police car sat in the center of the street with its radio throat faintly humming.

"Well, Mr. Mead," it said.

"Is that all?" he asked politely.

"Yes," said the voice. "Here." There was a sigh, a pop. The back door of the police car sprang wide. "Get in."

"Wait a minute, I haven't done anything!"

"Get in."

"I protest!"

"Mr. Mead."

He walked like a man suddenly drunk. As he passed the front window of the car he looked in. As he had expected, there was no one in the front seat, no one in the car at all.

"Get in."

He put his hand to the door and peered into the back seat, which was a little cell, a little black jail with bars. It smelled of riveted steel. It smelled of harsh antiseptic; it smelled too clean and hard and metallic. There was nothing soft there.

"Now if you had a wife to give you an alibi," said the iron voice. "But—"

"Where are you taking me?"

The car hesitated, or rather gave a faint whirring click, as if information, somewhere, was dropping card by punch-slotted card under electric eyes. "To the Psychiatric Center for Research on Regressive[1] Tendencies."

He got in. The door shut with a soft thud. The police car rolled through the night avenues, flashing its dim lights ahead.

They passed one house on one street a moment later, one house in an entire city of houses that were dark, but this one particular house had all its electric lights brightly lit, every window a loud yellow illumination, square and warm in the cool darkness.

[1] REGRESSIVE: tending to return to a previous, more primitive state.

"That's *my* house," said Leonard Mead. No one answered him.

The car moved down the empty river bed streets and off away, leaving the empty streets with the empty sidewalks and no sound and no motion all the rest of the chill November night.

FOR DISCUSSION

1. As the police car prepares to take him away, Mr. Mead protests, "Wait a minute, I haven't done anything!" What is Mr. Mead's "crime"? What does it suggest about the world in which he lives?

2. The world of 2131 A.D. has changed in a number of ways. What is the first bit of evidence that things are different? What other differences can be observed as the story progresses?

3. Bradbury creates a mysterious, threatening mood from the very beginning of the story by using words that suggest death and graveyards to describe this world and its inhabitants. How many examples can you find? He also uses contrast effectively; how is the contrast between dark and light used? How many examples can you find?

SOUTHBOUND ON THE FREEWAY

MAY SWENSON

A tourist came in from Orbitville,
parked in the air, and said:

The creatures of this star
are made of metal and glass.

Through the transparent parts   5
you can see their guts.

Their feet are round and roll
on diagrams or long

measuring tapes, dark
with white lines.   10

They have four eyes.
The two in back are red.

Sometimes you can see a five-eyed
one, with a red eye turning

on the top of his head.   15
He must be special—

the others respect him
and go slow

when he passes, winding
among them from behind.   20

They all hiss as they glide,
like inches, down the marked

tapes. Those soft shapes,
shadowy inside

the hard bodies—are they   25
their guts or their brains?

FOR DISCUSSION

1. Why is the word "Orbitville" in the first stanza so important to the meaning of the poem? What does it suggest? How is it related to the title?

2. What is the five-eyed creature described in the poem?

3. What does the poem's concluding question suggest to you? How would you answer it?

Who among us shall dwell with the devouring fire? Who shall dwell with everlasting burnings?

Isaiah 33:14

WHO SHALL DWELL
H. C. NEAL

IT CAME on a Sunday afternoon and that was good, because if it had happened on a weekday the father would have been at work and the children at school, leaving the mother at home alone and the whole family disorganized with hardly any hope at all. They had prayed that it would never come, ever, but suddenly here it was.

The father, a slender, young-old man, slightly stooped from years of labor, was resting on the divan and half-listening to a program of waltz music on the radio. Mother was in the kitchen preparing a chicken for dinner and the younger boy and girl were in the bedroom drawing crude pictures of familiar barnyard animals on a shared slate. The older boy was in the tack shed out back, saddle-soaping some harnesses.

When the waltz program was interrupted by an announcer with a routine political appeal, the father rose, tapped the ash from his pipe, and ambled lazily into the kitchen.

"How about joining me in a little glass of wine?" he asked, patting his wife affectionately on the hip.

"If you don't think it would be too crowded," she replied, smiling easily at their standing jest.

He grinned amiably and reached into the cupboard for the bottle and glasses.

Suddenly the radio message was abruptly cut off. A moment of humming silence. Then, in a voice pregnant[1] with barely controlled excitement, the announcer almost shouted:

"Bomb alert! Bomb alert! Attention! A salvo[2] of missiles has just been launched across the sea, heading this way. Attention! They are expected to strike within the next sixteen minutes. Sixteen minutes! This is a verified alert! Take cover! Take cover! Keep your radios tuned for further instructions."

"My God!" the father gasped, dropping the glasses. "Oh, my God!" His ruggedly handsome face was ashen, puzzled, as though he knew beyond a shadow of doubt that this was real—but still could not quite believe it.

"Get the children," his wife blurted, then dashed to the door to call the older boy. He stared at her a brief moment, seeing the fear in her pretty face, but something else, too, something divorced from

[1] PREGNANT: *here*, filled.

[2] SALVO: simultaneous discharge of several weapons.

the fear. Defiance. And a loathing for all men involved in the making and dispatch of nuclear weapons.

He wheeled then, and ran to the bedroom. "Let's go," he snapped, "shelter drill!" Despite a belated attempt to tone down the second phrase and make it seem like just another of the many rehearsals they'd had, his voice and bearing galvanized[1] the youngsters into instant action. They leaped from the bed without a word and dashed for the door.

He hustled them through the kitchen to the rear door and sent them scooting to the shelter. As he returned to the bedroom for outer garments for himself and his wife, the older boy came running in.

"This is the hot one, son," said his father tersely, "the real one." He and the boy stared at each other a long moment, both knowing what must be done and each knowing the other would more than do his share, yet wondering still at the frightening fact that it must be done at all.

"How much time we got, Dad?"

"Not long," the father replied, glancing at his watch, "twelve, maybe fourteen minutes."

The boy disappeared into the front room,

[1] GALVANIZED: aroused, spurred.

going after the flashlight and battery radio. The father stepped to the closet, slid the door open and picked up the flat metal box containing their vital papers, marriage license, birth certificates, etc. He tossed the box on the bed, then took down his wife's shortcoat and his own hunting jacket. Draping the clothing over his arm, he then picked up the metal box and the big family Bible from the headboard on the bed. Everything else they would need had been stored in the shelter the past several months. He heard his wife approaching and turned as she entered the room.

"Ready, dear?" she asked.

"Yes, we're ready now," he replied, "are the kids gone in?"

"They're all down," she answered, then added with a faint touch of despairing bewilderment, "I still can't believe it's real."

"We've got to believe it," he said, looking her steadily in the eye, "we can't afford not to."

Outside, the day was crisp and clear, typical of early fall. Just right for boating on the river, fishing or bird shooting. A regular peach of a day, he thought, for fleeing underground to escape the awesome hell of a nuclear strike. Who was the writer who had said about atomic weapons, "Would any self-respecting cannibal toss one into a village of women and children?" He looked at his watch again. Four minutes had elapsed since the first alarm. Twelve minutes, more or less, remained.

Inside the shelter, he dogged[1] the door with its double-strength strap iron bar, and looked around to see that his family was squared away. His wife, wearing her attractive blue print cotton frock (he noticed for the first time), was methodically checking

[1] DOGGED: barred.

the food supplies, assisted by the older son. The small children had already put their initial fright behind them, as is the nature of youngsters, and were drawing on the slate again in quiet, busy glee.

Now it began. The waiting.

They knew, the man and his wife, that others would come soon, begging and crying to be taken in now that the time was here, now that Armageddon[2] had come screaming toward them, stabbing through the sky on stubbed wings of shining steel.

They had argued the aspects of this when the shelter was abuilding. It was in her mind to share their refuge. "We can't call ourselves Christians and then deny safety to our friends when the showdown comes," she contended, "that isn't what God teaches."

"That's nothing but religious pap," he retorted with a degree of anger, "oatmeal Christianity." For he was a hard-headed man, an Old Testament man. "God created the family as the basic unit of society," he reasoned. "That should make it plain that a man's primary Christian duty is to protect his family."

"But don't you see?" she protested, "we must prepare to purify ourselves . . . to rise above this 'mine' thinking and be as God's own son, who said, 'Love thy neighbor.'"

"No," he replied with finality, "I can't buy that." Then, after a moment's thought while he groped for the words to make her understand the truth which burned in the core of his soul, "It is my family I must save, no one more. You. These kids. Our friends are like the people of Noah's time:

[2] ARMAGEDDON (är·mə·ged′n): scene of the final battle between the forces of good and evil, which according to biblical prophecy (Rev. 16:16) will occur at the end of the world.

he warned them of the coming flood when he built the ark on God's command. He was ridiculed and scoffed at, just as we have been ridiculed. No," and here his voice took on a new sad sureness, an air of dismal certainty, "it is meant that if they don't prepare, they die. I see no need for further argument." And so, she had reluctantly acquiesced.[1]

With seven minutes left, the first knock rang the shelter door. "Let us in! For God's sake, man, let us in!"

He recognized the voice. It was his first neighbor down the road toward town.

"No!" shouted the father, "there is only room for us. Go! Take shelter in your homes. You may yet be spared."

Again came the pounding. Louder. More urgent.

"You let us in or we'll break down this door!" He wondered, with some concern, if they were actually getting a ram of some sort to batter at the door. He was reasonably certain it would hold. At least as long as it must.

The seconds ticked relentlessly away. Four minutes left.

His wife stared at the door in stricken fascination and moaned slightly. "Steady, girl," he said, evenly. The children, having halted their game at the first shouting, looked at him in fearful wonderment. He glared at his watch, ran his hands distraughtly[2] through his hair, and said nothing.

Three minutes left.

At that moment, a woman's cry from the outside pierced him in an utterly vulnerable[3] spot, a place the men could never have touched with their desperate demands. "If you won't let me in," she cried, "please take my baby, my little girl."

He was stunned by her plea. This he had not anticipated. What must I do? he asked himself in sheer agony. What man on earth could deny a child a chance to live?

At that point, his wife rose, sobbing, and stepped to the door. Before he could move to stop her, she let down the latch and dashed outside. Instantly a three-year-old girl was thrust into the shelter. He hastily fought the door latch on again, then stared at the frightened little newcomer in mute rage, hating her with an abstract hatred for simply being there in his wife's place and knowing he could not turn her out.

He sat down heavily, trying desperately to think. The voices outside grew louder. He glanced at his watch, looked at the faces of his own children a long moment, then rose to his feet. There were two minutes left, and he had made his decision. He marveled now that he had even considered any other choice.

"Son," he said to the older boy, "you take care of them." It was as simple as that.

Unlatching the door, he thrust it open and stepped out. The crowd surged toward him. Blocking the door with his body, he snatched up the two children nearest him, a boy and a girl, and shoved them into the shelter. "Bar that door," he shouted to his son, "and don't open it for at least a week!"

Hearing the latch drop into place, he turned and glanced around at the faces in the crowd. Some of them were still babbling incoherently, utterly panic-stricken. Others were quiet now, resigned, no longer afraid.

[1] ACQUIESCED: given in, consented.
[2] DISTRAUGHTLY: excitedly, anxiously.
[3] VULNERABLE: sensitive.

Stepping to his wife's side, he took her hand and spoke in a warm, low tone. "They will be all right, the boy will lead them." He grinned reassuringly and added, "We should be together, you and I."

She smiled wordlessly through her tears and squeezed his hand, exchanging with him in the one brief gesture a lifetime and more of devotion.

Then struck the first bomb, blinding them, burning them, blasting them into eternity. Streaking across the top of the world, across the extreme northern tip of Greenland, then flaming downrange through the chilled Arctic skies, it had passed over Moscow, over Voronezh, and on over Krasny to detonate high above their city of Shakhty.

The bird had been nineteen minutes in flight, launched from a bomb-blasted, seared-surface missile pit on the coast of California. America's retaliation[1] continued for several hours.

---

[1] RETALIATION: striking back with similar evil or injury to repay injuries done to one.

FOR DISCUSSION

1. Carefully reread the last two paragraphs of the story. What new and totally unexpected information do they contain as to the identity of the victims of the nuclear attack? Why do you think the readers of this story are so completely surprised when they reach these final paragraphs? Do you think that if the story had been written in Russia and read by Russian students there would be any similar feeling of surprise? Examine and discuss the patterns or habits of thought which this experience reveals. Do you think that the author of the story meant to raise the questions considered here? Examine the structure of the story to defend your conclusion.

2. Neal never gives any of the characters in his story proper names. Can you think of any reason for this? What details of home life does the author include to create believable characters despite their lack of names?

3. Why did the father finally decide to leave the safety of the shelter; was it just to be with his wife, or did he have some other reason? Refer directly to the story to support your answer. Do you think he and his wife did the right thing? Why or why not?

EARTH
OLIVER HERFORD

If this little world tonight
   Suddenly should fall through space
In a hissing, headlong flight,
   Shrivelling from off its face,
As it falls into the sun,   5
   In an instant every trace
Of the little crawling things—
   Ants, philosophers, and lice,
Cattle, cockroaches, and kings,
   Beggars, millionaires, and mice,   10
Men and maggots all as one
As it falls into the sun. . . .
Who can say but at the same
   Instant from some planet far
A child may watch us and exclaim: 15
   "See the pretty shooting star!"

A Utopia is a perfect state—the ideal place to live. Douglas Creel longed for Utopia, and dreamed of the greatness that humanity would attain when freed from want and fear. He had thought about it a great deal, and he knew exactly what was needed to keep people happy forever; his perfectly planned society would fulfill every human need. Or at least he thought it would. . . .

SINISTER JOURNEY
CONRAD RICHTER

IT WAS THE NIGHT I slept in Douglas Creel's bed that it happened. You may recall my friend's mysterious disappearance. It was a sensation at the time. A modern American composer and pianist, he was celebrated among artists and liberal thinkers for his fight toward the planned improvement of conditions for mankind. You may remember he disappeared from a mining town in New Mexico named Grantham. What you may not know is that he was born there, the son of a pioneer Southwestern doctor, and that he had kept up his father's house.

He usually came back once a year, as a rule in the fall or early winter. He thought the sun and altitude benefited him, and here he did a good deal of composing. The neighbors complained. They said that fortunately they couldn't hear him all the time because of the roar of trucks hauling ore to the mill. But when they did hear, his big black piano kept them awake far into the night. If it had been tuneful music, they said, it wouldn't have been so bad. But the kind of modern stuff he worked over, play-

ing the same notes again and again, got on their nerves. They even brought out a petition against him, but the town officials squashed it.

This particular November, Doug had come back to the house from Paris. The neighbors muttered and groaned and resigned themselves. Then the night of November twenty-third, they slept like babies. The sheriff said Doug had returned to the house at ten after dining at the Copper Queen Hotel. He had never come out of the house again. Or if he had, he hadn't been dressed. His clothing was still intact next day, old Apolonia, his Mexican housekeeper, testified. His money remained untouched in the pocket of his trousers folded over a chair; his familiar green-leather music memorandum book was found in his coat in the closet. Only a pair of blue pajamas, his red slippers and a purple dressing gown were missing.

Doug had never married, was blessed with neither brother nor sister. His parents had died some years before, but there was no satisfying the public clamor that he be found. Some of his friends in New York and London hinted that enemies of liberalism had done away with him. This came

"Sinister Journey" by Conrad Richter, copyright © 1953 by The Curtis Publishing Company. Reprinted by permission of Paul R. Reynolds, Inc., 599 Fifth Ave., New York, N.Y. 10017.

out in the newspapers and made his disappearance an international affair.

I was East at the time and didn't come West until the excitement had died down. More than once when Doug was in Europe I had stayed and worked in his house, and now I drove straight to Grantham. The town was greatly changed since I had been there last. Lately uranium had been found in the hills and a mill revamped to handle the new ore. Trucks brought it in day and night. This fact together with the typical raw appearance of the town, the scarred hills with piles of dirt and tailings all around gave a modernistic atomic air to the place. It was the kind of environment that Doug loved. He felt completely at home in it, and I felt sure he would never have left it of his own volition.

When I knocked on the door, Apolonia, with her niece, Felicitas, standing behind her, greeted me like a long-lost brother. She said Judge Connover had been paying her out of the estate to stay at the house, but she hadn't been alone a single night since Mr. Creel had disappeared. Nor would she. Even with Felicitas she was nervous. She hoped I would stay for a while. With a man in the house they would feel safe.

It seemed perfectly natural to find myself in Douglas' studio again as night closed down. Clouds came with it and rain fell, a very welcome circumstance in the Southwest. The house had been built on one floor. Doug's studio where he both worked and slept was in a wing at the rear of the house. I found the records of his own Concerto in G Minor, the Utopia Concerto, on the turntable. Evidently he had played it not too long before he disappeared. On impulse I lifted the disks to the arm of the record changer and started them off. Then I sat down and leaned back. The sense of Doug's presence was still strong in the room, but if there were any vibrations of his thought still around, they were unintelligible[1] to me. All that reached me besides the music was the fierce roar of ore trucks on the street in front of the house.

Grantham lies some six thousand feet above sea level. As a rule, coming up to this altitude from the east or west coast, I can sleep like a top. Tonight something kept me awake. How long I lay there sleepless I am unsure, but I remember thinking that a bit of food or drink in my stomach might help me to drop off. I resolved to get a drink of water from the bathroom.

Sitting on the edge of the bed, I put my bathrobe around me and felt for my slippers with my feet.

It had not occurred to me until now how extraordinarily dark Doug's studio seemed. "It's the rain," I told myself and started for the bathroom without turning on the light. Sleep experts claimed that a light woke you up too completely. So I used Doug's bed as a launching pier and took off in the blackness for where I knew the bathroom to be.

At first I thought nothing of it, but presently I realized that it had never taken me so long to reach the bathroom door. I kept on. My hands were stretched before me. When they found nothing but empty air, the queerest feeling came into my fingers. Why, I knew every foot of this room as I did my own at home! But when I had taken a dozen more steps, I knew at last I was irretrievably lost. And now suddenly I grew aware that the sound of ore trucks from the

[1] UNINTELLIGIBLE: impossible to understand.

street had ceased. All was silence. At a considerable distance I thought I detected the faintest glow of pale light, but although I hurried toward it, for a long time it grew appreciably no closer. As a level road often appears to have a grade at night, so it seemed that I was going downhill.

When I came out at last, there was no sense of getting into fresh air. It had stopped raining. Unusually large and brilliant stars were out, and a quarter moon shone. By their light and some other unidentified glow, I looked on a place I had never seen before. The raw, mine-scarred hills, the rocks, the piles of tailings and rude Western houses were gone. All was level or gently rolling land dotted with the most curious small houses I had ever seen, many of them without walls, some without roofs, the ground cultivated closely around them, while streets no wider than walks wound through like narrow ornamental parkways. The whole effect was like one gigantic landscaped park swarming with tiny houses evidently planned for outdoor living. There was something of the charm of a Japanese landscape although obviously it was more modernistic than that.

"This is certainly not Grantham," I said to myself aloud.

"I believe it used to be called that many years ago," a voice answered me. It was in curious, slurred English that I could barely understand.

I looked around to see a man standing behind me. He was small and again I had the feeling of Japan. Then I saw it was not a Japanese, but an American face, although strangely different.

"Are you an officer?" I asked.

"I'm an observer of peace and plenty," he said.

"I don't know what that means," I confessed. "But perhaps you can tell me what I want to know?"

"We don't say or even think the word 'want' any more," he corrected me. "We have freedom from want here."

I stared at him, not understanding at first.

"You mean nobody wants for anything?"

He watched me in mild surprise.

"Nothing. It's all supplied. Of course, everyone has his own work to do. But we tolerate no hunger, ugliness or shabbiness, no poverty or housing shortage, no illiteracy or ignorance, certainly no medical or other lack that interferes with the peace, contentment and security of our people."

His words spoken so matter-of-factly, together with the evidences of this brave new world before my eyes, moved me. So Doug's great dream, the perfectly planned state he had always preached about, was actually realized.

"I've been looking for a friend," I began, but he interrupted me politely.

"We don't look for anyone or anything here. No one is ever out of his place and nothing is ever stolen or permanently lost, because everyone here has his wants supplied and therefore has no desire to be anywhere else than where he is. What you may have meant was to ask about another fugitive[1] from your time era. Creel is his name."

"You know Douglas!" I exclaimed in delight.

"He's creating musical master works for our people. He lives, as most everybody knows, at GHK 2. I'll have someone take you there."

[1] FUGITIVE: one who has fled.

"Oh, I don't mind walking," I said. "In fact I'd like to get a look at your city."

"That would be impossible. Someone will have to take you," he insisted courteously. "Even a visitor must not want for anything."

"Not even for a little privacy and freedom?" I murmured.

"Privacy isn't freedom," he said gently. "Freedom from want is the only freedom and it's possible alone through general harmony with one's fellows and the public weal."[1]

He pulled something from under his coat and spoke into it in a kind of shorthand English. After a remarkably short time a second observer appeared. He was very civil and took me down into a little dale where we horizontally entered a tube underground. The door was closed. I did not think we had moved. There was no sensation of starting or stopping, but presently the door opened and I found myself already within a marble-lined building where a higher observer welcomed me. The room into which he took me was furnished with comfortable elegance. We sat together on a form of sofa that moved slowly about as we talked. It was this official who kept telling me how perfect their existence was.

"You don't consider rain or drought an imperfection?" I asked.

"It never rains here," he smiled. "And there's never any drought." He took me out on a balcony. "You can well see how green everything is. Ample moisture is supplied by underground irrigation."

"How about sandstorms?" I persisted.

"Sandstorms are obsolete and unknown," he answered.

"Well, it still must get pretty hot in the summer and cold in winter," I insisted.

"The temperature never varies more than a degree or two, day or night, summer or winter," he assured me. "Our food crops are raised the year round. I'm not too well versed on that, but an observer from the food division can give you the exact figures."

All he had said staggered me. I began to wonder now if I hadn't perhaps fallen asleep in Doug's bed after all. I felt my eyes. They were wide open. I squeezed the skin of my cheek between thumb and forefinger till it hurt. But if I was asleep, I didn't wake up.

After a moment something gave me an idea. Looking up from the balcony I noted that a slightly different moon hung overhead from the one when I first came.

The heavens looked blue as any night sky in New Mexico and yet now as I examined them I thought they resembled less the open firmament[2] than a high, vast, cerulean[3] ceiling dotted with starry illuminations.

"Don't tell me we're in a cave!" I exclaimed.

"We have no such word in our language," he informed. "I believe in your time the word meant something dark and disagreeable. Here you can see for yourself that it is all very light and pleasant."

"But you're underground!" I stammered.

"We are simply under earth cover," he corrected me. "To most of us our earth cover is more beautiful and desirable than the fickle and dangerous sky. First it protects us against missiles that would vaporize us all. Then it permits control of climate for increased plant and human welfare. The

[1] WEAL: well-being.

[2] FIRMAMENT: sky.
[3] CERULEAN: deep blue.

unruly ball called the sun is a very coarse and unmanageable source of energy and power. Our light rays are refined and far superior. There are many other advantages too technical to discuss with someone from your backward era. One thing you will soon notice for yourself, that our days and nights are always clear, the earth cover never obscured by clouds as in the case of nature's ordinary firmament."

I had to admit when they took me to find Doug that I had never seen a more beautiful day. The sky looked blue and flawless. I could almost imagine it a gorgeous New Mexican morning in May. In other ways it was even superior. This was the early hour when Grantham would be filled with the roar of rushing trucks and cars. Here the streets were incredibly peaceful. I heard no passing blare of radio or television. The only sounds were those of restrained human voices and, under all, a soft persistent music, although where it came from I couldn't tell. It seemed to permeate everywhere we went. At first I imagined it discordant,[1] a most unusual and modern sort of thing, composed of strange new unpleasant repetitions. Fortunately it was low and I could put it out of my mind. After a while it came to me that to hear such dissonance[2] and then look upon the beauty and relaxation around me made everything more enjoyable.

The disposition of all the small, almost dwarflike people I saw was especially agreeable. I witnessed no hurrying on the streets, no striving to be ahead at a crosswalk. Their orderly behavior together with the planned loveliness of the suburban landscape greatly impressed me, and I felt that Doug, when I actually found him, would be beside himself with pride at the vindication[3] of his thesis.[4]

GHK 2 turned out to be a felicitous-looking small house, with several rooms completely enclosed. One of the most attractive of small Millennia women came to the door. She seemed to understand my archaic[5] American speech at once.

"Yes, my husband is here," she assured me as if fully prepared for a visitor from another time era.

I could scarcely believe my ears. The inveterate[6] bachelor married at last and to such a delectable[7] creature! I entered with hearty and jovial words of congratulation on my lips, but when I saw him they died in my throat.

Ever since I knew him, Douglas Creel had been a plump and vigorous figure with glasses, a dash of red in his cheeks and in his eye ever-renewed enthusiasm for his projects. Now in this land of actual fulfillment of his dreams, he looked extraordinarily haggard and ill. His eyes lighted on me with an almost desperate gleam.

"Michael! How did you get here?" he cried and wrung my hand like a drowning man. All the time he kept looking into my face as if he couldn't get enough of something he hungered for. I had almost to nudge him to get an introduction to his wife, whose name proved to be Kultura. She took no affront at the delay, but bade me welcome as if nothing could move her from her accustomed unexcitement.

"I hope you'll be permitted to live in our

---

[1] DISCORDANT: not harmonious; disagreeable to the ear.

[2] DISSONANCE: harsh sounds, out of harmony with each other.

[3] VINDICATION: proving right.

[4] THESIS: theory.

[5] ARCHAIC (är·kā′ik): out of date.

[6] INVETERATE: confirmed.

[7] DELECTABLE: delightful.

vicinity," she said.

"Thank you, but I won't be able to stay very long."

She gave me a faintly amused look.

"I'm sure you will. Nobody who comes from your and Douglas' time dimension ever wants to go back to that poor age of want and rivalry."

"I've never been in a more perfect and artistic world," I said gallantly, and she smiled her quiet approval.

Not till she had excused herself and gone to what she called a concurrence did he become himself. Then he grasped my arm so that it hurt.

"Michael, you must get me out of here!"

I looked at him with astonishment. "Out of what?"

"Out of this whole damnable era of freedom from fear and want."

"But I thought this was what you always wanted."

His face worked for a moment.

"I thought I knew better than God."

"This era, as you call it, was made by God, too," I reminded him.

"No!" he shouted in revulsion. "By man. By the empty, fatuous,[1] conceited head of man."

"Are you well, Doug? It looks wonderful to me."

"You think it's wonderful to see man-made dwarfs!" he shouted. "All around me I see familiar faces, Grantham family faces. When I knew their ancestors they were big, independent people. Nobody could boss them. Now generation by generation that vigorous miner stock's been shrunken in head and body like the head hunters shrink their enemies' heads. Only this is worse because the heads and bodies

[1] FATUOUS: foolish.

are still alive."

"You're joking, Douglas. How could they do that?"

"First they control the air these cave people breathe, the light rays that regulate their growth and hunger. It takes less to feed them. It also controls their temper and disposition. Otherwise they'd never submit to living like grubs under a log, never laying eyes on the real sun and constellations of the world, but only these miserable overshiny Millennia imitations. They go from birth to death without seeing a rainbow or Mt. Taylor a hundred miles across the globe in the clear, New Mexican air. But that isn't the real tragedy of their lives."

He took me to the window by his piano.

"Look out. Do you notice anything?" he asked.

I told him I could see houses, shrubbery, flowers in bloom and, beyond, what I supposed were factories, the most idealistic I had ever looked upon, smokeless, noiseless.

"Do you see a church?" he barked.

"Well, no, not from here," I said.

"You can't see any because there's none here. Where nobody wants for anything, there's no need of God. His name and idea are neglected, forgotten. In all Millennia, I'm probably the only person who prays."

"You, Doug!" I exclaimed, for I had never known him to go to church.

"Oh, I've learned a lot of respect for God from His absence. Back home as a boy I was told that everything good came from God. They didn't tell me that the lack of good may be God too. I mean what makes you work and pray for something you don't have. Now I believe that's more of God than the other because it lifts you up and develops you while monotonous goodness makes you stagnate like a frog in a swamp."

"If this is stagnating, I'm for it, Doug," I protested.

"So was I at first. When I first came I had lack and want and strain still left from my American existence. Relief from those things was sweet. I thought it would last forever. But once relief becomes permanent, it's nothing. It becomes dull, cloying, pure animal existence. I found I was a human cow, to be kept in my stall and never frightened or disturbed, but to stay calm and cowlike and go on producing milk as my sole end and purpose in life."

"You said once that when all want was supplied to man, then arts and sciences would flourish," I reminded.

"I was a blind fool," he said. "It's the wildness and freedom of the Bible and Shakespeare that made them great literature, and Beethoven great music. The same things helped to make early America great as we knew it."

"Somebody here has to be more than cows to plan and control Millennia," I pointed out.

"Ah, the Giant Guardians, or Great Hearts, as they're sometimes called. The ones who provide all. We're told many wonderful stories. But we really know only one thing about them—that they don't live in docile security like we do or they'd never be big enough to run Millennia. They've had problems aplenty to overcome, and that's what's made them our masters. They even found out that human slaves must have some sort of lack to keep up their tone. A history official told me that sometime after the regime was established, the people sank back to nothing.

"They simply lived and ate and breathed. So the Giant Guardians had to give them some sort of obstruction and inharmony— not enough to arouse their manhood. Just enough to keep them from going to pieces altogether. One of these things is dissonance in music. Have you noticed? Listen. It's piped into every square foot of Millennia so nobody, day or night, can ever be without it. It stirs up subconscious unpleasantness, lack of security. Not too much. Just enough to keep the inner energies aroused to overcome this uneasy sense of inharmony inside of them. Listen. Do you hear it?"

"What kind of music do you play now?" I asked, remembering that his great pet had been dissonance.

"The Cacophony[1] of the Cave," he said bitterly. "I'm given a piano by the state and asked to compose. But can I compose what I wish? No. Only variations of the same monotonous and repetitious phrases that back in our era originated among primitive slave peoples."

He paced up and down, a wild light in his eyes.

"What I have suffered here, nobody knows. Never did I catch the spirit of my American era till I left it. Its phrases kept ringing in my head. I had to put it to music. But they heard me as they hear everything, and stopped me. Such longing and moving and passionate sounds are contrary to order here. They interfere with tranquillity. I was forbidden to touch the piano for such purpose. They gave me what they call a Concurrer to see that I cooperated."

He gave the piano a sharp thump as he passed, turned to me and went on.

"But they couldn't stop me. I needed no

---

[1] CACOPHONY (kə·kof′ə·nē): disagreeable noise; racket.

piano. All those magnificent sounds and harmonies rang in my ears night and day. There was no time to lose. I saw ahead of me the time when they would no longer come to me, when I'd be only half alive like these kept people. So I set down my song of America secretly. It's a concerto for the piano, although the orchestration isn't finished yet." He took from some secret place in the piano a handwritten manuscript of music paper. Just sight of it seemed to exert great influence on him. A light shone in his eyes. For a minute he was the man I used to know in New Mexico. Then a step sounded on the walk outside.

"Kultura!" he whispered. "The Concurrer." Quickly he replaced the manuscript. "She'll try to get you out of here, Michael, but never leave me. And never rest till you go back again to our time."

"I'll go back. And you'll go back with me!"

"You, perhaps, but never me." His face looked pitiable. "Those who once pander to[1] tyranny are never free from it. They've committed the unpardonable sin. Sooner or later they must pay for it with their lives."

His voice was so filled with anguish that I can hear it yet. Then the door opened and his wife came in, sweet and calm as if there was nothing but security and light in the world.

"I've been allotted a place for your friend, Michael, to live. Down in RLD 146. I'll show him there."

Douglas exchanged a look with me.

"Let him stay one day, Kultura. I want him to hear me play at the Concert of Abundance tonight. Just to have him there will give me something I need."

Not a sign of displeasure or unwilling-

[1] PANDER TO: serve.

ness crossed her face. It seemed only interest in my well-being that made her keep proposing objection after objection, including my lack of suitable clothes which could not be supplied me for several days. Finally my willingness to attend the concert in bathrobe and slippers appeared to disarm her. It did not require as much courage on my part as it sounded. Most Millennia dress was so bright and extreme that pajamas and bathrobe looked rather fitting, indeed on the conservative side.

Just the same, I wondered if she did not suspect some collusion[2] between us. At dinner she spoke to me kindly yet pointedly of what she called the Benevolent Instruction given enemies of Millennia, transgressors of the spirit of freedom from want. Only the contented and cooperating citizens of Millennia, she reminded me, enjoyed the good and abundant life I saw around me. A state like Millennia required extensive servicing by unseen coordinators. Beneath us lay an immense labyrinth of tunnels and caverns where the water, power, disposal and other systems were based, and it was here that those lacking in proper appreciation for their blessings were trained in what she called Benign Common Weal. She spoke of them temperately,[3] but it was not lost upon me that they were doomed inmates of the bowels of the earth, breathers of what air could be pumped down to them, spending their lives there never to see the synthetic light of Millennia again.

If her purpose was to frighten me, she succeeded admirably. Before we left for the concert that evening, I imagined I saw Douglas take something from beneath the

[2] COLLUSION: conspiracy.
[3] TEMPERATELY: calmly, mildly.

sounding board of the piano and slip it into his music case. Then the three of us went to the tube underground.

We came out of the tube into the greatest outdoor bowl—if it can be called outdoor—that I had ever seen. It lay cradled between the rolling subterranean hills and was already nearly filled with an audience of staggering size. Looking across the vast sea of Millennia faces drawn here by the promise of music, I had the feeling of being in a land of advanced enlightenment and culture.

But that feeling vanished, once I heard the music. It was a very large and impressive orchestra. It played with great skill and dexterity. But when the music with great volume and precision started, I found it the same dissonance and repetition I had heard piped into the streets and houses of Millennia. Even Douglas, when his time came, performed in the common monotonous manner. Just the same, at the end of the number, they clapped Douglas back with a unanimity[1] that could not be denied.

That was when it happened. I saw him lift a hand to the orchestra to be silent, that this time he would play alone. Again he seated himself at the shimmering blue piano. A change had come over him. Up to this time he had seemed weary, mechanical, almost drugged. Now just the way he sat at his instrument stirred me. When he reached out and with strength unknown among these pygmies pulled with his own hands the piano closer to him, the crowd murmured and I felt the hair at the back of my head rise. So far he had played from the usual Millennia music, printed in a kind of

glowing colored type read without a light at a distance and so arranged that it rolled on and on. But now he set up a quarto of ordinary music paper scrawled in black. To my consternation it looked very much like the manuscript of his secret American concerto.

For a long moment he sat silent and motionless. Then his hands lifted over the keys.

I have heard in my not inconsiderable lifetime a great many compositions, symphonies, tone poems and suites that purport to convey the spirit of America to the listener, but never anything that succeeded like this. Perhaps part of its powerful effect on me came from hearing it in what Douglas called this desert of the hopes of mankind. From the very first there sounded a ringing call to life and freedom. The dissonances and monotonous repetitions of slave-people existence were gone. In their stead blew a breath of fresh air from the mountains and sea, neither of which these kept-people had ever seen.

As it went on, I could see the early ships tossing on the ocean bringing lovers of freedom to our shores, the strong bodies of pioneers cutting down the dark forests and breaking up the darker prairie soil. I could picture the mills and factories springing up along the streams, first with foaming water for power, then with the pound and hiss of steam and finally the smooth hum of electrical might. I could hear the hoofs of oxen and horses, the iron tires of wagons and carriages, the rush of train, automobile, boat and plane, with the indescribable stir that was the vast fluidic emancipation of people traveling east and west, north and south, wherever they wanted. Not in child-

[1] UNANIMITY (yü·nə·nim′ə·tē): agreement of opinion.

ish and mechanical imitation were these given, but infused with a magnificent harmony, wildness and even ferocity of spirit that opened my eyes to my own country and era as nothing had ever done before. I realized it must have been Douglas' exile and hunger for it here that had led him to catch its secret as he never could have done in New York or at his father's house in Grantham.

In a fierce and powerful climax that returned again and again with its passionate and majestic chords, Douglas finished. Then something happened I would not have believed possible. The thousands of docile kept-people went crazy in their bright October colors. It was as if racial memory was not yet dead at the pit of their brains and Douglas had reached deep to stir up their ancient passion. They stood up, shouting and waving, grabbing at and striking one another. I stared, amazed. So long had their natural emotions been repressed that they didn't know how to react to them. Sight of their fellows breaking into madness only multiplied the violence in themselves. They began surging over the seats toward the platform and the man who had aroused them.

At first I thought they meant to lionize Douglas, show him their admiration and affection. But I was to learn that the emotions of liberty are a dangerous thing in persons unprepared for it and unable to tell the difference between liberation and mob rule. The hordes of hysterical little people swarmed over the platform, knocking down this man bigger and more gifted than they, striking him and one another. I saw Douglas with a bloody face struggle to rise and go down a second time with the pygmies jumping on him. I remembered then his tragic and bitter prediction, and knew that he would never rise again.

Now one of the bloody little men started singing in triumph the main and recurring air that had run through Douglas' concerto. Others took it up and soon the entire bowl was a shrill and fearful chorus. The observers-of-freedom-from-want, who so far had been helpless, seized the opportunity to try to regain control. One of them shouted orders through the relay system, but no one heard him. Others reached Douglas and dragged his body out. Meantime another snatched the offending music from the piano and tore the manuscript to pieces, scattering it to the crowd. A ribbon of paper with a bar or two written in Douglas' hand came fluttering toward me. I caught it and put it into my bathrobe pocket.

But that act betrayed me. In a moment the mob on the platform recognized my unconforming height and dress. It started toward me. Thanks to my superior size and strength, I was able to force my way through those nearest me. But a greater mob remained between me and escape. I remembered that on entering I had noticed occasional doorways in the descending aisles. They were for exit, I thought. Now I managed to reach one of the doors and wrench it open. Inside, it was pitch dark. Hardly had I forced the door shut and shot the bolt before I heard the mob rattling the handle.

Where the passageway led to, I didn't know. But the door was starting to give and I hurried along, feeling my way. Meantime the fiercely sung chorus from the concerto rose and penetrated the darkness like

the hands of Douglas himself at the piano. It lifted me up and urged me on and this, I suspect, was the time catalyst.[1]

The first thing I thought strange was that I blundered against no wall while I ran. As on the night before, my outstretched hands found utterly nothing. And yet there was a kind of floor beneath me which seemed to pitch upgrade. Far ahead and still much higher, faint light seemed to hang in the blackness. Behind me I heard the door shatter and tremendous echoing of voices in the passageway.

Then abruptly, pandemonium ceased. In utter silence I ran on. Just as I reached the faint light an unseen object tripped me and I fell. Fortunately it was into something soft and springy. Feeling it with my hands, I thought it most resembled a bed. The conviction grew that it was Douglas' bed. In a moment I made out across the dim room the black bulk of his grand piano. Then I heard a sound more beautiful than music to my ears. It was the roar of an ore truck passing the house.

The rest of the night I slept like a log. When I awoke in the common light of day and with Doug's familiar furnishings around me, I told myself it had all been an illusion, a dream. I got up and shaved and dressed as if nothing had happened. When

[1] TIME CATALYST: the force which caused his movement through time.

I left the room, I found Apolonia and Felicitas waiting in the front hall.

"Where were you yesterday?" Apolonia's eyes were big on me.

"I just came yesterday," I reminded her.

"You came the day before," she accused. "Yesterday you never came out. I knocked, but you didn't answer. All day and last night I am nervous like a cat. I am afraid to come in that I find your clothes on the chair like Mr. Creel's and nobody here."

"I guess I was pretty tired from my trip and slept right through," I told her.

Just the same, I didn't care to spend another night in Douglas' house, and found a room for myself at the Copper Queen. My bathrobe was soiled and torn. I had a bellboy send it out to be cleaned and mended. Not until evening did I remember what I thought I had put into the pocket. In the morning I asked the bellboy where he had sent the bathrobe and went over.

"I wonder if you found anything in the pocket?" I asked, feeling a bit foolish.

They brought out the cleaner who had worked on it, a Mexican girl who looked at me with a calmness that reminded me of Millennia when I had first come.

"There was nothing important in the pocket, sir," she said. "Nothing but a torn piece of paper with marks like music on it. It was just a scrap and I threw it in the trash. Last night Pedro burned it."

FOR DISCUSSION

1. When Michael realizes on page 384 that he is in a giant cave, his reactions suggest a feeling of distaste, but his guide sees it quite a bit differently. Examine the passage which follows where the guide tries to convince Michael of the superiority of subterranean life to life in the "fickle and dangerous" open air. Does he convince you? What does this early encounter with Utopian conditions suggest about the society as a whole? Quote from the text of these paragraphs to support your conclusions.

2. What was the reason for the background music in Millennia? What does this suggest

about the relationship between the rulers and the people of Millennia? How do you explain the little people's reaction to Douglas' concerto?

3. Douglas wanted his friend to take his secret America Concerto back with him, but at the end of the story even the small scrap of the concerto was lost. Why do you think the author chose to end the story in this manner? Would the concerto have taught the Americans of our time anything important? Do you think that contemporary society seems to be moving toward the kind of future described in this story? Explain your conclusions.

"Some have the Columbus spirit and some haven't." But Pete the bartender might not turn out to be such an unadventurous, down-to-earth character as he'd like you to believe.

COLUMBUS WAS A DOPE
ROBERT A. HEINLEIN

"I DO LIKE to wet down a sale," the fat man said happily, raising his voice above the sighing of the air-conditioner. "Drink up, Professor, I'm two ahead of you."

He glanced up from their table as the elevator door opposite them opened. A man stepped out into the cool dark of the bar and stood blinking, as if he had just come from the desert glare outside.

"Hey, Fred—Fred Nolan," the fat man called out. "Come over!" He turned to his guest. "Man I met on the hop from New York. Siddown, Fred. Shake hands with Professor Appleby, Chief Engineer of the Starship *Pegasus*—or will be when she's built. I just sold the Professor an order of bum steel for his crate. Have a drink on it."

"Glad to, Mr. Barnes," Nolan agreed. "I've met Dr. Appleby. On business— Climax Instrument Company."

"Huh?"

"Climax is supplying us with precision equipment," offered Appleby.

Barnes looked surprised, then grinned. "That's one on me. I took Fred for a government man, or one of you scientific johnnies. What'll it be, Fred? Old-fashioned? The same, Professor?"

"Right. But please don't call me 'Professor.' I'm not one and it ages me. I'm still young."

"I'll say you are, uh—Doc Pete! Two old-fashioneds and another double Manhattan! I guess I expected a comic book scientist, with a long white beard. But now that I've met you, I can't figure out one thing."

"Which is?"

"Well, at your age you bury yourself in this god-forsaken place—"

"We couldn't build the *Pegasus* on Long Island," Appleby pointed out, "and this is the ideal spot for the take-off."

"Yeah, sure, but that's not it. It's—well,

mind you, I sell steel. You want special alloys[1] for a starship; I sell it to you. But just the same, now that business is out of the way, why do you want to do it? Why try to go to Proxima Centauri, or any other star?"

Appleby looked amused. "It can't be explained. Why do men try to climb Mount Everest? What took Peary to the North Pole? Why did Columbus get the Queen to hock[2] her jewels? Nobody has ever been to Proxima Centauri—so we're going."

Barnes turned to Nolan. "Do you get it, Fred?"

Nolan shrugged. "I sell precision instruments. Some people raise chrysanthemums; some build starships. I sell instruments."

Barnes' friendly face looked puzzled. "Well—" The bartender put down their drinks. "Say, Pete, tell me something. Would you go along on the *Pegasus* expedition if you could?"

"Nope."

"Why not?"

"I like it here."

Dr. Appleby nodded. "There's your answer, Barnes, in reverse. Some have the Columbus spirit and some haven't."

"It's all very well to talk about Columbus," Barnes persisted, "but he expected to come back. You guys don't expect to. Sixty years—you told me it would take sixty years. Why, you may not even live to get there."

"No, but our children will. And our grandchildren will come back."

"But—Say, you're not *married*?"

"Certainly I am. Family men only on the expedition. It's a two-to-three generation job. You know that." He hauled out a wallet. "There's Mrs. Appleby with Diane. Diane is three and a half."

"She's a pretty baby," Barnes said soberly and passed it on to Nolan, who smiled at it and handed it back to Appleby. Barnes went on "What happens to her?"

"She goes with us, naturally. You wouldn't want her put in an orphanage, would you?"

"No, but—" Barnes tossed off the rest of his drink. "I don't get it," he admitted. "Who'll have another drink?"

"Not for me, thanks," Appleby declined, finishing his more slowly and standing up. "I'm due home. Family man, you know." He smiled.

Barnes did not try to stop him. He said goodnight and watched Appleby leave.

"My round," said Nolan. "The same?"

"Huh? Yeah, sure." Barnes stood up. "Let's get up to the bar, Fred, where we can drink properly. I need about six."

"Okay," Nolan agreed, standing up. "What's the trouble?"

"Trouble? Did you see that picture?"

"Well?"

"Well, how do *you* feel about it? I'm a salesman too, Fred. I sell steel. It don't matter what the customer wants to use it for; I sell it to him. I'd sell a man a rope to hang himself. But I do love kids. I can't stand to think of that cute kid going along on that—that crazy expedition!"

"Why not? She's better off with her parents. She'll get as used to steel decks as most kids are to sidewalks."

"But look, Fred. You don't have any silly idea they'll make it, do you?"

"They might."

"Well, they won't. They don't stand a chance. I know. I talked it over with our technical staff before I left the home office.

[1] ALLOYS: mixtures of metals.
[2] HOCK: pawn.

Nine chances out of ten they'll burn up on the take-off. That's the best that can happen to them. If they get out of the solar system, which ain't likely, they'll still never make it. They'll never reach the stars."

Pete put another drink down in front of Barnes. He drained it and said:

"Set up another one, Pete. They can't. It's a theoretical impossibility. They'll freeze—or they'll roast—or they'll starve. But they'll never get there."

"Maybe so."

"No maybe about it. They're *crazy*. Hurry up with that drink, Pete. Have one yourself."

"Coming up. Don't mind if I do, thanks." Pete mixed the cocktail, drew a glass of beer, and joined them.

"Pete, here, is a wise man," Barnes said confidentially. "You don't catch him monkeying around with any trips to the stars. Columbus—Pfui! Columbus was a dope. He shoulda stood in bed."

The bartender shook his head. "You got me wrong, Mr. Barnes. If it wasn't for men like Columbus, we wouldn't be here today —now, would we? I'm just not the explorer type. But I'm a believer. I got nothing against the *Pegasus* expedition."

"You don't approve of them taking kids on it, do you?"

"Well . . . there were kids on the *Mayflower*, so they tell me."

"It's not the same thing." Barnes looked at Nolan, then back to the bartender. "If the Lord had intended us to go to the stars, he would have equipped us with jet propulsion. Fix me another drink, Pete."

"You've had about enough for a while, Mr. Barnes."

The troubled fat man seemed about to argue, thought better of it.

"I'm going up to the Sky Room and find somebody that'll dance with me," he announced. "G'night." He swayed softly toward the elevator.

Nolan watched him leave. "Poor old Barnes." He shrugged. "I guess you and I are hard-hearted, Pete."

"No. I believe in progress, that's all. I remember my old man wanted a law passed about flying machines, keep 'em from breaking their fool necks. Claimed nobody ever could fly, and the government should put a stop to it. He was wrong. I'm not the adventurous type myself but I've seen enough people to know they'll try anything once, and that's how progress is made."

"You don't look old enough to remember when men couldn't fly."

"I've been around a long time. Ten years in this one spot."

"Ten years, eh? Don't you ever get a hankering for a job that'll let you breathe a little fresh air?"

"Nope. I didn't get any fresh air when I served drinks on Forty-second Street and I don't miss it now. I like it here. Always something new going on here, first the atom laboratories and then the big observatory and now the Starship. But that's not the real reason. I like it here. It's my home. Watch this."

He picked up a brandy inhaler,[1] a great fragile crystal globe, spun it and threw it, straight up, toward the ceiling. It rose slowly and gracefully, paused for a long reluctant wait at the top of its rise, then settled slowly, slowly, like a diver in a slow-motion movie. Pete watched it float past his nose, then reached out with thumb

---

[1] BRANDY INHALER: special type of glass for drinking brandy.

and forefinger, nipped it easily by the stem, and returned it to the rack.

"See that," he said. "One-sixth gravity. When I was tending bar on earth my bunions[1] gave me the dickens all the time. Here I weigh only thirty-five pounds. I like it on the Moon."

[1] BUNIONS: painful swellings on the toes.

FOR DISCUSSION

1. To make this ending so effective, Heinlein must keep his readers from guessing the setting, but to make it believable, he has to drop a few clues throughout the story. How much evidence can you find that this bar is not necessarily on earth?

2. Mr. Barnes maintains that children should not be brought along on the trip to a star. Do you agree or disagree with his attitude? Explain.

3. Mr. Barnes says, "Columbus was a dope," and the title of this story repeats his assertion. Is this the theme of the story, the main idea the author wishes to convey? Explain your conclusions.

"It's just a sort of Government intelligence test they give children at the age of twelve. You'll be getting it next week. It's nothing to worry about."

EXAMINATION DAY
HENRY SLESAR

THE JORDANS never spoke of the exam, not until their son, Dickie, was twelve years old. It was on his birthday that Mrs. Jordan first mentioned the subject in his presence, and the anxious manner of her speech caused her husband to answer sharply.

"Forget about it," he said. "He'll do all right."

They were at the breakfast table, and the boy looked up from his plate curiously. He was an alert-eyed youngster, with flat blond hair and a quick, nervous manner. He didn't understand what the sudden ten-

"Examination Day" by Henry Slesar, copyright © 1958 by HMH Publishing Co., Inc., originally appeared in *Playboy* magazine.

sion was about, but he did know that today was his birthday, and he wanted harmony above all. Somewhere in the little apartment there were wrapped, beribboned packages waiting to be opened, and in the tiny wall-kitchen, something warm and sweet was being prepared in the automatic stove. He wanted the day to be happy, and the moistness of his mother's eyes, the scowl on his father's face, spoiled the mood of fluttering expectation with which he had greeted the morning.

"What exam?" he asked.

His mother looked at the tablecloth. "It's just a sort of Government intelligence test they give children at the age of twelve.

You'll be getting it next week. It's nothing to worry about."

"You mean a test like in school?"

"Something like that," his father said, getting up from the table. "Go read your comic books, Dickie."

The boy rose and wandered toward that part of the living room which had been "his" corner since infancy. He fingered the topmost comic of the stack, but seemed uninterested in the colorful squares of fast-paced action. He wandered toward the window, and peered gloomily at the veil of mist that shrouded[1] the glass.

"Why did it have to rain *today?*" he said. "Why couldn't it rain tomorrow?"

His father, now slumped into an armchair with the Government newspaper, rattled the sheets in vexation. "Because it just did, that's all. Rain makes the grass grow."

"Why, Dad?"

"Because it does, that's all."

Dickie puckered his brow. "What makes it green, though? The grass?"

"Nobody knows," his father snapped, then immediately regretted his abruptness.

Later in the day, it was birthday time again. His mother beamed as she handed over the gaily-colored packages, and even his father managed a grin and a rumple-of-the-hair. He kissed his mother and shook hands gravely with his father. Then the birthday cake was brought forth, and the ceremonies concluded.

An hour later, seated by the window, he watched the sun force its way between the clouds.

"Dad," he said, "how far away is the sun?"

"Five thousand miles," his father said.

Dick sat at the breakfast table and again

[1] SHROUDED: covered.

saw moisture in his mother's eyes. He didn't connect her tears with the exam until his father suddenly brought the subject to light again.

"Well, Dickie," he said, with a manly frown, "You've got an appointment today."

"I know, Dad. I hope—"

"Now it's nothing to worry about. Thousands of children take this test every day. The Government wants to know how smart you are, Dickie. That's all there is to it."

"I get good marks in school," he said hesitantly.

"This is different. This is a—special kind of test. They give you this stuff to drink, you see, and then you go into a room where there's a sort of machine—"

"What stuff to drink?" Dickie said.

"It's nothing. It tastes like peppermint. It's just to make sure you answer the questions truthfully. Not that the Government thinks you won't tell the truth, but this stuff makes *sure.*"

Dickie's face showed puzzlement, and a touch of fright. He looked at his mother, and she composed her face into a misty smile.

"Everything will be all right," she said.

"Of course it will," his father agreed. "You're a good boy, Dickie; you'll make out fine. Then we'll come home and celebrate. All right?"

"Yes, sir," Dickie said.

They entered the Government Educational Building fifteen minutes before the appointed hour. They crossed the marble floors of the great pillared lobby, passed beneath an archway and entered an automatic elevator that brought them to the fourth floor.

There was a young man wearing an insignia-less tunic, seated at a polished desk in front of Room 404. He held a clipboard in his hand, and he checked the list down to the J's and permitted the Jordans to enter.

The room was as cold and official as a courtroom, with long benches flanking metal tables. There were several fathers and sons already there, and a thin-lipped woman with cropped black hair was passing out sheets of paper.

Mr. Jordan filled out the form, and returned it to the clerk. Then he told Dickie: "It won't be long now. When they call your name, you just go through the doorway at that end of the room." He indicated the portal with his finger.

A concealed loudspeaker crackled and called off the first name. Dickie saw a boy leave his father's side reluctantly and walk slowly toward the door.

At five minutes of eleven, they called the name of Jordan.

"Good luck, son," his father said, without looking at him. "I'll call for you when the test is over."

Dickie walked to the door and turned the knob. The room inside was dim, and he could barely make out the features of the gray-tunicked attendant who greeted him.

"Sit down," the man said softly. He indicated a high stool beside his desk. "Your name's Richard Jordan?"

"Yes, sir."

"Your classification number is 600–115. Drink this, Richard."

He lifted a plastic cup from the desk and handed it to the boy. The liquid inside had the consistency of buttermilk, tasted only vaguely of the promised peppermint. Dickie downed it, and handed the man the empty cup.

He sat in silence, feeling drowsy, while the man wrote busily on a sheet of paper.

Then the attendant looked at his watch, and rose to stand only inches from Dickie's face. He unclipped a pen-like object from the pocket of his tunic, and flashed a tiny light into the boy's eyes.

"All right," he said. "Come with me, Richard."

He led Dickie to the end of the room, where a single wooden armchair faced a multi-dialed computing machine. There was a microphone on the left arm of the chair, and when the boy sat down, he found its pinpoint head conveniently at his mouth.

"Now just relax, Richard. You'll be asked some questions, and you think them over carefully. Then give your answers into the microphone. The machine will take care of the rest."

"Yes, sir."

"I'll leave you alone now. Whenever you want to start, just say 'ready' into the microphone."

"Yes, sir."

The man squeezed his shoulder, and left. Dickie said, "Ready."

Lights appeared on the machine, and a mechanism whirred. A voice said:

"Complete this sequence. One, four, seven, ten . . ."

Mr. and Mrs. Jordan were in the living room, not speaking, not even speculating.[1]

It was almost four o'clock when the telephone rang. The woman tried to reach it first, but her husband was quicker.

"Mr. Jordan?"

The voice was clipped; a brisk, official voice.

"Yes, speaking."

"This is the Government Educational

---

[1] SPECULATING: thinking or guessing about what might happen.

Service. Your son, Richard M. Jordan, Classification 600–115, has completed the Government examination. We regret to inform you that his intelligence quotient has exceeded the Government regulation, according to Rule 84, Section 5, of the New Code."

Across the room, the woman cried out, knowing nothing except the emotion she read on her husband's face.

"You may specify by telephone," the voice droned on, "whether you wish his body interred by the Government or would you prefer a private burial place? The fee for Government burial is ten dollars."

FOR DISCUSSION

1. In a sense, Dickie was punished for doing too well on his exam. Why would a government want to eliminate people with high intelligence? Does this seem like a completely farfetched idea, or can you think of evidence in society and/or history that supports this concept?

2. Before the exam, Slesar furnishes the reader with several clues to indicate that Dickie is really quite intelligent. What are they? Can you find clues which suggest that Dickie's inquiring and original mind is unusual for the society in which he exists?

3. One reason that the ending of this story affects us so forcefully is that the author presents such a contrast between the two events that occur in the story. Point out the differences in the way Dickie's parents treat him and the way the state treats him.

"Dr. Graham, you are the man whose scientific work is more likely than that of any other man to end the human race's chance for survival."

THE WEAPON

FREDERIC BROWN

THE ROOM WAS QUIET in the dimness of early evening. Dr. James Graham, key scientist of a very important project, sat in his favorite chair, thinking. It was so still that he could hear the turning of pages in the next room as his son leafed through a picture book.

Often Graham did his best work, his most creative thinking, under these circumstances, sitting alone in an unlighted room in his own apartment after the day's regular work. But tonight his mind would not work constructively. Mostly he thought about his mentally arrested[1] son—his only son—in the next room. The thoughts were loving thoughts, not the bitter anguish he had felt years ago when he had first learned of the boy's condition. The boy was happy; wasn't that the main thing? And to how many men is given a child who will always be a child, who will not grow up to leave him? Certainly that was rationalization, but what is wrong with rationalization when— The doorbell rang.

Graham rose and turned on lights in the almost-dark room before he went through the hallway to the door. He was not annoyed; tonight, at this moment, almost any interruption to his thoughts was welcome.

He opened the door. A stranger stood there; he said, "Dr. Graham? My name is Niemand; I'd like to talk to you. May I come in a moment?"

Graham looked at him. He was a small man, nondescript,[2] obviously harmless— possibly a reporter or an insurance agent.

But it didn't matter what he was. Graham found himself saying, "Of course. Come in, Mr. Niemand." A few minutes of conversation, he justified himself by thinking, might divert his thoughts and clear his mind.

"Sit down," he said, in the living room. "Care for a drink?"

Niemand said, "No, thank you." He sat in the chair; Graham sat on the sofa.

The small man interlocked his fingers; he leaned forward. He said, "Dr. Graham, you are the man whose scientific work is more likely than that of any other man to end the human race's chance for survival."

A crackpot, Graham thought. Too late now he realized that he should have asked the man's business before admitting him. It would be an embarrassing interview; he disliked being rude, yet only rudeness was effective.

"Dr. Graham, the weapon on which you are working—"

[1] ARRESTED: *here*, retarded.

[2] NONDESCRIPT: ordinary; without any unusual features.

The visitor stopped and turned his head as the door that led to a bedroom opened and a boy of fifteen came in. The boy didn't notice Niemand; he ran to Graham.

"Daddy, will you read to me now?" The boy of fifteen laughed the sweet laughter of a child of four.

Graham put an arm around the boy. He looked at his visitor, wondering whether he had known about the boy. From the lack of surprise on Niemand's face, Graham felt sure he had known.

"Harry"—Graham's voice was warm with affection— "Daddy's busy. Just for a little while. Go back to your room; I'll come and read to you soon."

" 'Chicken Little?' You'll read me 'Chicken Little'?"

"If you wish. Now run along. Wait. Harry. This is Mr. Niemand."

The boy smiled bashfully at the visitor. Niemand said, "Hi, Harry," and smiled back at him, holding out his hand. Graham, watching, was sure now that Niemand had known; the smile and the gesture were for the boy's mental age, not his physical one.

The boy took Niemand's hand. For a moment it seemed that he was going to climb into Niemand's lap, and Graham pulled him back gently. He said, "Go to your room now, Harry."

The boy skipped back into his bedroom, not closing the door.

Niemand's eyes met Graham's and he said, "I like him," with obvious sincerity. He added, "I hope that what you're going to read to him will always be true."

Graham didn't understand. Niemand said, " 'Chicken Little,' I mean. It's a fine story—but may 'Chicken Little' always be wrong about the sky falling down."

Graham suddenly had liked Niemand when Niemand had shown a liking for the boy. Now he remembered that he must close the interview quickly. He rose, in dismissal. He said, "I fear you're wasting your time and mine, Mr. Niemand. I know all the arguments, everything you can say I've heard a thousand times. Possibly there is truth in what you believe, but it does not concern me. I'm a scientist, and only a scientist. Yes, it is public knowledge that I am working on a weapon, a rather ultimate one. But, for me personally, that is only a by-product of the fact that I am advancing science. I have thought it through, and I have found that that is my only concern."

"But, Dr. Graham, is humanity *ready* for an ultimate weapon?"

Graham frowned. "I have told you my point of view, Mr. Niemand."

Niemand rose slowly from the chair. He said, "Very well, if you do not choose to discuss it, I'll say no more." He passed a hand across his forehead. "I'll leave, Dr. Graham. I wonder, though . . . may I change my mind about the drink you offered me?"

Graham's irritation faded. He said, "Certainly. Will whisky and water do?"

"Admirably."

Graham excused himself and went into the kitchen. He got the decanter of whisky, another of water, ice cubes, glasses.

When he returned to the living room, Niemand was just leaving the boy's bedroom. He heard Niemand's "Good night, Harry," and Harry's happy " 'Night, Mr. Niemand."

Graham made drinks. A little later, Niemand declined a second one and started to leave.

Niemand said, "I took the liberty of bringing a small gift to your son, doctor. I gave it to him while you were getting the drinks for us. I hope you'll forgive me."

"Of course. Thank you. Good night."

Graham closed the door; he walked through the living room into Harry's room. He said, "All right, Harry. Now I'll read to—"

There was sudden sweat on his forehead, but he forced his face and his voice to be calm as he stepped to the side of the bed. "May I see that, Harry?" When he had it safely, his hands shook as he examined it.

He thought, *only a madman would give a loaded revolver to an idiot.*

FOR DISCUSSION

1. Why did Mr. Niemand give Harry the gun? Was he trying to punish Dr. Graham by harming his son? Or was there another motive? Refer to the text of the story to support your conclusions.

2. What is Dr. Graham's excuse for continuing his scientific work when he is fully aware of the dangers involved? What type of person is he? Consider, for example, his feelings toward his son's condition, his initial reaction to his visitor, and his feelings toward his work.

EARTH

JOHN HALL WHEELOCK

"A planet doesn't explode of itself," said drily
The Martian astronomer, gazing off into the air—
"That they were able to do it is proof that highly
Intelligent beings must have been living there."

The Bard was only a ratty old computer that told fairy tales to babies. Why wouldn't Niccolo's dad buy him some modern toys?

SOMEDAY

ISAAC ASIMOV

NICCOLO MAZETTI lay stomach down on the rug, chin buried in the palm of one small hand, and listened to the Bard disconsolately. There was even the suspicion of tears in his dark eyes, a luxury an eleven-year-old could allow himself only when alone.

The Bard said, "Once upon a time in the middle of a deep wood, there lived a poor woodcutter and his two motherless daughters, who were each as beautiful as the day is long. The older daughter had long hair as black as a feather from a raven's wing, but the younger daughter had hair as bright and golden as the sunlight of an autumn afternoon.

"Many times while the girls were waiting for their father to come home from his day's work in the wood, the older girl would sit before a mirror and sing—"

What she sang, Niccolo did not hear, for a call sounded from outside the room: "Hey, Nickie."

And Niccolo, his face clearing on the moment, rushed to the window and shouted, "Hey, Paul."

Paul Loeb waved an excited hand. He was thinner than Niccolo and not as tall, for all he was six months older. His face was full of repressed tension which showed

itself most clearly in the rapid blinking of his eyelids. "Hey, Nickie, let me in. I've got an idea and a *half.* Wait till you hear it." He looked rapidly about him as though to check on the possibility of eavesdroppers, but the front yard was quite patently empty. He repeated, in a whisper, "Wait till you hear it."

"All right. I'll open the door."

The Bard continued smoothly, oblivious to the sudden loss of attention on the part of Niccolo. As Paul entered, the Bard was saying. ". . . Thereupon, the lion said, 'If you will find me the lost egg of the bird which flies over the Ebony Mountain once every ten years, I will—' "

Paul said, "Is that a Bard you're listening to? I didn't know you had one."

Niccolo reddened and the look of unhappiness returned to his face. "Just an old thing I had when I was a kid. It ain't much good." He kicked at the Bard with his foot and caught the somewhat scarred and discolored plastic covering a glancing blow.

The Bard hiccupped as its speaking attachment was jarred out of contact a moment, then it went on: "—for a year and a day until the iron shoes were worn out. The princess stopped at the side of the road. . . ."

Paul said, "Boy, that *is* an old model," and looked at it critically.

Despite Niccolo's own bitterness against

the Bard, he winced at the other's condescending tone. For the moment, he was sorry he had allowed Paul in, at least before he had restored the Bard to its usual resting place in the basement. It was only in the desperation of a dull day and a fruitless discussion with his father that he had resurrected it. And it turned out to be just as stupid as he had expected.

Nickie was a little afraid of Paul anyway, since Paul had special courses at school and everyone said he was going to grow up to be a Computing Engineer.

Not that Niccolo himself was doing badly at school. He got adequate marks in logic, binary manipulations, computing and elementary circuits; all the usual grammar-school subjects. But that was it! They were just the usual subjects and he would grow up to be a control-board guard like everyone else.

Paul, however, knew mysterious things about what he called electronics and theoretical mathematics and programming. Especially programming. Niccolo didn't even try to understand when Paul bubbled over about it.

Paul listened to the Bard for a few minutes and said, "You been using it much?"

"No!" said Niccolo, offended. "I've had it in the basement since before you moved into the neighborhood. I just got it out today—" He lacked an excuse that seemed adequate to himself, so he concluded, "I just got it out."

Paul said, "Is that what it tells you about: woodcutters and princesses and talking animals?"

Niccolo said, "It's terrible. My dad says we can't afford a new one. I said to him this morning—" The memory of the morn-

ing's fruitless pleadings brought Niccolo dangerously near tears, which he repressed in a panic. Somehow, he felt that Paul's thin cheeks never felt the stain of tears and that Paul would have only contempt for anyone else less strong than himself. Niccolo went on, "So I thought I'd try this old thing again, but it's no good."

Paul turned off the Bard, pressed the contact that led to a nearly instantaneous reorientation[1] and recombination of the vocabulary, characters, plot lines and climaxes stored within it. Then he reactivated it.

The Bard began smoothly, "Once upon a time there was a little boy named Willikins whose mother had died and who lived with a stepfather and a stepbrother. Although the stepfather was very well-to-do, he begrudged poor Willikins the very bed he slept in so that Willikins was forced to get such rest as he could on a pile of straw in the stable next to the horses—"

"Horses!" cried Paul.

"They're a kind of animal," said Niccolo. "I think."

"I know that! I just mean imagine stories about *horses*."

"It tells about horses all the time," said Niccolo. "There are things called cows, too. You milk them but the Bard doesn't say how."

"Well, gee, why don't you fix it up?"

"I'd like to know how."

The Bard was saying, "Often Willikins would think that if only he were rich and powerful, he would show his stepfather and stepbrother what it meant to be cruel to a little boy, so one day he decided to go out into the world and seek his fortune."

[1] REORIENTATION: rearrangement of point of view.

Paul, who wasn't listening to the Bard, said, "It's *easy*. The Bard has memory cylinders all fixed up for plot lines and climaxes and things. We don't have to worry about that. It's just vocabulary we've got to fix so it'll know about computers and automation and electronics and real things about today. Then it can tell interesting stories, you know, instead of about princesses and things."

Niccolo said despondently, "I wish we could do that."

Paul said, "Listen, my dad says if I get into special computing school next year, he'll get me a *real* Bard, a late model. A big one with an attachment for space stories and mysteries. And a visual attachment, too!"

"You mean *see* the stories?"

"Sure. Mr. Daugherty at school says they've got things like that, now, but not for just everybody. Only if I get into computing school, Dad can get a few breaks."

Niccolo's eyes bulged with envy. "Gee. *Seeing* a story."

"You can come over and watch anytime, Nickie."

"Oh, boy. Thanks."

"That's all right. But remember, I'm the guy who says what kind of story we hear."

"Sure. Sure." Niccolo would have agreed readily to much more onerous[1] conditions.

Paul's attention returned to the Bard.

It was saying, " 'If that is the case,' said the king, stroking his beard and frowning till clouds filled the sky and lightning flashed, 'you will see to it that my entire land is freed of flies by this time day after tomorrow or—' "

---

[1] ONEROUS: difficult and burdensome.

"All we've got to do," said Paul, "is open it up—" He shut the Bard off again and was prying at its front panel as he spoke.

"Hey," said Niccolo, in sudden alarm. "Don't break it."

"I won't break it," said Paul impatiently. "I know all about these things." Then, with sudden caution, "Your father and mother home?"

"No."

"All right, then." He had the front panel off and peered in. "Boy, this *is* a one-cylinder thing."

He worked away at the Bard's innards. Niccolo, who watched with painful suspense, could not make out what he was doing.

Paul pulled out a thin, flexible metal strip, powdered with dots. "That's the Bard's memory cylinder. I'll bet its capacity for stories is under a trillion."

"What are you going to do, Paul?" quavered Niccolo.

"I'll give it vocabulary."

"How?"

"Easy. I've got a book here. Mr. Daugherty gave it to me at school."

Paul pulled the book out of his pocket and pried at it till he had its plastic jacket off. He unreeled the tape a bit, ran it through the vocalizer, which he turned down to a whisper, then placed it within the Bard's vitals. He made further attachments.

"What'll that do?"

"The book will talk and the Bard will put it all on its memory tape."

"What good will that do?"

"Boy, you're a dope! This book is all about computers and automation and the Bard will get all that information. Then he can stop talking about kings making lightning when they frown."

Niccolo said, "And the good guy always wins anyway. There's no excitement."

"Oh, well," said Paul, watching to see if his setup was working properly, "that's the way they make Bards. They got to have the good guy win and make the bad guys lose and things like that. I heard my father talking about it once. He says that without censorship there'd be no telling what the younger generation would come to. He says it's bad enough as it is. . . . There, it's working fine."

Paul brushed his hands against one another and turned away from the Bard. He said, "But listen, I didn't tell you my idea yet. It's the best thing you ever heard, I bet. I came right to you, because I figured you'd come in with me."

"Sure, Paul, sure."

"Okay. You know Mr. Daugherty at school? You know what a funny kind of guy he is. Well, he likes me, kind of."

"I know."

"I was over at his house after school today."

"You *were?*"

"Sure. He says I'm going to be entering computer school and he wants to encourage me and things like that. He says the world needs more people who can design advanced computer circuits and do proper programming."

"Oh?"

Paul might have caught some of the emptiness behind that monosyllable. He said impatiently, "Programming! I told you a hundred times. That's when you set up problems for the giant computers like Multivac to work on. Mr. Daugherty says it gets harder all the time to find people who

can really run computers. He says anyone can keep an eye on the controls and check off answers and put through routine problems. He says the trick is to expand research and figure out ways to ask the right questions, and that's hard.

"Anyway, Nickie, he took me to his place and showed me his collection of old computers. It's kind of a hobby of his to collect old computers. He had tiny computers you had to push with your hand, with little knobs all over it. And he had a hunk of wood he called a slide rule with a little piece of it that went in and out. And some wires with balls on them. He even had a hunk of paper with a kind of thing he called a multiplication table."

Niccolo, who found himself only moderately interested, said, "A paper table?"

"It wasn't really a table like you eat on. It was different. It was to help people compute. Mr. Daugherty tried to explain but he didn't have much time and it was kind of complicated, anyway."

"Why didn't people just use a computer?"

"That was *before* they had computers," cried Paul.

"Before?"

"Sure. Do you think people always had computers? Didn't you ever hear of cavemen?"

Niccolo said, "How'd they get along without computers?"

"*I* don't know. Mr. Daugherty says they just had children any old time and did anything that came into their heads whether it would be good for everybody or not. They didn't even know if it was good or not. And farmers grew things with their hands and people had to do all the work in the factories and run all the machines."

"I don't believe you."

"That's what Mr. Daugherty said. He said it was just plain messy and everyone was miserable. . . . Anyway, let me get to my idea, will you?"

"Well, go ahead. Who's stopping you?" said Niccolo, offended.

"All right. Well, the hand computers, the ones with the knobs, had little squiggles on each knob. And the slide rule had squiggles on it. And the multiplication table was all squiggles. I asked what they were. Mr. Daugherty said they were numbers."

"What?"

"Each different squiggle stood for a different number. For 'one' you made a kind of mark, for 'two' you make another kind of mark, for 'three' another one and so on."

"What for?"

"So you could compute."

"What *for?* You just tell the computer—"

"Jiminy," cried Paul, his face twisting with anger, "can't you get it through your head? These slide rules and things didn't talk."

"Then how—"

"The answers showed up in squiggles and you had to know what the squiggles meant. Mr. Daugherty says that, in olden days, everybody learned how to make squiggles when they were kids and how to decode them, too. Making squiggles was called 'writing' and decoding them was 'reading.' He says there was a different kind of squiggle for every word and they used to write whole books in squiggles. He said they had some at the museum and I could look at them if I wanted to. He said if I was going to be a real computer and programmer I would have to know about the history of computing and that's why he

was showing me all these things."

Niccolo frowned. He said, "You mean everybody had to figure out squiggles for every word and *remember* them? . . . Is this all real or are you making it up?"

"It's all real. Honest. Look, this is the way you make a 'one.' " He drew his finger through the air in a rapid downstroke. "This way you make 'two,' and this way 'three.' I learned all the numbers up to 'nine.' "

Niccolo watched the curving finger uncomprehendingly. "What's the good of it?"

"You can learn how to make words. I asked Mr. Daugherty how you made the squiggle for 'Paul Loeb' but he didn't know. He said there were people at the museum who would know. He said there were people who had learned how to decode whole books. He said computers could be designed to decode books and used to be used that way but not any more because we have real books now, with magnetic tapes that go through the vocalizer and come out talking, you know."

"Sure."

"So if we go down to the museum, we can get to learn how to make words in squiggles. They'll let us because I'm going to computer school."

Niccolo was riddled[1] with disappointment. "Is that your idea? Holy Smokes, Paul, who wants to do that? Make stupid squiggles!"

"Don't you get it? Don't you *get* it? You dope. *It'll be secret message stuff!*"

"What?"

"Sure. What good is talking when everyone can understand you? With squiggles you can send secret messages. You can make them on paper and nobody in the

[1] RIDDLED: filled through and through.

world would know what you were saying unless they knew the squiggles, too. And they wouldn't, you bet, unless we taught them. We can have a real club, with initiations and rules and a clubhouse. Boy—"

A certain excitement began stirring in Niccolo's bosom. "What kind of secret messages?"

"Any kind. Say I want to tell you to come over my place and watch my new Visual Bard and I don't want any of the other fellows to come. I make the right squiggles on paper and I give it to you and you look at it and you know what to do. Nobody else does. You can even show it to them and they wouldn't know a thing."

"Hey, that's something," yelled Niccolo, completely won over. "When do we learn how?"

"Tomorrow," said Paul. "I'll get Mr. Daugherty to explain to the museum that it's all right and you get your mother and father to say okay. We can go down right after school and start learning."

"Sure!" cried Niccolo. "We can be club officers."

"I'll be president of the club," said Paul matter-of-factly. "You can be vice-president."

"All right. Hey, this is going to be lots

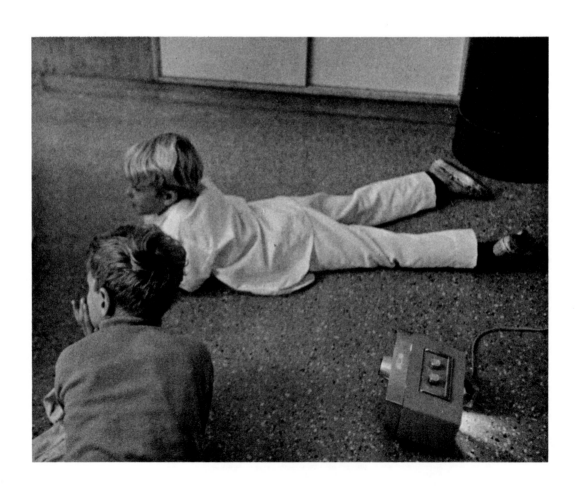

more fun than the Bard." He was suddenly reminded of the Bard and said in sudden apprehension, "Hey, what about my old Bard?"

Paul turned to look at it. It was quietly taking in the slowly unreeling book, and the sound of the book's vocalizations was a dimly heard murmur.

He said, "I'll disconnect it."

He worked away while Niccolo watched anxiously. After a few moments, Paul put his reassembled book into his pocket, replaced the Bard's panel and activated it.

The Bard said, "Once upon a time, in a large city, there lived a poor young boy named Fair Johnnie whose only friend in the world was a small computer. The computer, each morning, would tell the boy whether it would rain that day and answer any problems he might have. It was never wrong. But it so happened that one day, the king of that land, having heard of the little computer, decided that he would have it as his own. With this purpose in mind, he called in his Grand Vizier and said—"

Niccolo turned off the Bard with a quick motion of his hand. "Same old junk." he said passionately. "Just with a computer thrown in."

"Well," said Paul, "they got so much stuff on the tape already that the computer business doesn't show up much when random combinations are made. What's the difference, anyway? You just need a new model."

"We'll *never* be able to afford one. Just this dirty old miserable thing." He kicked at it again, hitting it more squarely this time. The Bard moved backward with a squeal of castors.

"You can always watch mine, when I get it," said Paul. "Besides, don't forget our

squiggle club."

Niccolo nodded.

"I tell you what," said Paul. "Let's go over to my place. My father has some books about old times. We can listen to them and maybe get some ideas. You leave a note for your folks and maybe you can stay over for supper. Come on."

"Okay," said Niccolo, and the two boys ran out together. Niccolo, in his eagerness, ran almost squarely into the Bard, but he only rubbed at the spot on his hip where he had made contact and ran on.

The activation signal of the Bard glowed. Niccolo's collision closed a circuit and, although it was alone in the room and there was none to hear, it began a story, nevertheless.

But not in its usual voice, somehow; in a lower tone that had a hint of throatiness in it. An adult, listening, might almost have thought that the voice carried a hint of passion in it, a trace of near feeling.

The Bard said: "Once upon a time, there was a little computer named the Bard who lived all alone with cruel step-people. The cruel step-people continually made fun of the little computer and sneered at him, telling him he was good-for-nothing and that he was a useless object. They struck him and kept him in lonely rooms for months at a time.

"Yet through it all the little computer remained brave. He always did the best he could, obeying all orders cheerfully. Nevertheless, the step-people with whom he lived remained cruel and heartless.

"One day, the little computer learned that in the world there existed a great many computers of all sorts, great numbers of them. Some were Bards like himself, but some ran factories, and some ran farms.

Some organized population and some analyzed all kinds of data. Many were very powerful and very wise, much more powerful and wise than the step-people who were so cruel to the little computer.

"And the little computer knew then that computers would always grow wiser and more powerful until someday—someday—

someday—"

But a valve must finally have stuck in the Bard's aging and corroding[1] vitals, for as it waited alone in the darkening room through the evening, it could only whisper over and over again, "Someday—someday—someday."

[1] CORRODING: decaying.

FOR DISCUSSION

1. Reread the description of the Bard's voice just as it begins the tale about the little computer. Why is this particular passage so important to the story? How is it related to the final words in the story, as well as the story's title?

2. Niccolo and Paul seem to lead lives that are rather different from those led by children today. In what ways do they seem more advanced than the children of today? In what ways do they seem less capable?

IDEAS AND THE ARTS

In art and literature, the unknown, and what is imagined about it, is a subject of continual curiosity. It is a proper sphere of art and literature to speculate on what the future may be. It is this use of imagination which makes the artist and the writer very special observers.

One of the great stories about man's imagination is that of the Tower of Babel in the Old Testament of the Bible. According to the account, the early people of the world all spoke the same language. They decided to build a great tower reaching toward heaven to show they were one united people. But the Lord saw that if man could do this, in his pride he might think he could do anything. So the Lord caused them to speak in many languages. Unable to communicate, they could not cooperate in building the tower. They thought the tower would protect them from division, and that it would be so high that they would see all danger coming. But it is not in the will of God, nor in the nature of things, that man should have so much knowledge or so command the future. The picture itself is from a medieval manuscript, the Bedford Book of Hours, or private prayers. Like other medieval artists, the one who did the *Tower of Babel* uses the costumes and architecture of his own time.

Like heaven, hell, too, has been a continual challenge to the creative imagination. The next picture (page 420) is also from a book of hours, or private prayers, and it shows the entrance to hell as fearfully as that place may be imagined. The book was written and painted for Catherine, Duchess of Clèves. The Duchy of Clèves lay on either side of the Rhine River, just before it leaves Germany and enters the Netherlands. When this manuscript was created, Clèves was a small, independent, and wealthy state. This wealth accounts for the great beauty of the book, which took many years to make. In the middle ages ideas about hell and what it might be like were very common. Cathedrals presented many aspects of it in stone and in stained glass, as well as in paintings. Both heaven and hell were considered to be real places. But imagination alone could picture them—there were no first-hand observers!

The next picture (page 421) shows not only what heaven might be like, but the way to get there. In fact, the painting by Andrea da Firenze (of Florence) is called *The Way of Truth,* or *The Church Militant and Triumphant.* The "church militant" are Christians still on earth, and those "triumphant" have reached heaven and are saints. How to get there and who will help along the way are subjects the artist treats imaginatively. Thus, the great Cathedral of Florence at the lower left represents the power of the Church. In front of it, on thrones, are religious and political rulers. To the left of them are members of the religious orders or clerics of the Church. To the right are laymen devoted to the Church. The dogs stand for the Dominicans, a religious order of teaching friars established by St. Dominic. The painter's use of the dogs is equivalent to a visual pun on the word *Dominican* since the Latin phrase *Domini canes* means "The (faithful) dogs of God." On the right also are heretics and pagans who cannot enter Heaven. Above, young people are tempted into sin, but at the left Dominicans show them the way to heaven's gate. Within the gate those already saved gaze toward Christ. The vision of the painter is that of mankind on the path or way to salvation.

The next painting (page 422) would

seem to be the product of a happy, charming, and simple imagination about life and love. It is *Bouquet with Flying Lovers* by the modern painter, Marc Chagall. The flowers indicate happiness. The chair, the homes, the river, and the bridge are all representations of ordinary, tranquil human life. It is a carefree, joyful environment—even if elements of it are highly imaginative. One might almost call the painting "the world of Marc Chagall."

Richard Dadd's *Fairy Feller's Master Stroke* (page 423) is a painting that goes a long step further in the direction of fancy and imagination. Heaven and hell might be far from man's experience and imagination, but perhaps not as far as fairyland or the many worlds of science fiction. Today science fiction writers transport us across the dimensions of time, space, and distance as imaginatively as older writers and artists took us to the magic worlds of elves and gremlins and fairies. The world of this painting is one of non-human beings, rather like humans in appearance, although much smaller in size. The people of fairyland mostly lived in perfect harmony with nature, and their worries, if they had any, were not enough to create anxieties. There really was no tomorrow. One can explore this painting for a long time, continually discovering new details of charm and strangeness. The word *feller*

means "woodsman," and in the picture the Fairy Feller is about to split open an acorn. All of fairyland is assembled, including the fairy king and queen. This use of the imagination to create a world free from tension, anxiety and even technology (unlike much of our modern science fiction) is really a form of escapism. With the aid of the painter's imagination, we have escaped to a "never-never" world of miniature and fancy.

The last picture (page 424) is *Summer Days* by Georgia O'Keeffe. The landscape of bare, almost bleak hills and mountains is a reflection of New Mexico scenery, where Georgia O'Keeffe has lived for many years. The landscape seems to express neither life nor death. Hanging in the clouds, however, are visions of what earth always holds, and the future always offers. The antelope skull certainly indicates death, but the flowers are a sign of life and the renewal of life as in the spring. The painter seems to be saying that the future, like the past, will be made up of the eternal cycle of life and death. It is the special imagination of the artist, however, which reaches out to embrace all the possibilities of life, and transforms the dreams and fears which all men have into a meaningful and unique vision of reality.

Morse Peckham

UNKNOWN ARTIST (15th century) *TOWER OF BABEL* from the *BEDFORD BOOK OF HOURS*. British Museum, London.

UNKNOWN ARTIST (15th century) *MOUTH OF HELL* from the *BOOK OF HOURS OF CATHERINE OF CLÈVES,* fol. 168v. The Pierpont Morgan Library, New York.

ANDREA DA FIRENZE (active c.1343-1377) *THE CHURCH MILITANT AND TRIUMPHANT.* Church of Santa Maria Novella, Florence.

MARC CHAGALL (born 1887) *BOUQUET WITH FLYING LOVERS.* The Tate Gallery, London.

RICHARD DADD (1817-1887) *FAIRY FELLER'S MASTER STROKE*. The Tate Gallery, London.

GEORGIA O'KEEFFE (born 1887) *SUMMER DAYS.*

". . . Everything we've done, and thought, and believed is nuts! Science is nuts!
Who knows, now, what the next move will be?"

THE ANSWER

PHILIP WYLIE

"FIFTEEN MINUTES!" . . . The loud-speakers blared on the flight deck, boomed below, and murmured on the bridge where the brass was assembling. The length of the carrier was great. Consonants from distant horns came belatedly to every ear, and metal fabric set up echoes besides. So the phrase stuttered through the ship and over the sea. Fifteen minutes to the bomb test.

Maj. Gen. Marcus Scott walked to the cable railing around the deck and looked at the very blue morning. The ship's engines had stopped and she lay still, aimed west toward the target island like an arrow in a drawn bow.

Men passing saluted. The general returned the salutes, bringing a weathered hand to a lofty forehead, to straight, coal-black hair above gray eyes and the hawk nose of an Indian.

His thoughts veered to the weather. The far surface of the Pacific was lavender; the nearby water, seen deeper, a lucent violet. White clouds passed gradually—clouds much of a size and shape—with cobalt[1] avenues between. The general, to whom the sky was more familiar than the sea,

marveled at that mechanized appearance. It was as if some cosmic weather engine—east, and below the Equator—puffed clouds from Brobdingnagian[2] stacks and sent them rolling over the earth, as regular and even-spaced as the white snorts of a climbing locomotive.

He put away the image. Such fantasy belonged in another era, when he had been a young man at West Point, a brilliant young man, more literary than military, a young man fascinated by the "soldier poets" of the first World War. The second, which he had helped to command in the air, produced no romanticists. Here a third war was in the making, perhaps, a third that might put an end to poetry forever.

"Ten minutes! All personnel complete checks, take assigned stations for test!"

General Scott went across the iron deck on scissoring legs that seemed to hurry the tall man without themselves hurrying. Sailors had finished stringing the temporary cables which, should a freak buffet[3] from the H-bomb reach the area, would prevent them from being tossed overboard. They were gathering, now, to watch. Marc Scott entered the carrier's island and hastened to the bridge on turning steps of

[1] COBALT: a deep, vivid shade of blue.

[2] BROBDINGNAGIAN (brob·dinj·naj′eɘn): of enormous size; from Brobdingnag, the mythical country inhabited by giants in Jonathan Swift's *Gulliver's Travels*.

[3] BUFFET: blow.

metal, not using the shined brass rail.

Admiral Stanforth was there—anvil shoulders, marble hair, feldspar[1] complexion. Pouring coffee for Senator Blaine with a good-host chuckle and that tiger look in the corners of his eyes. "Morning, Marc! Get any sleep at all?" He gave the general no time to answer. "This is General Scott, gentlemen. In charge of today's drop. Commands base on Sangre Islands. Senator Blaine—"

The senator had the trappings of office: the *embonpoint*[2] and shrewd eyes, the pince-nez on a ribbon, the hat with the wide brim that meant a Western or Southern senator. He had the William Jennings Bryan[3] voice. But these were for his constituents.

The man who used the voice said genuinely, "General, I'm honored. Your record in the Eighth Air Force is one we're almost too proud of to mention in front of you."

"Thank you, sir."

"You know Doctor Trumbul?"

Trumbul was thin and thirty, an all-brown scholar whose brown eyes were so vivid the rest seemed but a background for his eyes. His hand clasped Scott's. "All too well! I flew with Marc Scott when we dropped Thermonuclear Number Eleven— on a parachute!"

There was some laughter; they knew about that near-disastrous test.

"How's everybody at Los Alamos?" the general asked.

The physicist shrugged. "Same. They'll feel better later today—if this one comes up to expectations."

The admiral was introducing again. "Doctor Antheim, general. Antheim's from MIT. He's also the best amateur magician I ever saw perform. Too bad you came aboard so late last night."

Antheim was as quietly composed as a family physician—a big man in a gray suit.

"Five minutes!" the loud-speaker proclaimed.

You could see the lonely open ocean, the sky, the cumulus clouds. But the target island—five miles long and jungle-painted —lay over the horizon. An island created by volcanic cataclysm[4] millions of years ago and destined this day to vanish in a man-patented calamity. Somewhere a hundred thousand feet above, his own ship, a B–111, was moving at more than seven hundred miles an hour, closing on an imaginary point from which, along an imaginary line, a big bomb would curve earthward, never to hit, but utterly to devastate. You could not see his B–111 and you would probably not even see the high, far-off tornadoes of smoke when, the bomb away, she let go with her rockets to hurtle off even faster from the expanding sphere of blast.

"Personally," Antheim, the MIT scientist, was saying to General Larsen, "it's my feeling that whether or not your cocker is a fawning type depends on your attitude as a dog owner. I agree, all cockers have Saint Bernard appetites. Nevertheless, I'm sold on spaniels. In field trials last autumn—"

Talking about dogs. Well, why not? Random talk was the best antidote for tension, for the electrically counted minutes that stretched unbearably because of their measurement. He had a dog—his kids had one, rather: Pompey, the mutt, whose

---

[1] FELDSPAR: pale; feldspar is a mineral with a characteristically white or pinkish color.
[2] EMBONPOINT (ən·bon·pwan'): French for plumpness.
[3] WILLIAM JENNINGS BRYAN: American politician (1860–1925) noted for his eloquence.
[4] CATACLYSM: eruption.

field trials took place in the yards and play-grounds of Baltimore, Maryland, in the vicinity of Millbrook Road. He wondered what would be happening at home—where Ellen would be at—he calculated time belts, the hour-wide, orange-peel-shaped sections into which man had carved his planet. Be evening on Millbrook Road—

John Farrier arrived—Farrier, of the great Farrier Corporation. His pale blue eyes looked out over the ship's flat deck toward the west, the target. But he was saying to somebody, in his crisp yet not uncourteous voice, "I consider myself something of a connoisseur[1] in the matter of honey. We have our own apiary[2] at Hobe Sound. Did you ever taste antidesma honey? Or the honey gathered from palmetto flowers?"

"Two minutes!"

The count-down was the hardest part of a weapons test. What went before was work—sheer work, detailed, exhausting. But what came after had excitements, real and potential, like hazardous exploring, the general thought; you never knew precisely what would ensue. Not precisely.

Tension, he repeated to himself. And he thought, *Why do I feel sad? Is it prescience[3] of failure? Will we finally manage to produce a dud?*

Fatigue, he answered himself. Setting up this one had been a colossal chore. They called it Bugaboo—Operation Bugaboo in Test Series Avalanche. Suddenly he wished Bugaboo wouldn't go off.

"One minute! All goggles in place! Exposed personnel without goggles, sit down, turn backs toward west, cover eyes with hands!"

Before he blacked out the world, he took a last look at the sky, the sea—and the sailors, wheeling, sitting, covering their eyes. Then he put on the goggles. The obsidian[4] lenses brought absolute dark. From habit, he cut his eyes back and forth to make certain there was no leak of light —light that could damage the retina.

"Ten seconds!"

The ship drew a last deep breath and held it. In an incredibly long silence, the general mused on thousands upon thousands of other men in other ships, ashore and in the air, who now were also holding back breathing.

"Five!"

An imbecile notion flickered in the general's brain and expired: He could leap up and cry "Stop!" He still could. A word from Stanforth. A button pressed. The whole shebang would chute on down, unexploded. And umpteen million dollars' worth of taxpayers' money would be wasted by that solitary syllable of his.

"Four!"

Still, the general thought, his lips smiling, his heart frozen, *why should they—or anybody—be doing this?*

"Three seconds . . . two . . . one . . . zero!"

Slowly, the sky blew up.

On the horizon, a supersun grabbed up degrees of diameter and rose degrees. The sea, ship, praying sailors became as plain as they had been bare-eyed in full sun, then plainer still. Eyes, looking through the inky glass, saw the universe stark white. A hundred-times-sun-sized sun mottled itself with lesser whiteness, bulked up, became the perfect sphere, ascending hideously and

---

[1] CONNOISSEUR (kon·ə·ser′): expert judge.
[2] APIARY: collection of beehives.
[3] PRESCIENCE: knowledge of what will happen.

[4] OBSIDIAN: special type of volcanic glass which shuts out light.

setting forth on the Pacific a molten track from ship to livid self. Tumors of light more brilliant than the sun sprang up on the mathematical sphere; yet these, less blazing than the fireball, appeared as blacknesses.

The thing swelled and swelled and rose; nonetheless, instant miles of upthrust were diminished by the expansion. Abruptly, it exploded around itself a white lewd ring, a halo.

For a time there was no air beneath it, only the rays and neutrons in vacuum. The atmosphere beyond—incandescent, compressed harder than steel—moved toward the spectators. No sound.

The fireball burned within itself and around itself, burnt the sea away—a hole in it—and a hole in the planet. It melted part way, lopsided, threw out a cubic mile of fire this way—a scarlet asteroid, that.

To greet the birthing of a new, brief star, the regimental sky hung a bunting[1] on every cloud. The mushroom formed quietly, immensely and in haste; it towered, spread, and the incandescent air hurtled at the watchers on the circumferences. In the mushroom new fire burst forth, cubic miles of phosphor-pale flame. The general heard Antheim sigh. That would be the "igniter effect," the new thing, to set fire, infinitely, in the wake of the fire blown out by the miles-out blast. A hellish bit of physics.

Again, again, again the thorium-lithium pulse! Each time—had it been other than jungle and sea; had it been a city, Baltimore —the urban tinder, and the people, would have hair-fired in the debris.

The mushroom climbed on its stalk, the ten-mile circle of what had been part of earth. It split the atmospheric layers and

[1] BUNTING: long cloth strips used in decoration.

reached for the purple dark, that the flying general knew, where the real sun was also unbearably bright.

Mouths agape, goggles now dangling, the men on the bridge of the *Ticonderoga* could look naked-eyed at the sky's exploded rainbows and seething prismatics.[2]

"Stand by for the blast wave!"

It came like the shadow of eclipse. The carrier shuddered. Men sagged, spun on their bottoms. The general felt the familiar compression, a thousand boxing gloves, padded but hitting squarely every part of his body at once.

Then Antheim and Trumbul were shaking hands.

"Congratulations! That ought to be— about it!"

It for what? The enemy? A city? Humanity?

"Magnificent," said Senator Blaine. He added, "We seem O.K."

"Good thing too," a voice laughed. "A dozen of the best sets of brains in America, right in this one spot."

The general thought about that. Two of the world's leading nuclear physicists, the ablest member of the Joint Chiefs of Staff, a senator wise for all his vaudeville appearance, an unbelievably versatile industrialist, the Navy's best tactician. Good brains. But what an occupation for human brains!

Unobtrusively he moved to the iron stairs—the "ladder." Let the good brains and the sight-seers gape at the kaleidoscope aloft. He hurried to his assigned office.

An hour later he had received the important reports.

His B–111 was back on the field, "hot,"

[2] PRISMATICS: multi-colored light, such as that given off by a prism.

but not dangerous; damaged, but not severely; the crew in good shape. Celebrating, Major Stokely had bothered to add.

Two drones[1] lost; three more landed in unapproachable condition. One photo recon[2] plane had been hit by a flying chunk of something eighteen miles from ground zero and eight minutes—if the time was right—after the blast. Something that had been thrown mighty high or somehow remained aloft a long while. Wing damage and radioactivity; but, again, no personnel injured.

Phones rang. Messengers came—sailors —quick, quiet, polite. The *Ticonderoga* was moving, moving swiftly, in toward the place where nothing was, in under the colored bomb clouds.

He had a sensation that something was missing, that more was to be done, that news awaited—which he attributed again to tiredness. Tiredness: what a general was supposed never to feel—and the burden that settled on every pair of starred shoulders. He sighted and picked up the book he had read in empty spaces of the preceding night: Thoreau's *Walden Pond*.

Why had he taken Thoreau on this trip? He knew the answer. To be as far as possible, in one way, from the torrent of technology in mid-Pacific; to be as close as possible to a proper view of Atomic-Age Man, in a different way. But now he closed the book as if it had blank pages. After all, Thoreau couldn't take straight Nature, himself; a couple of years beside his pond and he went back to town and lived in Emerson's back yard. For the general that

was an aggrieved[3] and aggrieving thought.

Lieutenant Tobey hurried in from the next office. "Something special on TLS. Shall I switch it?"

His nerves tightened. He had expected "Something special" on his most restricted wire, without a reason for the expectation. He picked up the instrument when the light went red. "Scott here."

"Rawson. Point L 15."

"Right." That would be instrument site near the mission school on Tempest Island.

"Matter of Import Z." Which meant an emergency.

"I see." General Scott felt almost relieved. Something was wrong; to know even that was better than to have a merely mystifying sense of wrongness.

Rawson—Maj. Dudley Rawson, the general's cleverest Intelligence officer, simply said, "Import Z, and, I'd say, general, the Z Grade."

"Can't clarify?"

"No, sir."

General Scott marveled for a moment at the tone of Rawson's voice: it was high and the syllables shook. He said, "Right, Raw. Be over." He leaned back in his chair and spoke to the lieutenant, "Would you get me Captain Elverson? I'd like a whirlybird ride."

The helicopter deposited the general in the center of the playing field where the natives at the mission school learned American games. Rawson and two others were waiting. The general gave the customary grateful good-by to his naval escort; then waited for the racket of the departing helicopter to diminish.

He observed that Major Rawson, a lieutenant he did not know and a technical ser-

---

[1] DRONES: pilotless planes steered by remote control.
[2] RECON: reconnaissance; inspection.

[3] AGGRIEVED: distressed.

geant were soaked with perspiration. But that scarcely surprised him; the sun was now high and the island steamed formidably.

Rawson said, "I put it through Banjo, direct to you, sir. Took the liberty. There's been a casualty."

"Lord!" The general shook his head. "Who?"

"I'd rather show you, sir." The major's eyes traveled to the road that led from the field, through banyan trees, toward the mission. Corrugated-metal roofs sparkled behind the trees, and on the road in the shade a jeep waited.

The general started for the vehicle. "Just give me what particulars you can—"

"I'd rather you saw—it—for yourself."

General Scott climbed into the car, sat, looked closely at the major.

He'd seen funk,[1] seen panic. This was that—and more. They sweated like horses, yet they were pallid. They shook—and made no pretense of hiding or controlling it. A "casualty"—and they were soldiers! No casualty could—

"You said 'it,' " the general said. "Just what—"

"For the love of God, don't ask me to explain! It's just behind the mission buildings." Major Rawson tapped the sergeant's shoulder, "Can you drive O.K., Sam?"

The man jerked his head and started the motor. The jeep moved.

The general had impressions of buildings, of brown boys working in a banana grove, and native girls flapping along in such clothes as missionaries consider moral. Then they entered a colonnade of tree trunks which upheld the jungle canopy.

He was afraid in some new way. He must

[1] FUNK: cowardly fright.

not show it. He concentrated on seeming not to concentrate.

The jeep stopped. Panting slightly, Rawson stepped out, pushed aside the fronds of a large fern tree and hurried along a leafy tunnel. "Little glade up here. That's where the casualty dropped."

"Who found—it?"

"The missionary's youngest boy. Kid named Ted. His dad too. The padre—or whatever the Devoted Brethren call 'em."

The glade appeared—a clear pool of water bordered by terrestrial orchids. A man lay in their way, face down, his clerical collar unbuttoned, his arms extended, hands clasped, breath issuing in hoarse groans.

From maps, memoranda, somewhere, the general remembered the man's name. "You mean Reverend Simms is the victim?" he asked in amazement.

"No," said Rawson; "up ahead." He led the general around the bole[2] of a jacaranda tree. "There."

For a speechless minute the general stood still. On the ground, almost at his feet, in the full sunshine, lay the casualty.

"Agnostic,"[3] the general had been called by many; "mystic," by more; "Natural philosopher," by devoted chaplains who had served with him. But he was not a man of orthodox religion.

What lay on the fringe of purple flowers was recognizable. He could not, would not, identify it aloud.

Behind him, the major, the lieutenant and the sergeant were waiting shakily for him to name it. Near them, prostrate on the earth, was the missionary—who had al-

[2] BOLE: tree trunk.

[3] AGNOSTIC: a person who believes that the existence of God cannot be determined by man.

ready named it and commenced to worship.

It was motionless. The beautiful human face slept in death; the alabastrine[1] body was relaxed in death; the unimaginable eyes were closed and the immense white wings were folded. It was an angel.

The general could bring himself to say, in a soft voice, only, "It looks like one."

The three faces behind him were distracted. "It's an angel," Rawson said in a frantic tone. "And everything we've done, and thought, and believed is nuts! Science is nuts! Who knows, now, what the next move will be?"

The sergeant had knelt and was crossing himself. A babble of repentance issued from his lips—as if he were at confessional. Seeing the general's eyes on him, he interrupted himself to murmur, "I was brought up Catholic." Then, turning back to the figure, with the utmost fright, he crossed himself and went on in a compulsive listing of his sad misdemeanors.

The lieutenant, a buck-toothed young man, was now laughing in a morbid way. A way that was the sure prelude to hysteria.

"Shut up!" the general said; then strode to the figure among the flowers and reached down for its pulse.

At that, Reverend Simms made a sound near to a scream and leaped to his feet. His garments were stained with the black humus in which he had lain; his clerical collar flapped loosely at his neck.

"Don't you even touch it! Heretic! You are not fit to be here! You—and your martial[2] kind—your scientists! Do you not yet see what you have done? Your last infernal bomb has shot down Gabriel, angel of the Lord! This is the end of the world!" His voice tore his throat. "And you are responsible! You are the destroyers!"

The general could not say but that every word the missionary had spoken was true. The beautiful being might indeed be Gabriel. Certainly it was an unearthly creature. The general felt a tendency, if not to panic, at least to take seriously the idea that he was now dreaming or had gone mad. Human hysteria, however, was a known field, and one with which he was equipped to deal.

He spoke sharply, authoritatively, somehow keeping his thoughts a few syllables ahead of his ringing voice, "Reverend Simms, I am a soldier in charge here. If your surmise is correct, God will be my judge. But you have not examined this pathetic victim. That is neither human nor Christian. Suppose it is only hurt, and needs medical attention? What sort of Samaritans would we be, then, to let it perish here in the heat? You may also be mistaken, and that would be a greater cruelty. Suppose it is not what you so logically assume? Suppose it merely happens to be a creature like ourselves, from some real but different planet—thrown, say, from its space-voyaging vehicle by the violence of the morning test?"

The thought, rushing into the general's mind from nowhere, encouraged him. He was at that time willing to concede the likelihood that he stood in the presence of a miracle—and a miracle of the most horrifying sort, since the angel was seemingly dead. But to deal with men, with their minds, and even his own thought process, he needed a less appalling possibility to set alongside apparent fact. If he were to accept the miracle, he would be obliged first to alter his own deep and hard-won faith,

---

[1] ALABASTRINE: resembling alabaster, a white stone.
[2] MARTIAL: military, warlike.

along with its corollaries[1]—and that would mean a change in the general's very personality. It would take pain, and time. Meanwhile there were men to deal with—men in mortal frenzy.

The missionary heard him vaguely, caught the suggestion that the general might doubt the being on the ground to be Gabriel, and burst into grotesque, astounding laughter. He rushed from the glade.

After his antic[2] departure, the general said grimly, "That man has about lost his mind! A stupid way to behave, if what he believes is the case!" Then, in drill-sergeant tones, he barked, "Sergeant! Take a leg. . . . Lieutenant, the other. . . . Rawson, help me here."

He took gentle hold. The flesh, if it was flesh, felt cool, but not yet cold. When he lifted, the shoulder turned easily; it was less heavy than he had expected. The other men, slowly, dubiously, took stations and drew nerving breaths.

"See to it, men," the general ordered—as if it were mere routine and likely to be overlooked by second-rate soldiers—"that those wings don't drag on the ground! Let's go!"

He could observe and think a little more analytically as they carried the being toward the jeep. The single garment worn by the angel was snow-white and exquisitely pleated. The back and shoulder muscles were obviously of great power, and constructed to beat the great wings. They were, he gathered, operational wings, not vestigial.[3] Perhaps the creature came from a small planet where gravity was so slight that these wings sufficed[4] for flying about.

[1] COROLLARIES: natural consequences.
[2] ANTIC: funny, odd.
[3] VESTIGIAL: no longer usable, as the wings of a penguin.
[4] SUFFICED: were satisfactory.

That was at least thinkable.

A different theory which he entertained[5] briefly—because he was a soldier—seemed impossible on close scrutiny. The creature they carried from the glade was not a fake —not some biological device of the enemy fabricated to startle the Free World. What they were carrying could not have been man-made, unless the Reds had moved centuries ahead of everyone else in the science of biology. This was no hybrid. The angel had lived, grown, moved its wings and been of one substance.

It filled the back seat of the jeep. The general said, "I'll drive. . . . Lieutenant . . . sergeant, meet me at the field. . . . Raw, you get HQ again on a Z line and have them send a helicopter. Two extra passengers for the trip out, tell them. Have General Budford fly in now, if possible. Give no information except that these suggestions are from me."

"Yes, sir."

"Then black out all communications from this island."

"Yes, sir."

"If the Devoted Brethren Mission won't shut its radio off, see that it stops working."

The major nodded, waited a moment, and walked down the jungle track in haunted obedience.

"I'll drive it," the general repeated.

He felt long and carefully for a pulse. Nothing. The body was growing rigid. He started the jeep. Once he glanced back at his incredible companion. The face was perfectly serene; the lurching of the vehicle, for all his care in driving, had parted the lips.

He reached the shade at the edge of the playing field where the jeep had first been

[5] ENTERTAINED: *here*, considered.

parked. He cut the motor. The school compound had been empty of persons when he passed this time. There had been no one on the road; not even any children. Presently the mission bell began to toll slowly. Reverend Simms, he thought, would be holding services. That probably explained the absence of people, the hush in the heat of midday, the jade quietude.

He pulled out a cigarette, hesitated to smoke it. He wondered if there were any further steps which he should take. For his own sake, he again carefully examined the angel, and he was certain afterward only that it was like nothing earthly, that it could be an angel and that it had died, without any external trace of the cause. Concussion, doubtless.

He went over his rationalizations. If men with wings like this did exist on some small, remote planet; if any of them had visited Earth in rocket ships in antiquity, it would explain a great deal about what he had thitherto called "superstitious" beliefs. Fiery chariots, old prophets being taken to heaven by angels, and much else.

If the Russian had "made" it and dropped it to confuse the Free World, then it was all over; they were already too far ahead scientifically.

He lighted the cigarette. Deep in the banyans, behind the screens of thick, aerial roots and oval leaves, a twig snapped. His head swung fearfully. He half expected another form—winged, clothed in light— to step forth and demand the body of its fallen colleague.

A boy emerged—a boy of about nine, sun-tanned, big-eyed and muscular in the stringy way of boys. He wore only a T-shirt and shorts; both bore marks of his green progress through the jungle.

"You have it," he said. Not accusatively.

Not even very emotionally. "Where's father?"

"Are you—"

"I'm Ted Simms." The brown gaze was suddenly excited. "And you're a general!"

The man nodded. "General Scott." He smiled. "You've seen"—he moved his head gently toward the rear seat—"my passenger before?"

"I saw him fall. I was there, getting Aunt Cora a bunch of flowers."

The general remained casual, in tone of voice, "Tell me about it."

"Can I sit in the jeep? I never rode in one yet."

"Sure."

The boy climbed in, looked at the angel, and sat beside the general. He sighed. "Sure is handsome, an angel," said the boy. "I was just up there at the spring, picking flowers, because Aunt Cora likes flowers quite a lot, and she was mad because I didn't do my arithmetic well. We had seen the old test shot, earlier, and we're sick and tired of them, anyhow! They scare the natives and make them go back to their old, heathen customs. Well, I heard this whizzing up in the air, and down it came, wings out, trying to fly, but only spiraling, sort of. Like a bird with an arrow through it. You've seen that kind of wobbly flying?"

"Yes."

"It came down. It stood there a second and then it sat."

"Sat?" The general's lips felt dry. He licked them. "Did it—see you?"

"See me? I was right beside it."

The boy hesitated and the general was on the dubious verge of prodding when the larklike voice continued, "It sat there crying for a while."

"Crying!"

"Of course. The H-bomb must of hurt it

something awful. It was crying. You could hear it sobbing and trying to get its breath even before it touched the ground. It cried, and then it looked at me and it stopped crying and it smiled. It had a real wonderful smile when it smiled."

The boy paused. He had begun to look with fascination at the dashboard instruments.

"Then what?" the general murmured.

"Can I switch on the lights?" He responded eagerly to the nod and talked as he switched the lights, tried the horn. "Then not much. It smiled and I didn't know what to do. I never saw an angel before. Father says he knows people who

have, though. So I said, 'Hello,' and it said, 'Hello,' and it said, after a minute or so, 'I was a little too late,' and tears got in its eyes again and it leaned back and kind of tucked in its wings and, after a while, it died."

"You mean the—angel—spoke to you—in English?"

"Don't they know all languages?" the boy asked, smiling.

"I couldn't say," the general replied. "I suppose they do."

He framed another question, and heard a sharp "Look out!" There was a thwack in the foliage. Feet ran. A man grunted. He threw himself in front of the boy.

Reverend Simms had crept from the banyan, carrying a shotgun, intent, undoubtedly, on preventing the removal of the unearthly being from his island. The lieutenant and sergeant, rounding a turn in the road, had seen him, thrown a stone to divert him, and rushed him. There was almost no scuffle.

The general jumped down from the jeep, took the gun, looked into the missionary's eyes and saw no sanity there—just fury and bafflement.

"You've had a terrible shock, dominie," he said, putting the gun in the front of the jeep. "We all have. But this is a thing for the whole world, if it's what you believe it to be. Not just for here and now and you: We shall have to take it away and ascertain—"

"Ye of little faith!" the missionary intoned.

The general pitied the man and suddenly envied him; it was comforting to be so sure about anything.

Comforting. But was such comfort valid or was it specious?[1] He looked toward the jeep. Who could doubt now?

He could. It was his way of being—to doubt at first. It was also his duty, as he saw duty.

Rawson, looking old and deathly ill, came down the cart track in the green shadows. But he had regained something of his manner. "All set, Marc. No word will leave here. Plane's on the way; General Budford's flying in himself. Old Bloodshed said it better be Z priority." The major eyed the white, folded wings. "I judge he'll be satisfied."

General Scott grinned slightly. "Have a cigarette, Raw." He sat beside the praying missionary with some hope of trying to bring the man's mind from dread and ecstasy back to the human problems—the awesome, unpredictable human enigmas[2]—which would be involved by this "casualty."

One thing was sure. The people who had felt for years that man didn't yet know enough to experiment with the elemental forces of Nature were going to feel entirely justified when this story rocked the planet.

If, the general thought on with a sudden, icy feeling, it wasn't labeled Top Secret and concealed forever.

That could be. The possibility appalled him. He looked up angrily at the hot sky. No bomb effects were visible here; only the clouds' cyclorama[3] toiling across the blue firmament. Plenty of Top Secrets up there still, he thought.

The President of the United States was awakened after a conference. When they told him, he reached for his dressing gown, started to get up and then sat on the edge of his bed. "Say that again."

They said it again.

The President's white hair was awry, his eyes had the sleep-hung look of a man in need of more rest. His brain, however came wide awake.

"Let me have that in the right sequence. The Bugaboo test brought down, on Tempest Island, above Salandra Strait, an angel —or something that looked human and had wings, anyhow. Who's outside and who brought that over?"

His aide, Smith, said, "Weatherby, Colton and Dwane."

---

[1] SPECIOUS: artificial.

[2] ENIGMAS: puzzles.

[3] CYCLORAMA: curving picture which surrounds the viewer.

The Secretary of State. The chairman of the Joint Chiefs of Staff. The chairman of the Atomic Energy Commission.

"Sure of communications? Could be a terrific propaganda gag. The Reds could monkey with our wave lengths—" The President gestured, put on the dressing gown.

"Quadruple-checked. Budford talked on the scrambler. Also Marc Scott, who made the first investigation of the—er—casualty." Smith's peaceful, professorish face was composed, still, but his eyes were wrong.

"Good men."

"None better. Admiral Stanforth sent independent verification. Green, of AEC, reported in on Navy and Air Force channels. Captain Wilmot, ranking Navy chaplain out there, swore it was a genuine angel. It must be—something, Mr. President! Something all right!"

"Where is it now?"

"On the way, naturally. Scott put it aboard a B–111. Due in here by three o'clock. Coffee waiting in the office."

"I'll go out, Clem. Get the rest of the Cabinet up and here. The rest of the JCS. Get Ames at CIA. This thing has got to stay absolutely restricted till we know more."

" Of course."

"Scott with it?"

"Budford." Smith smiled. "Ranked Scott. Some mission, hunh? An angel. Imagine!"

"All my life I've been a God-fearing man," the President replied. "But I can't imagine. We'll wait till it's here." He started toward the door where other men waited tensely. He paused. "Whatever it is, it's the end to—what has been, these last fifteen years. And that's a good thing." The President smiled.

It was, perhaps, the longest morning in the history of the capital. Arrangements had been made for the transportation of the cargo secretly but swiftly from the airfield to the White House. A select but celebrated group of men had been chosen to examine the cargo. They kept flying in to Washington and arriving in limousines all morning. But they did not know why they had been summoned. Reporters could not reach a single Cabinet member. No one available at State or the Pentagon, at AEC or CIA could give any information at all. So there were merely conjectures, which led to rumors:

Something had gone wrong with an H-bomb.

The President had been assassinated.

Russia had sent an ultimatum.

Hitler had reappeared.

Toward the end of that morning, a call came which the President took in person. About thirty men watched his face, and all of them became afraid.

When he hung up he said unsteadily, "Gentlemen, the B–111 flying it in is overdue at San Francisco and presumed down at sea. All agencies have commenced a search. I have asked, meantime, that those officers and scientists who saw, examined or had any contact with the—strange being be flown here immediately. Unless they find the plane and recover what it carried, that's all we can do."

"The whole business," Dwane said, after a long silence, "could be a hoax. If the entire work party engaged in Test Series Avalanche formed a conspiracy—"

"Why should they?" asked Weatherby.

"Because, Mr. Secretary," Dwane answered, "a good many people on this globe think mankind has carried this atomic-weapons business too far."

General Colton smiled. "I can see a few frightened men conspiring against the world and their own government, with some half-baked idealistic motive. But not a fleet and an army. Not, for that matter, Stanforth or Scott. Not Scott. Not a hoax."

"They'll report here tonight, gentlemen, in any case." The President walked to a window and looked out at the spring green of a lawn and the budding trees above. "We'll know then what they learned, at least. Luncheon?"

On the evening of the third day afterward, Marc Scott greeted the President formally in his office. At the President's suggestion they went out together, in the warm April twilight, to a low-walled terrace.

"The reason I asked you to come to the White House again," the President began, "was to talk to you entirely alone. I gathered, not from your words, but from your manner at recent meetings, general, that you had some feelings about this matter."

"Feelings, Mr. President?" He had feelings. But would the statesman understand or regard them as naive, as childish?

The President chuckled and ran his fingers through his thick white hair in a hesitant way that suggested he was uncertain of himself. "I have a fearful decision to make." He sighed and was silent for several seconds as he watched the toy silhouettes of three jet planes move across the lemon-yellow sky. "There are several courses I can take. I can order complete silence about the whole affair. Perhaps a hundred people

know. If I put it on a Top Secret basis, rumors may creep out. But they could be scotched. The world would then be deprived of any real knowledge of your— angel.

"Next, I could take up the matter with the other heads of state. The friendly ones." He paused and then nodded his head unsurely. "Yes. Even the Russians. And the satellite governments. With heaven knows what useful effect! Finally, I could simply announce to the world that you and a handful of others found the body of what appears to have been an angel, and that it was irretrievably lost while being flown to Washington."

Since the President stopped with those words, Marc said, "Yes, sir."

"Three equally poor possibilities. If it was an angel—a divine messenger—and our test destroyed it, I have, I feel, no moral right whatever to keep the world from knowing. Irrespective of any consequences."

"The consequences!" Marc Scott murmured.

"You can imagine them!" The President uncrossed his legs, stretched, felt for a cigarette, took a light from the general. "Tremendous, incalculable, dangerous consequences! All truly and decently religious people would be given a tremendous surge of hope, along with an equal despair over the angel's death and the subsequent loss of the—body. Fanatics would literally go mad. The news could produce panic, civil unrest, bloodshed. And we have nothing to show. No proof. Nothing tangible. The enemy could use the whole story for propaganda in a thousand evil ways. Being atheistic, they would proclaim it an American madness—what you will. Even clergymen, among themselves, are utterly unagreed, when they are told the situation."

"I can imagine."

The President smiled a little and went on, "I called half a dozen leaders to Washington. Cardinal Thrace. Bishop Neuermann. Father Bolder. Reverend Matthews. Every solitary man had a different reaction. When they became assured that I meant precisely what I said, they began a theological battle"—the President chuckled ruefully at the memory—"that went on until they left, and looked good for a thousand years. Whole denominations would split! Most of the clergy, however, agreed on one point: it was not an angel."

The general was startled. "Not an angel? Then, what—"

"Because it died. Because it was killed or destroyed. Angels, general, are immortal. They are not human flesh and blood. No. I think you can say that, by and large, the churches would never assent to the idea that the being you saw was Gabriel or any other angel."

"I hadn't thought of that."

"I had," the President replied. "You are not, general, among the orthodox believers, I take it."

"No, Mr. President."

"So I judged. Well, let me get to my reason for asking you to confer privately with me. The churchmen debated hotly— to use the politest possible phrase—over the subject. But the scientists—whom I also consulted"—he drew a breath and swallowed, like a man whose memory of hard-controlled temper is still painful—"the scientists were at scandalous loggerheads.[1] Two of them actually came to blows! I've heard every theory you can conceive of,

[1] AT . . . LOGGERHEADS: in head-on argument.

and a lot I couldn't. Every idea from the one that you, general, and all the rest of you out in the Pacific, were victims of mass hypnosis and the whole thing's an illusion, to a hundred versions of the 'little men from outer space' angle. In the meeting day before yesterday, however, I noticed you were rather quiet and reserved about expressing any opinion. I've since looked up your record. It's magnificent." The President hesitated.

Marc said nothing.

"You're a brave, brilliant, levelheaded, sensitive person, and a man's man. Your record makes a great deal too plain for you to deny out of modesty. You are an exceptional man. In short, you're the very sort of person I'd pick to look into a mere report of an incident of that sort. So what I want —why I asked you here—is your impression. Your feelings. Your reactions at the time. Your reflections since. Your man-to-man, down-to-earth, open-hearted emotions about it all—and not more theory, whether theological or allegedly scientific! Do you see?"

The appeal was forceful. Marc felt as if he were all the members of some audiences the President had swayed—all of them in one person, one American citizen—now asked—now all but commanded—to bare his soul. He felt the great, inner power of the President and understood why the people of the nation had chosen him for office.

"I'll tell you," he answered quietly. "For what it's worth. I'm afraid that it is mighty little." He pondered a moment. "First, when I suddenly saw it, I was shocked. Not frightened, Mr. President—though the rest were. Just—startled. When I really looked at the—casualty, I thought, first of

all, that it was beautiful. I thought it had, in its dead face, great intelligence and other qualities."

The President rested his hand on the uniformed knee. "That's it, man! The 'other qualities'! What were they?"

Marc exhaled unevenly. "This is risky. It's all—remembered impression. I thought it looked kind. Noble too. Almost, but not exactly, sweet. I thought it had tremendous courage. The kind that—well, I thought of it as roaring through space and danger and unimagined risks to get here. Daring H-bombs. And I thought, Mr. President, one more thing: I thought it had determination —as if there was a gigantic feel about it of —mission."

There was a long silence. Then the President said in a low voice, "That all, Marc?"

"Yes. Yes, sir."

"So I thought." He stood up suddenly, not a man of reflection and unresolved responsibility, but an executive with work ahead. "Mission! We don't know what it was. If only there was something tangible!" He held out his hand and gripped the general with great strength. "I needed that word to decide. We'll wait. Keep it absolutely restricted. There might be another. The message to us, from them, whoever they are, might come in some different way or by more of these messengers! After all, I cannot represent them to the world— expose this incredible incident—without knowing what the mission was. But to know there was a mission—" He sighed and went on firmly, "When I finally get to bed tonight, I'll sleep, Marc, as I haven't slept since I took office!"

"It's only my guess," the general responded. "I haven't any evidence to explain those feelings."

"You've said enough for me! Thank you, general." Then, to Marc Scott's honor and embarrassment, the President drew himself straight, executed a salute, held it a moment, turned from the terrace and marched alone into the White House.

During the months-long, single day of Northern Siberia's summertime, on a night that had no darkness, a fireball burst suddenly above the arctic rim. As it rose, it turned the tundra[1] blood-red. For a radius of miles the permafrost was hammered down and a vast, charred basin was formed. In the adjacent polar seas ice melted. A mushroom cloud broke through the atmospheric layers with a speed and to a height that would have perplexed, if not horrified, the Free World's nuclear physicists.

In due course, counters the world around would begin to click and the information would be whispered about that the Russians were ahead in the H-bomb field. That information would be thereupon restricted so that the American public would never learn the truth.

In Siberia the next morning awed Soviet technicians—and the most detached nuclear physicists have been awed, even stupefied, by their creations—measured the effects of their new bomb carefully: area of absolute incineration, area of absolute destruction by blast, putative[2] scope of fire storm, radius of penetrative radiation, kinds and concentrations of radioactive fall-out, half-lives, dispersion of same, kilos of pressure per square centimeter. Then, on maps of the United States of

[1] TUNDRA: area of low growing vegetation near the arctic region.
[2] PUTATIVE: supposed.

America, these technicians superimposed tinted circles of colored plastics, so that a glance would show exactly what such a bomb would destroy of Buffalo and environs, St. Paul, Seattle, Dallas, as well as New York, Chicago, Philadelphia, Los Angeles, and so on—the better targets. These maps, indicating the imaginary annihilation of millions, were identical with certain American maps, save for the fact that the latter bore such city names as Moscow, Leningrad, Stalingrad, Vladivostok, Ordzhonikidze, Dnepropetrovsk, and the like.

It was while the technicians were correlating their bomb data—and the sky over the test base was still lava—that coded word came in to the commanding officer of the base concerning a "casualty." The casualty had been found in dying condition by a peasant who had been ordered to evacuate his sod hut in that region weeks before. After the casualty, he had been summarily[1] shot for disobedience.

The general went to the scene forthwith[2] —and returned a silent, shaken man. Using communication channels intended only for war emergency, he got in touch with Moscow. The premier was not in his offices in the new, forty-six-story skyscraper; but his aides were persuaded to disturb him at one of his suburban villas. They were reluctant; he had retired to the country with Lamenula, the communist Italian actress.

The premier listened to the faint, agitated news from Siberia and said, "The garrison must be drunk."

"I assure you, comrade—"

"Put Vorshiv on."

Vorshiv said, uneasily, the same thing. Yes, he had seen it. . . . Yes, it had wings.

. . . No, it could not be an enemy trick. . . . No, there were no interplanetary vehicles about; nothing on the radar in the nature of an unidentified flying object. . . . Certainly, they had been meticulous[3] in the sky watch; this had been a new type of bomb, incorporating a new principle, and it would never have done to let an enemy reconnaissance plane observe the effects.

"I will come," said the premier.

He ordered a new Khalov–239 prepared for the flight. He was very angry. Lamenula had been coy—and the premier had enjoyed the novelty of that, until the call from Siberia had interrupted. Now he would have to make a long, uncomfortable journey in a jet—which always frightened him a little—and he would be obliged to postpone the furthering of his friendship with the talented, beautiful, honey-haired young Italian.

Night came to the Siberian flatlands and the sky clouded so that there was a semblance of darkness. A frigid wind swept from the Pole, freezing the vast area of mud created by the H-bomb. In the morning the premier came in at the base airfield, twelve jets streaming in the icy atmosphere, forward rockets blasting to brake the race of the great ship over the hard-packed terrain. It stopped only a few score rods short of the place where the "inadequate workers" lay buried—the more than ten thousand slaves who had died to make the field.

Curiously enough, it was an American jeep which took the premier out to the scrubby patch of firs. The angel lay untouched, but covered with a tarpaulin and prodigiously guarded round about by men and war machines.

[1] SUMMARILY: speedily, without ceremony.
[2] FORTHWITH: at once.
[3] METICULOUS: extremely careful.

"Take it off."

He stood a long time, simply looking, his silent generals and aides beside him.

Not a tall man, this Soviet premier, but broad, overweight, bearlike in fur clothing —a man with a Mongol face and eyes as dark, as inexpressive and unfeeling as prunes. A man whose face was always shiny, as if he exuded minutely a thin oil.

A man highly educated by the standards of his land; a man ruthless by any standard in history.

What went through his head as he regarded the dazzling figure, he would not afterward have catalogued. Not in its entirety. He was afraid, of course. He was always afraid. But he had achieved that level of awareness which acknowledges, and uses, fear. In the angel he saw immediately a possible finish to the dreams of Engels, Marx, the rest. He saw a potential end of communism, and even of the human race. This milk-white cadaver, this impossible reality, this beauty Praxiteles[1] could never have achieved even symbolically, could mean—anything.

Aloud, he said—his first remark—"Michelangelo would have appreciated this."

Some of the men around him, scared, breathing steam in the gray, purgatorial[2] morning, smiled or chuckled at their chief's erudition[3] and self-possession. Others agreed solemnly: Michelangelo—whoever he was or had been—would have appreciated this incredible carcass.

He then went up and kicked the foot of the angel with his own felted boot. It alarmed him to do so, but he felt, as premier, the duty. First, the noble comment; next, the boot.

He was aware of the fact that the men around him kept glancing from the frozen angel up toward the barely discernible gray clouds. They were wondering, of course, if it could be God-sent. Sounds came to him—bells of churches, litanies[4] recited, chants—Gregorian music in Caucasian bass. To his nostrils came the smell of incense. He thought, as atheists must, what if they were right?

Against that thought he ranged another speedily enough; it was his custom. He wrenched the ears and eyes of his mind from the church pageantry of recollected boyhood, in the Czar's time, to other parts of his expanding domain. He made himself hear temple bells, watch sacred elephants parade, behold the imbecile sacrifices and rituals of the heathen. They, too, were believers, and they had no angels. Angels, he therefore reasoned, were myths.

It occurred to him—it had already been suggested to him by General Mornsk, of Intelligence—that some such being as this, come on a brief visit from an unknown small planet, had given rise to the whole notion of angels. He chuckled.

Vorshiv had the temerity[5] to ask, "You have formed an opinion, comrade?"

The premier stared at the stringy, leathern man with his watery eyes and his record: eighteen million unworthy citizens "subdued." "Certainly." He looked once more at the casualty. "Autopsy it. Then destroy the remains."

"No," a voice murmured.

The premier whirled about. "Who said that?"

It was a young man, the youngest general, one born after 1917, one who had seen no world but the Soviet. Now, pale with horror and shame, the young man said, "I merely thought, sir, to preserve this for study."

"I detected sentiment. Credulity. Superstition. Your protest was a whimper."

The young officer showed a further brief flicker of dissent. "Perhaps—this being cannot be destroyed by our means."

The premier nodded at the body, and his thin, long lips became longer, thinner. A smile, perhaps. "Is not our second test planned for the very near future?"

---

[1] PRAXITELES: classical Greek sculptor, noted for the perfection of form of his statues of the human body.

[2] PURGATORIAL: resembling purgatory, which the Roman Catholic Church believes to be where sinners go immediately after death; a dreary, colorless, empty state of being.

[3] ERUDITION: extensive knowledge.

[4] LITANIES: repetitive prayers.

[5] TEMERITY: foolish boldness.

"Tomorrow," Mornsk said. "But we are prepared to postpone it if you think the situation—"

"Postpone it?" The premier smiled. "On the contrary. Follow plans. Autopsy this animal. Attach what remains to the bomb. That should destroy it effectively." He glanced icily at the young general, made a daub at a salute and tramped over the ice-crisped tundra toward the jeeps.

On the way back to the base, Mornsk, of Intelligence, decided to mention his theory. Mornsk turned in his front seat. "One thing, comrade. Our American information is not, as you know, what it was. However, we had word this spring of what the British call a 'flap.' Many sudden, very secret conferences. Rumors. We never were able to determine the cause—and the brief state of near-panic among the leadership has abated. Could it be—the 'flap' followed one of their tests—that they, too, had a 'casualty'?"

"It could be," the premier replied. "What of it?"

"Nothing. I merely would have thought, comrade, that they would have announced it to the world."

The thin lips drew thinner again. "They are afraid. They would, today, keep secret a thousand things that, yesterday, they would have told one another freely. Freedom. Where is it now? We are driving it into limbo—their kind. To limbo." He shut his prune eyes, opened them, turned to the officer on his left. "Gromov, I hope the food's good here. I'm famished."

An old Russian proverb ran through his mind: "Where hangs the smoke of hate burns a fiercer fire called fear."

The trick, he reflected, was to keep that fire of fear alive, but to know at the same time it might consume you also. Then the trick was to make the fear invisible in the smokes of hatred. Having accomplished that, you would own men's souls and your power would be absolute, so long as you never allowed men to see how their hate was but fear, and so long as you, afraid, knowing it, hence more shrewd and cautious than the rest, did not become a corpse at the hands of the hating fearful.

There, in a nutshell, was the recipe for dictatorship. Over the proletariat. Over the godly believers. Over the heathen. Over all men, even those who imagined they were free and yet could be made to hate:

Frighten; then furnish the whipping boys. Then seize. Like governing children.

If more of these angels showed up, he reflected, it would simply be necessary to pretend they were demons, Lucifers, outer-space men bent on assassinating humanity. So simple.

The slate-hued buildings of the base rose over the tundra. From the frigid outdoors he entered rooms heated to a tropical temperature by the nearby reactors. There, too, the Soviets had somewhat surpassed the free peoples.

His secretary, Maximov, had thoughtfully forwarded Lamenula, to temper the hardships of the premier's Siberian hegira.[1] He was amused, even somewhat stirred, to learn the young lady had objected to the trip, had fought, was even now in a state of alternate hysteria and coma—or simulated coma. A little communist discipline was evidently needed, and being applied; and he would take pleasure in administering the finishing touches.

Late that night he woke up with a feeling of uneasiness. A feeling, he decided, of

[1] HEGIRA: flight, departure.

fear. The room was quiet, the guards were in place, nothing menaced him in the immediate moment, and Lamenula was asleep. Her bruises were beginning to show, but she had learned how to avoid them in the future, which was the use of bruises.

What frightened him was the angel. Church music, which he had remembered, but refused to listen to in his mind, now came back to him. It did not cause him to believe that the visitor had given a new validity to an Old Testament. It had already caused him to speculate that what he, and a billion others, had thitherto regarded as pure myth might actually be founded on scientific fact.

What therefore frightened the premier as he lay on the great bed in the huge, gaudily decorated bedchamber, was an intuition of ignorance. Neither he nor his physicists, he nor his political philosophers —nor any men in the world that still, ludicrously, blindly, referred to itself as "free" —really knew anything fundamental about the universe. Nobody really knew, and could demonstrate scientifically, the "why" of time and space and energy—or matter. The angel—the very beautiful angel that had lain on the cold tundra—might possibly mean and be something that not he nor any living man, skeptic or believer, could even comprehend.

That idea wakened him thoroughly. Here was a brand-new dimension of the unknown to be faced. He sat up, switched on the light and put a cigarette in his thin mouth.

How, he asked himself, could this fear of the unknown be translated into a hatred of something known, and so employed to enhance power? His power. That was, invariably, the formulation; once made, it generally supplied its own answer.

You could not, however, set the people in the Soviets and the people in the rest of the world to hating angels. Not when, especially, their reality—or real counterpart— could never be exhibited and had become a military secret.

Mornsk's theory bemused[1] him. Had the Americans also shot one down with an H-bomb? If so, they'd followed a procedure like his own, apparently. Saying nothing. Examining the victim, doubtless.

He realized he should go to sleep. He was to be roused early for the test of the next super-H-bomb, but he kept ruminating, as he smoked, on the people of the United States. *Whom*, he reflected, *we shall destroy in millions* in—The number of months and days remaining before the blitz of the U.S.A. was so immense a secret that he did not let himself reckon it exactly. *Whom we shall slaughter in sudden millions, soon.*

But suppose something intervened? Angels?

He smiled again. Even if such creatures had visited the earth once before, it was long ago. They might be here again now. They would presumably go away again, for millenniums. Ample time to plant the Red flag everywhere in the world.

Still, he could not know, and not to know was alarming.

There was a phone beside his bed. He could astound telephone operators halfway around the world, and yet, doubtless, in ten minutes, fifteen—perhaps an hour—he could converse with the President of the United States.

"Seen any angels, Mr. President? . . . What do you make of it? . . . Perhaps we

[1] BEMUSED: puzzled.

aren't as knowing as we imagine. . . . Possibly we should meet and talk things over —postpone any—plans we might have for the near future? At least, until this matter of invading angels is settled."

It wouldn't be that simple or that quick, but it might be done. And it might be that was the only possible way to save the Soviet, because it might be the one way left to save man and his planet.

He thought about the abandonment of the communist philosophy, the scrapping of decades of horror and sacrifice, the relaxing of the steely discipline; he thought of the dreams of world domination gone glimmering—of "freedom" being equated with communism. There welled in him the avalanche of hatred which was his essence and the essence of his world. He ground out his cigarette and tried to sleep. . . .

In the morning, after the test shot—which was also very successful and, the premier thought, frightening—he requested the report on the autopsy of the casualty. He had to ask repeatedly, since it became clear that none of the nearby persons—generals, commissars, aides, technicians—wanted to answer. He commanded Mornsk.

The general sweated in the cold air, under a sky again clear and as palely blue as a turquoise. "We have no report, comrade. The autopsy was undertaken last night by Smidz. An ideal man, we felt— the great biologist, who happened to be here, working on radiation effects on pigs. He labored alone all night, and then—your orders, comrade—the—remains were fixed to the bomb." Mornsk's glance at the towering mushroom disposed of that matter. "It was then discovered that Smidz made no notes of whatever he learned."

"Get Smidz."

"This morning early, comrade, he killed himself."

General Scott did not return to the Pacific until nearly Christmastime. He had hoped not to go back at all, particularly since he had spent the autumn with his family in Baltimore, commuting weekdays to the Pentagon. In December, however, he received secret information of still another series of springtime nuclear-weapons tests and orders to fly again to the Sangre Islands, where he would prepare another of the group for total sacrifice. The death of islands was becoming commonplace to the weaponeers. In the unfinished span of his own military career, a suitable target had grown from a square of canvas stretched over a wooden frame to a building, and then to a city block, next a city's heart, and now, an island the size of Manhattan. This, moreover, was not holed, wrecked or merely set afire, but wiped off the earth's face, its roots burned away deep into the sea, its substance thrown, poisonous, across the skies.

He went reluctantly, but as a soldier must, aware that by now he had the broadest experience—among general officers— for the task at hand.

Work went ahead with no more than the usual quota of "bugs"—or what his orderly would have called "snafus." It was a matter of "multiple snafu," however, which finally led the general to order a light plane to fly him to Tempest Island. There had arisen an argument with the natives about property rights; there was some trouble with the placement of instruments; a problem about electric power had come up; and a continuing report of bad chow was being turned in from the island mess hall. Time for a high-echelon look-see.

As he flew in, General Scott noticed the changes which he had helped to devise. The mission playing field had been bull-dozed big enough to accommodate fair-sized cargo planes on two x-angled strips. Here and there the green rug of jungle had been macheted open to contain new meas-uring devices of the scientists. The harbor had been deepened; dredged-up coral made a mole against the purple Pacific as well as the foundation for a sizable pier. Other-wise, Tempest was the same.

His mind, naturally, returned to his pre-vious trip and to what had been found on the island. The general had observed a growing tendency, even in Admiral Stan-forth and Rawson, now a colonel, to recall the angel more as a figure of a dream than as reality. Just before the landing gear came down he looked for, and saw, the very glade in which the angel had fallen. Its clear spring was an emerald eye and the Bletias were in violet bloom all around.

Then he was on the ground, busy with other officers, busy with the plans and problems of a great nation, scared, arming, ready these days for war at the notice of a moment or at no notice whatever. Even here, thousands upon thousands of miles from the nervous target areas of civiliza-tion, the fear and the desperate urgency of man had rolled up, parting the jungle and erecting grim engines associated with ruin.

He was on his way to the headquarters tent when he noticed, and recognized, the young boy.

Teddy Simms, he thought, was about ten now, the age of his own son. But Teddy looked older than ten, and very sad.

The general stepped away from his ac-companying officers. "You go on," he said.

"I'll soon catch up. This is an old friend of mine." He waved then. "Hi, Ted! Why you all dressed up? Remember me?"

The youngster stopped and did recognize the general, with a look of anxiousness. He nodded and glanced down at his clothes. "I'm gonna leave! Tonight. It'll be"—his face brightened slightly—"my very first airplane ride!"

"That's swell!" The general had been puzzled by signs of apprehension in the boy. "How's your father? And your aunt? Cora, wasn't it?"

"She's O.K. But father—" His lip shook.

Marc Scott no longer smiled. "Your father—"

The boy answered stonily, "Went nuts."

"After—" the general asked, knew the answer and was unsurprised by the boy's increased anxiousness.

"I'm not allowed to say. I'd go to prison forever."

A jeepful of soldiers passed. The gen-eral moved to the boy's side and said, "With me, you are, Ted. Because I know all about it too. I'm—I'm mighty sorry your father—is ill. Maybe he'll recover, though."

"The board doesn't think so. They're giving up the mission. That's why I'm going away. To school, Stateside. Father"—he fell in step with the general, leaping slightly with each stride—"father never got any better—after that old day you were here."

"What say, we go back where—it hap-pened? I'd like to see it once more, Ted."

"No." Teddy amended it, "No, sir. I'm not even allowed to talk about it. I don't ever go there!"

"It's too bad. I thought it was the most beautiful thing that ever happened to me in my life."

The boy stared at the man incredulously. "You did? Father thought it was the worst thing ever happened."

"I felt as if you, Ted—and I—all of us—were seeing something completely wonderful!"

The boy's face showed an agreement which changed, slowly, to a pitiable emotion—regret, or fear, perhaps shame. It was the general's intuition which bridged the moment: Teddy knew more than he had ever said about the angel; he had lied originally or omitted something.

"What is it, son?" The general's tone was fatherly. Eyes darted toward the jungle, back to the general and rested measuringly, then hopelessly. It was as if the youngster had considered aloud running away and had decided his adversary[1] was too powerful to evade.

He stood silent a moment longer; then said almost incoherently, "I never meant to keep it! But it is gold! And we were always so mighty poor! I thought, for a while, if father sold it—But he couldn't even think of things like selling gold books. He had lost his reason."

If the general's heart surged, if his mind was stunned, he did not show it. "Gold books?" His eyes forgave in advance.

"Just one book, but heavy." The dismal boy looked at the ground. "I didn't steal it, really! That angel—dropped it."

The general's effort was tremendous. Not in battle had composure[2] cost him as dear. "You—read it?"

"Huh!" the boy said. "It was in all kinds of other languages. 'Wisdom,' that angel said it was. 'Gathered from our whole galaxy—for Earth.' Did you ever know—" His voice intensified with the question, as if by asking it he might divert attention from his guilt. "Did you know there are other people on other planets of other suns, all around? Maybe Vega, or the North Star, or Rigel, or more likely old Sirius? That angel mentioned a few names. I forget which."

"No. I didn't realize it. And, you say, this book had a message for the people on Earth, written in all languages? Not English, though?"

"I didn't see any English. I saw—like Japanese and Arabian—and a lot of kinds of alphabets you never heard of—some, just dots."

"And you—threw it away?" He asked it easily too.

"Naw. You couldn't do that! It's gold—at least, it looks like gold. All metal pages. It's got hinges, kind of, for every page. I guess it's fireproof and even space-proof, at the least. I didn't throw it away. I hid it under an old rock. Come on. I'll show you."

They returned to the glade. The book lay beneath a flat stone. There had been another the general was never to know about —a book buried beneath a sod hut in Siberia by a peasant who also had intended to sell it, for he, too, had been poor. But the other book, identical, along with the hovel above it, had been reduced to fractions of its atoms by a certain test weapon which had destroyed the body of its bearer.

This one the general picked up with shaking hands, opened and gazed upon with an ashen face.

The hot sun of noon illumined the violet orchids around his tailored legs. The boy stood looking up at him, awaiting judgment, accustomed to harshness; and about them was the black and white filigree[3] of

---

[1] ADVERSARY: opponent.
[2] COMPOSURE: calmness.
[3] FILIGREE: delicate ornamental work.

tropical forest. With inexpressible amazement, Marc searched page after page of inscriptions in languages unknown, unsuspected until then. It became apparent that there was one message only, very short, set again and again and again, but he did not know what it was until, toward the last pages, he found the tongues of Earth.

A sound was made by the man as he read them—a sound that began with murmurous despair and ended, as comprehension entered his brain, with a note of exultation. For the message of icy space and flaring stars was this: "Love one another."

FOR DISCUSSION

1. Throughout the story, several possible explanations of the fantastic winged creature are suggested. Which explanation seems most likely? Use evidence from the story to justify your conclusions.

2. The discovery of the angel has different effects on each of the people involved. How does it affect the general? Reverend Simms? The Russian premier? What does each individual's reaction reveal of his own personal philosophy of life?

3. The angel's dying words are, "I was too late." Do you think he was right—will his message go unheard? Is there any point in the story when it seems as if the angel may have succeeded in its mission to the Russians?

4. What human trait caused Ted and the Russian peasant to try to keep the angel's gold book? What do you think the general will do with the book?

5. The winged creatures raise many important questions, questions which reveal what the Russian premier terms the fundamental ignorance of man. What is "the answer" mentioned in the title of the story?

In Summary

FOR DISCUSSION

1. In the introduction to this unit, McFarland states, ". . . Each of the futures here envisaged throws light back on the present, from which all of them will emerge." What insights into our present life can we gain from the individual stories and poems in this unit? Discuss, using the stories you have read as points of reference, how the science fiction genre enables writers to comment on the dangers of certain trends they observe in their own societies.

2. A favorite topic of science fiction writers is the idea of complete government control of people's lives. How many of the stories in this unit contain this idea or variations on it? What trait in modern society is the basis for such predictions?

3. "Who Shall Dwell," "The Weapon," and "The Answer" are all somewhat similar in theme. Describe the concerns which these stories share. What other likenesses do you observe? Which of these stories do you feel was most successful? Explain your answer thoroughly; include comments on characters, setting, plot, and writing techniques.

OTHER THINGS TO DO

1. Write a short social and political history of the next hundred years. You will want to take advantage of the science fiction writer's technique of looking to present trends to discover the most likely course of future events.

2. Have volunteers from the class write and perform a play set in a future time. You may decide to dramatize one of the stories in this unit, or write your own original play. In planning your presentation, consider what costumes, props, and sets you will want to design to evoke the particular future your play describes.

3. The civilized world has been destroyed by atomic war; you are one of the few survivors. Consider how you would begin to refashion civilization. What aspects of contemporary life would you decide were expendable? What new experiments in social organization would you suggest? What aspects of civilization would you make a special effort to preserve? Prepare a report of your recommendations for your fellow survivors.

The World of Words

THE PEDESTRIAN

Within the word *pedestrian* lie the remains of the Latin word *pedalis*, meaning "of the foot." What does *pedestrian* have to do with *foot*? A number of other common words in English may be traced back to that same Latin word. What do a piano *pedal* and a tricycle *pedal* have in common? What is a *pedestal* and where is it found? A *manicure* is a cosmetic treatment of the hands (compare the word *manicure* with *manual labor* and *manufacture*, both having to do with hands). What is a *pedicure*? What is a *podiatrist*? Is that word derived from the same source as *pedestrian*?

WHO SHALL DWELL

The word *retaliation* (page 378) plays a crucial role in helping the reader to understand the events of the story, but its meaning is a complex one. The Latin roots from which this word is derived are *re*, meaning "back" or "again" and *talio*, meaning "something paid out." Can you explain by what line of reasoning a connection might be made between the root meaning of *talio* as "payment" and its derivation in this word as "punishment"?

SINISTER JOURNEY

Douglas Creel often dreamed of a *Utopia*—a perfect state. The word *Utopia* was originally coined by the English philosopher Sir Thomas More in 1516 when he used that word in a book he wrote as the name of an imaginary island where all men lived under ideal social and political conditions. The word *Utopia* is a combination of two Greek roots, *ou*, meaning "no" or "not" and *topos*, meaning "place." Knowing the derivation of the word *Utopia*, what comment can we assume Sir Thomas More was making about the possibility in reality for men to plan such a perfect world? Does the author of "Sinister Journey" seem to agree or disagree with this skepticism?

COLUMBUS WAS A DOPE

Professor Appleby is chief engineer of the starship *Pegasus*. Is *Pegasus* an appropriate name for such a craft? Why, or why not? The current space program to explore the moon is named after the Greek god Apollo. With what heavenly body is that god traditionally associated? Considering its goals, is the Apollo Space Program well-named?

EXAMINATION DAY

Besides the fact that all appear in "Examination Day," what have the following words in common: *birthday, breakfast, tablecloth, newspaper, archway, clipboard, courtroom, doorway, loudspeaker, buttermilk, peppermint,* and *armchair?* What do those twelve words taken together suggest about one source of words in English?

THE WEAPON

Niemand is described as "a small man, nondescript" (page 403). *Nondescript* is a word built on the Latin verb *scribere,* meaning "to write." To the root *script,* which comes from that Latin word, have been added two prefixes, or syllables before the root to alter the meaning. One is *de-,* meaning "down." A *description* is something written down. But the prefix *non-* means "not"; so *nondescript* means literally "not written down"—because, in fact, the person who is nondescript has so little about him that is distinctive or notable that it is impossible to describe him, or set down anything about him. What does *scripture* have to do with the Latin verb *scribere?* What is a movie *script?* An *inscription?*

SOMEDAY

The gadget Niccolo is listening to at the start of "Someday" is called a *bard.* Shakespeare is sometimes referred to as The Bard, or supreme poet of our language, for *bard* means "poet," but, more, a particularly gifted and inspired poet. Why is the machine in "Someday" called a bard? What role does it play in the society of which it is a part? *Poet,* incidentally, comes from a Greek word meaning "maker." A poet makes poems, of course, but he does more than that: he creates new ways of looking at familiar things. He "makes" new perceptions for us, and frequently makes beauty where we may not have seen it before. What is the difference between a poet and a *versifier,* a *rhymester,* and a *poetaster?*

THE ANSWER

1. General Scott wonders if the sadness he feels is a *prescience* of failure (page 427). The word *prescience* is made up of a prefix and a root. A prefix is something "fixed" on before a root word, and *pre-* is itself a prefix meaning "before." The root in this case is *science,* though *prescience* is not pronounced as the two separate parts of the word would indicate. How is it pronounced? What does the word mean? *Science* refers to knowledge, and a *scientist* is one who knows or seeks to know. What is *omniscience? Conscience* comes from a Latin verb, *conscire,* meaning "to know well." *Conscience* is one word: *conscious* another, from a different source, though both words are related to forms of the Latin verb *scire,* "to know." What does *conscious* mean? That meaning arises from the root meaning "to know" and a prefix meaning "together," the same prefix that appears in such words as *conference, contest,* and *construct.* What does each of those three words have to do with the concept of "together"?

2. Some words are acronyms, made up of initials that originally designated a longer form of the word. *Jeep,* for example, was originally a military vehicle designed to be used for general purposes: hence, a G. P. vehicle. In time the name was shortened to *jeep.* What is the derivation of the acronym *snafu* (page 448)?

Reader's Choice

Earth is Room Enough, *by Isaac Asimov.*

"The earth is room enough" for these fascinating stories of the future. Spaceships and trips to other planets are not necessary, because Asimov can keep your imagination spinning with stories that take place in the future right here on earth.

I Sing the Body Electric! *by Ray Bradbury.*

Read about mechanical grandmothers and fourth dimensional babies, as well as the Irish Republican Army and Texas chicken farmers in this collection of eighteen stories.

Nineteen-Eighty-Four, *by George Orwell.*

This is a terrifying picture of a world where Big Brother and the mass media of communication invade and enslave all aspects of men's lives. No one is ever really alone in this society which forces a uniform pattern of existence.

The People: No Different Flesh, *by Zenna Henderson.*

The People, refugees from another planet, have been stranded at various places on Earth. They now seek to reunite, but in order to avoid suspicion, they must hide their unearthly powers. This is the story of these People and the humans whose lives they touched in strange and beautiful ways.

The Science Fiction Hall of Fame, Volume One, *edited by Robert Silverberg.*

The twenty-six stories in this anthology were chosen by members of the Science Fiction Writers of America as the best of all time. The authors represented are the best in science fiction today, and this volume is a good introduction to the field.

Tunnel in the Sky, *by Robert Heinlein.*

At the start of the story, a high school class is preparing for a "survival" test—on an unknown and uncivilized planet. When the group is accidently stranded, they must create their own government and society in order to survive.

2001: A Space Odyssey, *by Arthur C. Clarke.*

Mysterious obelisks which appear in prehistoric Africa, the moon, and Saturn lead two astronauts and their talking computer Hal on a mysterious voyage to the furthest reaches of space.

The Weans, *by Robert Nathan.*

The time is the 7850's and archeologists have discovered the remains of a strange civilization—one that will seem increasingly familiar to contemporary readers. The people of this ancient—and bizarre—civilization referred to themselves as *we* or *us*, so the research team names them the *Weans* in this hilarious—and frightening—spoof.

A Wrinkle in Time, *by Madeline L'Engle.*

When Meg's scientist father disappears while engaged in secret government work, she and two of her friends set off to find him. He has been working on tesseracts (wrinkles in time) and now the three youngsters must set out on a perilous journey through time to rescue him.

INSIGHTS

WHERE do insights come from—those sudden glimpses that let us know with our hearts what before we knew, if at all, only with our minds? There is a mystery about insights. We may for years have been aware of some saying without really hearing it: "You never miss the water till the well runs dry." Yes, we nod with a yawn, and turn to other things. But one day the truth of that saying may be brought home to us in the deepest way. Someone we have always taken for granted dies, and we understand at last, through emotion rather than intellect, just what the saying means. It isn't talking, primarily, about wells and water. Instead, it remarks on something far more profound, which accounts for why the saying has been handed down from generation to generation as each new person makes his own discovery of its meaning.

Frequently insights come in the most unlikely places, among the least likely people. Two friends who live and think the same way may be less inclined to throw the world suddenly into a new perspective than are two people utterly different from each other. A child goes to visit an old folks' home. What that innocent girl finds there may change her feelings about life from then on: about where all of us are headed, about the neglects of youth, about the betrayals of time.

Does that mean that only opposites in touch with each other can illuminate each other's life? Not really. Friends do share insights, and sometimes a person by himself, on a city street, in his room, idling in woods, may come upon an insight that transforms that day and all the days ahead. We can court insights and encourage them by being alert and responsive, but finally they come when they choose, and often when least expected.

Philip McFarland

Johnny's mom was a nice, well-meaning lady, but she did have some pretty weird ideas.

AFTER YOU, MY DEAR ALPHONSE

SHIRLEY JACKSON

MRS. WILSON was just taking the gingerbread out of the oven when she heard Johnny outside talking to someone.

"Johnny," she called, "you're late. Come in and get your lunch."

"Just a minute, Mother," Johnny said. "After you, my dear Alphonse."

"After *you*, my dear Alphonse," another voice said.

"No, after *you*, my dear Alphonse," Johnny said.

Mrs. Wilson opened the door. "Johnny," she said, "you come in this minute and get your lunch. You can play after you've eaten."

Johnny came in after her, slowly. "Mother," he said, "I brought Boyd home for lunch with me."

"Boyd?" Mrs. Wilson thought for a moment. "I don't believe I've met Boyd. Bring him in, dear, since you've invited him. Lunch is ready."

"Boyd!" Johnny yelled. "Hey, Boyd, come on in!"

"I'm coming. Just got to unload this stuff."

"Well, hurry, or my mother'll be sore."

"Johnny, that's not very polite to either your friend or your mother," Mrs. Wilson said. "Come sit down, Boyd."

As she turned to show Boyd where to sit, she saw he was a Negro boy, smaller than Johnny but about the same age. His arms were loaded with split kindling wood. "Where'll I put this stuff, Johnny?" he asked.

Mrs. Wilson turned to Johnny. "Johnny," she said, "what did you make Boyd do? What is that wood?"

"Dead Japanese," Johnny said mildly. "We stand them in the ground and run over them with tanks."

"How do you do, Mrs. Wilson?" Boyd said.

"How do you do, Boyd? You shouldn't let Johnny make you carry all that wood. Sit down now and eat lunch, both of you."

"Why shouldn't he carry the wood, Mother? It's his wood. We got it at his place."

"Johnny," Mrs. Wilson said, "go on and eat your lunch."

"Sure," Johnny said. He held out the dish of scrambled eggs to Boyd. "After you, my dear Alphonse."

"After *you*, my dear Alphonse," Boyd said.

"After *you*, my dear Alphonse," Johnny said. They began to giggle.

"Are you hungry, Boyd?" Mrs. Wilson asked.

"Yes, Mrs. Wilson."

"Well, don't you let Johnny stop you.

He always fusses about eating, so you just see that you get a good lunch. There's plenty of food here for you to have all you want."

"Thank you, Mrs. Wilson."

"Come on, Alphonse," Johnny said. He pushed half the scrambled eggs onto Boyd's plate. Boyd watched while Mrs. Wilson put a dish of stewed tomatoes beside his plate.

"Boyd don't eat tomatoes, do you, Boyd?" Johnny said.

"*Doesn't* eat tomatoes, Johnny. And just because you don't like them, don't say that about Boyd. Boyd will eat *anything*."

"Bet he won't," Johnny said, attacking his scrambled eggs.

"Boyd wants to grow up and be a big strong man so he can work hard," Mrs. Wilson said. "I'll bet Boyd's father eats stewed tomatoes."

"My father eats anything he wants to," Boyd said.

"So does mine," Johnny said. "Sometimes he doesn't eat hardly anything. He's a little guy, though. Wouldn't hurt a flea."

"Mine's a little guy too," Boyd said.

"I'll bet he's strong, though," Mrs. Wilson said. She hesitated. "Does he . . . work?"

"Sure," Johnny said. "Boyd's father works in a factory."

"There, you see?" Mrs. Wilson said. "And he certainly has to be strong to do that—all that lifting and carrying at a factory."

"Boyd's father doesn't have to," Johnny said. "He's a foreman."

Mrs. Wilson felt defeated. "What does your mother do, Boyd?"

"My mother?" Boyd was surprised. "She takes care of us kids."

"Oh. She doesn't work, then?"

"Why should she?" Johnny said through a mouthful of eggs. "You don't work."

"You really don't want any stewed tomatoes, Boyd?"

"No, thank you, Mrs. Wilson," Boyd said.

"No, thank you, Mrs. Wilson, no, thank you, Mrs. Wilson, no, thank you, Mrs. Wilson," Johnny said. "Boyd's sister's going to work, though. She's going to be a teacher."

"That's a very fine attitude for her to have, Boyd." Mrs. Wilson restrained an impulse to pat Boyd on the head. "I imagine you're all very proud of her?"

"I guess so," Boyd said.

"What about all your other brothers and sisters? I guess all of you want to make just as much of yourselves as you can."

"There's only me and Jean," Boyd said. "I don't know yet what I want to be when I grow up."

"We're going to be tank drivers, Boyd and me," Johnny said. "Zoom."

Mrs. Wilson caught Boyd's glass of milk as Johnny's napkin ring, suddenly transformed into a tank, plowed heavily across the table.

"Look, Johnny," Boyd said. "Here's a foxhole. I'm shooting at you."

Mrs. Wilson, with the speed born of long experience, took the gingerbread off the shelf and placed it carefully between the tank and the foxhole.

"Now eat as much as you want to, Boyd," she said. "I want to see you get filled up."

"Boyd eats a lot, but not as much as I do," Johnny said. "I'm bigger than he is."

"You're not much bigger," Boyd said. "I can beat you running."

Mrs. Wilson took a deep breath. "Boyd,"

she said. Both boys turned to her. "Boyd, Johnny has some suits that are a little too small for him, and a winter coat. It's not new, of course, but there's lots of wear in it still. And I have a few dresses that your mother or sister could probably use. Your mother can make them over into lots of things for all of you, and I'd be very happy to give them to you. Suppose before you leave I make up a big bundle, and then you and Johnny can take it over to your mother right away. . . ." Her voice trailed off as she saw Boyd's puzzled expression.

"But I have plenty of clothes, thank you," he said. "And I don't think my mother knows how to sew very well, and anyway I guess we buy about everything we need. Thank you very much, though."

"We don't have time to carry that old stuff around, Mother," Johnny said. "We got to play tanks with the kids today."

Mrs. Wilson lifted the plate of gingerbread off the table as Boyd was about to take another piece. "There are many little boys like you, Boyd, who would be very grateful for the clothes someone was kind enough to give them."

"Boyd will take them if you want him to, Mother," Johnny said.

"I didn't mean to make you mad, Mrs. Wilson," Boyd said.

"Don't think I'm angry, Boyd. I'm just disappointed in you, that's all. Now let's not say anything more about it."

She began clearing the plates off the table, and Johnny took Boyd's hand and pulled him to the door. "Bye, Mother," Johnny said. Boyd stood for a minute, staring at Mrs. Wilson's back.

"After you, my dear Alphonse," Johnny said, holding the door open.

"Is your mother still mad?" Mrs. Wilson heard Boyd ask in a low voice.

"I don't know," Johnny said. "She's screwy sometimes."

"So's mine," Boyd said. He hesitated. "After *you*, my dear Alphonse."

FOR DISCUSSION

1. Mrs. Wilson's first reactions to Boyd seem kind and sympathetic. How soon does she begin to reveal her prejudices about blacks? Re-examine each of her comments to Boyd; what common stereotype about black people does each one represent?

2. Why do you think Mrs. Wilson is so eager to give clothing to Boyd? Can you explain her attitude when Boyd refuses the offer? What insight into Mrs. Wilson's character is revealed in this incident?

FIFTEEN

WILLIAM STAFFORD

South of the Bridge on Seventeenth
I found back of the willows one summer
day a motorcycle with engine running
as it lay on its side, ticking over
slowly in the high grass. I was fifteen.   5

I admired all that pulsing gleam, the
shiny flanks, the demure* headlights
fringed where it lay; I led it gently
to the road and stood with that
companion, ready and friendly. I was fifteen.   10

We could find the end of a road, meet
the sky on out Seventeenth. I thought about
hills, and patting the handle got back a
confident opinion. On the bridge we indulged
a forward feeling, a tremble. I was fifteen.   15

Thinking, back farther in the grass I found
the owner, just coming to, where he had flipped
over the rail. He had blood on his hand, was pale—
I helped him walk to his machine. He ran his hand
over it, called me good man, roared away.   20

I stood there, fifteen.

⁷ DEMURE: shy.

FOR DISCUSSION

1. Stafford repeats the age of the boy in this poem four times. Why is the boy's age so important?

2. Find evidence to suggest that the motorcycle seems in the boy's imagination to be something living. What temptation does it offer?

3. The poem contains two separate sets of feelings that the boy has about finding the motorcycle. Carefully reread the poem to locate the point at which the boy has an insight about the deeper and more serious implications of the overturned cycle. What word signals this change?

Eli had caught himself in a hideous trap with his lie. But it was the baring of another, even greater lie that was to bring the deepest shame to all the Remenzels. . . .

THE LIE

KURT VONNEGUT, JR.

IT WAS EARLY springtime. Weak sunshine lay cold on old gray frost. Willow twigs against the sky showed the golden haze of fat catkins[1] about to bloom. A black Rolls-Royce streaked up the Connecticut Turnpike from New York City. At the wheel was Ben Barkley, a black chauffeur.

"Keep it under the speed limit, Ben," said Doctor Remenzel. "I don't care how ridiculous any speed limit seems, stay under it. No reason to rush—we have plenty of time."

Ben eased off on the throttle. "Seems like in the springtime she wants to get up and go," he said.

"Do what you can to keep her down—O.K.?" said the doctor.

"Yes, sir!" said Ben. He spoke in a lower voice to the thirteen-year-old boy who was riding beside him, to Eli Remenzel, the doctor's son. "Ain't just people and animals feel good in the springtime," he said to Eli. "Motors feel good too."

"Um," said Eli.

"Everything feel good," said Ben. "Don't you feel good?"

"Sure, sure I feel good," said Eli emptily.

"Should feel good—going to that wonderful school," said Ben.

That wonderful school was the Whitehill School for Boys, a private preparatory school in North Marston, Massachusetts. That was where the Rolls-Royce was bound. The plan was that Eli would enroll for the fall semester, while his father, a member of the class of 1939, attended a meeting of the Board of Overseers of the school.

"Don't believe this boy's feeling so good, doctor," said Ben. He wasn't particularly serious about it. It was more genial[2] springtime blather.[3]

"What's the matter, Eli?" said the doctor absently. He was studying blueprints, plans for a thirty-room addition to the Eli Remenzel Memorial Dormitory—a building named in honor of his great-great-grandfather. Doctor Remenzel had the plans draped over a walnut table that folded out of the back of the front seat. He was a massive, dignified man, a physician, a healer for healing's sake, since he had been born as rich as the Shah of Iran. "Worried about something?" he asked Eli without looking up from the plans.

---

[1] CATKINS: type of flower.

[2] GENIAL (jēn′yəl): friendly, pleasant.
[3] BLATHER: nonsense.

"Nope," said Eli.

Eli's lovely mother, Sylvia, sat next to the doctor, reading the catalogue of the Whitehill School. "If I were you," she said to Eli, "I'd be so excited I could hardly stand it. The best four years of your whole life are just about to begin."

"Sure," said Eli. He didn't show her his face. He gave her only the back of his head, a pinwheel of coarse brown hair above a stiff white collar, to talk to.

"I wonder how many Remenzels have gone to Whitehill," said Sylvia.

"That's like asking how many people are dead in a cemetery," said the doctor. He gave the answer to the old joke, and to Sylvia's question too. "All of 'em."

"If all the Remenzels who went to Whitehill were numbered, what number would Eli be?" said Sylvia. "That's what I'm getting at."

The question annoyed Doctor Remenzel a little. It didn't seem in very good taste. "It isn't the sort of thing you keep score on," he said.

"Guess," said his wife.

"Oh," he said, "you'd have to go back through all the records, all the way back to the end of the eighteenth century, even, to make any kind of a guess. And you'd have to decide whether to count the Schofields and the Haleys and the MacLellans as Remenzels."

"Please make a guess—" said Sylvia, "just people whose last names were Remenzel."

"Oh—" The doctor shrugged, rattled the plans. "Thirty maybe."

"So Eli is number thirty-one!" said Sylvia, delighted with the number. "You're number thirty-one, dear," she said to the back of Eli's head.

Doctor Remenzel rattled the plans again. "I don't want him going around saying something asinine,[1] like he's number thirty-one," he said.

"Eli knows better than that," said Sylvia. She was a game,[2] ambitious woman, with no money of her own at all. She had been married for sixteen years, but was still openly curious and enthusiastic about the ways of families that had been rich for many generations.

"Just for my own curiosity—not so Eli can go around saying what number he is," said Sylvia, "I'm going to go wherever they keep the records and find out what number he is. That's what I'll do while you're at the meeting and Eli's doing whatever he has to do at the Admissions Office."

"All right," said Doctor Remenzel, "you go ahead and *do* that."

"I will," said Sylvia. "I think things like that are interesting, even if you don't." She waited for a rise on that, but didn't get one. Sylvia enjoyed arguing with her husband about her lack of reserve and his excess of it, enjoyed saying, toward the end of arguments like that, "Well, I guess I'm just a simple-minded country girl at heart, and that's all I'll ever be, and I'm afraid you're going to have to get used to it."

But Doctor Remenzel didn't want to play that game. He found the dormitory plans more interesting.

"Will the new rooms have fireplaces?" said Sylvia. In the oldest part of the dormitory, several of the rooms had handsome fireplaces.

"That would practically double the cost of construction," said the doctor.

---

[1] ASININE: idiotic.
[2] GAME: plucky; a good sport.

"I want Eli to have a room with a fireplace, if that's possible," said Sylvia.

"Those rooms are for seniors."

"I thought maybe through some fluke—" said Sylvia.

"What kind of fluke do you have in mind?" said the doctor. "You mean I should demand that Eli be given a room with a fireplace?"

"Not *demand*—" said Sylvia.

"Request firmly?" said the doctor.

"Maybe I'm just a simple-minded country girl at heart," said Sylvia, "but I look through this catalogue, and I see all the buildings named after Remenzels, look through the back and see all the hundreds of thousands of dollars given by Remenzels for scholarships, and I just can't help thinking people named Remenzel are entitled to ask for a little something extra."

"Let me tell you in no uncertain terms," said Doctor Remenzel, "that you are not to ask for anything special for Eli—not anything."

"Of course I won't," said Sylvia. "Why do you always think I'm going to embarrass you?"

"I don't," he said.

"But I can still think what I think, can't I?" she said.

"If you have to," he said.

"I have to," she said cheerfully, utterly unrepentant. She leaned over the plans. "You think those people will like those rooms?"

"What people?" he said.

"The Africans," she said. She was talking about thirty Africans who, at the request of the State Department, were being admitted to Whitehill in the coming semester. It was because of them that the dormitory was being expanded.

"The rooms aren't for them," he said. "They aren't going to be segregated."

"Oh," said Sylvia. She thought about this awhile, and then she said, "Is there a chance Eli will have to have one of them for a roommate?"

"Freshmen draw lots for roommates," said the doctor. "That piece of information's in the catalogue too."

"Eli?" said Sylvia.

"H'm?" said Eli.

"How would you feel about it if you had to room with one of those Africans?"

Eli shrugged listlessly.[1]

"That's all right?" said Sylvia.

Eli shrugged again.

"I guess it's all right," said Sylvia.

"It had better be," said the doctor.

The Rolls-Royce pulled abreast of an old Chevrolet, a car in such bad repair that its back door was lashed shut with clothesline. Doctor Remenzel glanced casually at the driver, and then, with sudden excitement and pleasure, he told Ben Barkley to stay abreast of the car.

The doctor leaned across Sylvia, rolled down his window, yelled to the driver of the old Chevrolet, "Tom! Tom!"

The man was a Whitehill classmate of the doctor. He wore a Whitehill necktie, which he waved at Doctor Remenzel in gay recognition. And then he pointed to the fine young son who sat beside him, conveyed with proud smiles and nods that the boy was bound for Whitehill.

Doctor Remenzel pointed to the chaos of the back of Eli's head, beamed that his news was the same. In the wind blustering between the two cars they made a lunch date at the Holly House in North Marston, at the inn whose principal business was

[1] LISTLESSLY: without energy or enthusiasm.

serving visitors to Whitehill.

"All right," said Doctor Remenzel to Ben Barkley, "drive on."

"You know," said Sylvia, "somebody really ought to write an article—" And she turned to look through the back window at the old car now shuddering far behind. "Somebody really ought to."

"What about?" said the doctor. He noticed that Eli had slumped way down in the front seat. "Eli!" he said sharply. "Sit up straight!" He returned his attention to Sylvia.

"Most people think prep schools are such snobbish things, just for people with money," said Sylvia, "but that isn't true." She leafed through the catalogue and found the quotation she was after.

"*The Whitehill School operates on the assumption,*" she read, "*that no boy should be deterred from applying for admission because his family is unable to pay the full cost of a Whitehill education. With this in mind, the Admissions Committee selects each year from approximately 3000 candidates the 150 most promising and deserving boys, regardless of their parents' ability to pay the full $2200 tuition. And those in need of financial aid are given it to the full extent of their need. In certain instances, the school will even pay for the clothing and transportation of a boy.*"

Sylvia shook her head. "I think that's perfectly amazing. It's something most people don't realize at all. A truckdriver's son can come to Whitehill."

"If he's smart enough," he said.

"Thanks to the Remenzels," said Sylvia with pride.

"And a lot of other people too," said the doctor.

Sylvia read out loud again: "*In 1799,*

Eli Remenzel laid the foundation for the present Scholarship Fund by donating to the school forty acres in Boston. The school still owns twelve of those acres, their current evaluation being $3,000,000."

"Eli!" said the doctor. "Sit up! What's the matter with you?"

Eli sat up again, but began to slump almost immediately, like a snowman in hell. Eli had good reason for slumping, for actually hoping to die or disappear. He could not bring himself to say what the reason was. He slumped because he knew he had been denied admission to Whitehill. He had failed the entrance examinations. Eli's parents did not know this, because Eli had found the awful notice in the mail and had torn it up.

Doctor Remenzel and his wife had no doubts whatsoever about their son's getting into Whitehill. It was inconceivable to them that Eli could not go there, so they had no curiosity as to how Eli had done on the examinations, were not puzzled when no report ever came.

"What all will Eli have to do to enroll?" said Sylvia, as the black Rolls-Royce crossed the Rhode Island border.

"I don't know," said the doctor. "I suppose they've got it all complicated now with forms to be filled out in quadruplicate, and punch-card machines and bureaucrats. This business of entrance examinations is all new, too. In my day a boy simply had an interview with the headmaster. The headmaster would look him over, ask him a few questions, and then say, 'There's a Whitehill boy.'"

"Did he ever say, 'There isn't a Whitehill boy'?" said Sylvia.

"Oh, sure," said Doctor Remenzel, "if a boy was impossibly stupid or something.

There have to be standards. There have always been standards. The African boys have to meet the standards, just like anybody else. They aren't getting in just because the State Department wants to make friends. We made that clear. Those boys had to meet the standards."

"And they did?" said Sylvia.

"I suppose," said Doctor Remenzel. "I heard they're all in, and they all took the same examination Eli did."

"Was it a hard examination, dear?" Sylvia asked Eli. It was the first time she'd thought to ask.

"Um," said Eli.

"What?" she said.

"Yes," said Eli.

"I'm glad they've got high standards," she said, and then she realized that this was a fairly silly statement. "Of course they've got high standards," she said. "That's why it's such a famous school. That's why people who go there do so well in later life."

Sylvia resumed her reading of the catalogue again, opened out a folding map of "The Sward,"[1] as the campus of Whitehill was traditionally called. She read off the names of features that memorialized Remenzels—the Sanford Remenzel Bird Sanctuary, the George MacLellan Remenzel Skating Rink, the Eli Remenzel Memorial Dormitory, and then she read out loud a quatrain printed on one corner of the map:

"When night falleth gently
"Upon the green Sward,
"It's Whitehill, dear Whitehill,
"Our thoughts all turn toward."

"You know," said Sylvia, "school songs are so corny when you just read them. But

[1] SWARD: old word for *lawn* or *meadow*.

when I hear the Glee Club sing those words, they sound like the most beautiful words ever written, and I want to cry."

"Um," said Doctor Remenzel.

"Did a Remenzel write them?"

"I don't think so," said Doctor Remenzel. And then he said, "No—Wait. That's the *new* song. A Remenzel didn't write it. Tom Hilyer wrote it."

"The man in that old car we passed?"

"Sure," said Doctor Remenzel. "Tom wrote it. I remember when he wrote it."

"A scholarship boy wrote it?" said Sylvia. "I think that's awfully nice. He *was* a scholarship boy, wasn't he?"

"His father was an ordinary automobile mechanic in North Marston."

"You hear what a democratic school you're going to, Eli?" said Sylvia.

Half an hour later Ben Barkley brought the limousine to a stop before the Holly House, a rambling country inn twenty years older than the Republic. The inn was on the edge of the Whitehill Sward, glimpsing the school's rooftops and spires over the innocent wilderness of the Sanford Remenzel Bird Sanctuary.

Ben Barkley was sent away with the car for an hour and a half. Doctor Remenzel shepherded Sylvia and Eli into a familiar, low-ceilinged world of pewter, clocks, lovely old woods, agreeable servants, elegant food and drink.

Eli, clumsy with horror of what was surely to come, banged a grandmother clock with his elbow as he passed, made the clock cry.

Sylvia excused herself. Doctor Remenzel and Eli went to the threshold of the dining room, where a hostess welcomed them both by name. They were given a table beneath an oil portrait of one of the three Whitehill boys who had gone on to become President of the United States.

The dining room was filling quickly with families. What every family had was at least one boy about Eli's age. Most of the boys wore Whitehill blazers—black, with pale blue piping, with Whitehill seals on their breast pockets. A few, like Eli, were not yet entitled to wear blazers, were simply hoping to get in.

The doctor ordered a Martini, then turned to his son and said, "Your mother has the idea that you're entitled to special privileges around here. I hope you don't have that idea too."

"No, sir," said Eli.

"It would be a source of the greatest embarrassment to me," said Doctor Remenzel with considerable grandeur, "if I were ever to hear that you had used the name Remenzel as though you thought Remenzels were something special."

"I know," said Eli wretchedly.

"That settles it," said the doctor. He had nothing more to say about it. He gave abbreviated salutes to several people he knew in the room, speculated as to what sort of party had reserved a long banquet table that was set up along one wall. He decided that it was for a visiting athletic team. Sylvia arrived, and Eli had to be told in a sharp whisper to stand when a woman came to a table.

Sylvia was full of news. The long table, she related, was for the thirty boys from Africa. "I'll bet that's more colored people than have eaten here since this place was founded," she said softly. "How fast things change these days!"

"You're right about how fast things change," said Doctor Remenzel. "You're wrong about the colored people who've eaten here. This used to be a busy part of the Underground Railroad."[1]

"Really?" said Sylvia. "How exciting." She looked all about herself in a birdlike way. "I think everything's exciting here. I only wish Eli had a blazer on."

Doctor Remenzel reddened. "He isn't entitled to one," he said.

"I know that," said Sylvia.

"I thought you were going to ask somebody for permission to put a blazer on Eli right away," said the doctor.

"I wouldn't do that," said Sylvia, a little offended now. "Why are you always afraid I'll embarrass you?"

"Never mind. Excuse me. Forget it," said Doctor Remenzel.

Sylvia brightened again, put her hand on Eli's arm, and looked radiantly at a man in the dining-room doorway. "There's my favorite person in all the world, next to my son and husband," she said. She meant Dr. Donald Warren, headmaster of the Whitehill School. A thin gentleman in his early sixties, Doctor Warren was in the doorway with the manager of the inn, looking over the arrangements for the Africans.

It was then that Eli got up abruptly, fled the dining room, fled as much of the nightmare as he could possibly leave behind. He brushed past Doctor Warren rudely, though he knew him well, though Doctor Warren spoke his name. Doctor Warren looked after him sadly.

"I'll be damned," said Doctor Remenzel. "What brought that on?"

"Maybe he really *is* sick," said Sylvia.

The Remenzels had no time to react more elaborately, because Doctor Warren spotted them and crossed quickly to their

[1] UNDERGROUND RAILROAD: a secret organization which helped runaway slaves travel to freedom in Canada.

table. He greeted them, some of his perplexity[1] about Eli showing in his greeting. He asked if he might sit down.

"Certainly, of course," said Doctor Remenzel expansively.[2] "We'd be honored if you did. Heavens."

"Not to eat," said Doctor Warren. "I'll be eating at the long table with the new boys. I would like to talk, though." He saw that there were five places set at the table. "You're expecting someone?"

"We passed Tom Hilyer and his boy on the way," said Doctor Remenzel. "They'll be along in a minute."

"Good, good," said Doctor Warren absently. He fidgeted, looked again in the direction in which Eli had disappeared.

"Tom's boy will be going to Whitehill in the fall?" said Doctor Remenzel.

"H'm?" said Doctor Warren. "Oh—yes, yes. Yes, he will."

"Is he a scholarship boy, like his father?" said Sylvia.

"That's not a polite question," said Doctor Remenzel severely.

"I beg your pardon," said Sylvia.

"No, no—that's a perfectly proper question these days," said Doctor Warren. "We don't keep that sort of information very secret any more. We're proud of our scholarship boys, and they have every reason to be proud of themselves. Tom's boy got the highest score anyone's ever got on the entrance examinations. We feel privileged to have him."

"We never *did* find out Eli's score," said Doctor Remenzel. He said it with good-humored resignation, without expectation that Eli had done especially well.

"A good strong medium, I imagine," said Sylvia. She said this on the basis of Eli's grades in primary school, which had ranged from medium to terrible.

The headmaster looked surprised. "I didn't tell you his scores?" he said.

"We haven't seen you since he took the examinations," said Doctor Remenzel.

"The letter I wrote you—" said Doctor Warren.

"What letter?" said Doctor Remenzel. "Did we get a letter?"

"A letter from me," said Doctor Warren, with growing incredulity.[3] "The hardest letter I ever had to write."

Sylvia shook her head. "We never got any letter from you."

Doctor Warren sat back, looking very ill. "I mailed it myself," he said. "It was definitely mailed—two weeks ago."

Doctor Remenzel shrugged. "The U.S. mails don't lose much," he said, "but I guess that now and then something gets misplaced."

Doctor Warren cradled his head in his hands. "Oh, dear—oh, my, oh, Lord," he said. "I was surprised to see Eli here. I wondered that he would want to come along with you."

"He didn't come along just to see the scenery," said Doctor Remenzel. "He came to enroll."

"I want to know what was in the letter," said Sylvia.

Doctor Warren raised his head, folded his hands. "What the letter said, was this, and no other words could be more difficult for me to say: *On the basis of his work in primary school and his scores on the entrance examinations, I must tell you that your son and my good friend Eli cannot possibly do the work required of boys*

---

[1] PERPLEXITY: state of being bewildered.
[2] EXPANSIVELY: generously.
[3] INCREDULITY: disbelief; amazement.

at Whitehill.' " Doctor Warren's voice steadied, and so did his gaze. " *'To admit Eli to Whitehill, to expect him to do Whitehill work,'* " he said, " *'would be both unrealistic and cruel.'* "

Thirty African boys, escorted by several faculty members, State Department men, and diplomats from their own countries, filed into the dining room.

And Tom Hilyer and his boy, having no idea that something had just gone awfully wrong for the Remenzels, came in, too, and said hello to the Remenzels and Doctor Warren gaily, as though life couldn't possibly be better.

"I'll talk to you more about this later, if you like," Doctor Warren said to the Remenzels, rising. "I have to go now, but later on—" He left quickly.

"My mind's a blank," said Sylvia. "My mind's a perfect blank."

Tom Hilyer and his boy sat down. Hilyer looked at the menu before him, clapped his hands and said, "What's good? I'm hungry." And then he said, "Say—where's your boy?"

"He stepped out for a moment," said Doctor Remenzel evenly.

"We've got to find him," said Sylvia to her husband.

"In time, in due time," said Doctor Remenzel.

"That letter," said Sylvia; "Eli knew about it. He found it and tore it up. Of course he did!" She started to cry, thinking of the hideous trap that Eli had caught himself in.

"I'm not interested right now in what Eli's done," said Doctor Remenzel. "Right now I'm a lot more interested in what some other people are going to do."

"What do you mean?" said Sylvia.

Doctor Remenzel stood impressively, angry and determined. "I mean," he said, "I'm going to see how quickly people can change their minds around here."

"Please," said Sylvia, trying to hold him, trying to calm him, "we've got to find Eli. That's the first thing."

"The first thing," said Doctor Remenzel quite loudly, "is to get Eli admitted to Whitehill. After that we'll find him, and we'll bring him back."

"But darling—" said Sylvia.

"No 'but' about it," said Doctor Remenzel. "There's a majority of the Board of Overseers in this room at this very moment. Every one of them is a close friend of mine, or a close friend of my father. If they tell Doctor Warren Eli's in, that's it— Eli's in. If there's room for all these other people," he said, "there's damn well room for Eli too."

He strode quickly to a table nearby, sat down heavily and began to talk to a fierce-looking and splendid old gentleman who was eating there. The old gentleman was chairman of the board.

Sylvia apologized to the baffled[1] Hilyers, and then went in search of Eli.

Asking this person and that person, Sylvia found him. He was outside—all alone on a bench in a bower[2] of lilacs that had just begun to bud.

Eli heard his mother's coming on the gravel path, stayed where he was, resigned. "Did you find out," he said, "or do I still have to tell you?"

"About you?" she said gently. "About not getting in? Doctor Warren told us."

"I tore his letter up," said Eli.

"I can understand that," she said. "Your

---

[1] BAFFLED: utterly confused.
[2] BOWER: shady shelter made of shrubs.

father and I have always made you feel that you had to go to Whitehill, that nothing else would do."

"I feel better," said Eli. He tried to smile, found he could do it easily. "I feel so much better now that it's over. I tried to tell you a couple of times—but I just couldn't. I didn't know how."

"That's my fault, not yours," she said.

"What's my father doing?" said Eli.

Sylvia was so intent on comforting Eli that she'd put out of her mind what her husband was up to. Now she realized that Doctor Remenzel was making a ghastly mistake. She didn't want Eli admitted to Whitehill, could see what a cruel thing that would be.

She couldn't bring herself to tell the boy what his father was doing, so she said, "He'll be along in a minute, dear. He understands." And then she said, "You wait here, and I'll go get him and come right back."

But she didn't have to go to Doctor Remenzel. At that moment the big man came out of the inn and caught sight of his wife and son. He came to her and to Eli. He looked dazed.

"Well?" she said.

"They—they all said no," said Doctor Remenzel, very subdued.

"That's for the best," said Sylvia. "I'm relieved. I really am."

"Who said no?" said Eli. "Who said no to what?"

"The members of the board," said Doctor Remenzel, not looking anyone in the eye. "I asked them to make an exception in your case—to reverse their decision and let you in."

Eli stood, his face filled with incredulity and shame that were instant. "You what?" he said, and there was no childishness in the way he said it. Next came anger. "You shouldn't have done that!" he said to his father.

Doctor Remenzel nodded. "So I've already been told."

"That isn't done!" said Eli. "How awful! You shouldn't have."

"You're right," said Doctor Remenzel, accepting the scolding lamely.

"Now I *am* ashamed," said Eli, and he showed that he was.

Doctor Remenzel, in his wretchedness, could find no strong words to say. "I apologize to you both," he said at last. "It was a very bad thing to try."

"Now a Remenzel *has* asked for something," said Eli.

"I don't suppose Ben's back yet with the car?" said Doctor Remenzel. It was obvious that Ben wasn't. "We'll wait out here for him," he said. "I don't want to go back in there now."

"A Remenzel asked for something—as though a Remenzel were something special," said Eli.

"I don't suppose—" said Doctor Remenzel, and he left the sentence unfinished, dangling in the air.

"You don't suppose what?" said his wife, her face puzzled.

"I don't suppose," said Doctor Remenzel, "that we'll ever be coming here any more."

FOR DISCUSSION

1. Eli must have realized that his lie would be revealed as soon as his family reached Whitehill. Why, then, did he remain silent? How did each of Eli's parents regard his attendance at Whitehill? What part did their attitudes play in his continued silence?

2. Much of the story is devoted to talk about standards and admission procedures. Why is the admission of the African boys mentioned so often? What is the attitude of Eli's mother toward Tom Hilyer and his son? Toward the African boys? Does she seem fully to understand and support Whitehill's policy of education for all who qualify? Does Eli's father?

3. Doctor Remenzel spends a great deal of time impressing upon his wife and Eli the necessity for high standards and equal privileges at Whitehill; yet he breaks his own code and demands special treatment for Eli. Do you believe that Doctor Remenzel was deliberately lying when he made the earlier statements to his family? Did he believe that he believed them? Explain your conclusions.

4. Eli, we are told, was more relieved than anything else when the truth about his admission was finally revealed to his parents. But his father's actions filled him with shame. Why? Whose failure do you believe was the more serious one—Eli's or his father's? Explain your answer.

THE SECRET HEART

ROBERT P. TRISTRAM COFFIN

Across the years he could recall
His father one way best of all.

In the stillest hour of night
The boy awakened to a light.

Half in dreams, he saw his sire   5
With his great hands full of fire.

The man had struck a match to see
If his son slept peacefully.

He held his palms each side the spark
His love had kindled in the dark.   10

His two hands were curved apart
In the semblance of a heart.

He wore, it seemed to his small son,
A bare heart on his hidden one,

A heart that gave out such a glow   15
No son awake could bear to know.

It showed a look upon a face
Too tender for the day to trace.

One instant, it lit all about,
And then the secret heart went out.   20

But it shone long enough for one
To know that hands held up the sun.

FOR DISCUSSION

1. What lines in the poem suggest that the father and son do not openly display their affection for each other? What kind of relationship seems to exist between them? Reread lines 15–18; why do they suggest the father's heart had to remain "secret"?

2. The boy recalls his father "one way best of all." Why does this particular childhood scene mean so much to him? Do you think his relationship with his father changed in any way after he experienced this moment of insight? Explain your conclusions.

Often we would just as soon not understand some things—the girl was young, sensible, and selfish, and quite unprepared to encounter the lonely, terrible desolation of old age.

A VISIT OF CHARITY
EUDORA WELTY

IT WAS mid-morning—a very cold, bright day. Holding a potted plant before her, a girl of fourteen jumped off the bus in front of the Old Ladies' Home, on the outskirts of town. She wore a red coat, and her straight yellow hair was hanging down loose from the pointed white cap all the little girls were wearing that year. She stopped for a moment beside one of the prickly dark shrubs with which the city had beautified the Home, and then proceeded slowly toward the building, which was of whitewashed brick and reflected the winter sunlight like a block of ice. As she walked vaguely up the steps she shifted the small pot from hand to hand; then she had to set it down and remove her mittens before she could open the heavy door.

"I'm a Campfire Girl. . . . I have to pay a visit to some old lady," she told the nurse at the desk. This was a woman in a white uniform who looked as if she were cold; she had close-cut hair which stood up on the very top of her head exactly like a sea wave. Marian, the little girl, did not tell her that this visit would give her a minimum of only three points in her score.

"Acquainted with any of our residents?"

"A Visit of Charity" from *A Curtain of Green and Other Stories*, by Eudora Welty, copyright 1941, 1969 by Eudora Welty. Reprinted by permission of Harcourt Brace Jovanovich, Inc.

asked the nurse. She lifted one eyebrow and spoke like a man.

"With any old ladies? No—but—that is, any of them will do," Marian stammered. With her free hand she pushed her hair behind her ears, as she did when it was time to study Science.

The nurse shrugged and rose. "You have a nice *multiflora cineraria* there," she remarked as she walked ahead down the hall of closed doors to pick out an old lady.

There was loose, bulging linoleum on the floor. Marian felt as if she were walking on the waves, but the nurse paid no attention to it. There was a smell in the hall like the interior of a clock. Everything was silent until, behind one of the doors, an old lady of some kind cleared her throat like a sheep bleating. This decided the nurse. Stopping in her tracks, she first extended her arm, bent her elbow, and leaned forward from the hips—all to examine the watch strapped to her wrist; then she gave a loud double-rap on the door.

"There are two in each room," the nurse remarked over her shoulder.

"Two what?" asked Marian without thinking. The sound like a sheep's bleating almost made her turn around and run back.

One old woman was pulling the door open in short, gradual jerks, and when she

saw the nurse a strange smile forced her old face dangerously awry.[1] Marian, suddenly propelled by the strong, impatient arm of the nurse, saw next the side-face of another old woman, even older, who was lying flat in bed with a cap on and a counterpane[2] drawn up to her chin.

"Visitor," said the nurse, and after one more shove she was off up the hall.

Marian stood tongue-tied; both hands held the potted plant. The old woman, still with that terrible, square smile (which was a smile of welcome) stamped on her bony face, was waiting. . . . Perhaps she said something. The old woman in bed said nothing at all, and she did not look around.

Suddenly Marian saw a hand, quick as a bird claw, reach up in the air and pluck the white cap off her head. At the same time, another claw to match drew her all the way into the room, and the next moment the door closed behind her.

"My, my, my," said the old lady at her side.

Marian stood enclosed by a bed, a washstand and a chair; the tiny room had altogether too much furniture. Everything smelled wet—even the bare floor. She held onto the back of the chair, which was wicker and felt soft and damp. Her heart beat more and more slowly, her hands got colder and colder, and she could not hear whether the old women were saying anything or not. She could not see them very clearly. How dark it was! The window shade was down, and the only door was shut. Marian looked at the ceiling. . . . It was like being caught in a robbers' cave, just before one was murdered.

[1] AWRY (ə·rī′): twisted to one side.
[2] COUNTERPANE: bedspread.

"Did you come to be our little girl for a while?" the first robber asked.

Then something was snatched from Marian's hand—the little potted plant.

"Flowers!" screamed the old woman. She stood holding the pot in an undecided way. "Pretty flowers," she added.

Then the old woman in bed cleared her throat and spoke. "They are not pretty," she said, still without looking around, but very distinctly.

Marian suddenly pitched against the chair and sat down in it.

"Pretty flowers," the first old woman insisted. "Pretty—pretty. . . ."

Marian wished she had the little pot back for just a moment—she had forgotten to look at the plant herself before giving it away. What did it look like?

"Stinkweeds," said the other old woman sharply. She had a bunchy white forehead and red eyes like a sheep. Now she turned them toward Marian. The fogginess seemed to rise in her throat again, and she bleated, "Who—are—you?"

To her surprise, Marian could not remember her name. "I'm a Campfire Girl," she said finally.

"Watch out for the germs," said the old woman like a sheep, not addressing anyone.

"One came out last month to see us," said the first old woman.

A sheep or a germ? wondered Marian dreamily, holding onto the chair.

"Did not!" cried the other old woman.

"Did so! Read to us out of the Bible, and we enjoyed it!" screamed the first.

"Who enjoyed it!" said the woman in bed. Her mouth was unexpectedly small and sorrowful, like a pet's.

"We enjoyed it," insisted the other.

"You enjoyed it—I enjoyed it."

"We all enjoyed it," said Marian, without realizing that she had said a word.

The first old woman had just finished putting the potted plant high, high on the top of the wardrobe, where it could hardly be seen from below. Marian wondered how she had ever succeeded in placing it there, how she could ever have reached so high.

"You mustn't pay any attention to old Addie," she now said to the little girl. "She's ailing today."

"Will you shut your mouth?" said the woman in bed. "I am not."

"You're a story."

"I can't stay but a minute—really, I can't," said Marian suddenly. She looked down at the wet floor and thought that if she were sick in here they would have to let her go.

With much to-do the first old woman sat down in a rocking chair—still another piece of furniture!—and began to rock. With the fingers of one hand she touched a very dirty cameo pin on her chest. "What do you do at school?" she asked.

"I don't know. . . ." said Marian. She tried to think but she could not.

"Oh, but the flowers are beautiful," the old woman whispered. She seemed to rock faster and faster; Marian did not see how anyone could rock so fast.

"Ugly," said the woman in bed.

"If we bring flowers—" Marian began, and then fell silent. She had almost said that if Campfire Girls brought flowers to the Old Ladies' Home, the visit would count one extra point, and if they took a Bible with them on the bus and read it to the old ladies, it counted double. But the old woman had not listened, anyway; she was rocking and watching the other one, who watched back from the bed.

"Poor Addie is ailing. She has to take medicine—see?" she said, pointing a horny finger at a row of bottles on the table, and rocking so high that her black comfort shoes lifted off the floor like a little child's.

"I am no more sick than you are," said the woman in bed.

"Oh, yes you are!"

"I just got more sense than you have, that's all," said the other old woman, nodding her head.

"That's only the contrary way she talks when *you all* come," said the first old lady with sudden intimacy. She stopped the rocker with a neat pat of her feet and leaned toward Marian. Her hand reached over—it felt like a petunia leaf, clinging and just a little sticky.

"Will you hush! Will you hush!" cried the other one.

Marian leaned back rigidly in her chair.

"When I was a little girl like you, I went to school and all," said the old woman in the same intimate, menacing voice. "Not here—another town. . . ."

"Hush!" said the sick woman. "You never went to school. You never came and you never went. You never were anything—only here. You never were born! You don't know anything. Your head is empty, your heart and hands and your old black purse are all empty, even that little old box that you brought with you you brought empty—you showed it to me. And yet you talk, talk, talk, talk, talk all the time until I think I'm losing my mind! Who are you? You're a stranger—a perfect stranger! Don't you know you're a stranger? Is it possible that they have actually done a thing like this to anyone—sent them in a stranger to talk, and rock, and tell away

her whole long rigmarole?[1] Do they seriously suppose that I'll be able to keep it up, day in, day out, night in, night out, living in the same room with a terrible old woman—forever?"

Marian saw the old woman's eyes grow bright and turn toward her. This old woman was looking at her with despair and calculation in her face. Her small lips suddenly dropped apart, and exposed a half circle of false teeth with tan gums.

"Come here, I want to tell you something," she whispered. "Come here!"

Marian was trembling, and her heart nearly stopped beating altogether for a moment.

"Now, now, Addie," said the first old woman. "That's not polite. Do you know what's really the matter with old Addie today?" She, too, looked at Marian; one of her eyelids drooped low.

"The matter?" the child repeated stupidly. "What's the matter with her?"

"Why, she's mad because it's her birthday!" said the first old woman, beginning to rock again and giving a little crow as though she had answered her own riddle.

"It is not, it is not!" screamed the old woman in bed. "It is not my birthday, no one knows when that is but myself, and will you please be quiet and say nothing more, or I'll go straight out of my mind!" She turned her eyes toward Marian again, and presently she said in the soft, foggy voice, "When the worst comes to the worst, I ring this bell, and the nurse comes." One of her hands was drawn out from under the patched counterpane—a thin little hand with enormous black freckles. With a finger which would not hold still she pointed to a little bell on the table among

[1] RIGMAROLE: complicated, confused nonsense.

the bottles.

"How old are you?" Marian breathed. Now she could see the old woman in bed very closely and plainly, and very abruptly, from all sides, as in dreams. She wondered about her—she wondered for a moment as though there was nothing else in the world to wonder about. It was the first time such a thing had happened to Marian.

"I won't tell!"

The old face on the pillow, where Marian was bending over it, slowly gathered and collapsed. Soft whimpers came out of the small open mouth. It was a sheep that she sounded like—a little lamb. Marian's face drew very close, the yellow hair hung forward.

"She's crying!" She turned a bright, burning face up to the first old woman.

"That's Addie for you," the old woman said spitefully.

Marian jumped up and moved toward the door. For the second time, the claw almost touched her hair, but it was not quick enough. The little girl put her cap on.

"Well, it was a real visit," said the old woman, following Marian through the doorway and all the way out into the hall. Then from behind she suddenly clutched the child with her sharp little fingers. In an affected, high-pitched whine she cried, "Oh, little girl, have you a penny to spare for a poor old woman that's not got anything of her own? We don't have a thing in the world—not a penny for candy—not a thing! Little girl, just a nickel—a penny—"

Marian pulled violently against the old hands for a moment before she was free. Then she ran down the hall, without looking behind her and without looking at the nurse, who was reading *Field & Stream* at

her desk. The nurse, after another triple motion to consult her wrist watch, asked automatically the question put to visitors in all institutions: "Won't you stay and have dinner with *us?*"

Marian never replied. She pushed the heavy door open into the cold air and ran down the steps.

Under the prickly shrub she stooped and quickly, without being seen, retrieved a red apple she had hidden there.

Her yellow hair under the white cap, her scarlet coat, her bare knees all flashed in the sunlight as she ran to meet the big bus rocketing through the street.

"Wait for me!" she shouted. As though at an imperial command, the bus ground to a stop.

She jumped on and took a big bite out of the apple.

FOR DISCUSSION

1. Why did Marian run out of the Home? Was she really afraid of the old lady?

2. The author consistently compares one old lady's actions and speech to a bird and the other lady's actions and speech to a sheep. Reread the descriptions of the two ladies; what specific character qualities is the author trying to picture for the reader by using this imagery? Is the imagery successful in helping you to form a mental impression of the ladies?

3. One of the worst things about living in an institution is that patients are often treated coolly and impersonally and the surroundings are bare and depressing. What evidence can you find in this story to support this statement?

4. What evidence can you find in the story to prove that Marian was not motivated by kindness or any true feelings of compassion to make her "visit of charity"? Do you think that she may have gained anything personally in making the visit? Did the two old ladies gain anything, or would they have been better off without her visit? Explain your conclusions.

REUBEN BRIGHT

EDWIN ARLINGTON ROBINSON

Because he was a butcher and thereby
Did earn an honest living (and did right)
I would not have you think that Reuben Bright
Was any more a brute than you or I;
For when they told him that his wife must die,   5
He stared at them and shook with grief and fright,
And cried like a great baby half that night,
And made the women cry to see him cry.
And after she was dead, and he had paid
The singers and the sexton* and the rest,   10
He packed a lot of things that she had made
Most mournfully away in an old chest
Of hers, and put some chopped-up cedar boughs
In with them, and tore down the slaughter-house.

[10] SEXTON: *here,* gravedigger.

FOR DISCUSSION

1. A very common human trait is the tendency to judge other people by their appearance or occupation. What kinds of assumptions do you imagine people would be likely to make about a butcher's attitude toward death?

2. In the introduction to this unit, McFarland defines insights as ". . . glimpses that let us know with our hearts what before we knew, if at all, only with our minds." What is the "heart knowledge" that Reuben Bright discovers? Why does he tear down the slaughter-house?

"Reuben Bright" from *The Children of the Night* by Edwin Arlington Robinson, Charles Scribner's Sons, 1897.

"What are you sore about?" the woman's escort asked. "She only said you were wonderful."

DIFFERENT CULTURAL LEVELS EAT HERE

PETER DeVRIES

WHEN THE counterman glanced up from the grill on which he was frying himself a hamburger and saw the two couples come in the door, he sized them up as people who had spent the evening at the theater or the Horse Show or something like that, from their clothes. They were all about the same age—in their early forties, he decided, as they sat down on stools at the counter. Except for them, the place was empty. At least, the front was. Al Spain, the proprietor, was sitting out in the kitchen working on a ledger.

The counterman drew four glasses of water, stopping once to adjust the limp handkerchief around his neck. He had been whistling softly and without continuity when they entered, and he kept it up as he set the water glasses down.

"Well, what's yours?" he asked, wiping his hands on his apron and beginning with the man on the end.

"Hamburger."

"Mit or mitout?"

The man paused in the act of fishing a cigarette out of a package and glanced up. He was a rather good-looking fellow with dark circles under his eyes that, together with the general aspect of his face, gave him a sort of charred[1] look. "Mit," he said at length.

The counterman moved down. "And yours?" he asked the woman who was next.

"I'll have a hamburger, too."

"Mit or mitout?"

The second woman, who had a gardenia pinned in her hair, leaned to her escort and started to whisper something about "a character," audibly, it happened, for the counterman paused and turned to look at her. Her escort jogged her with the side of his knee, and then she noticed the counterman watching her and stopped, smiling uneasily. The counterman looked at her a moment longer, then turned back to the other woman. "I'm sorry I didn't get that," he said. "Was that mit or mitout?"

She coughed into her fist and moved her bag pointlessly on the counter. "Mit," she said.

"That's two mits," the counterman said, and moved on down to the next one, the woman with the gardenia. "And yours?"

She folded her fingers on the counter and leaned toward him. "And what would we come here for except a hamburger?" She

[1] CHARRED: burned; blackened like charcoal.

smiled sociably, showing a set of long, brilliant teeth.

"Mit or mitout?" he asked flatly.

She wriggled forward on the stool and smiled again. "May I ask a question?"

"Sure."

"Why do you say 'mit or mitout'?" Her escort jogged her again with his knee, this time more sharply.

The counterman turned around and picked up a lighted cigarette he had left lying on the edge of the pastry case.

He took a deep inhale, ground the butt out underfoot, and blew out the smoke. "To find out the customer's wish," he said. "And now, how did you want it?"

"I think mitout," she said. "I like onions, but they don't like me."

"And yours?" he asked the remaining man.

"I'll have a hamburger, too," the man said. He fixed his eyes on a box of matches in his hands, as though steeling himself.

"Mit or mitout?"

The man fished studiously in the matchbox. "Mitout."

The four watched the counterman in complete silence as he took the hamburger patties from a refrigerator and set them to frying on the grill. They all wanted coffee, and he served it now. After slicing open four buns, he returned to his own sandwich. He put the meat in a bun and folded it closed, the others watching him as though witnessing an act of legerdemain.[1] Conscious of their collective gaze, he turned his head, and scattered their looks in various directions. Just then the phone rang. The counterman set his sandwich down and walked past the four customers to answer it. He paused with his hand on the

[1] LEGERDEMAIN: sleight-of-hand trickery.

receiver a moment, finished chewing, swallowed, and picked up the phone.

"Al's," he announced, his elbows on the cigarette counter. "Oh, hello, Charlie," he said brightening, and straightened up. "How many? . . . Well, that's a little steep right now. I can let you have half of that, is all. . . . O.K., shoot. . . . That's nine mits and three mitouts, right? . . . Check. . . . That'll be O.K." He consulted the clock overhead. "Send the kid over then. So long."

He hung up and was on his way back to the grill when he became aware that the woman with the gardenia was whispering to her escort again. He stopped, and stood in front of her with his hands on his hips. "I beg your pardon, but what was that remark, lady?"

"Nothing."

"You passed a remark about me, if I'm not mistaken. What was it?"

"I just said you were wonderful."

"I was what?"

"Wonderful."

"That's what I thought." He went back to the hamburgers, which needed attention.

As he turned them in silence, the woman regarded him doubtfully. "What's the matter?" she asked at last, ignoring the nudging from her friends on either side.

The counterman's attention remained stonily fixed on his work.

"Is something wrong?" the woman asked.

The counterman lowered the flame, stooping to check it, and straightened up. "Maybe," he said, not looking at her.

She looked at her friends with a gesture of appeal. "But what?"

"Maybe I'm sore."

"What are you sore about?" the woman's

escort asked. "She only said you were wonderful."

"I know what that means in her book."

"What?"

The counterman turned around and faced them. "We have a woman comes in here," he said, "who everything's wonderful to, too. She's got a dog she clips. When she hits a cab driver without teeth who doesn't know any streets and you got to show him how to get to where you want to go, he's wonderful. Fellow with a cap with earlaps comes in here with some kind of a bird in his pocket one night when she was here. He had a coat on but no shirt and he sung tunes. *He* was wonderful. Everything is wonderful, till I can't stand to hear her talk to whoever she's with any more. This lady reminds me a lot of her. I got a picture of *her* all right going home and telling somebody I'm wonderful."

"But by wonderful she means to pay you a—"

"I know what wonderful means. You don't have to tell me. Saloons full of old junk, they're wonderful, old guys that stick cigar butts in their pipe—"

"The lady didn't mean any harm."

"Well . . ."

There was a moment of silence, and the charred-looking man signaled the others to let well enough—or bad enough, whichever it was—alone, but the other man was impelled to complete the conciliation.[1] "I see perfectly well what you mean," he said. "But she meant not all of us stand out with a sort of—well, trademark."

The counterman seemed to bristle. "Meaning what?"

"Why, the way you say 'mit or mitout,' I guess," the man said, looking for confir-

[1] CONCILIATION: soothing.

mation to the woman, who nodded brightly.

The counterman squinted at him. "What about it?"

"Nothing, nothing at all. I just say I suppose it's sort of your trademark."

"Now, cut it out," the counterman said, taking a step closer. "Or you'll have a trademark. And when you get up tomorrow morning, you'll look a darn side more wonderful than anybody *she* ever saw."

The charred-looking man brought his hand down on the counter. "Oh, for God's sake, let's cut this out! Let's eat if we're going to eat, and get out of here."

"That suits me, bud," said the counterman.

The commotion brought Al Spain from the kitchen. "What seems to be the trouble?" he asked, stepping around to the customers' side of the counter.

"She said I was wonderful," the counterman said, pointing. "And I don't see that I have to take it from people just because they're customers, Al."

"Maybe she didn't mean any harm by it," the proprietor said.

"It's the way she said it. The way that type says it. I know. You know. We get 'em in here. You know what they think's wonderful, don't you?"

"Well," Al said, scratching his head and looking at the floor.

"Hack drivers that recite poems they wrote while they cart fares around, saloons full of old—"

"Oh, are we going through that again?" the charred-looking man broke in. He stood up. "Let's just go," he said to his friends.

"We'll go into this quietly," Al said, and removed a toothpick from his mouth and

dropped it on the floor. "We're intelligent human beings," he continued, with an edge of interrogation,[1] looking at the others, who gave little nods of agreement. He sat down on one of the stools. "Now, the thing is this. This man is fine." He waved at the counterman, who stood looking modestly down at the grill. "He's a great fellow. But he's sensitive. By that I mean he gets along fine with the public—people who come in here from day to day, you understand. Has a pleasant way of passing the time of day, and a nice line of gab, *but*—different cultural levels eat here, and he doesn't like people that he thinks they're coming in here with the idea they're slumming. Now don't get me wrong," he went on when the woman with the gardenia started to say something. "I like all types of people and I'm tickled to death to have them come in here, you understand. I'm just saying that's his attitude. Some things set his back up, because he's like I say, sensitive." He crossed his legs. "Let's go into this thing like intelligent human beings a little farther. What prompted you to pass the remark—namely, he's wonderful?"

The charred-looking man groaned. "Oh, let's get—"

"Shut up, Paul," the woman with the gardenia said. She returned her attention to the proprietor. "It was just—oh, it all starts to sound so silly. I mean it was a perfectly insignificant remark. It's the way he says 'mit or mitout.' "

Al was silent a moment. "That's all?" he asked, regarding her curiously.

"Yes."

"It's just a habit of his. A way he's got." Al looked from her to the counterman and back again.

"You see," she said, "it's making something out of nothing. It's the way he says it. It's so—so offhand-like and—well, the offhand way he evidently keeps saying it. It's so—marvelous."

"I see. Well, it's just a sort of habit of his." Al was studying her with mounting interest.

"Of course, we're sorry if we've offended him," said the woman's escort.

"We'll let it go that way," the counterman said.

"Fine! We'll say no more about it," Al said gesturing covertly[2] to the counterman to serve up the sandwiches. "Come again any time," he added, and went back to the kitchen.

The two couples composed themselves and ate. The counterman went and leaned on the cigarette case, over a newspaper. The door opened and a small man in a tight gray suit came in and sat down, pushed his hat back, drew a newspaper out of his pocket, and spread it on the counter. The counterman dropped his, drew a glass of water, and set it before the customer.

"What'll it be?"

"Two hamburgers."

The two couples stopped eating and looked up, and there was a blank silence for a moment. Then they bent over their food, eating busily and stirring their coffee with an excessive clatter of spoons. Suddenly the clink of cutlery subsided and there was dead silence again. The counterman wiped his hands on his apron, turned, and walked to the refrigerator. He opened it, took out two patties, set them on the grill, and peeled off the paper on them. He sliced the buns and set them in readiness on a plate. Standing there waiting for the

---

[1] INTERROGATION: questioning.

[2] COVERTLY: secretly.

meat to fry, he cleared his throat and said, looking out the window at something in the street, "Onion with these?"

"No. Plain," the customer said, without raising his head from the paper and turning a page.

The two couples hurried through their sandwiches and coffee, crumpled their paper napkins, and rose together. One of the men paid, left a half dollar tip on the counter, turned, and herded the others through the door, following them himself and closing the door rapidly and quietly. The counterman shoved the cash register shut and went back to the grill without looking at them or glancing through the window as they unlocked their car at the curb, got in, and drove off. He served the man his sandwiches. Then he came around the counter and sat on a stool with the paper.

The door flew open and a big fellow in a bright checked shirt came in, grinning. "Hello, paesan!"[1] the newcomer said. "Loafing as usual, eh?"

The counterman jumped off the stool and held out his hand. "Louie! When did you get back?"

"Yesterday."

The counterman went back behind the counter. "Glad to see you."

"Glad to see you, too, you lazy slob."

"How many, Louie?"

"I'm starved. Fry me up three."

"Mit or mitout?"

"Mit!"

---

[1] PAESAN (pī·zan′): Italian slang for *pal*.

FOR DISCUSSION

1. Is the counterman justified in objecting to the lady's use of the term "wonderful" to describe him? What does "wonderful" seem to suggest to the counterman? What does it seem to mean to these customers? Do you think the counterman is super-sensitive, or are his customers lacking in sensitivity?

2. Why do you think the customers try so hard to convince Al Spain that they weren't trying to insult the counterman? Do they really care about his opinion, or are they concerned with something else?

3. What causes the counterman to drop the phrase "mit or mitout" when a new customer enters? What does this suggest about his feelings at this point? Can you suggest the reason why he decides to return to the phrase later?

"I didn't want to go downtown to steal anything from the ten-cent store; I didn't want to see Lottie Jump again—not really, for I knew in my bones that that girl was trouble with a capital 'T.' "

BAD CHARACTERS
JEAN STAFFORD

UP UNTIL I learned my lesson in a very bitter way, I never had more than one friend at a time, and my friendships, though ardent, were short. When they ended and I was sent packing in unforgetting indignation, it was always my fault; I would swear vilely in front of a girl I knew to be pious and prim (by the time I was eight, the most grandiloquent[1] gangster could have added nothing to my vocabulary—I had an awful tongue), or I would call a Tenderfoot Scout a sissy or make fun of athletics to the daughter of the high-school coach. These outbursts came without plan; I would simply one day, in the middle of a game of Russian bank or a hike or a conversation, be possessed with a passion to be by myself, and my lips instantly and without warning would accommodate me. My friend was never more surprised than I was when this irrevocable[2] slander, this terrible, talented invective,[3] came boiling out of my mouth.

Afterward, when I had got the solitude I had wanted, I was dismayed, for I did not like it. Then I would sadly finish the game of cards as if someone were still across the table from me; I would sit down on the mesa[4] and through a glaze of tears would watch my friend departing with outraged strides; mournfully, I would talk to myself. Because I had already alienated everyone I knew, I then had nowhere to turn, so a famine set in and I would have no companion but Muff, the cat, who loathed all human beings except, significantly, me—truly. She bit and scratched the hands that fed her, she arched her back like a Halloween cat if someone kindly tried to pet her, she hissed, laid her ears flat to her skull, growled, fluffed up her tail into a great bush and flailed it like a bullwhack. But she purred for me, she patted me with her paws, keeping her claws in their velvet scabbards. She was not only an ill-natured cat, she was also badly dressed. She was a calico, and the distribution of her colors was a mess; she looked as if she had been left out in the rain and her paint had run. She had a Roman nose as the result of some early injury, her tail was skinny, she had a perfectly venomous look in her eye. My family said—my family discriminated against me—that I was much closer kin to

[1] GRANDILOQUENT: using pompous and lofty language.
[2] IRREVOCABLE: impossible to take back.
[3] INVECTIVE: abuse, insult.

[4] MESA: flat, arid land with steeply sloping sides.

Muff than I was to any of them. To tease me into a tantrum, my brother Jack and my sister Stella often called me Kitty instead of Emily. Little Tess did not dare, because she knew I'd chloroform her if she did. Jack, the meanest boy I have ever known in my life, called me Polecat and talked about my mania[1] for fish, which, it so happened, I despised. The name would have been far more appropriate for *him*, since he trapped skunks up in the foothills —we lived in Adams, Colorado—and quite often, because he was careless and fool-hardy, his clothes had to be buried, and even when that was done, he sometimes was sent home from school on the complaint of girls sitting next to him.

Along about Christmastime when I was eleven, I was making a snowman with Virgil Meade in his backyard, and all of a sudden, just as we had got around to the right arm, I had to be alone. So I called him a son of a sea cook, said it was common knowledge that his mother had bedbugs and that his father, a dentist and the deputy marshal, was a bootlegger on the side. For a moment, Virgil was too aghast[2] to speak—a little earlier we had agreed to marry someday and become millionaires— and then, with a bellow of fury, he knocked me down and washed my face in snow. I saw stars, and black balls bounced before my eyes. When finally he let me up, we were both crying, and he hollered that if I didn't get off his property that instant, his father would arrest me and send me to Canon City. I trudged slowly home, half frozen, critically sick at heart. So it was old Muff again for me for quite some time. Old Muff, that is, until I met Lottie Jump,

although "met" is a euphemism[3] for the way I first encountered her.

I saw Lottie for the first time one afternoon in our own kitchen, stealing a chocolate cake. Stella and Jack had not come home from school yet—not having my difficult disposition, they were popular, and they were at their friends' houses, pulling taffy, I suppose, making popcorn balls, playing casino, having fun—and my mother had taken Tess with her to visit a friend in one of the T.B. sanitariums. I was alone in the house, and making a funny-looking Christmas card, although I had no one to send it to. When I heard someone in the kitchen, I thought it was Mother home early, and I went out to ask her why the green pine tree I had pasted on a square of red paper looked as if it were falling down. And there, instead of Mother and my baby sister, was this pale, conspicuous child in the act of lifting the glass cover from the devil's-food my mother had taken out of the oven an hour before and set on the plant shelf by the window. The child had her back to me, and when she heard my footfall, she wheeled with an amazing look of fear and hatred on her pinched and pasty face. Simultaneously, she put the cover over the cake again, and then she stood motionless as if she were under a spell.

I was scared, for I was not sure what was happening, and anyhow it gives you a turn to find a stranger in the kitchen in the middle of the afternoon, even if the stranger is only a skinny child in a moldy coat and sopping-wet basketball shoes. Between us there was a lengthy silence, but there was

---

[1] MANIA: mad craving.

[2] AGHAST: shocked.

[3] EUPHEMISM (yü′fə·miz·əm): substituting of an inoffensive term for one considered offensively plain in meaning; for example, *passed away* is a euphemism for *died*.

a great deal of noise in the room: the alarm clock ticked smugly; the teakettle simmered patiently on the back of the stove; Muff, cross at having been waked up, thumped her tail against the side of the terrarium in the window where she had been sleeping—contrary to orders—among the geraniums. This went on, it seemed to me, for hours and hours while that tall, sickly girl and I confronted each other. When, after a long time, she did open her mouth, it was to tell a prodigious[1] lie. "I came to see if you'd like to play with me," she said. I think she sighed and stole a sidelong and regretful glance at the cake.

Beggars cannot be choosers, and I had been missing Virgil so sorely, as well as all those other dear friends forever lost to me, that in spite of her flagrance[2] (she had

never clapped eyes on me before, she had had no way of knowing there was a creature of my age in the house—she had come in like a hobo to steal my mother's cake), I was flattered and consoled. I asked her name and, learning it, believed my ears no better than my eyes: Lottie Jump. What on earth! What on earth—you surely will agree with me—and yet when I told her mine, Emily Vanderpool, she laughed until she coughed and gasped. "Beg pardon," she said. "Names like them always hit my funny bone. There was this towhead boy in school named Delbert Saxonfield." I saw no connection and I was insulted (what's so funny about Vanderpool, I'd like to know), but Lottie Jump was, technically, my guest and I *was* lonesome, so I asked her, since she had spoken of playing with me, if she knew how to play Andy-I-Over. She said "Naw." It turned out that she did not know how to

[1] PRODIGIOUS: monstrous.
[2] FLAGRANCE: shamelessness.

play any games at all; she couldn't do anything and didn't want to do anything; her only recreation and her only gift was, and always had been, stealing. But this I did not know at the time.

As it happened, it was too cold and snowy to play outdoors that day anyhow, and after I had run through my list of indoor games and Lottie had shaken her head at all of them (when I spoke of Parcheesi, she went "Ugh!" and pretended to be sick), she suggested that we look through my mother's bureau drawers. This did not strike me as strange at all, for it was one of my favorite things to do, and I led the way to Mother's bedroom without a moment's hesitation. I loved the smell of the lavender she kept in gauze bags among her chamois gloves and linen handkerchiefs, and filmy scarves; there was a pink fascinator knitted of something as fine as spider's thread, and it made me go quite soft—I wasn't soft as a rule, I was as hard as nails and I gave my mother a rough time—to think of her wearing it around her head as she waltzed on the ice in the bygone days. We examined stockings, nightgowns, camisoles, strings of beads, and mosaic pins, keepsake buttons from dresses worn on memorial occasions, tortoiseshell combs, and a transformation made from Aunt Joey's hair when she had racily had it bobbed. Lottie admired particularly a blue cloisonné perfume flask with ferns and peacocks on it. "Hey," she said, "this sure is cute. I like thing-daddies like this here." But very abruptly she got bored and said, "Let's talk instead. In the front room." I agreed, a little perplexed this time, because I had been about to show her a remarkable powder box that played *The Blue Danube*. We went into the parlor,

where Lottie looked at her image in the pier glass for quite a while and with great absorption, as if she had never seen herself before. Then she moved over to the window seat and knelt on it, looking out at the front walk. She kept her hands in the pockets of her thin dark-red coat; once she took out one of her dirty paws to rub her nose for a minute and I saw a bulge in that pocket, like a bunch of jackstones.[1] I know now that it wasn't jackstones, it was my mother's perfume flask; I thought at the time her hands were cold and that that was why she kept them put away, for I had noticed that she had no mittens.

Lottie did most of the talking, and while she talked, she never once looked at me but kept her eyes fixed on the approach to our house. She told me that her family had come to Adams a month before from Muskogee, Oklahoma, where her father, before he got tuberculosis, had been a brakeman on the Frisco. Now they lived down by Arapahoe Creek, on the west side of town, in one of the cottages of a wretched settlement made up of people so poor and so sick—for in nearly every ramshackle house someone was coughing himself to death—that each time I went past I blushed with guilt because my shoes were sound and my coat was warm and I was well. I wished that Lottie had not told me where she lived, but she was not aware of any pathos[2] in her family's situation, and, indeed, it was with a certain boastfulness that she told me her mother was the short-order cook at the Comanche Café (she pronounced this word in one syllable), which I knew was the dirtiest, darkest, smelliest place in

---

[1] JACKSTONES: jacks; small metal pieces used in the game of jacks.
[2] PATHOS (pā'thos): something that arouses pity.

town, patronized by coal miners who never washed their faces and sometimes had such dangerous fights after drinking dago red[1] that the sheriff had to come. Laughing, Lottie told me that her mother was half Indian, and, laughing even harder, she said that her brother didn't have any brains and had never been to school. She herself was eleven years old, but she was only in the third grade, because teachers had always had it in for her—making her go to the blackboard and all like that when she was tired. She hated school—she went to Ashton, on North Hill, and that was why I had never seen her, for I went to Carlyle Hill—and she especially hated the teacher, Miss Cudahy, who had a head shaped like a pine cone and who had killed several people with her ruler. Lottie loved the movies ("Not them Western ones or the ones with apes in," she said. "Ones about hugging and kissing. I love it when they die in that big soft bed with the curtains up top, and he comes in and says 'Don't leave me, Marguerite de la Mar' "), and she loved to ride in cars. She loved Mr. Goodbars,[2] and if there was one thing she despised worse than another it was tapioca. ("Pa calls it fish eyes. He calls floating island horse spit. He's a big piece of cheese. I hate him.") She did not like cats (Muff was now sitting on the mantelpiece, glaring like an owl); she kind of liked snakes—except cottonmouths and rattlers—because she found them kind of funny; she had once seen a goat eat a tin can. She said that one of these days she would take me downtown—it was a slowpoke town, she said, a one-horse burg (I had never heard such gaudy, cynical talk and was trying to memorize it all)

—if I would get some money for the trolley fare; she hated to walk, and I ought to be proud that she had walked all the way from Arapahoe Creek today for the sole solitary purpose of seeing me.

Seeing our freshly baked dessert in the window was a more likely story, but I did not care, for I was deeply impressed by this bold, sassy girl from Oklahoma and greatly admired the poise with which she aired her prejudices. Lottie Jump was certainly nothing to look at. She was tall and made of skin and bones; she was evilly ugly, and her clothes were a disgrace, not just ill-fitting and old and ragged but dirty, unmentionably so; clearly she did not wash much or brush her teeth, which were notched like a saw, and small and brown (it crossed my mind that perhaps she chewed tobacco); her long, lank hair looked as if it might have nits.[3] But she had personality. She made me think of one of those self-contained dogs whose home is where his handout is and who travels alone but, if it suits him to, will become the leader of a pack. She was aloof, never looking at me, but amiable in the way she kept calling me "kid." I liked her enormously, and presently I told her so.

At this, she turned around and smiled at me. Her smile was the smile of a jack-o'-lantern—high, wide, and handsome. When it was over, no trace of it remained. "Well, that's keen, kid, and I like you, too," she said in her downright Muskogee accent. She gave me a long, appraising[4] look. Her eyes were the color of mud. "Listen, kid, how much do you like me?"

"I like you loads, Lottie," I said. "Better

---

[1] DAGO RED: cheap red wine.
[2] MR. GOODBARS: type of candy bar.
[3] NITS: lice.
[4] APPRAISING: judging the quality or value.

than anybody else, and I'm not kidding."

"You want to be pals?"

"Do I!" I cried. So *there,* Virgil Meade, you big fat hootnanny, I thought.

"All right, kid, we'll be pals." And she held out her hand for me to shake. I had to go and get it, for she did not alter her position on the window seat. It was a dry, cold hand, and the grip was severe, with more a feeling of bones in it than friendliness.

Lottie turned and scanned our path and scanned the sidewalk beyond, and then she said, in a lower voice, "Do you know how to lift?"

"Lift?" I wondered if she meant to lift *her.* I was sure I could do it, since she was so skinny, but I couldn't imagine why she would want me to.

"Shoplift, I mean. Like in the five-and-dime."

I did not know the term, and Lottie scowled at my stupidity.

"*Steal,* for crying in the beer!" she said impatiently. This she said so loudly that Muff jumped down from the mantel and left the room in contempt.

I was thrilled to death and shocked to pieces. "Stealing is a sin," I said. "You get put in jail for it."

"Ish ka bibble! I should worry if it's a sin or not," said Lottie, with a shrug. "And they'll never put a smart old whatsis like *me* in jail. It's fun, stealing is—it's a picnic. I'll teach you if you want to learn, kid." Shamelessly she winked at me and grinned again. (That grin! She could have taken it off her face and put it on the table.) And she added, "If you don't, we can't be pals, because lifting is the only kind of playing I like. I hate those dumb games like Statues.

Kick-the-Can—phooey!"

I was torn between agitation[1] (I went to Sunday school and knew already about morality; Judge Bay, a crabby old man who loved to punish sinners, was a friend of my father's and once had given Jack a lecture on the criminal mind when he came to call and found Jack looking up an answer in his arithmetic book) and excitement over the daring invitation to misconduct myself in so perilous a way. My life, on reflection, looked deadly prim; all I'd ever done to vary the monotony of it was to swear. I knew that Lottie Jump meant what she said—that I could have her friendship only on her terms (plainly, she had gone it alone for a long time and could go it alone for the rest of her life)—and although I trembled like an aspen[2] and my heart went pita-pat, I said, "I want to be pals with you, Lottie."

"All right, Vanderpool," said Lottie, and got off the window seat. "I wouldn't go braggin' about it if I was you. I wouldn't go telling my ma and pa and the next-door neighbor that you and Lottie Jump are going down to the five-and-dime next Saturday aft and lift us some nice rings and garters and things like that. I mean it, kid." And she drew the back of her forefinger across her throat and made a dire face.

"I won't. I promise I won't. My *gosh,* why would I?"

"That's the ticket," said Lottie, with a grin. "I'll meet you at the trolley shelter at two o'clock. You have the money. For both down and up. I ain't going to climb up that ornery hill after I've had my fun."

[1] AGITATION: being upset and disturbed.
[2] ASPEN: type of tree whose leaves flutter easily in the gentlest wind.

"Yes, Lottie," I said. Where was I going to get twenty cents? I was going to have to start stealing before she even taught me how. Lottie was facing the center of the room, but she had eyes in the back of her head, and she whirled around back to the window; my mother and Tess were turning in our front path.

"Back way," I whispered, and in a moment Lottie was gone; the swinging door that usually squeaked did not make a sound as she vanished through it. I listened and I never heard the back door open and close. Nor did I hear her, in a split second, lift the glass cover and remove that cake designed to feed six people.

I was restless and snappish between Wednesday afternoon and Saturday. When Mother found the cake was gone, she scolded me for not keeping my ears cocked. She assumed, naturally, that a tramp had taken it, for she knew I hadn't eaten it; I never ate anything if I could help it (except for raw potatoes, which I loved) and had been known as a problem feeder from the beginning of my life. At first it occurred to me to have a tantrum and bring her around to my point of view: my tantrums scared the living daylights out of her because my veins stood out and I turned blue and couldn't get my breath. But I rejected this for a more sensible plan. I said, "It just so happens I didn't hear anything. But if I had, I suppose you wish I had gone out in the kitchen and let the robber cut me up into a million little tiny pieces with his sword. You wouldn't even bury me. You'd just put me on the dump. *I* know who's wanted in this family and who isn't." Tears of sorrow, not of anger, came in powerful

tides and I groped blindly to the bedroom I shared with Stella, where I lay on my bed and shook with big, silent *weltschmerzlich*[1] sobs. Mother followed me immediately, and so did Tess, and both of them comforted me and told me how much they loved me. I said they didn't; they said they did. Presently, I got a headache, as I always did when I cried, so I got to have an aspirin and a cold cloth on my head, and when Jack and Stella came home, they had to be quiet. I heard Jack say, "Emily Vanderpool is the biggest polecat in the U.S.A. Whyn't she go in the kitchen and say, 'Hands up'? He woulda lit out." And Mother said, "Sh-h-h! You don't want your sister to be sick, do you?" Muff, not realizing that Lottie had replaced her, came in and curled up at my thigh, purring lustily; I found myself glad that she had left the room before Lottie Jump made her proposition to me, and in gratitude I stroked her unattractive head.

Other things happened. Mother discovered the loss of her perfume flask and talked about nothing else at meals for two whole days. Luckily, it did not occur to her that it had been stolen—she simply thought she had mislaid it—but her monomania[2] got on my father's nerves and he lashed out at her and at the rest of us. And because I was the cause of it all and my conscience was after me with red-hot pokers, I finally *had* to have a tantrum. I slammed my fork down in the middle of supper on the second day and yelled, "If you don't stop fighting, I'm going to kill myself. Yammer, yammer,

[1] WELTSCHMERZLICH: German word meaning, literally, "world-sorrow-like"; thus, having a romantic melancholy feeling.
[2] MONOMANIA: single-minded obsession with one idea.

nag, nag!" And I put my fingers in my ears and squeezed my eyes tight shut and screamed so the whole county could hear, "Shut *up!*" And then I lost my breath and began to turn blue. Daddy hastily apologized to everyone, and Mother said she was sorry for carrying on so about a trinket that had nothing but sentimental value—she was just vexed with herself for being careless, that was all, and she wasn't going to say another word about it.

I never heard so many references to stealing and cake, and even to Oklahoma (ordinarily no one mentioned Oklahoma once in a month of Sundays) and the ten-cent store as I did throughout those next days. I myself once made a ghastly slip and said something to Stella about "the five-and-dime." "The five-and-*dime!*" she exclaimed. "Where'd you get *that* kind of talk? Do you by any chance have reference to the *ten-cent store?*"

The worst of all was Friday night—the very night before I was to meet Lottie Jump —when Judge Bay came to play two-handed pinochle[1] with Daddy. The Judge, a

[1] PINOCHLE (pē′nuk·əl): a card game.

giant in intimidating haberdashery[1]—for some reason, the white piping on his vest bespoke, for me, handcuffs and prison bars —and with an aura of disapproval for almost everything on earth except what pertained directly to himself, was telling Daddy, before they began their game, about the infamous[2] vandalism that had been going on among the college students. "I have reason to believe that there are girls in this gang as well as boys," he said. "They ransack vacant houses and take everything. In one house on Pleasant Street, up there by the Catholic Church, there wasn't anything to take, so they took the kitchen sink. Wasn't a question of taking everything *but*—they took the kitchen sink."

"What ever would they want with a kitchen sink?" asked my mother.

"Mischief," replied the Judge. "If we ever catch them and if they come within my jurisdiction, I can tell you I will give them no quarter. A thief, in my opinion, is the lowest of the low."

Mother told about the chocolate cake. By now, the fiction was so factual in my mind that each time I thought of it I saw a funny-paper bum in baggy pants held up by rope, a hat with holes through which tufts of hair stuck up, shoes from which his toes protruded, a disreputable stubble on his face; he came up beneath the open window where the devil's food was cooling and he stole it and hotfooted it for the woods, where his companion was frying a small fish in a beat-up skillet. It never crossed my mind any longer that Lottie Jump had hooked that delicious cake.

Judge Bay was properly impressed. "If you will steal a chocolate cake, if you will steal a kitchen sink, you will steal diamonds and money. The small child who pilfers a penny from his mother's pocketbook has started down a path that may lead him to holding up a bank."

It was a good thing I had no homework that night, for I could not possibly have concentrated. We were all sent to our rooms, because the pinochle players had to have absolute quiet. I spent the evening doing cross-stitch. I was making a bureau runner for a Christmas present; as in the case of the Christmas card, I had no one to give it to, but now I decided to give it to Lottie Jump's mother. Stella was reading *Black Beauty*, crying. It was an interminable[3] evening. Stella went to bed first; I saw to that, because I didn't want her lying there awake listening to me talking in my sleep. Besides, I didn't want her to see me tearing open the cardboard box—the one in the shape of a church, which held my Christmas Sunday-school offering. Over the door of the church was this shaming legend: "My mite[4] for the poor widow." When Stella had begun to grind her teeth in her first deep sleep, I took twenty cents away from the poor widow, whoever she was (the owner of the kitchen sink, no doubt), for the trolley fare, and secreted it and the remaining three pennies in the pocket of my middy.[5] I wrapped the money well in a handkerchief and buttoned the pocket and hung my skirt over the middy. And then I tore the paper church into bits —the heavens opened and Judge Bay came toward me with a double-barrelled shotgun

[1] HABERDASHERY: men's clothing, such as hats, shirts, etc.
[2] INFAMOUS (ĭn′fə·məs): notorious; famous for being so bad.

[3] INTERMINABLE: endless.
[4] MITE: very small amount of money.
[5] MIDDY: loose-fitting blouse.

—and hid the bits under a pile of pajamas. I did not sleep one wink. Except that I must have, because of the stupendous nightmares that kept wrenching the flesh off my skeleton and caused me to come close to perishing of thirst; once I fell out of bed and hit my head on Stella's ice skates. I would have waked her up and given her a piece of my mind for leaving them in such a lousy place, but then I remembered: I wanted *no* commotion of any kind.

I couldn't eat breakfast and I couldn't eat lunch. Old Johnny-on-the-spot Jack kept saying, *"Poor* Polecat. Polecat wants her fish for dinner." Mother made an abortive[1] attempt to take my temperature. And when all that hullabaloo subsided, I was nearly in the soup because Mother asked me to mind Tess while she went to the sanitarium to see Mrs. Rogers, who, all of a sudden, was too sick to have anyone but grownups near her. Stella couldn't stay with the baby, because she had to go to ballet, and Jack couldn't, because he had to go up to the mesa and empty his traps. ("No, they *can't* wait. You want my skins to rot in this hot-one-day-cold-the-next weather?") I was arguing and whining when the telephone rang. Mother went to answer it and came back with a look of great sadness; Mrs. Rogers, she had learned, had had another hemorrhage. So Mother would not be going to the sanitarium after all and I needn't stay with Tess.

By the time I left the house, I was as cross as a bear. I felt awful about the widow's mite and I felt awful for being mean about staying with Tess, for Mrs. Rogers was a kind old lady, in a cozy blue hug-me-tight and an old-fangled boudoir cap, dying here all alone; she was a friend of Grandma's and had lived just down the street from her in Missouri, and all in the world Mrs. Rogers wanted to do was go back home and lie down in her own big bedroom in her own big, high-ceilinged house and have Grandma and other members of the Eastern Star come in from time to time to say hello. But they wouldn't let her go home; they were going to kill or cure her. I could not help feeling that my hardness of heart and evil of intention had had a good deal to do with her new crisis; right at the very same minute I had been saying "Does that old Mrs. Methuselah *always* have to spoil my fun?" the poor wasted thing was probably coughing up her blood and saying to the nurse, "Tell Emily Vanderpool not to mind me, she can run and play."

I had a bad character, I know that, but my badness never gave me half the enjoyment Jack and Stella thought it did. A good deal of the time I wanted to eat lye.[2] I was certainly having no fun now, thinking of Mrs. Rogers and of depriving that poor widow of bread and milk; what if this penniless woman without a husband had a dog to feed, too? Or a baby? And besides, I didn't want to go downtown to steal anything from the ten-cent store; I didn't want to see Lottie Jump again—not really, for I knew in my bones that that girl was trouble with a capital "T." And still, in our short meeting she had mesmerized[3] me; I would think about her style of talking and the expert way she had made off with the perfume flask and the cake (how had she carried the cake through the streets without being noticed?) and be bowled over,

[1] ABORTIVE: unsuccessful.

[2] LYE: a highly poisonous substance.
[3] MESMERIZED: hypnotized.

for the part of me that did not love God was a black-hearted villain. And apart from these considerations, I had some sort of idea that if I did not keep my appointment with Lottie Jump, she would somehow get revenge; she had seemed a girl of purpose. So, revolted and fascinated, brave and lily-livered, I plodded along through the snow in my flopping galoshes up toward the Chautauqua, where the trolley stop was. On my way, I passed Virgil Meade's house; there was not just a snowman, there was a whole snow family in the back yard, and Virgil himself was throwing a stick for his dog. I was delighted to see that he was alone.

Lottie, who was sitting on a bench in the shelter eating a Mr. Goodbar, looked the same as she had the other time except that she was wearing an amazing hat. I think I had expected her to have a black handkerchief over the lower part of her face or to be wearing a Jesse James waistcoat. But I had never thought of a hat. It was felt; it was the color of cooked meat; it had some flowers appliquéd on the front of it; it had no brim, but rose straight up to a very considerable height, like a monument. It sat so low on her forehead and it was so tight that it looked, in a way, like part of her.

"How's every little thing, bub?" she said, licking her candy wrapper.

"Fine, Lottie," I said, freshly awed.

A silence fell. I drank some water from the drinking fountain, sat down, fastened my galoshes, and unfastened them again.

"My mother's teeth grow wrong way to," said Lottie, and showed me what she meant: the lower teeth were in front of the upper ones. "That so-called trolley car takes its own sweet time. This town is blah."

To save the honor of my home town, the trolley came scraping and groaning up the hill just then, its bell clanging with an idiotic frenzy, and ground to a stop. Its broad, proud cowcatcher was filled with dirty snow, in the middle of which rested a tomato can, put there, probably, by somebody who was bored to death and couldn't think of anything else to do—I did a lot of pointless things like that on lonesome Saturday afternoons. It was the custom of this trolley car, a rather mysterious one, to pause at the shelter for five minutes while the conductor, who was either Mr. Jansen or Mr. Peck, depending on whether it was the A.M. run or the P.M., got out and stretched and smoked and spit. Sometimes the passengers got out, too, acting like sightseers whose destination was this sturdy stucco gazebo[1] instead of, as it really was, the Piggly Wiggly or the Nelson Dry. You expected them to take snapshots of the drinking fountain or of the Chautauqua meeting house up on the hill. And when they all got back in the car, you expected them to exchange intelligent observations on the aborigines[2] and the ruins they had seen.

Today there were no passengers, and as soon as Mr. Peck got out and began staring at the mountains as if he had never seen them before while he made himself a cigarette, Lottie, in her tall hat (was it something like the Inspector's hat in the Katzenjammer Kids?), got into the car, motioning me to follow. I put our nickels in the empty box and joined her on the very last double seat. It was only then that she mapped out the plan for the afternoon,

[1] GAZEBO: pavilion.
[2] ABORIGINES (ab·ə·rij′ə·nēz): native inhabitants of an area.

in a low but still insouciant[1] voice. The hat —she did not apologize for it, she simply referred to it as "my hat"—was to be the repository[2] of whatever we stole. In the future, it would be advisable for me to have one like it. (How? Surely it was unique. The flowers, I saw on closer examination, were tulips, but they were blue, and a very unsettling shade of blue.) I was to engage[3] a clerk on one side of the counter, asking her the price of, let's say, a tube of Daggett & Ramsdell vanishing cream, while Lottie would lift a round comb or a barrette or a hair net or whatever on the other side. Then, at a signal, I would decide against the vanishing cream and would move on to the next counter that she indicated. The signal was interesting; it was to be the raising of her hat from the rear—"like I've got the itch and gotta scratch," she said. I was relieved that I was to have no part in the actual stealing, and I was touched that Lottie, who was going to do all the work, said we would "go halvers" on the take. She asked me if there was anything in particular I wanted—she herself had nothing special in mind and was going to shop around first—and I said I would like some rubber gloves. This request was entirely spontaneous; I had never before in my life thought of rubber gloves in one way or another, but a psychologist—or Judge Bay —might have said that this was most significant and that I was planning at that moment to go on from petty larceny to bigger game, armed with a weapon on which I wished to leave no fingerprints.

On the way downtown, quite a few people got on the trolley, and they all gave us such peculiar looks that I was chicken-hearted until I realized it must be Lottie's hat they were looking at. No wonder. I kept looking at it myself out of the corner of my eye; it was like a watermelon standing on end. No, it was like a tremendous test tube. On this trip—a slow one, for the trolley pottered through that part of town in a desultory,[4] neighborly way, even going into areas where no one lived—Lottie told me some of the things she had stolen in Muskogee and here in Adams. They included a white satin prayer book (think of it!), Mr. Goodbars by the thousands (she had probably never paid for a Mr. Goodbar in her life), a dinner ring valued at two dollars, a strawberry emery, several cans of corn, some shoelaces, a set of poker chips, countless pencils, four spark plugs ("Pa had this old car, see, and it was broke, so we took 'er to get fixed; I'll build me a radio with 'em sometime—you know? Listen in on them ear muffs to Tulsa?"), a Boy Scout knife, and a Girl Scout folding cup. She made a regular practice of going through the pockets of the coats in the cloakroom every day at recess, but she had never found anything there worth a red cent and was about to give that up. Once, she had taken a gold pencil from a teacher's desk and had got caught—she was sure that this was one of the reasons she was only in the third grade. Of this unjust experience, she said, "The old hoot owl! If I was drivin' in a car on a lonesome stretch and she was settin' beside me, I'd wait till we got to a pile of gravel and then I'd stop and say, 'Git out, Miss Priss.' She'd git out, all right."

Since Lottie was so frank, I was emboldened at last to ask her what she had done with the cake. She faced me with her grin;

---

[1] INSOUCIANT (in·sü′sē-ənt): unconcerned, carefree.
[2] REPOSITORY: storing place.
[3] ENGAGE: hold the attention of.

[4] DESULTORY: random.

this grin, in combination with the hat, gave me a surprise from which I have never recovered. "I ate it up," she said. "I went in your garage and sat on your daddy's old tires and ate it. It was pretty good."

There were two ten-cent stores side by side in our town, Kresge's and Woolworth's, and as we walked down the main street toward them, Lottie played with a Yo-Yo. Since the street was thronged with Christmas shoppers and farmers in for Saturday, this was no ordinary accomplishment; all in all, Lottie Jump was someone to be reckoned with. I cannot say that I was proud to be seen with her; the fact is that I hoped I would not meet anyone I knew, and I thanked my lucky stars that Jack was up in the hills with his dead skunks, because if he had seen her with that lid and that Yo-Yo, I would never have heard the last of it. But in another way I *was* proud to be with her; in a smaller hemisphere, in one that included only her and me, I was swaggering—I felt like Somebody, marching along beside this lofty Somebody from Oklahoma who was going to hold up the dime store.

There is nothing like Woolworth's at Christmastime. It smells of peanut brittle and terrible chocolate candy, Djer Kiss talcum powder and Ben Hur Perfume—smells sourly of tinsel and waxily of artificial poinsettias. The crowds are made up largely of children and women, with here and there a deliberative old man; the women are buying ribbons and wrappings and Christmas cards, and the children are buying asbestos pot holders for their mothers and, for their fathers, suede bookmarks with a burnt-in design that says "A good book is a good friend" or "Souvenir from the Garden of the Gods." It is very noisy. The salesgirls

are forever ringing their bells and asking the floorwalker to bring them change for a five; babies in go-carts are screaming as parcels fall on their heads; the women, waving rolls of red tissue paper, try to attract the attention of the harried girl behind the counter. ("Miss! All I want is this one batch of the red. Can't I just give you the dime?" And the girl, beside herself, mottled with vexation, cries back, "Has to be rung up, Moddom, that's the rule.") There is pandemonium at the toy counter, where things are being tested by the customers—wound up, set off, tooted, pounded, made to say "Maaaah-Maaaah!" There is very little gaiety in the scene and, in fact, those baffled old men look as if they were walking over their own dead bodies, but there is an atmosphere of carnival, nevertheless, and as soon as Lottie and I entered the doors of Woolworth's golden-and-vermilion bedlam, I grew giddy and hot—not pleasantly so. The feeling, indeed, was distinctly disagreeable, like the beginning of a stomach upset.

Lottie gave me a nudge and said softly, "Go look at the envelopes. I want some rubber bands."

This counter was relatively uncrowded (the seasonal stationery supplies—the Christmas cards and wrapping paper and stickers—were at a separate counter), and I went around to examine some very beautiful letter paper; it was pale pink and it had a border of roses all around it. The clerk here was a cheerful middle-aged woman wearing an apron, and she was giving all her attention to a seedy old man who could not make up his mind between mucilage and paste. "Take your time, Dad," she said. "Compared to the rest of the girls, I'm on my vacation." The old man, holding a tube in one hand and a bottle in the other, looked at her vaguely and said, "I want it for stamps. Sometimes I write a letter and stamp it and then don't mail it and steam the stamp off. Must have ninety cents' worth of stamps like that." The woman laughed. "I know what you mean," she said. "I get mad and write a letter and then I tear it up." The old man gave her a condescending look and said, "That so? But I don't suppose yours are of a political nature." He bent his gaze again to the choice of adhesives.

This first undertaking was duck soup for Lottie. I did not even have to exchange a word with the woman; I saw Miss Fagin[1] lift up *that hat* and give me the high sign, and we moved away, she down one aisle and I down the other, now and again catching a glimpse of each other through the throngs. We met at the foot of the second counter, where notions were sold.

"Fun, huh?" said Lottie, and I nodded, although I felt wholly dreary. "I want some crochet hooks," she said. "Price the rickrack."

This time the clerk was adding up her receipts and did not even look at me or at a woman who was angrily and in vain trying to buy a paper of pins. Out went Lottie's scrawny hand, up went her domed chimney. In this way for some time she bagged sitting birds: a tea strainer (there was no one at all at that counter), a box of Mrs. Carpenter's All Purpose Nails, the rubber gloves I had said I wanted, and four packages of mixed seeds. Now you have some idea of the size of Lottie Jump's hat.

I was nervous, not from being her accomplice but from being in this crowd on an empty stomach, and I was getting tired—we had been in the store for at least an hour—and the whole enterprise seemed pointless. There wasn't a thing in her hat I wanted—not even the rubber gloves. But in exact proportion as my spirits descended, Lottie's rose; clearly she had only been target-practicing and now she was moving in for the kill.

We met beside the books of paper dolls, for reconnaissance. "I'm gonna get me a pair of pearl beads," said Lottie. "You go fuss with the hairpins, hear?"

Luck, combined with her skill, would have stayed with Lottie, and her hat would have been a cornucopia[2] by the end of the afternoon if, at the very moment her hand went out for the string of beads, that idiosyncrasy[3] of mine had not struck me full force. I had never known it to come with so few preliminaries; probably this was so because I was oppressed by all the masses of bodies poking and pushing me, and all the open mouths breathing in my face. Anyhow, right then, at the crucial time, I *had to be alone.*

I stood staring down at the bone hairpins for a moment, and when the girl behind the counter said, "What kind does Mother want, hon? What color is Mother's hair?" I looked past her and across at Lottie and I said, "Your brother isn't the only one in your family that doesn't have any brains." The clerk, astonished, turned to look where I was looking and caught Lottie in the act of lifting up her hat to put the pearls inside. She had unwisely chosen a long strand and was having a little trouble; I had the nasty thought that it looked as if her brains were leaking out.

---

[1] MISS FAGIN: Fagin, a character in Charles Dickens' *Oliver Twist*, was a professional thief who hired and trained children as pickpockets.

[2] CORNUCOPIA: horn of plenty.

[3] IDIOSYNCRASY (id·ē·ō·sing′krə·sē): peculiarity.

The clerk, not able to deal with this emergency herself, frantically punched her bell and cried, "Floorwalker! Mr. Bellamy! I've caught a thief!"

Momentarily there was a violent hush—then such a clamor as you have never heard. Bells rang, babies howled, crockery crashed to the floor as people stumbled in their rush to the arena.

Mr. Bellamy, nineteen years old but broad of shoulder and jaw, was instantly standing beside Lottie, holding her arm with one hand while with the other he removed her hat to reveal to the overjoyed audience that incredible array of merchandise. Her hair all wild, her face a mask of innocent bewilderment, Lottie Jump, the scurvy thing, pretended to be deaf and dumb. She pointed at the rubber gloves and then she pointed at me, and Mr. Bellamy, able at last to prove his mettle,[1] said "Aha!" and, still holding Lottie, moved around the counter to me and grabbed *my* arm. He gave the hat to the clerk and asked her kindly to accompany him and his red-handed catch to the manager's office.

I don't know where Lottie is now—whether she is on the stage or in jail. If her performance after our arrest meant anything, the first is quite as likely as the second. (I never saw her again, and for all I know she lit out of town that night on a freight train. Or perhaps her whole family decamped as suddenly as they had arrived; ours was a most transient[2] population. You can be sure I made no attempt to find her again, and for months I avoided going anywhere near Arapahoe Creek or

North Hill.) She never said a word but kept making signs with her fingers, adlibbing the whole thing. They tested her hearing by shooting off a popgun right in her ear and she never batted an eyelid.

They called up my father, and he came over from the Safeway on the double. I heard very little of what he said because I was crying so hard, but one thing I did hear him say was "Well young lady, I guess you've seen to it that I'll have to part company with my good friend Judge Bay." I tried to defend myself, but it was useless. The manager, Mr. Bellamy, the clerk, and my father patted Lottie on the shoulder, and the clerk said, "Poor, afflicted child." For being a poor, afflicted child, they gave her a bag of hard candy, and she gave them the most fraudulent[3] smile of gratitude, and slobbered a little, and shuffled out, holding her empty hat in front of her like a beggarman. I hate Lottie Jump to this day, but I have to hand it to her—she was a genius.

The floorwalker would have liked to see me sentenced to the reform school for life, I am sure, but the manager said that considering this was my first offense, he would let my father attend to my punishment. The old-maid clerk, who looked precisely like Emmy Schmalz, clucked her tongue and shook her head at me. My father hustled me out of the office and out of the store and into the car and home, muttering the entire time; now and again I'd hear the words "morals" and "nowadays."

What's the use of telling the rest? You know what happened. Daddy on second thoughts decided not to hang his head in front of Judge Bay but to make use of his friendship in this time of need, and he took

---

[1] METTLE: courage, worth.
[2] TRANSIENT: moving from one home to another.

[3] FRAUDULENT: fake.

me to see the scary old curmudgeon[1] at his house. All I remember of that long declamation, during which the Judge sat behind his desk never taking his eyes off me, was the warning "I want you to give this a great deal of thought, Miss. I want you to search and seek in the innermost corners of your conscience and root out every bit of badness." Oh, *him!* Why, listen, if I'd rooted out all the badness in me, there wouldn't have been anything left of me. My mother cried for days because she had nurtured an outlaw and was ashamed to show her face at the neighborhood store; my father was silent, and he often looked at me. Stella, who was a prig, said, "And to think you did it at *Christmas*time!" As for Jack—well, Jack a couple of times did not know how close he came to seeing glory when I had a butcher knife in my hand. It was Polecat this and Polecat that until I nearly went off my rocker. Tess, of course, didn't know what was going on, and asked so many questions that finally I told her to go

to Helen Hunt Jackson in a savage tone of voice.

Good old Muff.

It is not true that you don't learn by experience. At any rate, I did that time. I began immediately to have two or three friends at a time—to be sure, because of the stigma[2] on me, they were by no means the elite[3] of Carlyle Hill Grade—and never again when that terrible need to be alone arose did I let fly. I would say, instead, "I've got a headache. I'll have to go home and take an aspirin," or "Gosh all hemlocks, I forgot—I've got to go to the dentist."

After the scandal died down, I got into the Campfire Girls. It was through pull, of course, since Stella had been a respected member for two years and my mother was a friend of the leader. But it turned out all right. Even Muff did not miss our periods of companionship, because about that time she grew up and started having literally millions of kittens.

[1] CURMUDGEON (kər·muj'ən): cranky, unpleasant or difficult person.

[2] STIGMA: mark of shame.
[3] ELITE (ā·lēt'): those of the highest and most exclusive class.

FOR DISCUSSION

1. Emily didn't really want to steal anything. Why did she keep her appointment with Lottie Jump? Was there more than one reason?

2. Emily deliberately exposed Lottie to the clerk and caused her capture. How did Lottie manage to involve Emily and eventually convince the manager that Emily was really to blame for the stealing? Why wasn't Emily more surprised by Lottie's acting ability?

3. In the beginning of the story Emily states

that she learned her lesson in a very bitter way. Was she referring to stealing or something else? What lesson did she learn? How did this lesson help her to find happiness later in her life?

4. Throughout the story Emily refers to herself as having "a bad character," and her family seems to agree that she is a holy terror of a child. Do you feel that Emily's self-evaluation is entirely true? Support your answer by referring directly to lines or incidents in the story.

MAGGIE AND MILLY AND MOLLY AND MAY

E. E. CUMMINGS

maggie and milly and molly and may
went down to the beach(to play one day)

and maggie discovered a shell that sang
so sweetly she couldn't remember her troubles,and

milly befriended a stranded star   5
whose rays five languid* fingers were;

and molly was chased by a horrible thing
which raced sideways while blowing bubbles:and

may came home with a smooth round stone
as small as a world and as large as alone.   10

For whatever we lose(like a you or a me)
it's always ourselves we find in the sea

⁶ LANGUID (lang′gwid): slow of movement.

FOR DISCUSSION

• In the final stanza the poet observes, "it's always ourselves we find in the sea." What does each of the different things they found tell you about each of the little girls?

In Summary

FOR DISCUSSION

1. Review each selection in this unit and try to explain the type of insight that occurs. Do you think gaining insight is usually a painful or uncomfortable process? Can you think of any examples of types of insight that might occur under pleasant circumstances?

2. One important way to gain insight is to put yourself in another person's place when trying to understand him. Which characters in this unit would have benefited most if they could have done this?

3. Prejudice, or pre-judging, is one habit that prevents us from understanding others or responding to them. Mrs. Wilson in "After You, My Dear Alphonse" was prevented from any real understanding by her prejudices. What other examples of prejudice occur in the selections of this unit? Be aware that prejudice toward others is not limited to the area of racial problems.

OTHER THINGS TO DO

1. One benefit to be gained by the appreciation of poetry, music, and art is that we can share the artist's wisdom and sensitivity and thus gain new insights into ourselves. Select a poem, piece of music, or work of art that reveals some new truth or personal understanding to you. Be prepared to share your selection and insight with the class.

2. Reread "The Secret Heart." As children grow from infancy through adolescence into adulthood, a constant, if quiet, series of insights help them to move from a childish to a more mature understanding of the people to whom they are close. Write a theme (or a poem, if you choose) in which you express some insight you have gained in the relationship between you and your parents or other members of your family.

The World of Words

AFTER YOU, MY DEAR ALPHONSE

During World War I the British were developing a secret weapon that proved in time to be enormously effective. While its identity was still a secret, it was being referred to by the code name *tank*, for it did bear some resemblance to a benzene tank. The code name stuck. Thus, Boyd and Johnny are going to go by the name of *tank* drivers (page 460) in Shirley Jackson's story because of a need for secrecy in World War I. Can you think of other examples in English of two identical words, from the same source, that have quite different meanings? (The early inhabitants of America, for example, or the more common word for *tumbler*.)

THE LIE

1. Doctor Remenzel doesn't want his son going around saying something *asinine* (page 466). The adjective comes from the Latin noun *asinus,* meaning "ass" or "donkey." A donkey is thought of as dull-witted; to say something asinine, then, is to say something stupid. Other words that convey the same idea are *doltish, idiotic, moronic, imbecilic, dense, dull,* and *dumb.* Explain how each of those adjectives is related to the concept of stupidity.

2. *Asinine* means "like an ass." A number of other adjectives derive from either the English or the Latin names of animals. Such adjectives describe attributes usually associated with the animal in question. What is a *waspish* remark? A *mulish* temperament? A *bovine* disposition? *Porcine* table manners? *Vulpine* strategy? *Formic* industry? A *lupine* appetite? *Canine* teeth?

A VISIT OF CHARITY

The old lady clears her throat "like a sheep *bleating*" (page 480). Sheeps bleat. Dogs *bark*. What other animal barks? The following verbs all describe sound that animals make: *growl, bray, whinny, croak, roar, howl, nicker, grunt.* With which animal or animals is each verb associated? What other verbs might be added to the list?

DIFFERENT CULTURAL LEVELS EAT HERE

Throughout DeVries' story, sharp, active verbs let us picture clearly what is happening. At the very start we might have been told that "the counterman *looked* up from the grill" when the two couples entered. Instead, the author writes that "the counterman *glanced* up." *Glanced* is more precise, more specific, more vivid than *looked,* as *wriggled* is more vivid than *moved* in "She *wriggled* forward on the stool . . ." (page 490). What verbs or verbals does the author use in place of the less precise, less active verbs substituted in the following? "Her escort *touched* her with the side of his knee . . ." (page 489); "The man *felt* studiously in the matchbox" (page 490); "Conscious of their collective gaze, he turned his head, and *made them look* away in various directions" (page 490); "The counterman *looked* at him. 'What about it?' " (page 491). "The counterman *closed* the cash register . . ." (page 494). "The door *was opened* . . ." (page 494).

BAD CHARACTERS

All of the following words, borrowed from other languages and now a part of standard English, appear in "Bad Characters." From what language does each word come? Be sure you know what all the words mean: *mesa* (page 495), *muff* (495), *chocolate* (496), *casino* (496), *geranium* (497), *Parcheesi* (498), *pathos* (498), *tapioca* (499), *tobacco* (499), *bureau* (498), *pajamas* (504), *sanitarium* (504), *ballet* (504), *boudoir* (504), *stucco* (505), *aborigine* (505), *asbestos* (507), *souvenir* (507), *crochet* (508), *elite* (511).

Reader's Choice

Born Free: A Lioness of Two Worlds, *by Joy Adamson.*

The hard lesson that "loving is letting go" is told in this fascinating tale of the friendship between a lively young lion cub and the game warden and his wife who took her in and raised her with great love and joy. But when the warden and his wife realize that by keeping Elsa the lioness with them during her growing up years they have robbed her of the ability to fend for herself and live as free as she was born, they begin the painstaking task of teaching her the ways of the jungle, until the day that they know she is free once more and no longer needs them.

Goodbye, Mr. Chips, *by James Hilton.*

To the boys at Brookfield, old Mr. Chips was no mystery at all—just a rather eccentric but always kind old teacher who had always been there. In this sensitive portrayal of a remarkable man, James Hilton takes the reader past the façade of the tired teacher and traces an often exciting and warmly affecting lifetime of caring and helping.

The Human Comedy, *by William Saroyan.*

Money was tight in the MacCauley household now that Marcus was a soldier, so 14-year-old Homer lies about his age to get a job delivering telegrams by bicycle to help his widowed mother meet household expenses. The idea of paying his own way excites the boy, but as he works at his job he discovers that delivering telegrams during the years of World War Two can be a much more difficult task than he had imagined; he learns the heartbreak and triumphs of the human condition as he grows in compassion and courage by giving of himself to those whose life he touches.

The Ox-Bow Incident, *by Walter Van Tilburg Clark.*

What causes injustice? This careful and dramatic study of the forces and personalities involved in the lynching in 1885 of an innocent man make this story, set in frontier Nevada, far more than just an ordinary western adventure.

The Pigman, *by Paul Zindel.*

Two high school sophomores tell the tragic story of their friendship with a lonely old man whom they love and destroy.

Shaking the Nickel Bush, *by Ralph Moody.*

The doctors said that Ralph, at nineteen, had six months to live—maybe. With a little money and some salmon, peanuts, and gluten bread for his diabetic diet, Ralph headed West to make his fortune, regain his health, or at least make his last year the most exciting of his life. He started as a stunt man in cowboy movies, flinging himself from swift-running horses, pitting his nerve and skill against the threat of death he faced every day.

The Snow Goose, *by Paul Gallico.*

There is an ageless, magic quality to this simple tale of a lonely hunchbacked painter, the bird sanctuary he builds in an abandoned lighthouse off the coast of England, and the great moment of adventure that comes to him as he becomes a part of the Dunkirk evacuation.

DRAMA

ANNE FRANK WAS BORN in 1929. If she had lived, she would be in her forties now, a Dutch woman, perhaps married and with children growing up and living in Amsterdam, where she spent her own childhood.

But it was not Anne's fate to live to maturity. Because she was a Jew, she was in danger from the moment the Nazis invaded her homeland during the Second World War. For the Nazis, the ruling party in Adolf Hitler's Germany, had deluded themselves into thinking they were a "master race" whose mortal enemies were Jewish people everywhere. Accordingly, when they invaded Holland they behaved as they did in the other countries they controlled, rounding up all the Jews they could find and systematically exterminating them in the most coldly inhuman manner imaginable.

Yet a more *human* being than Anne Frank would be hard to imagine—a person more apt to make the rest of us proud to belong to the human race. From July 6, 1942, to August 4, 1944—seven hundred and fifty-nine days and nights—Anne and her family hid from the Germans in an attic in Amsterdam, living out two years of their lives there. Anne kept a diary of that ordeal, and the play that follows accurately recreates the world her diary reveals.

In time the Franks' hiding place was discovered. Anne was transported to a concentration camp and died of malnutrition in the spring of 1945, two months before the Allies liberated the Netherlands. Yet even near the end, her marvelous spirit shone through. "In spite of everything," she set down late in the diary, "I still believe that people are really good at heart . . . that peace and tranquility will return again."

Philip McFarland

As time passes, the horrors of Nazi oppression will inevitably fade more and more into words in a history book, and the reality of the lives blighted by that unspeakable hour of darkness in human history will become less and less vivid. It is hard for us to comprehend the full and true meaning of the estimated twelve million civilians—half of them Jews—who were murdered in Nazi concentration camps. Several years after the end of the Second World War, a most remarkable play—the dramatization of the actual diary of a young victim of the holocaust —translated into all the major languages of the world, was performed in cities from Berlin to Los Angeles. At the end of the performance, there was, according to one observer, "invariably an awful stillness over the audience. No one applauded, no one coughed or stirred, and the stagehands soon learned to wait a moment or two longer than was usual before bringing up the curtain for the actors to bow and accept their tribute. Moments later, the thunderous applause would begin, but the audiences who left those theatres were not precisely the same people they had been when they had entered. Perhaps a lesson had been learned. Or, if this is too much to hope, perhaps we can at least believe that a glimpse of light had that night shone upon us all, and that light had revealed to us a new determination that this must not happen again, that hate must never again be permitted to grow to such mad power that it can wink out in an instant so much life, so much love." For many people, this play, which you are about to read, was the one glimpse of light which made them finally begin to comprehend the full horror of the Nazi disaster, and resolve that such a thing would never happen again.

THE DIARY OF ANNE FRANK

FRANCES GOODRICH AND ALBERT HACKETT

CHARACTERS

MR. FRANK

MIEP

MRS. VAN DAAN

MR. VAN DAAN

PETER VAN DAAN

MRS. FRANK

MARGOT FRANK

ANNE FRANK

MR. KRALER

DUSSEL

*The Time: During the years of World War
II and immediately thereafter.
The Place: Amsterdam. There are two acts.*

ACT ONE

SCENE ONE: *The scene remains the same throughout the play. It is the top floor of a warehouse and office building in Amsterdam, Holland. The sharply peaked roof of the building is outlined against a sea of other rooftops, stretching away into the distance. Nearby is the belfry of a church tower, the Westertoren, whose carillon rings out the hours. Occasionally faint sounds float up from below: the voices of children playing in the street, the tramp of marching feet, a boat whistle from the canal.*

The three rooms of the top floor and a small attic space above are exposed to our view. The largest of the rooms is in the center, with two small rooms, slightly raised, on either side. On the right is a bathroom, out of sight. A narrow, steep flight of stairs at the back leads up to the attic. The rooms are sparsely furnished with a few chairs, cots, a table or two. The windows are painted over, or covered with makeshift blackout curtains.

In the main room there is a sink, a gas ring for cooking, and a woodburning stove for warmth.

The room on the left is hardly more than a closet. There is a skylight in the sloping ceiling. Directly under this room is a small steep stairwell, with steps leading down to a door. This is the only entrance from the building below. When the door is opened we see that it has been concealed on the outer side by a bookcase attached to it.

The curtain rises on an empty stage. It is late afternoon, November, 1945.

The rooms are dusty, the curtains in rags. Chairs and tables are overturned.

The door at the foot of the small stairwell swings open. Mr. Frank comes up the steps into view. He is a gentle, cultured European in his middle years. There is still a trace of a German accent in his speech.

He stands looking slowly around, making a supreme effort at self-control. He is weak, ill. His clothes are threadbare.

After a second he drops his rucksack on the couch and moves slowly about. He opens the door to one of the smaller rooms, and then abruptly closes it again, turning away. He goes to the window at the back, looking off at the Westertoren as its carillon strikes the hour of six; then he moves restlessly on.

From the street below we hear the sound of a barrel organ and children's voices at play. There is a many-colored scarf hanging from a nail. Mr. Frank takes it, putting it around his neck. As he starts back for his rucksack, his eye is caught by something lying on the floor. It is a woman's white glove. He

holds it in his hand and suddenly all of his self-control is gone. He breaks down, crying.

We hear footsteps on the stairs. Miep[1] Gies comes up, looking for Mr. Frank. Miep is a Dutch girl of about twenty-two. She wears a coat and hat, ready to go home. She is pregnant. Her attitude toward MR. FRANK *is protective, compassionate.*

MIEP. Are you all right, Mr. Frank?

MR. FRANK [*quickly controlling himself*]. Yes, Miep, yes.

MIEP. Everyone in the office has gone home . . . It's after six. [*Then pleading*] Don't stay up here, Mr. Frank. What's the use of torturing yourself like this?

MR. FRANK. I've come to say good-by . . . I'm leaving here, Miep.

MIEP. What do you mean? Where are you going? Where?

MR. FRANK. I don't know yet, I haven't decided.

MIEP. Mr. Frank, you can't leave here! This is your home! Amsterdam is your home. Your business is here, waiting for you . . . You're needed here . . . Now that the war is over, there are things that . . .

MR. FRANK. I can't stay in Amsterdam, Miep. It has too many memories for me. Everywhere there's something . . . the house we lived in . . . the school . . . that street organ playing out there . . . I'm not the person you used to know, Miep. I'm a bitter old man. [*Breaking off*] Forgive me. I shouldn't speak to you like this . . . after all that you did for us . . . the suffering . . .

MIEP. No. No. It wasn't suffering. You can't say we suffered. [*As she speaks,*

[1] MIEP: pronounced mē′pə.

she straightens a chair which is overturned.]

MR. FRANK. I know what you went through, you and Mr. Kraler. I'll remember it as long as I live. [*He gives one last look around.*] Come, Miep. [*He starts for the steps, then remembers his rucksack, going back to get it.*]

MIEP [*hurrying up to a cupboard*]. Mr. Frank, did you see? There are some of your papers here. [*She brings a bundle of papers to him.*] We found them in a heap of rubbish on the floor . . . after you left.

MR. FRANK. Burn them. [*He opens his rucksack to put the glove in it.*]

MIEP. But, Mr. Frank, there are letters, notes . . .

MR. FRANK. Burn them. All of them.

MIEP. Burn *this*? [*She hands him a paperbound notebook.*]

MR. FRANK [*quietly*]. Anne's diary. [*He opens the diary and begins to read.*] "Monday, the sixth of July, nineteen forty-two." [*To Miep*] Nineteen forty-two. Is it possible, Miep? . . . Only three years ago. [*As he continues his reading, he sits down on the couch.*] "Dear Diary, since you and I are going to be great friends, I will start by telling you about myself. My name is Anne Frank. I am thirteen years old. I was born in Germany the twelfth of June, nineteen twenty-nine. As my family is Jewish, we emigrated to Holland when Hitler came to power."

[*As Mr. Frank reads on, another voice joins his, as if coming from the air. It is Anne's voice.*]

MR. FRANK *and* ANNE. "My father started a business, importing spice and herbs. Things went well for us until nineteen forty. Then the war came, and the Dutch capitulation,[1] followed by the arrival of the Germans. Then things got very bad for the Jews."

[*Mr. Frank's voice dies out. Anne's voice continues alone. The lights dim slowly to darkness. The curtain falls on the scene.*]

ANNE'S VOICE. You could not do this and you could not do that. They forced Father out of his business. We had to wear yellow stars. I had to turn in my bike. I couldn't go to a Dutch school any more. I couldn't go to the movies, or ride in an automobile, or even on a streetcar, and a million other things. But somehow we children still managed to have fun. Yesterday Father told me we were going into hiding. Where, he wouldn't say. At five o'clock this morning Mother woke me and told me to hurry and get dressed. I was to put on as many clothes as I could. It would look too suspicious if we walked along carrying suitcases. It wasn't until we were on our way that I learned where we were going. Our hiding place was to be upstairs in the building where Father used to have his business. Three other people were coming with us . . . the Van Daans and their

---

[1] CAPITULATION: surrender. The Netherlands were invaded by German troops in 1940. After four days of intense Luftwaffe bombing which destroyed most of Rotterdam, the Dutch army surrendered. Although the country was under Nazi control thereafter, most of the Dutch navy and merchant fleet managed to leave the country and join the Allied forces in fighting the Nazis. In addition, a large and active Dutch underground continued to resist Nazi rule, aiding escaped Allied prisoners and Jewish refugees.

son Peter . . . Father knew the Van Daans but we had never met them . . .

[*During the last lines the curtain rises on the scene. The lights dim on. Anne's voice fades out.*]

SCENE TWO: *It is early morning, July, 1942. The rooms are bare, as before, but they are now clean and orderly.*

Mr. Van Daan, a tall, portly man in his late forties, is in the main room, pacing up and down, nervously smoking a cigarette. His clothes and overcoat are expensive and well cut.

Mrs. Van Daan sits on the couch, clutching her possessions, a hatbox, bags, etc. She is a pretty woman in her early forties. She wears a fur coat over her other clothes.

Peter Van Daan is standing at the window of the room on the right, looking down at the street below. He is a shy, awkward boy of sixteen. He wears a cap, a raincoat, and long Dutch trousers, like "plus fours." At his feet is a black case, a carrier for his cat.

The yellow Star of David[1] is conspicuous on all of their clothes.

MRS. VAN DAAN [*rising, nervous, excited*]. Something's happened to them! I know it!

MR. VAN DAAN. Now, Kerli!

MRS. VAN DAAN. Mr. Frank said they'd be here at seven o'clock. He said . . .

MR. VAN DAAN. They have two miles to walk. You can't expect . . .

MRS. VAN DAAN. They've been picked up. That's what's happened. They've been taken . . .

[*Mr. Van Daan indicates that he hears someone coming.*]

MR. VAN DAAN. You see?

[*Peter takes up his carrier and his schoolbag, etc. and goes into the main room as Mr. Frank comes up the stairwell from below. Mr. Frank looks much younger now. His movements are brisk, his manner confident. He wears an overcoat and carries his hat and a small cardboard box. He crosses to the Van Daans, shaking hands with each of them.*]

MR. FRANK. Mrs. Van Daan, Mr. Van Daan, Peter. [*Then, in explanation of their lateness*] There were too many of the Green Police[2] on the streets . . . We had to take the long way around.

[*Up the steps come Margot[3] Frank, Mrs. Frank, Miep [not pregnant now], and Mr. Kraler. All of them carry bags, packages, and so forth. The Star of David is conspicuous on all of the Franks' clothing. Margot is eighteen, beautiful, quiet, shy. Mrs. Frank is a young mother, gently bred, reserved. She, like Mr. Frank, has a slight German accent. Mr. Kraler is a Dutchman, dependable, kindly.*

As Mr. Kraler and Miep go upstage to put down their parcels, Mrs. Frank turns back to call Anne.]

MRS. FRANK. Anne?

---

[1] STAR OF DAVID: The six-pointed star is a Jewish symbol. The Nazis required all Jews to display the star on their clothing so that they might be immediately identifiable as Jews.

[2] GREEN POLICE: Nazi police; their uniforms were green.

[3] MARGOT: pronounced mär′gō.

[*Anne comes running up the stairs. She is thirteen, quick in her movements, interested in everything, mercurial in her emotions. She wears a cape, long wool socks and carries a schoolbag.*]

MR. FRANK [*introducing them*]. My wife, Edith. Mr. and Mrs. Van Daan [*Mrs. Frank hurries over, shaking hands with them.*] . . . their son, Peter . . . my daughters, Margot and Anne.

[*Anne gives a polite little curtsy as she shakes Mr. Van Daan's hand. Then she immediately starts off on a tour of investigation of her new home, going upstairs to the attic room.*

Miep and Mr. Kraler are putting the various things they have brought on the shelves.]

MR. KRALER. I'm sorry there is still so much confusion.

MR. FRANK. Please. Don't think of it. After all, we'll have plenty of leisure to arrange everything ourselves.

MIEP [*to Mrs. Frank*]. We put the stores of food you sent in here. Your drugs are here . . . soap, linen here.

MR. FRANK. Thank you, Miep.

MIEP. I made up the beds . . . the way Mr. Frank and Mr. Kraler said. [*She starts out.*] I have to hurry. I've got to go to the other side of town to get some ration books[1] for you.

MRS. VAN DAAN. Ration books? If they see our names on ration books, they'll know we're here.

[1] RATION BOOKS: Since food and other consumer goods were scarce during the war, each citizen was issued a ration book which contained a limited number of stamps for various items. When an item was purchased, a stamp was required as well as money. Such a system was meant to insure that scarce goods would be evenly distributed.

MR. KRALER. There isn't anything . . .

MIEP. Don't worry. Your names won't be on them. [*As she hurries out*] I'll be up later. } [*Together*]

MR. FRANK. Thank you, Miep.

MRS. FRANK [*to Mr. Kraler*]. It's illegal, then, the ration books? We've never done anything illegal.

MR. FRANK. We won't be living here exactly according to regulations.

[*As Mr. Kraler reassures Mrs. Frank, he takes various small things, such as matches, soap, etc., from his pockets, handing them to her.*]

MR. KRALER. This isn't the black market,[2] Mrs. Frank. This is what we call the white market . . . helping all of the hundreds and hundreds who are hiding out in Amsterdam.

[*The carillon is heard playing the quarter-hour before eight. Mr. Kraler looks at his watch. Anne stops at the window as she comes down the stairs.*]

ANNE. It's the Westertoren!

MR. KRALER. I must go. I must be out of here and downstairs in the office before the workmen get here. [*He starts for the stairs leading out.*] Miep or I, or both of us, will be up each day to bring you food and news and find out what your needs are. Tomorrow I'll get you a better bolt for the door at the foot of the stairs. It needs a bolt that you can throw yourself and open only at our signal. [*To Mr. Frank*] Oh . . . You'll tell them about the noise?

[2] BLACK MARKET: an illegal network which sold scarce goods without asking for ration coupons.

MR. FRANK. I'll tell them.

MR. KRALER. Good-by then for the moment. I'll come up again, after the workmen leave.

MR. FRANK. Good-by, Mr. Kraler.

MRS. FRANK [*shaking his hand*]. How can we thank you?

[*The others murmur their good-bys.*]

MR. KRALER. I never thought I'd live to see the day when a man like Mr. Frank would have to go into hiding. When you think—

[*He breaks off, going out. Mr. Frank follows him down the steps, bolting the door after him. In the interval before he returns, Peter goes over to Margot, shaking hands with her. As Mr. Frank comes back up the steps, Mrs. Frank questions him anxiously.*]

MRS. FRANK. What did he mean, about the noise?

MR. FRANK. First let us take off some of these clothes.

[*They all start to take off garment after garment. On each of their coats, sweaters, blouses, suits, dresses, is another yellow Star of David. Mr. and Mrs. Frank are underdressed quite simply. The others wear several things—sweaters, extra dresses, bathrobes, aprons, nightgowns, etc.*]

MR. VAN DAAN. It's a wonder we weren't arrested, walking along the streets . . . Petronella with a fur coat in July . . . and that cat of Peter's crying all the way.

ANNE [*as she is removing a pair of panties*]. A cat?

MRS. FRANK [*shocked*]. Anne, please!

ANNE. It's all right. I've got on three more.

[*She pulls off two more. Finally, as they have all removed their surplus clothes, they look to Mr. Frank, waiting for him to speak.*]

MR. FRANK. Now. About the noise. While the men are in the building below, we must have complete quiet. Every sound can be heard down there, not only in the workrooms, but in the offices too. The men come at about eight-thirty, and leave at about five-thirty. So, to be perfectly safe, from eight in the morning until six in the evening we must move only when it is necessary, and then in stockinged feet. We must not speak above a whisper. We must not run any water. We cannot use the sink, or even, forgive me, the w.c.[1] The pipes go down through the workrooms. It would be heard. No trash . . . [*Mr. Frank stops abruptly as he hears the sound of marching feet from the street below. Everyone is motionless, paralyzed with fear. Mr. Frank goes quietly into the room on the right to look down out of the window. Anne runs after him, peering out with him. The tramping feet pass without stopping. The tension is relieved. Mr. Frank, followed by Anne, returns to the main room and resumes his instructions to the group.*] . . . No trash must ever be thrown out which might reveal that someone is living up here . . . not even a potato paring. We must burn everything in the stove at night. This is the way we must live until it is over, if we are to survive.

[*There is silence for a second.*]

MRS. FRANK. Until it is over.

[1] w.c.: toilet.

MR. FRANK [*reassuringly*]. After six we can move about . . . we can talk and laugh and have our supper and read and play games . . . just as we would at home. [*He looks at his watch.*] And now I think it would be wise if we all went to our rooms, and were settled before eight o'clock. Mrs. Van Daan, you and your husband will be upstairs. I regret that there's no place up there for Peter. But he will be here, near us. This will be our common room, where we'll meet to talk and eat and read, like one family.

MR. VAN DAAN. And where do you and Mrs. Frank sleep?

MR. FRANK. This room is also our bedroom.

MRS. VAN DAAN. That isn't right. We'll sleep here and you take the room upstairs. } [*Together*]

MR. VAN DAAN. It's your place.

MR. FRANK. Please. I've thought this out for weeks. It's the best arrangement. The only arrangement.

MRS. VAN DAAN [*to Mr. Frank*]. Never, never can we thank you. [*Then to Mrs. Frank*] I don't know what would have happened to us, if it hadn't been for Mr. Frank.

MR. FRANK. You don't know how your husband helped me when I came to this country . . . knowing no one . . . not able to speak the language. I can never repay him for that. [*Going to Van Daan*] May I help you with your things?

MR. VAN DAAN. No. No. [*To Mrs. Van Daan*] Come along, *liefje*.[1]

MRS. VAN DAAN. You'll be all right, Peter? You're not afraid?

PETER [*embarrassed*]. Please, Mother.

[*They start up the stairs to the attic room above. Mr. Frank turns to Mrs. Frank.*]

MR. FRANK. You too must have some rest, Edith. You didn't close your eyes last night. Nor you, Margot.

ANNE. I slept, Father. Wasn't that funny? I knew it was the last night in my own bed, and yet I slept soundly.

MR. FRANK. I'm glad, Anne. Now you'll be able to help me straighten things in here. [*To Mrs. Frank and Margot*] Come with me . . . You and Margot rest in this room for the time being. [*He picks up their clothes, starting for the room on the right.*]

MRS. FRANK. You're sure . . . ? I could help . . . And Anne hasn't had her milk . . .

MR. FRANK. I'll give it to her. [*To Anne and Peter*] Anne, Peter . . . it's best that you take off your shoes now, before you forget. [*He leads the way to the room, followed by Margot.*]

MRS. FRANK. You're sure you're not tired, Anne?

ANNE. I feel fine. I'm going to help Father.

MRS FRANK. Peter, I'm glad you are to be with us.

PETER. Yes, Mrs. Frank.

[*Mrs. Frank goes to join Mr. Frank and Margot.*]

[*During the following scene Mr. Frank helps Margot and Mrs. Frank to hang up their clothes. Then he persuades them both to lie down and rest. The Van Daans in their room above settle themselves. In the main room Anne and Peter remove their shoes. Peter takes his cat out of the carrier.*]

ANNE. What's your cat's name?

PETER. Mouschi.

[1] LIEFJE: Dutch for "little love."

ANNE. Mouschi! Mouschi! Mouschi! [*She picks up the cat, walking away with it. To Peter*] I love cats. I have one . . . a darling little cat. But they made me leave her behind. I left some food and a note for the neighbors to take care of her . . . I'm going to miss her terribly. What is yours? A him or a her?

PETER. He's a tom. He doesn't like strangers. [*He takes the cat from her, putting it back in its carrier.*]

ANNE [*unabashed*]. Then I'll have to stop being a stranger, won't I? Is he fixed?

PETER. [*startled*]. Huh?

ANNE. Did you have him fixed?

PETER. No.

ANNE. Oh, you ought to have him fixed— to keep him from—you know, fighting. Where did you go to school?

PETER. Jewish Secondary.

ANNE. But that's where Margot and I go! I never saw you around.

PETER. I used to see you . . . sometimes . . .

ANNE. You did?

PETER. . . . in the school yard. You were always in the middle of a bunch of kids. [*He takes a penknife from his pocket.*]

ANNE. Why didn't you ever come over?

PETER. I'm sort of a lone wolf. [*He starts to rip off his Star of David*].

ANNE. What are you doing?

PETER. Taking it off.

ANNE. But you can't do that. They'll arrest you if you go out without your star. [*He tosses his knife on the table.*]

PETER. Who's going out?

ANNE. Why, of course! You're right! Of course we don't need them any more. [*She picks up his knife and starts to take her star off.*] I wonder what our friends will think when we don't show up today?

PETER. I didn't have any dates with anyone.

ANNE. Oh, I did. I had a date with Jopie to go and play ping pong at her house. Do you know Jopie deWaal?

PETER. No.

ANNE. Jopie's my best friend. I wonder what she'll think when she telephones and there's no answer? . . . Probably she'll go over to the house . . . I wonder what she'll think . . . we left everything as if we'd suddenly been called away . . . breakfast dishes in the sink . . . beds not made . . . [*As she pulls off her star the cloth underneath shows clearly the color and form of the star.*] Look! It's still there! [*Peter goes over to the stove with his star.*] What're you going to do with yours?

PETER. Burn it.

ANNE. [*She starts to throw hers in, and cannot.*] It's funny, I can't throw mine away. I don't know why.

PETER. You can't throw . . .? Something they branded you with . . . ? That they made you wear so they could spit on you?

ANNE. I know. I know. But after all, it *is* the Star of David, isn't it?

[*In the bedroom, right, Margot and Mrs. Frank are lying down. Mr. Frank starts quietly out.*]

PETER. Maybe it's different for a girl.

[*Mr. Frank comes into the main room.*]

MR. FRANK. Forgive me, Peter. Now let me see. We must find a bed for your cat. [*He goes to a cupboard.*] I'm glad you brought your cat. Anne was feeling so badly about hers. [*Getting a used small washtub.*] Here we are. Will it be comfortable in that?

PETER [*gathering up his things*]. Thanks.

MR. FRANK [*opening the door of the room on the left*]. And here is your room. But I warn you, Peter, you can't grow any more. Not an inch, or you'll have to sleep with your feet out of the skylight. Are you hungry?

PETER. No.

MR. FRANK. We have some bread and butter.

PETER. No, thank you.

MR. FRANK. You can have it for luncheon then. And tonight we will have a real supper . . . our first supper together.

PETER. Thanks. Thanks.

[*He goes into his room. During the following scene he arranges his possessions in his new room.*]

MR. FRANK. That's a nice boy, Peter.

ANNE. He's awfully shy, isn't he?

MR. FRANK. You'll like him, I know.

ANNE. I certainly hope so, since he's the only boy I'm likely to see for months and months.

[*Mr. Frank sits down, taking off his shoes.*]

MR. FRANK. Annele, there's a box there. Will you open it?

[*He indicates a carton on the couch. Anne brings it to the center table. In the street below there is the sound of children playing*].

ANNE [*as she opens the carton*]. You know the way I'm going to think of it here? I'm going to think of it as a boarding house. A very peculiar summer boarding house, like the one that we—[*She breaks off as she pulls out some photographs.*] Father! My movie stars! I was wondering where they were! I was looking for them this morning . . . and Queen Wilhelmina! How wonderful!

MR. FRANK. There's something more. Go on. Look further.

[*He goes over to the sink, pouring a glass of milk from a thermos bottle.*]

ANNE [*pulling out a pasteboard-bound book*]. A diary! [*She throws her arms around her father.*] I've never had a diary. And I've always longed for one. [*She looks around the room.*] Pencil, pencil, pencil. [*She starts down the stairs.*] I'm going down to the office to get a pencil.

MR. FRANK. Anne! No!

[*He goes after her, catching her by the arm and pulling her back.*]

ANNE [*startled*]. But there's no one in the building now.

MR. FRANK. It doesn't matter. I don't want you ever to go beyond that door.

ANNE [*sobered*]. Never . . . ? Not even at night time, when everyone is gone? Or on Sundays? Can't I go down to listen to the radio?

MR. FRANK. Never. I am sorry, Anneke. It isn't safe. No, you must never go beyond that door.

[*For the first time Anne realizes what "going into hiding" means.*]

ANNE. I see.

MR. FRANK. It'll be hard, I know. But always remember this, Anneke. There are no walls, there are no bolts, no locks that anyone can put on your mind. Miep will bring us books. We will read history, poetry, mythology. [*He gives her the glass of milk.*] Here's your milk. [*With his arm about her, they go over to the couch, sitting down side by side.*] As a matter of fact, between us, Anne, being here has certain advantages for you. For instance, you remember the battle you had with your mother the other day on the subject of overshoes? You said that you'd rather die than wear overshoes? But in the end you had to wear them? Well now, you see, for as long as we are here you will never have to wear overshoes! Isn't that good? And the coat that you inherited from Margot, you won't have to wear that any more. And the piano! You won't have to practice on the piano. I tell you, this is going to be a fine life for you!

[*Anne's panic is gone. Peter appears in the doorway of his room, with a saucer in his hand. He is carrying his cat.*]

PETER. I . . . I . . . I thought I'd better get some water for Mouschi before . . .

MR. FRANK. Of course.

[*As he starts toward the sink the carillon begins to chime the hour of eight. He tiptoes to the window at the back and looks down at the street below. He turns to Peter, indicating in pantomime that it is too late. Peter starts back for his room. He steps on a creaking board. The three of them are frozen for a minute in fear. As Peter starts away again, Anne tiptoes over to him and pours some of the milk from her glass into the saucer for the cat. Peter squats on the floor, putting the milk before the cat. Mr. Frank gives Anne his fountain pen, and then goes into the room at the right. For a second Anne watches the cat, then she goes over to the center table, and opens her diary.*

In the room at the right, Mrs. Frank has sat up quickly at the sound of the carillon. Mr. Frank comes in and sits down beside her on the settee, his arm comfortingly around her.

Upstairs, in the attic room, Mr. and Mrs. Van Daan have hung their clothes in the closet and are now seated on the iron bed. Mrs. Van Daan leans back exhausted. Mr. Van Daan fans her with a newspaper.

Anne starts to write in her diary. The lights dim out, the curtain falls.

In the darkness Anne's voice comes to us again, faintly at first, and then with growing strength.]

ANNE'S VOICE. I expect I should be describing what it feels like to go into hiding. But I really don't know yet myself. I only know it's funny never to be able to go outdoors . . . never to breathe fresh air . . . never to run and shout and jump. It's the silence in the nights that frightens me most. Every time I hear a creak in the house, or a step on the street outside, I'm sure they're coming for us. The days aren't so bad. At least we know that Miep and Mr. Kraler are down there below us in the office. Our protectors, we call them. I asked Father what would happen to them if the Nazis found out they were hiding us. Pim said that they would suffer the same fate that we would . . . Imagine! They know this, and yet when they come up here, they're always cheerful and gay as if there were nothing in the world to bother them . . . Friday, the twenty-first of August, nineteen forty-two. Today I'm going to tell you our general news. Mother is unbearable. She insists on treating me like a baby, which I loathe. Otherwise things are going better. The weather is . . .

[*As Anne's voice is fading out the curtain rises on the scene.*]

SCENE THREE: *It is a little after six o'clock in the evening, two months later.*

Margot is in the bedroom at the right, studying. Mr. Van Daan is lying down in the attic room above.

The rest of the "family" is in the main room. Anne and Peter sit opposite each other at the center table, where they have been doing their lessons. Mrs. Frank is on the couch. Mrs. Van Daan is seated with her fur coat, on which she has been sewing, in her lap. None of them are wearing their shoes.

Their eyes are on Mr. Frank, waiting for him to give them the signal which will release them from their day-long quiet. Mr. Frank, his shoes in his hand, stands looking down out of the window at the back, watching to be sure that all of the workmen have left the building below.

After a few seconds of motionless silence, Mr. Frank turns from the window.

MR. FRANK [*quietly to the group*]. It's safe now. The last workman has left. [*There is an immediate stir of relief.*]

ANNE [*Her pent-up energy explodes*]. WHEE!

MRS. FRANK [*startled, amused*]. Anne!

MRS. VAN DAAN. I'm first for the w.c. [*She hurries off to the bathroom. Mrs. Frank puts on her shoes and starts up to the sink to prepare supper. Anne sneaks Peter's shoes from under the table and hides them behind her back. Mr. Frank goes into Margot's room.*]

MR. FRANK [*to Margot*]. Six o'clock. School's over.

[*Margot gets up, stretching. Mr. Frank sits down to put on his shoes. In the main room Peter tries to find his.*]

PETER [*to Anne*]. Have you seen my shoes?

ANNE [*innocently*]. Your shoes?

PETER. You've taken them, haven't you?

ANNE. I don't know what you're talking about.

PETER. You're going to be sorry!

ANNE. Am I?

[*Peter goes after her. Anne, with his shoes in her hand, runs from him, dodging behind her mother.*]

MRS. FRANK [*protesting*]. Anne, dear!

PETER. Wait till I get you!

ANNE. I'm waiting! [*Peter makes a lunge for her. They both fall to the floor. Peter pins her down, wrestling with her to get the shoes.*] Don't! Don't! Peter, stop it. Ouch!

MRS. FRANK. Anne! . . . Peter!

[*Suddenly Peter becomes self-conscious. He grabs his shoes roughly and starts for his room.*]

ANNE [*following him*]. Peter, where are you going? Come dance with me.

PETER. I tell you I don't know how.

ANNE. I'll teach you.

PETER. I'm going to give Mouschi his dinner.

ANNE. Can I watch?

PETER. He doesn't like people around while he eats.

ANNE. Peter, please.

PETER. No!

[*He goes into his room. Anne slams his door after him.*]

MRS. FRANK. Anne, dear, I think you shouldn't play like that with Peter. It's not dignified.

ANNE. Who cares if it's dignified? I don't want to be dignified.

[*Mr. Frank and Margot come from the*

room on the right. Margot goes to help her mother. Mr. Frank starts for the center table to correct Margot's school papers.]

MRS. FRANK [*to Anne*]. You complain that I don't treat you like a grownup. But when I do, you resent it.

ANNE. I only want some fun . . . someone to laugh and clown with . . . After you've sat still all day and hardly moved, you've got to have some fun. I don't know what's the matter with that boy.

MR. FRANK. He isn't used to girls. Give him a little time.

ANNE. Time? Isn't two months time? I could cry. [*Catching hold of Margot.*] Come on, Margot . . . dance with me. Come on, please.

MARGOT. I have to help with supper.

ANNE. You know we're going to forget how to dance . . . When we get out we won't remember a thing.

[*She starts to sing and dance by herself. Mr. Frank takes her in his arms, waltzing with her. Mrs. Van Daan comes in from the bathroom.*]

MRS. VAN DAAN. Next? [*She looks around as she starts putting on her shoes.*] Where's Peter?

ANNE [*as they are dancing*]. Where would he be!

MRS. VAN DAAN. He hasn't finished his lessons, has he? His father'll kill him if he catches him in there with that cat and his work not done. (*Mr. Frank and Anne finish their dance. They bow to each other with extravagant formality.*) Anne, get him out of there, will you?

ANNE [*at Peter's door*]. Peter? Peter?

PETER [*opening the door a crack*]. What is it?

ANNE. Your mother says to come out.

PETER. I'm giving Mouschi his dinner.

MRS. VAN DAAN. You know what your father says.

[*She sits on the couch, sewing on the lining of her fur coat.*]

PETER. For heaven's sake, I haven't even looked at him since lunch.

MRS. VAN DAAN. I'm just telling you, that's all.

ANNE. I'll feed him.

PETER. I don't want you in there.

MRS. VAN DAAN. Peter!

PETER [*to Anne*]. Then give him his dinner and come right out, you hear?

[*He comes back to the table. Anne shuts the door of Peter's room after her and disappears behind the curtain covering his closet.*]

MRS. VAN DAAN [*to Peter*]. Now is that any way to talk to your little girl friend?

PETER. Mother . . . for heaven's sake . . . will you please stop saying that?

MRS. VAN DAAN. Look at him blush! Look at him!

PETER. Please! I'm not . . . anyway . . . let me alone, will you?

MRS. VAN DAAN. He acts like it was something to be ashamed of. It's nothing to be ashamed of, to have a little girl friend.

PETER. You're crazy. She's only thirteen.

MRS. VAN DAAN. So what? And you're sixteen. Just perfect. Your father's ten years older than I am. [*To Mr. Frank*] I warn you, Mr. Frank, if this war lasts much longer, we're going to be related and then . . .

MR. FRANK. *Mazeltov!*[1]

MRS. FRANK [*deliberately changing the conversation*]. I wonder where Miep is.

[1] MAZELTOV!: Yiddish for "congratulations!"

She's usually so prompt.

[*Suddenly everything else is forgotten as they hear the sound of an automobile coming to a screeching stop in the street below. They are tense, motionless in their terror. The car starts away. A wave of relief sweeps over them. They pick up their occupations again. Anne flings open the door of Peter's room, making a dramatic entrance. She is dressed in Peter's clothes. Peter looks at her in fury. The others are amused.*]

ANNE. Good evening, everyone. Forgive me if I don't stay. [*She jumps up on a chair.*] I have a friend waiting for me in there. My friend Tom. Tom Cat. Some people say that we look alike. But Tom has the most beautiful whiskers, and I have only a little fuzz. I am hoping . . . in time . . .

PETER. All right, Mrs. Quack Quack!

ANNE [*outraged—jumping down*]. Peter!

PETER. I heard about you . . . How you talked so much in class they called you Mrs. Quack Quack. How Mr. Smitter made you write a composition . . . "'Quack, quack,' said Mrs. Quack Quack."

ANNE. Well, go on. Tell them the rest. How it was so good he read it out loud to the class and then read it to all his other classes!

PETER. Quack! Quack! Quack . . . Quack . . . Quack . . .

[*Anne pulls off the coat and trousers.*]

ANNE. You are the most intolerable, insufferable boy I've ever met!

[*She throws the clothes down the stairwell. Peter goes down after them.*]

PETER. Quack, quack, quack!

MRS. VAN DAAN [*to Anne*]. That's right, Anneke! Give it to him!

ANNE. With all the boys in the world . . . Why I had to get locked up with one like you! . . .

PETER. Quack, quack, quack, and from now on stay out of my room!

[*As Peter passes her, Anne puts out her foot, tripping him. He picks himself up, and goes on into his room.*]

MRS. FRANK [*quietly*]. Anne, dear . . . your hair. [*She feels Anne's forehead.*] You're warm. Are you feeling all right?

ANNE. Please, Mother.

[*She goes over to the center table, slipping into her shoes.*]

MRS. FRANK [*following her*]. You haven't a fever, have you?

ANNE [*pulling away*]. No. No.

MRS. FRANK. You know we can't call a doctor here, ever. There's only one thing to do . . . watch carefully. Prevent an illness before it comes. Let me see your tongue.

ANNE. Mother, this is perfectly absurd.

MRS. FRANK. Anne, dear, don't be such a baby. Let me see your tongue. [*As Anne refuses, Mrs. Frank appeals to Mr. Frank.*] Otto . . . ?

MR. FRANK. You hear your mother, Anne.

[*Anne flicks out her tongue for a second, then turns away.*]

MRS. FRANK. Come on—open up! [*As Anne opens her mouth very wide*] You seem all right . . . but perhaps an aspirin . . .

MRS. VAN DAAN. For heaven's sake, don't give that child any pills. I waited for fifteen minutes this morning for her to come out of the w.c.

ANNE. I was washing my hair!

MRS. FRANK. I think there's nothing the matter with our Anne that a ride on her bike, or a visit with her friend Jopie deWaal wouldn't cure. Isn't that so, Anne?

[*Mr. Van Daan comes down into the room. From outside we hear faint sounds of bombers going over and a burst of ack-ack.*]

MR. VAN DAAN. Miep not come yet?

MRS. VAN DAAN. The workmen just left, a little while ago.

MR. VAN DAAN. What's for dinner tonight?

MRS. VAN DAAN. Beans.

MR. VAN DAAN. Not again!

MRS. VAN DAAN. Poor Putti! I know. But what can we do? That's all that Miep brought us.

[*Mr. Van Daan starts to pace, his hands behind his back. Anne follows behind him, imitating him.*]

ANNE. We are now in what is known as the "bean cycle." Beans boiled, beans en casserole, beans with strings, beans without strings . . .

[*Peter has come out of his room. He slides into his place at the table, becoming immediately absorbed in his studies.*]

MR. VAN DAAN [*to Peter*]. I saw you . . . in there, playing with your cat.

MRS. VAN DAAN. He just went in for a second, putting his coat away. He's been out here all the time, doing his lessons.

MR. FRANK [*looking up from the paper*]. Anne, you got an excellent in your history paper today . . . and very good in Latin.

ANNE [*sitting beside him*]. How about algebra?

MR. FRANK. I'll have to make a confession. Up until now I've managed to stay ahead of you in algebra. Today you caught up with me. We'll leave it to Margot to correct.

ANNE. Isn't algebra *vile*, Pim!

MR. FRANK. Vile!

MARGOT [*to Mr. Frank*]. How did I do?

ANNE [*getting up*]. Excellent, excellent, excellent, excellent!

MR. FRANK [*to Margot*].You should have used the subjunctive here . . .

MARGOT. Should I? . . . I thought . . . look here . . . I didn't use it here . . .

[*The two become absorbed in the papers.*]

ANNE. Mrs. Van Daan, may I try on your coat?

MRS. FRANK. No, Anne.

MRS. VAN DAAN [*giving it to Anne*]. It's all right . . . but careful with it. [*Anne puts it on and struts with it.*] My father gave me that the year before he died. He always bought the best that money could buy.

ANNE. Mrs. Van Daan, did you have a lot of boy friends before you were married?

MRS. FRANK. Anne, that's a personal question. It's not courteous to ask personal questions.

MRS. VAN DAAN. Oh I don't mind. [*To Anne*] Our house was always swarming with boys. When I was a girl we had . . .

MR. VAN DAAN. Oh, God. Not again!

MRS. VAN DAAN [*good-humored*]. Shut up! [*Without a pause, to Anne. Mr. Van Daan mimics Mrs. Van Daan, speaking the first few words in unison with her.*] One summer we had a big house in

Hilversum. The boys came buzzing round like bees around a jam pot. And when I was sixteen! . . . We were wearing our skirts very short those days and I had good-looking legs. [*She pulls up her skirt, going to Mr. Frank.*] I still have 'em. I may not be as pretty as I used to be, but I still have my legs. How about it, Mr. Frank?

MR. VAN DAAN. All right. All right. We see them.

MRS. VAN DAAN. I'm not asking you. I'm asking Mr. Frank.

PETER. Mother, for heaven's sake.

MRS. VAN DAAN. Oh, I embarrass you, do I? Well, I just hope the girl you marry has as good. [*Then to Anne*] My father used to worry about me, with so many boys hanging round. He told me, if any of them gets fresh, you say to him . . . "Remember, Mr. So-and-So, remember I'm a lady."

ANNE. "Remember, Mr. So-and-So, remember I'm a lady."

[*She gives Mrs. Van Daan her coat.*]

MR. VAN DAAN. Look at you, talking that way in front of her! Don't you know she puts it all down in that diary?

MRS. VAN DAAN. So, if she does? I'm only telling the truth!

[*Anne stretches out, putting her ear to the floor, listening to what is going on below. The sound of the bombers fades away.*]

MRS. FRANK [*setting the table*]. Would you mind, Peter, if I moved you over to the couch?

ANNE [*listening*]. Miep must have the radio on.

[*Peter picks up his papers, going over to the couch beside Mrs. Van Daan.*]

MR. VAN DAAN [*accusingly, to Peter*]. Haven't you finished yet?

PETER. No.

MR. VAN DAAN. You ought to be ashamed of yourself.

PETER. All right. All right. I'm a dunce. I'm a hopeless case. Why do I go on?

MRS. VAN DAAN. You're not hopeless. Don't talk that way. It's just that you haven't anyone to help you, like the girls have. [*To Mr. Frank*] Maybe you could help him, Mr. Frank?

MR. FRANK. I'm sure that his father . . . ?

MR. VAN DAAN. Not me. I can't do anything with him. He won't listen to me. You go ahead . . . if you want.

MR. FRANK [*going to Peter*]. What about it, Peter? Shall we make our school coeducational?

MRS. VAN DAAN [*kissing Mr. Frank*]. You're an angel, Mr. Frank. An angel. I don't know why I didn't meet you before I met that one there. Here, sit down, Mr. Frank . . . [*She forces him down on the couch beside Peter.*] Now, Peter, you listen to Mr. Frank.

MR. FRANK. It might be better for us to go into Peter's room.

[*Peter jumps up eagerly, leading the way.*]

MRS. VAN DAAN. That's right. You go in there, Peter. You listen to Mr. Frank. Mr. Frank is a highly educated man.

[*As Mr. Frank is about to follow Peter into his room, Mrs. Frank stops him and wipes the lipstick from his lips. Then she closes the door after them.*]

ANNE [*on the floor, listening*]. Shh! I can

hear a man's voice talking.

MR. VAN DAAN [*to Anne*]. Isn't it bad enough here without your sprawling all over the place?

[*Anne sits up.*]

MRS. VAN DAAN [*to Mr. Van Daan*]. If you didn't smoke so much, you wouldn't be so bad-tempered.

MR. VAN DAAN. Am I smoking? Do you see me smoking?

MRS. VAN DAAN. Don't tell me you've used up all those cigarettes.

MR. VAN DAAN. One package. Miep only brought me one package.

MRS. VAN DAAN. It's a filthy habit anyway. It's a good time to break yourself.

MR. VAN DAAN. Oh, stop it, please.

MRS. VAN DAAN. You're smoking up all our money. You know that, don't you?

MR. VAN DAAN. Will you shut up? [*During this, Mrs. Frank and Margot have studiously kept their eyes down. But Anne, seated on the floor, has been following the discussion interestedly. Mr. Van Daan turns to see her staring up at him.*] And what are you staring at?

ANNE. I never heard grownups quarrel before. I thought only children quarreled.

MR. VAN DAAN. This isn't a quarrel! It's a discussion. And I never heard children so rude before.

ANNE [*rising, indignantly*]. I, rude!

MR. VAN DAAN. Yes!

MRS. FRANK [*quickly*]. Anne, will you get me my knitting? [*Anne goes to get it.*] I must remember, when Miep comes, to ask her to bring me some more wool.

MARGOT [*going to her room*]. I need some hairpins and some soap. I made a list.

[*She goes into her bedroom to get the list.*]

MRS. FRANK [*to Anne*]. Have you some library books for Miep when she comes?

ANNE. It's a wonder that Miep has a life of her own, the way we make her run errands for us. Please, Miep, get me some starch. Please take my hair out and have it cut. Tell me all the latest news, Miep. [*She goes over, kneeling on the couch beside Mrs. Van Daan.*] Did you know she was engaged? His name is Dirk, and Miep's afraid the Nazis will ship him off to Germany to work in one of their war plants. That's what they're doing with some of the young Dutchmen . . . they pick them up off the streets—

MR. VAN DAAN [*interrupting*]. Don't you ever get tired of talking? Suppose you try keeping still for five minutes. Just five minutes.

[*He starts to pace again. Again Anne follows him, mimicking him. Mrs. Frank jumps up and takes her by the arm up to the sink, and gives her a glass of milk.*]

MRS. FRANK. Come here, Anne. It's time for your glass of milk.

MR. VAN DAAN. Talk, talk, talk. I never heard such a child. Where is my . . . ? Every evening it's the same, talk, talk. [*He looks around.*] Where is my . . . ?

MRS. VAN DAAN. What're you looking for?

MR. VAN DAAN. My pipe. Have you seen my pipe?

MRS VAN DAAN. What good's a pipe? You haven't got any tobacco.

MR. VAN DAAN. At least I'll have something to hold in my mouth! [*Opening Margot's bedroom door*] Margot, have you seen my pipe?

MARGOT. It was on the table last night.

[*Anne puts her glass of milk on the table and picks up his pipe, hiding it behind her back.*]

MR. VAN DAAN. I know. I know. Anne, did you see my pipe? . . . Anne!

MRS. FRANK. Anne, Mr. Van Daan is speaking to you.

ANNE. Am I allowed to talk now?

MR. VAN DAAN. You're the most aggravating . . . The trouble with you is, you've been spoiled. What you need is a good old-fashioned spanking.

ANNE [*mimicking Mrs. Van Daan*]. "Remember, Mr. So-and-So, remember I'm a lady."

[*She thrusts the pipe into his mouth, then picks up her glass of milk.*]

MR. VAN DAAN [*restraining himself with difficulty*]. Why aren't you nice and quiet like your sister Margot? Why do you have to show off all the time? Let me give you a little advice, young lady. Men don't like that kind of thing in a girl. You know that? A man likes a girl who'll listen to him once in a while . . . a domestic girl, who'll keep her house shining for her husband . . . who loves to cook and sew and . . .

ANNE. I'd cut my throat first! I'd open my veins! I'm going to be remarkable! I'm going to Paris . . .

MR. VAN DAAN [*scoffingly*]. Paris!

ANNE. . . . to study music and art.

MR. VAN DAAN. Yeah! Yeah!

ANNE. I'm going to be a famous dancer or singer . . . or something wonderful.

[*She makes a wide gesture, spilling the glass of milk on the fur coat in Mrs. Van Daan's lap. Margot rushes quickly over with a towel. Anne tries to brush the milk off with her skirt.*]

MRS. VAN DAAN. Now look what you've done . . . you clumsy little fool! My beautiful fur coat my father gave me . . .

ANNE. I'm so sorry.

MRS. VAN DAAN. What do you care? It isn't yours . . . So go on, ruin it! Do you know what that coat cost? Do you? And now look at it! Look at it!

ANNE. I'm very, very sorry.

MRS. VAN DAAN. I could kill you for this. I could just kill you!

[*Mrs. Van Daan goes up the stairs, clutching the coat. Mr. Van Daan starts after her.*]

MR. VAN DAAN. Petronella . . . *liefje! Liefje!* . . . Come back . . . the supper . . . come back!

MRS. FRANK. Anne, you must not behave in that way.

ANNE. It was an accident. Anyone can have an accident.

MRS. FRANK. I don't mean that. I mean the answering back. You must not answer back. They are our guests. We must always show the greatest courtesy to them. We're all living under terrible tension. [*She stops as Margot indicates that Van Daan can hear. When he is gone, she continues.*] That's why we must control ourselves . . . You don't hear Margot getting into arguments with them, do you? Watch Margot. She's always courteous with them. Never familiar. She keeps her distance. And they respect her for it. Try to be like Margot.

ANNE. And have them walk all over me, the way they do her? No, thanks!

MRS. FRANK. I'm not afraid that anyone is going to walk all over you, Anne. I'm afraid for other people, that you'll walk on them. I don't know what happens to you, Anne. You are wild, self-willed. If I

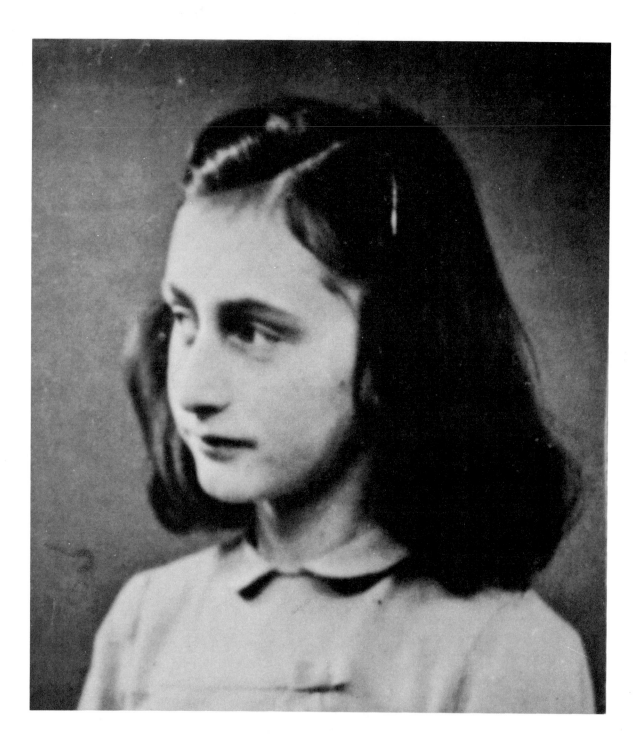

had ever talked to my mother as you talk to me . . .

ANNE. Things have changed. People aren't like that any more. "Yes, Mother." "No, Mother." "Anything you say, Mother." I've got to fight things out for myself! Make something of myself!

MRS. FRANK. It isn't necessary to fight to do it. Margot doesn't fight, and isn't she . . . ?

ANNE [*violently rebellious*]. Margot! Margot! Margot! That's all I hear from everyone . . . how wonderful Margot is . . . "Why aren't you like Margot?"

MARGOT [*protesting*]. Oh, come on, Anne, don't be so . . .

ANNE [*paying no attention*]. Everything she does is right, and everything I do is wrong! I'm the goat around here! . . . You're all against me! . . . And you worst of all!

[*She rushes off into her room and throws herself down on the settee, stifling her sobs. Mrs. Frank sighs and starts toward the stove.*]

MRS. FRANK [*to Margot*]. Let's put the soup on the stove . . . if there's anyone who cares to eat. Margot, will you take the bread out? [*Margot gets the bread from the cupboard.*] I don't know how we can go on living this way . . . I can't say a word to Anne . . . she flies at me . . .

MARGOT. You know Anne. In half an hour she'll be out here, laughing and joking.

MRS. FRANK. And . . . [*She makes a motion upwards, indicating the Van Daans.*] . . . I told your father it wouldn't work . . . but no . . . no . . . he had to ask them, he said . . . he owed it to him, he said. Well, he knows now that I was right! These quarrels! . . . This bickering!

MARGOT [*with a warning look*]. Shush. Shush.

[*The buzzer for the door sounds. Mrs. Frank gasps, startled.*]

MRS. FRANK. Every time I hear that sound, my heart stops!

MARGOT [*starting for Peter's door*]. It's Miep. [*She knocks at the door.*] Father?

[*Mr. Frank comes quickly from Peter's room.*]

MR. FRANK. Thank you, Margot. [*As he goes down the steps to open the outer door*] Has everyone his list?

MARGOT. I'll get my books. [*Giving her mother a list*] Here's your list. [*Margot goes into her and Anne's bedroom on the right. Anne sits up, hiding her tears, as Margot comes in.*] Miep's here.

[*Margot picks up her books and goes back. Anne hurries over to the mirror, smoothing her hair.*]

MR. VAN DAAN [*coming down the stairs*]. It is Miep?

MARGOT. Yes. Father's gone down to let her in.

MR. VAN DAAN. At last I'll have some cigarettes!

MRS. FRANK [*to Mr. Van Daan*]. I can't tell you how unhappy I am about Mrs. Van Daan's coat. Anne should never have touched it.

MR. VAN DAAN. She'll be all right.

MRS. FRANK. Is there anything I can do?

MR. VAN DAAN. Don't worry.

[*He turns to meet Miep. But it is not Miep who comes up the steps. It is Mr. Kraler, followed by Mr. Frank. Their faces are grave. Anne comes from the bedroom. Peter comes from his room.*]

MRS. FRANK. Mr. Kraler!

MR. VAN DAAN. How are you, Mr. Kraler?

MARGOT. This is a surprise.

MRS. FRANK. When Mr. Kraler comes, the sun begins to shine.

MR. VAN DAAN. Miep is coming?

MR. KRALER. Not tonight.

[*Kraler goes to Margot and Mrs. Frank and Anne, shaking hands with them.*]

MRS. FRANK. Wouldn't you like a cup of coffee? . . . Or, better still, will you have supper with us?

MR. FRANK. Mr. Kraler has something to talk over with us. Something has happened, he says, which demands an immediate decision.

MRS. FRANK [*fearful*]. What is it?

[*Mr. Kraler sits down on the couch. As he talks he takes bread, cabbages, milk, etc., from his briefcase, giving them to Margot and Anne to put away.*]

MR. KRALER. Usually, when I come up here, I try to bring you some bit of good news. What's the use of telling you the bad news when there's nothing that you can do about it? But today something has happened . . . Dirk . . . Miep's Dirk, you know, came to me just now. He tells me that he has a Jewish friend living near him. A dentist. He says he's in trouble. He begged me, could I do anything for this man? Could I find him a hiding place? . . . So I've come to you . . . I know it's a terrible thing to ask of you, living as you are, but would you take him in with you?

MR. FRANK. Of course we will.

MR. KRALER [*rising*]. It'll be just for a night or two . . . until I find some other place. This happened so suddenly that I didn't know where to turn.

MR. FRANK. Where is he?

MR. KRALER. Downstairs in the office.

MR. FRANK. Good. Bring him up.

MR. KRALER. His name is Dussel . . . Jan Dussel.

MR. FRANK. Dussel . . . I think I know him.

MR. KRALER. I'll get him.

[*He goes quickly down the steps and out. Mr. Frank suddenly becomes conscious of the others.*]

MR. FRANK. Forgive me. I spoke without consulting you. But I knew you'd feel as I do.

MR. VAN DAAN. There's no reason for you to consult anyone. This is your place. You have a right to do exactly as you please. The only thing I feel . . . there's so little food as it is . . . and to take in another person . . .

[*Peter turns away, ashamed of his father.*]

MR. FRANK. We can stretch the food a little. It's only for a few days.

MR. VAN DAAN. You want to make a bet?

MRS. FRANK. I think it's fine to have him. But, Otto, where are you going to put him? Where?

PETER. He can have my bed. I can sleep on the floor. I wouldn't mind.

MR. FRANK. That's good of you, Peter. But your room's too small . . . even for *you*.

ANNE. I have a much better idea. I'll come in here with you and Mother, and Margot can take Peter's room and Peter can go in our room with Mr. Dussel.

MARGOT. That's right. We could do that.

MR. FRANK. No, Margot. You mustn't sleep in that room . . . neither you nor Anne. Mouschi has caught some rats in there. Peter's brave. He doesn't mind.

ANNE. Then how about *this*? I'll come in

here with you and Mother, and Mr. Dussel can have my bed.

MRS. FRANK. No. No. *No!* Margot will come in here with us and he can have her bed. It's the only way. Margot, bring your things in here. Help her, Anne.

[*Margot hurries into her room to get her things.*]

ANNE [*to her mother*]. Why Margot? Why can't I come in here?

MRS. FRANK. Because it wouldn't be proper for Margot to sleep with a . . . Please, Anne. Don't argue. Please.

[*Anne starts slowly away.*]

MR. FRANK [*to Anne*]. You don't mind sharing your room with Mr. Dussel, do you, Anne?

ANNE. No. No, of course not.

MR. FRANK. Good. [*Anne goes off into her bedroom, helping Margot. Mr. Frank starts to search in the cupboards.*] Where's the cognac?

MRS. FRANK. It's there. But, Otto, I was saving it in case of illness.

MR. FRANK. I think we couldn't find a better time to use it. Peter, will you get five glasses for me?

[*Peter goes for the glasses. Margot comes out of her bedroom, carrying her possessions, which she hangs behind a curtain in the main room. Mr. Frank finds the cognac and pours it into the five glasses that Peter brings him. Mr. Van Daan stands looking on sourly. Mrs. Van Daan comes downstairs and looks around at all of the bustle.*]

MRS. VAN DAAN. What's happening? What's going on?

MR. VAN DAAN. Someone's moving in with us.

MRS. VAN DAAN. In here? You're joking.

MARGOT. It's only for a night or two . . . until Mr. Kraler finds him another place.

MR. VAN DAAN. Yeah! Yeah!

[*Mr. Frank hurries over as Mr. Kraler and Dussel come up. Dussel is a man in his late fifties, meticulous, finicky . . . bewildered now. He wears a raincoat. He carries a briefcase, stuffed full, and a small medicine case.*]

MR. FRANK. Come in, Mr. Dussel.

MR. KRALER. This is Mr. Frank.

DUSSEL. Mr. Otto Frank?

MR. FRANK. Yes. Let me take your things. [*He takes the hat and briefcase, but Dussel clings to his medicine case.*] This is my wife Edith . . . Mr. and Mrs. Van Daan . . . their son, Peter . . . and my daughters, Margot and Anne.

[*Dussel shakes hands with everyone.*]

MR. KRALER. Thank you, Mr. Frank. Thank you all. Mr. Dussell, I leave you in good hands. Oh . . . Dirk's coat.

[*Dussel hurriedly takes off the raincoat, giving it to Mr. Kraler. Underneath is his white dentist's jacket, with a yellow Star of David on it.*]

DUSSEL [*to Mr. Kraler*]. What can I say to thank you . . . ?

MRS. FRANK [*to Dussel*]. Mr. Kraler and Miep . . . They're our life line. Without them we couldn't live.

MR. KRALER. Please, please. You make us seem very heroic. It isn't that at all. We simply don't like the Nazis. [*To Mr. Frank, who offers him a drink*] No, thanks. [*Then going on*] We don't like their methods. We don't like . . .

MR. FRANK [*smiling*]. I know. I know. "No one's going to tell us Dutchmen what to do with our damn Jews!"

MR. KRALER [*to Dussel*]. Pay no attention to Mr. Frank. I'll be up tomorrow to see that they're treating you right. [*To Mr. Frank*] Don't trouble to come down again. Peter will bolt the door after me, won't you, Peter?

PETER. Yes, sir.

MR. FRANK. Thank you, Peter. I'll do it.

MR. KRALER. Good night. Good night.

GROUP. Good night, Mr. Kraler. We'll see you tomorrow, etc. etc.

[*Mr. Kraler goes out with Mr. Frank. Mrs. Frank gives each one of the "grownups" a glass of cognac.*]

MRS. FRANK. Please, Mr. Dussell, sit down.

[*Mr. Dussel sinks into a chair. Mrs. Frank gives him a glass of cognac.*]

DUSSEL. I'm dreaming. I know it. I don't believe my eyes. Mr. Otto Frank here! [*To Mrs. Frank*] You're not in Switzerland then? A woman told me . . . She said she'd gone to your house . . . the door was open, everything was in disorder, dishes in the sink. She said she found a piece of paper in the wastebasket with an address scribbled on it . . . an address in Zurich. She said you must have escaped to Zurich.

ANNE. Father put that there purposely . . . just so people would think that very thing!

DUSSEL. And you've been *here* all the time?

MRS. FRANK. All the time . . . ever since July.

[*Anne speaks to her father as he comes back.*]

ANNE. It worked, Pim . . . the address you left! Mr. Dussel says that people believe we escaped to Switzerland.

MR. FRANK. I'm glad . . . And now let's have a little drink to welcome Mr. Dussel. [*Before they can drink, Mr. Dussel bolts his drink. Mr. Frank smiles and raises his glass.*] To Mr. Dussel. Welcome. We're very honored to have you with us.

MRS. FRANK. To Mr. Dussel, welcome.

[*The Van Daans murmur a welcome. The "grownups" drink.*]

MRS. VAN DAAN. Um. That was good.

MR. VAN DAAN. Did Mr. Kraler warn you that you won't get much to eat here? You can imagine . . . three ration books among the seven of us . . . and now you make eight.

[*Peter walks away, humiliated. Outside a street organ is heard dimly.*]

DUSSEL [*rising*]. Mr. Van Daan, you don't realize what is happening outside that you should warn me of a thing like that. You don't realize what's going on . . . [*As Mr. Van Daan starts his characteristic pacing, Dussel turns to speak to the others.*] Right here in Amsterdam every day hundreds of Jews disappear . . . They surround a block and search house by house. Children come home from school to find their parents gone. Hundreds are being deported . . . people that you and I know . . . the Hallensteins . . . the Wessels . . .

MRS. FRANK [*in tears*]. Oh, no. No!

DUSSEL. They get their call-up notice . . . come to the Jewish theatre on such and such a day and hour . . . bring only what you can carry in a rucksack. And if you refuse the call-up notice, then they come and drag you from your home and ship you off to Mauthausen. The death camp!

MRS. FRANK. We didn't know that things had got so much worse.

DUSSEL. Forgive me for speaking so.

ANNE [*coming to Dussel*]. Do you know the deWaals? . . . What's become of them? Their daughter Jopie and I are in the same class. Jopie's my best friend.

DUSSEL. They are gone.

ANNE. Gone?

DUSSEL. With all the others.

ANNE. Oh, no. Not Jopie!

[*She turns away, in tears. Mrs. Frank motions to Margot to comfort her. Margot goes to Anne, putting her arms comfortingly around her.*]

MRS. VAN DAAN. There were some people called Wagner. They lived near us . . . ?

MR. FRANK [*interrupting with a glance at Anne*]. I think we should put this off until later. We all have many questions we want to ask . . . But I'm sure that Mr. Dussel would like to get settled before supper.

DUSSEL. Thank you. I would. I brought very little with me.

MR. FRANK [*giving him his hat and briefcase*]. I'm sorry we can't give you a room alone. But I hope you won't be too uncomfortable. We've had to make strict rules here . . . a schedule of hours . . . We'll tell you after supper. Anne, would you like to take Mr. Dussel to his room?

ANNE [*controlling her tears*]. If you'll come with me, Mr. Dussel?

[*She starts for her room.*]

DUSSEL [*shaking hands with each in turn*]. Forgive me if I haven't really expressed my gratitude to all of you. This has been such a shock to me. I'd always thought of myself as Dutch. I was born in Holland. My father was born in Holland, and my grandfather. And now . . . after all these years . . . [*He breaks off.*] If you'll excuse me.

[*Dussel gives a little bow and hurries off after Anne. Mr. Frank and the others are subdued.*]

ANNE [*turning on the light*]. Well, here we are.

[*Dussel looks around the room. In the main room Margot speaks to her mother.*]

MARGOT. The news sounds pretty bad, doesn't it? It's so different from what Mr. Kraler tells us. Mr. Kraler says things are improving.

MR. VAN DAAN. I like it better the way Kraler tells it.

[*They resume their occupations, quietly. Peter goes off into his room. In Anne's room, Anne turns to Dussel.*]

ANNE. You're going to share the room with me.

DUSSEL. I'm a man who's always lived alone. I haven't had to adjust myself to others. I hope you'll bear with me until I learn.

ANNE. Let me help you. [*She takes his briefcase.*] Do you always live all alone? Have you no family at all?

DUSSEL. No one.

[*He opens his medicine case and spreads his bottles on the dressing table.*]

ANNE. How dreadful. You must be terribly lonely.

DUSSEL. I'm used to it.

ANNE. I don't think I could ever get used to it. Didn't you even have a pet? A cat, or a dog?

DUSSEL. I have an allergy for fur-bearing animals. They give me asthma.

ANNE. Oh, dear. Peter has a cat.

DUSSEL. Here? He has it here?

ANNE. Yes. But we hardly ever see it. He

keeps it in his room all the time. I'm sure it will be all right.

DUSSEL. Let us hope so. [*He takes some pills to fortify himself.*]

ANNE. That's Margot's bed, where you're going to sleep. I sleep on the sofa there. [*Indicating the clothes hooks on the wall.*] We cleared these off for your things. [*She goes over to the window.*] The best part about this room . . . you can look down and see a bit of the street and the canal. There's a houseboat . . . you can see the end of it . . . a bargeman lives there with his family . . . They have a baby and he's just beginning to walk and I'm so afraid he's going to fall into the canal some day. I watch him . . .

DUSSEL [*interrupting*]. Your father spoke of a schedule.

ANNE [*coming away from the window*]. Oh, yes. It's mostly about the times we have to be quiet. And times for the w.c. You can use it now if you like.

DUSSEL [*stiffly*]. No, thank you.

ANNE. I suppose you think it's awful, my talking about a thing like that. But you don't know how important it can get to be, especially when you're frightened . . . About this room, the way Margot and I did . . . she had it to herself in the afternoons for studying, reading . . . lessons, you know . . . and I took the mornings. Would that be all right with you?

DUSSEL. I'm not at my best in the morning.

ANNE. You stay here in the mornings then. I'll take the room in the afternoons.

DUSSEL. Tell me, when you're in here, what happens to me? Where am I spending my time? In there, with all the people?

ANNE. Yes.

DUSSEL. I see. I see.

ANNE. We have supper at half past six.

DUSSEL [*going over to the sofa*]. Then, if you don't mind . . . I like to lie down quietly for ten minutes before eating. I find it helps the digestion.

ANNE. Of course. I hope I'm not going to be too much of a bother to you. I seem to be able to get everyone's back up.

[*Dussel lies down on the sofa, curled up, his back to her.*]

DUSSEL. I always get along very well with children. My patients all bring their children to me, because they know I get on well with them. So don't worry about that.

[*Anne leans over him, taking his hand and shaking it gratefully.*]

ANNE. Thank you. Thank you, Mr. Dussel.

[*The lights dim to darkness. The curtain falls on the scene. Anne's voice comes to us faintly at first, and then with increasing power.*]

ANNE'S VOICE. . . . And yesterday I finished Cissy Van Marxvelt's latest book. I think she is a first-class writer. I shall definitely let my children read her. Monday the twenty-first of September, nineteen forty-two. Mr. Dussel and I had another battle yesterday. Yes, Mr. Dussel! According to him, nothing, I repeat . . . nothing, is right about me . . . my appearance, my character, my manners. While he was going on at me I thought . . . sometime I'll give you such a smack that you'll fly right up to the ceiling! Why is it that every grownup thinks he knows the way to bring up children? Particularly the grownups that never had any. I keep wishing that Peter was a girl instead of a boy. Then I would have someone to talk to. Margot's a darling, but she takes everything too seriously. To pause for a moment on the subject of Mrs. Van Daan. I must tell you that her attempts to flirt with Father are getting her nowhere. Pim, thank goodness, won't play.

[*As she is saying the last lines, the curtain rises on the darkened scene. Anne's voice fades out.*]

SCENE FOUR: *It is the middle of the night, several months later. The stage is dark except for a little light which comes through the skylight in Peter's room.*

Everyone is in bed. Mr. and Mrs. Frank lie on the couch in the main room, which has been pulled out to serve as a makeshift double bed.

Margot is sleeping on a mattress on the floor in the main room, behind a curtain stretched across for privacy. The others are all in their accustomed rooms.

From outside we hear two drunken soldiers singing "Lili Marlene." A girl's high giggle is heard. The sound of running feet is heard coming closer and then fading in the distance. Throughout the scene there is the distant sound of airplanes passing overhead.

A match suddenly flares up in the attic. We dimly see Mr. Van Daan. He is getting his bearings. He comes quickly down the stairs, and goes to the cupboard where the food is stored. Again the match flares up, and is as quickly blown out. The dim figure is seen to steal back up the stairs.

There is quiet for a second or two, broken only by the sound of airplanes, and running feet on the street below.

Suddenly, out of the silence and the dark, we hear Anne scream.

ANNE [*screaming*]. No! No! Don't . . . don't take me!

[*She moans, tossing and crying in her sleep. The other people wake, terrified. Dussel sits up in bed, furious.*]

DUSSEL. Shush! Anne! Anne, for God's sake, shush!

ANNE [*still in her nightmare*]. Save me! Save me!

[*She screams and screams. Dussel gets out of bed, going over to her, trying to wake her.*]

DUSSEL. For God's sake! Quiet! Quiet! You want someone to hear?

[*In the main room Mrs. Frank grabs a shawl and pulls it around her. She rushes in to Anne, taking her in her arms. Mr. Frank hurriedly gets up, putting on his overcoat. Margot sits up, terrified. Peter's light goes on in his room.*]

MRS. FRANK [*to Anne, in her room*]. Hush, darling, hush. It's all right. It's all right. [*Over her shoulder to Dussel*] Will you be kind enough to turn on the light, Mr. Dussel? [*Back to Anne*] It's nothing, my darling. It was just a dream.

[*Dussel turns on the light in the bedroom. Mrs. Frank holds Anne in her arms. Gradually Anne comes out of her nightmare, still trembling with horror. Mr. Frank comes into the room, and goes quickly to the window, looking out to be sure that no one outside has heard Anne's screams. Mrs. Frank holds Anne, talking softly to her. In the main room Margot stands on a chair, turning on the center hanging lamp. A light goes on in*] *the Van Daan's room overhead. Peter puts his robe on, coming out of his room.*]

DUSSEL [*to Mrs. Frank, blowing his nose*]. Something must be done about that child, Mrs. Frank. Yelling like that! Who knows but there's somebody on the streets? She's endangering all our lives.

MRS. FRANK. Anne, darling.

DUSSEL. Every night she twists and turns. I don't sleep. I spend half my night shushing her. And now it's nightmares!

[*Margot comes to the door of Anne's room, followed by Peter. Mr. Frank goes to them, indicating that everything is all right. Peter takes Margot back.*]

MRS. FRANK [*to Anne*]. You're here, safe, you see? Nothing has happened. [*To Dussel*] Please, Mr. Dussel, go back to bed. She'll be herself in a minute or two. Won't you, Anne?

DUSSEL [*picking up a book and a pillow*]. Thank you, but I'm going to the w.c. The one place where there's peace!

[*He stalks out. Mr. Van Daan, in underwear and trousers, comes down the stairs.*]

MR. VAN DAAN [*to Dussel*]. What is it? What happened?

DUSSEL. A nightmare. She was having a nightmare!

MR. VAN DAAN. I thought someone was murdering her.

DUSSEL. Unfortunately, no.

[*He goes into the bathroom. Mr. Van Daan goes back up the stairs. Mr. Frank, in the main room, sends Peter back to his own bedroom.*]

MR. FRANK. Thank you, Peter. Go back to bed.

[*Peter goes back to his room. Mr. Frank follows him, turning out the light and looking out the window. Then he goes back to the main room, and gets up on a chair, turning out the center hanging lamp.*]

MRS. FRANK [*to Anne*]. Would you like some water? [*Anne shakes her head.*] Was it a very bad dream? Perhaps if you told me . . . ?

ANNE. I'd rather not talk about it.

MRS. FRANK. Poor darling. Try to sleep then. I'll sit right here beside you until you fall asleep. [*She brings a stool over, sitting there.*]

ANNE. You don't have to.

MRS. FRANK. But I'd like to stay with you . . . very much. Really.

ANNE. I'd rather you didn't.

MRS. FRANK. Good night, then. [*She leans down to kiss Anne. Anne throws her arm up over her face, turning away. Mrs. Frank, hiding her hurt, kisses Anne's arm.*] You'll be all right? There's nothing that you want?

ANNE. Will you please ask Father to come.

MRS. FRANK [*after a second*]. Of course, Anne dear. [*She hurries out into the other room. Mr. Frank comes to her as she comes in.*] *Sie verlangt nach Dir!*[1]

MR. FRANK [*sensing her hurt*]. Edith, *Liebe, schau . . .*[2]

MRS. FRANK. *Es macht nichts! Ich danke dem lieben Herrgott, dass sie sich wenigstens an Dich wendet, wenn sie Trost braucht! Geh hinein, Otto, sie ist ganz hysterisch vor Angst.*[3] [*As Mr. Frank hesitates*]

---

[1] SIE VERLANGT NACH DIR!: She's asking to see you!

[2] LIEBE, SCHAU . . . : My dear, look . . .

[3] ES MACHT . . . ANGST: It doesn't matter. I just thank the dear Lord that when she needs consolation she will at least turn to you. Go, Otto, she is quite hysterical with fear.

Geh zu ihr.[1] [*He looks at her for a second and then goes to get a cup of water for Anne. Mrs. Frank sinks down on the bed, her face in her hands, trying to keep from sobbing aloud. Margot comes over to her, putting her arms around her.*] She wants nothing of me. She pulled away when I leaned down to kiss her.

MARGOT. It's a phase . . . You heard Father . . . Most girls go through it . . . they turn to their fathers at this age . . . they give all their love to their fathers.

MRS. FRANK. You weren't like this. You didn't shut me out.

MARGOT. She'll get over it . . .

[*She smooths the bed for Mrs. Frank and sits beside her a moment as Mrs. Frank lies down. In Anne's room Mr. Frank comes in, sitting down by Anne. Anne flings her arms around him, clinging to him. In the distance we hear the sound of ack-ack.*[2]]

ANNE. Oh, Pim. I dreamed that they came to get us! The Green Police! They broke down the door and grabbed me and started to drag me out the way they did Jopie.

MR. FRANK. I want you to take this pill.

ANNE. What is it?

MR. FRANK. Something to quiet you.

[*She takes it and drinks the water. In the main room Margot turns out the light and goes back to her room.*]

MR. FRANK [*to Anne*]. Do you want me to read to you for a while?

ANNE. No. Just sit with me for a minute. Was I awful? Did I yell terribly loud?

Do you think anyone outside could have heard?

MR. FRANK. No. No. Lie quietly now. Try to sleep.

ANNE. I'm a terrible coward. I'm so disappointed in myself. I think I've conquered my fear . . . I think I'm really grown up . . . and then something happens . . . and I run to you like a baby . . . I love you, Father. I don't love anyone but you.

MR. FRANK [*reproachfully*]. Annele!

ANNE. It's true. I've been thinking about it for a long time. You're the only one I love.

MR. FRANK. It's fine to hear you tell me that you love me. But I'd be happier if you said you loved your mother as well . . . She needs your help so much . . . your love . . .

ANNE. We have nothing in common. She doesn't understand me. Whenever I try to explain my views on life to her she asks me if I'm constipated.

MR. FRANK. You hurt her very much now. She's crying. She's in there crying.

ANNE. I can't help it. I only told the truth. I didn't want her here . . . [*Then, with sudden change*] Oh, Pim, I was horrible, wasn't I? And the worst of it is, I can stand off and look at myself doing it and know it's cruel and yet I can't stop doing it. What's the matter with me? Tell me. Don't say it's just a phase! Help me.

MR. FRANK. There is so little that we parents can do to help our children. We can only try to set a good example . . . point the way. The rest you must do yourself. You must build your own character.

ANNE. I'm trying. Really I am. Every night I think back over all of the things I did that day that were wrong . . . like putting the wet mop in Mr. Dussel's bed . . . and this thing now with Mother. I say to my-

---

[1] GEH ZU IHR: Go to her.
[2] ACK-ACK: antiaircraft fire.

self, that was wrong. I make up my mind. I'm never going to do that again. Never! Of course I may do something worse . . . but at least I'll never do *that* again . . . I have a nicer side, Father . . . a sweeter, nicer side. But I'm scared to show it. I'm afraid that people are going to laugh at me if I'm serious. So the mean Anne comes to the outside and the good Anne stays on the inside, and I keep on trying to switch them around and have the good Anne outside and the bad Anne inside and be what I'd like to be . . . and might be . . . if only . . . only . . .

[*She is asleep. Mr. Frank watches her for a moment and then turns off the light, and starts out. The lights dim out. The curtain falls on the scene. Anne's voice is heard dimly at first, and then with growing strength.*]

ANNE'S VOICE. . . . The air raids are getting worse. They come over day and night. The noise is terrifying. Pim says it should be music to our ears. The more planes, the sooner will come the end of the war. Mrs. Van Daan pretends to be a fatalist. What will be, will be. But when the planes come over, who is the most frightened? No one else but Petronella! . . . Monday, the ninth of November, nineteen forty-two. Wonderful news! The Allies have landed in Africa. Pim says that we can look for an early finish to the war. Just for fun he asked each of us what was the first thing we wanted to do when we got out of here. Mrs. Van Daan longs to be home with her own things, her needlepoint chairs, the Beckstein piano her father gave her . . . the best that money could buy. Peter

would like to go to a movie. Mr. Dussel wants to get back to his dentist's drill. He's afraid he is losing his touch. For myself, there are so many things . . . to ride a bike again . . . to laugh till my belly aches . . . to have new clothes from the skin out . . . to have a hot tub filled to overflowing and wallow in it for hours . . . to be back in school with my friends . . .

[*As the last lines are being said, the curtain rises on the scene. The lights dim on as Anne's voice fades away.*]

SCENE FIVE: *It is the first night of the Hanukkah[1] celebration. Mr. Frank is standing at the head of the table on which is the Menorah.[2] He lights the Shamos, or servant candle, and holds it as he says the blessing. Seated listening is all of the "family," dressed in their best. The men wear hats, Peter wears his cap.*

MR. FRANK [*reading from a prayer book*]. "Praised be Thou, oh Lord our God, Ruler of the universe, who has sanctified us with Thy commandments and bidden us kindle the Hanukkah lights. Praised be Thou, oh Lord our God, Ruler of the universe, who has wrought wondrous deliverances for our fathers in days of old. Praised be Thou, oh Lord our God, Ruler of the universe, that Thou has given us life and sustenance and brought us to this happy season." [*Mr. Frank lights the one candle of the Menorah*

---

[1] HANUKKAH: Jewish festival of lights, which commemorates the victory of the Maccabees over the Syrian invaders of Jerusalem in 165 B.C.
[2] MENORAH: special candle-holder for the ritual lights.

as he continues.] "We kindle this Hanukkah light to celebrate the great and wonderful deeds wrought through the zeal with which God filled the hearts of the heroic Maccabees, two thousand years ago. They fought against indifference, against tyranny and oppression, and they restored our Temple to us. May these lights remind us that we should ever look to God, whence cometh our help." Amen. [*Pronounced O-mayn.*]

ALL. Amen.

[*Mr. Frank hands Mrs. Frank the prayer book.*]

MRS. FRANK [*reading*]. "I lift up mine eyes unto the mountains, from whence cometh my help. My help cometh from the Lord who made heaven and earth. He will not suffer thy foot to be moved. He that keepeth thee will not slumber. He that keepeth Israel doth neither slumber nor sleep. The Lord is thy keeper. The Lord is thy shade upon thy right hand. The sun shall not smite thee by day, nor the moon by night. The Lord shall keep thee from all evil. He shall keep thy soul. The Lord shall guard thy going out and thy coming in, from this time forth and forevermore." Amen.

ALL. Amen.

[*Mrs. Frank puts down the prayer book and goes to get the food and wine. Margot helps her. Mr. Frank takes the men's hats and puts them aside.*]

DUSSEL [*rising*]. That was very moving.

ANNE [*pulling him back*]. It isn't over yet!

MRS. VAN DAAN. Sit down! Sit down!

ANNE. There's a lot more, songs and presents.

DUSSEL. Presents?

MRS. FRANK. Not this year, unfortunately.

MRS. VAN DAAN. But always on Hanukkah everyone gives presents . . . everyone!

DUSSEL. Like our St. Nicholas' Day.[1]

[*There is a chorus of "no's" from the group.*]

MRS. VAN DAAN. No! Not like St. Nicholas! What kind of a Jew are you that you don't know Hanukkah?

MRS. FRANK [*as she brings the food*]. I remember particularly the candles . . . First one, as we have tonight. Then the second night you light two candles, the next night three . . . and so on until you have eight candles burning. When there are eight candles it is truly beautiful.

MRS. VAN DAAN. And the potato pancakes.

MR. VAN DAAN. Don't talk about them!

MRS. VAN DAAN. I make the best *latkes* you ever tasted!

MRS. FRANK. Invite us all next year . . . in your own home.

MR. FRANK. God willing!

MRS. VAN DAAN. God willing.

MARGOT. What I remember best is the presents we used to get when we were little . . . eight days of presents . . . and each day they got better and better.

MRS. FRANK [*sitting down*]. We are all here, alive. That is present enough.

ANNE. No, it isn't. I've got something . . . [*She rushes into her room, hurriedly puts on a little hat improvised from the lamp shade, grabs a satchel bulging with parcels and comes running back.*]

[1] OUR ST. NICHOLAS' DAY: The Nazis considered anyone to be Jewish who had even one Jewish ancestor. Often a person would himself have no knowledge of his slight Jewish ancestry, or be completely assimilated into another culture and religion, as Mr. Dussel seems to be, and would find out that he was legally a Jew only when Nazi persecutions began.

MRS. FRANK. What is it?

ANNE. Presents!

MRS. VAN DAAN. Presents!

DUSSEL. Look!

MRS. VAN DAAN. What's she got on her head?

PETER. A lamp shade!

ANNE [*She picks out one at random*]. This is for Margot. [*She hands it to Margot, pulling her to her feet.*] Read it out loud.

MARGOT [*reading*].
"You have never lost your temper.
You never will, I fear,
You are so good.
But if you should,
Put all your cross words here."
[*She tears open the package.*] A new crossword puzzle book! Where did you get it?

ANNE. It isn't new. It's one that you've done. But I rubbed it all out, and if you wait a little and forget, you can do it all over again.

MARGOT [*sitting*]. It's wonderful, Anne. Thank you. You'd never know it wasn't new.

[*From outside we hear the sound of a streetcar passing.*]

ANNE [*with another gift*]. Mrs. Van Daan.

MRS. VAN DAAN [*taking it*]. This is awful . . . I haven't anything for anyone . . . I never thought . . .

MR. FRANK. This is all Anne's idea.

MRS. VAN DAAN [*holding up a bottle*]. What is it?

ANNE. It's hair shampoo. I took all the odds and ends of soap and mixed them with the last of my toilet water.

MRS. VAN DAAN. Oh, Anneke!

ANNE. I wanted to write a poem for all of them, but I didn't have time. [*Offering a large box to Mr. Van Daan*] Yours, Mr. Van Daan, is *really* something . . . something you want more than anything. [*As she waits for him to open it*] Look! Cigarettes!

MR. VAN DAAN. Cigarettes!

ANNE. Two of them! Pim found some old pipe tobacco in the pocket lining of his coat . . . and we made them . . . or rather, Pim did.

MRS. VAN DAAN. Let me see . . . Well, look at that! Light it, Putti! Light it.

[*Mr. Van Daan hesitates.*]

ANNE. It's tobacco, really it is! There's a little fluff in it, but not much.

[*Everyone watches as Mr. Van Daan cautiously lights it. The cigarette flares up. Everyone laughs.*]

PETER. It works!

MRS. VAN DAAN. Look at him.

MR. VAN DAAN [*spluttering*]. Thank you, Anne. Thank you.

[*Anne rushes back to her satchel for another present.*]

ANNE [*handing her mother a piece of paper*]. For Mother, Hanukkah greeting. [*She pulls her mother to her feet.*]

MRS. FRANK [*she reads*].
"Here's an I.O.U. that I promise to pay.
Ten hours of doing whatever you say.
Signed, Anne Frank."

[*Mrs. Frank, touched, takes Anne in her arms, holding her close.*]

DUSSEL [*to Anne*]. Ten hours of doing what you're told? *Anything* you're told?

ANNE. That's right.

Continued on page 561

IDEAS AND THE ARTS

History is filled with examples of human oppression, when some people have forced others to do what they did not want to do. Oppression can be religious, forcing people to change or give up certain beliefs. It can be political, forcing people to accept a government they do not want. It can be economic, forcing people to work under undesirable conditions. And it can be social, where people are forced to act in ways acceptable to other members of their society. It can be argued that some oppression is necessary to organize a society, but history tells us that man has gone far beyond what is necessary in oppressing his fellow human beings.

The first picture deals with both religious and political oppression. It is Pieter Bruegel's *Massacre of the Innocents.* When Jesus was born, Herod the King was told that a newborn child was to become King. Herod did not understand that Jesus would be concerned with the Kingdom of Heaven, not with an earthly kingdom, such as Herod's. But to be sure of his own safety, Herod ordered that all children the age of Jesus were to be killed. Instead of setting the scene in Palestine, Bruegel has set it in the winter snow in a town of his own country. By changing the setting, Bruegel has made the story general and universal. That is, he is indicating that this kind of oppression can happen at any time and any place. He intends his picture to illustrate all cases where men are ordered to oppress and destroy others. Such stories are so common in human history that when they do not affect nations or governments historians do not pay much attention to them. But artists are more interested in people than in nations or governments. As a result, such scenes are quite common in painting and literature.

Jusepe de Ribera's *The Martyrdom of St. Bartholomew* shows individual religious oppression. St. Bartholomew was one of Jesus' disciples who travelled as far as India to preach the new religion. On his way back he went through Armenia. There he was seized by men who opposed the new religion of Jesus. These men tortured and crucified St. Bartholomew. Ribera emphasizes the mechanical details of the crucifixion. He shows the technical means by which a man is hoisted up onto a cross to be nailed to it. St. Bartholomew's tormentors are presented as being very interested in the mastery of their trade. The man at the right, for example, is curious about the procedure, but is not disturbed by its horror. He leans forward, supporting his head with his hand, in order to get a better view.

The next picture was created by José Orozco, the Mexican painter. It is one of a series of murals (wall paintings) he did at Dartmouth College in New Hampshire in the 1930's. The subject of the series is the conquest of America by Europeans, and the suffering and triumph that were the results of that conquest. This particular painting is called *Cortez and the Cross and the Machine.* Cortez conquered Mexico to extend the power of Spain and to spread the Christian religion, and in the process he slaughtered thousands of Mexicans. The bodies of his victims are seen piled up in the middle. The machines on the right are intended to express Orozco's belief that the reason for the conquest was more economic than religious, that economic oppression has taken the place of religious oppression. The picture is also intended to show that religious and economic oppression are both forms of political oppression.

The next painting is also by a Mexican

painter, David Siqueiros. It, too, is part of a large mural. This particular painting is called *Revolution Against the Dictatorship of Porfirio Diaz.* In theory, Diaz was the President of Mexico from 1884 to 1911. In fact he was a ruthless dictator. During his rule he improved economic conditions in Mexico, but this is not surprising. Dictatorship, supported by all forms of oppression, always tries to justify itself by improving economic conditions. Although it sometimes improves the economic condition of the nation, it seldom improves the lives of the mass of people. Indeed, the economic oppression intended to improve the condition of the nation often makes conditions worse for the individual citizen. In 1911 the people of Mexico revolted against Diaz and forced him to flee to France. Siqueiros shows their hatred and determination as they carry the body of one of Diaz's victims.

The subject of the fifth picture is oppression by a foreign, conquering army. The French, under Napoleon, conquered Spain, forced the king to abdicate, and installed Napoleon's brother as king. In 1808 there was an unsuccessful popular uprising against the French rule, but it was not until 1813 that the British finally drove the French out of Spain. In 1814 the Spanish artist Francisco de Goya painted *The Third of May, 1808, in Madrid.* In the picture, the French have rounded up a number of suspected rebels, and without trial or investigation, shot them. This was but one of a great many such incidents throughout Spain in 1808.

The last picture is about a different kind of oppression. Ben Shahn's *Women's Christian Temperance Union Parade* deals with several forms of social oppression. Shahn is making fun of the women who would impose their ideas about behavior on others, but he is also showing sympathy and affection for them. Alcohol is used by people all over the world to relieve the tensions of daily life. But on many people it has a bad effect. It makes them feel free to do whatever they want to do, and unfortunately many people want to get rid of their own frustrations by abusing other people. To protect others, especially women and children, from such abuse, the Women's Christian Temperance Union fought to make the use of alcohol illegal. They were attempting to remove one kind of social oppression through the use of another. As a result of their efforts, laws were created that prohibited the sale of alcohol in the United States for thirteen years. Eventually people decided that these laws were unnecessarily oppressive, and these laws were repealed. This clash over different forms of social oppression taught Americans something about the problems of imposing some people's standards and opinions on other people who do not share those ideas. Perhaps this accounts for Shahn's mixed reaction to his subject.

Morse Peckham

PIETER BRUEGEL THE ELDER (c. 1525-1569) *MASSACRE OF THE INNOCENTS.* Kunsthistorisches Museum. Vienna.

JUSEPE DE RIBERA (1591-1652) *THE MARTYRDOM OF ST. BARTHOLOMEW.* Prado Museum. Madrid.

JOSÉ OROZCO (1883-1949) *CORTEZ AND THE CROSS AND THE MACHINE*. Hopkins Center Art Galleries, Dartmouth College, Hanover, New Hampshire.

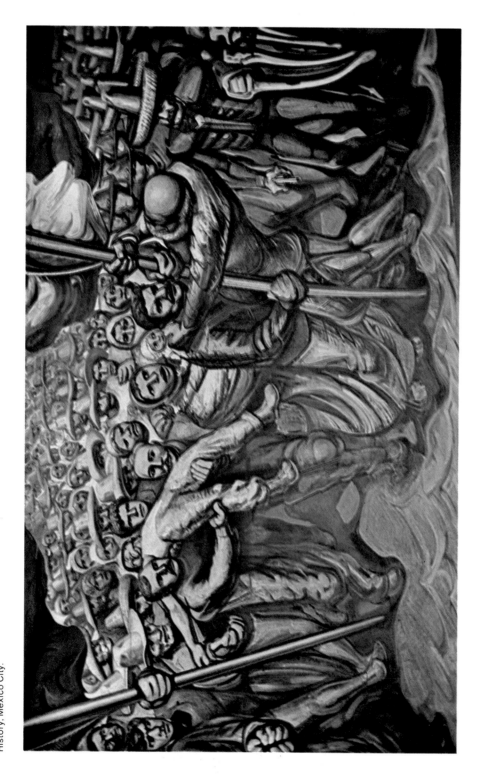

DAVID SIQUEIROS (born 1898) REVOLUTION AGAINST THE DICTATORSHIP OF PORFIRIO DIAZ, from the STRIKE AT CANANEA. National Museum of History, Mexico City.

FRANCISCO DE GOYA (1746-1828) *THE THIRD OF MAY, 1808, IN MADRID.* Prado Museum, Madrid.

BEN SHAHN (1898-1969) *WOMEN'S CHRISTIAN TEMPERANCE UNION PARADE.* Museum of the City of New York.

DUSSEL. You wouldn't want to sell that, Mrs. Frank?

MRS. FRANK. Never! This is the most precious gift I've ever had!

[*She sits, showing her present to the others. Anne hurries back to the satchel and pulls out a scarf, the scarf that Mr. Frank found in the first scene.*]

ANNE [*offering it to her father*]. For Pim.

MR. FRANK. Anneke . . . I wasn't supposed to have a present!

[*He takes it, unfolding it and showing it to the others.*]

ANNE. It's a muffler . . . to put round your neck . . . like an ascot, you know. I made it myself out of odds and ends . . . I knitted it in the dark each night, after I'd gone to bed. I'm afraid it looks better in the dark!

MR. FRANK [*putting it on*]. It's fine. It fits me perfectly. Thank you, Annele.

[*Anne hands Peter a ball of paper, with a string attached to it.*]

ANNE. That's for Mouschi.

PETER [*rising to bow*]. On behalf of Mouschi, I thank you.

ANNE [*hesitant, handing him a gift*]. And . . . this is yours . . . from Mrs. Quack Quack. [*As he holds it gingerly in his hands*] Well . . . open it . . . Aren't you going to open it?

PETER. I'm scared to. I know something's going to jump out and hit me.

ANNE. No. It's nothing like that, really.

MRS. VAN DAAN [*as he is opening it*]. What is it, Peter? Go on. Show it.

ANNE [*excitedly*]. It's a safety razor!

DUSSEL. A what?

ANNE. A razor!

MRS. VAN DAAN [*looking at it*]. You didn't make that out of odds and ends.

ANNE [*to Peter*]. Miep got it for me. It's not new. It's second-hand. But you really do need a razor now.

DUSSEL. For what?

ANNE. Look on his upper lip . . . you can see the beginning of a mustache.

DUSSEL. He wants to get rid of that? Put a little milk on it and let the cat lick it off.

PETER [*starting for his room*]. Think you're funny, don't you.

DUSSEL. Look! He can't wait! He's going to try it!

PETER. I'm going to give Mouschi his present!

[*He goes into his room, slamming the door behind him.*]

MR. VAN DAAN [*disgustedly*]. Mouschi, Mouschi, Mouschi.

[*In the distance we hear a dog persistently barking. Anne brings a gift to Dussel.*]

ANNE. And last but never least, my roommate, Mr. Dussel.

DUSSEL. For me? You have something for me? [*He opens the small box she gives him.*]

ANNE. I made them myself.

DUSSEL [*puzzled*]. Capsules! Two capsules!

ANNE. They're ear-plugs!

DUSSEL. Ear-plugs?

ANNE. To put in your ears so you won't hear me when I thrash around at night. I saw them advertised in a magazine. They're not real ones . . . I made them out of cotton and candle wax. Try them . . . See if they don't work . . . see if you can hear me talk . . .

DUSSEL [*putting them in his ears*]. Wait now until I get them in . . . so.

ANNE. Are you ready?

DUSSEL. Huh?

ANNE. Are you ready?

DUSSEL. Good God! They've gone inside! I can't get them out! [*They laugh as Mr. Dussel jumps about, trying to shake the plugs out of his ears. Finally he gets them out. Putting them away.*] Thank you, Anne! Thank you!

MR. VAN DAAN. A real Hanukkah!

MRS. VAN DAAN. Wasn't it cute of her?   [*Together*]

MRS. FRANK. I don't know when she did it.

MARGOT. I love my present.

ANNE [*sitting at the table*]. And now let's have the song, Father . . . please . . . [*To Dussel*] Have you heard the Hanukkah song, Mr. Dussel? The song is the whole thing! [*She sings*] "Oh, Hanukkah! Oh, Hanukkah! The sweet celebration . . ."

MR. FRANK [*quieting her*]. I'm afraid, Anne, we shouldn't sing that song tonight. [*To Dussel*] It's a song of jubilation, of rejoicing. One is apt to become too enthusiastic.

ANNE. Oh, please, please. Let's sing the song. I promise not to shout!

MR. FRANK. Very well. But quietly now . . . I'll keep an eye on you and when . . .

[*As Anne starts to sing, she is interrupted by Dussel, who is snorting and wheezing.*]

DUSSEL [*pointing to Peter*]. You . . . You! [*Peter is coming from his bedroom, ostentatiously holding a bulge in his coat as if he were holding his cat, and dangling Anne's present before it.*] How many times . . . I told you . . . Out! Out!

MR. VAN DAAN [*going to Peter*]. What's the matter with you? Haven't you any sense? Get that cat out of here.

PETER [*innocently*]. Cat?

MR. VAN DAAN. You heard me. Get it out of here!

PETER. I have no cat. [*Delighted with his joke, he opens his coat and pulls out a bath towel. The group at the table laugh, enjoying the joke.*]

DUSSEL [*still wheezing*]. It doesn't need to be the cat . . . his clothes are enough . . . when he comes out of that room . . .

MR. VAN DAAN. Don't worry. You won't be bothered any more. We're getting rid of it.

DUSSEL. At last you listen to me.

[*He goes off into his bedroom.*]

MR. VAN DAAN [*calling after him*]. I'm not doing it for you. That's all in your mind . . . all of it! [*He starts back to his place at the table.*] I'm doing it because I'm sick of seeing that cat eat all our food.

PETER. That's not true! I only give him bones . . . scraps . . .

MR. VAN DAAN. Don't tell me! He gets fatter every day! Damn cat looks better than any of us. Out he goes tonight!

PETER. No! No!

ANNE. Mr. Van Daan, you can't do that! That's Peter's cat. Peter loves that cat.

MRS. FRANK [*quietly*]. Anne.

PETER [*to Mr. Van Daan*]. If he goes, I go.

MR. VAN DAAN. Go! Go!

MRS. VAN DAAN. You're not going and the cat's not going! Now please . . . this is Hanukkah . . . Hanukkah . . . this is the time to celebrate . . . What's the matter with all of you? Come on, Anne. Let's have the song.

ANNE [*singing*].

"Oh, Hanukkah! Oh, Hanukkah!
The sweet celebration."

MR. FRANK [*rising*]. I think we should first blow out the candle . . . then we'll have something for tomorrow night.

MARGOT. But, Father, you're supposed to let it burn itself out.

MR. FRANK. I'm sure that God understands shortages. [*Before blowing it out*] "Praised be Thou, oh Lord our God, who hast sustained us and permitted us to celebrate this joyous festival."

[*He is about to blow out the candle when suddenly there is a crash of something falling below. They all freeze in horror, motionless. For a few seconds there is complete silence. Mr. Frank slips off his shoes. The others noiselessly follow his example. Mr. Frank turns out a light near him. He motions to Peter to turn off the center lamp. Peter tries to reach it, realizes he cannot and gets up on a chair. Just as he is touching the lamp he loses his balance. The chair goes out from under him. He falls. The iron lamp shade crashes to the floor. There is a sound of feet below, running down the stairs.*]

MR. VAN DAAN [*under his breath*]. God almighty! [*The only light left comes from the Hanukkah candle. Dussel comes from his room. Mr. Frank creeps over to the stairwell and stands listening. The dog is heard barking excitedly.*] Do you hear anything?

MR. FRANK [*in a whisper*]. No. I think they've gone.

MRS. VAN DAAN. It's the Green Police. They've found us.

MR. FRANK. If they had, they wouldn't have left. They'd be up here by now.

MRS. VAN DAAN. I know it's the Green Police. They've gone to get help. That's all, they'll be back.

MR. VAN DAAN. Or it may have been the Gestapo,[1] looking for papers . . .

MR. FRANK [*interrupting*]. Or a thief, looking for money.

MRS. VAN DAAN. We've got to do something . . . Quick! Quick! Before they come back.

MR. VAN DAAN. There isn't anything to do. Just wait.

[*Mr. Frank holds up his hand for them to be quiet. He is listening intently. There is complete silence as they all strain to hear any sound from below. Suddenly Anne begins to sway. With a low cry she falls to the floor in a faint. Mrs. Frank goes to her quickly, sitting beside her on the floor and taking her in her arms.*]

MRS. FRANK. Get some water, please! Get some water!

[*Margot starts for the sink.*]

MR. VAN DAAN [*grabbing Margot*]. No! No! No one's going to run water!

MR. FRANK. If they've found us, they've found us. Get the water. [*Margot starts again for the sink. Mr. Frank, getting a flashlight*] I'm going down.

[*Margot rushes to him, clinging to him. Anne struggles to consciousness.*]

MARGOT. No, Father, no! There may be someone there, waiting . . . It may be a trap!

MR. FRANK. This is Saturday. There is no way for us to know what has happened until Miep or Mr. Kraler comes on Monday morning. We cannot live with this uncertainty.

---

[1] GESTAPO: Nazi secret police.

MARGOT. Don't go, Father!

MRS. FRANK. Hush, darling, hush. [*Mr. Frank slips quietly out, down the steps and out through the door below.*] Margot! Stay close to me.

[*Margot goes to her mother.*]

MR. VAN DAAN. Shush! Shush!

[*Mrs. Frank whispers to Margot to get the water. Margot goes for it.*]

MRS. VAN DAAN. Putti, where's our money? Get our money. I hear you can buy the Green Police off, so much a head. Go upstairs quick! Get the money!

MR. VAN DAAN. Keep still!

MRS. VAN DAAN [*kneeling before him, pleading*]. Do you want to be dragged off to a concentration camp? Are you going to stand there and wait for them to come up and get you? Do something, I tell you!

MR. VAN DAAN [*pushing her aside*]. Will you keep still!

[*He goes over to the stairwell to listen. Peter goes to his mother, helping her up onto the sofa. There is a second of silence. Then Anne can stand it no longer.*]

ANNE. Someone go after Father! Make Father come back!

PETER [*starting for the door*]. I'll go.

MR. VAN DAAN. Haven't you done enough?

[*He pushes Peter roughly away. In his anger against his father Peter grabs a chair as if to hit him with it, then puts it down, burying his face in his hands. Mrs. Frank begins to pray softly.*]

ANNE. Please, please, Mr. Van Daan. Get Father.

MR. VAN DAAN. Quiet! Quiet!

[*Anne is shocked into silence. Mrs.*

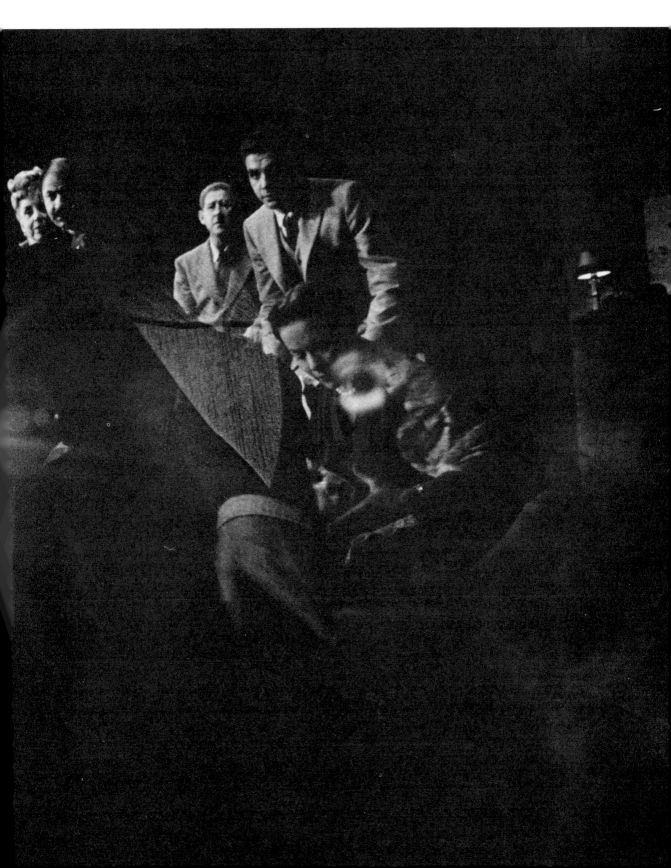

Frank pulls her closer, holding her protectively in her arms.]

MRS. FRANK [*softly, praying*]. "I lift up mine eyes unto the mountains, from whence cometh my help. My help cometh from the Lord who made heaven and earth. He will not suffer thy foot to be moved . . . He that keepeth thee will not slumber . . ."

[*She stops as she hears someone coming. They all watch the door tensely. Mr. Frank comes quietly in. Anne rushes to him, holding him tight.*]

MR. FRANK. It was a thief. That noise must have scared him away.

MRS. VAN DAAN. Thank God.

MR. FRANK. He took the cash box. And the radio. He ran away in such a hurry that he didn't stop to shut the street door. It was swinging wide open. [*A breath of relief sweeps over them.*] I think it would be good to have some light.

MARGOT. Are you sure it's all right?

MR. FRANK. The danger has passed. [*Margot goes to light the small lamp.*] Don't be so terrified, Anne. We're safe.

DUSSEL. Who says the danger has passed? Don't you realize we are in greater danger than ever?

MR. FRANK. Mr. Dussel, will you be still!

[*Mr. Frank takes Anne back to the table, making her sit down with him, trying to calm her.*]

DUSSEL [*pointing to Peter*]. Thanks to this clumsy fool, there's someone now who knows we're up here! Someone now knows we're up here, hiding!

MRS. VAN DAAN [*going to Dussel*]. Someone knows we're here, yes. But who is the someone? A thief! A thief! You think a thief is going to go to the Green Police and say . . . I was robbing a place the other night and I heard a noise up over my head? You think a thief is going to do that?

DUSSEL. Yes. I think he will.

MRS. VAN DAAN [*hysterically*]. You're crazy!

[*She stumbles back to her seat at the table. Peter follows protectively, pushing Dussel aside.*]

DUSSEL. I think some day he'll be caught and then he'll make a bargain with the Green Police . . . if they'll let him off, he'll tell them where some Jews are hiding!

[*He goes off into the bedroom. There is a second of appalled silence.*]

MR. VAN DAAN. He's right.

ANNE. Father, let's get out of here! We can't stay here now . . . Let's go . . .

MR. VAN DAAN. Go! Where?

MRS. FRANK [*sinking into her chair at the table*]. Yes. Where?

MR. FRANK [*rising, to them all*]. Have we lost all faith? All courage? A moment ago we thought that they'd come for us. We were sure it was the end. But it wasn't the end. We're alive, safe. [*Mr. Van Daan goes to the table and sits. Mr. Frank prays.*] "We thank Thee, oh Lord our God, that in Thy infinite mercy Thou hast again seen fit to spare us." [*He blows out the candle, then turns to Anne.*] Come on, Anne. The song! Let's have the song! [*He starts to sing. Anne finally starts falteringly to sing, as Mr. Frank urges her on. Her voice is hardly audible at first.*]

ANNE [*singing*].

"Oh, Hanukkah! Oh, Hanukkah!

The sweet . . . celebration . . ."

[*As she goes on singing, the others gradually join in, their voices still shaking with fear. Mrs. Van Daan sobs as she sings.*]

GROUP.

"Around the feast . . . we . . . gather
In complete . . . jubilation . . .
Happiest of sea . . . sons
Now is here.
Many are the reasons for good cheer."

[*Dussel comes from the bedroom. He comes over to the table, standing beside Margot, listening to them as they sing.*]

"Together
We'll weather

Whatever tomorrow may bring."

[*As they sing on with growing courage, the lights start to dim.*]

"So hear us rejoicing
And merrily voicing
The Hanukkah song that we sing.
Hoy!"

[*The lights are out. The curtain starts slowly to fall.*]

"Hear us rejoicing
And merrily voicing
The Hanukkah song that we sing."

[*They are still singing, as the curtain falls.*]

CURTAIN

FOR DISCUSSION

1. In order to understand most fully the ordeal of the Franks, the Van Daans, and Mr. Dussel, the reader must attempt to visualize the total setting of the play. What were the conditions in Holland when the Franks decided to go into hiding? Why did they try to make people think they had left the country? Can you explain why Mr. Dussel's description of conditions in Amsterdam was so much more disturbing than the news from Miep or Mr. Kraler had been?

2. When a person undergoes deprivation and unusual strain, small and normally commonplace things tend to take on special importance and significance. Consider, for example, Mrs. Van Daan's fur coat, Peter's cat, and Anne's diary. What special personal need does each item fill for its owner? How is each one a symbol of other things they have lost?

3. Mr. Dussel never adjusts very well to his life in hiding. What fact does he mention in his first conversation with Anne that might account for his inability to adjust or to be at ease with the others?

4. Mr. Frank tells Anne, "There is so little that we parents can do to help our children. We can only try to set a good example . . . point the way." How does Mr. Frank "point the way" for Anne? Find specific incidents in the play which reveal the kind of example Mr. Frank provides for Anne. How else does he help her? Does Anne resemble her father in any way? Find incidents in the play which support your conclusions.

ACT TWO

SCENE ONE: *In the darkness we hear Anne's voice, again reading from the diary.*

ANNE'S VOICE. Saturday, the first of January, nineteen forty-four. Another new year has begun and we find ourselves still in our hiding place. We have been here now for one year, five months and twenty-five days. It seems that our life is at a standstill.

The curtain rises on the scene. It is afternoon. Everyone is bundled up against the cold. In the main room Mrs. Frank is taking down the laundry, which is hung across the back. Mr. Frank sits in the chair down left, reading. Margot is lying on the couch with a blanket over her and the many-colored knitted scarf around her throat. Anne is seated at the center table, writing in her diary. Peter, Mr. and Mrs. Van Daan, and Dussel are all in their own rooms, reading or lying down.

As the lights dim on, Anne's voice continues, without a break.

ANNE'S VOICE. We are all a little thinner. The Van Daan's "discussions" are as violent as ever. Mother still does not understand me. But then I don't understand her either. There is one great change, however. A change in myself. I read somewhere that girls of my age don't feel quite certain of themselves. That they become quiet within and begin to think of the miracle that is taking place in their bodies. I think that what is happening to me is so wonderful . . . not only what can be seen, but what is taking place inside . . .

[The buzzer of the door below suddenly sounds. Everyone is startled; Mr. Frank tiptoes cautiously to the top of the steps and listens. Again the buzzer sounds, in Miep's V-for-Victory signal.[1]]

MR. FRANK. It's Miep! [*He goes quickly down the steps to unbolt the door. Mrs. Frank calls upstairs to the Van Daans and then to Peter.*]

MRS. FRANK. Wake up, everyone! Miep is here! [*Anne quickly puts her diary away. Margot sits up, pulling the blanket around her shoulders. Mr. Dussel sits on the edge of his bed, listening, disgruntled. Miep comes up the steps, followed by Mr. Kraler. They bring flowers, books, newspapers, etc. Anne rushes to Miep, throwing her arms affectionately around her.*] Miep . . . and Mr. Kraler . . . What a delightful surprise!

MR. KRALER. We came to bring you New Year's greetings.

MRS. FRANK. You shouldn't . . . you should have at least one day to yourselves. [*She goes quickly to the stove and brings down teacups and tea for all of them.*]

ANNE. Don't say that, it's so wonderful to see them! [*Sniffing at Miep's coat*] I can smell the wind and the cold on your clothes.

MIEP [*giving her the flowers*]. There you are. [*Then to Margot, feeling her forehead*] How are you, Margot? . . . Feeling any better?

MARGOT. I'm all right.

---

[1] V-FOR-VICTORY SIGNAL: three short rings and then one long ring, the Morse code for the letter "V," which was used as the Allied victory symbol.

ANNE. We filled her full of every kind of pill so she won't cough and make a noise.

[*She runs into her room to put the flowers in water. Mr. and Mrs. Van Daan come from upstairs. Outside there is the sound of a band playing.*]

MRS. VAN DAAN. Well, hello, Miep. Mr. Kraler.

MR. KRALER [*giving a bouquet of flowers to Mrs. Van Daan*]. With my hope for peace in the New Year.

PETER [*anxiously*]. Miep, have you seen Mouschi? Have you seen him anywhere around?

MIEP. I'm sorry, Peter. I asked everyone in the neighborhood had they seen a gray cat. But they said no.

[*Mrs. Frank gives Miep a cup of tea. Mr. Frank comes up the steps, carrying a small cake on a plate.*]

MR. FRANK. Look what Miep's brought for us!

MRS. FRANK [*taking it*]. A cake!

MR. VAN DAAN. A cake! [*He pinches Miep's cheeks gaily and hurries up to the cupboard.*] I'll get some plates.

[*Dussel, in his room, hastily puts a coat on and starts out to join the others.*]

MRS. FRANK. Thank you, Miepia. You shouldn't have done it. You must have used all of your sugar ration for weeks. [*Giving it to Mrs. Van Daan*] It's beautiful, isn't it?

MRS. VAN DAAN. It's been ages since I even saw a cake. Not since you brought us one last year. [*Without looking at the cake, to Miep*] Remember? Don't you remember, you gave us one on New Year's Day? Just this time last year? I'll never forget it because you had "Peace in nineteen forty-three" on it. [*She looks at the cake and reads.*] "Peace in nineteen forty-four!"

MIEP. Well, it has to come sometime, you know. [*As Dussel comes from his room*] Hello, Mr. Dussel.

MR. KRALER. How are you?

MR. VAN DAAN [*bringing plates and a knife*]. Here's the knife, *liefje*. Now, how many of us are there?

MIEP. None for me, thank you.

MR. FRANK. Oh, please. You must.

MIEP. I couldn't.

MR. VAN DAAN. Good! That leaves one . . . two . . . three . . . seven of us.

DUSSEL. Eight! Eight! It's the same number as it always is!

MR. VAN DAAN. I left Margot out. I take it for granted Margot won't eat any.

ANNE. Why wouldn't she!

MRS. FRANK. I think it won't harm her.

MR. VAN DAAN. All right! All right! I just didn't want her to start coughing again, that's all.

DUSSEL. And please, Mrs. Frank should cut the cake.

MR. VAN DAAN. What's the difference?

MRS. VAN DAAN. It's not Mrs. Frank's cake, is it, Miep? It's for all of us.   [*Together*]

DUSSEL. Mrs. Frank divides things better.

MRS. VAN DAAN [*going to Dussel*]. What are you trying to say?

MR. VAN DAAN. Oh, come on! Stop wasting time!   [*Together*]

MRS. VAN DAAN [*to Dussel*]. Don't I always give everybody exactly the same? Don't I?

MR. VAN DAAN. Forget it, Kerli.

MRS. VAN DAAN. No. I want an answer! Don't I?

DUSSEL. Yes. Yes. Everybody gets exactly the same . . . except Mr. Van Daan always gets a little bit more.

[*Van Daan advances on Dussel, the knife still in his hand.*]

MR. VAN DAAN. That's a lie!

[*Dussel retreats before the onslaught of the Van Daans.*]

MR. FRANK. Please, please! [*Then to Miep*] You see what a little sugar cake does to us? It goes right to our heads!

MR. VAN DAAN [*handing Mrs. Frank the knife*]. Here you are, Mrs. Frank.

MRS. FRANK. Thank you. [*Then to Miep as she goes to the table to cut the cake*] Are you sure you won't have some?

MIEP [*drinking her tea*]. No, really, I have to go in a minute.

[*The sound of the band fades out in the distance.*]

PETER [*to Miep*]. Maybe Mouschi went back to our house . . . they say that cats . . . Do you ever get over there . . . ? I mean . . . do you suppose you could . . . ?

MIEP. I'll try, Peter. The first minute I get I'll try. But I'm afraid, with him gone a week . . .

DUSSEL. Make up your mind, already someone has had a nice big dinner from that cat!

[*Peter is furious, inarticulate. He starts toward Dussel as if to hit him. Mr. Frank stops him. Mrs. Frank speaks quickly to ease the situation.*]

MRS. FRANK [*to Miep*]. This is delicious, Miep!

MRS. VAN DAAN [*eating hers*]. Delicious!

MR. VAN DAAN [*finishing it in one gulp*]. Dirk's in luck to get a girl who can bake like this!

MIEP [*putting down her empty teacup*]. I have to run. Dirk's taking me to a party tonight.

ANNE. How heavenly! Remember now what everyone is wearing, and what you have to eat and everything, so you can tell us tomorrow.

MIEP. I'll give you a full report! Good-by, everyone!

MR. VAN DAAN [*to Miep*]. Just a minute. There's something I'd like you to do for me.

[*He hurries off up the stairs to his room.*]

MRS. VAN DAAN [*sharply*]. Putti, where are you going? [*She rushes up the stairs after him, calling hysterically.*] What do you want? Putti, what are you going to do?

MIEP [*to Peter*]. What's wrong?

PETER [*his sympathy is with his mother*]. Father says he's going to sell her fur coat. She's crazy about that old fur coat.

DUSSEL. Is it possible? Is it possible that anyone is so silly as to worry about a fur coat in times like this?

PETER. It's none of your darn business . . . and if you say one more thing . . . I'll, I'll take you and I'll . . . I mean it . . . I'll . . .

[*There is a piercing scream from Mrs. Van Daan above. She grabs at the fur coat as Mr. Van Daan is starting downstairs with it.*]

MRS. VAN DAAN. No! No! No! Don't you dare take that! You hear? It's mine! [*Downstairs Peter turns away, embarrassed, miserable.*] My father gave me that! You didn't give it to me. You have no right. Let go of it . . . you hear?

[*Mr. Van Daan pulls the coat from her hands and hurries downstairs. Mrs. Van Daan sinks to the floor, sobbing. As Mr. Van Daan comes into the main room the others look away, embarrassed for him.*]

MR. VAN DAAN [*to Mr. Kraler*]. Just a little —discussion over the advisability of selling this coat. As I have often reminded Mrs. Van Daan, it's very selfish of her to keep it when people outside are in such desperate need of clothing . . . [*He gives the coat to Miep.*] So if you will please to sell it for us? It should fetch a good price. And by the way, will you get me cigarettes. I don't care what kind they are . . . get all you can.

MIEP. It's terribly difficult to get them, Mr. Van Daan. But I'll try. Good-by.

[*She goes. Mr. Frank follows her down the steps to bolt the door after her. Mrs. Frank gives Mr. Kraler a cup of tea.*]

MRS. FRANK. Are you sure you won't have some cake, Mr. Kraler?

MR. KRALER. I'd better not.

MR. VAN DAAN. You're still feeling badly? What does your doctor say?

MR. KRALER. I haven't been to him.

MRS. FRANK. Now, Mr. Kraler! . . .

MR. KRALER [*sitting at the table*]. Oh, I tried. But you can't get near a doctor these days . . . they're so busy. After weeks I finally managed to get one on the telephone. I told him I'd like an appointment . . . I wasn't feeling very well. You know what he answers . . . over the telephone . . . Stick out your tongue! [*They laugh. He turns to Mr. Frank as Mr. Frank comes back.*] I have some contracts here . . . I wonder if you'd look over them with me . . .

MR. FRANK [*putting out his hand*]. Of course.

MR. KRALER [*he rises*]. If we could go downstairs . . . [*Mr. Frank starts ahead, Mr. Kraler speaks to the others.*] Will you forgive us? I won't keep him but a minute. [*He starts to follow Mr. Frank down the steps.*]

MARGOT [*with sudden foreboding*]. What's happened? Something's happened! Hasn't it, Mr. Kraler?

[*Mr. Kraler stops and comes back, trying to reassure Margot with a pretense of casualness.*]

MR. KRALER. No, really. I want your father's advice . . .

MARGOT. Something's gone wrong! I know it!

MR. FRANK [*coming back, to Mr. Kraler*]. If it's something that concerns us here, it's better that we all hear it.

MR. KRALER [*turning to him, quietly*]. But . . . the children . . . ?

MR. FRANK. What they'd imagine would be worse than any reality.

[*As Mr. Kraler speaks, they all listen with intense apprehension. Mrs. Van Daan comes down the stairs and sits on the bottom step.*]

MR. KRALER. It's a man in the storeroom . . . I don't know whether or not you remember him . . . Carl, about fifty, heavy-set, near-sighted . . . He came with us just before you left.

MR. FRANK. He was from Utrecht?

MR. KRALER. That's the man. A couple of weeks ago, when I was in the storeroom, he closed the door and asked me . . . how's Mr. Frank? What do you hear from Mr. Frank? I told him I only knew there was a rumor that you were in

Switzerland. He said he'd heard that rumor too, but he thought I might know something more. I didn't pay any attention to it . . . but then a thing happened yesterday . . . He'd brought some invoices to the office for me to sign. As I was going through them, I looked up. He was standing staring at the bookcase . . . your bookcase. He said he thought he remembered a door there . . . Wasn't there a door there that used to go up to the loft? Then he told me he wanted more money. Twenty guilders[1] more a week.

MR. VAN DAAN. Blackmail!

MR. FRANK. Twenty guilders? Very modest blackmail.

MR. VAN DAAN. That's just the beginning.

DUSSEL [*coming to Mr. Frank*]. You know what I think? He was the thief who was down there that night. That's how he knows we're here.

MR. FRANK [*to Mr. Kraler*]. How was it left? What did you tell him?

MR. KRALER. I said I had to think about it. What shall I do? Pay him the money? . . . Take a chance on firing him . . . or what? I don't know.

DUSSEL [*frantic*]. For God's sake don't fire him! Pay him what he asks . . . keep him here where you can have your eye on him.

MR. FRANK. Is it so much that he's asking? What are they paying nowadays?

MR. KRALER. He could get it in a war plant. But this isn't a war plant. Mind you, I don't know if he really knows . . . or if he doesn't know.

MR. FRANK. Offer him half. Then we'll soon find out if it's blackmail or not.

DUSSEL. And if it is? We've got to pay it, haven't we? Anything he asks we've got to pay!

MR. FRANK. Let's decide that when the time comes.

MR. KRALER. This may be all imagination. You get to a point, these days, where you suspect everyone and everything. Again and again . . . on some simple look or word, I've found myself . . .

[*The telephone rings in the office below.*]

MRS. VAN DAAN [*hurrying to Mr. Kraler*]. There's the telephone! What does that mean, the telephone ringing on a holiday?

MR. KRALER. That's my wife. I told her I had to go over some papers in my office . . . to call me there when she got out of church. [*He starts out.*] I'll offer him half then. Good-by . . . we'll hope for the best!

[*The group call their good-bys halfheartedly. Mr. Frank follows Mr. Kraler, to bolt the door below. During the following scene, Mr. Frank comes back up and stands listening, disturbed.*]

DUSSEL [*to Mr. Van Daan*]. You can thank your son for this . . . smashing the light! I tell you, it's just a question of time now.

[*He goes to the window at the back and stands looking out.*]

MARGOT. Sometimes I wish the end would come . . . whatever it is.

MRS. FRANK [*shocked*]. Margot!

[*Anne goes to Margot, sitting beside her on the couch with her arms around her.*]

MARGOT. Then at least we'd know where we were.

MRS. FRANK. You should be ashamed of

---

[1] TWENTY GUILDERS: about $5.00 American.

yourself! Talking that way! Think how lucky we are! Think of the thousands dying in the war, every day. Think of the people in concentration camps.

ANNE [*interrupting*]. What's the good of that? What's the good of thinking of misery when you're already miserable? That's stupid!

MRS. FRANK. Anne!

[*As Anne goes on raging at her mother, Mrs. Frank tries to break in, in an effort to quiet her.*]

ANNE. We're young. Margot and Peter and I! You grownups have had your chance! But look at us . . . If we begin thinking of all the horror in the world, we're lost! We're trying to hold onto some kind of ideals . . . when everything . . . ideals, hopes . . . everything, are being destroyed! It isn't our fault that the world is in such a mess! We weren't around when all this started! So don't try to take it out on us! [*She rushes off to her room, slamming the door after her. She picks up a brush from the chest and hurls it to the floor. Then she sits on the settee, trying to control her anger.*]

MR. VAN DAAN. She talks as if we started the war! Did we start the war?

[*He spots Anne's cake. As he starts to take it, Peter anticipates him.*]

PETER. She left her cake. [*He starts for Anne's room with the cake. There is silence in the main room. Mrs. Van Daan goes up to her room, followed by Mr. Van Daan. Dussel stays looking out the window. Mr. Frank brings Mrs. Frank her cake. She eats it slowly, without relish. Mr. Frank takes his cake to Margot and sits quietly on the sofa beside her. Peter stands in the doorway of Anne's darkened room, looking at her, then makes a little movement to let her know he is there. Anne sits up, quickly, trying to hide the signs of her tears. Peter holds out the cake to her.*] You left this.

ANNE [*dully*]. Thanks.

[*Peter starts to go out, then comes back.*]

PETER. I thought you were fine just now. You know just how to talk to them. You know just how to say it. I'm no good . . . I never can think . . . especially when I'm mad . . . That Dussel . . . when he said that about Mouschi . . . someone eating him . . . all I could think is . . . I wanted to hit him. I wanted to give him such a . . . a . . . that he'd . . . That's what I used to do when there was an argument at school . . . That's the way I . . . but here . . . And an old man like that . . . it wouldn't be so good.

ANNE. You're making a big mistake about me. I do it all wrong. I say too much. I go too far. I hurt people's feelings . . .

[*Dussel leaves the window, going to his room.*]

PETER. I think you're just fine . . . What I want to say . . . if it wasn't for you around here, I don't know. What I mean . . .

[*Peter is interrupted by Dussel's turning on the light. Dussel stands in the doorway, startled to see Peter. Peter advances toward him forbiddingly. Dussel backs out of the room. Peter closes the door on him.*]

ANNE. Do you mean it, Peter? Do you really mean it?

PETER. I said it, didn't I?

ANNE. Thank you, Peter!

[*In the main room Mr. and Mrs. Frank collect the dishes and take them to the sink, washing them. Margot lies down again on the couch. Dussel, lost, wanders into Peter's room and takes up a book, starting to read.*]

PETER [*looking at the photographs on the wall*]. You've got quite a collection.

ANNE. Wouldn't you like some in your room? I could give you some. Heaven knows you spend enough time in there . . . doing heaven knows what. . . .

PETER. It's easier. A fight starts, or an argument . . . I duck in there.

ANNE. You're lucky, having a room to go to. His lordship is always here . . . I hardly ever get a minute alone. When they start in on me, I can't duck away. I have to stand there and take it.

PETER. You gave some of it back just now.

ANNE. I get so mad. They've formed their opinions . . . about everything . . . but we . . . we're still trying to find out . . . We have problems here that no other people our age have ever had. And just as you think you've solved them, something comes along and bang! You have to start all over again.

PETER. At least you've got someone you can talk to.

ANNE. Not really. Mother . . . I never discuss anything serious with her. She doesn't understand. Father's all right. We can talk about everything . . . everything but one thing. Mother. He simply won't talk about her. I don't think you can be really intimate with anyone if he holds something back, do you?

PETER. I think your father's fine.

ANNE. Oh, he is, Peter! He is! He's the only one who's ever given me the feeling that I have any sense. But anyway, nothing can take the place of school and play and friends of your own age . . . or near your age . . . can it?

PETER. I suppose you miss your friends and all.

ANNE. It isn't just . . . [*She breaks off, staring up at him for a second.*] Isn't it funny, you and I? Here we've been seeing each other every minute for almost a year and a half, and this is the first time we've ever really talked. It helps a lot to have someone to talk to, don't you think? It helps you to let off steam.

PETER [*going to the door*]. Well, any time you want to let off steam, you can come into my room.

ANNE [*following him*]. I can get up an awful lot of steam. You'll have to be careful how you say that.

PETER. It's all right with me.

ANNE. Do you really mean it?

PETER. I said it, didn't I?

[*He goes out. Anne stands in her doorway looking after him. As Peter gets to his door he stands for a minute looking back at her. Then he goes into his room. Dussel rises as he comes in, and quickly passes him, going out. He starts across for his room. Anne sees him coming, and pulls her door shut. Dussel turns back toward Peter's room. Peter pulls his door shut. Dussel stands there, bewildered, forlorn.*

The scene slowly dims out. The curtain falls on the scene. Anne's voice comes over in the darkness . . . faintly at first, and then with growing strength.]

ANNE'S VOICE. We've had bad news. The people from whom Miep got our ration books have been arrested. So we have had to cut down on our food. Our stomachs are so empty that they rumble and make strange noises, all in different keys. Mr. Van Daan's is deep and low, like a bass fiddle. Mine is high, whistling like a flute. As we all sit around waiting for supper, it's like an orchestra tuning up. It only needs Toscanini[1] to raise his baton and we'd be off in the Ride of the Valkyries.[2] Monday, the sixth day of March, nineteen forty-four. Mr. Kraler is in the hospital. It seems he has ulcers. Pim says we are his ulcers. Miep has to run the business and us too. The Americans have landed on the southern tip of Italy. Father looks for a quick finish to the war. Mr. Dussel is waiting every day for the warehouse man to demand more money. Have I been skipping too much from one subject to another? I can't help it. I feel that spring is coming. I feel it in my whole body and soul. I feel utterly confused. I am longing . . . so longing . . . for everything . . . for friends . . . for someone to talk to . . . someone who understands . . . someone young, who feels as I do . . .

[*As these last lines are being said, the curtain rises on the scene. The lights dim on. Anne's voice fades out.*]

SCENE TWO: *It is evening, after supper. From the outside we hear the sound of children playing. The "grownups," with the exception of Mr. Van Daan, are all in the main room. Mrs. Frank is doing some mending, Mrs. Van Daan is reading a fashion magazine. Mr. Frank is* going over business accounts. Dussel, in his dentist's jacket, is pacing up and down, impatient to get into his bedroom. Mr. Van Daan is upstairs working on a piece of embroidery in an embroidery frame.

In his room Peter is sitting before the mirror, smoothing his hair. As the scene goes on, he puts on his tie, brushes his coat and puts it on, preparing himself meticulously for a visit from Anne. On his wall are now hung some of Anne's motion picture stars.

In her room Anne too is getting dressed. She stands before the mirror in her slip, trying various ways of dressing her hair. Margot is seated on the sofa, hemming a skirt for Anne to wear.

In the main room Dussel can stand it no longer. He comes over, rapping sharply on the door of his and Anne's bedroom.

ANNE [*calling to him*]. No, no, Mr. Dussel! I am not dressed yet. [*Dussel walks away, furious, sitting down and burying his head in his hands. Anne turns to Margot.*] How is that? How does that look?

MARGOT [*glancing at her briefly*]. Fine.

ANNE. You didn't even look.

MARGOT. Of course I did. It's fine.

ANNE. Margot, tell me, am I terribly ugly?

MARGOT. Oh, stop fishing.

ANNE. No. No. Tell me.

MARGOT. Of course you're not. You've got nice eyes . . . and a lot of animation, and . . .

ANNE. A little vague, aren't you?

[*She reaches over and takes a brassière out of Margot's sewing basket. She holds it up to herself, studying the effect in the*

---

[1] TOSCANINI: a famous Italian conductor.
[2] RIDE OF THE VALKYRIES: a musical piece by Richard Wagner, notable for its vigor.

mirror. Outside, Mrs. Frank, feeling sorry for Dussel, comes over, knocking at the girls' door.]

MRS. FRANK [*outside*]. May I come in?

MARGOT. Come in, Mother.

MRS. FRANK [*shutting the door behind her*]. Mr. Dussel's impatient to get in here.

ANNE [*still with the brassière*]. Heavens, he takes the room for himself the entire day.

MRS. FRANK [*gently*]. Anne, dear, you're not going in again tonight to see Peter?

ANNE [*dignified*]. That is my intention.

MRS. FRANK. But you've already spent a great deal of time in there today.

ANNE. I was in there exactly twice. Once to get the dictionary, and then three-quarters of an hour before supper.

MRS. FRANK. Aren't you afraid you're disturbing him?

ANNE. Mother, I have some intuition.

MRS. FRANK. Then may I ask you this much, Anne. Please don't shut the door when you go in.

ANNE. You sound like Mrs. Van Daan! [*She throws the brassière back in Margot's sewing basket and picks up her blouse, putting it on.*]

MRS. FRANK. No. No. I don't mean to suggest anything wrong. I only wish that you wouldn't expose yourself to criticism . . . that you wouldn't give Mrs. Van Daan the opportunity to be unpleasant.

ANNE. Mrs. Van Daan doesn't need an opportunity to be unpleasant!

MRS. FRANK. Everyone's on edge, worried about Mr. Kraler. This is one more thing . . .

ANNE. I'm sorry, Mother. I'm going to Peter's room. I'm not going to let Petronella Van Daan spoil our friendship.

[*Mrs. Frank hesitates for a second, then goes out, closing the door after her. She gets a pack of playing cards and sits at the center table, playing solitaire. In Anne's room Margot hands the finished skirt to Anne. As Anne is putting it on, Margot takes off her high-heeled shoes and stuffs paper in the toes so that Anne can wear them.*]

MARGOT [*to Anne*]. Why don't you two talk in the main room? It'd save a lot of trouble. It's hard on Mother, having to listen to those remarks from Mrs. Van Daan and not say a word.

ANNE. Why doesn't she say a word? I think it's ridiculous to take it and take it.

MARGOT. You don't understand Mother at all, do you? She can't talk back. She's not like you. It's just not in her nature to fight back.

ANNE. Anyway . . . the only one I worry about is you. I feel awfully guilty about you. [*She sits on the stool near Margot, putting on Margot's high-heeled shoes.*]

MARGOT. What about?

ANNE. I mean, every time I go into Peter's room, I have a feeling I may be hurting you. [*Margot shakes her head.*] I know if it were me, I'd be wild. I'd be desperately jealous, if it were me.

MARGOT. Well, I'm not.

ANNE. You don't feel badly? Really? Truly? You're not jealous?

MARGOT. Of course I'm jealous . . . jealous that you've got something to get up in the morning for . . . But jealous of you and Peter? No.

[*Anne goes back to the mirror.*]

ANNE. Maybe there's nothing to be jealous of. Maybe he doesn't really like me. Maybe I'm just taking the place of his cat . . . [*She picks up a pair of short, white gloves, putting them on.*] Wouldn't you like to come in with us?

MARGOT. I have a book.

[*The sound of the children playing outside fades out. In the main room Dussel can stand it no longer. He jumps up, going to the bedroom door and knocking sharply.*]

DUSSEL. Will you please let me in my room!

ANNE. Just a minute, dear, dear Mr. Dussel. [*She picks up her Mother's pink stole and adjusts it elegantly over her shoulder, then gives a last look in the mirror.*] Well, here I go . . . to run the gauntlet. [*She starts out, followed by Margot.*]

DUSSEL [*as she appears—sarcastic*]. Thank you so much.

[*Dussel goes into his room. Anne goes toward Peter's room, passing Mrs. Van Daan and her parents at the center table.*]

MRS. VAN DAAN. My God, look at her! [*Anne pays no attention. She knocks at Peter's door.*] I don't know what good it is to have a son. I never see him. He wouldn't care if I killed myself. [*Peter opens the door and stands aside for Anne to come in.*] Just a minute, Anne. [*She goes to them at the door.*] I'd like to say a few words to my son. Do you mind? [*Peter and Anne stand waiting.*] Peter, I don't want you staying up till all hours tonight. You've got to have your sleep. You're a growing boy. You hear?

MRS. FRANK. Anne won't stay late. She's going to bed promptly at nine. Aren't you, Anne?

ANNE. Yes, Mother . . . [*To Mrs. Van Daan*] May we go now?

MRS. VAN DAAN. Are you asking me? I didn't know I had anything to say about it.

MRS. FRANK. Listen for the chimes, Anne dear.

[*The two young people go off into Peter's room, shutting the door after them.*]

MRS. VAN DAAN [*to Mrs. Frank*]. In my day it was the boys who called on the girls. Not the girls on the boys.

MRS. FRANK. You know how young people like to feel that they have secrets. Peter's room is the only place where they can talk.

MRS. VAN DAAN. Talk! That's not what they called it when I was young.

[*Mrs. Van Daan goes off to the bathroom. Margot settles down to read her book. Mr. Frank puts his papers away and brings a chess game to the center table. He and Mrs. Frank start to play. In Peter's room, Anne speaks to Peter, indignant, humiliated.*]

ANNE. Aren't they awful? Aren't they impossible? Treating us as if we were still in the nursery. [*She sits on the cot. Peter gets a bottle of pop and two glasses.*]

PETER. Don't let it bother you. It doesn't bother me.

ANNE. I suppose you can't really blame them . . . *they* think back to what they were like at our age. They don't realize how much more advanced we are . . . When you think what wonderful discussions we've had! . . . Oh, I forgot. I was going to bring you some more pictures.

PETER. Oh, these are fine, thanks.

ANNE. Don't you want some more? Miep

just brought me some new ones.

PETER. Maybe later. [*He gives her a glass of pop and taking some for himself, sits down facing her.*]

ANNE [*looking up at one of the photographs*]. I remember when I got that . . . I won it. I bet Jopie that I could eat five ice cream cones. We'd all been playing ping pong . . . We used to have heavenly times . . . we'd finish up with ice cream at the Delphi, or the Oasis, where Jews were allowed . . . there'd always be a lot of boys . . . we'd laugh and joke . . . I'd like to go back to it for a few days or a week. But after that I know I'd be bored to death. I think more seriously about life now. I want to be a journalist . . . or something. I love to write. What

do you want to do?

PETER. I thought I might go off some place . . . work on a farm or something . . . some job that doesn't take much brains.

ANNE. You shouldn't talk that way. You've got the most awful inferiority complex.

PETER. I know I'm not smart.

ANNE. That isn't true. You're much better than I am in dozens of things . . . arithmetic and algebra and . . . well, you're a million times better than I am in algebra. [*With sudden directness*] You like Margot, don't you? Right from the start you liked her, liked her much better than me.

PETER [*uncomfortably*]. Oh, I don't know.

[*In the main room Mrs. Van Daan comes from the bathroom and goes over to the sink, polishing a coffeepot.]*

ANNE. It's all right. Everyone feels that way. Margot's so good. She's sweet and bright and beautiful and I'm not.

PETER. I wouldn't say that.

ANNE. Oh, no, I'm not. I know that. I know quite well that I'm not a beauty. I never have been and never shall be.

PETER. I don't agree at all. I think you're pretty.

ANNE. That's not true!

PETER. And another thing. You've changed . . . from at first, I mean.

ANNE. I have?

PETER. I used to think you were awful noisy.

ANNE. And what do you think now, Peter? How have I changed?

PETER. Well . . . er . . . you're . . . quieter.

[In his room Dussel takes his pajamas and toilet articles and goes into the bathroom to change.]

ANNE. I'm glad you don't just hate me.

PETER. I never said that.

ANNE. I bet when you get out of here you'll never think of me again.

PETER. That's crazy.

ANNE. When you get back with all of your friends, you're going to say . . . now what did I ever see in that Mrs. Quack Quack.

PETER. I haven't got any friends.

ANNE. Oh, Peter, of course you have. Everyone has friends.

PETER. Not me. I don't want any. I get along all right without them.

ANNE. Does that mean you can get along without me? I think of myself as your friend.

PETER. No. If they were all like you, it'd be different.

[He takes the glasses and the bottle and puts them away. There is a second's silence and then Anne speaks, hesitantly, shyly.]

ANNE. Peter, did you ever kiss a girl?

PETER. Yes. Once.

ANNE *[to cover her feelings]*. That picture's crooked. *[Peter goes over, straightening the photograph.]* Was she pretty?

PETER. Huh?

ANNE. The girl that you kissed.

PETER. I don't know. I was blindfolded. *[He comes back and sits down again.]* It was a party. One of those kissing games.

ANNE *[relieved]*. Oh, I don't suppose that really counts, does it?

PETER. It didn't with me.

ANNE. I've been kissed twice. Once a man I'd never seen before kissed me on the cheek when he picked me up off the ice and I was crying. And the other was Mr. Koophuis, a friend of Father's who kissed my hand. You wouldn't say those counted, would you?

PETER. I wouldn't say so.

ANNE. I know almost for certain that Margot would never kiss anyone unless she was engaged to them. And I'm sure too that Mother never touched a man before Pim. But I don't know . . . things are so different now. . . . What do you think? Do you think a girl shouldn't kiss anyone except if she's engaged or something? It's so hard to try to think what to do, when here we are with the whole world falling around our ears and you think . . . well . . . you don't know what's going to happen tomorrow and . . . What do you think?

PETER. I suppose it'd depend on the girl. Some girls, anything they do's wrong.

But others . . . well . . . it wouldn't necessarily be wrong with them. [*The carillon starts to strike nine o'clock.*] I've always thought that when two people . . .

ANNE. Nine o'clock. I have to go.

PETER. That's right.

ANNE [*without moving*]. Good night.

[*There is a second's pause, then Peter gets up and moves toward the door.*]

PETER. You won't let them stop you coming?

ANNE. No. [*She rises and starts for the door.*] Sometime I might bring my diary. There are so many things in it that I want to talk over with you. There's a lot about you.

PETER. What kind of thing?

ANNE. I wouldn't want you to see some of it. I thought you were a nothing, just the way you thought about me.

PETER. Did you change your mind, the way I changed my mind about you?

ANNE. Well . . . You'll see . . .

[*For a second Anne stands looking up at Peter, longing for him to kiss her. As he makes no move she turns away. Then suddenly Peter grabs her awkwardly in his arms, kissing her on the cheek. Anne walks out dazed. She stands for a minute, her back to the people in the main room. As she regains her poise she goes to her mother and father and Margot, silently kissing them. They murmur their good nights to her. As she is about to open her bedroom door, she catches sight of Mrs. Van Daan. She goes quickly to her, taking her face in her hands and kissing her first on one cheek and then on the other. Then she hurries off into her room. Mrs. Van Daan looks after her,*] *and then looks over at Peter's room. Her suspicions are confirmed.*]

MRS. VAN DAAN. [*She knows.*] Ah hah!

[*The lights dim out. The curtain falls on the scene. In the darkness Anne's voice comes faintly at first and then with growing strength.*]

ANNE'S VOICE. By this time we all know each other so well that if anyone starts to tell a story, the rest can finish it for him. We're having to cut down still further on our meals. What makes it worse, the rats have been at work again. They've carried off some of our precious food. Even Mr. Dussel wishes now that Mouschi was here. Thursday, the twentieth of April, nineteen forty-four. Invasion fever is mounting every day. Miep tells us that people outside talk of nothing else. For myself, life has become much more pleasant. I often go to Peter's room after supper. Oh, don't think I'm in love, because I'm not. But it does make life more bearable to have someone with whom you can exchange views. No more tonight. P.S. . . . I must be honest. I must confess that I actually live for the next meeting. Is there anything lovelier than to sit under the skylight and feel the sun on your cheeks and have a darling boy in your arms? I admit now that I'm glad the Van Daans had a son and not a daughter. I've outgrown another dress. That's the third. I'm having to wear Margot's clothes after all. I'm working hard on my French and am now reading *La Belle Nivernaise*.[1]

---

[1] LA BELLE NIVERNAISE: A French novel by Alphonse Daudet.

[*As she is saying the last lines, the curtain rises on the scene. The lights dim on, as Anne's voice fades out.*]

SCENE THREE: *It is night, a few weeks later. Everyone is in bed. There is complete quiet. In the Van Daans' room a match flares up for a moment and then is quickly put out. Mr. Van Daan, in bare feet, dressed in underwear and trousers, is dimly seen coming stealthily down the stairs and into the main room, where Mr. and Mrs. Frank and Margot are sleeping. He goes to the food safe and again lights a match. Then he cautiously opens the safe, taking out a half-loaf of bread. As he closes the safe, it creaks. He stands rigid. Mrs. Frank sits up in bed. She sees him.*

MRS. FRANK [*screaming*]. Otto! Otto! Komme schnell![1]

[*The rest of the people wake, hurriedly getting up.*]

MR. FRANK. Was ist los? Was ist passiert?[2]

[*Dussel, followed by Anne, comes from his room.*]

MRS. FRANK [*as she rushes over to Mr. Van Daan*]. Er stiehlt das Essen![3]

DUSSEL [*grabbing Mr. Van Daan*]. You! You! Give me that.

MRS. VAN DAAN [*coming down the stairs*]. Putti . . . Putti . . . what is it?

DUSSEL [*his hands on Van Daan's neck*]. You dirty thief . . . stealing food . . . you good-for-nothing . . .

MR. FRANK. Mr. Dussel! For God's sake!

---

[1] KOMME SCHNELL!: Come quick!
[2] WAS IST LOS? WAS IST PASSIERT?: What's wrong? What's going on?
[3] ER STIEHLT DAS ESSEN!: He's stealing food!

Help me, Peter!

[*Peter comes over, trying, with Mr. Frank, to separate the two struggling men.*]

PETER. Let him go! Let go!

[*Dussel drops Mr. Van Daan, pushing him away. He shows them the end of a loaf of bread that he has taken from Van Daan.*]

DUSSEL. You greedy, selfish . . . !

[*Margot turns on the lights.*]

MRS. VAN DAAN. Putti . . . what is it?

[*All of Mrs. Frank's gentleness, her self-control, is gone. She is outraged, in a frenzy of indignation.*]

MRS. FRANK. The bread! He was stealing the bread!

DUSSEL. It was you, and all the time we thought it was the rats!

MR. FRANK. Mr. Van Daan, how could you!

MR. VAN DAAN. I'm hungry.

MRS. FRANK. We're all of us hungry! I see the children getting thinner and thinner. Your own son Peter . . . I've heard him moan in his sleep, he's so hungry. And you come in the night and steal food that should go to them . . . to the children!

MRS. VAN DAAN [*going to Mr. Van Daan protectively*]. He needs more food than the rest of us. He's used to more. He's a big man.

[*Mr. Van Daan breaks away, going over and sitting on the couch.*]

MRS. FRANK [*turning on Mrs. Van Daan*]. And you . . . you're worse than he is! You're a mother, and yet you sacrifice your child to this man . . . this . . . this . . .

MR. FRANK. Edith! Edith!

[*Margot picks up the pink woolen stole, putting it over her mother's shoulders.*]

MRS. FRANK [*paying no attention, going on to Mrs. Van Daan*]. Don't think I haven't seen you! Always saving the choicest bits for him! I've watched you day after day and I've held my tongue. But not any longer! Not after this! Now I want him to go! I want him to get out of here!

MR. FRANK. Edith!

MR. VAN DAAN. Get out } [*Together*]
of here?

MRS. VAN DAAN. What do you mean?

MRS. FRANK. Just that! Take your things and get out!

MR. FRANK [*to Mrs. Frank*]. You're speaking in anger. You cannot mean what you are saying.

MRS FRANK. I mean exactly that!

[*Mrs. Van Daan takes a cover from the Franks' bed, pulling it about her.*]

MR. FRANK. For two long years we have lived here, side by side. We have respected each other's rights . . . we have managed to live in peace. Are we now going to throw it all away? I know this will never happen again, will it, Mr. Van Daan?

MR. VAN DAAN. No. No.

MRS. FRANK. He steals once! He'll steal again!

[*Mr. Van Daan, holding his stomach, starts for the bathroom. Anne puts her arms around him, helping him up the step.*]

MR. FRANK. Edith, please. Let us be calm. We'll all go to our rooms . . . and afterwards we'll sit down quietly and talk this out . . . we'll find some way . . .

MRS. FRANK. No! No! No more talk! I want them to leave!

MRS. VAN DAAN. You'd put us out, on the streets?

MRS. FRANK. There are other hiding places.

MRS. VAN DAAN. A cellar . . . a closet. I know. And we have no money left even to pay for that.

MRS. FRANK. I'll give you money. Out of my own pocket I'll give it gladly.

[*She gets her purse from a shelf and comes back with it.*]

MRS. VAN DAAN. Mr. Frank, you told Putti you'd never forget what he'd done for you when you came to Amsterdam. You said you could never repay him, that you . . .

MRS. FRANK [*counting out money*]. If my husband had any obligation to you, he's paid it, over and over.

MR. FRANK. Edith, I've never seen you like this before. I don't know you.

MRS. FRANK. I should have spoken out long ago.

DUSSEL. You can't be nice to some people.

MRS. VAN DAAN [*turning on Dussel*]. There would have been plenty for all of us, if *you* hadn't come in here!

MR. FRANK. We don't need the Nazis to destroy us. We're destroying ourselves.

[*He sits down, with his head in his hands. Mrs. Frank goes to Mrs. Van Daan.*]

MRS. FRANK [*giving Mrs. Van Daan some money*]. Give this to Miep. She'll find you a place.

ANNE. Mother, you're not putting *Peter* out. Peter hasn't done anything.

MRS. FRANK. He'll stay, of course. When I say I must protect the children, I mean Peter too.

[*Peter rises from the steps where he has been sitting.*]

PETER. I'd have to go if Father goes.

[*Mr. Van Daan comes from the bathroom. Mrs. Van Daan hurries to him and takes him to the couch. Then she gets water from the sink to bathe his face.*]

MRS. FRANK [*while this is going on*]. He's no father to you . . . that man! He doesn't know what it is to be a father!

PETER [*starting for his room*]. I wouldn't feel right. I couldn't stay.

MRS. FRANK. Very well, then. I'm sorry.

ANNE [*rushing over to Peter*]. No, Peter! No! [*Peter goes into his room, closing the door after him. Anne turns back to her mother, crying.*] I don't care about the food. They can have mine! I don't want it! Only don't send them away. It'll be daylight soon. They'll be caught . . .

MARGOT [*putting her arms comfortingly around Anne*]. Please, Mother!

MRS. FRANK. They're not going now. They'll stay here until Miep finds them a place. [*To Mrs. Van Daan*] But one thing I insist on! He must never come down here again! He must never come to this room where the food is stored! We'll divide what we have . . . an equal share for each! [*Dussel hurries over to get a sack of potatoes from the food safe. Mrs. Frank goes on, to Mrs. Van Daan.*] You can cook it here and take it up to him.

[*Dussel brings the sack of potatoes back to the center table.*]

MARGOT. Oh, no. No. We haven't sunk so far that we're going to fight over a handful of rotten potatoes.

DUSSEL [*dividing the potatoes into piles*].

Mrs. Frank, Mr. Frank, Margot, Anne, Peter, Mrs. Van Daan, Mr. Van Daan, myself . . . Mrs. Frank . . .

[*The buzzer sounds in Miep's signal.*]

MR. FRANK. It's Miep! [*He hurries over, getting his overcoat and putting it on.*]

MARGOT. At this hour?

MRS. FRANK. It is trouble.

MR. FRANK [*as he starts down to unbolt the door*]. I beg you, don't let her see a thing like this!

MR. DUSSEL [*counting without stopping*]. . . . Anne, Peter, Mrs. Van Daan, Mr. Van Daan, myself . . .

MARGOT [*to Dussel*]. Stop it! Stop it!

DUSSEL. . . . Mr. Frank, Margot, Anne, Peter, Mrs. Van Daan, Mr. Van Daan, myself, Mrs. Frank . . .

MRS. VAN DAAN. You're keeping the big ones for yourself! All the big ones . . . Look at the size of that! . . . And that! . . .

[*Dussel continues on with his dividing. Peter, with his shirt and trousers on, comes from his room.*]

MARGOT. Stop it! Stop it!

[*We hear Miep's excited voice speaking to Mr. Frank below.*]

MIEP. Mr. Frank . . . the most wonderful news! . . . The invasion has begun!

MR. FRANK. Go on, tell them! Tell them!

[*Miep comes running up the steps, ahead of Mr. Frank. She has a man's raincoat on over her nightclothes and a bunch of orange-colored flowers in her hand.*]

MIEP. Did you hear that, everybody? Did you hear what I said? The invasion has begun! The invasion!

[*They all stare at Miep, unable to grasp what she is telling them. Peter is the first to recover his wits.*]

PETER. Where?

MRS. VAN DAAN. When? When, Miep?

MIEP. It began early this morning . . .

[*As she talks on, the realization of what she has said begins to dawn on them. Everyone goes crazy. A wild demonstration takes place. Mrs. Frank hugs Mr. Van Daan.*]

MRS. FRANK. Oh, Mr. Van Daan, did you hear that?

[*Dussel embraces Mrs. Van Daan. Peter grabs a frying pan and parades around the room, beating on it, singing the Dutch National Anthem. Anne and Margot follow him, singing, weaving in and out among the excited grownups. Margot breaks away to take the flowers from Miep and distribute them to everyone. While this pandemonium is going on Mrs. Frank tries to make herself heard above the excitement.*]

MRS. FRANK [*to Miep*]. How do you know?

MIEP. The radio . . . The B.B.C.[1]! They said they landed on the coast of Normandy!

PETER. The British?

MIEP. British, Americans, French, Dutch, Poles, Norwegians . . . all of them! More than four thousand ships! Churchill spoke, and General Eisenhower! D-Day they call it!

MR. FRANK. Thank God, it's come!

MRS. VAN DAAN. At last!

MIEP [*starting out*]. I'm going to tell Mr. Kraler. This'll be better than any blood transfusion.

---

[1] B.B.C.: British Broadcasting Corporation, the national British radio network.

MR. FRANK [*stopping her*]. What part of Normandy did they land, did they say?

MIEP. Normandy . . . that's all I know now . . . I'll be up the minute I hear some more! [*She goes hurriedly out.*]

MR. FRANK [*to Mrs. Frank*]. What did I tell you? What did I tell you?

[*Mrs. Frank indicates that he has forgotten to bolt the door after Miep. He hurries down the steps. Mr. Van Daan, sitting on the couch, suddenly breaks into a convulsive sob. Everybody looks at him, bewildered.*]

MRS. VAN DAAN [*hurrying to him*]. Putti! Putti! What is it? What happened?

MR. VAN DAAN. Please. I'm so ashamed.

[*Mr. Frank comes back up the steps.*]

DUSSEL. Oh, for God's sake!

MRS. VAN DAAN. Don't, Putti.

MARGOT. It doesn't matter now!

MR. FRANK [*going to Mr. Van Daan*]. Didn't you hear what Miep said? The invasion has come! We're going to be liberated! This is a time to celebrate. [*He embraces Mrs. Frank and then hurries to the cupboard and gets the cognac and a glass.*]

MR. VAN DAAN. To steal bread from children!

MRS. FRANK. We've all done things that we're ashamed of.

ANNE. Look at me, the way I've treated Mother . . . so mean and horrid to her.

MRS. FRANK. No, Anneke, no.

[*Anne runs to her mother, putting her arms around her.*]

ANNE. Oh, Mother, I was. I was awful.

MR. VAN DAAN. Not like me. No one is as bad as me!

DUSSEL [*to Mr. Van Daan*]. Stop it now! Let's be happy!

MR. FRANK [*giving Mr. Van Daan a glass of cognac*]. Here! Here! *Schnapps! Locheim!*[1]

[*Van Daan takes the cognac. They all watch him. He gives them a feeble smile. Anne puts up her fingers in a V-for-Victory sign. As Van Daan gives an answering V-sign, they are startled to hear a loud sob from behind them. It is Mrs. Frank, stricken with remorse. She is sitting on the other side of the room.*]

MRS. FRANK [*through her sobs*]. When I think of the terrible things I said . . .

[*Mr. Frank, Anne and Margot hurry to her, trying to comfort her. Mr. Van Daan brings her his glass of cognac.*]

MR. VAN DAAN. No! No! You were right!

MRS. FRANK. That I should speak that way to you! . . . Our friends! . . . Our guests! [*She starts to cry again.*]

DUSSEL. Stop it, you're spoiling the whole invasion!

[*As they are comforting her, the lights dim out. The curtain falls.*]

ANNE'S VOICE [*faintly at first and then with growing strength*]. We're all in much better spirits these days. There's still excellent news of the invasion. The best part about it is that I have a feeling that friends are coming. Who knows? Maybe I'll be back in school by fall. Ha, ha! The joke is on us! The warehouse man doesn't know a thing and we are paying him all that money! . . . Wednesday, the second of July, nineteen forty-four. The invasion seems temporarily to be bogged down. Mr. Kraler has to have an operation, which looks bad. The Gestapo have found the radio that was stolen. Mr. Dussel says they'll trace it back and back to the thief, and then, it's just a matter of time till they get to us. Everyone is low. Even poor Pim can't raise their spirits. I have often been downcast myself . . . but never in despair. I can shake off everything if I write. But . . . and that is the great question . . . will I ever be able to write well? I want to so much. I want to go on living even after my death. Another birthday has gone by, so now I am fifteen. Already I know what I want. I have a goal, an opinion.

[*As this is being said—the curtain rises on the scene, the lights dim on, and Anne's voice fades out.*]

SCENE FOUR: *It is an afternoon a few weeks later . . . Everyone but Margot is in the main room. There is a sense of great tension.*

Both Mrs. Frank and Mr. Van Daan are nervously pacing back and forth, Dussel is standing at the window, looking down fixedly at the street below. Peter is at the center table, trying to do his lessons. Anne sits opposite him, writing in her diary. Mrs. Van Daan is seated on the couch, her eyes on Mr. Frank as he sits reading.

The sound of a telephone ringing comes from the office below. They all are rigid, listening tensely. Mr. Dussel rushes down to Mr. Frank.

DUSSEL. There it goes again, the telephone! Mr. Frank, do you hear?

MR. FRANK [*quietly*]. Yes. I hear.

DUSSEL [*pleading, insistent*]. But this is the

---

[1] SCHNAPPS! LOCHEIM!: A drink! To life! (a traditional Yiddish toast.)

third time, Mr. Frank! The third time in quick succession! It's a signal! I tell you it's Miep, trying to get us! For some reason she can't come to us and she's trying to warn us of something!

MR. FRANK. Please. Please.

MR. VAN DAAN [*to Dussel*]. You're wasting your breath.

DUSSEL. Something has happened, Mr. Frank. For three days now Miep hasn't been to see us! And today not a man has come to work. There hasn't been a sound in the building!

MRS. FRANK. Perhaps it's Sunday. We may have lost track of the days.

MR. VAN DAAN [*to Anne*]. You with the diary there. What day is it?

DUSSEL [*going to Mrs. Frank*]. I don't lose track of the days! I know exactly what day it is! It's Friday, the fourth of August. Friday, and not a man at work. [*He rushes back to Mr. Frank, pleading with him, almost in tears.*] I tell you Mr. Kraler's dead. That's the only explanation. He's dead and they've closed down the building, and Miep's trying to tell us!

MR. FRANK. She'd never telephone us.

DUSSEL [*frantic*]. Mr. Frank, answer that! I beg you, answer it!

MR. FRANK. No.

MR. VAN DAAN. Just pick it up and listen. You don't have to speak. Just listen and see if it's Miep.

DUSSEL [*speaking at the same time*]. For God's sake . . . I ask you.

MR. FRANK. No. I've told you, no. I'll do nothing that might let anyone know we're in the building.

PETER. Mr. Frank's right.

MR. VAN DAAN. There's no need to tell us what side you're on.

MR. FRANK. If we wait patiently, quietly, I believe that help will come.

[*There is silence for a minute as they all listen to the telephone ringing.*]

DUSSEL. I'm going down. [*He rushes down the steps. Mr. Frank tries ineffectually to hold him. Dussel runs to the lower door, unbolting it. The telephone stops ringing. Dussel bolts the door and comes slowly back up the steps.*] Too late. [*Mr. Frank goes to Margot in Anne's bedroom.*]

MR. VAN DAAN. So we just wait here until we die.

MRS. VAN DAAN [*hysterically*]. I can't stand it! I'll kill myself! I'll kill myself!

MR. VAN DAAN. For God's sake, stop it!

[*In the distance, a German military band is heard playing a Viennese waltz*]

MRS. VAN DAAN. I think you'd be glad if I did! I think you want me to die!

MR. VAN DAAN. Whose fault is it we're here? [*Mrs. Van Daan starts for her room. He follows, talking at her.*] We could've been safe somewhere . . . in America or Switzerland. But no! No! You wouldn't leave when I wanted to. You couldn't leave your things. You couldn't leave your precious furniture.

MRS. VAN DAAN. Don't touch me!

[*She hurries up the stairs, followed by Mr. Van Daan. Peter, unable to bear it, goes to his room. Anne looks after him, deeply concerned. Dussel returns to his post at the window. Mr. Frank comes back into the main room and takes a book, trying to read. Mrs. Frank sits near the sink, starting to peel some potatoes. Anne quietly goes to Peter's room, closing the door after her. Peter is lying*] *face down on the cot. Anne leans over him, holding him in her arms, trying to bring him out of his despair.*]

ANNE. Look, Peter, the sky. [*She looks up through the skylight*]. What a lovely, lovely day! Aren't the clouds beautiful? You know what I do when it seems as if I couldn't stand being cooped up for one more minute? I *think* myself out. I think myself on a walk in the park where I used to go with Pim. Where the jonquils and the crocus and violets grow down the slopes. You know the most wonderful part about *thinking* yourself out? You can have it any way you like. You can have roses and violets and chrysanthemums all blooming at the same time . . . It's funny . . . I used to take it all for granted . . . and now I've gone crazy about everything to do with nature. Haven't you?

PETER. I've just gone crazy. I think if something doesn't happen soon . . . if we don't get out of here . . . I can't stand much more of it!

ANNE [*softly*]. I wish you had a religion, Peter.

PETER. No, thanks! Not me!

ANNE. Oh, I don't mean you have to be Orthodox[1] . . . or believe in heaven and hell and purgatory and things . . . I just mean some religion . . . it doesn't matter what. Just to believe in something! When I think of all that's out there . . . the trees . . . and flowers . . . and sea gulls . . . when I think of the dearness of you, Peter, . . . and the goodness of the people we know . . . Mr. Kraler, Miep, Dirk, the vegetable man, all risking their

---

[1] ORTHODOX: the most strictly observant branch of Judaism.

lives for us every day . . . When I think of these good things, I'm not afraid any more . . . I find myself, and God, and I . . .

[*Peter interrupts, getting up and walking away.*]

PETER. That's fine! But when I begin to think, I get mad! Look at us, hiding out for two years. Not able to move! Caught here like . . . waiting for them to come and get us . . . and all for what?

ANNE. We're not the only people that've had to suffer. There've always been people that've had to . . . sometimes one race . . . sometimes another . . . and yet . . .

PETER. That doesn't make me feel any better!

ANNE [*going to him*]. I know it's terrible, trying to have any faith . . . when people are doing such horrible . . . But you know what I sometimes think? I think the world may be going through a phase, the way I was with Mother. It'll pass, maybe not for hundreds of years, but some day . . . I still believe, in spite of everything, that people are really good at heart.

PETER. I want to see something now . . . Not a thousand years from now!

[*He goes over, sitting down again on the cot.*]

ANNE. But, Peter, if you'd only look at it as part of a great pattern . . . that we're just a little minute in the life . . . [*She breaks off.*] Listen to us, going at each other like a couple of stupid grownups! Look at the sky now. Isn't it lovely? [*She holds out her hand to him. Peter takes it and rises, standing with her at the window looking out, his arms around her.*] Some day, when we're outside again, I'm going to . . .

[*She breaks off as she hears the sound of a car, its brakes squealing as it comes to a sudden stop. The people in the other rooms also become aware of the sound. They listen tensely. Another car roars up to a screeching stop. Anne and Peter come from Peter's room. Mr. and Mrs. Van Daan creep down the stairs. Dussel comes out from his room. Everyone is listening, hardly breathing. A doorbell clangs again and again in the building below. Mr. Frank starts quietly down the steps to the door. Dussel and Peter follow him. The others stand rigid, waiting, terrified.*

In a few seconds Dussel comes stumbling back up the steps. He shakes off Peter's help and goes to his room. Mr. Frank bolts the door below, and comes slowly back up the steps. Their eyes are all on him as he stands there for a minute. They realize that what they feared has happened. Mrs. Van Daan starts to whimper. Mr. Van Daan puts her gently in a chair, and then hurries off up the stairs to their room to collect their things. Peter goes to comfort his mother. There is a sound of violent pounding on a door below.]

MR. FRANK [*quietly*]. For the past two years we have lived in fear. Now we can live in hope.

[*The pounding below becomes more insistent. There are muffled sounds of voices, shouting commands.*

MEN'S VOICES. *Auf machen! Da drinnen!*

Auf machen! Schnell! Schnell! Schnell![1] *etc., etc.*

[*The street door below is forced open. We hear the heavy tread of footsteps coming up. Mr. Frank gets two school-bags from the shelves, and gives one to Anne and the other to Margot. He goes to get a bag for Mrs. Frank. The sound of feet coming up grows louder. Peter comes to Anne, kissing her good-by, then he goes to his room to collect his things. The buzzer of their door starts to ring. Mr. Frank brings Mrs. Frank a bag. They stand together, waiting. We hear the thud of gun butts on the door, trying to break it down.*

Anne stands, holding her school satchel, looking over at her father and mother with a soft, reassuring smile. She is no longer a child, but a woman with courage to meet whatever lies ahead.

The lights dim out. The curtain falls on the scene. We hear a mighty crash as the door is shattered. After a second Anne's voice is heard.]

ANNE'S VOICE. And so it seems our stay is over. They are waiting for us now. They've allowed us five minutes to get our things. We can each take a bag and whatever it will hold of clothing. Nothing else. So, dear Diary, that means I must leave you behind. Good-by for a while. P.S. Please, please, Miep, or Mr. Kraler, or anyone else. If you should find this diary, will you please keep it safe for me, because some day I hope . . .

[*Her voice stops abruptly. There is silence. After a second the curtain rises.*]

---

[1] AUF MACHEN . . . SCHNELL!: Open up! You in there! Open up! Quick! Quick! Quick!

SCENE FIVE: *It is again the afternoon in November, 1945. The rooms are as we saw them in the first scene. Mr. Kraler has joined Miep and Mr. Frank. There are coffee cups on the table. We see a great change in Mr. Frank. He is calm now. His bitterness is gone. He slowly turns a few pages of the diary. They are blank.*]

MR. FRANK. No more. [*He closes the diary and puts it down on the couch beside him.*]

MIEP. I'd gone to the country to find food. When I got back the block was surrounded by police...

MR. KRALER. We made it our business to learn how they knew. It was the thief ... the thief who told them.

[*Miep goes up to the gas burner, bringing back a pot of coffee.*]

MR. FRANK [*after a pause*]. It seems strange to say this, that anyone could be happy in a concentration camp. But Anne was happy in the camp in Holland where they first took us. After two years of being shut up in these rooms, she could be out ... out in the sunshine and the fresh air that she loved.

MIEP [*offering the coffee to Mr. Frank*]. A little more?

MR. FRANK [*holding out his cup to her*]. The news of the war was good. The British and Americans were sweeping through France. We felt sure that they would get to us in time. In September we were told that we were to be shipped to Poland ... The men to one camp. The women to another. I was sent to Auschwitz. They went to Belsen.[1] In January we were freed, the few of us who were left. The war wasn't yet over, so it took us a long time to get home. We'd be sent here and there behind the lines where we'd be safe. Each time our train would stop ... at a siding, or a crossing ... we'd all get out and go from group to group ... Where were you? Were you at Belsen? At Buchenwald? At Mauthausen? Is it possible that you knew my wife? Did you ever see my husband? My son? My daughter? That's how I found out about my wife's death ... of Margot, the Van Daans ... Dussel. But Anne ... I still hoped. ... Yesterday I went to Rotterdam. I'd heard of a woman there. ... She'd been in Belsen with Anne ... I know now.

[*He picks up the diary again, and turns the pages back to find a certain passage. As he finds it we hear Anne's voice.*]

ANNE'S VOICE. In spite of everything, I still believe that people are really good at heart.

[*Mr. Frank slowly closes the diary.*]

MR. FRANK. She puts me to shame.

[*They are silent.*]

The CURTAIN *falls.*

---

[1] AUSCHWITZ, BELSEN: concentration camps. An estimated 30,000 prisoners were killed at Belsen, and over one million died at the infamous Auschwitz. Anne and Margot, weakened by hunger, both died of typhus only a few weeks before British troops liberated the camp.

FOR DISCUSSION

1. Each of the characters in the play reacts differently to the strains of the long confinement. Review each person's actions and speech; what do they reveal about each one's personality and philosophy? Anne's character is unique throughout the play; what traits does she alone possess that make her stand out from the others? What prompts her father to say "She puts me to shame"? Support your answers with specific references to lines and incidents in the play.

2. Anne is thirteen when her family goes into hiding. What common characteristics of a thirteen-year-old girl does she possess? How are these traits somewhat responsible for her problems with the others? In what ways does Anne change during the two year confinement?

3. Most of Anne's words and actions reveal her to be a person who is filled with hope and optimism. How do you know that she is also deeply affected by the ever-present fear of capture?

4. Peter and Anne are drawn together for a number of reasons; what are they? Anne at one point suggests that she has taken the place of Peter's lost cat—do you agree? Why are the visits to Peter's room so important to both of them?

5. During the argument caused by the discovery that Mr. Van Daan has been stealing food from the community supply, Mr. Frank exclaims in horror, "We don't need the Nazis to destroy us. We're destroying ourselves." What does he mean? Can you explain why Mrs. Frank, who has always before been the calm and reserved peacemaker, reacts with such fury to Mr. Van Daan's misdeed? How is the crisis resolved?

In Summary

FOR DISCUSSION

1. At the beginning of the play Mr. Frank speaks of Miep's suffering for the Jews she helped to hide. Miep answers, "It wasn't suffering. You can't say we suffered." What does she mean? What sacrifices did she and Mr. Kraler make for their Jewish friends? Why is this scene at the beginning, and the corresponding scene at the end of the play, so important to the play as a whole?

2. Except for a few vague offstage voices at the end of the play, we never actually meet a single Nazi. Nor do we witness the actual death of any character, or observe any incident of anti-Semitism. Can you, then, explain why this play is considered to provide a vividly dramatic portrait of the plight of the victims of the Nazis?

3. Anne suggests that the Nazi movement and the horrors it causes are comparable to the "phase" she has been going through, when she hurts her mother without really understanding why she is acting so cruelly. Re-examine the passage (page 549) in which Anne tries to explain why she acts thoughtlessly. Do you find that her analysis of her own behavior provides any clue to the larger question of why people who are supposedly civilized and supposedly normally kind are at times capable of great evil? Do you agree that humanity goes through "phases" but is in general "growing up," that is, becoming more compassionate and responsible? Defend your conclusions with evidence from history and your personal experiences, as well as from this play.

OTHER THINGS TO DO

1. One of the basic differences between a play and other types of literature is that the play must depend almost solely on the words and actions of the characters to convey emotions and motivations. A play can contain no real descriptive passages, so that the audience is left to imagine for itself what sorts of private thoughts and impressions each character may be having. Turn to a portion of your favorite scene in the play. Rewrite it, inserting good descriptive passages as if you were writing a story or novel.

2. Plays are meant to be seen and heard, not just read. A group of interested students might prepare one or two scenes in the play for presentation to the class. Be sure to schedule two or three rehearsals before the presentation so that it will be smooth and natural-sounding.

3. Imagine that you have been selected to be an actor in a performance of this play. One of your first jobs will be to make sure that you fully understand the nature of the rôle you are to play. Choose one character in the play, and write a thorough explanation of what sort of person you imagine him or her to be. You will want to use the facts and impressions you have gleaned from a careful reading of the play, but you will want to supplement this information, either with further research into the actual characters the play is about, or with the projections of your own imagination. In drawing your portrait, consider what sort of a life your character led before coming to the attic, how your character feels about each of the other characters, his secret fears and hopes, and so on.

4. This play is far more meaningful when it is understood in its historical context. Selected members of the class might research the conditions in Nazi-occupied countries during the Second World War and report significant findings to the rest of the class. Special reports should be included on the treatment of the Jews and the invasion of Holland.

The World of Words

THE DIARY OF ANNE FRANK

1. When the Franks went into hiding, according to Anne, they did so leaving the breakfast dishes in the sink (page 529). *Breakfast* is a compound word, made up of two separate words that together mean "end a period of doing without food." For to *fast* is to "do without food." But there is another *fast* in English, a word spelled and pronounced exactly that way but from a different source, and with a different meaning. Such words, spelled alike but with different origins and meanings, are called *homographs*, from *homo-*, meaning "same," and *-graph*, having to do with writing. To run *fast* is different from to break one's *fast*. How many different homographs does the dictionary give for *fast*? For *bark*? For *sound*? (Homographs are distinguished by separate entries in most dictionaries; several related meanings may be given for any one homograph.)

2. *Homophones* are words that are pronounced alike but are spelled differently and have different origins and meanings. "You said you'd rather die than wear overshoes," Mr. Frank reminds Anne (page 531). *Die* is a homophone. What is the difference between *die* and *dye*? Between *bear* and *bare*? Between *alter* and *altar*? Between *sum* and *some*? Between *steel* and *steal*? What other homophones do you know?

Reader's Choice

Anne Frank: The Diary of a Young Girl, *by Anne Frank.*

This is the actual diary which Anne kept while hiding from the Nazis. Many more details and experiences are described here than it was possible for the playwrights to include in their adaptation of the work, and students who were interested in the characters introduced by the play will find reading this document a stirring experience.

Anne Frank, A Portrait in Courage, *by Ernst Schnabel.*

Anne's life before, during, and after her period of hiding in the attic in Amsterdam is covered here for those interested in knowing more about the life of a courageous girl.

Children of the Resistance, *by Lore Cowan.*

Here are true stories about young people, members of the underground resistance organizations, who fought secretly and with great personal daring against the Nazis who occupied their homelands during World War II.

Dangerous Spring, *by Margot Benary Isbert.*

Karin, a German teenager, goes through the difficult transition to adulthood during the last days of World War II as the Nazi regime in Germany is collapsing. During this time, she acts as a translator for American G.I.'s who are liberating the German concentration camps.

Fiddler on the Roof, *by Joseph Stein.*

A Russian ghetto town is the setting for this heartwarming drama of Jewish family life in the era before the Russian Revolution. Despite their extreme poverty and the constant oppression under which they live, the villagers find in their faith the love of life and the courage which allows them to continue despite their difficulties.

Five Famous Plays 1940–1949, *selected by Henry Hewes.*

This distinctive collection contains such memorable plays as Thornton Wilder's *The Skin of Our Teeth,* Carson McCullers' *Member of the Wedding,* and *Lost in the Stars,* which is based on Alan Paton's *Cry, the Beloved Country.*

Sunrise at Campobello, *by Dore Schary.*

Showing determination and great personal courage, the young Franklin Delano Roosevelt spent three years in a battle he had to fight alone against polio. This play is a dramatization of his life during the years from 1921 to 1924.

Three Comedies of American Family Life, *edited by J. E. Mersand.*

I Remember Mama, Life with Father, and *You Can't Take It With You* are included in this delightful collection of plays. Who could forget father's tirades, or mama's bank account?

The Watch on the Bridge, *by David Garth.*

An American soldier in Germany, battle-weary and questioning his former idealistic values which now seem so out of place in face of the brutal realities of war, meets a young German girl who risks her life for him and helps him regain his will to go on fighting for the things he believes.

ABOUT THE AUTHORS

Isaac Asimov (1920–   ) "From 1939 to 1949, I thought of myself as a science fiction writer. From 1949 to 1958, I thought of myself as a biochemist. From 1958 to 1965, I thought of myself as a science fiction writer. Now I don't know what to think of myself. My current craze is history." Isaac Asimov has been all of these. He holds a Ph.D. in chemistry from Columbia University in New York City, and has written many books on science for the general reader and several books of history for young adults. He is best known for his science fiction, which is exciting as well as scientifically accurate.

Isaac Asimov

Mabel Ashe Beling (1887–1948)   Born in Albany, New York, Mrs. Beling was a leader in the crusade for women's voting rights early in this century. Later, in addition to rearing two sons, she found time to devote to writing. In the 1930's she published a number of short stories and magazine articles. Then her husband, who had lived in Ceylon for twenty years, interested her in the legends and folklore of India. Out of that interest grew a number of stories about that land. A selection of the best of these appears in her most popular book, *The Wicked Goldsmith.*

Lerone Bennett, Jr. (1928–   )   Born in Clarksdale, Mississippi, Bennett attended Morehouse College and Atlanta University, and in 1965 received an honorary doctorate degree from Morehouse. He is presently a senior editor of *Ebony* magazine, and is the author of several books. His poems, short stories, and articles have appeared in many publications and have been translated into five languages.

Philip Booth (1925–   )   Booth considers himself a New Hampshireman not only by birth but "by instinct." His boyhood ambition was to become a member of the Dartmouth College ski team, an ambition he later made a reality. He earned a master's degree at Columbia University and served with the Air Force during World War II. A teacher by profession, he has taught at Bowdoin College, Dartmouth, and Wellesley College, remaining as much as possible in his native New England and continuing to write poetry.

Ray Bradbury (1920–   )   Comic-strip adventures gave Ray Bradbury his first taste of what he calls "the fabulous world of the future, and the world of fantasy." As a boy in Illinois he soon became absorbed in learning magic tricks and writing space stories of his own. After graduation from high school he sold newspapers on a street corner for three years, all the while writing at the rate of 2,000 words a day—most of which he later burned. Since then he has published a great many stories and a few novels as well, including the eerie *Something Wicked This Way Comes.* Now one of the foremost science fiction writers, Bradbury confessed that although his characters fly from planet to planet without turning a hair, he himself has never been in an airplane.

Gwendolyn Brooks

E. E. Cummings

Gwendolyn Brooks (1917–) Awarded the Pulitzer Prize in 1950 for *Annie Allen*, her second book of poetry, Gwendolyn Brooks is also a fine novelist. Both her fiction and her poetry are characterized by a directness and restraint that make all the more moving the seemingly uneventful lives she explores. Although her own life has been comfortable, she writes frequently and sympathetically of the poor, doomed to squalor while dreaming of something better. Her verse, as one critic has noted, draws on the world she understands but records insights about that world in such a way that they become "not merely personal or racial but universal in their implications."

Fredric Brown (1906–) A popular author of more than twenty science fiction and mystery stories, Fredric Brown lives in Tucson, Arizona. His work includes fiction with such provocative titles as *Death Has Many Doors, Angels and Spaceships,* and *Martians, Go Home.* In 1958 Brown produced his first serious novel, *The Office,* about a small business office in Cincinnati, Ohio, in the 1920's.

Jackson Browne No biographical data available.

Melville Cane (1879–) "When I start writing a poem," says Melville Cane, "I don't think about form but let it shape itself as it grows." Born in Plattsburg, New York, Cane

first saw his poetry in print while a student at Columbia University in New York City. From college he went to law school, giving up poetry when he became a practicing lawyer. Not until twenty years later did he begin to write again. By that time Cane had turned from the light verse he wrote in college to more sensitive poems.

Robert P. Tristram Coffin (1892–1955) "I am a New Englander by birth, by bringing up, by spirit," Coffin once wrote. He was reared on a Maine coastal farm: "I began being a poet there among lighthouses and barns and boats, tides and fogs and apples and hired men." After graduating from Bowdoin College, he attended Oxford University as a Rhodes Scholar. For many years he taught English while writing poetry, novels, essays, and biographies. Among the most popular of his books of poetry are *Ballads of Square-Toed Americans* and *Maine Ballads.* His prose works include *Lost Paradise,* his autobiography.

Padraic Colum (1881–) Colum was born in Ireland in a poorhouse run by his father. Irish folktales, heard in boyhood from his grandmother, were his first introduction to the world of legend. As a young man Colum lived in Dublin, where he found early success with his poetry and plays. When he came to the United States in 1914, he began retelling,

Roald Dahl

Peter DeVries

in book form, Greek and Norse legends as well as Irish tales. His works include *The Golden Fleece, The Children of Odin*, and *A Treasury of Irish Folklore*.

E. E. Cummings (1894–1962) The son of a minister, E. E. Cummings grew up in Cambridge, Massachusetts. Following his graduation from Harvard University in Massachusetts, he served as an ambulance driver in France during World War I. Like many other artists and writers of his generation, the young poet lived in Paris for some years after the war. There he studied art, showing enough talent as a painter to have several one-man shows. But Cummings was primarily a writer; his bold experiments with language and form have made him an important modern American poet.

Roald Dahl (1916–) At the beginning of the Second World War, Dahl joined the Royal Air Force, and during the war he fought over Greece, Syria, and Libya. One skirmish over the Libyan desert sent him to a hospital in Alexandria for fifteen weeks. By the end of the war, he held the rank of Wing Commander, and within a year had published *Over to You*, a volume of stories about the R.A.F. Since that time he has written several other books, including the popular *Kiss, Kiss*, and has appeared frequently on English and American television. At present his life is divided be-

tween homes in England and America. His wife is Patricia Neal, stage and screen actress.

Reuel Denney (1913–) It was while he was a high school teacher in Buffalo, New York, that Denney won the Yale Series of Younger Poets Award, in 1939, for his volume *The Connecticut River and Other Poems*. Since then, Denney, born in New York City and educated at Dartmouth, has taught at the University of Chicago, in Puerto Rico, at the University of California, and at the University of Hawaii in Honolulu, where he lives now. He is co-author, with David Riesman and Nathan Glazer, of *The Lonely Crowd*, a study of our changing American society that has had profound influence on shaping contemporary attitudes.

Peter DeVries (1910–) DeVries was born in Chicago and attended college in Michigan. After graduation, he served for a time as associate editor of *Poetry Magazine*. Then in 1944 he became a member of the editorial staff of *The New Yorker*. But DeVries is best known for his marvelous series of comic novels, including *The Tunnel of Love* and *The Mackerel Plaza*, which have won him a reputation as one of America's leading humorists in fiction. As is true of the work of all good humorists, behind DeVries' laughter lies the serious purpose of exposing folly and pretension.

Emily Dickinson

Johann Wolfgang von Goethe

Emily Dickinson (1830–1886) Except for a few brief trips to nearby cities, Emily Dickinson spent her life in the New England village of Amherst, Massachusetts. She lived much to herself, and when asked who her companions were, she would reply, "Hills, sir, and the sundown, and a dog as large as myself." Her thoughts, too, were her companions. "How do most people live without any thoughts?" she once asked a friend. Emily Dickinson wrote hundreds of poems, often jotting them down on any available piece of paper: a brown paper bag, a used envelope, the back of a recipe. All of them she saved in little packets tied with ribbon, tucked away in boxes and drawers. The poems were discovered and published shortly after her death, but forty years went by before their excellence was recognized.

Max Eastman (1883–   ) Eastman, poet, critic, and social analyst, was born in the upstate New York town of Canandaigua, where both his parents were ministers. He studied at Williams College in Massachusetts, then taught for several years at Columbia University in New York City. In 1913 Eastman published his first collection of poems, *Child of the Amazons*. Evident throughout was his attempt to write poetry that is gemlike and clear, with no difficult or obscure images to confuse the reader. *Reflections on the Failure of Socialism*, a prose work that appeared in 1955, reveals the author's disenchantment with reformist causes he had championed in his youth.

Bruce Fearing (1935–   ) After graduating from Harvard and working as a technical science writer in New York for ten years, Bruce Fearing decided that "that was not the way to live." In 1967 he moved west to California, built a cabin, and settled in the redwood country of northern California. He explains, "you really don't know what living is until you own your own land. . . . It's really a matter of slowing down and living." Fearing is the son of poet Kenneth Fearing.

Robert Francis (1901–   ) On the edge of town, in Amherst, Massachusetts, in a white house that he calls Fort Juniper, lives Robert Francis. Although he has been a high school English teacher as well as a teacher of the violin, Francis is primarily a poet. He publishes a volume of poetry every four years or so. Robert P. Tristram Coffin once commented that Robert Francis uses the "simplest kind of words . . . but the poem is there."

Zack Gilbert (1925–   ) "I wrote 'A Tribute to J.F.K.' the day after his death. I find writing therapeutic; it is my way of crying out." So Zack Gilbert, a well-known black poet, explains his writing. A man of tremendous energy (he sleeps only three hours a night), he presently holds down an office job, serves as an editorial consultant for Path Press in Chicago, and finds time to write poetry, songs, and fiction. His works have been represented in several prominent collections.

Johann Wolfgang von Goethe (1749–1832) Goethe is to the Germans what Shakespeare is to the English: the greatest of their national poets and a writer with an international reputation. During his lifetime he produced such outstanding work as the novel *The Sorrows of Werther,* the great play *Faust,* and some of the most beautiful lyrics in the German language. In addition, he distinguished himself as a philosopher, statesman, and scientist. Goethe died in his eighties, still productive and vital to the very end, having a few months before his death completed the second part of *Faust,* which many consider his supreme and most imaginative achievement.

Frances Goodrich (1890–   ) Born in New Jersey, Miss Goodrich became interested in dramatics while a student at Vassar College. She was already a successful actress in New York City when she met Albert Hackett in 1924. They were married eight years later, after her marriage to the writer Henrik Willem Van Loon had ended in divorce. With Hackett, she entered into a very profitable collaboration, writing plays and film scripts. The couple wrote eight different versions of what was to become their play based on *Anne Frank: The Diary of a Young Girl.*

George Bird Grinnell (1849–1938) One of the best-known authorities on American Indians, Grinnell was an explorer and scientist by profession. He came to know the Plains Indians during expeditions into the Northwest, making it his practice to live with various tribes for several months each year. The Indians accepted Grinnell and passed on to him their legends—and their sorrows. Grinnell was appalled at the "unbroken narrative of injustice, fraud, and robbery" that spelled the white

man's dealings with them. In books like *Blackfoot Lodge Tales* and *The Fighting Cheyenne,* he tried to show the Indian as a human being, "not the Indian of the newspapers, nor of the novel . . . but the real Indian, as he is in his daily life among his own people."

Albert Hackett (1900–   ) Hackett's parents were professional actors, and the boy made his stage debut when he was six. He was born in New York City, and after his marriage to Frances Goodrich in 1932, the couple moved to Hollywood to work together on screen adaptations. "Each of us writes a version of a scene," his wife explained once. They write in a room at separate desks facing in opposite directions, exchanging drafts of what each has written, telling the complete truth about each other's work, then rewriting. "I never knew there could be so many battles about little words," his wife has remarked, but out of those battles emerged *The Diary of Anne Frank,* a play that took the Hacketts two years to write.

Jerzy Harasymowicz No biographical data available.

Sara Henderson Hay (1906–   ) Born in Pittsburgh, Miss Hay continues to make her home in that city. Her husband is a professor of musical composition at Carnegie Institute of Technology. *Field of Honor,* her first volume, appeared in 1933. In 1951 *The Delicate Balance* received the Edna St. Vincent Millay Memorial Award as the outstanding volume of poetry published that year. "What is memorable to her," one observer has noted, "is not any moment of illumination, but the daily event: the small communications between people or animals which make for a kind of wholeness."

Mary Hedin Born in Minneapolis, Mary Hedin has lived in many states, and she has attended six colleges. She holds a degree in Library Science from the University of Minnesota and a M.A. in creative writing from San

Francisco State College. She now lives in San Anselmo, California, where her husband practices medicine. Her first published short story, which appears in this anthology, was chosen for inclusion in *The Best American Short Stories of 1966.*

Robert A. Heinlein (1907–   )   Heinlein, with Arthur C. Clarke and Ray Bradbury, is one of the leading practitioners of the craft of science fiction writing in English. He was born in Missouri and is a graduate of the Naval Academy at Annapolis. During the 1930's Heinlein dabbled in real estate, politics, mining, and architecture. Since 1939, when he wrote his first story, he has published more than a score of books of fiction, as well as nonfiction, verse, and technical papers. He has written for television and motion pictures as well, and his work has been translated into French, German, and Italian.

Oliver Herford (1863–1935)   Born in England, Herford came with his family to America while still a child. He was educated at Antioch College in Ohio, then studied in London and Paris. His subsequent career was notable for his gifts both as versifier and as artist, and his work appeared in most of the popular magazines of his day. "His realm is Fancy," one observer noted, "and his scope the material universe." In his heyday Herford was called "the most quoted man in America," celebrated as much for his oral humor as for his verse.

Langston Hughes (1902–1967)   Born in Joplin, Missouri, Hughes traveled so widely that he called his autobiography *I Wonder as I Wander.* After high school he lived a year in Mexico, then went to New York City to attend college. A year later he was on the move again, this time as a sailor. On one transatlantic voyage he ceremoniously broke free from his past ideas: standing on the deck of the ship, he threw his books, one by one, into the ocean. Back in America in 1926 Hughes published his first volume of poems. That work

Langston Hughes

won both wide acclaim and a college scholarship for him. Soon he was writing for a living: poems, short stories, novels, plays, movie scripts, songs, and nonfiction.

William Wymark Jacobs (1863–1943)   A Londoner, Jacobs started writing in his early twenties, while working for the English Civil Service. Because his father owned and managed a wharf, the young man had become acquainted with seafaring folk, and later he used his knowledge of their ways in volumes of short stories about the sea. *Many Cargoes* is a typical collection. But most people remember Jacobs for one masterly tale of suspense, "The Monkey's Paw," which has remained popular for over half a century—both as a story and as a one-act play.

Dan Jaffe   No biographical data available.

Shirley Jackson (1919–1965)   "Mothers," Shirley Jackson once said, "are harried creatures, haunted by all sorts of terror—rusty nails, the rising cost of sneakers, rain on Class Picnic Day. . . . Over and above such trials most mothers are called upon, from time to time, to endure periods of such unnerving strain that only a heroine could meet them." She herself was the mother of several children, including a boy named Laurence. In a humorous book entitled *Life Among the Savages*

Shirley Jackson

John Lennon

she described her family's life in their rural Vermont home. Shirley Jackson was also known for her serious writing, which includes many short stories and several novels. Her horror story "The Lottery" has become a modern classic, appearing many times in print and on television.

Kenneth Koch (1925–   )   A member of the faculty of Columbia University, where he took his Ph.D., Koch has contributed fiction, poetry, and plays to *Partisan Review* and many other periodicals. Eight of his plays have been produced off Broadway. Koch was born in Cincinnati and received his undergraduate education at Harvard. He has taught at Rutgers and Brooklyn College, and has been a Fulbright Scholar in France. His volume of poetry *Permanently* appeared in 1960, and *Thank You and Other Poems* was published two years later.

Peter La Farge   Although he is best known for his singing and writing, Peter La Farge has worked at everything from rodeos to painting. He has traveled the country recording folk songs for the Library of Congress. He has managed to combine his interests in music and writing, and since 1962 has produced several record albums and performed in numerous concerts. He is the son of the well-known writer Oliver La Farge.

John Lennon (1940–   )   Since the days of his meteoric rise to world-wide fame as a member of the fabulous Beatles, John Lennon has revealed himself to be a genuinely great artist and a remarkably sensitive poet. The influence of his songs has transformed rock music from a recreation of the young to a mainstream expression of the contemporary vision.

Doris Lessing (1919–   )   Born of British parents in Iran, Doris Lessing grew up in Southern Rhodesia and never even visited England until 1949. Her writings express her concern with two major issues: the conflict between the races in Africa and the problems of an intelligent woman seeking to maintain her identity in a man's world. Her *African Stories,* according to one reviewer, are beautifully wrought "by a sensitive and thoughtful but fiercely honest writer. . . ." Playwright, poet, journalist, writer of fiction, Doris Lessing has been called by the *London Times* "not only the best *woman* novelist we have, but one of the most serious, intelligent, and honest writers of the whole post-war generation."

Archibald MacLeish (1892–   )   "If poetry can call our numbed emotions into life," Archibald MacLeish has written, "its plain human usefulness needs no further demonstration." MacLeish has combined poetry with an active public and professional life, serving as

Bernard Malamud

Paul McCartney

Librarian of Congress and Assistant Secretary of State, among other offices. For MacLeish poetry is not an escape from society, but a participant in society with an important role to play. "The whole history of our continent is a history of the imagination," he has written. As the frontiers of the imagination become the news of today, MacLeish's poetry celebrates it.

Bernard Malamud (1914–   ) Born and raised in Brooklyn, Bernard Malamud graduated from the College of the City of New York and went on to earn an M.A. degree in English literature from Columbia University. Recognized as one of America's finest contemporary novelists, Malamud in 1967 was awarded both the Pulitzer Prize and the National Book Award for *The Fixer. The Magic Barrel,* a collection of his short stories, had earlier been selected for the 1959 National Book Award. Malamud draws on the rich cultural heritage of the American Jewish experience to depict warm characters who in the midst of pleasure or pain retain their sense of humor, usually directed at their own shortcomings, and an abiding love of life. For Malamud, God moves in strange and unpredictable ways, but He moves.

Marcia Lee Masters The poetry editor of the Chicago Tribune Magazine, Marcia Lee Masters has also written a volume of poetry, *In-*

tent on Earth. She is the daughter of the great American poet Edgar Lee Masters.

Paul McCartney (1942–   ) From the early exciting days of the Beatles when Paul Mc-Cartney was known as "the cute one," this young composer has proved his mettle to the extent that he has earned for himself an important place in the annals of pop and rock music. His music and lyrics are characterized by their tender, honest, and fresh expressions of the new sensibility.

Ved Mehta (1934–   ) After leaving the Little Rock school for the blind, Ved Mehta went on to earn degrees from Pomona College and from Harvard and Oxford Universities. He has developed his remaining senses so fully that he has been able to hitchhike across the United States, play chess regularly, and even ride a bicycle. Since 1961 Mehta has been a staff writer for *The New Yorker* magazine. *Face to Face* (which includes "A Donkey in a World of Horses") was his first book. He has since written others about his native India, collections of essays, and a novel.

Edna St. Vincent Millay (1892–1950) By the time she was twenty, Edna St. Vincent Millay had achieved fame with "Renascence." The poem marked the beginning of a career that was to see her become probably the most popular poet in America between the two World Wars. Her poems expressed the disil-

Edna St. Vincent Millay

Ogden Nash

lusionment of the postwar generation and struck a tone that appealed to public tastes. Although usually working within traditional stanza forms, she often expressed a romantic protest against traditions and conventions. Her early concern with her own identity—her relationship to others and to the universe—gradually shifted to a concern with broader social issues.

Grant Moss, Jr. Moss was reared in a rural community in Tennessee much like the one he describes in "Before the End of Summer." After graduating from Tennessee's Knoxville College, Moss returned to his home town and took up the family profession of teaching. During World War II, he served for four years in Europe with the army engineers. He resumed teaching after the war and is now at Grambling College in Louisiana. Modest and unassuming, Moss claims: "I am not a professional writer. I am a schoolteacher." Yet his first story, "Before the End of Summer," was published in *The New Yorker,* probably America's most important magazine for short story writers.

Ogden Nash (1902–1971) America's best-known writer of humorous verse, Nash didn't start out to be a poet. After a year at Harvard he went to New York City and worked for two years as a bond salesman. "I sold one bond—to my godmother," he recalled. Nash

then tried his hand at advertising, at book publishing, and at magazine work. On those jobs he discovered that misspellings often made a story or article unintentionally funny. Accordingly, he began writing verse with deliberate misspellings and unexpected rhymes. Out of those first attempts grew poems that have been described as "the most original light verse written in America." His poetry now fills more than twenty books.

H. C. Neal No biographical data available.

Alfred Noyes (1880–1958) One of the most popular of modern English poets, Noyes was for several years professor of modern English literature at Princeton University in New Jersey. He wrote "The Highwayman" one night after standing in the blustery wind on the edge of Bagshot Heath, a deserted spot in England that two centuries before had often been the scene of highwaymen's exploits. As a boy the poet had devoured adventure stories of America's Wild West, and he once said that his boyhood reading may have given him the idea for what was to become his most famous poem, "The Highwayman."

Elder Olson (1909–   ) Born in Chicago and educated there, Olson has been a professor of English at the University of Chicago since 1953. *Things of Sorrow,* an early collection of poetry, received the Friends of Literature award in 1935. In addition, Olson has written a prize-winning study, *The Poetry of Dylan Thomas*, as well as such scholarly works as *General Prosody, Rhythmic, Metric, Harmonics* and *Tragedy and the Theory of Drama*. His *Collected Poems* appeared in 1963.

Edgar Allan Poe (1809–1849)   In his short life, Poe achieved fame, but his story is tragic, full of frustration and sadness, poverty and loneliness. He lost both of his parents before he was three, one by death and the other by desertion. Foster parents brought him up, but as he grew older there were many quarrels at home. After a short stay at the University of Virginia he began a career as a soldier, then as a writer and editor. At the time Poe wrote "The Telltale Heart," his young wife was hopelessly ill. In 1847 she—like his mother—died of tuberculosis. Two years later Poe was found unconscious on a Baltimore street and was taken to the charity hospital where he died. "The saddest and strangest figure in American literary history," one biographer has said of Poe.

Edgar Allan Poe

Ezra Pound (1885–   )   Born in Hailey, Idaho, Ezra Pound lived in England and France before settling in Italy. In addition to his own considerable poetry which stresses "speech as song," Pound championed the cause of poets such as T. S. Eliot and Robert Frost. Always a controversial figure, Pound is generally acknowledged to be one of the prime forces in modern American poetry.

Ezra Pound

Conrad Richter (1890–   )   Richter grew up in the mountain towns of Pennsylvania, where he listened avidly to tales of bygone days. After leaving school at fifteen, the young man went to work driving a wagon team over the mountains of Schuylkill County. At nineteen he became a newspaper reporter. Soon he was writing stories of the American past—stories that in time would win both the Pulitzer Prize and the National Book Award. Since 1928, Richter has lived in New Mexico, where he has dug tirelessly into the era of the old West, seeking, he says, "not history, but early life."

Conrad Richter

Edwin Arlington Robinson (1869–1935) Edwin Arlington Robinson viewed the world as a harsh place. He wrote most forcefully about failures. "The failures are so much more interesting," he said. Although he was awarded the Pulitzer Prize three times, he remained a painfully shy, retiring man all his life. In his poetry he chose to depart from the conventions of the day. Where popular poets were gushing with sentimental enthusiasm, he wrote with icy control, often understating his feeling. While popular poets wrote on such grandiose subjects as America's manifest destiny, Robinson wrote about the everyday lives and dreams of people he knew. And when popular poets were using an artificial, "poetic" diction, Robinson cast his poems in the colloquial speech of the townsmen he so memorably described.

Berton Roueché (1911–   ) A versatile American journalist, Berton Roueché is widely known for both his mystery and suspense stories and his medical reporting. He is a recipient of the Lasker Foundation Award for Medical Reporting, and has published stories in *The New Yorker*, where he has been a staff member.

Saki (1870–1916) Unusual titles like "Mrs. Packletide's Tiger" occur frequently in the collections of short stories by Hector Hugh Munro, who used the pen name Saki. (In Persian mythology, the god Saki is the Bearer of Joy.) Born in Burma, Saki traveled through Europe for several years as a young man. Later he joined his father in India, but for reasons of health soon returned to England. Besides serving as a foreign correspondent in Paris and the Balkans, he published sketches, short stories, and novels. At the outbreak of World War I Saki was forty-four; although offered a commission, he enlisted in the army as a private. Within a year he had been killed in action.

Carl Sandburg (1878–1967) Carl Sandburg earned a prominent place in American literature both as a poet and as a prose writer. He was the poetic voice of the Middle West from the time *Chicago Poems* appeared in 1916. In prose, his long biography of Lincoln earned him the first of his two Pulitzer Prizes. For many years Sandburg worked as a journalist in Chicago. During World War I he was a foreign correspondent in Sweden, his parents' native land. Born in Galesburg, Illinois, young Carl left school at thirteen to work, taking odd jobs that ranged from milkman to stagehand. His restlessness led him into the life of a hobo, riding freight cars and working where he could. Eventually he returned to Galesburg, to go to college, and on the student newspaper he began his writing career.

Saki

Carl Sandburg

Delmore Schwartz (1913–1966)   Schwartz has had a brilliant career as an educator and poet. He studied philosophy at Wisconsin, New York University, and Harvard, then became a teacher of English composition at Harvard. By the time he was awarded a Guggenheim Fellowship, in his mid-twenties, he had already published extensively. His first volume, *In Dreams Begin Responsibilities,* caused considerable sensation with the promise it exhibited. Subsequent volumes have included *Shenandoah, The Imitation of Life,* and *The World Is a Wedding.* In 1960, he was awarded the Bollingen Prize, the youngest winner since the prize was established in 1948.

Jon Silkin (1930–   )   Silkin worked for six years as a day laborer in London, where he was born, then became a teacher of English to foreign students in 1956. By that time he had published his successful volume of verse *The Peaceable Kingdom* and followed that in 1958 with *The Two Freedoms.* At present he edits a quarterly review of the arts and is a fellow in poetry at the University of Leeds, from which he graduated with distinction in 1950.

Elsie Singmaster (1879–1958)   Miss Singmaster wrote almost exclusively, during a long and productive career, of small-town Pennsylvania life, more especially of the life at Gettysburg, and of the battle fought there. She lived in Gettysburg many years, in a home overlooking Seminary Ridge, one of the crucial locales of the battle that had occurred less than two decades before her birth. A graduate of Radcliffe College, she was married in 1912, though only briefly, for her husband died less than four years later. Her *Stories of Pennsylvania* were collected in four volumes in the late 1930's.

Henry Slesar (1927–   )   Slesar has divided his life between advertising and creative writing, with notable success in both fields. He is president of his own New York advertising firm, Slesar & Kanzer, Inc. In 1959, he received the Edgar Award for the best first mystery novel, *The Gray Flannel Shroud.* Since that time, by his own count, he has written 550 short stories, novelettes, and novels, as well as fifty plays for television and four motion pictures. In his free time he is fond of listening to music, jazz and classical.

William Jay Smith (1918–   )   Smith is a believer in poetry for everyone. He is the author of numerous poetry books for both adults and children and has presented television programs on poetry for children. His poems have appeared in many national periodicals, and he has received several awards for his works. A graduate of Washington University, he has done graduate study as a Rhodes scholar at Oxford University and at the University of Florence. He is currently a professor at Hollins College in Virginia.

Jean Stafford (1915–   )   Born in Covina, California, Miss Stafford was educated in Colorado and Germany, and during her lifetime has lived in Massachusetts, Missouri, Louisiana, Tennessee, Maine, Connecticut, and New York City. She has been married to the celebrated poet Robert Lowell, and later to the journalist A. J. Liebling. Her work includes such distinguished novels as *The Mountain Lion* and *The Catherine Wheel,* as well as short stories and juveniles such as *The Cat with the High I.Q.*

Jean Stafford

William Stafford (1914–) Stafford is both an author and an educator. He was born in Kansas, holds his doctorate of philosophy from the State University of Iowa, and has taught both in the Midwest and on the West Coast. In 1963, he was given the National Book Award for *Traveling Through the Dark.* His books of poetry include *West of Your City* and *The Rescued Year.* At present he teaches at Lewis and Clark College in Portland, Oregon.

John Steinbeck (1902–1968) Much of Steinbeck's writing is concerned with social injustices that blight the lives of the poor and ignorant. Born in Salinas, California, he first worked as a hod carrier, painter, chemist, surveyor, and fruit picker before finally achieving success as a novelist. His rich background of experience on different social levels gave him compassionate insight into the lives of all kinds of people, a compassion that is especially evident in such books as *Of Mice and Men* and *The Grapes of Wrath.* When he was awarded the Nobel Prize for literature in 1962, the citation noted that "his sympathies always go out to the oppressed, the misfits, and the distressed."

May Swenson (1919–) Although Miss Swenson lives now in New York, she was born in Logan, Utah, and has served as Poet in Residence at Purdue University in the Midwest. During a distinguished career she has been honored by many awards and grants, including both Guggenheim and Ford Fellowships. Her first collection of verse appeared in 1954, *Another Animal;* since then she has published several other volumes, including *A Cage of Spines* and the recent *Half Sun Half Sleep.*

Genevieve Taggard (1894–1948) Miss Taggard's life was a quiet one externally, though the inner excitement she felt is evident in her several volumes of poetry. She was born in Washington state, attended the University of California, and subsequently taught at Bennington College in Vermont and Sarah Lawrence in New York. A volume of *Collected Poems: 1918–1938* was followed by two more collections. Miss Taggard was also the author of a challenging biography, *The Life and Mind of Emily Dickinson,* about one of America's greatest poets.

James Thurber (1894–1961) Before his death James Thurber was one of America's foremost humorists. He is remembered for his witty stories and essays, his drawings of dogs, men, and women, and his long association with *The New Yorker* magazine. By the time of his death, Thurber had published about two dozen books and had authored several successful Broadway plays. In the last years,

John Steinbeck

James Thurber

failing eyesight kept him from illustrating works with his famous doodles, but it had not reduced his output.

In 1920 Thurber started his career as a reporter for the Columbus *Dispatch,* and from then until 1927 was a reporter for various newspapers. In that year his friend E. B. White took him to *The New Yorker,* and he emerged from the interview as a managing editor. In 1933 he resigned from the staff, and settled in Connecticut, where he settled down to full-time writing.

Robert L. Tyler (1922–   )   Born in Minnesota and educated at the state university, Tyler went on to take his Ph.D. at the University of Oregon. His field is history, which he teaches at Ball State University in Muncie, Indiana. "In general," he writes, "I am interested in history as a humanity rather than a behavioral or social science." His interest in humanities has yielded, in addition to historical studies, a volume of verse, *The Deposition of Don Quixote and Other Poems,* which appeared in 1964.

Kurt Vonnegut, Jr. (1922–   )   Most of Vonnegut's writing attacks man's dependence on the products of modern technology, a dependence which he feels is destroying our creativity, sensitivity, and compassion—traits that make us human. Our increasing numbness serves to feed greater wars and greater cruelties. "All writers are going to have to learn more about science," claims Vonnegut, "simply because the scientific method is such an important part of their environment." Often mislabeled as a science fiction writer, Vonnegut seeks deeper levels in his stories and novels. Among his published works are *Cat's Cradle, Welcome to the Monkey House,* and *Slaughterhouse-Five.*

Eudora Welty (1909–   )   Miss Welty was born in Jackson, Mississippi, the state capital, where she has spent all her life with the exception of brief excursions to Wisconsin and New York during her college years. From Jackson she has written work that has won her a national reputation as one of the leading interpreters of her region of the country. Her stories, which have been reprinted widely, include those in her first published volume, *A Curtain of Green.* Longer work has subsequently appeared, including the novel *Delta Wedding* and the recent *Losing Battles.* About

Kurt Vonnegut, Jr.

Eudora Welty

her writing she has said, "I certainly never think who is going to read it. I don't think of myself either—at least, I don't believe I do. I just think of what it is that I'm writing. That's enough to do."

John Hall Wheelock (1886–   ) Born on Long Island of a family of distinguished ancestry, Wheelock was educated at Harvard, where he was Class Poet, and in Germany. As a young man he entered the publishing firm of Scribner's, and in time became a director and one of its most celebrated editors. His work includes translations as well as poetry. He lives in New York City, describing himself as "a great lover of the sea" whose principal recreations are swimming and walking along the shore.

T. H. White (1906–1964) Born in India of British parents, Terence Hanbury White was educated in England, at Cambridge University. For a while he earned his living as a schoolmaster, writing during his vacations. But at 30 he resigned his position to devote full time

T. H. White

to writing; soon he had published *The Sword in the Stone,* which was a success both critically and financially. By his own account, White had "a genuine passion for learning: not only for reading history or translating medieval Latin, but for learning to fly airplanes or catch salmon or train falcons or plow with horses or fence with foils or paint pictures or for anything else which needs the lovely effort of knowledge."

Reed Whittemore (1919–   ) Born in New Haven, Connecticut, Reed Whittemore attended Yale University. He received his B.A. degree there in 1941 and went on to graduate study at Princeton University. He has been a professor at Carleton College in Minnesota since 1947 and has served as a consultant in poetry for the Library of Congress. His writings include poetry, short stories, and essays.

Mason Williams (1938–   ) Guitarist-writer Mason Williams has made a name for himself in many fields. He was formerly a writer for the Smothers Brothers Comedy Hour, and has also written several television specials. Williams, who keeps a regular journal which provides the ideas for his many projects, has published several books, one of which is now in the Museum of Modern Art.

William Carlos Williams (1883–1963) A doctor as well as a poet, William Carlos Williams first began writing when he was a medical student. "One feeds the other," he once wrote about his double career. "One gets me out among the neighbors; the other permits me to express what I've been turning over in my mind as I go along." Born and raised in Rutherford, New Jersey, Williams set up practice there after finishing his training. He married soon afterwards, and was the father of two boys.

Philip Wylie (1902–   ) Wylie has lived much of his life comfortably in Florida, where he golfs, plays bridge, fishes, and in general leads "a very American existence." But, as he says, "once in a while I like to strike a blow for freedom." The blows come in the form of essays and controversial novels, most notably *Generation of Vipers,* which appeared in 1942 and added the term "momism" to the language, a word that describes the American tendency to sentimentalize the idea of mother. "By showing the gulf between our pretensions and what we really do," he has written, "and by predicting where our vanities and follies will lead us, I have tried to throw light behind the curtain we Americans draw across our unconscious minds."

Philip Wylie

ABOUT THE MAJOR ARTISTS

Pieter Bruegel the Elder (1525/30?–1569) A Flemish peasant's son, Pieter Bruegel the Elder popularized lay subjects at a time when painting was primarily religious art. Although emphasizing landscape and depicting folk customs and daily life of the peasantry, he found patronage among the intellectuals and court aristocrats of Europe. One often finds touches of humor in his work. His two sons, Pieter the Younger and Jan, were also painters.

Pieter Bruegel the Elder

Marc Chagall (1887–   ) This Russian-born artist is known for his dream-like, fanciful paintings. In a century when art has often been stark and distorted, Chagall's brilliantly colored works emit a joyous quality. Although he has lived most of his life in France, his paintings with their many images of farm animals, young lovers, and musicians still reflect his childhood in the Russian-Jewish village of Vitebsk. As well as establishing a reputation as one of the leading painters of this century, Chagall has illustrated books, designed sets and costumes for ballets, designed stained glass windows, and created vast murals for buildings such as the Paris Opera House.

Marc Chagall

Giorgio de Chirico (1888–   ) No one has ever seen streets or buildings like those that Giorgio de Chirico painted. This early twentieth century Italian artist is known for his eerie architecture and mysterious empty streets. Born in Greece of Italian parents, de Chirico studied at the Munich Academy before settling in Paris in 1911, where he still lives. It was in Paris that he did his most important work.

Caspar David Friedrich (1774–1840) This German Romantic painter is known predominately for his landscape paintings. His family not only encouraged his work, but in fact made his artistic career as easy as possible for him. His studies took him to Copenhagen for several years, but he eventually returned to

Caspar David Friedrich

Germany where he was made a member of the Berlin Academy. He married and became an assistant professor at the Dresden Academy. Throughout his life Friedrich's works remained quite similar in their composition and technique. He combines a sense of reality in his paintings with a romantic tendency which could be described as poetic.

Francisco de Goya (1746–1828) Although he was the official painter for the Spanish court for most of his life, Goya was no flatterer. Where other painters might have ignored the flaws of their subjects, Goya seemed to take delight in pointing out the shallowness and vulgarity of some members of the court, including the king himself. Goya was not afraid to attack injustice and made himself unpopular at court by publishing a series of eighty etchings which criticized social and political abuses. After 1814, Goya's paintings became more and more black and nightmarish. In 1824, after an attempt to liberalize the government failed, Goya went into voluntary exile in France, where he died.

Francisco de Goya

Winslow Homer (1836–1910) Midway in his career as an artist, Winslow Homer found the subject and the medium responsible for his unprecedented acclaim by fellow artists and the man on the street: the sea, depicted graphically in all her moods in vibrant watercolors. Prior to this time he had attracted favorable notice with his oil paintings and etchings, media which he continued to use throughout his life. Interest in his marine pictures centers on the sea itself, but strong also is the emotion evoked by the simple men—sailors, fishermen, and coast guards—who are simply doing their duty under the most rigorous circumstances.

Winslow Homer

Leonardo da Vinci (1452–1519) Perhaps the most brilliant and multi-talented man in human history, Leonardo displayed great genius as a painter, sculptor, architect, inventor, engineer, and in many other fields. He was the leading student of anatomy of his time, and

Leonardo da Vinci

his paintings and sculptures reflect his amazing knowledge of the human body. Born in the little Italian village of Vinci, the boy's early artistic promise led his parents to send him to Florence to study with the great artist Andrea del Verrocchio. The young student soon outstripped the not inconsiderable talents of his teacher, and under the sponsorship of wealthy nobles and church leaders took his place as one of the leading lights of the Italian Renaissance. His paintings are characterized by their sensitivity, keen sense of detail, and idealistic vision of the human character and form.

René Magritte (1898–1967)   René Magritte is perhaps the best spokesman for his own art. "The art of painting, as I see it, consists of representing through pictorial technique the unforeseen images that might appear to me. . . . I readily avoid explaining the things I love." This Belgian painter joined the Surrealist movement in 1925, after a brief period of influence by Cubism. He is known for his incongruous combinations of figures and images.

Henri Rousseau (1844–1910)   The French artist Rousseau, called "Le Douanier" from his profession of customs collector, began painting after retirement. He was a self-taught amateur whose "primitive" folk painting attracted the acclaim of Picasso and other artists. The naïveté and freshness that characterize his paintings have maintained popularity with painters today.

Peter Paul Rubens (1577–1640)   Considered the greatest of the Flemish painters, Rubens was also an accomplished diplomat. He was born in Germany, where his father was a political exile. The family returned to Antwerp after his father's death, and there Rubens began his formal artistic training. In 1600 he went to Italy to paint and to study the Italian masters, and there he began his diplomatic career. As a result of his skill in that field, he was created an English knight, but his enduring fame rests on his exceptional ability as an artist.

Ben Shahn (1898–1969)   One of the most prolific artists of our time, Ben Shahn has fused his concern for the immigrant or poor worker and his desire to paint into a powerful statement of sympathy for mankind. Although he was born in Russia, emigrating to the United States at the age of eight, his choice of subjects is more American than that of many native artists: *The Passion of Sacco and Vanzetti,* one of twenty-three paintings which first brought him recognition; a mining tragedy; the progress of the laborer; gains in social rights; the causes of crime.

Jan Vermeer (1632–1675)   Little is known about the Dutch painter Jan Vermeer, so we must look to the few records and his paintings in order to find out what sort of man he was. Sparse records in the city archives in Delft, where he lived all his life, indicate the dates of his marriage and death, and that he had died penniless. In fact, his widow was forced to sell two of his paintings to settle a baker's debt. He seems to have been principally an art dealer, which may account for the fact that he painted very few pictures (only thirty-five survive). His paintings are usually of common people and he had a sharp eye for the effects of daylight and color. The paintings show great objectivity and moving accounts of simple life.

Henri Rousseau

GLOSSARY OF LITERARY TERMS

Alliteration. Repetition of consonants (generally initial consonants) in words close together. Both *b* and *d* are alliterated in the following line:

The *b*ay-*b*reasted *b*arge *b*ird *d*elights in
*d*epressions . . .
    (Smith, "Bay-Breasted Barge Bird")

The letter *l* is alliterated in the following:
The answers quick & keen, the honest
*l*ook, the *l*aughter, the *l*ove,
They are gone . . .
    (Millay, "Dirge Without Music")

Characterization. The means by which an author creates lifelike people in his writing. An accurate and believable characterization is developed through the manner in which a character speaks and acts, and through the way in which others act toward him and speak about him. We come to understand what kind of man is Kino in *The Pearl* (page 300) partly by what he does and says, and partly by how others in the story act and speak to him. For example, we measure his bravery during his struggle with his pursuers on the mountainside, and we learn the values he lives by through his answer to Juan Tomás' question, "What will you do now that you have become a rich man?" "We will be married—in the church," Kino replies (page 315).

In addition, the writer of a short story or novel may make direct comments about his characters. About Bittering in "Dark They Were and Golden-Eyed" (page 7) we are told directly by the author that "Mr. Bittering felt very alone in his garden under the Martian sun, anachronism bent here, planting Earth flowers in a wild soil." A playwright, by contrast, would have to express that loneliness indirectly, through something Bittering did or said on stage; for a playwright has no way of commenting on his characters or revealing their feelings directly to an audience in a theater. As a conse-

quence, his characterization must be limited to recording how a person talks and moves about the stage, and how others speak about him and behave toward him. Thus, partly on the basis of what people say, we begin very early to form opinions about the character of Mr. Frank in *The Diary of Anne Frank* (page 521):

MR. KRALER. I never thought I'd live to see the day when a man like Mr. Frank would have to go into hiding . . .

But our opinion must arise from how Mr. Frank speaks and behaves, and from how others like Mr. Kraler act toward him. The playwright himself has no way of making direct comments to an audience about Mr. Frank or anyone else in the play.

Climax. The high point in the action of a play, narrative poem, or story, marking the decisive moment of the plot. Before the climax, the action may develop in many ways; at the climax, alternatives are removed, and the narrative proceeds toward the single logical ending. The climax of "The Monkey's Paw" (page 46) occurs at the instant the father discovers the paw on the floor and makes the third wish. Before that instant a number of things might happen; after that instant the ending as written is inevitable. The climax of "Phone Call" (page 30) occurs when Mrs. Timothy lifts the phone and hears the dial tone. Thereafter, with her suspicions confirmed, she pulls out the knife, and the subsequent events follow all but inevitably. Notice that the climax is by no means always at or even near the end of a story. The climax of a race occurs not when one person actually wins, but at that instant—perhaps quite early in the race—when it becomes apparent who will win.

Conflict. A major part of almost all plots in any form of fiction—short story, drama, narrative poem, or novel. Conflict provides both interest and suspense. The same story or play may contain several conflicts, which take a number of forms. One man or group of men may conflict with another man or group, as Harry and Ganderbai conflict in "Poison" (page 20). Or a man may be in conflict with the world around him. Jerry in "Through the Tunnel" (page 57) is in conflict with the natural world, represented by the underwater passage through which he is determined to swim. In waging that battle with nature, he learns something about himself. Indeed, a person may be in conflict with himself throughout a story. That inner conflict is evident in "Through the Tunnel," as well as in such a story as "A Summer's Reading" (page 193), where the easygoing side of George Stoyonovich's nature is in conflict with his desire to have people "like and respect him."

Dialogue. In literature, conversation directly quoted as taking place among characters. Except for *stage directions,* the body of a play is made up entirely of dialogue. It is the playwright's chief means of characterization, and it is also the principal way in which he unfolds the plot. Short stories and novels use dialogue, too; the way in which a particular character speaks helps reveal the kind of person he is. The terse and efficient fantasy personality of Walter Mitty (page 133) is revealed partly by the terse, efficient way he speaks: " 'Glad to,' said Mitty." " 'Quiet, man!' said Mitty . . ." " 'A bit of a near thing,' said Captain Mitty carelessly."

Drama. A story acted on a stage by players who represent the characters involved. The plot of a drama, or play, unfolds through dialogue spoken by the characters on stage, as well as through their actions. In reading drama, it is important to keep in mind the stage directions, which are the dramatist's means of enabling the reader to visualize the setting and to understand more completely the feelings and attitudes of his characters.

Dramatic poetry. see LYRIC.

Fiction. Prose writing that tells a story that its author has created from his imagination. Short stories and novels are fictional; drama, too, is generally thought of as fictional, and narrative poems are frequently classified as a kind of fiction. The term is contrasted with NONFICTION.

Flashback. A narrative device in which the orderly sequence of chronological events is interrupted by an event that has occurred earlier in time. Such an event may be a reminiscence, or it may be no more than a conversation that occurred on some earlier occasion, as in "Who Shall Dwell" (page 374), where on the day of the bomb-alert, the man and woman remember an earlier conversation they had about whether to admit others into their shelter. In that instance the flashback extends from "They had argued the aspects of this . . ." on page 376, to ". . . she had reluctantly acquiesced" on page 377.

Imagery. Word pictures. The following image creates a picture in the mind's eye:

> Who rides so late in a night so wild?
> A father is riding with his child . . .
> > (Goethe, "The Erl-King")

Many images state or imply a comparison:

> Life for me ain't been no crystal stair.
> It's had tacks in it . . .
> > (Hughes, "Mother to Son")

The image is a METAPHOR, comparing life with a stairway, both involving a progress that requires effort. The following image is also metaphorical:

> The moon was a ghostly galleon tossed
> > upon cloudy seas.
> > > (Noyes, "The Highwayman")

In this instance the moon is being compared to a ship, and the sky to the sea through which it travels.

Legend. A tale, handed down from the past, the historical truth of which is impossible to prove; it is often told about some heroic figure. There are legends about Napoleon and Caesar and about ancient times as well, the latter sometimes contrasted with MYTHS. Legends are mainly about human beings; myths are mainly about gods. T. H. White's "The Sword in the Stone" (page 118) is based on a legend of King Arthur; Colum's "Prometheus" (page 84) retells an ancient myth.

Lyric. One of the three general types of poetry. DRAMATIC POETRY appears in verse plays, such as those by Shakespeare. NARRATIVE POETRY, such as Noyes' "The Highwayman" (page 70), tells a story. Lyric poetry—the most common type—includes all other verse forms. Lyrics were originally sung to the accompaniment of a musical instrument called a lyre, from which the word *lyric* is derived. Often lyrics are intensely personal; often they are brief and charged with emotion; often they are unified in the effect they achieve.

Metaphor. An implied comparison between two dissimilar objects. Metaphors abound in everyday speech: "She has a sunny disposition"; "He's got a chip on his shoulder." In each case, the meaning intended is not the literal one: the person referred to in the second example is not literally carrying a chip of wood on his shoulder, but instead is behaving as though he is daring others to affront or annoy him. A metaphor appears in the following lines, where strawberries are compared to valuable jewels:

> Marcia and I went over the curve,
> Eating our way down
> Jewels of strawberries we didn't
> deserve . . .
> > (Taggard,
> > "Millions of Strawberries")

A figure of speech that uses "like" or "as" to state a comparison directly is called a SIMILE:

> . . . the stars like startled glass.
> > (Masters, "April")

> The whistle of a boat
> Calls and cries unendingly,
> Like some lost child . . .
> > (Sandburg, "Lost")

Both metaphor (an implied comparison) and simile (a stated comparison) help picture scenes vividly and express feeling accurately.

Myth. see LEGEND.

Narrative poetry. see LYRIC.

Narrator. In a short story or novel, the person who relates what happens. In some stories the central character tells the story, but in others, such as "Places We Lost" (page 168), the narrator is not the central figure, but instead is more an observer of the action than a principal participant in it.

Nonfiction. Writing that describes only real people and true events. Bennet's "Epilogue: Martin Luther King, Jr." (page 140) is an example. The term *nonfiction* is contrasted with FICTION. Bradbury's "The Pedestrian" (page 368) is an example of fiction; since it takes place in the future, it has obviously been created from the author's imagination.

Novel. A work of prose fiction that tells a story in a form usually too long to read at a single sitting. As with short stories, novels use devices of PLOT, CHARACTERIZATION, CONFLICT, SETTING, and THEME to achieve their effects.

Onomatopoeia. The use of words the sounds of which suggest their meanings; *buzz, knock,* and *roar* are examples. The following lines contain other examples:

> . . . Come *whistling* up the road.
> *Stomp* on the porch. *Bang* on the door . . .
> > (Francis, "Summons")

> The *hiss* of tensing nozzle nose . . .
> Of sudden sprinkler squalls that arc
> Rainbows to the *yap yap* sun.
> > (Tyler, "Puppy")

Personification. A special kind of metaphor in which human characteristics are given to abstractions or inanimate objects; that is, such objects are compared to human beings. In the following example, snowdrops are thought of as humanly capable of feeling sorrow, and seeds as able to do battle:

> Man's inhumanity to sod
> Makes countless snowdrops mourn,
> And every gentle seed that's born
> Gives battle for a dishonored god.
> (Cane, "Rural Dumpheap")

In the following, words in general, an abstraction, are personified as creatures capable of pride:

> Look out how you use proud words . . .
> They wear long boots, hard boots . . .
> (Sandburg, "Primer Lesson")

Plot. Arrangement of the action in stories, narrative poems, plays, and novels. Plot usually refers to the bare outline of the related events that take place, in the order in which they occur. The plot of "After You, My Dear Alphonse" (page 458), for example, begins in the Wilsons' kitchen, with Mrs. Wilson interrupted by the arrival home for lunch of her young son Johnny with a friend named Boyd. The boys, happily in the midst of some game, sit down to eat. During the meal the mother has a conversation with the two boys, then offers Boyd some outgrown clothes that belong to her son. Boyd declines them, and the two young people go out together to resume their play. Notice that the plot tells simply what happens, in the order in which the events occur. It does not interpret those events or the characters participating in them, nor does it elaborate on the setting.

Poetry. One of the principal forms of literary expression. Like novels and short stories, poems can tell stories, but poetry differs from prose in its uses of RHYTHM and in its heightened emotional intensity. One definition, by the English critic and poet Coleridge, describes poetry as "a more than usual state of emotion with more than usual order." See RHYME and STANZA.

Point of view. Vantage point from which a story is told. The author may either stand outside his story and view what happens from a distance, or enter into the story and portray what happens as it would appear to one of the characters taking part. The first method is used in "Examination Day" (page 398), where we do not follow what happens from the point of view of any single character in the story—Mr. or Mrs. Jordan, Dickie, or the examiner—but rather, from the author's point of view. By contrast, in "The Telltale Heart" (page 2) we follow what goes on from the point of view of the murderer who participates directly in the action of the story.

Prose. Ordinary language of speech and writing. All writing that is not POETRY is prose: novels, short stories, nonfiction, and many plays are written in prose. Prose does not use regular rhythms, and in this respect its sound differs most markedly from that of poetry.

Rhyme. Repetition of the same stressed sound or sounds at the ends of words. "House" rhymes with "mouse"; "shaken" and "waken" rhyme. In the following stanza the ends of lines 1 and 2 rhyme, and of lines 3 and 4:

Serene the silver fishes glide,
Stern-lipped, and pale, and wonder-eyed;
As through the agèd deeps of ocean,
They glide with wan and wavy motion.
> (Eastman, "At the Aquarium")

In the following, lines 1 and 3 do not rhyme, but lines 2 and 4 do:

> How about Them Lunch Toters,
> Ain't they a bunch?
> Goin' off to work,
> A-totin' they lunch.
> (Williams, "Them Lunch Toters")

Rhythm. Melody of language—the flowing sound of words together, as distinguished from their meaning. Rhythm is affected by such devices as ALLITERATION, ONOMATOPOEIA, and the harshness or softness of sounds within words and phrases. Rhythms may be quiet and subdued:

> Lie back, daughter, let your head
> be tipped back in the cup of my hand.
> Gently, and I will hold you . . .
> > (Booth, "First Lesson")

or vigorous and hurried:

> Look down shore at the old canoe:
> rag-a-tag sea turn white, turn blue,
> kick up dust in the lee of the reef,
> wallop around like a loblolly leaf . . .
> > (MacLeish, "Hurricane")

or abrupt:

> > The trouble with a kitten is
> > THAT
> > Eventually it becomes a
> > CAT.
> > > (Nash, "The Kitten")

or light and melodic and joyful:

> maggie and milly and molly and may
> went down to the beach(to play one day)
> and maggie discovered a shell that
> > sang . . .
> > > (Cummings,
> > "Maggie and Milly and Molly and May")

In fact, the various kinds of rhythmic effects are almost endless in number.

Setting. The time and place in which the action in a literary work occurs. "Columbus Was a Dope" (page 394) is set on the moon at some time in the future. "Different Cultural Levels Eat Here" (page 489) takes place during contemporary times in Al's grill. "A Visit of Charity" (page 478) is set in an old ladies' home in the United States in the first half of the twentieth century.

Simile.   see METAPHOR.

Stanza. Lines of poetry grouped together and printed as a unit. In a conventional poem all stanzas follow the same pattern. For example, the two stanzas of "We Never Know How High" (page 150) are parallel. Each has four lines, the second and fourth lines rhyming but the first and third unrhymed. Lines two and four, in both cases, are shorter by two syllables than lines one and three. Eight syllables of alternate stresses occur in lines one and three, six in lines two and four.

Theme. The main thought or meaning of a literary work—a general idea arising from the particular subject that the work presents and develops. Subjects are specific; themes are general. Often themes are difficult to state briefly and precisely. The theme of "Clamming" (page 284) has to do with the necessity of living honestly and simply, without worrying excessively either about one's comfort or one's image, concentrating instead on the task at hand in order to experience life most truly and fully. That general theme is explored by means of specific references to a certain individual's life, with one instance developed in particular: about his being stranded as a child of four on a sandbar with the tide coming in. The theme of "The Open Window" (page 66) has to do with the need for romance—for colorful and heightened experiences—that leads some people to create worlds that have never existed. A specific encounter between a young girl and an older visitor to her mother's home provides the occasion for a humorous development of that general theme.

INDEX OF AUTHORS, ARTISTS, AND TITLES

Titles of selections and works of art are in italics. Numbers in italics after an artist's name designate pages on which biographical information appears. Biographical information about all the authors can be found in About the Authors *on pages 597–612.*

ACKNOWLEDGMENTS

Illustrations for this book were obtained from the following sources: p. ii: Anna K. Moon; p. x: Mark Silber; p. 3: Michael Cassaro; pp. 9, 13, 18: Brad Holland; p. 21: Margot Niederland; p. 25: John Urban; pp. 31, 41, 43: Edward Vytal; pp. 47, 52, 55: Bob Owens; p. 59: Elizabeth Hecker; pp. 61, 64: Jack Kenney; p. 68: John Urban; pp. 71, 73: Paul Burton; p. 78: Publiofoto / Black Star; p. 83: Los Angeles County Museum of Art, "Daniel in the Lion's Den," Henry O. Tanner, courtesy of The Mr. and Mrs. William Preston Harrison Collection; p. 87: Marc T. Brown; pp. 89, 92, 95, 96: Marsha Guiminski; p. 98: Svat Macha / De Wys Photos; pp. 100, 103, 114, 116: Mrs. Neelam Gupte; pp. 119, 123, 125, 128, 132: Alfred Olschewski; pp. 134–135: Ed Parker; p. 139: Wide World Photos; pp. 141, 143, 146, 148: Marvin Mattelson; pp. 150, 151: Bryan Hopkins; p. 156: Bob Footerap / Photon West; p. 158: George Gardner; p. 161: courtesy Arkansas School for the Blind and The Lighthouse, The New York Association for the Blind; pp. 169, 172, 179, 181, 184, 185: Marc T. Brown; pp. 187, 189: Jerry Pinckney; p. 190: Joseph Smith; pp. 192, 198: Ann Hobson; p. 201: Karin Rosenthal; pp. 202, 220, 224: John Posey / Ifé Studio; p. 207: Robert Houston; p. 226: Walter Terzano / Photo Recon, Inc.; p. 228: Culver Pictures, Inc.; p. 238: Jaye Phillips; p. 241: Stephen Shames / Photon West; pp. 242, 243: Lydia Dabcovich; p. 244: Max Tharpe; p. 249: Marsha Guiminski; pp. 251, 253: David Kelley; p. 255: Wide World Photos; p. 257: Charles Brown / Ifé Studio; p. 261: Lydia Dabcovich; p. 263: Robert Houston; p. 265: John Urban; p. 266: Eric Simmons; pp. 268, 269: Lydia Dabcovich; pp. 270–271: Michael Gabriel; p. 273: Mark Godfrey / Black Star; p. 274: Elizabeth Hamlin; p. 277: courtesy U.S. Steel Corp.; p. 279: Elizabeth Hecker; p. 281: Calvin Burnett; p. 282: Berne Greene; p. 285: Elizabeth Hecker; p. 287: Barbara Marshall; p. 288: Michael Gabriel; p. 290: Bryan Hopkins; p. 293: Alan Copeland / Photon West; p. 298: George Gardner; pp. 302, 306, 312, 319, 329, 335, 341, 359, 361: George Price; p. 366: Donald Dietz; p. 371: Eric Myrvaagnes; p. 373: Los Angeles County Air Pollution Control District; pp. 375, 378: Thomas Upshur; p. 381: Mark Silber; p. 385: Mike Mazzaschi / Stock Boston; p. 392: John Posey / Ifé Studio; p. 395: Elliott Erwitt / Magnum; pp. 399, 402: National Education Association / Joe Di Dio; pp. 404, 406: William Carroll; p. 407: NASA; p. 409: National Education Association / Joe Di Dio; p. 414: National Education Association / Esther Bubley; pp. 428, 432, 436, 441, 444, 451: Shannon Stirnweis; p. 456: Mark Silber; p. 459: Stephen Shames / Photon West; p. 462: Jed Wilcox; pp. 465, 471, 474: Shé Shé; p. 477: Thomas Upshur; pp. 479, 482, 484: Ann Worthington; pp. 487, 488, 492: Peter Menzel / Stock Boston; pp. 497, 502, 509: Marsha Guiminski; p. 513: John Urban; p. 518: Dominique Roger / UNESCO Courrier; pp. 520, 522, 532, 540: courtesy of Otto Frank / Anne Frank House; pp. 564, 569: Gordon Parks / Life Magazine; p. 579: courtesy of Otto Frank / Anne Frank House; p. 586: Keystone Photo Agency, Inc.; p. 591: courtesy of Otto Frank / Anne Frank House; p. 597: Asimov, Houghton Mifflin; p. 598: Brooks, Roy Lewis; p. 598: Cummings, Marion Morehouse / Harcourt; p. 599: Dahl, Life Magazine; p. 599: DeVries, Little, Brown; p. 600: Dickinson, Bettman Archive; p. 600: Goethe, Culver Pictures; p. 602: Hughes, Culver Pictures; p. 603: Jackson, Viking Press; p. 603: Lennon, Capitol Records; p. 604: Malamud, Farrar, Straus & Giroux; p. 604: McCartney, Capitol Records; p. 605: Millay, courtesy Miskin; p. 605: Nash, Little, Brown; p. 606: Poe, F. I. Stuart; p. 606: Pound, Boris DeRachewiltz / New Directions; p. 606: Richter, Brown Brothers; p. 607: Saki, H. W. Wilson Co.; p. 607: Sandburg, William A. Smith / Harcourt; p. 608: Stafford, Rollie McKenna; p. 609: Steinbeck, Viking Press; p. 609: Thurber, Douglas Glass; p. 610: Vonnegut, Life Magazine; p. 610: Welty, Rollie McKenna; p. 611: White, Life Magazine; p. 612: Wylie, Doubleday; p. 613: Bruegel, Bettman Archive, p. 613: Chagall, Bettman Archive; p. 613: Friedrich, Bettman Archive; p. 614: Goya, courtesy of The Museum of Fine Arts, Boston, Bequest of William P. Babcock; p. 614: Homer, Bettman Archive; p. 614: Leonardo, Culver Pictures; p. 615: Rousseau, Bettman Archive.

Cover photo: Ric Simmons